THE CAMBRIDGE HISTORY OF INDIA

THE CAMBRIDGE HISTORY OF INDIA

The Mughul Period

PLANNED BY

WOLSELEY HAIG

EDITED BY

RICHARD BURN

IN SIX VOLUMES
VOLUME IV

GYAN

Published by

GYAN

Gyan Publishing House
5, Ansari Road
Daryaganj, New Delhi-110002
Phone: 011-47034999, 9811692060
E-mail: books@gyanbooks.com

Distribution Network
gyanbooks.com
India, USA, Canada, UK, Australia

ISBN: 978-93-6433-283-5 (Set)
978-93-6433-261-3 (PB)
First Published, 1937

2nd Impression 2024

Printed at: Gyan Press, Delhi.

THE CAMBRIDGE HISTORY OF INDIA, VOLUME IV
Editor: RICHARD BURN

THE CAMBRIDGE HISTORY OF INDIA

IN SIX VOLUMES

VOLUME IV

The Mughul Period

THE CAMBRIDGE HISTORY OF INDIA

VOLUME IV

The Mughul Period

PLANNED BY

LT.-COLONEL SIR WOLSELEY HAIG

K.C.I.E., C.S.I., C.M.G., C.B.E., M.A.

EDITED BY

SIR RICHARD BURN

C.S.I., F.R.A.S.B., M.A.

CAMBRIDGE

AT THE UNIVERSITY PRESS

1937

PREFACE

THIS VOLUME was planned by Sir Wolseley Haig, whose serious illness unfortunately disabled him from editorial work on any of the material which he had received, and even from revising finally all the chapters to which his name is attached. Thus while Chapters III, IV and V were completed by him in final form and appear as he left them, Chapters IX, XII and XV have been re-written from his full notes.

In the preceding volume the history terminated, in the case of Delhi at 1526, and in the case of the other Muslim kingdoms of northern and southern India and of the Hindu kingdom of Vijayanagar at later dates between 1565 and 1600 which marked their extinction or definite stages in their history. The narrative is carried on here to the accession of Shāh 'Ālam II, during whose nominal rule Delhi was to be included in British territory. As the volume deals primarily with Mughul India references to the European powers which obtained a footing in the country are incidental, and fuller accounts of their progress or varying fortunes will be found in Volumes V and VI.

Disappointed of his hopes to recover the seat of his ancestors in Central Asia Bābur had already raided India, when he was invited to penetrate farther, and succeeded in founding a new empire there owing to the mutual distrust of each other which characterised the Afghān chiefs in northern India, and to the superiority of his small but trained force. His son Humāyūn, whose character shows alternate energy and sloth, bravery and indecision, conquered areas and lost them during ten years, till he was driven into exile by Sher Shāh, the single Afghān ruler in India who could hold Afghāns together, and who had had practical experience of administration in lower grades. Sher Shāh's early death and the incompetence of his successors led to Humāyūn's return, but an accident cut short his life after a few months.

Akbar, succeeding as a boy to a much smaller area than his grandfather had held, left at his death an empire extending from Qandahār to the Bay of Bengal and from the Hindu Kush to the Deccan; and apart from mere territorial acquisition he had realised as none of his predecessors had done that successful government is bound up with consent by the governed as well as with domination by the ruler. His methods of administration remained the ideal throughout the Mughul period, though neglected or distorted, and some of them still survive. Political success too often feeds egotism, and in Akbar's case illiteracy withheld restraint so that his religious speculations bred derision.

At his death reaction was certain and under Jahāngīr, whose temperament was artistic rather than practical and in whom generosity degenerated into self-indulgence, administration declined. For a time there was a revival under Shāh Jahān, whose success in India led him to attempt the traditional enterprise of his line for the recovery of Central Asia. But a century of life in India had produced Mughul princes disinclined for the rigours and solitudes to be endured north of the Hindu Kush and the effort failed.

Succession to Bābur and his descendants had not taken place without jealousy or open dispute, and Jahāngīr and Shāh Jahān had each rebelled in his father's lifetime. The serious illness of Shāh Jahān kindled the smouldering envy of his four sons and war ensued from which Aurangzīb emerged successful, having killed or exiled his three brothers, and made his father a prisoner in the fort of Āgra, to survive there for eighteen years. Aurangzīb's reign falls into two periods. From 1658 to 1681 he remained in northern India, where his narrow-minded efficiency and religious intolerance caused the alienation of the warlike frontier tribes and destroyed the loyalty of the Rājputs to the empire which had been won by Akbar and maintained by Jahāngīr and Shāh Jahān. Having, as he believed, subdued these discordant elements, he left for southern India to extinguish the remaining Muslim powers there and to quell the rising activities of the Marāthās. Success in the former enterprise increased his difficulties in the latter and after ceaseless strife his life ended with the limits of the empire extended, but its resources squandered and its army ruined, while in the north the Sikhs and Jāts were also showing rebellious tendencies.

Aurangzīb's dying efforts to prevent his sons from repeating the fratricidal war for which he had set them an example failed. His son Shāh 'Ālam Bahādur defeated his brothers, but was old and tired and reigned only a few years. The Delhi empire now becomes the subject of contests between nobles who set up puppet rulers, establish a new hereditary rule of succession to public office, and carve out principalities for themselves which are independent of the emperor in all but name, and of which Hyderābād, Bengal, Oudh and Rohilkhand are the chief. The Marāthās, first enlisted by the Deccan kingdoms to oppose Jahāngīr's invading army, and gradually turning into a compact nation in their homeland, later engage in guerrilla expeditions beyond its limits. The Nizām of Hyderābād, to protect himself, diverts them against Delhi, and the Nawāb of Oudh rashly invites their assistance against his rival the Nawāb of Farrukhābād and thus brings them into the Dūāb. Weakened by the shattering raid of Nādir Shāh the Delhi empire cannot withstand them and they advance far into the Punjab. With a stable and effective administration at home their activities outside the Deccan are chiefly predatory till their military officers in Gujarāt, Mālwā and Nāgpur assume independence.

The story is ended in this volume by the temporary union of the disintegrating Muslim powers with the Afghān invader Ahmad Shāh Abdālī, who delivers a shattering blow to Marāthā pretentions at Pānīpat, while the Rājputs, who have also suffered, hold aloof, and Shāh 'Ālam II succeeds to a shrunken territory, hemmed in by Hindu states on three sides and the new Rohilla and Oudh rulers on the other.

For the first time in Indian history the politics of Burma and India clash, largely owing to acts of piracy committed by Arakanese and refugees from Portuguese settlements. Chapter xvii also describes the separate dynasties which held power in Burma till Alaungpaya founded the latest.

For the revenue system of the Mughuls more information is available than was the case with their predecessors. Its importance justifies the allotment of a separate chapter, xvi. As in Volume iii, the monuments are the subject of a chapter, xviii, with numerous illustrations, including references to the buildings of Bijāpur, Khāndesh, Sind and the Rājputs dating from the Mughul period. Permission to reproduce Figs. 24 and 25 has been generously given by the authorities of the Victoria and Albert Museum, London, and Fig. 67 by the Archaeological Survey of India, which retains the copyright. Prints for the other plates were obtained from the following sources: Messrs Johnston and Hoffman, Calcutta: Figs. 7, 17, 37, 45, 46, 57, 61, 63, 83. Messrs Plâte, Ltd., Colombo: Figs. 18, 36, 44, 60, 62, 85. Messrs Bourne and Shepherd, Calcutta: Figs. 38, 43, 47, 52, 73, 86.

Sir Wolseley Haig's scheme of transliteration in Volume iii has been mainly followed though *hamza* has been more sparingly marked in words such as *ta'rīkh* and *Sha'n*, which are pronounced in India today as *tārīkh* and *Shān*. Names of places are usually spelt as in the *Imperial Gazetteer of India*, for which special enquiries were made to ascertain the correct modern vernacular form. That form was transliterated according to a uniform plan except in cases where official or English literary usage had established a corruption, such as Calcutta, Bombay or Cawnpore. The index contains a number of alternative forms, sometimes not used in the book, for names often spelt differently or for names newly identified in it.

Personal names cause greater difficulty. Those of Hindus are usually derived from Sanskrit, but in the modern vernaculars have assumed differing forms, so that a single Sanskrit name may have even more spellings in its modern dress than "Philip" has in the languages of Europe, and a still larger number of pronunciations. While names of Muslims are more regular an additional complication arises from the use of titles, especially during the seventeenth and eighteenth centuries, when we find a series of individuals each with the title of Khān Jahān or Fīrūz Jang, or on the other hand an individual bearing different titles in succession. In the text an attempt has been made to reduce confusion by using the appellation held for the longest period, while the index includes other titles and cross-references to them.

In rendering official designations into English it is desirable to avoid terms which have a specialised sense in European countries. This applies particularly to the term *jāgīr*, which appears as "assignment". Many writers have translated it by "fief", which is not appropriate for several reasons. The system is explained at pp. 455–456, and the reason for discarding the term "fief" is that the "assignment" of an official was always liable to change, was not hereditary, and was not necessarily within the area of the official's jurisdiction. The largest administrative division of the empire (*sūba*) has been called a province, and the officer in charge (*sipāh sālār* or *sūbadār*) a viceroy. The term "commandant" represents the officer in executive charge of a smaller area (*Faujdār*) or of a fort (*qila'dār*).

One of the maps has been adapted from a map in Volume III, and three are taken with small changes from maps in the *Cambridge Shorter History of India*. Map V has been redrawn, by permission of Messrs Longmans, from the map facing p. 152, *History of Burma*, by G. E. Harvey. Map VI has been specially prepared to show the more important places mentioned in the book.

The index is not exhaustive of all references to well-known places such as Āgra which are frequently mentioned, but it includes indications of important items concerning them.

Dates of the Hijra year have been converted into the Christian era by using New Style from 1583, when Pope Gregory XIII reformed the Christian calendar, though Britain did not adopt the new reckoning till 1752.

Acknowledgments are due to all the contributors to this volume for their readiness to co-operate in obliterating the differences which arise when the same series of events has to be dealt with by a number of writers and in all other matters connected with the book. Special assistance outside his own chapter has been received from Mr W. H. Moreland, C.S.I., C.I.E., and Sir Jadunath Sarkar undertook at very short notice Chapter XIII, which Sir Wolseley Haig had intended to write. I am also indebted to Sir Verney Lovett, K.C.S.I., for instructive criticism, and to Mr C. E. A. W. Oldham, C.S.I., Mr Ghulam Yazdani, Director of Archaeology, Hyderābād State, and to the late S. Ahmad Hasan, C.I.E., for throwing light on a number of obscurities. During the printing of the volume the University Press has given invaluable help to reconcile discrepancies and avoid blemishes.

R. B.

January 1937

TABLE OF CONTENTS

GENERAL PLAN

CHAPTER I

BĀBUR

By Sir E. Denison Ross, C.I.E., Ph.D., D.Litt., Director of the School of Oriental Studies, London.

CHAPTER II

HUMĀYŪN

By Sir Richard Burn, C.S.I., F.R.A.S.B., M.A.

CHAPTER III

SHER SHĀH AND THE SŪR DYNASTY. THE RETURN OF HUMĀYŪN

By Lt.-Colonel Sir Wolseley Haig, K.C.I.E., C.S.I., C.M.G., C.B.E., M.A.

CHAPTER IV

AKBAR, 1556–1573

By Lt.-Colonel Sir Wolseley Haig.

CHAPTER V

AKBAR, MYSTIC AND PROPHET

By Lt.-Colonel Sir Wolseley Haig.

CHAPTER VI

JAHĀNGĪR

By Sir Richard Burn.

CHAPTER VII

SHĀH JAHĀN

By Sir Richard Burn.

CHAPTER VIII

AURANGZĪB (1658–1681)

By SIR JADUNATH SARKAR, C.I.E., D.Litt.

CHAPTER IX

THE KINGDOMS OF THE DECCAN DURING THE REIGNS OF JAHĀNGĪR, SHĀH JAHĀN AND AURANGZĪB, AND THE RISE OF THE MARĀTHĀ POWER

By Lt.-Colonel Sir Wolseley Haig.

CHAPTER X

AURANGZĪB (1681–1707)

By Sir Jadunath Sarkar.

CHAPTER XI

BAHĀDUR SHĀH, JAHĀNDĀR SHĀH, FARRUKH-SIYAR, RAFĪ'-UD-DARAJĀT AND RAFĪ'-UD-DAULA

By Sir Jadunath Sarkar.

CHAPTER XII

MUHAMMAD SHĀH

By Lt.-Colonel Sir Wolseley Haig.

CHAPTER XIII

THE HYDERĀBĀD STATE (1724–1762)

By Sir Jadunath Sarkar.

CHAPTER XIV

THE RISE OF THE MARĀTHĀ EMPIRE (1707–1761)

By H. G. Rawlinson, C.I.E., M.A., F.R.Hist.S.
(Late Indian Educational Service.)

CHAPTER XV

AHMAD SHĀH, 'ĀLAMGĪR II AND SHĀH 'ĀLAM

By Lt.-Colonel Sir Wolseley Haig.

CHAPTER XVI

THE REVENUE SYSTEM OF THE MUGHUL EMPIRE

By W. H. Moreland, C.S.I., C.I.E.

CHAPTER XVII

BURMA (1531–1782)

By G. E. Harvey, Indian Civil Service (*retired*).

CHAPTER XVIII

MONUMENTS OF THE MUGHUL PERIOD

By Percy Brown, A.R.C.A., F.R.A.S.B., Secretary and Curator, Victoria Memorial Hall, Calcutta, formerly Principal of the Government School of Art and Keeper of the Government Art Gallery, Calcutta.

LIST OF BIBLIOGRAPHIES

CHRONOLOGICAL TABLES

DYNASTIC LISTS AND GENEALOGICAL TABLES

LIST OF MAPS

PLATES

(at end of book)

(*For acknowledgments see also p.* vii *of Preface.*)

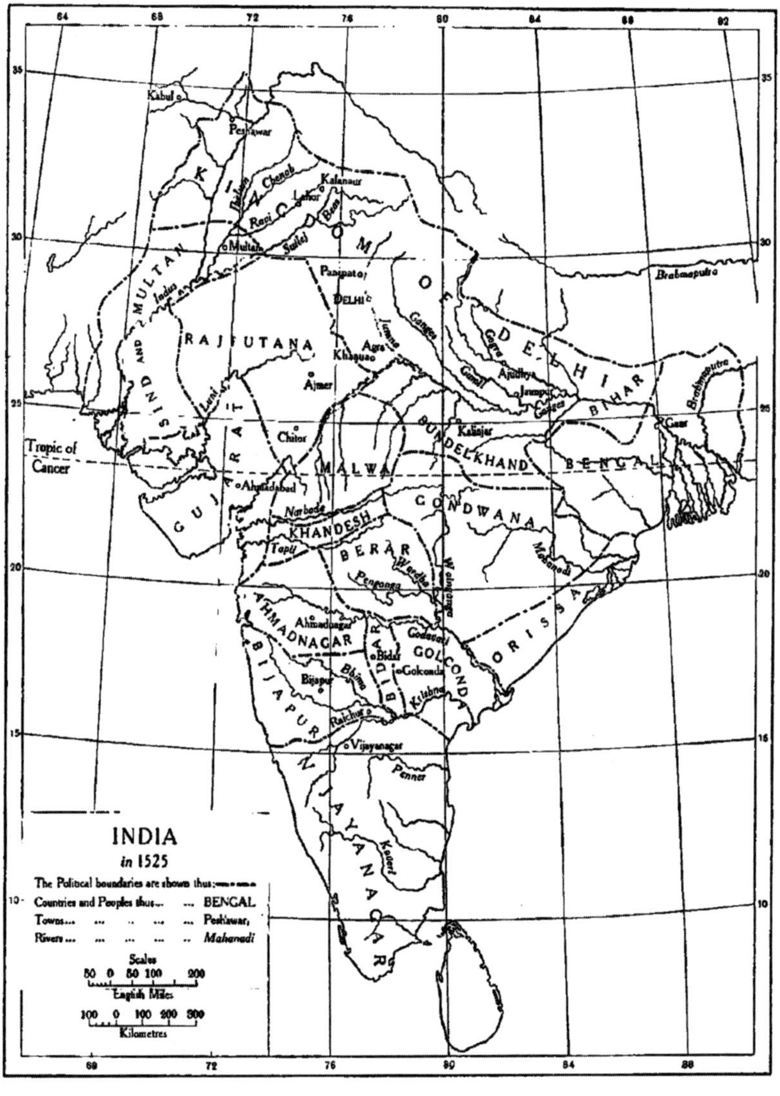
INDIA
in 1525
The Political boundaries are shown thus:
Countries and Peoples thus ... BENGAL
Towns ... Peshawar,
Rivers ... Mahanadi
Scales
English Miles
Kilometres
Tropic of Cancer
KINGDOM OF DELHI
MULTAN
SIND AND
RAJPUTANA
GUJARAT
MALWA
KHANDESH
BERAR
GONDWANA
BUNDELKHAND
BIHAR
BENGAL
ORISSA
AHMADNAGAR
BIDAR
GOLCONDA
BIJAPUR
VIJAYANAGAR
Kabul
Peshawar
Kalanaur
Lahor
Multan
Panipat
DELHI
Agra
Khanua
Ajmer
Chitor
Ahmadabad
Kalinjar
Ajudhya
Jaunpur
Gaur
Ahmadnagar
Bidar
Golconda
Bijapur
Raichur
Vijayanagar
Jhelam
Chenab
Ravi
Beas
Sutlej
Indus
Luni
Jumna
Ganges
Gogra
Gumti
Brahmaputra
Narbada
Tapti
Penganga
Wardha
Wainganga
Mahanadi
Godavari
Bhima
Kistna
Penner
Kaveri

CHAPTER I

BĀBUR

I

IN chapter IX of volume III, which dealt with the Lodī dynasty, the narrative was brought down to the revolts of the Afghān chiefs in Lucknow and Bihār against Ibrāhīm Shāh Lodī, and the intrigues of Daulat Khān, the semi-independent governor of Lahore. In the present chapter will be described the events which led to the expulsion of the Lodīs from upper India by the emperor Bābur.

It would have sufficed for the purposes of an Indian history if the narrative had been resumed at the point where the disaffected Afghāns first began to intrigue with the Timurid ruler of Kābul in the year 1523. But the early life of the emperor Bābur offers so strange and engrossing a subject that it would be improper not to present the reader with a summary at least of the previous career of the man who founded the Mughul Empire of Delhi. We must, therefore, momentarily focus our attention on the country situate between Persia and Turkestān, in which Bābur was born and where he spent the first thirty years of his life. Since Tamerlane's invasion of India in 1398 (see vol. III, chap. VII) this country never seems to have attracted the attention of his descendants, for though these included men of rare gifts none of them were great soldiers or statesmen. The two we remember best are Ulugh Beg, Tīmūr's grandson, who was an eminent astrologer, and Sultān Husain Baiqara, Tīmūr's great-great-grandson, who for fifty-four years made Herāt one of the greatest centres of literature and art that the world has ever seen—a veritable cinquecento Florence in the heart of Asia. But between 1405, when Tīmūr died, and 1500 (by which time Tīmūr's central Asian kingdoms had been divided between the Uzbegs and the Safavids) among all the Timurid princes—who are known to Muslim historians as the Mīrzās—there was none capable of consolidating their common heritage. The hereditary instinct for great adventures seems to have lain dormant in the Timurid stock, until it suddenly revealed itself again in the person of the emperor Bābur. The whole result of Tamerlane's invasion of India had been the appointment of a governor of Multān, who, although he founded the short-lived dynasty of Sayyids, never even assumed the title of king. Of the other lands conquered by Tīmūr nothing remained to his immediate successors except Transoxiana, most of the modern Afghānistān, Khurāsān, and part of Persia, and his conquest of Delhi counted for no more when he died than his defeat of the Ottoman Sultān Bāyazīd.

At the time of Bābur's birth, in 1483, these countries were no longer a single empire, but were broken up into a number of separate states large and small ruled over by Timurid princes among whom there was constant rivalry and warfare. Among these princes was Bābur's father, 'Umar Shaikh Mīrzā, who had inherited the kingdom of Farghāna. In 1494 'Umar Shaikh died and was succeeded by Bābur, then a child of eleven. For the next twenty years he was engaged in continual struggles with his cousins, in which his main objective was always the kingdom of Transoxiana with its capital Samarqand, for, like his great ancestor Tīmūr, Bābur had a deep-seated affection for this city. His only lasting success during this period was his occupation in 1504 of Kābul, a Timurid state, which then became his headquarters. It was to Kābul that he withdrew after his defeat by the Uzbegs at the battle of Ghazdawān in 1512, when he finally abandoned all hope of realising his chief ambition; but there, instead of resigning himself to the relative obscurity of a minor principality, he began to contemplate what neither Chingīz Khān nor Tīmūr had been able to achieve, namely the conquest of Hindūstān. Nothing could have seemed less probable when Bābur at the age of eleven inherited his father's small kingdom of Farghāna than that he should one day become emperor of Hindūstān; and in the first thirty years of his active career, in spite of his untiring energy and indomitable courage, he achieved nothing beyond turning his cousins out of Badakhshān, Kābul and Ghaznī.

It is almost impossible in a brief survey to infuse life and interest into the petty wars and intrigues in which young Bābur found himself involved in his early career. The bones of contention were the various towns in Transoxiana and Khurāsān, notably Samarqand, Bukhārā and Herāt, and the protagonists were the Timurid Mīrzās and the Mughul Khāns. These years are packed with incidents and adventures, forming a panorama in which the outstanding figure is the youthful prince who was destined to found a great empire in a land far removed and greatly differing in climate, population and culture from his own. The history of the country lying between the Oxus and the Jaxartes between 1494 and 1512 can only be made interesting if told in great detail; that is to say, if one concentrates on the principal personalities, their ambitions and quarrels. Sketched briefly these events have little meaning, and simply offer a number of names, many of which are quite confusing on account of their similarity and sometimes even their identity with each other. Since, however, it is with the founding of the Mughul dynasty of Delhi that this chapter is concerned, it is clear that we must pass quite rapidly over Bābur's career in the north and only deal fully with his great Indian adventure.

In the history of the first twenty years of Bābur's career the scene changes so rapidly and the protagonists are so numerous that even in the briefest account something in the nature of a list of *dramatis personae* is required, for without such a list there must be confusion in the reader's mind.

Zahīr-ud-Dīn Muhammad Bābur, the founder of the Mughul Empire in Hindūstān, was born in Farghāna on 14 February, 1483. His father, 'Umar Shaikh Mīrzā, was descended in the fourth generation from the great Tamerlane, and his mother, Qutluq Nigār Khānum, the daughter of Yūnus Khān, was descended from Chagatāi Khān, the son of Chingīz Khān. 'Umar Shaikh Mīrzā was one of the nine sons of Sultān Abū Sa'īd Khān, who, in 1452, had succeeded to what yet remained of Tamerlane's vast empire, thanks very largely to the support of the Uzbegs of Turkestān under their Qipchaq leader, Abu-'l-Khair Khān. On the death of Sultān Abū Sa'īd Khān in 1469 his empire was divided among his sons.

The eldest son Ahmad had obtained Transoxiana with its capital Samarqand, and the second son Mahmūd became lord of Badakhshān and Hisār. The fourth son of Abū Sa'īd Mīrzā, Ulugh Beg, became lord of Kābul and Ghaznī, and he had a son called 'Abdur-Razzāq. The fifth son 'Umar Shaikh, the father of Bābur, inherited the kingdom of Farghāna with its capital Andijān. The most powerful of the Timurids at this time was, however, Sultān Husain Baiqara, who belonged to the Mīrān-Shāh branch of Tamerlane's family, and was ruling Khurāsān from Herāt. His territories included in the east, Balkh; in the west, Bistām and Dāmaghān; in the north, Khwārazm (Khiva); and in the south, Qandahār. He had a son named Badī'-uz-Zamān Mīrzā. Bābur had two brothers, Jahāngīr Mīrzā and Nāsir Mīrzā. Such were the chief Timurid princes or Mīrzās. The most prominent chiefs and nobles outside the family of Tamerlane were Khusrav Shāh, a Qipchaq Mongol, who was minister of Mahmūd Mīrzā and for a time governor of Qunduz; and Zū-'n-Nūn Arghūn, also a Mongol, who was governor of Qandahār on behalf of Sultān Husain Baiqara—he claimed descent from Arghūn Khān, son of Abāqa, son of Hulāgū, Īl-khānī rulers of Persia two centuries earlier. His two sons, Shāh Beg and Muhammad Muqīm Khān, both play a prominent part in this story. The great chiefs of the Uzbegs who ultimately usurped the eastern possessions of the Timurids, were Abu-'l-Khair Khān; his grandson Muhammad Shaibānī Khān (also known as Shāhībeg or Shaibak, a corruption of Shāhbakht); and 'Ubaid-ullah Khān, the nephew of Shaibānī. Amongst the Chaghatāi Chingīz-Khānids were Sultān Ahmad Khān and Sultān Mahmūd Khān, the sons of Yūnus Khān, the father of Bābur's mother. Ahmad had several sons of whom we hear at this time, notably Mansūr Sultān, Sa'īd Khān and Chīn-Tīmūr. Finally, mention may be made of Mīrzā Haidar Dughlāt, Bābur's cousin and friend, the author of the famous *Tārīkh-i-Rashīdī*.

In order to follow the career of Bābur we must first familiarise our-

which includes on the north the Sea of Aral, on and Kirmān), on the south upper India, and on the east Kashmir, Tibet, and Chinese Turkestān. We must think of various countries in the terms of the sixteenth century. Transoxiana, or Māvarā-un-nahr, comprised most of the country between the Oxus and the Jaxartes, including Samarqand and Bukhārā. In the south-east is Farghāna with its capital Andijān. Khurāsān included Marv, Balkh, Herāt, Qandahār and Khwārazm (Khiva). Kābul (which included Ghaznī) was independent. Hisār and Qunduz were included in Badakhshān.

In 1494 Ahmad, the son of Yūnus Khān, died, and was succeeded by his brother Mahmūd, who died in the following year, when his territories were divided between his two sons, Baisunqur and Mas'ūd. 'Umar Shaikh also died in 1494, and his kingdom of Farghāna was inherited by his son Bābur, then only eleven years of age. From the very outset of his career the young prince found himself the object of external foes and of internal intrigues; for he had inherited his father's quarrels as well as his insecure throne. The first years of Bābur's reign were mainly occupied in fighting against his cousin Baisunqur, from whom he captured Samarqand in 1497, after a siege of seven months.

At this stage we hear of the arrival in Transoxiana of Shaibānī Khān, chief of the Uzbegs, who was destined to play a great part in the early history both of Bābur and of Shāh Isma'īl, the founder of the Safavid dynasty of Persia. Baisunqur Mīrzā had invited Shaibānī Khān to come and help him against his cousin Bābur. The Khān of the Uzbegs came but again withdrew without rendering any assistance, having seen enough to make him realise, as Erskine says: "the richness of the prey and the weakness of its defenders." In 1501, after suffering a defeat at Sar-i-pul, Bābur withdrew to Samarqand which, after a protracted siege, he surrendered to Shaibānī Khān. Bābur himself only obtained his freedom by a promise that his sister should marry the Uzbeg Khān. He now withdrew to Tāshkent, which had been given to Sultān Mahmūd Khān, son of Yūnus Khān, by 'Umar Shaikh; and there Bābur spent three years in hiding and misery. In June 1504 we find him accompanied by a handful of men and women, a refugee without a home and without a destination. Shaibānī Khān, the Uzbeg, in the meanwhile had become master of Transoxiana, and had put to flight Khusrav Shāh, the governor of Qunduz. This disaster and the consequent dispersal of Khusrav's army came as a blessing to Bābur, to whose camp large numbers of deserters fled. Those chiefs who now attached themselves to Bābur were called the "Guest Begs". Bābur now found himself at the head of a force of over four thousand men (according to Mīrzā Haidar, twenty thousand) and he was obliged to choose between marching to help in the defence of Herāt which

taining taunting references to the possible visit of the former to Meshed and of the latter to Mecca). Isma'īl, having overrun Khurāsān as far as Meshed, went in pursuit of Shaibānī in the direction of Marv, where the latter shut himself up. Isma'īl, in order to bring him out into the open, gave out that he was returning home after paying a ceremonial visit to the Holy City of Meshed. The ruse had the desired result, and on 2 December, 1510, a battle was engaged outside Marv, in which Shaibānī was defeated and slain. The Uzbegs now withdrew from Khurāsān into Transoxiana, and Isma'īl wintered in Herāt. News of the victory at Marv was brought to Bābur, who, with hopes revived of regaining his lost territories, set out with all possible speed *via* Bāmiān and reached Qunduz in January, 1511. Shāh Isma'īl sent an embassy, laden with rich presents and bringing Bābur's sister Khānzāda Begam, who had, as we have seen, been given in marriage to Shaibānī Khān. On the approach of Bābur, however, fearing the results of her devotion to her brother, Shaibānī had divorced her and married her to a man who afterwards fell in the battle near Marv. Bābur sent Khān Mīrzā to thank Isma'īl and to congratulate him on his victory over their common enemy; he further suggested that Isma'īl might help him to recover Transoxiana. The latter consented and began to invade this country but, owing to affairs in Āzarbaijān which required his personal attention, he accepted proposals of peace made by certain Uzbeg chiefs, and withdrew again to Herāt. In the meanwhile Bābur learnt that his cousin Mīrzā Haidar had driven the Uzbegs out of Farghāna. Not long after, Bābur with the help of some Qizilbāsh troops took Bukhārā and Samarqand, and the Uzbegs withdrew to Turkestān. In October, 1511, he was proclaimed king at Samarqand. His dominions now included Tāshkent and Kābul, Qunduz and Hisār, Samarqand, Bukhārā and Farghāna.

When the Uzbegs, who had retired beyond the Jaxartes, learnt that Shāh Isma'īl had withdrawn, they resolved to attempt the recovery of Transoxiana. 'Ubaid-ullah Khān, who had succeeded his uncle Shaibānī Khān, now attacked Bukhārā; whereupon Bābur moved out of Samarqand to meet him. In May, 1512, an encounter took place at Kul-i-Malik, in which Bābur was defeated, and, finding it impossible to remain in Samarqand, he withdrew to Hisār, whither the Uzbegs followed him in August. In the meanwhile Najm Beg (Najm-i-Sānī), who had been despatched to help Bābur by Shāh Isma'īl on reaching the frontier of Khurāsān, hearing of Bābur's defeat at Kul-i-Malik, collected further troops from Herāt, advanced on Balkh and in October met Bābur at the Darband-i-Āhanīn. The combined armies took Khuzar and moved on Qarshī, whose inhabitants were put mercilessly to the sword, much to the disgust of Bābur who desired them to be spared. Najm Beg now advanced on Bukhārā. The Uzbegs entrenched themselves in the fort of Ghazdawān where they were besieged by Bairam Beg and Najm Beg, but it was winter and, while the Uzbegs were well provisioned, Najm Beg was unable to feed his troops. Bābur and others advised him to withdraw to Qarshī till the winter was over, and then to return with plentiful supplies. Najm Beg agreed, but on the morrow the Uzbegs attacked and utterly defeated the Persians. Bābur, who was at this time thirty, now abandoned all hope of reascending the throne of Samarqand, which he had won and lost no less than three times. His Mughul allies turned against him and, barely escaping in his sleeping attire from a sudden attack made on his camp, he withdrew first to Hisār and then to Qunduz, and finally he again crossed the Hindu Kush and returned to Kābul. Khān Mīrzā (Wais Mīrzā), the son of Mahmūd Mīrzā, was left in Badakhshān, which Bābur still possessed and Nāsir Mīrzā, who had been left in charge of Kābul, was on Bābur's return appointed to Ghaznī. His death, due to intemperate habits which shortly after intervened, led to a revolt among the Mughul chiefs. Bābur, having disposed of this rebellion, now settled down for four years (1515–18) to what was the nearest approach to a "quiet life" that he had ever known. Müller says "Bābur dedicated the next four years to ceaseless wars in every direction, for without them it was not possible to teach the mountain dwellers of Kābul and Ghaznī the respect due to his overlordship"—which means that he conducted a series of punitive expeditions. Grenard states that these expeditions were "merely an Asiatic method of advertising the advantages of obedience". His raids were "shopping expeditions". For example, Bābur himself writes in one place: "We resolved that, since grain was plentiful in Hashtnagar, it was expedient to lead a raid against the Afghāns there." At any rate, during these years Bābur undertook nothing in the nature of military expeditions on a larger scale.

II

We may now turn to the second phase of Bābur's career, namely his invasions and conquest of Hindūstān. In this part of his history we shall encounter many names already familiar to the student of these volumes; it may, nevertheless, be useful to enumerate some of those persons with whom the narrative is mostly concerned. Hitherto Bābur had been dealing with men of his own race or of races closely connected with it, either Mongols or Turks. That is, of course, only true in regard to the chiefs and leaders; for the population of Khurāsān, Badakhshān and Kābul were more Iranian than Turkish. Not till he crossed the Sind or Indus river did Bābur encounter rulers and chiefs of Indo-Aryan stock, and whereas the first twenty years of his active life were spent in competition with Tatar chiefs, his last years (1524–30) were passed in fighting against Afghāns and Hindus. Hindūstān was as foreign to him and to his army—in spite of the bond of Islam—as Egypt was to Napoleon and his French troops.

Although the Punjab had been overrun by Tamerlane in 1398–9 this event had only caused a temporary interruption in the Turko-Afghān period, which had begun with Qutb-ud-dīn Aibak in 1206. This period had witnessed the rise and fall of six dynasties, none of which lasted a full century. When Tamerlane invaded India he brought to an end the Tughluq dynasty, which had ruled over Delhi for nearly a hundred years. He left no prince to continue his conquest; all he did was to appoint Khizr Khān governor of Multān, and for nearly forty years this man and his descendants ruled in Delhi under the name of the Sayyid dynasty, the last of whom, 'Alā-ud-Dīn (1444–50), abdicated in favour of Buhlūl Lodī. On his passage to India, however, Tamerlane had established his rule in all the country between the Oxus and the Indus, and when at the beginning of the sixteenth century his descendant Bābur crossed the Hindu Kush, he regarded not merely Kābul and Ghaznī as his lawful heritage, but even the Punjab. Recalling the precedent set by the Mongols in the thirteenth century and by Tamerlane in the fourteenth, it came as a complete surprise both to the Afghāns and to the Hindu rajas when Bābur made it clear that he had come to stay. But though he made the way ready for the Mughul Empire of Delhi, it was only a military preparation, and his own son having failed to put these gains on a lasting basis, it fell to the lot of his grandson, Akbar, to turn all these advantages to permanent account.

When Buhlūl Lodī, the elected head of a confederacy of Afghān chiefs, appeared on the scene, the old empire of Delhi had really ceased to exist. His grandfather had been governor of Multān under Fīrūz Tughluq, and his father and several of his uncles had served under the Sayyids. Buhlūl annexed the Punjab to Delhi; his son Sikandar Lodī during a reign of thirty years added considerably to the kingdom he had inherited from his father. But the Delhi kingdom was actually a congeries of semi-independent governorships mostly held by Afghāns (Lodīs, Farmūlīs or Lohānīs). Bābur himself says that when he first entered Hindūstān this country was governed by five Muslim and two pagan rulers, namely the Lodīs in the Delhi empire which extended from Bhera to Bihār; Sultān Muhammad Muzaffar in Gujarāt; the Bahmanīs in the Deccan; Mahmūd Khaljī in Mālwā; Nusrat Shāh in Bengal; the Raja of Vijayanagar, and Rānā Sanga in Chitor. In order to make himself master of Hindūstān, Bābur would have to dispose of the Lodīs and of Rānā Sanga. The leading *dramatis personae* in this Indian episode are Ibrāhīm Lodī—the son of Sikandar Lodī, the son of Buhlūl Lodī—who came to the throne in 1517; and 'Ālam Khān or 'Alā-ud-Din—another son of Buhlūl Lodī. Outside the ruling house were Daulat Khān, governor of Lahore, the son of Tātār Khān, who held Sirhind and all the countries of the Punjab to the north of the Sutlej; Dilāwar Khān, Ghāzī Khān and Hājji Khān, his sons; Hasan Khān Mewātī, Biban—an Afghān chief, king of Oudh—and Rānā Sangram Singh, or Rānā Sanga of Chitor, who was the acknowledged head of the Hindu chiefs.

The Four Invasions

There has been some disagreement among the Muslim historians regarding the various invasions of Hindūstān by Bābur. Bābur himself, writing in 1526 after the battle of Pānīpat, says that from the time of his conquest of Kābul in 1505 his desire for Hindūstān had been constant, but that until 1519 it had not, for a variety of reasons, been possible to make a move on that country, and so its territories had remained unsubdued. At the beginning of this year, however, Bābur made a sudden descent on Bājaur which he captured after a short siege. At the same time with a view to winning over the people he concluded an alliance with the Yūsufzāīs by marrying the daughter of one of their chiefs; and when shortly after the fort of Bhera on the Jhelum submitted without offering resistance Bābur gave orders that no violence should be done to the inhabitants or to their flocks and crops. Bābur himself evidently regarded his occupation of Bājaur and Bhera as his first Indian expedition. "From then till now we laboriously held tight to Hindūstān, five times leading an army into it. The fifth time...made Hindūstān our conquest and possession."[1] Abu-'l-Fazl also reckons that Bābur made five expeditions, but he regards the abortive expeditions of January, 1505, and of September, 1507, as the first and second, and the successful invasion in January, 1519, as the third. Abu-'l-Fazl confesses he could get no information about his fourth expedition; the fifth is, of course, that which led to the battle of Pānīpat. Unfortunately there is a gap in the *Memoirs* between 2 January, 1520, and 16 November, 1525, so that we cannot know precisely which expeditions Bābur regarded as the second, third and fourth.

In January, 1505, Bābur took Kohāt and Tarbila in Multān, and returned in May of that year without having crossed the Indus. In September, 1507, he turned back owing to disagreement among his chiefs after reaching Mandrāwar.

In order to understand the circumstances which facilitated the ultimate conquest of India by Bābur, we must take up the narrative where it broke off in chapter IX of vol. III of this series.

Ibrāhīm Shāh Lodī, in 1523, was confronted with rebellion and risings in all the outlying parts of his kingdom. His relations had one and all turned against him, but his most serious rivals were his uncle, 'Ālam Khān (also known as 'Alā-ud-dīn) who had been living

[1] *Memoirs*, translated by Mrs Beveridge, p. 479.

under the protection of Sultān Muzaffar of Gujarāt (see vol. III, p. 321), and Daulat Khān Lodī, the governor of Lahore. During the revolts against Shāh Ibrāhīm, Daulat Khān, who had formed the confederacy, sent his son Ghāzī Khān to Delhi in order to ascertain the position of affairs at headquarters, and on his return to Lahore Ghāzī Khān warned his father that Ibrāhīm intended to deprive him of his governorship. Daulat Khān was determined to resist, but doubting his power to do so unaided he sent messengers to Kābul, offering to acknowledge Bābur as his sovereign in return for assistance. Bābur readily agreed, although 'Ālam Khān, the uncle of Shāh Ibrāhīm, who had recently fled to Kābul, was at the time begging Bābur to place him on the throne of Delhi.

The Lodī army sent against Daulat Khān under the leadership of Bihār Khān encountered Bābur's army near Lahore and was utterly defeated, and Bābur found himself master of that city, a victory which he quickly followed up by the capture of Dīpālpur, where he was joined by Daulat Khān and his two sons Ghāzī and Dilāwar. Instead of handing over Lahore to Daulat Khān, Bābur only presented him with Jullundur and Sultānpur as assignments. Daulat Khān was naturally disgusted and went into hiding with his son Ghāzī, intending to take the first opportunity which might offer of regaining what he had lost. Dilāwar Khān, who had acted treacherously towards his father, was now given Sultānpur and the title of Khān Khānān.

'Ālam, who still aspired to the throne of Delhi, now offered Bābur the formal cession of Lahore if he would help him to achieve this end. This offer on the part of a leading Lodī prince naturally appealed to Bābur, as it would give him a legitimate right to what he had only taken by force. He therefore instructed his generals whom he had left in Lahore to assist 'Ālam Khān in his attack on Delhi. That Bābur himself could not take part in this expedition was due to the fact that the Uzbegs were laying siege to Balkh, and as the safety of this city was almost as vital to himself as to Shāh Isma'īl, to whom it now belonged, he felt it incumbent upon him to go to the aid of his Persian ally. 'Ālam Khān now felt that the sooner he acted the better, as it would not only be to his own advantage if he could defeat his nephew Ibrāhīm without the personal aid of Bābur, but also because there was the risk that if things did not go well with Bābur, the Indian contingent might at any moment be recalled. Daulat Khān, as soon as Bābur left India, emerged from his hiding-place, and with a view to the possible recovery of Lahore offered to help 'Ālam Khān to conquer Delhi. Bābur's officers, however, could not agree to this arrangement, in that Daulat Khān was no longer on friendly terms with Bābur. After much discussion it was finally agreed that Daulat and his son Ghāzī were to remain in charge of the Punjab, while his other sons Dilāwar and Hājjī were to accompany 'Ālam Khān in his attack on Delhi. The attack came to nothing—chiefly owing to treachery on both sides—and Ibrāhīm still remained lord of Delhi. But Bābur, who had disposed of his troubles in the north, was not far off.

Leaving Mīrzā Kāmrān, then a mere child, in nominal charge of Kābul and Qandahār, Bābur set out over the Indus river to Siālkot. On his march he was joined first by Humāyūn with the troops from Badakhshān, and later on the same day by Khvāja Kilān with the Ghaznī troops. It was at Siālkot that Bābur heard of 'Ālam Khān's failure to take Delhi. Daulat Khān and Ghāzī, on learning of Bābur's approach, fled to the fortress of Milwat (Malot) north of Lahore. Bābur blockaded Milwat on every side and Daulat Khān, seeing no hope of escape, capitulated.[1] Daulat Khān died on the way to Bhera, where he was to have been imprisoned. 'Ālam Khān again fled to Bābur, bringing with him a certain number of his scattered troops, who had suffered severely at the hands of Ibrāhīm. He arrived on foot and nearly destitute.

Lahore and its dependent provinces being practically subdued, Bābur was now able to devote his whole attention to the capture of Delhi. Realising the political importance of having an Afghān prince in his camp, he paid every attention to 'Ālam Khān suitable to his rank; and, although the latter had everything to lose by Bābur's success, he was entrusted with a command both at Pānīpat and at Khānua. The opposing parties were now both advancing to an encounter. Ibrāhīm marched his main forces due north from Delhi along the right bank of the Jumna, while a secondary force under Hāmid Khān moved up from Hissār Fīrūza in the south-west. This force, coming into contact with Bābur's right wing, was totally routed by Humāyūn, who was then eighteen years of age. This was Humāyūn's first experience of battle. Bābur marched to Ambāla, and following the river Jumna arrived at Pānīpat, which he occupied. Here Bābur, whose forces probably numbered some 25,000, took up a defensive position, drawing up his army in a long line. On his extreme right were the town and suburbs of Pānīpat. His centre was protected by rows of movable carts (*arāba*), seven hundred in number, connected by twisted bull-hides; between every pair of guns there were six or seven movable breastworks (*tura*) for the protection of the matchlock men. In the centre (*ghul*) was Bābur himself. His left was protected by ditches and branches of trees. His principal officers were Humāyūn and Khvāja Kilān on the right, Muhammad Sultān Mīrzā and Mahdī Khvāja on the left, Chīn Tīmūr Sultān on the right centre (*ung-ghul*), and Mīr 'Alī Khalīfa—the Prime Minister—on the left centre (*sul-ghul*). On the extreme right and left of the whole line were strong flanking parties (*tulghama*), ready at a moment's notice

[1] Ghāzī Khān seems to have been a man of culture and taste, for Bābur speaks of his library where he found precious books, which he divided between Humāyūn and Kāmrān.

to wheel round and take the enemy in the flank or rear. On 12 April Bābur was ready to receive Ibrāhīm's attack, but for eight days nothing happened, except for the attempts of small parties of the emperor's troops to vex the enemy by riding up to their camp and shooting arrows among them. On 20 April Bābur, growing impatient, sent out a force of four or five thousand men to make a night attack, which though badly conducted had the desired effect of making Ibrāhīm move. On 21 April at daybreak the Afghāns were seen to approach. Ibrāhīm had with him 100,000 men and nearly 1000 elephants. It seemed that the main attack was to be made on the emperor's right. At first they moved forward at a quick pace in the manner of shock troops, and the first slackening of their speed when they came near Bābur's defences caused confusion with the lines which were following close on their heels. Bābur at once took advantage of this check to use his flanking parties, which wheeled round and attacked the enemy in the rear. In the meanwhile the emperor's left wing under Mahdī Khvāja had been faring badly at the hands of the Afghāns, but strong support being sent from the centre, the Mughuls were able to repel them. At this juncture Bābur ordered his gunners to open fire, and then the main attacking force of the Afghāns found themselves exposed to arrows on either flank and to shot or bullets in front. The battle lasted till noon and was throughout most hotly contested, but the superior strategy and experience of the Timurid prince enabled him to bring confusion among the vastly superior numbers of the Afghāns, who finally took to flight leaving, it is said, over 15,000 dead on the field, including Sultān Ibrāhīm himself and Vikramājīt the old Rājā of Gwalior, who had fought nobly on the side of the man who had but lately deprived him of his principality. Bābur's first care now was to secure the public treasures of Delhi and Āgra, and to prevent plundering by his victorious army. He himself entered Delhi and Humāyūn was sent forward to Āgra, which still held out: and though he was not able at once to enter the forts, he prevented any treasure being carried off. An incident now occurred which has its place among the romantic anecdotes of Indian history. The wives and children of the Rājā of Gwalior, who had been left in the fort of Āgra, were seized, while attempting to escape, by Humāyūn's men. Humāyūn, hearing of this, treated them with the utmost courtesy and protected them from their captors. In order to show their gratitude to the young prince they presented him with jewels and precious stones; among these was a diamond of enormous value, which has been identified with the famous *Koh-i-Nūr* now in the Tower of London. Humāyūn handed over this diamond by way of homage to his father, who returned it to him as a gift. On the Friday following Bābur's arrival in Delhi (27 April, 1526[1]) his name was read in the Grand

[1] Hodivala, *Historical Studies in Mughal Numismatics*, pp. 261–2.

Mosque as "Emperor of Hindūstān" and his highest ambition was at last attained. In his *Memoirs* Bābur compares his own success to the similar achievements of Sultān Mahmūd of Ghaznī and of Sultān Shihāb-ud-Dīn Ghūrī, and points out that though he owed everything to divine favour, his own performance was infinitely superior to theirs for they had had at their disposal enormous resources in men and money.

The Indian summer having now set in, Bābur's most devoted chiefs and followers were beginning to murmur, including the loyal Khvāja Kilān, who, advocating that Bābur should follow the example of Tamerlane and abandon Hindūstān, was allowed to withdraw and become governor of Ghaznī; to others was offered the choice of staying or returning.

No chapter in the *Memoirs* is more interesting than that containing Bābur's description of India and its fauna and flora, which follows his description of the battle of Pānīpat. It is fitting in this place to quote his general impressions of this country:

> Hindūstān is a country of few charms. Its people have no good looks; of social intercourse, paying and receiving visits there is none; of genius and capacity none; of manners none; in handicraft and work there is no form or symmetry, method or quality; there are no good horses, no good dogs, no grapes, musk-melons or first-rate fruits, no ice or cold water, no good bread or cooked food in the *bazars*, no hot-baths, no colleges, no candles, torches or candlesticks.
>
> In place of candle and torch they have a great dirty gang they call lamp-men (*diwālī*), who in the left hand hold a smallish wooden tripod to one corner of which a thing like the top of a candlestick is fixed, having a wick in it about as thick as the thumb. In the right hand they hold a gourd, through a narrow slit made in which oil is let trickle in a thin thread when the wick needs it. Great people keep a hundred or two of these lamp-men. This is the Hindūstān substitute for lamps and candlesticks! If their rulers and begs have work at night needing candles, these dirty lamp-men bring these lamps, go close up and there stand.
>
> Except their large rivers and their standing-waters which flow in ravines or hollows (there are no waters). There are no running-waters in their gardens or residences (*'imāratlar*). These residences have no charm, air (*hawā*), regularity or symmetry.
>
> Peasants and people of low standing go about naked. They tie on a thing called *langūta*, a decency-clout which hangs two spans below the navel. From the tie of this pendant decency-clout, another clout is passed between the thighs and made fast behind. Women also tie on a cloth (*lang*), one-half of which goes round the waist, the other is thrown over the head.
>
> Pleasant things of Hindūstān are that it is a large country and has masses of gold and silver. Its air in the Rains is very fine. Sometimes it rains 10, 15 or 20 times a day; torrents pour down all at once and rivers flow where no water had been. While it rains and through the Rains, the air is remarkably fine, not to be surpassed for healthiness and charm. The fault is that the air becomes very soft and damp. A bow of those (Transoxanian) countries after going through the Rains in Hindūstān, may not be drawn even; it is ruined; not only the bow, everything is affected, armour, book, cloth, and utensils all; a house even does not last long. Not only in the Rains but also in the cold and the hot seasons, the airs are excellent; at these times, however, the north-west wind constantly gets up laden with dust and earth. It gets up in great strength every year in the heats, under the Bull and Twins, when the Rains are near; so strong and carrying so much dust and earth that there is no seeing one another. People call this wind Darkener of the

Sky (H. *āndhī*). The weather is hot under the Bull and Twins, but not intolerably so, not so hot as in Balkh and Qandahār and not for half so long.

Another good thing in Hindūstān is that it has unnumbered and endless workmen of every kind. There is a fixed caste (*jam'i*) for every sort of work and for every thing, which has done that work or that thing from father to son till now. Mulla Sharaf, writing in the *Zafar-nāma* about the building of Tīmūr Beg's Stone Mosque, lays stress on the fact that on it 200 stone-cutters worked, from Āzarbaijān, Fārs, Hindūstān and other countries. But 680 men worked daily on my buildings in Āgra and of Āgra stone-cutters only; while 1491 stone-cutters worked daily on my buildings in Āgra, Sīkrī, Biāna (Bayāna), Dholpur, Gwāliar and Kol. In the same way there are numberless artisans and workmen of every sort in Hindūstān. (*Memoirs*, pp. 518–20.)

The difficulties with which Bābur was now confronted cannot be better described than in his own words:

On our first coming to Āgra, there was remarkable dislike and hostility between its people and mine, the peasantry and soldiers running away in fear of our men. Delhi and Āgra excepted, not a fortified town but strengthened its defences and neither was in obedience nor submitted. Qāsim Sambhalī was in Sambhal; Nizām Khān was in Biāna; in Mewāt was Hasan Khān Mewāti himself—impious mannikin!—who was the sole leader of the trouble and mischief. Muhammad Zaitūn was in Dholpur; Tātār Khān Sarang-khānī was in Gwāliar; Husain Khān Nūhānī was in Rāprī; Qutb Khān was in Itāwa (Etawa); 'Ālam Khān (Kālpī) was in Kālpī. Qanauj and the other side of Gang (Ganges) was all held by Afghans in independent hostility, such as Nāsir Khān Nūhānī, Ma'rūf Farmūlī and a crowd of other amīrs. These had been in rebellion for three or four years before Ibrāhīm's death and when I defeated him, were holding Qanauj and the whole country beyond it. At the present time they were lying two or three marches on our side of Qanauj and had made Bihār Khān the son of Daryā Khān Nūhānī their pādshāh, under the style Sultān Muhammad. Marghūb the slave was in Mahawin [Mahāban]; he remained there, thus close, for some time but came no nearer.

It was the hot-season when we came to Āgra. All the inhabitants had run away in terror. Neither grain for ourselves nor corn for our horses was to be had. The villages, out of hostility and hatred to us, had taken to thieving and highway-robbery; there was no moving on the roads. There had been no chance since the treasure was distributed to send men in strength into the parganas and elsewhere. Moreover the year was a very hot one; violent pestilential winds struck people down in heaps together; masses began to die off.

On these accounts the greater part of the begs and best braves became unwilling to stay in Hindūstān, indeed set their faces for leaving it. It is no reproach to old and experienced begs if they speak of such matters; even if they do so, this man (Bābur) has enough sense and reason to get at what is honest or what is mutinous in their representations, to distinguish between loss and gain. But as this man had seen his task whole, for himself, when he resolved on it, what taste was there in their reiterating that things should be done differently? What recommends the expression of distasteful opinions by men of little standing? Here is a curious thing: This last time of our riding out from Kābul, a few men of little standing had just been made begs; what I looked for from them was that if I went through fire and water and came out again, they would have gone in with me unhesitatingly, and with me have come out, that wherever I went, there at my side would they be—not that they would speak against my fixed purpose, not that they would turn back from any task or great affair on which, all counselling, all consenting, we had resolved, so long as that counsel was not abandoned. Badly as these new begs behaved, Secretary Ahmadī and Treasurer Walī behaved still worse. Khwāja Kilān had done well in the march out from Kābul, in Ibrāhīm's defeat and until Āgra was occupied; he had spoken bold words and shewn ambitious views. But a few days after the capture of Āgra, all his views changed—the one zealous for departure at any price was Khwāja Kilān.

When I knew of this unsteadiness amongst (my) people, I summoned all the begs and took counsel. Said I, "There is no supremacy and grip on the world without means and resources; without lands and retainers sovereignty and command are impossible. By the labours of several years, by encountering hardship, by long travel, by flinging myself and the army into battle, and by deadly slaughter, we, through God's grace, beat these masses of enemies in order that we might take their broad lands. And now what force compels us, what necessity has arisen that we should, without cause, abandon countries taken at such risk of life? Was it for us to remain in Kābul, the sport of harsh poverty? Henceforth, let no well-wisher of mine speak of such things! But let not those turn back from going who, weak in strong persistence, have set their faces to depart!" By these words, which recalled just and reasonable views to their minds, I made them, willy-nilly, quit their fears. (*Memoirs*, pp. 523–5.)

Meanwhile, some of the Afghān chiefs set up Ibrāhīm's brother, Mahmūd, but most of them, seeing that Bābur, who had made Āgra his headquarters, had come to stay and did not, like Tamerlane, intend to withdraw, laid down their arms. While Bābur was in Kābul, Rānā Sanga of Chitor (the modern Udaipur), who was at this time recognised as head of all the Rājputs, had exchanged friendly embassies with him, and had even offered to help him against Ibrāhīm. His life had been one of constant wars, in the course of which he had defeated Sultān Mahmūd Khaljī, and captured the provinces of Bhīlsa, Sārangpur, Chanderī and Ranthambhor. He is said to have been so often wounded in battle that in addition to having eighty scars he had but one eye and one arm and was a cripple. He is said to have had at his disposal when necessary seven rajas and one hundred and four chiefs. But Bābur as emperor of Delhi and Bābur as a leader of raids from Kābul were two different people, and Rānā Sanga now declared war against him, and for the first time Bābur found himself engaged in a *jihād* or Holy War against the idolator. Humāyūn meanwhile was sent on a punitive expedition against the various amīrs in the east, who under Nāsir Khān Nūhānī and Ma'rūf Farmūlī had taken Kanauj. During this expedition Humāyūn took Jaunpur and Ghāzīpur. Gwalior was also taken by a stratagem, of which Bābur gives a vivid account. It may be mentioned that after the capture of Gwalior, Bābur had a narrow escape from death by poisoning, for which Sultān Ibrāhīm's mother was responsible. Rānā Sanga now marched on Bayāna, where Mahdī Khvāja was governor, but the troops who came out to oppose the Rānā, being unable to withstand him, turned back. The Rānā, who had now been joined by a number of powerful chiefs including Silahdi (Silāh-ud-Dīn) of Rāisen (30,000 horse) and Hasan Khān, the renegade raja of Mewāt (12,000 horse), advanced with 100,000 horse to a hill near Khānua, a village in the Bharatpur state thirty-seven miles west of Āgra. Bābur was at this moment in a highly precarious position, being practically surrounded in his camp on all sides by an enemy in possession of the open country. As he himself confesses, he was at this crisis overwhelmed by religious compunction.

He had on many occasions intended to give up wine drinking, and now he issued a *farmān* on the subject, and having disposed of all his gold and silver wine vessels he poured his wine into a well. He further vowed that he would remit the *tamgha* or stamp duty to all Muslims. As before the battle of Pānīpat, he found it necessary to speak stirring words of encouragement to his troops, who were even more dejected than their master. On 16 March, 1527, was fought the battle of Khānua. Bābur again adopted the *arāba* formation. He himself was in the centre; Chīn Tīmūr and Khusrav Kūkiltash were on the right; Humāyūn (who had returned from his successful campaign in the east), Dilāwar Khān Khānān and other Indian nobles were also on the right wing; Sayyid Mahdī Khvāja was on the left; and on the right and left were flanking parties; the artillery line was commanded by Nizām-ud-dīn 'Alī Khalīfa. The Rānā's left wing opened the battle by attacking Bābur's right, but was driven back by Chīn Tīmūr. Mustafā Rūmī, the Turkish gunner, brought forward the carts and guns from the centre of Humāyūn's division, and broke the enemy's ranks. Then followed an attack by the Rānā's right wing, which was repulsed, and finally Bābur led his centre forward. After ten hours' fighting Bābur's forces were victorious, and the Rānā took to flight. Hasan Khān Mewātī was among the slain. Sultān Mahmūd Lodī who was present at the battle escaped. After his victory over Rānā Sanga, Bābur proceeded to reduce Mewāt, and on 7 April, 1527, he entered its capital Alwar in triumph. By the end of 1527 Bābur's authority was established everywhere except in Oudh.

Meanwhile Medinī Rāi, a Rajput chief, had established himself in Chanderī on the borders of Bundelkhand and Mālwā. Here he was besieged by Bābur. The garrison on the second day gave up all hope of resistance, and having put their women to death they rushed out naked to perish, but not to be captured (29 January, 1528). Humāyūn with a large contingent, taking advantage of Bābur's promise made before the battle of Khānua that all who pleased might go on leave to Kābul, was now despatched to Badakhshān, while Bābur himself set out to punish Biban, who had repulsed the Mughul army in Oudh and captured Lucknow. Crossing the Ganges Bābur speedily defeated Biban and drove him into Bengal. Sultān Mahmūd Lodī, the brother of Ibrāhīm, had meanwhile occupied Bihār, and he now with a force of 100,000 men advanced on Benares, where he was put to flight. On 6 May, 1529, Bābur won his third great battle in India, at the junction of the Ganges and its tributary the Gogra, whence it has come to be known as the battle of the Gogra. In this engagement he was opposed by the Afghān chiefs who had taken up the cause of Sultān Mahmūd Lodī. Bābur gives a very detailed account of the campaign leading up to this battle, which reads like a diary kept from day to day. The progress of the battle itself, in which much use was made both of boats and of artillery, is, however, by no means easy to follow. As a result of this victory Bābur was joined by nearly all the Afghān chiefs and amīrs; and was able to conclude a treaty of peace with Nusrat Shāh, king of Bengal, by which he himself became sovereign of Bihār.

Humāyūn having spent a year in Badakhshān, where in obedience to his father's commands he had refrained from attempting the recapture of Samarqand, set out for Kābul and thence for Āgra. He was next sent to his *jāgīr* Sambhal. At the end of six months he was suddenly attacked by fever. This caused Bābur so much anxiety that he caused Humāyūn to be brought to Āgra. The most learned doctors were at a loss for a remedy. A famous saint, Mīr Abū Baqā, being called in to advise, said that when physicians were at a loss, the patient should give in alms the most valuable thing he had and should seek remedy from God. Bābur thereupon said: "I am the most valuable thing that Humāyūn possesses.. . .I shall make myself a sacrifice for him. May God the Creator accept it."[1] Bābur was shortly after taken ill, and Humāyūn recovered: as he lay dying, Bābur appointed Humāyūn his successor. Mīr Khalīfa, having formed a bad opinion of Humāyūn, desired to place Mahdī Khvāja, Bābur's brother-in-law, on the throne, but he changed his mind, it would seem, on account of the arrogant behaviour of the Khvāja. Bābur died in Āgra on 26 December, 1530.[2]

The Indian career of the Turkī prince Bābur did not actually begin till his capture of Lahore in 1524, and he died in 1530. It therefore took him only six years to lay the foundations of a vast empire the rulers of which, real or nominal, continued down to the middle of the nineteenth century. It is interesting to recall that his famous ancestor Tīmūr had, in 1397, invaded northern India, and entered Delhi in 1398 as a conqueror. But Tamerlane's ambitions were too great for him to treat his Indian campaign as more than a raid. That Bābur should have confined his conquering activities to northern India, after consolidating his power between the Oxus and Kashmīr, was, no doubt, partly due to the fact that he had been helped by the powerful founder of the Safavid kingdom, Shāh Isma'īl, with whom, much against his better Sunnī feelings, he had made an alliance which had lasted twenty months (A.H. 917–18—A.D. 1511–12). There could, therefore, be no question of attacking Persia, even had he been strong enough to do so. It was as lord of Kābul that he cast longing glances across the Hindu Kush.

The question naturally presents itself: how did Bābur keep such a detailed record of his own doings from the age of eleven (A.H. 899)? Not only his own doings, but those of his relations are recorded in full detail. And whence did he derive all this information, biographical and geographical? Mīrzā Haidar Dughlāt had the same

[1] *Akbar-nāma*, p. 276.

[2] *Hodivala*, p. 262.

gift: he tells us he wrote the *Tārīkh-i-Rashīdī* because the memory of the Mughuls and their Khāns—i.e. the eastern branch of the Chaghatāi—stood in danger of being altogether lost through want of a chronicler. The earlier Mongols, Chingīz and his descendants, had been fortunate in their chroniclers in their own day. It was the descendants of Tamerlane, however, Bābur, Mīrzā Haidar, Gulbadan Begam, who first among princes undertook to write autobiographies, while Humāyūn, Jahāngīr (for part of his reign) and Shāh Jahān were content to have their memoirs written by personal attendants. There are very few examples in history of a great conqueror who was also an eminent poet, though many soldiers, like Julius Caesar and Xenophon, have been men of letters. Bābur was a sufficiently good poet (in Turkī) to have become famous on that account alone, had he achieved no fame as a soldier or ruler.

In writing an epitome of the emperor Bābur's career, having in view only the part he played in the history of his times, the romantic side of this remarkable man's personal character has perforce been relegated to the background: but in conclusion a few words may be said regarding his private life.

Bābur was one of those men who are so active in mind and body that they are never idle and always find time for everything. Excepting during the three years when he was hiding in Tāshkent under the protection of the Sultān of Kāshghar he knew no rest, and he himself says towards the end of his life that he had never kept the Fast of Ramazān twice in any one place. He was pre-eminently human, and has drawn a picture of himself in his memoirs in which no attempt is made to hide either his virtues or his vices. He was a rigid Sunnī Muslim, and both orthodox and superstitious in his beliefs. When in order to please the Shiah Shāh Isma'īl he adopted the Qizilbāsh head-dress for himself and his soldiers, he showed a form of moral courage reminding one of his grandson Akbar, who while still professing Islam displayed the utmost leniency towards Hindus and Christians: and if Bābur's motive was purely political, it required no little self-reliance to face the sarcasm and derision which this head-dress provoked among the zealous Sunnīs of Transoxiana: not to mention the hatred in which the name of Shāh Isma'īl was held by reason of his cruelty towards the Sunnīs of Khurāsān.

As a soldier Bābur was, like most of his race, fearless in battle, and as a general he was a great tactician with a keen eye to detect any mistake on the part of his opponents. He was also one of the first military commanders in Asia to appreciate the value of artillery.

As a diplomatist he seems to have shown much more cunning and skill in dealing with the Afghāns than with his own people: and the manner in which he played off the rebellious amīrs of Sultān Ibrāhīm against each other was worthy of a Machiavelli.

While inheriting a savagery common to all the Mongols and

Turks, and a total disregard for human life, he was capable of great generosity in forgiving those who had behaved ill towards him. Like all his family he was strongly addicted to intemperance, though his drinking bouts were always followed by very sincere repentance. He had a love for the beauties of nature probably rare in his day, something apart from a delight in the artificial beauties of poetry, which was common to all his co-religionists whether Turks or Persians. His careful descriptions of the animals and plants of India reveal great powers of observation. These portions of his memoirs read like the notes of a peace-loving naturalist rather than those of a restless warrior.

The *Memoirs* of Bābur must be reckoned among the most enthralling and romantic works in the literature of all time. They were written in that form of Turkish known as Turkī, which was Bābur's mother-tongue. As we possess them they are not complete; all the copies known to us contain gaps from 1508 to 1519, from 1520 to 1525 and from 1529 to 1530. A more complete copy was apparently known to his cousin Mīrzā Haidar, the author of the *Tārīkh-i-Rashīdī*; but the translation into Persian made in 1589 by Khān Khānān 'Abdur-Rahīm, the son of Bairam Khān, contains the same gaps as the Haidarabad Codex, from which Mrs Annette Beveridge made her admirable English translation.

Bābur was a real poet, and apart from the incidental verses introduced in his memoirs we have from his pen a small collection of Turkī lyrics, which bear comparison with the best poetry of his day.[1] He also wrote a religious poem called the *Mubayyin*, and about two years before his death he wrote a versified rendering of the *Risāla-i-Wālidiyya*, a pious tract written by the famous Khvāja Ahrār in honour of his parents.

[1] See *Dīvān-i-Bābur Pādishāh*, edited with facsimile by E. Denison Ross, *Journal of the Asiatic Society of Bengal*, 1910. This edition was based on a unique MS. in the library of the Nawāb of Rāmpur.

CHAPTER II

HUMĀYŪN

ALTHOUGH Bābur had recognised his eldest son Humāyūn as successor to the large territory he had acquired, the new ruler's position was extremely insecure. As he lay dying Bābur had warned Humāyūn of the possibility of claims by the three other brothers and had charged him always to forgive their faults.

By force of arms the Mughuls had imposed themselves on northern India, but they had been so occupied in fighting that they had hardly begun to rule, and India was still only an outlying portion of the realm, Kābul being the proper capital and centre. Their generals were still soldiers and not administrators, and, as Bābur had said on his first conquest of Kābul, the scheme of government was still *saifī* (by the sword) not *qalamī* (by the pen). To strengthen his position Bābur had invited members of the families of Tīmūr and Chingīz freely to join him. Not a few with royal blood in their veins were possible claimants to the throne recently vacated.[1] In the occupied area were many turbulent elements excited by the century of chaos which had followed Tīmūr's invasion, and among these, especially towards the east, were many Afghāns belonging to the last dynasty which had ruled. Bābur had met and defeated the Rājputs, but had not subdued them, and they, more than the other sections of Indians in the north, had a strong national instinct. South-west of Rājputāna lay Gujarāt, where Bahādur Shāh was reviving and extending the kingdom of his predecessors.[2]

Humāyūn, taking his insecure seat on the throne four days after his father's death, assigned the westerly Punjab, Kābul and Qandahār to be governed by his brother Kāmrān, and made smaller provisions for the two younger brothers. He then proceeded early in 1531 to besiege the strong fortress of Kālinjar in Bundelkhand, which might be used as a base for attacks on the lower Dūāb. During these operations he received news that Mahmūd Lodī, brother of the late king Ibrāhīm Lodī, who had received support in Bengal, had invaded the east of his territory and taken Jaunpur. Humāyūn marched rapidly towards Jaunpur and defeated the Afghāns.[3] They were scattered for a time, but Sher Khān,[4] who was reported to have failed to support Mahmūd Lodī at the critical time and was the ablest

[1] There was even a plot in favour of Mahdī Khvāja, brother-in-law of Bābur. (*Humāyūn-nāma*, pp. 25 and 298.)

[2] See vol. III, chap. XIII.

[3] The site of the battle was probably in the Daunrūā estate, on the banks of the Sāī river, 15 miles east of Jaunpur.

[4] For Sher Khān's earlier history see chap. III.

leader among them, began a fresh concentration. In order to break this up Humāyūn despatched an army to invest the stronghold of Chunār on the Ganges south of Benares, and followed it himself. Before any results could be obtained other embarrassments led him to arrange a peace by which Sher Khān was left to continue his plans for an Afghān supremacy in the east. Kāmrān, since his father's death, had cherished hopes of gaining the whole of Bābur's territory in spite of the ample provision he had received. Leaving his brother 'Askarī in charge of Qandahār he advanced with an army to Lahore which he secured by a cunning stratagem, as the governor refused to be false to his trust. At the same time he continued to assure Humāyūn of his loyalty and actually received a further grant of territory round Hissār Fīrūza which had been Humāyūn's own governorship and for some generations to come was regarded as the holding of the Mughul heir apparent.

While his hold over his own territory was thus weakened through the claims of a treacherous brother and the open attempts of the Afghāns, Humāyūn was forced to take notice of affairs outside. Suspecting the loyalty of Muhammad Zamān Mīrzā, who was not only his brother-in-law but was also descended like himself from Tīmūr, and had been appointed by Bābur governor of Bihār, he removed him from office in 1533 and placed him in confinement at Bayāna. Muhammad Zamān escaped and offered his services to Bahādur Shāh, king of Gujarāt, while a cousin named Muhammad Sultān and his sons who had been plotting with him were seized and sentenced to be blinded. The peaceful relations which existed between Gujarāt and Āgra were broken by the refusal of Bahādur Shāh to turn away the fugitives and by the terms of the letter sent in his name to Humāyūn.[1] His continued extension of authority towards central India and Rājputāna also aroused jealousy and some alarm. Humāyūn received an application for help from the Rānā of Chitor who was in danger of being crushed by his ambitious neighbour, and although Humāyūn's religious principles would not allow him to aid an unbeliever against an enemy of his own faith, he marched to Gwalior late in 1534 and called on Bahādur Shāh to stop his enterprise against the Rānā and again demanded the fugitives. Despairing of help from Āgra the Rānā came to terms with Bahādur Shāh and Humāyūn hoped to be able to attend to his eastern possessions where Afghān intrigue was most dangerous.

Peace between Chitor and Gujarāt was, however, short, and Bahādur Shāh not only renewed his attack but also sent a strong force to resist the Mughul power. This army was commanded by Tātār Khān Lodī, whose father 'Alā-ud-dīn was one of the Afghān kings of Delhi, and had himself, after two unsuccessful attempts on the throne, been banished by Bābur to Badakhshān, and escaping

[1] See vol. III, p. 329.

thence was one of the refugees in Gujarāt. While 'Alā-ud-dīn took one force towards Kālinjar and another threatened the Punjab, Tātār Khān moved directly on Āgra. He was successful in taking Bayāna and his advance troops even raided the suburbs of Āgra.

Humāyūn now displayed better qualities of determination than hitherto. He directed his brothers Hindāl and 'Askarī who were at Āgra to attack the invaders and himself moved through eastern Mālwā to Sārangpur, receiving the capitulation of the strong fortress of Rāisen on the way. Tātār Khān's army, in spite of its initial success, did not await the Mughul forces under 'Askarī. Most of his troops abandoned him with their booty and having only a few thousand horse remaining with him he was overwhelmed and slain by 'Askarī at Mandrel. 'Alā-ud-dīn's force, threatened by Humāyūn himself, withdrew to Gujarāt, and the army which had marched towards the Punjab also returned.

When Humāyūn reached Sārangpur Chitor had not fallen, and a council was held in the Gujarāt camp to decide whether the siege should be pressed or the Mughul enemy met. It was correctly guessed that Humāyūn would not fight a Muslim king while he was engaged against an unbeliever like the Rānā, and efforts were redoubled to take the fortress. The Gujarāt artillery prevailed at last, and while the women of the city perished voluntarily in flames the remnant of the garrison hurled themselves to death against the weapons of the besiegers. As the end of the siege was approaching Humāyūn had moved on into Gujarāt territory till he reached Mandasor only 60 miles from Chitor, and once again Bahādur Shāh had to make choice of his plan of campaign. This time he rejected the advice of his most acute councillor who wished him to attack Humāyūn at once with troops elated by their recent success. He decided to remain on the defensive and rely on his superior artillery to repel the Mughuls. An entrenched camp in such a position was merely a trap. When the besieged made a sally they were easily defeated in the open field by the Mughuls even with odds in their favour, and rarely succeeded in drawing them close enough to bring them under artillery fire. As the siege continued supplies ran short and could not be replaced. The garrison was dying of starvation and Bahādur Shāh decided to escape. With a few attendants he left the camp in the night (March, 1535) and made his way to Māndū with Mallū Qādir Khān, the governor of that place, while some of the surviving troops either followed him or were led by Muhammad Zamān Mīrzā to cause revolt in the Punjab.

The tumult of departure added to the explosion of cannon made the Mughuls believe that they were about to be attacked and their forces were drawn up in readiness. As daylight appeared the truth was known and they broke into the camp and divided the spoil. A body of horse was sent in pursuit of the fugitives and Humāyūn followed it to Māndū. This vast fortress with a battlemented wall 23 miles in length stands on an isolated plateau 2079 feet above the sea. Its size and the length of its defences have frequently enabled surprise attacks to penetrate its walls, though later it held out for six months when besieged by Akbar.[1] Bahādur Shāh opened negotiations for peace in which the cession of Mālwā to Humāyūn was proposed, but while the terms were still being discussed a small body of Mughuls forced their way over an unguarded part of the walls and opened the nearest gate. Mallū Khān at once warned Bahādur Shāh, who tried to escape and meeting a Mughul force cut his way through and reached the citadel. Despairing of his ability to hold this he ordered his horses to be raised and lowered over the wall and fled to Chāmpāner[2] while the Mughul army sacked Māndū. For the time being the whole of Mālwā lay at the mercy of Humāyūn, who followed up his success by a hasty pursuit of Bahādur Shāh. As the Mughul troops reached Chāmpāner, Bahādur Shāh, after setting fire to the town, fled north to Cambay where he halted only to destroy the fleet he had prepared to combat the Portuguese, and escaped thence to Diu, evading Humāyūn by only a few hours and outstripping the force which pursued him. Humāyūn at Cambay was the first of his house to see the ocean. During his halt there his small escort had a narrow escape from being overwhelmed by the local chieftains who were tributary to Bahādur Shāh, and who planned a night attack. Though they were able to plunder the camp during the night Humāyūn had been warned of the design by an old woman of the neighbourhood whose son had been enslaved by the Mughuls and who hoped by this service to gain his release. As light appeared the marauders were attacked and driven off with great slaughter.

When Bahādur Shāh had fled from Humāyūn before Chitor, his chief artillery officer, a Turk called Rūmī Khān, had deserted to the Mughul side and had remained with Humāyūn. He was now approached by an emissary from Bahādur Shāh, who by a skilful mixture of abuse and persuasion induced him to dissuade Humāyūn from an attack on Diu. Humāyūn was convinced that the air of the seashore did not suit him and he returned to Chāmpāner which was being stoutly defended by Ikhtiyār Khān, a Gujarāt general.

Though this magnificent city had been laid in ashes after an existence of only 50 years the citadel was still intact, well equipped for a siege, and situated in difficult jungle through the concealed paths of which the people of the country could take fresh supplies. The Mughul army was not well supplied for siege operations and four months passed without any progress being made. Success was finally due to the intelligence of the emperor fortified by his personal bravery. While reconnoitring the position he saw some villagers come

[1] For a description see G. Yazdani, *Mandū*, 1929.
[2] In 22° 29′ N., 73° 32′ E.

out of the woods and as their explanations were not satisfactory he had them beaten. They then guided the Mughuls to the foot of the walls. Though these could not be breached Humāyūn at once devised a means of scaling them by driving spikes into the mortar between the stones, and on a moonlight night, while a furious attack was made on other parts of the fortress 300 men climbed the wall, Humāyūn himself being the fortieth. This unexpected attack inside the citadel, with the news that the emperor himself was in command, terrified the defenders, who allowed Humāyūn's party to capture a gate. Ikhtiyār Khān although safe in the upper fort had not sufficient munitions there to prolong his resistance and was forced to surrender on 9 August, 1535. Since its foundation Chāmpāner had been a repository for the treasure of the Gujarāt kings and Humāyūn's army was enriched by great booty. One of Bahādur Shāh's officers whom Humāyūn plied with drink, instead of putting to the torture as his counsellors advised, revealed great treasures hidden in a reservoir and well. The capture of the two celebrated forts at Māndū and Chāmpāner so delighted Humāyūn that he commemorated his victories by striking coin at these places.

While Humāyūn had thus beaten down open resistance, had taken strongholds and had assumed the outward appearance of sovereignty, he took no steps to consolidate his rule and wasted months in revelry and enjoyment of his booty. An army sent by Shāh Husain of Sind to help in his campaign against Gujarāt was diverted by a bribe offered by the governor of Pātan in the north of the kingdom who still held out for Bahādur Shāh, and it finally returned as Shāh Husain feared that his troops might be corrupted by the luxury of the imperial army. Bahādur Shāh in his retreat at Diu was approached by the chiefs in the north of his lost kingdom, who offered to remit their land revenue to him as the Mughuls were taking no steps to collect it. He commissioned 'Imād-ul-Mulk to march to Ahmadābād with full powers over collection and remission. As the new governor progressed, taking steps to restore administration, he was joined by considerable forces and was able to recruit more by using the funds he had collected. Humāyūn, though he easily fell into habits of sloth and luxury during success, could always rouse himself when danger was apparent. He marshalled forces and sending his brother 'Askarī in advance went to meet 'Imād-ul-Mulk. Although the latter was able to surprise 'Askarī at a disadvantage and plunder his camp, the Mughul army reformed and won the battle which ensued. Humāyūn then advanced to and occupied Ahmadābād and at last took steps to organise the newly acquired province. He placed 'Askarī in charge as viceroy with Hindū Beg, an experienced general, to aid him and appointed officials to other posts. His advisers pressed him in view of the disturbances and rebellion which were taking part in the east of his realm to restore Gujarāt to Bahādur Shāh. So far was he from taking this sound advice that he planned to attack Diu where Bahādur Shāh was sheltering.

Mālwā had been left in such haste, with no arrangements for the proper government of the province, that it had been invaded by former officials and the Mughul troops had been driven to Ujjain. Humāyūn decided to return to Māndū which had greatly attracted him, and his arrival there was sufficient for the time to quell opposition. His departure from Gujarāt was, however, the signal for disaster in that tract; Bahādur Shāh still had a fleet, and his people held one or two ports on the coast. With help from the Portuguese and a body of African slaves he was able to re-establish a stronger footing and took town after town. There was no master mind to direct the sending of reinforcements and 'Askarī showed more disposition to call in troops to ensure his own safety than to help his subordinates. Moreover, detachments of Gujarāt forces left scattered in the north and east when Bahādur Shāh abandoned Chitor were now coming together. Ghazanfar, who was a foster brother of 'Askarī, deserted after being confined for a rude jest at the viceroy and offered to disclose to Bahādur Shāh full details of the Mughul position at Ahmadābād, which he described as so precarious that 'Askarī would fly if attacked. The local chiefs in Gujarāt, who had found no reason to prefer the new rulers, also urged their former king to return, promising him their assistance.

While Bahādur Shāh was rallying his former subjects, collecting troops and approaching Ahmadābād, his opponent 'Askarī began to lose heart. No help was to be expected from Humāyūn, and a section of 'Askarī's advisers urged him to declare himself independent of his brother in the hope that such a measure would be popular in the locality and an encouragement to the troops. Bahādur Shāh had arrived within a few miles of Ahmadābād and the Mughul army moved out to meet him. Although 'Askarī was not prepared to set himself up against Humāyūn he was convinced that retreat was necessary, and his counsellors planned to take what treasure was left in Chāmpāner and to make for Āgra where they still hoped to persuade 'Askarī to assume the royal title. After a bombardment which nearly led Bahādur Shāh to execute Ghazanfar, as he had foretold no opposition, the Mughuls abandoned their camp and even their private baggage and hastened towards Chāmpāner. Their flight encouraged Bahādur Shāh to pursue them rapidly and even to attack the rear-guard. This, however, turned on the Gujarāt forces with such bravery that the Mughuls were able to reach the Māhī river, and to cross it, though not without loss owing to the hastiness of their flight. Thirty miles beyond it lay Chāmpāner where 'Askarī hoped to secure treasure and supplies. In this he was disappointed, as Tārdī Beg, the governor, was faithful to Humāyūn, to whom he had already sent news of the plan for 'Askarī's independence. Accordingly, while he refreshed the troops he gave no access to the fort and in reply to demands for its contents urged that he must await Humāyūn's orders. Hindered in their plans the officers of the army now proposed to seize Tārdī Beg by stratagem, to take the treasure, and to proclaim 'Askarī. Tārdī Beg, however, evaded capture and bade them move. As their camp still surrounded the fort he used his artillery and drove them off towards Āgra. News of their departure drew on Bahādur Shāh, who had halted at the river. Tārdī Beg, either on instructions from Humāyūn or unwilling in the circumstances to stand a siege, then carried off as much of the treasure as he could to Māndū where he was praised for his bravery by the emperor. Thus ended for the time the Mughul occupation of Gujarāt which had lasted barely more than a year (1535–6).

Impressed by the fuller news which Tārdī Beg was able to give him Humāyūn was convinced of the necessity for action to save the centre of his precarious rule. He hastily left Māndū and made for Āgra through Chitor territory where he met the disorganised force of 'Askarī. It was not a suitable time for recriminations and punishment of disaffection. A sterner character might have swept aside a father's dying injunctions, but Humāyūn knew that during his idle sojourn in Mālwā rebellion had broken out in the eastern provinces. A fratricidal struggle would end all his hopes of restoring peace. He therefore affected forgiveness and even rewarded the plotters, before he marched with them to Āgra. Very soon after his departure from Mālwā that province was seized by Mallū Khān who had once been in the service of the kings of Mālwā, and later governor after the annexation by Gujarāt.[1] Mughul domination in western India thus ceased entirely.

In the eastern provinces it was also becoming insecure. Muhammad Sultān, who had been confined, with the additional sentence of blinding, when he revolted with his cousin Muhammad Zamān Mīrzā, had evaded the operation and later made his escape from prison. He then established himself beyond the Ganges at Bilgrām, a few miles north of Kanauj, which he also took, while one of his sons secured the country along the river as far as Mānikpur and another marched on Jaunpur. The danger of losing a rich province led Hindāl, the youngest brother of Humāyūn, who had been left in charge at Āgra, to proceed against the rebels. He soon retook Kanauj, and though his crossing there was opposed he discovered a ford higher up the river and passing over it unobserved met Muhammad Sultān and defeated him before his sons could rejoin their father. He then pursued the flying rebels as far as Ajodhya and halted as he felt himself unable to attack the rebel whose forces had been strengthened by the recall of his sons from their various enterprises. The deadlock was relieved by news that Humāyūn was

[1] See vol. IV, p. 369.

approaching Āgra on his return from Mālwā, and Muhammad Sultān Mīrzā decided that his best chance of success was to fight before the emperor's forces arrived. In the battle which ensued the rebels fared the worse and being a collection of mercenaries with no common bond except the hope of success they lost heart and began to desert. Muhammad Sultān himself fled with his sons far into Bengal and Hindāl was able to occupy Jaunpur, where he stayed till Humāyūn arrived at Āgra and then joined him.

When Humāyūn had made his peace with Sher Khān after his fruitless siege of Chunār, so that he might be free to pursue his expedition against Gujarāt he had taken with him by way of guarantee a son of Sher Khān variously known as Qutb Khān or 'Abdur-Rashīd with a small force of Afghāns. The alliance was short and Qutb Khān had deserted with his followers to join his father. And while the emperor was engaged in what did not amount to more than military promenades, or was sitting still to enjoy the temporary gains of his enterprises, Sher Khān had consolidated his hold on south Bihār without the slightest opposition by Mughul forces,[1] whose able commander Sultān Junaid Barlās was dead. Humāyūn after his return to Āgra remained there for a wasted year, at times meditating the recovery of Gujarāt and Mālwā, where he had an offer of help from the king of Ahmadnagar, but usually occupied with the pleasures of social life, which were always apt to distract him from serious affairs. It was not till the rainy season of 1537 had set in that he started out to crush or at least check Sher Khān, having made some attempt to settle the administration of the provinces he still held. His naturally forgiving disposition, aided by the persuasion of his sister, led him on the way to accept the submission of her husband Muhammad Zamān, who after his unsuccessful attempt to rouse the Punjab had also failed to seize the throne of Gujarāt after the death of Bahādur Shāh.[2] Travelling by boat along the Jumna and Ganges, Humāyūn reached the strong fortress of Chunār which he besieged. This ancient castle, founded on a steep rock jutting into the Ganges, was built by the Hindus and strengthened by successive Muslim rulers. It had come into Sher Khān's possession through his marriage to a daughter of a governor and was held for him at this time by his son Qutb Khān. As Humāyūn approached Qutb Khān withdrew part of his forces to the forest-covered hills in the neighbourhood from which he could harass the Mughuls. A siege of several months ensued during which Rūmī Khān, the Turkish gunner who had deserted from the Gujarāt army to join Humāyūn, made many unsuccessful attempts to force an entry. Finally he obtained certain information about the state of the defences by stratagem. An African slave possessed of some ability and willing to endure hardship was savagely flogged in the Mughul camp and then managed to enter

[1] See chap. III, p. 50. [2] Vol. III, p. 334.

the fort, where he showed his wounds and offered to help the garrison by advice on their defence in revenge for the treatment he had received. He was thus allowed to inspect the fortifications, and escaping after a few days was able to tell Rūmī Khān where to direct his fire. A floating battery was moved close to the fort and a breach made. Though the first assault was driven back the garrison, seeing the battery being repaired for further work, lost heart and yielded under a promise of amnesty, but this was broken by one of the Mughul leaders who had the hands of several hundred gunners struck off. Rūmī Khān who was appointed commandant for his services held his post for only a few days, when he died suddenly, probably poisoned at the instance of jealous rivals.

As an isolated military exploit the capture of Chunār was notable, but it commanded no land routes and the time occupied in its reduction was wasted. Sher Khān, having strengthened his position in Bihār while Humāyūn was in western India, had advanced into Bengal. He was held up for a time at the pass of Teliyāgarhī by the forces of Ghiyās-ud-dīn Mahmūd of Bengal, but finally compelled him to retreat to his capital at Gaur. During the blockade Mahmūd sought help from Humāyūn and receiving none fled by boat to Hājīpur and the city was taken soon after. Pursued by Sher Khān's troops Mahmūd barely escaped with his life and reached Humāyūn's camp severely wounded. Humāyūn, after moving the short distance from Chunār to Benares and halting there, had at last made up his mind to prevent Sher Khān from acquiring further territory. He therefore began his march eastwards and met Mahmūd near the confluence of the Son and Ganges (1538). Even now, though he knew that Sher Khān had seized the capital and treasure of Bengal, he first sent an envoy to Sher Khān offering him a governorship near his home if he would surrender his new gains. When the envoy after some delay returned he brought the news that Sher Khān was already removing his booty to the hills of south Bihār. The rainy season having set in Humāyūn's officers suggested a halt until the country could be more easily traversed but the emperor accepted the suggestion of Mahmūd that it was best to attack before Sher Khān had consolidated his power. Accordingly the Mughul forces advanced into a trap devised by the strategy of Sher Khān. When they reached the difficult pass at Teliyāgarhī they found it strongly defended by Jalāl Khān, a son of Sher Khān. Halting to reconnoitre they were attacked by Jalāl Khān, who had orders from his father to delay the advance till the treasure was secured, and who observed that the Mughul forces were carelessly disposed. He inflicted considerable loss and drove the van back on the main army at Kahalgāon.[1] A heavy storm which sank Humāyūn's barge and flooded the country prevented advance for several days. When a scouting

[1] Colgong in 25° 16′ N. and 87° 14′ E.

party was able to move it was discovered that Jalāl Khān, who had now received news of his father's safe arrival in the fastnesses of south Bihār, had abandoned the defence. Sher Khān had in fact gained by stratagem the fort of Rohtās as a place of refuge for his family and treasure now that Chunār was lost.

While the emperor was at Kahalgāon Mahmūd received news that two of his sons had been killed by the Afghāns, and still suffering from his wounds he died from the effects of this last shock. Humāyūn now pressed on to seize what he hoped would be a rich prize. But Gaur, though entered without further opposition, was a desolate place with corpses still lying in the streets, and the rich granaries which Mahmūd had promised him were wasted. In spite of these warnings of the vanity of his hopes, Humāyūn liked the attractive fertility of the place and gave it the name of Jannatābād, or abode of Paradise, on the coins he struck to commemorate his success. The former government having been destroyed there was no opposition in the country-side to his officers or to his parcelling out the districts among his followers. Once more reaction set in after an apparently successful enterprise, and the whole force from emperor to private soldier devoted itself to ease and pleasure.

Gaur is about 350 miles east of Benares which was the nearest place really within the Mughul occupation. To secure communications and supplies Humāyūn left his brother Hindāl on the north bank of the Ganges, neglecting all precaution on the south, where the level alluvial plain soon meets the Kaimur range and its eastern extension. In these hills covered with thorny jungle and hence known as Jhārkhand, Sher Khān found a convenient base from which to develop his plan of cutting off Humāyūn from his capital. Hindāl soon deserted his post in north Bihār and there were grounds for suspecting his loyalty, while Sher Khān rapidly overran the south as far as the river, and crossing it took Benares. He sent his son Jalāl Khān to besiege Jaunpur, arrested and imprisoned the families of the leading men in the district, and invested Chunār. Though the governor of Jaunpur still held the city, reinforcements which arrived from Oudh were roughly handled by Jalāl Khān owing to the rashness of their leader.

Humāyūn's officers, who for a time had successfully concealed from him the serious events which were taking place, were now alarmed. He himself realised that further delay would entail complete loss of his position, and he was spurred by finding that the officer whom he designated to hold Bengal while he attempted to cut his way through Sher Khān's forces regarded such promotion as equivalent to a sentence of death. Delay had once more placed him in the unfavourable position of a campaign during the rainy season and as his force laboured through the adhesive mud of the Ganges valley in 1539, he received news that his vanguard had been taken in the town of Monghyr and its leader captured. In doubt as to the best method of advance he offered through his brother 'Askarī to grant any boons to those who could suggest suitable plans. 'Askarī would have asked for money, silks, slaves and eunuchs, but the officers of the army, impressed by their critical situation and perhaps less corrupted by the recent period of sensuality and luxury, were content with rank, and better pay for themselves and their troops. When 'Askarī advanced he found that Sher Khān had not only gained the victories already reported, but had also sent troops as far as Kanauj and had styled himself Shāh or King. Humāyūn now joined 'Askarī on the north bank of the Ganges opposite Monghyr, and would have been wise to pursue his march on that side. Accepting, however, the advice of an unworthy favourite against that of more experienced and reliable officers, he crossed to the south bank, which was the more usual route. When the Mughul army reached the confluence of the Son and Ganges the Afghān forces of Sher Khān were in sight, and the great gun made by Rūmī Khān for the siege of Chunār was taken by them in the boat which was conveying it up the river. So far only slight opposition had been met with and the army was able to reach Chausa, a short distance from the Karamnāsa which divides Bihār from the territory of Benares.

Here it was necessary to halt in view of the uncertainty as to Sher Khān's exact position. His near approach was certain and he had in fact withdrawn his troops from the siege of Jaunpur and arrived near the western bank of the river as Humāyūn reached the eastern. Once again Humāyūn rejected the sound advice of his officers who pointed out that his troops were that day comparatively fresh after a short march, while Sher Khān's cavalry had ridden many miles. An immediate attack might have given him victory. But he preferred his favourite's plan merely to cross the river and postpone the struggle. The delay favoured Sher Khān, who set about fortifying his camp, knowing that the Mughul army would deteriorate and was already weakened by its long march and absence of the stimulus of success.

From his brothers Humāyūn could rely on no help. Hindāl had abandoned his post on the line of communications when Humāyūn advanced into Bengal, and was living in the palace at Āgra where he enjoyed the outward forms of power without using them for the benefit of the state. But while his immediate advisers traded on his youth and inexperience other officers saw more clearly the dangers which threatened. Faqr 'Alī, the governor of Delhi, with difficulty persuaded Hindāl to mobilise the troops available at Āgra and to move them east. He also visited Yādgār Nāsir at Kālpī lower down the Jumna and planned a concentration in southern Oudh which would threaten Sher Khān's designs on Jaunpur. These wise designs were, however, ruined by the arrival at Kanauj of Mughul officers who had abandoned Humāyūn in Bengal, including Zāhid Beg, who had declined to remain there as governor. They found Nūr-ud-dīn Muhammad, who was in charge of Kanauj, favourable to their disloyal proposals though he was married to Humāyūn's sister. Offering their services to Hindāl they at once advanced to Kol ('Alīgarh), where they would be in a position to join Hindāl or to move farther west to Kāmrān in the Punjab if Hindāl did not meet their wishes. Hindāl, though he received their message graciously, was not yet prepared to declare his own independence and despatched news of their arrival to Yādgār Mīrzā. Before it reached its destination the rebels informed Hindāl that while they were prepared to give him support if he would stand forth as emperor they would join Kāmrān if he declined. Hindāl now decided to revolt, but was for a few days held back by the remonstrances of Shaikh Phūl,[1] whom Humāyūn sent from Gaur on first hearing of Hindāl's departure from his post. The Shaikh, like his more celebrated brother Muhammad Ghaus, was a renowned religious teacher and was Humāyūn's own spiritual adviser. His message of remonstrance accompanied by offers of forgiveness and affection seemed at first likely to recall Hindāl to allegiance. Orders were issued to equip and despatch forces to raise the siege of Jaunpur. Unfortunately Nūr-ud-dīn arrived while these measures were being expedited and he was able to destroy the whole effect of the Shaikh's mission, and Hindāl was persuaded once more to accept the support of the rebel nobles, for which they demanded the sacrifice of Shaikh Phūl as he had caused Hindāl to break his former promises to them. They hoped that Hindāl, involved in such a disgraceful crime, would be irretrievably separated from Humāyūn, whom they hated and despised. A frivolous charge of conspiracy with Sher Khān[2] was laid and the Shaikh was executed under the orders of Nūr-ud-dīn. Such a crime revolted the ladies of the palace and all officers who still remained faithful to Humāyūn. It marked indeed the destruction of Hindāl's ambitious designs, for when he advanced on Delhi instead of marching to assist the emperor, Yādgār Nāsir and Faqr 'Alī forestalled him by hasty marches and reached that city before he arrived. While Hindāl was unsuccessfully besieging Delhi Kāmrān arrived from the Punjab. Humāyūn's generosity had placed him in a commanding position which he had improved by successful expeditions. The capture of Qandahār completed his domination over practically the whole of Afghānistān and the Punjab. He now moved towards Humāyūn's territory and Hindāl, uncertain as to his intentions, abandoned the siege of Delhi and withdrew to Āgra. If Kāmrān had really exerted himself and pressed on to attack Sher Khān it is possible that the emperor might have come out of his difficulties with some success. But although Kāmrān was persuaded to leave Delhi untouched and to follow Hindāl to Āgra his

[1] Buhlūl, according to some writers.
[2] He was said to have secretly collected military stores; *Humāyūn-nāma*, p. 135.

intentions were completely selfish. On Kāmrān's approach Hindāl withdrew to his own government at Alwar, but soon was persuaded to offer his submission, together with the rebel officers who were almost his sole adherents. The brothers did indeed set out as if to march to Humāyūn's help, but the ambition of Kāmrān and the weakness of Hindāl made them yield to the suggestion of the nobles that if Sher Khān defeated Humāyūn the empire would fall to his brother and that if the emperor won he could be persuaded to forgive them. So after a few marches they turned back to Āgra just as Humāyūn's affairs reached a crisis.

He was indeed in a critical position, having missed his first opportunity to engage in battle before Sher Khān was ready. During more than two months of scorching weather he had lain in an open camp and now the rainy season had arrived which made military tactics difficult. Before him was the strongly entrenched camp of the Afghāns; on his right flank lay the Ganges, its stream swelling as the snows melted in the Himālayas and the monsoon rains added to its volume; on the left were the hills with Sher Khān's stronghold of Rohtās. No help was to be expected from his brothers and after some fruitless skirmishing he made overtures for peace. Sher Khān at first replied that while the Mughul army wished for peace the emperor had made war. He himself also desired peace but his army was for fighting. Later he sent his own spiritual adviser who entered on negotiations, the terms of which are variously stated. Humāyūn was to give up Bihār and, according to some accounts, Bengal and also the prized fortress of Chunār but was to retain sovereignty, as shown by the right to strike coin. With their affairs settled to outward appearance the Mughul forces were negligently disposed, and Sher Khān had beaten off a Hindu ally who was supporting Humāyūn. Seizing his opportunity for destroying his opponent Sher Khān sent a force across the Karamnāsa as if to occupy Bihār and secretly instructed his main army to attack the Mughul camp in two places and also to prevent escape across the Ganges. Their surprise was complete and the attack was well developed before Humāyūn was awake (26 June, 1539). He sprang on a horse and collected a small guard, endeavouring to save his empress, but was unable to reach the tents and would have been killed but for his own personal bravery. The royal harem, crowded with fugitive wives of Mughul officers, was captured and protected by Sher Khān, while Humāyūn, attempting to cross the Ganges on horseback, was forced to use the inflated skin offered him by a water-carrier when he had lost his seat. The rout was complete and the Mughul army practically destroyed.

Exulting in his victory Sher Khān related that it had been foretold in a dream the night before, and he promised a safe-conduct to the ladies of the Mughul court, a promise which he honoured later. While Humāyūn and 'Askarī made their way with difficulty to Āgra, Sher

Khān advanced into Bengal and there defeated the governor left by Humāyūn and scattered his small force completely. While he was thus engaged the four brothers had come together. Humāyūn either through a sense of the weakness of his own position or through genuine fraternal love had forgiven, at once, Kāmrān's failure to come to his help and, after a formal rebuke, Hindāl's open rebellion. He still hoped to defeat Sher Khān and refused to accept Kāmrān's offer, prompted by ambitious and selfish aims, to lead the fresh troops from the Punjab against the enemy. Kāmrān, seeing the failure of his design to become the master of Hindūstān, wished to return to the Punjab where his rule was undisputed, and in spite of Humāyūn's opposition was at last able to depart owing to ill-health which he attributed openly to the climate of Āgra, but secretly believed was due to poison administered by Bābur's widows at the instigation of Humāyūn.

Sher Khān, having now consolidated his position in Bengal, returned along the north bank of the Ganges and felt himself strong enough to attack the Mughuls. A preliminary expedition led by his son Qutb Khān against Yādgār Mīrzā, who still held Kālpī, was a failure and Qutb Khān lost his life. Excited by this success, Humāyūn advanced early in 1540 from Āgra towards the Ganges and Sher Khān retreated across it. The Mughul army though probably twice the size of Sher Khān's was no longer the equal of Bābur's trained forces. Many of its best soldiers had perished in the fruitless expedition to Bengal. As the force drew near the enemy it was abandoned by numbers of experienced leaders, especially those who had joined from Kāmrān's troops. An exception was that of Mīrzā Haidar Dughlāt, a first cousin of Bābur, who had been greatly trusted by Kāmrān and had been left by him in charge of Lahore when he made his successful raid on Qandahār. Both the brothers sought to retain his services and he finally decided to serve Humāyūn, who had treated him as a brother, in the honest belief that if Sher Khān were not defeated he would drive all the Mughuls, including Kāmrān, out of India. The two armies lay facing each other near Kanauj with the broad bed of the Ganges between. As defections continued it was clear that Humāyūn must fight or would find himself a leader without an army. Accordingly the river was crossed and small engagements took place. Before any general battle had occurred the rainy season began unduly early and the Mughul camp in the low land near the river was flooded. Mīrzā Haidar suggested a bold manœuvre to mask a change to a better position near the enemy. This was difficult to carry out as the camp was thronged with many thousands of followers and the army would be an easy prey if attacked during the confusion of a move. On 17 May, 1540, the Mughul artillery was sent to the front and the guns and wagons were chained together, so that the camp followers could march behind their protection if an attack was made. Sher Khān moved out his forces against them, while the Mughuls were still in confusion with their numerous non-combatants pressing on behind the guns in such masses that the chains were broken. The leaders were incapable and cowardly and many of them fled for their lives as they saw the Afghān troops arrive. Humāyūn with his usual personal bravery tried to rally his men, but was forced to fly. Mīrzā Haidar laments that 40,000 men in armour fled before 10,000 without a single cannon being fired. A few miles behind them lay the river in which many perished, encumbered by their armour. Humāyūn crossed with difficulty on an elephant but only a few[1] of the thousand men immediately accompanying him succeeded in escaping. As the small band rode towards Āgra it was attacked by Chauhān Thākurs at Bhongāon[2] and the refusal of 'Askarī to help in chastising the assailants moved Humāyūn's wrath. At Āgra, the capital, there was no chance of a rally. So great was their distress that Humāyūn, who had lost a daughter after the battle of Chausa, discussed with Hindāl the question of killing their female relations to avoid capture by the Afghāns, but was dissuaded and Hindāl conducted them to Lahore, often having to beat off attacks by the villagers on the route. The emperor's small party rode in confusion towards Delhi till the news that a party of Afghāns was following roused Humāyūn to instil some order into his small following. After a couple of days' halt at Delhi he hurried on to Lahore, forced to cross rivers swollen by rain without the help of boats. Close behind them came the Afghāns, who occupied Āgra and Delhi without opposition. At Lahore all four brothers met, Hindāl and 'Āskarī having visited the headquarters of their charges on the way to collect what treasure could be recovered. Even in the presence of imminent danger from the Afghāns concord was impossible. With Humāyūn driven out of Hindūstān Kāmrān saw that he was likely to have to give up his own possessions in the Punjab and Afghānistān, and the danger of this made him disinclined to join in a hazardous resistance to Sher Khān which might involve the waste of his own resources.

As Sher Khān overran the Punjab the need for action increased. Humāyūn sent him a request to allow Sirhind to be the boundary and received a contemptuous warning that he should withdraw to Kābul. Kāmrān hoped that he could at least maintain his hold on the west if he held the rugged tribal country between India and Afghānistān. Humāyūn, while brave in tactical affairs, failed himself to produce any strategical plan. He was pressed by Mīrzā Haidar to withdraw to the Punjab hills and shelter in Kashmīr, while Hindāl and Yādgār Mīrzā suggested a movement through Sind to reconquer Gujarāt from which Hindūstān might be again invaded. While the brothers wrangled, Kāmrān treacherously sent

[1] The manuscripts read variously *hasht* = eight, or *shast* = sixty.
[2] In 27° 17′ N. and 79° 14′ E.

a message to offer his assistance to Sher Khān if he were left alone. An ambassador from Sher Khān was received as if he had come to the court of Humāyūn, while secret negotiations continued. Sher Khān crossed the Beās and the brothers abandoned Lahore in a rout described as being as confused as the Day of Resurrection. The treachery of Kāmrān was now so well known in the Mughul camp that Humāyūn was urged to have him killed, but the memory of Bābur's dying wishes was still too fresh on his mind to allow him to agree to fratricide. He determined to adopt Mīrzā Haidar's scheme for the conquest of Kashmīr and moved in that direction. Before he had advanced far a threatening movement by Kāmrān was reported and his army, disgusted with the treachery of the latter, was eager to oppose him by arms. Humāyūn in his anxiety to avoid a contest which could only have weakened the Mughul strength refused to show a hostile appearance to his brother, and the meeting was thus peaceful. It ended with the departure of Kāmrān for his governorship at Kābul accompanied by his brother 'Askarī. But Humāyūn's clemency convinced Hindāl that his brother was wanting in the firmness which at that time was necessary for one who sought to rule in India. And just as Kāmrān had pursued his self-seeking aims by leaving the emperor when most in need of help, so Hindāl abandoned him and set out on a vain expedition to pursue his scheme of conquering Sind and then Gujarāt again and making it a base for further attacks on Hindūstān. In this expedition he was joined by still more adherents from Humāyūn's shrinking forces.

Mīrzā Haidar's plan for capturing Kashmīr was sound in every way. His previous experience in 1533, when he had raided the country as a general of the king of Kāshghar,[1] had shown him what little resistance could be expected in a country torn by faction, and he knew and pointed out that a determined force holding it could repel any army of men from the plains, hampered by the difficulty of travel and the absence of supplies. He was, moreover, sure of support from one of the parties in the state. It had been arranged that he should enter Kashmīr from Naushahra and he marched in advance of Humāyūn. When the emperor followed him and reached Bhera, where he hoped to obtain the assistance of the local governor, he found that Kāmrān had already preceded him and forestalled his hopes. Once more he was urged to assert himself and brush Kāmrān from his path, but refused as he had done at Lahore. A proposal that he should retreat through Kābul to Badakhshān was rejected by Kāmrān, whose treacherous nature led him to suspect that Humāyūn might dispossess him from Kābul and advance no farther. The road to Naushahra being blocked and it being impossible for Humāyūn to stay between an envious and unscrupulous brother on one hand and the victorious Sher Khān who was pressing on from Lahore, he

[1] Vol. III, p. 287.

decided to abandon the hope of Kashmīr and to follow Hindāl to Sind (end of 1540). He had hardly started when again a collision with Kāmrān was imminent. Their forces met in a defile of the Salt Range near Khushāb, at the end of which the roads towards Sind and Kābul diverged, and a dispute arose as to which should pass through it first. Kāmrān's thinly veiled intention of assuming the headship of the family appeared more clearly than ever when he asserted his own right of precedence, and for once Humāyūn's pride was stung and battle seemed inevitable. It was averted only by the remonstrances of a man of saintly reputation in the train of Kāmrān.

Thus began a wearying exile which lasted for nearly 15 years and was endured only by the greatest fortitude and perseverance, though it was constantly prolonged by Humāyūn's inability to command respect and faithful allegiance. Before he could join Hindāl news came that the country round Multān, which had been ceded to Bābur by the Arghūn ruler of Sind, was in a state of anarchy. Hindāl's force had met and overwhelmed a small escort of Afghāns accompanying Kāmrān's messenger to Sher Khān, but was unable to face the Baloch raiders who had overrun the country and cut off what scanty supplies were available. Hindāl was thus compelled to return and the brothers met, but were almost immediately faced with the danger of attack by Khavāss Khān, an Afghān general who had taken Multān and was searching for them, but retired to headquarters as he could get no news of them. While Humāyūn thus marched or lay in great discomfort in the most inhospitable part of the Indian plain his faithful general Mīrzā Haidar had carried out the plan of seizing Kashmīr with a minute force, and was so successful in establishing himself that he ruled till his death in action ten years later.

Humāyūn's first experiences in Sind illustrate his lack of skill in the conduct of a difficult campaign, against an opponent so able as Shāh Husain, the ruler of the country. Making his toilsome journey down the Indus he reached Rohrī on the left bank not far from the island fortress of Bhakkar. Shāh Husain had strengthened the garrison and bidden the governor lay waste the country round so that the Mughul forces would be unable to obtain supplies. This was easily effected as population was scanty and cultivation sparse and only possible where land could be irrigated from the river. To relieve the pressure of want Humāyūn divided his troops, himself remaining in fairly comfortable quarters to prosecute the siege, while Hindāl and Yādgār advanced towards Sehwān where they hoped to obtain better supplies. In reply to the emperor's summons to surrender the fortress the governor replied that he was subordinate to Shāh Husain and could obey only him, though he sent a small supply of grain to relieve the immediate wants of Humāyūn's camp. Envoys were then despatched to Shāh Husain, who detained them for months by holding out promises he had no intention of fulfilling. He thus reduced the

Mughul forces to such extreme want that many of the soldiers killed their horses and camels for food. When the emperor at last made up his mind to recall the envoys Shāh Husain sent with them an ambassador with the cunning suggestion that Humāyūn should occupy a tract described as rich which lay east of Sind and would prove a convenient place from which Gujarāt could be conquered. Though Humāyūn was easily dazzled by this prospect, his followers realised that it wanted in substance, as the inhabitants of the area named had never been subdued by Shāh Husain and were not likely to allow the Mughuls to occupy their country. Humāyūn's delay at Bhakkar and the indulgence of hopes which were patently empty in the eyes of all his advisers disgusted Hindāl, who had long been demanding permission to attack Sehwān, a richer portion of Sind lying south of Bhakkar, and had some intentions of deserting his brother and capturing Qandahār. When finally Hindāl was allowed to move against Sehwān Shāh Husain had strengthened its garrison and repeated his scheme of destroying the villages and cultivation in its neighbourhood. To ensure his brother's good faith Humāyūn marched to join him and while in his camp nearly caused an irrevocable breach by insisting on marrying (in 1541) Hamīda Begam, the daughter of Hindāl's spiritual guide, who afterwards became the mother of the emperor Akbar. The girl was probably in love with somebody else and herself displayed the strongest objection to the match. Sickness breaking out in the camp, Humāyūn left it to return to Bhakkar, and Hindāl in disgust abandoned his task and left for Qandahār, sending messages to Yādgār Mīrzā to invite him to follow. Once more Humāyūn's vacillation had brought him into serious trouble and to secure Yādgār Mīrzā's adherence he made promises of considerable grants to be conferred when he regained power. Realising too late that Shāh Husain had been merely playing with him, he decided to attack Shāh Husain's capital city Tatta near the mouth of the Indus, and set out on this enterprise. But on the way he was again persuaded to turn aside and besiege Sehwān, a hopeless task in view of the defensive plans which had been carried out. As he entered on this futile operation Shāh Husain, judging that the time had arrived for a more active policy, collected a fleet of boats and advanced up the river. Humāyūn's unwieldy force, swollen by fugitives of his own race who had fled from the Afghān supremacy in Hindūstān, was driven to great extremities by the lack of food. An appeal made to Hindāl for assistance was disregarded. Yādgār Mīrzā, who was also directed to attack Shāh Husain, had already been seduced by that astute monarch, and had received favourably a suggestion that he should himself become emperor by conquering Gujarāt with help from Sind and might have the reversion of Sind itself by marrying Shāh Husain's daughter. Thus deprived of any hope of assistance and alarmed by the proximity of Shāh

Husain, Humāyūn gave up his siege operations so suddenly that his retreat towards Bhakkar was almost a rout, and much loss was experienced on the march. With the connivance of Yādgār Mīrzā all the boats on the river near Bhakkar had been seized or sunk by Sind officers and on his arrival at the bank Humāyūn was forced to kill cattle and prepare skin floats for rafts to make the crossing. He now perceived that Yādgār Mīrzā was no longer faithful and his followers, already reduced in number, began to desert either to Yādgār Mīrzā or to more distant supporters. When finally Yādgār Mīrzā proposed to attack Humāyūn openly, and was only dissuaded after he had actually left his camp, the emperor's despair almost impelled him to resign all hope and withdraw to a religious exile in Mecca. As a last resource he accepted an invitation from Rājā Māldeo of Mārwār, who promised him assistance, and made his way to Rājputāna, suffering great privations on the march.

The raja's object in offering help to Humāyūn is doubtful. Since the battle of Khānua the Rājputs had had no desire for friendship with the Mughuls. But Sher Khān's success had increased the possible danger of further incursions into Rājputāna and Māldeo appears to have hoped that aid to Humāyūn, who had shown himself generous, if not mighty, would be repaid. From the miserable handful of refugees who were now painfully approaching his capital he saw that he could expect nothing, and he therefore decided to seize and give up Humāyūn to Sher Khān. Humāyūn discovered this intention through his spies and again retreated, suffering even greater hardships than before. On one occasion the small band of fugitives had to march for more than three days without water as the wells had been filled in or destroyed. Their sufferings in the Indian desert at the hottest period of the year were terrible and many died of thirst. So reduced in circumstances was the emperor himself that he had to play a disgraceful trick on his own few officers by having their baggage searched in their absence in order to obtain a few presents for the Rānā of 'Umarkot, who gave him shelter on his arrival there.

For a time prosperity seemed about to dawn, as the Rānā offered help to conquer the south-eastern part of Sind, which had once belonged to his ancestors. An expedition started in November, 1542, and a few days later news came that the empress, who had remained at 'Umarkot, had borne a son who later became the emperor Akbar. So poor had Humāyūn become that he had to borrow from his brother the means to provide a meagre feast for his nobles. While the attack on what was a rich area succeeded at first it was soon met by Shāh Husain with his powerful resources of diplomacy and arms. The arrogance of the Mughuls towards Hindus also operated in his favour, and Humāyūn lost the support of his new allies. Though he was now joined by Bairam Khān, one of the best and most faithful soldiers of the time, who had escaped from Sher Khān with great difficulty, his staff had decreased, and a fresh disaster impelled him to make up his mind to risk all on a final decisive battle. Shāh Husain, though stronger in every way, preferred negotiation and offered Humāyūn passage through his country to Qandahār with supplies and money for the journey. The terms were accepted and the emperor departed (1543).

Any hopes he had entertained of safety in his brother's territory were soon destroyed. Kāmrān assumed the royal title, and struck coin in his own name at Kābul and Qandahār, invaded Badakhshān, as the ruler of that tract still recognised Humāyūn, and when his governor at Qandahār made over that place to Hindāl on his flight from Sind, he besieged the town and on obtaining its surrender despatched Hindāl as prisoner to Kābul and appointed 'Askarī as ruler in his place. He even tried to establish relationship with Shāh Husain by proposing to marry the Shāh's daughter. With these unfavourable prospects before him Humāyūn entered on a difficult wintry march in no way rendered easier by the transport and guides whom Shāh Husain had sent with him. Many of the camels supplied were untrained and threw off their loads or riders at the start; while the guides misled the troops. 'Askarī set the defences of Qandahār in order and wrote to the Baloch chiefs to arrest the emperor, who had a narrow escape and was obliged to abandon his infant son to the precarious mercy of faithless brothers. Avoiding Qandahār he made his way into Persia with many doubts whether a friendless Sunnī ruler who had lost every vestige of sovereignty would find refuge with a bigoted Shiah.

His reception, though splendid, was in fact more designed to exhibit the magnificence of his host than to do honour to an emperor of India, and when he joined the Shāh's camp he was subjected to many insults and hardly veiled threats of violence if he did not change his religious practices.[1] These were borne with quiet patience and at last in 1545 Shāh Tahmāsp offered him a force with which to contend against Kāmrān, a condition of success being the promise to restore Qandahār to Persia. Passing through Sīstān he laid siege to Qandahār and sent Bairam Khān to Kābul to gain adherents there. After an obstinate resistance for several months 'Askarī surrendered Qandahār. He and his amīrs came out with swords hanging round their necks to show their complete submission. Humāyūn forgave his brother as usual, but at the feast to celebrate the capture of the town he had 'Askarī's letters to the Baloches placed in front of him. Qandahār was reluctantly made over to the Persians and designs begun for an attack on Kābul. The Persian allies, however, having attained their object, declined to advance and the cold of winter and the smallness of his force prevented Humāyūn from

[1] His sister's account in the *Humāyūn-nāma* omits all mention of this ill-treatment.

moving, though Kāmrān had been deserted by many adherents. Pressed by his necessity he overcame his reluctance to break his promises to the Shāh, and when the Persian prince died who had accompanied him in command of his allies, he reoccupied Qandahār and was at last able to set out for Kābul. During the absence of Kāmrān in the Hazāra country Yādgār and Hindāl escaped from Kābul and joined the emperor. Though he was impeded and faced near the city by Kāmrān he pressed on, gaining more and more deserters, and was able to enter the camp of Kāmrān, who fled into Kābul and then escaped towards Ghaznī and finally into Sind, so that Humāyūn was able to enter the city and again meet his son Akbar (November, 1544).

He spent the rest of the winter in settling the affairs of southern Afghānistān, which now recognised his rule, and some advance in a spirit of resolution is marked by his directing the execution of his cousin Yādgār Mīrzā who had been so faithless in Sind. In the spring of 1545 he crossed the Hindū Kush to reduce the northern part of the country and made a successful campaign. While here an unfortunate illness in which his life was despaired of gave the signal for plots and insubordination. Although his recovery stopped these dissensions among his immediate adherents Kāmrān took advantage of his absence north of the mountains to surprise Kābul with help from Shāh Husain (1546). Arriving unexpectedly in the early morning he found the garrison off their guard and slipped in with the crowd of early grass-cutters and water-carriers. There he behaved with great cruelty towards all who had helped the emperor and fell into his hands. Humāyūn hastened to recover his capital, crossing the mountains with difficulty, and again losing many officers who deserted, fearing that Kāmrān would massacre their families in Kābul. The town was blockaded and warfare continued with greater bitterness than had yet been shown in the contests between the brothers. It is even stated by some writers that the infant Akbar was exposed on the ramparts to the fire of his father's cannon. The siege was pressed so strongly that Kāmrān contemplated surrender but was persuaded that his brother's patience must now be exhausted and he escaped in the hope of avoiding death (1547). As he fled he was actually captured by Hindāl but was allowed to escape. He sought refuge with Sulaimān the ruler of Badakhshān and, being spurned by one who had already suffered at the hands of the Mughuls, fled to the Uzbegs in Balkh who received him favourably in the hope of keeping alive dissensions between the brothers. For a time it appeared probable that Kāmrān would again rise to power. With Uzbeg help he invaded Badakhshān and gaining some success was joined by many of his former supporters, who were always more disposed to side with a successful prince than to keep faith with one who seemed to be losing power. It was too late in the year for

Humāyūn to cross the passes and in the following spring he was delayed by a foolish quarrel between high officers at Kābul, which led to other defections. When he did advance the Uzbegs, who had no wish to see any of the brothers supreme, refused to give further help to Kāmrān and after some inconclusive fighting Kāmrān submitted (1548), relying on Humāyūn's generosity to forgive him. He was received in public audience and hung a whip round his neck to signify his sense of criminal guilt and began to express regret. Humāyūn cut short his confessions and calling him brother seized him in his arms and wept. Kāmrān was then appointed to govern a tract north of the Oxus, and was disgusted with its remoteness and inadequacy.

When in the following year (1549) Humāyūn marched into Balkh Kāmrān was summoned to join with his forces against the Uzbegs, but failed to attend. The emperor gained some successes and actually reached the city of Balkh which he probably would have taken. But a sudden panic seized his army through fear that Kāmrān might slip past them and again occupy Kābul. A hasty withdrawal became a rout and the shattered army reached Kābul with difficulty. Once more Kāmrān abandoned his post, attacked Badakhshān and failing there tried to seduce Hindāl from allegiance to the emperor, but failed and was severely handled by the Uzbegs. Though he withdrew he was invited to Kābul by malcontents in Humāyūn's army and marched towards it making false professions of fealty to his brother. These were at first accepted by Humāyūn till the advice of his officers convinced him of their unreliability, and Humāyūn made up his mind to capture Kāmrān. In the battle which ensued Humāyūn's troops failed him. He was severely wounded and had to fly while Kāmrān was able to occupy Kābul and enrich himself by plundering the treasury and country. After several months' painful convalescence in the mountains during which he was believed at Kābul to be dead, Humāyūn took the field again with the help of a force raised by the wife of Sulaimān, ruler of Badakhshān. He attempted to bind his adherents by a solemn oath of fealty. Advancing to Kābul he met Kāmrān in battle and defeated him. 'Askarī, who had sided with Kāmrān, was captured and after confinement for a time was sent on pilgrimage and never returned,[1] while Kāmrān escaped to pursue for some time his schemes for power.

Humāyūn had now realised the folly of indiscriminate forgiveness of rebels, and set himself to consolidate his position in Afghānistān. In this he was ably helped by Bairam Khān who received the title of Khān Khānān. Kāmrān was followed up as he tried to rouse the country between Kābul and India and in a night attack Hindāl was killed by an Afghān. It was characteristic of the attitude of Mughul princes to each other that the news of the death caused a

[1] He died in Mecca in 1558.

paroxysm of grief to Kāmrān though Hindāl was then opposing him. For some time Kāmrān suffered hardships wandering among the border Afghān tribes and then he sought refuge with Islām Shāh in India (1552), where his reception was as contemptuous as that of Humāyūn during his exile in Persia. Escaping to the Khokar country he was surrendered to Humāyūn, who had come in pursuit of him. And now the emperor was strongly pressed by all his advisers, military, civil and religious, to execute his brother to prevent further evil to the state. Though his heart had become tougher during his recent trials Humāyūn was still far from seeking his brother's life, but he agreed so far that he ordered him to be blinded. An affecting farewell took place between the brothers in which Humāyūn expressed his sympathy with Kāmrān's sufferings and Kāmrān admitted his own misconduct and fault. Abandoned by all his nearest friends but accompanied by a faithful wife Kāmrān travelled to Sind and thence to Mecca where he died (1557).

Humāyūn was now free from the most dangerous rivals of his own house and the generals of his race who had aided or opposed him as seemed most to their personal interests were dead or scattered. How he regained some part of his former possession in India will be related in the next chapter. Like most Mughul princes Humāyūn, who was born in 1508, was placed in nominal charge of a province at an early age. He was only twelve when Badakhshān was made over to him in 1520, and he remained there almost continuously till he assisted in Bābur's conquest of northern India, after which he was allowed to return. On his journey back an incident occurred which throws light on his character. Halting at Delhi he robbed the government treasury though he had been amply rewarded by his father and had received a territorial grant. His experience of the pleasures to be enjoyed in India then made the isolation of Badakhshān irksome to him, and Bābur in his *Memoirs* records a letter rebuking his son for his discontent, and criticising the carelessness of his spelling and composition. When Bābur's strenuous mode of living had sapped his health Humāyūn abandoned his post and came to India to be near his father.

The defects thus noted in his early life, carelessness, unreliability and self-indulgence, persisted in his maturity. They were accompanied by an excess of kindliness which often led to lack of decision, when promptness and even ruthlessness were needed. The tradition of his race was one of conquest rather than consolidation or administrative development. Transoxiana and Afghānistān were hard schools in which a rigorous climate and barren soil bred warriors who excelled in forays but developed no skill in peaceful administration. It was not till his final recovery of India that he really planned a scheme for ruling it, and his death occurred before it could be carried out. Though possessed of high personal courage and endurance in distress Humāyūn, like many of his descendants, found the softer climate of

India corrupting. He could fight against odds and show skill in devising methods of taking a difficult fort. But when a battle was won or a city stormed he would sit down to consume the captured treasure, sharing it generously with his whole army, which thus became enervated and corrupted. At times indulgence in opium sapped his power of action still further, and he wasted months of his life in feasting or in a drugged stupor.

Some latent pettiness of nature would cause him as much anger when the ladies of the court were late for a pleasure excursion as the revolt of a brother which threatened his sovereignty and life. In the one case he would insist on letters of apology, while in the other the appearance of the culprit with professions of regret was sufficient to dispel his anger and cause tears of joy at the reconciliation. Humanity carried to an extreme brought misery not only to him but to the people who looked to him as a ruler. With rare exceptions his best generals deserted him again and again, confident that they would be forgiven if the tide changed in his favour and they offered to serve him once more. There is a well-known story that the water-carrier, who saved his life in the crossing of the Ganges after the battle of Chausa, was allowed to occupy the throne at Āgra for a day and to exercise all imperial power, which illustrates Humāyūn's lack of proportion.

His unsettled life and wanderings made it impossible that he could gather round him cultured men of learning, but like most of the Mughuls he was fond of literature. His reliance on astrology gave him some interest in astronomy and this was indirectly the cause of his death, as he fell while descending from the roof of his library where he had been directing his astronomers to observe a transit of Venus, with a view to issuing orders at a lucky moment.

CHAPTER III

SHER SHĀH AND THE SŪR DYNASTY THE RETURN OF HUMĀYŪN

DURING his long struggle with the kings of the Sharqī dynasty of Jaunpur,[1] Sultān Buhlūl Lodī recruited his forces with bodies of Afghāns from Roh, the highlands of the Sulaimān range, whose leaders received assignments in India for the maintenance of their followers. Among them was one Ibrāhīm Khān, of the Sūr tribe, a horse-dealer according to Abu-'l-Fazl, who is ever ready to disparage those who drove his master's father from his throne. Whether Ibrāhīm Khān ever sold horses is uncertain, but he was a soldier who received assignments as a reward for his services. He is said to have claimed descent from the Shansabānids of Ghūr,[2] but probably without grounds.

Ibrāhīm had at least three sons, and one of them, Hasan Khān, had eight sons, of whom the eldest, Farīd, was born some years before 1489. Ibrāhīm held assignments at first in the Punjab, but afterwards in the *pargana* of Nārnaul, under the Afghān Jamāl Khān, who held the large assignment of Hissār, and on his death his son Hasan Khān succeeded; when Sikandar Lodī defeated his rebellious brother Bārbak, but permitted him to retain the government of Jaunpur,[3] Jamāl Khān was transferred to that province, and received there large assignments which enabled him to prevent Bārbak from again disturbing the peace of the realm. With him he took all the members of the Sūr tribe or clan serving in Hissār and Nārnaul, and Hasan Khān received the *parganas* of Sasarām,[4] Hājīpur[5] and Khavāsspur Tāndā[6] for the maintenance of 500 horse. Of Hasan's eight sons only four are of any importance, Farīd and Nizām, the two eldest, born of his senior wife, an Afghān, and Sulaimān and Ahmad, the two youngest, born of a Hindu concubine. He had wearied of his Afghān wife, and was entirely submissive to his concubine. She was devoted to the interests of her own sons and so resented any favour shown to her stepsons that Farīd, while yet a lad, chafing under his father's coldness to him, fled from their home at Sasarām, and took refuge with Jamāl Khān at Jaunpur. Jamāl Khān urged Farīd to return to his father and to pursue his studies, but Farīd refused to return as Jaunpur was a better place for study than Sasarām. Such progress did he make that his father, when he visited

[1] See vol. III, pp. 229–34 and 254–9.
[2] See vol. III, pp. 38–48 and 689.
[3] See vol. III, p. 236.
[4] 24° 57′ N., 84° 1′ E.
[5] 25° 41′ N., 85° 12′ E.
[6] In Tirhūt.

Jaunpur, invited him to return and placed him in charge of the two *parganas*, Hājīpur and Khavāsspur Tāndā.

The administration of these two *parganas* was Farīd's initiation, and he mastered all the details of revenue and customary law, and rigorously suppressed bribery, extortion, brigandage and disaffection.

But Hasan was still subservient to his concubine, who was so enraged by his praise of her stepson that she ceased to admit him to intercourse with her, and thus compelled him to promise that he would make over the administration of Farīd's *parganas* to her son, Sulaimān. Farīd, after vainly reproaching his father with breach of faith, as he had promised that he would not in future neglect Farīd, left the district and sought service in Āgra, at the court of Ibrāhīm Lodī. He found a patron in Daulat Khān, who held the command of 12,000 horse, and earned his approbation and an offer of assistance. Farīd complained of his father's injustice and begged that the king might be moved to confer on him the two *parganas* of which his father had deprived him, but Ibrāhīm Lodī was in a bad humour and refused to do anything for an undutiful son. Daulat Khān temporarily satisfied Farīd by promoting him in his own service, and shortly afterwards, on his father's death, obtained for him a royal grant in succession to his father. This land was now in possession of his half-brother, Sulaimān, who fled when Farīd came to take possession of it and took refuge with another of the tribe, Muhammad Khān Sūr, who held the *pargana* of Chaund,[1] and who, having been on bad terms with Hasan, welcomed the opportunity of fomenting the quarrels of his sons. He proposed to Farīd a division of the assignment, but Farīd replied that while he was prepared to share his father's property with his brothers he would not give up any share in the administration of the area granted to him by the king.

Meanwhile Bābur had invaded India, and Farīd resolved to await the result of the contest between him and Ibrāhīm Lodī, confident that if Ibrāhīm prevailed his assignment would be confirmed, and resolved, should Bābur prevail, to enlist the aid of Bihār Khān, the governor of Bihār, against his half-brother and his patron Muhammad Sūr.

Bihār Khān, on receipt of the news of the defeat and death of Ibrāhīm at Pānīpat, assumed the title of Sultān Muhammad, as independent sovereign of Bihār, and received Farīd when he waited upon him. Farīd soon gained the good opinion of his new master, as he had gained that of all others whom he had served, and rose to high rank in his service. One day, while hunting with him, he slew a tiger and received the title of Sher (tiger) Khān, by which he will henceforth be described. The Sultān, at the same time, appointed him tutor to his young son, Jalāl Khān.

[1] Also transliterated Jaund. Now Chainpur in Shāhābād district, see Oldham, *Journal of F. Buchanan*, p. 122, n. 3.

Sher Khān after some time sought leave to return for a period to his assignment, which, though administered by his own brother, Nizām Khān, required his personal attention. Muhammad belonged to the Lohānī tribe of Afghāns, and most of his courtiers and officials, who were of the same tribe, resented the intrusion of one of the Sūr tribe, so that Muhammad Sūr found little difficulty in rousing ill-will against Sher Khān during his absence. Mahmūd Lodī, the brother of Ibrāhīm, who had taken refuge in Rājputāna, was expected in Bihār, and it was suggested that Sher Khān would side with Mahmūd against Sultān Muhammad. Sultān Muhammad, however, took no action against him, but appointed Muhammad Sūr arbiter in the dispute between Sher Khān and his half-brother, Sulaimān. Thus empowered, Muhammad Sūr directed Sher Khān to share the assignment equally with all his brothers, but he, citing the royal order, refused to comply, and Muhammad sent his troops to seize the estate. Sher Khān's agent was defeated and slain and the remnant of his troops fled to Sher Khān at Sasarām.

Sher Khān's position was now difficult. He would not appeal to Sultān Muhammad, who he knew was unwilling to quarrel with Muhammad Sūr. He therefore opened negotiations with Sultān Junaid Birlās, Bābur's governor of Karā and Mānikpur, and, with his brother Nizām, sought aid in recovering his assignment which he promised to hold as the subordinate of Junaid. Junaid welcomed this opportunity of extending Bābur's influence and supplied Sher Khān with a force, by the help of which he not only recovered his own assignment but expelled Muhammad Sūr from Chaund and drove him into the Rohtās hills. This success so enhanced his reputation that large numbers of Afghāns entered his service, and he returned the contingent placed at his service by Junaid with a handsome reward and thanks for the assistance. He then sought reconciliation with his kinsman, Muhammad Sūr, inviting him to return and resume his estates, as it behoved all Afghāns to unite. Muhammad Sūr returned to Chaund, and Sher Khān, having, as he believed, gained his good will, visited Junaid at Āgra where he was presented to Bābur. He now temporarily entered Bābur's service, really with the object of studying Bābur's system and ascertaining how he could be expelled from India. He accompanied Bābur on an expedition to Chanderī, but is said to have been indiscreet in his criticism of the system of administration and of the army, and to have caused offence by his behaviour at the royal table. Bābur was disposed to imprison him had he not been dissuaded by Junaid and his brother Mīr Khalīfa, the minister, who warned him of the danger of making enemies of the Afghāns. Sher Khān, perceiving how matters stood, fled with his contingent from the royal camp, and excused his departure in a letter to Junaid, feigning that local affairs urgently required his presence. He had also incurred the suspicions of his former master, Sultān Muhammad, by entering Bābur's service, and Muhammad Sūr was endeavouring to obtain permission to eject Nizām Khān from Sasarām. Sher Khān had seen enough of Bābur, and from now onwards sought to unite the Afghāns against the Mughuls. He repaired once more to the court of Sultān Muhammad, who welcomed and again appointed him tutor and guardian of Jalāl Khān. The Sultān died very shortly after this and, his son being yet a minor, his mother assumed the regency and appointed Sher Khān her agent, so that he became the ruler of Bihār and, when Jalāl Khān's mother died, king in all but name. He strengthened his position by entering into a close alliance with the governor of Hājipur on behalf of Sultān Mahmūd of Bengal, perceiving that unless Bihār and Bengal united to oppose Bābur both might fall into his hands. The king of Bengal, however, desiring to acquire Bihār, sent a force to invade it which was defeated with great loss of treasure, horses and elephants.

Meanwhile the hostility of most of the Lohānīs at Jalāl Khān's court against Sher Khān grew, and a plot was formed to assassinate him, but he was informed of it in time and warned Jalāl Khān, who had been privy to the plot, that Mahmūd of Bengal was intent on conquering Bihār and would certainly succeed if its chief defender were removed. Jalāl Khān, apparently convinced, promised to dismiss the conspirators but took no step in that direction, and two hostile parties were formed in Bihār, one consisting of Jalāl Khān and the majority of the Lohānīs, the other of Sher Khān, some of the Lohānīs, and his own and other Afghān tribes. Sher Khān attempted to restore unity by reminding his enemies that the great fault of the Afghāns was treachery to those of their own race, which had cost the Lodīs the dominion of Hindūstān, but his words fell upon deaf ears.

Sultān Mahmūd now sent a fresh army to avenge the earlier defeat. The jealousies of the Lohānī tribe blinded them to their own interests as well as to those of their sovereign and they persuaded Jalāl Khān to rid himself of Sher Khān at all costs. He therefore ordered Sher Khān to return to his charge, on the pretext that the Lohānīs were unwilling to fight under his orders. Sher Khān retired to Sasarām, and Jalāl Khān allowed himself to be persuaded to join the army of Mahmūd of Bengal, and ceased to be king of Bihār. Sher Khān rejoiced at the news. There were now, he said, no divisions in the army of Bihār, and the land, by Jalāl Khān's desertion, was his. He enlisted more troops and advanced against the army of Bengal, but, owing to his numerical inferiority, entrenched himself and refrained from attacking the enemy in force. Reinforcements were summoned from Bengal, and Sher Khān found it necessary to give battle before these should arrive. By the well-known stratagem of a feigned flight his first line drew the enemy's cavalry away from his artillery and elephants, and Sher Khān then fell on it with his reserves and routed it. The commander was slain while attempting to flee, Jalāl Khān escaped with great difficulty into Bengal, and the treasure, the elephants and the artillery of Bengal fell into the hands of Sher Khān, who was now the unquestioned sovereign of Bihār.

He next acquired possession of the strong fortress of Chunār, on the Ganges, from the widow of its commandant, whom he married at the suggestion of her principal officer. The acquisition of the fortress and of the great treasure which it contained added greatly to Sher Khān's power and influence as well as to his resources, but he was now seriously embarrassed.

Mahmūd Lodī, the brother of Ibrāhīm Lodī, had been expected to arrive in Bihār a few years before this time, but he had taken refuge with Sangrām Singh, the Rānā of Chitor, and had taken part with him in the battle of Khānua. After the battle he had returned to Chitor, but he now left Rājputāna, and, at the invitation of some of the nobles of the Lodī court, who had settled in Patna, made that city his headquarters. He was a mere fugitive, but he represented the old Afghān royal house and assumed royal state. Sher Khān was summoned to appear before him and could not refuse to obey without belying all the principles of unity which he had so persistently preached. He was informed that his assignment was confirmed but that in order to provide for Mahmūd's nobles and retinue he was obliged to resume, for the present, the rest of Bihār, which would be restored to Sher Khān when the prince had established himself on the throne. Sher Khān submitted and retired to Sasarām, ostensibly in order to prepare forces to accompany the prince in a projected expedition into Oudh.

When the prince summoned Sher Khān to bring his contingent, he replied that his troops were not yet ready and that he would join him later. Mahmūd Lodī's officers pointed out that Sher Khān had already once served the Mughuls, and suggested that he was now temporising. They advised a line of march by way of Sasarām so as to compel him to accompany the army. Sher Khān made the best of his failure and, after giving Mahmūd a royal reception, accompanied him.

Humāyūn's officers fled from Jaunpur on the approach of the Afghāns, and Mahmūd sent his forces forward and occupied Lucknow. When the news of the loss of Lucknow reached Āgra Humāyūn marched towards Jaunpur, and his army and that of Mahmūd Lodī met at Daunrūā, where the latter was severely defeated and compelled to retire into Bihār. Being unable to raise a fresh army there, he withdrew into Orissa, where he passed the few remaining years of his life, in sensual pleasures, until his death in 1542.

After the battle Humāyūn demanded the surrender of the important fortress, Chunār, from Sher Khān, who had failed to support Mahmūd

Lodī, and had promised obedience to the Mughuls. On his refusal Humāyūn prepared to besiege Chunār, but was diverted by news of the raid made by Tātār Khān as related in chapter II (p. 23) and set out for Gujarāt accompanied by Qutb Khān, son of Sher Khān, with a small force.

During Humāyūn's absence in Gujarāt, Sher Khān spared no efforts in consolidating his power in Bihār, and was joined by his son Qutb Khān, who deserted Humāyūn's camp in Gujarāt, and by most of the leading Afghāns in Bahādur's service, who abandoned him when he was in difficulties. Sher Khān then attacked the kingdom of Bengal and annexed all of its territory which lay to the west of Teliyāgarhī.

When Humāyūn returned from Gujarāt to Āgra he was warned that Sher Khān had grown so powerful as to have become a danger to the empire, but he contented himself with sending Hindū Beg to Jaunpur with orders to report on the situation. Hindū Beg had ever been favourably disposed to Sher Khān, and was easily induced to report that the emperor had nothing to fear from him.

Sher Khān, having thus, as he believed, set the emperor's mind at rest, sent an army under his son, Jalāl Khān, to complete the annexation of Bengal, and Sultān Mahmūd, too weak to meet the invaders in the field, appealed to Humāyūn and took refuge in Gaur where he was besieged by Jalāl Khān and Khavāss Khān, who had now become Sher Khān's most capable, loyal and enterprising officer.

Sher Khān's son, Jalāl Khān, leaving Khavāss Khān in charge of the siege of Gaur, marched to hold Teliyāgarhī, "the gate of Bengal". Gaur was obliged, by lack of provisions, to surrender to Khavāss Khān, and Sultān Mahmūd of Bengal took refuge with Humāyūn. Sher Khān had found an asylum in the strong fortress of Rohtās. The Mughul historians tell an absurd story, invented in order to besmirch the character of Sher Khān, of his gaining possession of Rohtās by smuggling into the fortress, in litters, as though they had been veiled ladies, a large number of his men-at-arms; but the true story is discreditable enough to him. He first obtained from Churāman, the raja's Brāhman minister, a promise of shelter in the fort. The raja prudently objected that it was dangerous to admit a force strong enough to overpower the garrison, but Churāman insisted that his word had been passed and that nothing was to be feared from Sher Khān. The raja yielded against his better judgement, the Afghāns were admitted, and Sher Khān in a short time expelled the garrison and took possession of the fortress.

Then, while Humāyūn was making an easy conquest of a defenceless but devastated area, Sher Khān, who had hitherto carefully avoided facing him in the field, set about cutting his communications. He besieged Benares and sent Khavāss Khān, whom he had recalled from Gaur, to Monghyr with instructions to seize the officer whom

Humāyūn had left in command of that city. Khavāss Khān captured this officer and carried him to Benares, which city Sher Khān shortly afterwards took, putting nearly the whole garrison to the sword. He then sent forces to Jaunpur, Sambhal and Bahraich, each of which towns was captured, the imperial garrison being expelled, and ordered the force which had captured Jaunpur to march on Āgra, where Humāyūn's brother, Hindāl Mīrzā, had rebelled after slaying the envoy whom Humāyūn himself had sent to urge him to remain loyal.

Sher Khān now assembled all his forces in the neighbourhood of Rohtās and awaited an opportunity of attacking Humāyūn as he attempted to extricate his demoralised army from Bengal. The pretext was that Humāyūn, who had promised him the kingdom of Bengal, had broken faith with him and taken the kingdom for himself. At the battle of Chausa on 26 June, 1539, Humāyūn was completely defeated and fled to Āgra.

Sher Khān now struck coin[1] and caused the *khutba* to be recited in his own name and assumed the royal title, styling himself Farīd-ud-dīn Sher Shāh. A force sent to Gaur defeated and slew the officer whom Humāyūn had left to hold that city, and Sher Shāh, following Humāyūn towards Āgra, occupied the country as far west as Kanauj and Kālpī, and sent a mission to Mālwā and Gujarāt promising help if they menaced Humāyūn from the west. Gujarāt was too disturbed to take part in a general attack on the emperor, but Mallū Khān of Māndū, who had assumed the title of Qādir Shāh,[2] returned a favourable reply, though he aroused the wrath of Sher Shāh by writing after the manner of a sovereign prince.

News was received that Humāyūn was marching towards Kanauj in order to meet the Afghān army there, and Sher Shāh sent his son Qutb Khān towards Māndū to urge Qādir Shāh to fulfil his promise. Qādir Shāh, however, showed no sign of support and Humāyūn despatched his brothers 'Askarī and Hindāl against him. Qutb Khān was defeated and slain by them on his way from Kālpī to Chanderī, and the two princes rejoined their brother. Humāyūn reached Kanauj in April 1540, and found Sher Shāh encamped on the east bank of the Ganges over against him. Crossing the river he again encountered Sher Shāh on 17 May, again sustained a crushing defeat (chap. II, p. 34), and fled through Āgra to the north.

Sher Shāh despatched a force to besiege Gwalior, sent another to Sambhal, to secure and pacify the country to the east of the Ganges, and pursued Humāyūn first to Āgra and thence, as he continued his flight, to Lahore. From Lahore Kāmrān Mīrzā retired to Kābul, and Humāyūn into Sind, and Sher Shāh, having pursued him for some distance, returned to Lahore. He had now driven his foes from Bengal, Bihār, Hindūstān and the Punjab, had received the submission of the Baloch chiefs on the frontier, and was at leisure to turn his

[1] Earliest known date 945 A.H. (May 1538–May 1539 A.D.). [2] See vol. III, p. 369.

attention to domestic affairs. To guard his northern frontier he selected the site of a great fortress in the hills ten miles north of Jhelum, which he named Rohtās, after his stronghold in the hills of Bihār.

Sher Shāh now learned that his governor of Bengal had married a daughter of Sultān Mahmūd of that country, and was meditating rebellion, so he set out at once for Gaur. Here he punished the governor, by imprisonment in chains, for his presumption in marrying without leave, and for having held courts in the royal manner. Sher Shāh then remodelled the administration of Bengal to avert the danger of rebellion. He divided the country into a number of charges but appointed no governor or viceroy, and gave to no official authority over another, but appointed a jurist as supervisor of all, with instructions to see that the charges were properly administered, that all money due to the treasury was regularly remitted, and that the officials abstained from conspiracy. He then returned to Āgra.

In 1542 he invaded Mālwā with a view to punishing Qādir Shāh for having assumed the royal title and for having failed to support his son Qutb Khān. On his way he halted at Gwalior and received the submission of the governor of that fortress, who had promised that he would surrender when Sher Shāh arrived. He then marched on to Sārangpur, where Qādir Shāh appeared before him, made his submission, and was kindly received and honourably treated, and accompanied Sher Shāh to Ujjain. Here Sher Shāh promised him the government of a province instead of that of Mālwā, of which he had been deprived, but he became apprehensive of the king's intentions towards him, and made his escape, taking refuge with Mahmūd III of Gujarāt.

On his way back to Āgra from Mālwā, Sher Shāh persuaded the commandant of Ranthambhor to surrender that fortress to him, and after his return he remained for a year in Āgra, engaged in reorganising the administration of his empire, in the laying out of roads, and the erection of public buildings. Sher Shāh then paid a visit of inspection to Bihār and Bengal, in the course of which he suffered so severely from malaria as to believe himself to be at the point of death, and to vow that if God spared his life and restored him to health he would punish Pūran Mal for his offences against Islām.[1]

Pūran Mal of Rāisen had, not long before this time, attacked and captured Chanderī, put its inhabitants to the sword, added to his territory the country around that town, and enslaved many women, Muslims as well as Hindus, some of whom he employed as dancing girls. The punishment of such offences as these was incumbent on a faithful Muslim, and Sher Shāh, when sufficiently recovered, returned to Āgra and in 1543 set out for Māndū, whence he marched to Rāisen.

[1] See vol. III, p. 370.

The siege of the fortress was protracted until the Hindus were reduced to distress, and at length Pūran Mal came forth on receiving a solemn oath that the lives and property of himself and his relations would be safe. For a while, he and his clansmen were lodged in peace, but the widows of the slaughtered Muslims of Chanderī assembled and, waiting by the roadside, assailed Sher Shāh with loud lamentations. Sher Shāh's blood boiled, but he was perplexed by the oath on the Qur'ān which had enticed Pūran Mal from his stronghold. The Muslim casuists set his mind at rest by declaring that an oath which should never have been sworn bound none, and Sher Shāh prepared for the deed which has left the deepest blot on his memory.

The elephants were collected as for a march on the following day, and during the night the troops were posted round the Rājput camp. At sunrise Pūran Mal saw that his fate was sealed. He severed his wife's head from her body, and, bearing it in his hands, commanded his clansmen to follow his example. The Afghān troops fell on them while they were engaged in the ghastly task of slaughtering their wives and daughters, and they fought gallantly, "like hogs at bay" as a Muslim historian records, but they were cut down by the Afghāns and trampled to death by the elephants and not a man escaped. A few women and children were taken alive; a daughter of Pūran Mal was given to some minstrels to be trained as a dancing girl, and three sons of his elder brother were castrated.

Sher Shāh, after reaching Rāisen, had received a message from Khavāss Khān to the effect that he and Haibat Khān who had been left at Rohtās could not agree. That two Afghān chiefs should thus seek arbitration, even of their king, rather than settle their differences by the sword, speaks volumes for Sher Shāh's influence over his quarrelsome fellow-countrymen. Sher Shāh recalled Khavāss Khān from the Punjab and left Haibat Khān in the government of that province, with instructions to reduce it to order. Since the flight of Humāyūn, Fath Khān Jāt had been in rebellion and had preyed upon travellers on the high roads between Delhi and Lahore, while the Baloch had been governing the city and district of Multān solely in their own interests. Haibat Khān dealt first with the Jāt, who had established himself in Ajudhan (Pāk Pattan) but fled and retired into a mud fort where he was besieged. In a few days' time he surrendered himself and was imprisoned, but there still remained in the fort Hindū Baloch and Bakhshū Langāh, whose men cut their way through the besiegers, leaving their leaders in Haibat Khān's hands. Haibat Khān then marched on Multān and induced some of its citizens and husbandmen to return. He reported his success to Sher Shāh, who rewarded him and at the same time commanded him to repeople Multān, "to observe the customs of the Langāhs",[1] and not to measure the land, but to content himself with one-fourth of its gross

[1] See vol. III, pp. 503–5.

produce. Fath Khān Jāt and Hindū Baloch were put to death, but Sher Shāh ordered Haibat Khān to spare the lives of Bakhshū Langāh and his son, to restore to them their lands, and to retain one of them always with him as a hostage. Haibat Khān returned to Lahore, leaving in Multān Fath Jang Khān, who completely restored the prosperity of the city and the province so that they flourished even more than under the Langāhs. These references to the prosperity of Multān under the Langāhs are instructive, both as to the character of that dynasty, of which little is known, but which evidently identified itself with the interests of its subjects, and as to the justice of Sher Shāh and the historians of his line in admitting that a dynasty which had been in rebellion against Afghān Sultāns of Delhi had left behind it a reputation worthy of emulation.

Before leaving Rāisen Sher Shāh had wisely rejected the advice of some of his counsellors to invade the Deccan. For years past the Rājputs had been a persistent menace to Muslim rule in northern India. Sangrām Singh of Mewār had defeated and captured Mahmūd II of Mālwā though he was aided by a contingent of 10,000 horse from Gujarāt, and had later borne a part in inviting Bābur to India with the object of profiting by the dissensions of the Muslims. At Khānua he had wellnigh succeeded in subverting Muslim rule in Hindūstān, and, though the capture of Chitor by Bahādur of Gujarāt in 1534 had broken the power of Mewār, other chiefs had taken the place of the Rānā. Pūran Mal, who had taken advantage of the hostilities between Sher Shāh and Humāyūn to found an independent principality in Mālwā, had been crushed, but the great state of Mārwār had become dangerous to Sher Shāh's rule. Its sovereign, Māldeo the Rāthor, had established his influence in Mewār, had recovered Ajmer and Nāgaur, and while Bābur and Humāyūn were establishing their dominion over Hindūstān proper had annexed fortresses and districts which had been held by officers of the Lodī dynasty. Sher Shāh had good reason to be alarmed by the growth of a hostile power on the borders of his dominions, and in the autumn of 1543 marched from Āgra with the greatest army which he had ever led in the field to attack Māldeo. He adopted his usual precaution of entrenching his camp at every halt, but on entering the sandy desert of Rājāsthān found it impossible to throw up a parapet. His grandson, Mahmūd Khān, said to have been only seven years of age, suggested that the parapet should be constructed of sacks filled with sand, and this precocious young soldier seems to have been the inventor of sandbags in the East.

Sher Shāh, with his army of 80,000 horse, came into contact with Māldeo in the neighbourhood of Ajmer but hesitated to attack though opposed by only 50,000 horse. For a month the two armies lay opposite to one another and Sher Shāh's situation had become critical, owing to lack of supplies, before he used a device not infrequently employed in eastern warfare. Causing letters to be written to himself, as from Māldeo's *thākurs*, or nobles, promising that they would deliver their master into his hands, he had them enclosed in a silken bag which was dropped, as though by accident, near Māldeo's tent. It was picked up and carried to Māldeo, who was dismayed by what he deemed the treachery of his *thākurs*. He countermanded the general action which he had ordered, and would not trust their protestations of fidelity. As the Muslims advanced, 12,000 Rājput horse, led by *thākurs* bent on proving their loyalty, charged them, and cut their way almost to the centre of the royal camp, but were overwhelmed by numbers and almost annihilated. Māldeo saw too late that he had been deceived and could no longer withstand the invader. His army dispersed but its valour had so impressed Sher Shāh that he exclaimed that he had wellnigh lost the empire of India for a handful of millet. He left Khavāss Khān and 'Īsā Khān Niyāzī to establish his authority in Mārwār and marched to Chitor, the keys of which were sent to him by the officer who held it on behalf of Rānā Uday Singh of Mewār.

His next objective was the fortress of Kālinjar.[1] Rājā Bīr Singh Bundelā[2] had been summoned to court and, instead of obeying the summons, had taken refuge with Rājā Kīrat Singh of Kālinjar, who had refused to surrender him. Sher Shāh determined to reduce Kīrat Singh to obedience and, on reaching Kālinjar, invested the fortress. The siege lasted for nearly a year, and at length, when the parallels had approached the walls, Sher Shāh ascended a high tower in the line of circumvallation, ordered one of his officers to bring a supply of loaded shells, or, more probably, rockets, and amused himself in the meantime by shooting arrows into the town. When the rockets were brought one of them was fired against the gate of the town, but rebounded and fell into and ignited a heap of ammunition by which the king was standing. Sher Shāh was most severely burned by the explosion and was carried to his tent. Here he summoned his nobles and commanded them to capture the fortress while he yet lived. About the time of the evening prayer it was reported to him that Kālinjar had been taken by storm and its garrison put to the sword, and on learning this he died content on 22 May, 1545.

He has received scant justice from historians. The annalists of the Timurids have been obliged to admit, ungraciously, his merits as a soldier and a statesman, but to them he was ever Sher Khān, the Afghān rebel, and their works have chiefly supplied the material for European histories of India. He was, however, the greatest of the Muslim rulers of India and was entirely free from, and active in the correction of, the faults usually associated with his race. In youth

[1] 25° 1′ N., 80° 29′ E.

[2] It was more probably Bīr Bhān the Bāghel Rājā of Rewah, a friend of Humāyūn, see Memoir 21, *Arch. Survey of India*, p. 3 [Ed.].

and early manhood he had sedulously devoted himself to the acquisition of learning and the study of the art of government, and found an opportunity of putting his knowledge into practice in the administration of the *parganas* which his father placed under his charge, where, also in the suppression of rebellion and organised brigandage, he gained practical experience of the art of war, and thenceforward, for a short time in Bābur's service, then in that of Sultān Muhammad of Bihār, and then as independent ruler of that kingdom, he devoted the whole of his time to affairs of state, allowing himself no leisure, and by the time he attained to supreme authority he was ultimately acquainted with all the details of civil administration, as no other Indian ruler, before or since, has been.

The basis of Indian administration is the assessment and collection of the land revenue, and Sher Shāh's system was his own. To each *pargana* he appointed an *amīn* responsible for the general administration, a *shiqqdār*, his assistant, who supervised the assessment and collection of the revenue, a treasurer, and two clerks, or secretaries, to keep the records or accounts, one in Persian and the other in Hindī. The cultivated land was measured every harvest, and the revenue was assessed in cash on the value of the produce.[1] To each *sarkār*, or revenue district, were appointed a chief *shiqqdār* and a chief *munsif*, whose duty it was to see that the revenue was collected in full, but that the cultivators were not oppressed.

There was, however, one weak point in his system, which facilitated peculation and illicit profits. It was his custom to transfer his revenue officials every year or two, his reason for this measure being that all his old and loyal servants might profit by the charge of a revenue district. This pernicious practice encouraged officials to make all that they could in the short time during which they held office.

The administration of the army was even more efficient. The system of branding the horses of the contingents which assignees were bound to supply, to prevent them from borrowing horses for the muster-parades, had been invented by the Saljūqs in the twelfth century but the only Indian ruler who had hitherto been able to enforce it had been 'Alā-ud-dīn Khaljī. Sher Shāh enforced it rigorously. The great Akbar after him attempted, but failed, and his secretary Abu-'l-Fazl contemptuously observes that Sher Shāh sought the applause of posterity by reviving the regulation of 'Alā-ud-dīn, of which he had read, but the remark is typical of Akbar's panegyrist, whose bitterness may perhaps be explained by his master's failure.

Among the graver difficulties overcome by Sher Shāh was that offered by the character of his own people, proud, turbulent, disobedient and vindictive, ever ready to prefer family and tribal to national interests. Buhlūl Lodī had been content with the position of leader of a confederacy of tribal chiefs, *primus inter pares*, but Sher

[1] See chap. xvi, p. 456.

Shāh perceived that to expel the Timurids from India and prevent their return the authority of a tribal chief would not suffice, and that he must wield that of a sovereign. He constantly warned his nobles that it was owing to the feuds and quarrels of the Afghāns and to their lack of a national spirit that Bābur had been able to invade and establish himself in India, and his admonitions, enforced by sterner measures, were so effective that, perhaps for the only time in history, he, an Afghān himself, established and ruled an Afghān kingdom in which none was for a party and all were for the state.

The Afghān sovereign who surmounted so many difficulties and raised himself from the condition of a petty assignee to that of ruler of a great empire was also a builder and a road-maker. Of his four great roads one ran from Sonārgāon in Bengal through Āgra, Delhi and Lahore to the Indus, one from Āgra to Māndū, one from Āgra to Jodhpur and Chitor, and one from Lahore to Multān. On either side of all were planted fruit trees, and beside them were erected 1700 caravanserais, with separate lodgings for Muslims and Hindus and servants to supply food to those of each religion. Grain and fodder were supplied for horses and cattle, and each caravanserai contained a well and a mosque of burnt brick, with a *mu'azzin* and an *imām* in attendance. A police official kept the peace and prevented crime, and two post-horses were stabled in each building for the use of riders conveying the royal mail. Of these caravanserais no trace remains, for the Timurids were not careful to maintain memorials of the Afghān rebel.

Besides building Rohtās, near Jhelum, Sher Shāh built two forts at Delhi, extended the city towards the Jumna, and built forts at Kanauj and elsewhere. Crime was rigorously suppressed and the headmen of villages were held responsible for the surrender of those who committed crimes in their villages or of criminals who took refuge in them. Even the historians of the Timurids admit that in the Afghān's reign an old woman with a basket of gold could safely sleep in the open plain at night without a guard, and the historian Badāūnī, born in 1540, imitates the founder of his faith by thanking God that he was born the subject of so just a king. It was India's grave misfortune that this great king did not, as he himself once exclaimed when observing his grey hairs in a mirror, ascend the throne until the time of evening prayer. His body was borne to Sasarām and there a splendid mausoleum, which still stands, was raised above it. He was a pious and rigidly orthodox Muslim, but was liberal and tolerant. The most flagrant act of his life was his breach of faith with Pūran Mal and the massacre of the Hindus after the surrender of Rāisen; but those Hindus had committed the gravest of all offences against Islam, and Sher Shāh was convinced that his faith required the violation of a pledge which should never have been given.

He left two sons, 'Ādil Khān and Jalāl Khān. The nobles, eager to avoid strife by filling the throne with the least possible delay, summoned Jalāl Khān from Patna and enthroned him at Kālinjar on 26 May, 1545, only four days after his father's death, under the title of Islām Shāh, a title corrupted by some historians, by the figure known as *imāla*, into Islīm Shāh and again into Salīm Shāh, but the new king's correct title, as appears from his coins, was Islām Shāh.

Islām Shāh wrote to his elder brother in Ranthambhor promising to surrender the crown, and urged him to hasten to Āgra, but 'Ādil Khān was suspicious and required the guarantee and the personal escort of four great nobles. His request was granted and Islām Shāh, who at Kālinjar had put to death Kīrat Singh and seventy of his chief followers, marched to meet his brother. They met near Fathpur Sīkrī and marched to Āgra, where Islām Shāh's behaviour, though he feigned to offer the throne to his brother, was so suspicious that 'Ādil Khān declared that he required no more than a subordinate charge and permission to depart in peace. Islām Shāh was loth to let him go free, but the four great nobles who had guaranteed his safety insisted that faith should be kept, and 'Ādil Khān went to Bayāna, the charge selected by him. Two months later 'Ādil Khān fled from Bayāna in consequence of an attempt made by Islām Shāh to arrest and bring him to court. He took refuge with Khavāss Khān, who had always been a partisan of 'Ādil Khān, and now openly declared for him. They marched on Āgra where they had hopes of support, but delayed on the way. In the meantime Islām Shāh had discovered the plot and marched against the rebels. Meeting them at a village about ten miles to the west of the city he defeated them, and 'Ādil Khān fled, alone and unattended, towards Patna, where he disappeared. Khavāss Khān retired into Mewāt, and defeated at Fīrūzpur[1] an army sent in pursuit of him by Islām Shāh, but, being well aware that he could not long resist all the power of the crown, retired to his former assignment, Sirhind. Islām Shāh sent an officer in pursuit with 40,000 horse, but he and Khavāss Khān understood one another, and Khavāss Khān was permitted to retire through Katehr (Rohilkhand) to find a refuge on the lower slopes of the Kumāūn hills.

The extent of the conspiracy to raise 'Ādil Khān to the throne filled Islām Shāh with suspicion of all his nobles. Some were stripped of their possessions and imprisoned, others were confined in Gwalior and drugged with a preparation of poppy-heads until they became imbecile, and many were put to death. The place of the old nobles slain or imprisoned was taken by the officers of the troops which Islām Shāh had commanded before ascending the throne, and many of the private soldiers of that contingent were promoted to fill their places.

[1] 27° 41′ N., 76° 56′ E.

These measures seriously alarmed those who remained, and revived tribal jealousies, especially in the Niyāzī tribe. Sa'īd Khān fled to his brother, Haibat Khān Niyāzī, governor of Lahore, and persuaded him to head a revolt against the tyrant. Qutb Khān, who had been implicated in the attempt to raise 'Ādil Khān to the throne, joined them, and Islām Shāh demanded his surrender. So little were the tribal chiefs capable of a common course that Haibat Khān, actuated probably by some private grudge, surrendered him, and he was imprisoned in Gwalior with fourteen of the other old nobles.

The attitude of the rebels in the Punjab was now so menacing that Islām Shāh marched against them and was joined at Delhi by Shujā'at Khān. The rebels, meanwhile, advanced to Ambāla and there the armies met.

The night before the battle Haibat Khān and Khavāss Khān, who had joined him from the Kumāūn hills, held a council to decide who should be raised to the throne in the event of their defeating Islām Shāh. Khavāss Khān remained loyal to the Sūr tribe and maintained that the right of 'Ādil Khān, whose whereabouts he seems to have known, was indefeasible, but Haibat Khān, placing his personal ambition before loyalty to the family of his old master, declared that the crown was the prize of the sword. The next day, when the forces met, Khavāss Khān, refusing to aid the Niyāzī chief to gain a crown, withdrew his contingent and retired into Kumāūn. The Niyāzīs were defeated, but before they fled an unsuccessful attempt was made to murder the king.

Islām Shāh pursued the Niyāzīs as far as New Rohtās and then returned towards Āgra, leaving a force to continue the pursuit. This force was defeated at Dungot[1] on the Indus and retired to Sirhind, while the Niyāzīs took refuge with the Gakkhars and finally in Kashmīr.

Islām Shāh now, having failed to persuade the Rājā of Kumāūn to surrender Khavāss Khān, entered into communication with Khavāss Khān himself and, after recording a solemn oath that he had forgiven him all his offences, begged him to attend at court and proceed against the Rānā of Mewār who had plundered the royal territories and carried off the wives and daughters of Muslims. At the same time he sent orders to the governor of Sambhal to put Khavāss Khān to death so soon as he should come within reach. Khavāss Khān, disregarding the warning of his host, the Rājā, obeyed the summons and was met at Sirsī, only six miles from Sambhal, by the governor, who, although he owed advancement to him, caused him to be assassinated in his tent at night, and sent his head, on a spear, and his body, stuffed with straw, to Islām Shāh. Thus perished the noblest and the ablest of the adherents of the Sūr dynasty (1546).

[1] 71° 40′ E., 32° 58′ N.

Islām Shāh still persisted in attempts to destroy men who had served his father well and might have served him equally well, had they been trusted. He secretly employed an Afghān to stab Shujā'at Khān of Mālwā on his way to court. The wounded noble, though visited by the king who professed great concern, as soon as his wound was healed, hastily left the court at Gwalior, without permission, and retired into Mālwā (1547). The king pursued him, and Shujā'at Khān might have defeated him, but refused to attack his sovereign and withdrew into the rugged tract of Bānswārā, and Islām Shāh, having nominally dismissed him from the government of Mālwā, was obliged to turn towards the Punjab, where the Niyāzīs yet defied his authority. The rebels had again established themselves in Dungot, but a royal force defeated them and captured the mother and daughters of Haibat Khān, who for two years were exhibited once a week in a state of nudity in Islām Shāh's hall of public audience and at the end of that time were put to death. The remnant of the Niyāzīs again took refuge with the Gakkhars whom Islām Shāh endeavoured for two years to subdue. Their chief successfully eluded him, but he took one of their principal leaders, flayed him alive and imprisoned his son in Gwalior.

It was not only the old nobles of Sher Shāh's court who were harassed by persecution. In an attempt made on the king's life at this time his assailant was overpowered and slain, but the sword with which he was armed was found to be one which Islām Shāh had himself presented to Iqbāl Khān, an infantry soldier whom he had ennobled. Iqbāl Khān's complicity was not fully proved, and his life was spared, but he was again reduced to the condition of a private soldier.

The wretched king now learned of a plot to remove him and raise to the throne his cousin and brother-in-law, Mubāriz Khān Sūr, but, fearful of arousing the suspicion and resentment of his wife, sister of Mubāriz Khān, he refrained from disclosing his knowledge, and contented himself with the precaution of increasing the guard over his tents.

The Niyāzīs, finding that the Gakkhars could no longer afford them a secure refuge, retreated to Kashmīr and there intervened in the dispute between Mīrzā Haidar, the conqueror and ruler of Kashmīr, and the Chakk tribe. The Chakk tribe was eventually victorious and afterwards attacked Haibat Khān and his force of Niyāzīs. The Niyāzīs, though they defended themselves valiantly, Bībī Rābi'a, Haibat Khān's wife, fighting like a man, were outnumbered and overpowered and all were slain.

Islām Shāh, in camp near the Chenāb, was thus relieved of the menace of this long-standing rebellion, and he now received at his court Kāmrān Mīrzā, fleeing before his brother Humāyūn. The prince was haughtily received, was obliged to humiliate himself before his host, and became the butt of the Afghān nobles, who ridiculed him in Hindī, which he did not understand. Thus goaded he uttered some Persian verses reflecting on the king, and was placed in open arrest, but succeeded in making his escape and took refuge with Sultān Ādam the Gakkhar, who surrendered him to Humāyūn on receiving an assurance that his life should be spared.

After returning to Delhi Islām Shāh learned that Humāyūn had crossed the Indus, and, though seriously ill, tore off some leeches which had been applied to his neck and set out for Lahore, but on arriving there learned that his enemy had gone back to Kābul, so he returned to Gwalior, his favourite place of residence. Here he spent his time chiefly in sport but continued so to harass his nobles that they conspired to assassinate him. He escaped by good fortune, and the chief conspirators were put to death and others were imprisoned. He now suggested to his wife that her brother, whose partisans increased in number, should be removed lest his pretensions should injure the interests of their son, but she insisted that her brother was a mere nonentity who cared for nothing but music, pleasure and dissipation, to which he was devoting his time in order to avert suspicion. The known partisans of Mubāriz Khān meanwhile refused to attend court together, lest they should be seized and put to death, and the king dared not proceed against those who attended singly lest the remainder should rise against him. His health now failed but he concealed his malady from others and cauterized with his own hand a growth from which he suffered, so injuring himself that he fell mortally sick. He made a final appeal to his wife to remove her brother, and, as she merely burst into tears, turned his face to the wall and died on 22 November, 1554.

At this period there was much unrest among Muslims in India. The millennium of Muhammad's flight from Mecca was approaching and there was a belief, not universal, but widely current, that the manifestation of the Mahdī, who was to convert the whole world to Islam, to fill the earth with equity and justice as it had been filled with tyranny and oppression, and to reign for seven years, was about to take place. In 1504, in the reign of Ibrāhīm Lodī, one Sayyid Muhammad of Jaunpur had given definite form to this doctrine, and had at length claimed to be the Mahdī, but had died on his return from the pilgrimage to Mecca. In Sher Shāh's reign Shaikh 'Alā'ī, son of Shaikh Hasan, one of the most highly respected religious teachers in Bengal, made the pilgrimage to Mecca, and on his return established himself in Bayāna as his father's successor, but after a time fell under the influence of Shaikh 'Abdullah Niyāzī, an Afghān who had been a follower of Sayyid Muhammad of Jaunpur. The two leaders confined their teaching and preaching, the distinctive mark of which was rigid puritanism, to the poor. They kept no goods or means of livelihood, but they and their followers always went armed, and made it their business to enforce as well as to make the laws. They admonished any whom they found in the city or in the market doing an act which they judged to be unlawful or irreligious, and, if he paid no need to their warnings, administered chastisement, and they permitted no interference with their actions by officials, though they aided all magistrates who acted in accordance with their tenets and principles. This defiance of constituted authority rendered 'Alā'ī so obnoxious to the magistracy and the public that by the advice of 'Abdullah Niyāzī he set out once more for Mecca, but, on reaching Khavāsspur, near Jodhpur, he succeeded in converting Khavāss Khān, then governor of Sher Shāh's territories in Rājāsthān, to his views. His fanatical condemnation of all worldly enjoyment soon, however, disgusted Khavāss Khān, and 'Alā'ī returned to Bayāna, where he was living when Islām Shāh ascended the throne. He was summoned to Āgra, appeared at court with a large band of ragged and dirty armed followers, saluted the king as an equal and bore himself most insolently. Maulānā 'Abdullah of Sultānpur, entitled Makhdūm-ul-Mulk, of whom more will be heard in Akbar's reign, held the office of *Sadr-us-Sudūr*, or chief jurist, and unsparingly condemned 'Alā'ī as a schismatic.

Shaikh 'Alā'ī continued, however, to preach, and the learned Shaikh Mubārak of Nāgaur, who played a very prominent part in Akbar's reign and was ever in search of something new in the way of religion, attached himself to 'Alā'ī and became a Mahdavī. Many of the courtiers too, who had at first jeered at the uncouth preacher, became, to the king's indignation, his disciples. Islām Shāh hesitated to follow the advice of the orthodox theologians, who decreed that the heretic should be put to death, and banished him to the Deccan where the Mahdavī doctrines had many adherents, but 'Alā'ī travelled no further than Handiya, the frontier-town on the Narbadā, where he converted the governor, Bihār Khān, and the greater number of his troops. 'Alā'ī was then recalled.

Islām Shāh, on his way to the Punjab to suppress the rebellion of the Niyāzīs, halted at Bhasāwar, near Bayāna, and ordered the governor of Bayāna, Miyān Bahwā Lohānī, to produce Shaikh 'Abdullah. Bahwā, who was his disciple, was unwilling to deliver his spiritual guide to the king. 'Abdullah, though he voluntarily appeared, refused to salute the king, and Islām Shāh angrily asked, "Is this the master of Shaikh 'Alā'ī?" Makhdūm-ul-Mulk replied, "The very man", whereupon Shaikh 'Abdullah was so severely beaten that he fell as if dead, but he recovered from his punishment and after wandering for some time settled at Sirhind, where he renounced the Mahdavī creed, preached against the doctrines of the sect, and became an orthodox teacher. He received a grant of land from Akbar, and died in 1592 in the ninetieth year of his age.

Shaikh 'Alā'ī was sent to Shaikh Budh, a learned and orthodox physician in Bihār, who was commanded to examine him and to issue a *fatwā*, or authoritative decree, regarding his doctrines and the punishment due to one who held them, but although 'Alā'ī behaved arrogantly and insolently Shaikh Budh shrank from the responsibility of condemning him. His sons, however, wrote a letter in his name, recommending that the decision of Makhdūm-ul-Mulk, *Sadr-us-Sudūr*, the most discriminating of the jurists of the day, should be enforced, and sent it, with 'Alā'ī, to the royal camp in the Punjab. Here 'Alā'ī refused to recant, and was made over to Makhdūm-ul-Mulk, who sentenced him to a flogging. His weakness, owing to bad health and the fatigue of his journey, was so great that at the third stripe he succumbed and died (1548). His body was trampled on by an elephant, and was left unburied. After his death the Mahdavī movement in northern India died down, but it flourished longer in the Deccan.

Islām Shāh had no share of the great qualities of his father, who stood alone among the Afghāns, while the son had all the faults attributed to them. He was suspicious, cruel, vindictive and narrow-minded, unable to "think imperially" and dominated by clan or family feeling. His treatment of his nobles recalls the folly of another Afghān ruler, Ibrāhīm Lodī, but his cruelty exceeded Ibrāhīm's. During his father's life he had been closely associated with the greatest of his nobles, Khavāss Khān, whose services, eclipsing those of the prince, aroused his jealousy, and whose experience of the prince's character decided him to adopt the cause of his elder brother, 'Ādil Khān. Even after 'Ādil Khān's disappearance Islām Shāh's suspicions of his nobles remained alive, and it was his treatment of them that caused the Niyāzīs to rebel, and alienated them from his house. He was unable, in spite of his cruelty, to control the tribal chieftains, and the clan feuds which Sher Shāh had suppressed broke out afresh and made it clear that empire was not for the Afghāns.

Islām Shāh's jealousy of his father's reputation betrayed the meanness of his character. Between each two of the caravanserais which his father had built on the main roads he built another caravanserai, wholly unnecessary, and instead of distributing alms in the imperial camp, as his father had done, he followed the wasteful course of permitting them to be distributed, under inefficient supervision, at all the caravanserais. He remodelled the army, dividing the cavalry into troops and squadrons of 50, 200, 250 and 500. Two other measures angered the old nobles and aroused in them that hostility which drew upon them his suspicion. The first was the special favour shown to his personal troops, a force of 6000 cavalry which had been under his command during his father's life. After his accession the private soldiers of this force were promoted to the rank of officers, and the officers to that of *amīr* or noble. The second was the arbitrary substitution of cash payments for assignments and of assignments for cash payments among officers holding high command in the army. None of these measures, either civil or military, was necessary; some led to wasteful expenditure of public funds, others aroused discontent, and all were introduced merely with the object of advancing their author's reputation as an administrator and legislator.

On the death of Islām Shāh the nobles enthroned in Gwalior, on 22 November, 1554, his son Fīrūz, then aged only twelve years. The minister and regent was Tāj Khān Kararānī, the murderer of Khavāss Khān, and the power which he wielded excited the envy of the other nobles, who, by arousing the suspicions of the young king's mother against him, induced her to remove him and appoint him to the government of Mālwā.

About a month after his departure Mubāriz Khān, who had assured himself of the support of many of the disaffected nobles, arrived at Gwalior at the head of a large force. He was the son of Nizām Khān, the younger brother of Sher Shāh, and brother of the young king's mother, who, as already described, had twice saved his life when her husband wished to remove him as a danger to their son. On the pretext of offering his congratulations to the young king he forced his way, all travel-stained as he was, into his presence, and the boy's mother, divining his intentions, besought him, as she had saved his life, to spare that of her son, but the monster seized his nephew, severed his head from his body, and seven days later ascended the throne under the title of 'Ādil Shāh or Muhammad 'Ādil.

He appointed as his minister Shamsher Khān, a younger brother of the murdered Khavāss Khān, and as his *vakīl*, or deputy minister, Daulat Khān, a Hindu converted to Islam, but confided in and chiefly depended upon Hīmū, a Hindu of the Dhūnsar caste. This man had originally sold salt in the streets of Rewārī, and, having been appointed weighman in the market, had come under the notice of Islām Shāh, who had received him at his court and employed him in a confidential capacity. At the court of 'Ādil Shāh he gradually acquired great influence, and, though a Hindu of a non-fighting race, proved, like the barber of Tilak, who commanded the Indian cavalry of Mas'ūd of Ghaznī, that he possessed both military and administrative ability.

'Ādil Shāh, in order to conciliate those of the nobles and the army who were likely to resent his barbarous murder of his nephew, distributed treasure freely, and conferred titles on those who desired them. Having thus, to some extent, allayed disaffection, he marched to Chunār and took possession of such of the treasure of Sher Shāh as yet remained there. Salīm Khān, one of the Sūr clan, rose in rebellion to avenge the murder of Fīrūz Shāh, but his rebellion was crushed and he fled into the hills.

'Ādil Shāh made Chunār his residential capital. During Islām Shāh's reign he had simulated imbecility, probably without much effort, for he was certainly of defective intellect. He devoted his time almost entirely to frivolous and sensual pleasure and was contemptuously known as 'Adlī, which is a contemptuous diminutive of his title. For the conduct of the public business of his kingdom he relied almost entirely upon Hīmū, thus alienating most of the Afghān nobles, many of whom withdrew from court to their districts where each behaved as an independent prince. Junaid Khān, governor of Bayāna, and his son, governor of Ajmer, rebelled, and defeated and plundered Jamāl Khān, governor of Gwalior, who was sent against them. Their success alarmed 'Ādil Shāh, but Hīmū offered to crush the rebels. The king was at first ill-disposed to trust the command of troops to a Hindu but finally allowed him to take the field with three or four thousand horse. Junaid Khān, not unnaturally, despised such an enemy, and sent against him one of his officers, whom Hīmū defeated. This was the Dhūnsar's first military success. Junaid Khān now took the field with his whole force, which far outnumbered Hīmū's, but Hīmū chose the perilous venture of a night attack. He fell on Junaid Khān's camp from two sides in the third watch of the night, throwing his troops into confusion so that many of them were slaughtering one another; the flying rebels were pursued and slain in great numbers, and Junaid Khān was fortunate to escape with his life. The plunder was great, and this victory, and Hīmū's modesty when he returned to his master at Gwalior, established his reputation.

Tāj Khān Kararānī had returned to court after the death of Fīrūz and was the leading Afghān noble there. Among the few remaining at court was Ibrāhīm Khān Sūr, a second cousin of the king, and also a brother-in-law. One day, on a ceremonial occasion, Ibrāhīm entered the hall of audience and all present rose to salute him, except Tāj Khān, who remained seated. A few days later an attempt was made on Tāj Khān's life, and Tāj Khān, convinced that the king and Ibrāhīm had instigated the attempt, assembled his followers, and as soon as he had recovered from his wound left Gwalior. Cutting his way through a force sent to intercept him, he succeeded in reaching Jaunpur, where the governor failed to persuade him to return to court. A force sent in pursuit defeated him but failed to arrest his flight.

'Ādil Shāh now grew suspicious of all his Afghān nobles, and aroused their fears by putting to death his two principal supporters. From Hīmū's subsequent career it seems probable that it was he who sowed dissension between the king and his leading nobles, but, however this may be, Ibrāhīm Khān Sūr was selected as the next victim. He, however, learned the design from his wife, the king's sister, and fled with his troops from Gwalior, defeating on the way a large force sent in pursuit. At Delhi he was joined by the governor of Sirhind and other Afghān nobles, assumed the royal title, and caused the *khutba* to be recited in his own name. 'Ādil Shāh, now at Chunār, was much perturbed by this news, and, returning hastily to Gwalior, released two nobles whom he had imprisoned and sent them against Ibrāhīm Shāh. On reaching Delhi, however, they joined Ibrāhīm.

'Ādil Shāh's attention was now diverted from his rival by the rebellion at Ujjain of a Hindu chieftain who marched on Gwalior. The king again hastened from Chunār to Gwalior and despatched troops against the rebel. The Hindu, after an initial success, was slain and his army fled. The Afghāns inflicted on them great slaughter and 'Ādil Shāh pursued the remnant of the Hindu force to Ujjain, where he captured its late commander's wives and children and took much plunder. After this success he lingered in Mālwā, and Ibrāhīm Shāh of Delhi took full advantage of his absence from Hindūstān by annexing many districts of the Punjab. After tarrying too long 'Ādil Shāh returned to Gwalior and determined to take the field in person against his brother-in-law; but before marching on Delhi he decided to blind or put to death Ahmad Khān, another cousin, who was married to the king's younger sister. She, like her sister, warned her husband of his danger, and Ahmad, who commanded 4000 horse, left Gwalior one day when the king was drunk and rode with his troops to Delhi. There he had an interview with Ibrāhīm Shāh of whom he demanded, as the price of his adherence, the government of the Punjab. Ibrāhīm hesitated to confer on a possible rival such an appointment. Ahmad broke off negotiations, withdrew, assembled his troops and prepared to attack Ibrāhīm. On 18 March, 1555, the armies of the two princes met at Farah, eighteen miles north-west of Āgra, and though Ahmad's troops were outnumbered in the proportion of nearly four to one, he defeated his cousin, who fled to Sambhal, while most of his troops transferred their services to the victor. Ahmad then occupied Delhi, where he was enthroned under the title of Sikandar Shāh, and caused the *khutba* to be recited and struck coins in his own name. His power increased rapidly, and Ibrāhīm, unable to face him in the field, withdrew eastwards. 'Ādil Shāh attempted to recover the territory which Sikandar had gained from Ibrāhīm but failed, and three kings now reigned in northern India. The authority of 'Ādil Shāh extended over Āgra and Mālwā and as far east as Jaunpur; that of Sikandar Shāh from Delhi to Rohtās in the Punjab; and that of Ibrāhīm Shāh from the foot of the Himālayas to Gujrāt in the Punjab.

Humāyūn had been preparing, since the death of Islām Shāh, to invade India and recover his throne, and now, hearing of the confusion which prevailed in the land, where three kings claimed supremacy, and of the dissensions between the Afghān princes and nobles, resolved to carry his project into effect. One day, while taking the air, he took an omen from the names of the first three men whom he met. The first was Daulat ("Empire"), the second Murād

("Desired"), and the third Sa'ādat ("Good Fortune"). A second omen, taken from the poems of Hāfiz, fell on the ode containing the couplet:

دولت از مرغ همایون طلب و سایهٔ او
ز انکه با زاغ و زغن شهپر دولت نبود

Seek fortune from the auspicious phoenix, and the shadow cast by him,
For the pinion of fortune is possessed neither by crow nor by kite.

The word rendered "auspicious" was Humāyūn's own name, and it is not surprising that the omen confirmed his decision. Leaving Kābul he reached Peshāwar on 25 December, 1554, and, after crossing the Indus, was joined nine days later by Bairam Khān and many other officers from Qandahār. Sultān Ādam, the Gakkhar, who had promised him support, failed to join him, but explained his absence by a treaty with Sikandar Shāh, who had compelled him to enter into it and to surrender his son as a hostage.

Humāyūn marched to Lahore and the Afghāns in that city fled on his approach. Tātār Khān Kāshī, who had held Rohtās for Sikandar, had already abandoned it, and Humāyūn was able to despatch from Lahore a force which occupied the districts of Jullundur, Sirhind and Hissār without striking a blow, while another force defeated at Dīpālpur, in March, 1555, an Afghān army and captured its camp and baggage and the wives and families of the officers.

The news of this defeat aroused Sikandar Shāh, who was in Delhi, to action, and he assembled an army of 30,000 horse and despatched it towards Sirhind, which city Humāyūn's advance guard had reached. Humāyūn's officers, assembled at Jullundur, decided, despite their numerical inferiority to the Afghān army, to give battle and crossed the Sutlej. The Afghāns pressed forward to oppose their passage of the river but did not reach the neighbourhood of the bank until the invaders had already crossed it. The armies met at sunset, and as the darkness fell the village before which the Afghān army was drawn up caught fire, so that the Mughul archers clearly saw their enemy by the blaze of the thatched roofs, and rained showers of arrows on them until they broke and fled, leaving their camp and baggage in the hands of the victors. Bairam Khān, who commanded the Mughul forces, then advanced to Sirhind and occupied and fortified the town, and the news of his victory was received with much joy in Humāyūn's court at Lahore.

Sikandar Shāh, on learning of the defeat of his troops, himself took the field, marched with 80,000 horse, and elephants and artillery, from Delhi to Sirhind. He entrenched himself before the city, and the Mughul officers strengthened its fortifications and sent a message to Humāyūn begging him to join his army without delay. He was indisposed, but sent his young son, Akbar, to represent him and left Lahore as soon as his health permitted, arriving at Sirhind on 27 May,

1555. Here he spent nearly a month in perfecting its defences, while occasional combats took place between his troops and those of Sikandar Shāh. On 22 June Khvāja Mu'azzam, Atga Khān and some other officers attacked the Afghāns with a considerable force, and though Humāyūn, as usual, was not prepared for a general action, other troops were drawn in, to support those already engaged, until the action became general. Sikandar Shāh had received reinforcements, but his army, now numbering nearly 100,000 horse, was defeated after a well-contested fight and fled, losing heavily in the retreat. Sikandar took refuge in the skirts of the Himālayas, and the leaders of the victorious army were received on their return with much honour, until the generals disturbed their master's ease by disputing one another's title to the credit of the victory. Humāyūn summarily settled their dispute by naming his son Akbar, in the despatch announcing the victory, as the commander of his army. It was now discovered that Khvāja Mu'azzam had been in treasonable correspondence with Sikandar Shāh, and he was imprisoned, but it seems difficult to believe that he can have had any object in aiding Sikandar's cause, and it is not improbable that his correspondence was designed to involve his dilatory master in a general action, and that his message to Sikandar had the same object as that of Themistocles to the Persians before Salamis.

After the battle Humāyūn marched to Samānā, whence he sent officers into the Punjab to check any attempt of Sikandar to emerge from the hills, and to establish order in that province; and another to occupy Delhi. He himself, finding the climate of Samānā pleasant, seemed to be inclined to loiter there indefinitely, until a message from Delhi, which had been occupied without opposition, urged him to take possession of his capital. He left Samānā, halted on 20 July at Salīmgarh on the Jumna, and on 23 July once more entered Delhi. Here he settled down to rest after his labours, appointing officers to various commands. In consequence of the misbehaviour of the governor of the Punjab Humāyūn sent the young prince Akbar in his place as titular governor of the Punjab, the duties of the office falling upon his tutor, Bairam Khān. Misgovernment in the Punjab had been Sikandar Shāh's opportunity. His forces increased, he emerged from his retreat, and he was menacing the Punjab, necessitating the movement of the imperial troops under Bairam Khān and Akbar against him.

At the same time a rebellion in the eastern provinces broke out. One Qambar Beg rose in rebellion, and so many adventurers from the Sambhal district and the Gangetic Dūāb joined him that the movement had the appearance of becoming serious. 'Alī Qulī Khān Shaibānī was deputed to suppress the rebellion, and besieged Qambar in Budaun. The siege did not last long; the city was taken and Qambar was put to death, his head being sent to Delhi.

This was the last of Humāyūn's earthly troubles, for on 24 January, 1556, he "stumbled out of life as he had stumbled through it". He was sitting on the roof of the palace library at Delhi at the time of evening prayer, conversing with astrologers and others, and rose to descend the steep stairs in order to attend the service of prayer. On hearing the *mu'azzin's* cry, he knelt in reverence, but his staff slipped and he tripped on the skirt of his robe, falling down the stairs and fracturing the base of his skull. He was carried within the palace and, on recovering consciousness, learned from the court physicians that his condition was serious and despatched a message to his son Akbar, now with Bairam Khān at Kalānaur,[1] informing him that he was likely to die and finally designating him as his heir. On 26 January he breathed his last, and the true report of his death was sent to Akbar and Bairam Khān. Owing to the condition of the country it was concealed from the general public, a man being dressed up to represent him on the occasions on which he had been in the habit of appearing in public, and the Turkish admiral Sīdī 'Alī Ra'īs, who was leaving the court for Lahore, being instructed to bear the news that the emperor yet lived.[2] The news of his death reached Akbar on or before 14 February, and on 14 February[3] Humāyūn's death was made known and Akbar was proclaimed in Delhi.

According to the official account Humāyūn's fatal fall was attributed to an act of reverence, but it has also been attributed, by less courtly chroniclers, to the effects of drugs or drink, to both of which he was addicted.

The empire which Humāyūn bequeathed to his young son consisted, in fact, of little more than the ground occupied by Bairam Khān's small army. Delhi and Āgra had indeed been occupied but events were soon to show how precarious was the tenure of these provinces. Certain districts in the Punjab and in the trans-Gangetic province of Katehr were held, but the army's loyalty was not wholly above suspicion, and three members of the Sūr clan still claimed the sovereignty of the whole of north-western India. One had been defeated, but not crushed, another was ready to take his place should he be defeated by Akbar's troops, and the third, with his capital at Chunār, had not yet been attacked. The economic condition of the land was even worse than the political. Its most fertile and populous provinces were devastated by a famine caused by failure of the rains combined with two years' destructive internecine warfare. "The capital was devastated and nothing remained but a few houses. An epidemic plague ensued and spread through most of the cities of Hindūstān. Multitudes died, and men were driven to feed on human flesh, parties being formed to seize and eat solitary victims."

[1] 32° 0′ N., 75° 10′ E.

[2] C. E. A. W. Oldham, *Indian Antiquary* (1930), pp. 219, 239, and (1931), pp. 5 and 26.

[3] For a discussion of the dates of Humāyūn's fall and death, and of the accession of Akbar, see Hodivala, *Mughal Numismatics*, pp. 264–6. [Ed.]

CHAPTER IV

AKBAR, 1556–1573

THE young emperor, who was only a few months more than thirteen years of age, was confronted with a situation scarcely less difficult than that in which his grandfather had found himself when his nobles were clamouring to be led back to Kābul, and in considering the difficulties which faced him it must be remembered that he was a precocious and masterful youth whom the jealousies of his courtiers compelled his guardian, Bairam Khān, to consult on all measures of importance. His father had returned to India and had possessed himself of Delhi and Āgra, but the recovery of these cities, immediately after his death, by his enemies reduced Akbar's inheritance to the Punjab.

The first difficulty with which Akbar and his guardian were called upon to deal was caused by the misconduct of Shāh Abu-'l-Ma'ālī, a noble of his father's court and a dangerous fanatic, whose pretensions, based on favours shown to him by Humāyūn, were obnoxious not only to the dignity of the courtiers but to the majesty of the throne. Resenting a fancied slight he at first refused to attend the young emperor's court and when he deigned to appear thrust himself forward into a place to which he had no claim and behaved with such gross disregard of propriety that it was necessary to arrest him. Bairam Khān believed him to be actively disloyal and advocated his immediate execution, but Akbar was loth to sully his hands, on the threshold of his reign, with the blood of one of his father's old servants, and the offender was sent to Lahore, where he was imprisoned.

Three princes of the Sūr clan still pretended to the throne of Delhi. These were Muhammad 'Ādil Shāh, who had occupied the throne for about a year, his cousin and brother-in-law Ibrāhīm, who had dethroned 'Ādil in 1553, and Ibrāhīm's cousin and brother-in-law Sikandar, who expelled Ibrāhīm in 1554 and was defeated by Humāyūn at Sirhind in 1555 and driven from Delhi and Āgra. 'Ādil had established himself at Chunār and was killed in 1557 in a battle with Bahādur Shāh of Bengal, and Ibrāhīm had withdrawn into Bengal. Bairam Khān, correctly estimating the character of the two surviving princes, considered Sikandar, who was still in arms in the Punjab, a more imminent menace than either of the others, and remained for some time after Akbar's enthronement at Kalānaur with the object of crushing Sikandar's resistance. He failed, however, owing to lack of information, to make sufficient provision to meet the attack of a foe more dangerous than any of the three princes.

This was Hīmū, "the Corn-chandler", a Hindu of Rewārī whom 'Ādil had made his minister, an able, energetic and ambitious soldier who was preparing to expel the Mughuls from India, nominally in the interests of 'Ādil, but actually in his own. Hīmū secretly cherished designs of seizing for himself the imperial throne and restoring the dominion to the Hindus. Hīmū was still in the field on behalf of 'Ādil and in his name could command the obedience of a large force of Afghāns.

It was believed that Iskandar Khān the Uzbeg at Āgra, Tārdī Beg Khān at Delhi, and 'Alī Qulī Khān Shaibānī at Sambhal were strong enough to repel any attacks from the south-east and to defend Hindūstān against both 'Ādil and his minister, but Hīmū's energy and determination were underrated. Bairam Khān, believing the situation to be secure, sent a force to Kābul to escort thence to India the ladies of Humāyūn's harem. Sulaimān Mīrzā of Badakhshān, who was then besieging that city, was forced by it to retire to his own dominions, and the ladies were safely conducted to India.

Hīmū now advanced from Gwalior on Āgra, and Iskandar Khān, instead of awaiting him, retired towards Delhi, losing between two and three thousand men in the course of his retreat. Hīmū followed him and encamped near Tughluqābād where Iskandar was joined by Tārdī Beg Khān, the governor of Delhi. The temporary success of the Mughul right wing hardly delayed Hīmū's complete victory over their centre and Tārdī Beg Khān, who, without making even an effort to hold Delhi, continued his rapid retreat towards Sirhind. Iskandar Khān perforce accompanied him and the retreating army was joined on its way by 'Alī Qulī Khān Shaibānī, who could no longer maintain himself at Sambhal after Hīmū's occupation of Delhi.

The news of the fall of Delhi reached Akbar and Bairam Khān at Jullundur and most of the courtiers and officers counselled an immediate retreat on Kābul, urging that it was folly to attempt to withstand Hīmū, now at the head of 100,000 men, with the 20,000 which were all that Akbar could muster. Bairam Khān decided, however, to risk all in the attempt to recover Delhi and had no difficulty in persuading the high-spirited and precocious Akbar to adopt his view. Khizr Khvāja Khān was left at Lahore to deal with Sikandar Sūr and on 13 October, 1556, the imperial army marched to Sirhind. Here it was met by the fugitives from Delhi, whose voices were added to those which clamoured for a retreat. This outburst was speedily silenced by Bairam Khān, who, having obtained from his youthful master "a sort of permission", caused Tārdī Beg Khān to be put to death.

The execution was a bold measure. Tārdī Beg Khān and Bairam Khān were outwardly on friendly terms, but were known to be rivals, and their rivalry was embittered by religious differences. Bairam cannot but have known that his action would be severely criticised, and his enemies, in fact, made it one of the articles in his impeachment when, a few years later, he fell from favour; but the murder was not the crime which they maintained it to be. Tārdī Beg Khān's disgraceful conduct at Delhi merited death according to the military codes of all ages and his advocacy of an immediate retreat from Sirhind rendered his death necessary. In fact credit is due to Bairam Khān for taking so promptly, at considerable risk to himself and his reputation, a step which alone could have restored and maintained the spirit and discipline of the army.

Hīmū was so elated by his victories and by the capture of Delhi as to believe that he had already reached the goal of his ambition. He made no pretence of restoring his master, but assumed the title of Rājā Vikramāditya and is said to have struck coin bearing his titles, though no specimen is known to exist. His Afghān officers were temporarily reconciled, by a liberal distribution of plunder, to the ascendancy of an infidel, and Hīmū sent forward his advance guard, with the greater part of his artillery, to meet that of Akbar, which, under the command of 'Alī Qulī Khān Shaibānī, had marched on Pānīpat. 'Alī Qulī Khān inflicted a severe defeat on Hīmū's advance guard, and captured his artillery.

Meanwhile the main bodies of the two armies were in motion and met, on 5 November, 1556, on the historic plain of Pānīpat. Bairam Khān detained Akbar at a safe distance from the field and entrusted the command of the centre to 'Alī Qulī Khān. Hīmū's army so greatly outnumbered that of Akbar that it was able almost to envelop it and threw both wings into confusion. Hīmū then attempted to decide the fate of the day by leading against the centre his 1500 elephants, on which he chiefly relied. 'Alī Qulī Khān and his officers, taking every advantage of the inequalities of the ground, fought with the utmost valour but would certainly have been overpowered had not Hīmū's eye been pierced by an arrow so well directed that its point projected from the back of his head. His troops at once dispersed.

Shāh Qulī Khān Mahram, a Bahārlū Turk in Bairam Khān's service, who afterwards attained to the command of 3500 horse, came up with Hīmū's elephant, *Hawāī*, as the driver was endeavouring to carry his master beyond the reach of danger. He begged Shāh Qulī not to slay him and told him who the elephant's wounded rider was. Shāh Qulī at once caused Hīmū to be led to Akbar, who had by now appeared on the field. When the wounded Hindu was placed before the young emperor Bairam Khān prayed him to earn the title of *Ghāzī* by slaying an infidel with his own sword, and the boy severed Hīmū's head from his body,[1] or according to another version merely touched the infidel, who was slain by those in attendance.

[1] *J.R.A.S.* 1916, p. 527.

Immediately after the victory Iskandar Khān the Uzbeg was sent in pursuit of the flying enemy, and followed them, with great slaughter, to the gates of the capital, which he entered and secured for the emperor. Two days later Akbar entered Delhi and 'Alī Qulī Khān and Iskandar Khān were rewarded for their services with the titles of Khān Zamān and Khān 'Ālam respectively.

The victory was complete. All of Hīmū's 1500 elephants had been captured and the broken remnant of his army was dispersed, but his wife had escaped from Delhi into Mewāt, taking with her all his treasure, and Pīr Muhammad Khān was sent in pursuit. He slew many fugitives and took much plunder, but Hīmū's wife made good her escape and much of the treasure was lost. His aged father was captured and, on refusing to accept Islam, was put to death.

Events had progressed less favourably in the Punjab. Sikandar Sūr had attacked Khizr Khvāja Khān at Chamiārī, about 35 miles north-east of Lahore, and had driven him into that city, and Khān 'Ālam was sent to his relief, followed, on 7 December, by the emperor and Bairam Khān, who could now safely leave imperial interests in Hindūstān in the hands of the nobles.

During their absence in the Punjab Khān Zamān reoccupied Sambhal and established his authority throughout the country between that town and Lucknow, and Qiyā Khān Gung, after occupying Āgra, drove away Rājā Rām Sāh, who was attempting to recover from Bahbal Khān, an officer in the service of 'Ādil, the fortress of Gwalior, which had belonged to his ancestors, and himself besieged the fortress.

On learning that Akbar had reached Jullundur, Sikandar Sūr retired from before Lahore and fled to Mānkot, a hill fortress which Islām Shāh had built to restrain the aggression of the Gakkhars, and here he was besieged by Akbar.

During the siege the ladies of Humāyūn's harem arrived at the camp from Kābul, and Akbar, who was not yet fifteen years of age, married his first wife, the daughter of his uncle Hindāl.

Sikandar Sūr had great confidence in the strength of Mānkot but relied chiefly on such diversion as could be created by his cousin 'Ādil, who still held Chunār, but who was now attacked by his cousin Khizr Khān Sūr, styling himself Jalāl-ud-dīn Bahādur Shāh of Bengal, and was slain. The news of his death so discouraged Sikandar that he surrendered in May, 1557, after enduring a siege of some months' duration, and by the interest of Atga Khān, the emperor's foster-father, received Bihār as an assignment. He died two years later.

Akbar marched in July to Lahore and in December to Delhi, halting on the way at Jullundur, where Bairam Khān married his cousin Salīma Begam, daughter of Humāyūn's sister.

On reaching the Sutlej Akbar learnt that Hājī Khān of Mewāt, who had fled to Nārnaul after the defeat of Hīmū, was marching on Hissār, and halted at Sirhind while Bairam Khān led the army against the rebel. Hājī Khān would not risk a conflict but fled and took refuge in Gujarāt, and three officers, one of whom was Sayyid Mahmūd Khān Bārha,[1] were sent to establish order in Ajmer and Rājputāna. Akbar reached Delhi on 14 April, 1558.

It is necessary, in order to convey a clear understanding of the intrigues which beset Akbar in the early years of his reign, to explain the state of parties at his court. There was, first, the protector's party consisting primarily of the greater number of the most loyal and able nobles.

Bairam Khān was a loyal and devoted servant but his disposition was arbitrary, haughty and jealous and he could not easily tolerate the presence of possible rivals near his young master. He was a staunch Shiah and his religion rendered him unpopular at a court composed chiefly of orthodox Sunnīs. He resented the decline of his influence as Akbar grew towards manhood, and his foibles were distorted by his enemies into evidence of a desire to subvert the emperor's authority.

The second great faction was the harem party, whose influence, as is so often the case in the East, was almost wholly evil. The interests of this party were served, beyond the walls of the harem, by Akbar's foster-relatives. The relationship existing between a child and the foster-mother who has suckled him is regarded by Turks, and by Muslims generally, as one of peculiar tenderness. It endures through life and extends to all the near relations of the foster-mother. The names of ten of Akbar's nurses are preserved, and it is recorded that there were others. The most influential of these was Jījī Anaga ("foster-mother"), whose husband, Shams-ud-dīn Khān, had saved Humāyūn from drowning and was honoured, after his wife's advancement, with the title of Atga ("foster-father") Khān. Of his two sons, the one who survived beyond the early years of Akbar's reign was known originally as Mīrzā 'Azīz *Kūka* ("foster-brother") but received the title of Khān A'zam and rose to the highest rank. Akbar excused the leniency with which he treated Khān A'zam's acts of disobedience and contumacy by saying, "Between me and 'Azīz is a river of milk which I cannot cross." The relationship extended to Atga Khān's elder brother, Mīr Muhammad Khān, entitled Khān Kalān ("Great", or elder Khān), to his younger brothers, Sharīf Khān and Qutb-ud-

[1] "'Sayyid Mahmūd was the first of the Bārha Sayyids that held office under the Tīmūrides.' He was with Sikandar Sūr in Mānkot but, seeing that the cause of the Afghāns was hopeless he left Sikandar and went over to Akbar" (*Āīn-i-Akbarī*, I, 389).

The Sayyids of Bārha, as distinguished for personal bravery as their kinsmen of Bilgrām are for their learning, derived their cognomen from twelve (*bāra*) villages which they held in the Muzaffarnagar District in the Upper Dūāb. Like the Sayyids of Bilgrām in Oudh they trace their origin to Sayyid Abu-'l-Farāh of Wāsit, who visited India in A.D. 1217. They reached the acme of their influence in the eighteenth century. See chaps. XIII and XIV of this volume, and W. Irvine, *J.A.S.B.* 1896, p. 175.

dīn Khān, and to their sons. Māham Anaga had been Akbar's chief nurse and though she never seems to have suckled him her son Adham Khān ranked as his foster-brother. These foster-relations are usually referred to by Muslim historians as *Atga Khail*, "the foster-father cohort".

The execution of Tārdī Beg Khān had excited much hostility against Bairam Khān, and an open breach occurred between him and "the foster-father cohort" on the march from Mānkot, when he suspected that the accidental finish of an elephant-fight near his tent was due to the machinations of Atga Khān and protested to Māham Anaga. The quarrel was patched up, but Pīr Muhammad Khān, formerly a servant of Bairam Khān, had gone over to the harem party, and his influence was ever directed towards the breeding of strife. The execution of Musāhib Beg, who had presumed on his father's services to Humāyūn to treat the protector with discourtesy and a similar exercise of arbitrary authority at Kābul by Mun'im Khān, which was approved by Bairam Khān, provided the enemies of the latter with further material for charges against him.

During Akbar's stay at Delhi the court was scandalised by a disgraceful affair between Khān Zamān and Shāham Beg, one of Humāyūn's pages, whom he enticed from Delhi. The details of this affair are of importance only as shedding some light on the morals of the great at the courts of the Mughul emperors, of which the less said the better. Khān Zamān was ordered to send Shāham Beg back to Delhi but instead of obeying sent an emissary to allay the wrath of "the foster-father cohort", which took the leading part in the proceedings against him. The emissary was slain by the brutal Pīr Muhammad Khān and Khān Zamān hurriedly dismissed Shāham Beg who, after leaving him, lodged with a man whose relations put him to death for attempting to seduce his host's wife.

After a stay of some months at Delhi the court left for Āgra, then a city of small importance, travelling by boat down the Jumna.

At Āgra Bairam Khān's chief anxiety was the education of his ward, who was devoted to manly exercises and field sports but, in spite of having been endowed with a vigorous intellect, could not be brought to pay any attention to what the ablest of his biographers calls "the usual apparatus of learning". In short, he was an idle boy who would not learn to read and write and he never acquired either of these arts. His father had urged him to mend his ways but it is doubtful whether Bairam Khān received any support from the harem party or "the foster-father cohort", whose interest lay in retarding the boy's progress as much as possible. After reaching man's estate Akbar atoned, as far as he could, for his boyish idleness by listening diligently to the reading of works on history, theology and philosophy, but it is unfortunate that in this respect he never rendered himself independent of the services of others, for the memory, however it may be cultivated, and Akbar's powers of memory, naturally immense, were developed by his illiteracy, can never supply the power of reference, and had he been able to use his eyes he might perhaps have been saved from the religious absurdities of his later years, which had their origin in his delight in listening to religious and philosophical discussions and found their expression in his confused recollections of these disputes.

Abu-'l-Fazl, on whose speculations Akbar in later years firmly relied, was, perhaps, the most subtle and the most fulsome adviser and flatterer that ever monarch had. Adulation is the business of the counsellor and of the historian of an eastern ruler, but Abu-'l-Fazl surpassed other historians and encomiasts as the light of the sun surpasses that of the moon. Most Eastern courtiers are content with assuring their masters that they are the best, the wisest and the greatest of mankind, but Abu-'l-Fazl's panegyrics contain the suggestion, if not the assertion, that his master is something more than man. His boyish idleness is attributed to a divinely inspired desire to remain behind a veil, concealing his powers from all, until the time came for him to reveal to a wondering world his divine commission. Similarly the emperor's devotion, in his maturer years, to the childish and futile diversion of pigeon-flying is represented as a form of worship. This fulsome adulation, which disgusts even those accustomed by long study to the flights of oriental encomiasts, had its motive. It was not self-advancement, but it may be suspected that it was revenge. This question will be discussed later.

The tutor whom Bairam Khān selected was Mīr 'Abdul-Latīf, the Persian, who failed, like his predecessors, to induce Akbar to learn to read, but was the first to teach him the principle of *sulh-i-kull*, or universal toleration, on which Abu-'l-Fazl so frequently descants. He came of a Sayyid family of Qazvīn, persecuted in Persia as Sunnīs, but was so moderate in his religious views as to be suspected, in India, of Shiah proclivities.

Party spirit was now inflamed by a serious quarrel between Pīr Muhammad Khān and his former master. Pīr Muhammad fell sick, and Bairam, who courteously visited him, was refused admission. Pīr Muhammad's excuse, that his servants had not recognised him, aggravated his offence and a few days later he was compelled to surrender his standards, kettledrums and other insignia of honour, was deprived of his title of Nāsir-ul-Mulk, and was imprisoned at Bayāna, whence he was sent, after a short interval, to Gujarāt with a view to his performing the pilgrimage to Mecca, which was regarded as banishment.

Bairam Khān's treatment of Pīr Muhammad was not his only crime in the eyes of the harem party. Almost immediately after this event he appointed Shaikh Gadāī, a Shaikh with no special qualifications, to the important post of *Sadr-us-Sudūr*, fourth in importance in the empire. The *Sadr* was the chief law officer and ecclesiastic and controlled all grants, endowments and allowances. The appointment raised a storm of protest from the orthodox, among the most prominent of whom was "the foster-father cohort", and contributed more than any other measure of Bairam Khān to his downfall.

It was probably with the object of diverting Akbar's attention from the discontent caused by these and other measures that Bairam Khān drew his attention to Gwalior, which Qiyā Khān Gung was still besieging but could not take for lack of support. He was reinforced and the fortress surrendered early in 1559. Qiyā Khān Gung was then sent into the eastern districts of Akbar's dominions, where Khān Zamān was still sulking, but made his peace and regained his master's favour by expelling Ibrāhīm Sūr from Jaunpur and surrendering Lucknow to Qiyā Khān.

Expeditions to Ranthambhor, held by Rāi Surjan on behalf of the Rānā of Chitor, and to Chunār, held by Jamāl Khān the Afghān, were less successful, and in each case the imperial troops were obliged to retreat without having effected their purpose. A third expedition, under Bahādur Khān Shaibānī, sent by Bairam Khān to annex Mālwā, was recalled early in 1560 from Siprī, owing to the strained relations between Akbar and his guardian.

Akbar was now in his eighteenth year and the restraint to which he was subjected by Bairam Khān galled him. The harem party did its utmost to widen the breach and on 28 March Akbar left Āgra on a hunting expedition. When he had reached Sikandra Rāo, about 45 miles north-east of the city, Māham Anaga urged him to visit his mother, who was lying sick at Delhi and longed to see him. Akbar rode at once to Delhi, thereby openly severing himself from his guardian, who remained at Āgra, and was ceremoniously received by Shihāb-ud-dīn Ahmad Khān, governor of the capital, who was in the plot and came out to some distance from the city to receive him. Having thus succeeded in separating him from the protector the conspirators confessed that they had incurred the resentment of Bairam Khān and appealed to his pride by throwing themselves on his protection, while Shihāb-ud-dīn Ahmad Khān began to put the defences of the city into a state of repair. Atga Khān marched from the Punjab to join him and Pīr Muhammad Khān returned from Gujarāt. Some correspondence passed between the protector and the emperor and when Akbar imprisoned Bairam Khān's emissaries the breach was irreparable.

The few adherents left to Bairam Khān urged him to attempt to recover the emperor's person by force, but he refused to turn his arms against his master, and left Āgra announcing that he proposed making a pilgrimage to Mecca. The harem party had gained its object and might well have been content with its victory, but it was certain that Bairam Khān intended to visit the Punjab to recover the private hoards which he had left at Lahore and Sirhind and his enemies assured Akbar that he intended to raise the standard of rebellion in that province. Akbar sent his tutor, Mīr 'Abdul-Latīf, to Bairam with a decree announcing that he had decided to take the management of affairs into his own hands and that he desired Bairam Khān to perform the pilgrimage to Mecca, and promising to make ample provision for his expenses. Bairam Khān promised obedience, but his movements were leisurely, and the harem party induced Akbar to send Pīr Muhammad Khān with a large force to hasten them. The selection of Pīr Muhammad for such a duty was deliberately provocative and Bairam Khān, after lodging his family at Bhatinda, turned towards Jullundur. Pīr Muhammad returned to court and reported his movements and a large force under Atga Khān which was sent against Bairam Khān defeated him at Jullundur and drove him towards the hills.

Akbar marched in person to Sirhind, where he was joined by Mun'im Khān and other nobles from Kābul. The grant of the protector's title of Khān Khānān to Mun'im Khān was a further indication, if any were needed, that Bairam Khān's day was over. He was pursued and was besieged at Tilwāra, a hill-fortress on the banks of the Beās, whence he sent a message to Akbar expressing contrition for his rebellion and offering to submit. He was assured, in return, that he would be well received and in October he appeared before Akbar in his camp at Hājīpur. His meeting with his master and former ward was affecting, but Akbar made the situation quite clear to him. He offered him one of three alternatives, the districts of Kālpī and Chanderī, the place of companion and confidential adviser to himself, or permission to depart for Mecca. Bairam Khān chose the last and left for Mecca by way of Gujarāt, where he was hospitably received by Mūsā Khān Fulādī, governor of Pātan, but was assassinated by a gang of Afghāns led by one Mubārak Khān, whose father had been killed in 1555 at the battle of Māchīwārā, where Bairam Khān had commanded the Mughul army. The Afghāns plundered his camp, and his family reached Ahmadābād almost destitute. Akbar sent for them and afterwards married as his second wife Salīma Begam, Bairam's widow, and charged himself with the education of his infant son, Mīrzā 'Abdur-Rahīm, known as Mīrzā Khān, who rose to the highest rank and in 1584 received his father's title of Khān Khānān.

It was chiefly to Bairam Khān, ably supported by Khān Zamān, that Akbar owed his throne. It was inevitable that a young man of Akbar's force of character should emerge from a state of tutelage, but he would have done well to wait, for he was not yet fit to assume sole charge of his empire and remained for four years more under the pernicious influence of the harem party. The means by which he escaped from Bairam's influence was probably the best which he could have adopted, but the insults and ungenerous treatment which drove the protector into rebellion would be a blot upon his memory were it not certain that they originated with Bairam's bitterest enemies in the harem party.

There could be no better testimony to Bairam Khān's worth than that recorded by the bigot Badāūnī, who could seldom see any good in a Shiah. "In wisdom, generosity, sincerity, goodness of disposition, submissiveness, and humility he surpassed all....The second conquest of Hindūstān and the building up of the empire were due to his strenuous efforts, his valour, and his wide policy....At last vile hypocrites poisoned the mind of His Majesty against him, until his affairs fell at length into the condition of which a brief description has been given."[1]

Mālwā still retained its independence under Bāz Bahādur, son of Shujā'at Khān, and early in 1561 Akbar sent an army to annex the province. Harem influence is traceable in the extremely injudicious selection of the commander of the force, Adham Khān, and of the second in command, Pīr Muhammad Khān.

Bāz Bahādur, a voluptuary devoted to music and to the society of dancers and singers, above all to that of his beloved mistress Rūp Matī, famed for her beauty and her devotion to her lover, now held his court at Sārangpur.[2] The imperial army invaded Mālwā, advancing by regular daily marches until it was within 20 miles of Sārangpur, and it was not until it had reached this point that Bāz Bahādur awoke from his dreams of love and music and bestirred himself to defend his kingdom. Marching from the city, he entrenched himself at a distance of three miles from it and awaited the attack of the imperial troops, but on 29 March he was induced, by feigned attacks from various directions, to leave his entrenched position and take the field. The battle was of short duration. His troops were outnumbered and his Afghān officers were disaffected and left the field early in the day. Bāz Bahādur saved his life by flight, but his women, his treasures and his elephants fell into the hands of the victors, and the devoted Rūp Matī took poison in order to escape the embraces of Adham Khān.

Pīr Muhammad Khān and Adham Khān sullied their victory by the most revolting cruelty. The historian Badāūnī, who was an eyewitness of their atrocities, describes them as follows:[3]

"On the day of the victory the two commanders were in their camp, and the prisoners were brought before them and were put to death by troops, so that their blood flowed in rivers."

Pīr Muhammad Khān cracked brutal jests on the wretched victims, and when Mihr 'Alī Beg Sildūz, at Badāūnī's instance, represented that whatever might be done with rebels taken in arms it was not

[1] *Bad.* III (trans. Haig), 265, 266.
[2] 23° 34′ N., 76° 29′ E.
[3] *Bad.* (text), II, 47.

lawful to put their wives and children to death Pīr Muhammad replied, "If we keep them for the night what will happen to them?"

"In that night the plundering marauders stowed away their Muslim captives, the wives of holy and learned men, Sayyids, and nobles, in boxes and saddlebags, and carried them off to Ujjain and in other directions. Sayyids and holy men came forth, bearing copies of the Korān, to welcome the conquerors, and Pīr Muhammad Khān slew and burnt them all."

Adham Khān sent to court, with the despatches announcing his victory, only a few elephants, and kept most of the spoils and all the women for himself. Māham Anaga's influence was powerless to restrain Akbar's resentment of such an insult to his authority, but she wrote to her son to warn him to look to himself and Akbar left Āgra on 27 April. After receiving, on his way, tribute from Surjan Rāi of Ranthambhor and the surrender of Gāgraun he reached Sārangpur on 13 May, to the consternation of Adham Khān, whose mother's letter had not yet reached him. The delinquent humbled himself before his sovereign, but his prayers and excuses were unavailing until his mother appeared to intercede for him. She arranged a reconciliation and attempted to conceal her son's crimes by causing to be put to death two of Bāz Bahādur's most beautiful concubines, whom he had ravished. The crime was discovered but as it was traced to Māham Anaga it went unpunished.

Adham Khān was permitted to remain in Mālwā as governor, with Pīr Muhammad Khān as his principal assistant, and Akbar returned to Āgra, slaying on the way, near Narwar, with one stroke of his sword, a tigress which had five cubs. He delighted in such feats of daring and took special pride in his mastery over elephants. One day he mounted, rode and controlled the vicious elephant *Hawāī*, probably the beast of that name which had been ridden by Hīmū at Pānīpat. Not content with this feat he commanded the servants of the elephant stables to bring forth another fierce brute, *Ran Bāghā*, "the Tiger in Battle", and continued to ride *Hawāī* while the two fought. *Hawāī* overcame *Ran Bāghā* who fled, pursued by the victor, across the bridge spanning the Jumna. The pontoons were submerged by the ponderous beasts, but both reached the further bank in safety, and there Akbar succeeded in bringing *Hawāī* to a stand.

"In later years Akbar explained more than once to Abu-'l-Fazl that his motive in undertaking such adventures was that God might end his life if he should knowingly have taken a step displeasing to the Most High, or cherished an aspiration contrary to his will, for, he said, 'We cannot support the burden of life under God's displeasure.'"

Such sentiments do little credit either to his heart or to his head. If, as is certain, he did not hold such views when he was nineteen he was lying, and the suggestion that God required his aid for the purpose of destroying him shows that in the maze of his religious speculations he had not found even the clue to the truth.

Before Akbar started for Mālwā a very serious rebellion had broken out in the eastern provinces of the empire. Sher Khān, the son of Muhammad 'Ādil, had assembled at Chunār an army of nearly 20,000 horse, 50,000 foot, and 500 elephants, and had marched on Jaunpur. Ibrāhīm Khān the Uzbeg, Majnūn Khān Qāqshāl, and Shāham Khān Jalāir had been ordered to support Khān Zamān, who, with his brother Bahādur and their troops, stood alone in the path of the invaders. The forces met in the neighbourhood of Jaunpur, and the Mughuls, though outnumbered, inflicted a crushing defeat on the Afghāns and dispersed their imposing array.

Khān Zamān, by repeating Adham Khān's offence, incurred the wrath of Akbar, who marched from Āgra by way of Kālpī and Karā towards Jaunpur. Khān Zamān and his brother Bahādur, on learning of his departure from Āgra, repented their contumacy and marched to Karā, where they offered to him all the elephants which they had taken from the Afghāns. Their timely submission disarmed his wrath and he permitted them to return to Jaunpur, and, having despatched Āsaf Khān to Chunār, which was still in the hands of the Afghāns, returned to Āgra, arriving there on 29 August. Chunār was surrendered to Āsaf Khān and became an outpost of the empire.

In November Atga Khān was summoned from Kābul and appointed minister of the empire, though the formality of dismissing Mun'im Khān, who had acted in that capacity ever since the fall of Bairam Khān, was not observed. The appointment was extremely distasteful, not only to Mun'im Khān but also to Māham Anaga, "who regarded herself as the virtual lieutenant of the empire", and she was still further annoyed by the recall of her son, Adham Khān, from Mālwā, where his sensuality and tyranny had rendered him obnoxious to all. His recall was welcome to none more than to the still less scrupulous ruffian Pīr Muhammad Khān, who desired freedom even from supervision so lax as Adham Khān's.

On 14 January, 1562, Akbar made his first pilgrimage to the shrine of the famous saint Mu'īn-ud-dīn Chishtī of Ajmer, of whose merits he had heard. This pilgrimage became an annual institution and was regularly performed by him while he remained a Muslim. On his way to Ajmer Rājā Bihārī Mal of Amber, who had been the first Rājput chief to be presented at his court, obeyed a summons to wait on him, attended the camp with his whole family, and begged Akbar's acceptance of his daughter in marriage. His offers were accepted and at Sāmbhar, on his return march, Akbar married the princess, who eventually became the mother of Jahāngīr, and received into his service Mān Singh, the nephew and adopted son of Bhagwān Dās, Bihārī Mal's heir.

This was the first fruits of Mīr 'Abdul-Latīf's teachings and the earliest indication of Akbar's noble resolve to be a father to all his people, Hindus as well as Muslims, to be emperor of India, in short, rather than the commander of a small garrison, alien in religion, and to a great extent in blood, to the mass of the people. Shaikh Abu-'l-Fazl is sometimes wrongly credited with having directed Akbar into the path of religious toleration, on which he descants much in his own pompous and artificial style, but Akbar deliberately adopted the policy and pursued it for years before he had ever seen his famous secretary.

Mīrzā Sharaf-ud-dīn Husain, whose assignment was in the neighbourhood of Ajmer, was sent to capture the fortress of Merta,[1] then held by Jaimal for the Rānā, Uday Singh of Chitor. The fortress was surrendered and quarter was given on the condition that it should be handed over intact, with its contents, to the imperial troops, but one Deo Dās violated this condition by setting fire to its stores and by offering a determined opposition to the troops as they entered, with the result that "he exalted several of the emperor's soldiers to the dignity of martyrdom and himself entered eternal fire, being accompanied to hell by 200 of his famous Rājputs",[2] and the fortress was occupied by Sharaf-ud-dīn Husain.

Akbar arrived at Āgra on 13 February, 1562, having married at Sāmbhar, as already related, the princess of Amber.

Pīr Muhammad Khān, who had remained in Mālwā as governor on the removal of Adham Khān, displayed great activity in clearing the country of the adherents of Bāz Bahādur. He besieged and captured Bījāgarh[3] and put the whole garrison to the sword, and as Bāz Bahādur had taken refuge in Khāndesh and was causing some trouble on the southern frontier of Mālwā he invaded that country and penetrated as far as Burhānpur, massacring the inhabitants without distinction as he advanced, and sparing neither Sayyids nor learned and holy men. Mubārak II of Khāndesh and Bāz Bahādur appealed for aid to Tufāl Khān, the actual ruler of Berār, and on his joining them fell upon Pīr Muhammad Khān, dispersed his troops and forced him to flee towards Māndū. As he was crossing the Narbadā his horse was overturned in the river by a camel and he was drowned, and thus, as a historian says, "he went to fire by way of water, and the sighs of the orphans, of the weak, and of the captives did their work with him".[4]

The pursuit was pressed and the imperial officers could make no stand in Mālwā but were forced to flee to Āgra, and Bāz Bahādur thus regained, for a short time, possession of his kingdom, but Akbar at once sent 'Abdullah Khān the Uzbeg of Kālpī and Ahmad Khān Farankhudī to recover the country, and Bāz Bahādur fled and took

[1] 26° 39′ N., 74° 2′ E.
[2] *Bad.* (text) II, 50.
[3] 21° 41′ N., 75° 20′ E.
[4] *Bad.* (text) II, 51.

refuge with Uday Singh of Chitor while 'Abdullah Khān occupied Māndū and re-established Mughul rule throughout the country.

In the hot weather of this year Akbar, while hunting near Sakīt, now in the Etah district of the United Provinces, heard complaints of a gang of Hindu brigands who infested that neighbourhood. He at once marched against them and they fled and took refuge in the village of Paraunkh, 15 miles south-east of Sakīt. At the head of his escort of 200 horse he attacked the brigands, who are said to have numbered 4000. He was not well supported, but pressed on, receiving twelve arrows in his shield and narrowly escaping death by his elephant stumbling into a grain pit. He succeeded, however, in forcing the animal through a wall of the buildings in which the brigands had taken refuge and they were set on fire, about a thousand of the wretches perishing in the flames. Akbar was ever ready for such perilous enterprises and we shall see that at a much later period of his life he displayed similar reckless courage in Gujarāt. These exploits, performed in the interests of his empire, stand on an entirely different footing from his foolish pranks with tigers and elephants.

A tragedy now enabled him to free himself for ever of the baleful influence of Māham Anaga and her ruffianly son. The discontent caused by the appointment of Atga Khān as minister has already been described. It was shared by Shihāb-ud-dīn Ahmad Khān as well as by those mentioned before, and the malcontents instigated the unscrupulous Adham Khān to remove the obstacle from their path. Authorities differ as to the details of the murder, but on 16 May, 1562, Adham Khān, attended by his followers, swaggered into the hall where Atga Khān was engaged either in public business or in reading the Korān and advanced towards him in a threatening manner, with his hand on his dagger. Whether he stabbed him himself is not certain, but two of his followers, at a signal from him, cut the minister down and he staggered out and fell dead in the courtyard. Adham Khān then attempted to force his way into the inner apartments where Akbar, who had been sleeping, was awakened by the tumult. His object does not appear to have been, as Dr Vincent Smith believed, "the last extremity of treason",[1] but to make his peace. The eunuch on duty, however, barred his way, and Akbar, armed with his sword, came out by another door. As his glance fell on the dead body of Atga Khān he cried to Adham Khān, "You son of a ——,[2] why have you killed my foster-father?" Adham Khān seized his hands and begged him to hear him, but Akbar, maddened by the restraint, wrenched himself free and felled him with a blow of his fist. He then ordered his attendants to throw him down from the terrace, and the order was obeyed, but as Adham Khān was

[1] *Akbar, the Great Mogul*, p. 60.

[2] For doubt as to his use of an epithet see Mrs Beveridge, *Humāyūn-nāma*, p. 62, n. 1. [Ed.]

seen to be breathing he was taken up and thrown down a second time, so that his neck was broken and his brains spattered the pavement. Akbar then returned to the inner apartments and broke the news, as quietly as he could, to the murderer's mother, who was ill. The sick woman said simply, "Your Majesty did well", and forty days later died of grief for her worthless son.

Mun'im Khān and Muhammad Qāsim Khān, another conspirator, fled across the Jumna and made for Rūpar and Māchīwārā, intending to escape to Kābul, where they hoped that Ghanī Khān, the former's son, would be able to protect them, but they were captured near Sarwat in the Dūāb and handed over to Sayyid Mahmūd Bārha, who sent them back to Āgra, whence an emissary had already been despatched to convey to them an assurance that they should not be molested. On their arrival at Āgra they were not only pardoned, but Mun'im Khān was permitted to retain his title of Khān Khānān and was reinstated as chief minister of the empire.

It has been plausibly conjectured[1] that there was an element of contempt in this reinstatement, for the post to which Mun'im Khān was restored was shorn of nearly all its former importance. Akbar had learnt his lesson and was resolved in future to be emperor in fact as well as in name. During Mun'im Khān's short absence he had discovered gross abuses in the administration of the crown lands and had appointed to the charge of those lands, under his own immediate control, the eunuch Buhlūl Malik, who had faithfully served Islām Shāh Sūr and was now entitled I'timād Khān. The selection was a wise one and the eunuch served his new master faithfully and well.

So it was to be in all other departments of state. The powers of the *Sadr-us-Sudūr* had already been greatly curtailed on the appointment of Muhammad Sālih of Herāt to that post earlier in the year, and the chief minister of the empire was henceforward to register and execute his master's decrees rather than to govern the empire.

The completion of Akbar's twentieth year was the turning point of his life. He had freed himself from all malign influences and was able to pursue his own high ideals. With all his faults and all his foibles, and they were many, he was a truly great ruler and was the first of the Muslim sovereigns of India to conceive the idea of dealing impartially with all his subjects, whether Hindus or Muslims. It may also be said that he was the last. Henceforward the chronicle of his reign is the story of the man, not of the influence of this or that minister or faction.

The province of Kābul was governed nominally by Akbar's younger brother, prince Muhammad Hakīm, but the management of its affairs was in the hands of his guardian, who at the beginning of the reign had been Mun'im Khān. When he came to court on the occasion of Bairam Khān's fall he left his son, Ghanī Khān, to

[1] *Akbar, the Great Mogul*, p. 63.

act for him, but the young man was unequal to the task. He could manage neither the turbulent populace of Kābul nor the prince's mother, who was a power in the state, and during a temporary absence from the town the gates were shut against him by the princess, Māh Chūchak Begam, and by his own uncle, Fāzil (or Fazāil) Beg. Ghanī Khān retired to Akbar's court and Fāzil Beg took his place, but left all business in the hands of his son, Abu-'l-Fath. Abu-'l-Fath's behaviour estranged him both from the old nobles of Kābul and from Māh Chūchak Begam, and he was assassinated. Fāzil Beg attempted to escape but was captured and shared the fate of his son.

Mun'im Khān was now reappointed to Kābul and, over-estimating his popularity, hastened thither with an inadequate force. He was attacked and defeated near Jalālābād by Māh Chūchak Begam and fled to the Gakkhar country, whence he wrote to Akbar begging that he might be permitted either to make the pilgrimage to Mecca or to hide his shame in the Punjab, but Akbar consoled him, recalled him to court, and made him governor of Āgra.

Affairs at Kābul were now thrown into greater confusion than ever by the arrival of the stormy petrel, Shāh Abu-'l-Ma'ālī, who, having escaped from his prison at Lahore, had performed the pilgrimage to Mecca, whence he returned ready to seize any opportunity of fomenting strife and stirring up sedition. At Jālor he had found Sharaf-ud-dīn Husain, one of the conspirators who had fled from court after the murder of Atga Khān, and at his instigation had taken possession of Nārnaul and had defeated and slain Ismā'īl Qulī and Ahmad Beg, who had been sent against him by Husain Qulī Khān, then engaged in an attempt to capture Sharaf-ud-dīn Husain. Ismā'īl Qulī and Ahmad Beg had, however, before their final defeat and death, driven Abu-'l-Ma'ālī from Nārnaul and captured his brother, Khān-zāda Muhammad, and as one imperial officer after another closed the gates of their fortresses against him and he heard that Akbar was marching from Āgra to Delhi he resolved to take refuge at Kābul, where he hoped to be able to obtain possession of the person of Muhammad Hakīm Mīrzā, whom he might set up as a pretender to the imperial throne in opposition to Akbar.

He fled through the Punjab, fruitlessly pursued by the imperial troops, and was kindly received at Kābul by Māh Chūchak Begam, who gave him her daughter, Fakhr-un-Nisa Begam, in marriage. She soon had reason to repent her courtesy to the turbulent and ambitious Sayyid, who formed a party of the malcontents in the state, put to death his benefactress and her agent, Haidar Qāsim Kūhbur, and took the management of affairs into his own hands. The young prince Muhammad Hakīm now secretly appealed for aid to Mīrzā Sulaimān of Badakhshān, who marched on Kābul. Shāh Abu-'l-Ma'ālī, carrying with him the prince, went forth to meet him, but during the battle which ensued the prince found an opportunity of escaping to the enemy and the Kābulīs, seeing that he had taken refuge with Mīrzā Sulaimān, dispersed. Shāh Abu-'l-Ma'ālī fled, but was pursued, taken and hanged on 13 May, 1564.

Mīrzā Sulaimān then married his daughter to Muhammad Hakīm, distributed the province among his own adherents, appointed Ummīd 'Alī guardian of the prince and returned to Badakhshān.

The "foster-father cohort" was importunate for vengeance on those who had been concerned in the murder of Atga Khān, but Akbar, who had pardoned and reinstated two and could not lay his hand on the third of the conspirators, did not meet their demand and found it necessary to divert their attention by active employment. A plausible pretext for interfering in the affairs of the Gakkhars offered him an opportunity. Sultān Sārang, who had been confirmed by Bābur as chief of the Gakkhars, had been put to death by Islām Khān Sūr and his son Kamāl Khān was in Akbar's service. The leadership of the tribe had been seized by Kamāl Khān's uncle, Sultān Ādam, and Kamāl, who had rendered distinguished services against the Afghāns at Jaunpur, begged Akbar to restore him to at least half of his inheritance. Akbar accordingly called upon Sultān Ādam to surrender to his nephew half of the tribal territory and, on his refusing to comply, fitted out an expedition the command of which he gave to Khān Kalān and Qutb-ud-dīn Khān, two of Atga Khān's three brothers. The expedition was successful. Sultān Ādam and his son Lashkarī were captured and Kamāl Khān was placed in possession of the Gakkhar country, which lay between the Indus and the frontier of Kashmīr. He put his uncle to death and threw his cousin into prison, where he shortly afterwards died.

Akbar was hunting at Muttra when he heard of the death of Ismā'īl Qulī and Ahmad Beg, near Nāgaur, at the hands of Shāh Abu-'l-Ma'ālī, and on receiving the news marched to Delhi with a view to cutting off the rebel, but the report of his movement so accelerated Abu-'l-Ma'ālī's flight that by the time the emperor reached Delhi arrest was impossible.

While at Muttra Akbar abolished the tax levied on Hindu pilgrims visiting the town, another instance of his clemency to his Hindu subjects.

At Delhi one of the most discreditable episodes of his life occurred. He chanced to see and to fall in love with an extremely beautiful woman, the wife of one Shaikh 'Abdul-Wasī, and sent a message to the Shaikh reminding him of the article in the code of Chingīz Khān to the effect that the husband of any woman whom the sovereign may desire is bound to divorce his wife and surrender her to his lord. The Shaikh was complaisant, divorced his wife and retired to Bīdar in the Deccan. The woman through whom Akbar had become acquainted with the Shaikh's wife now suggested that he should in like manner connect himself with the leading families of Delhi and

Āgra, and pandars and eunuchs were employed to inspect secretly the harems of the leading men of the city and report the discovery of any woman of special beauty. This invasion of the sanctity of the home caused much murmuring and discontent, and on 12 January, 1564, as Akbar was returning from a visit to the tomb of Shaikh Nizām-ud-dīn Auliya, a slave named Fulād shot an arrow at him which inflicted no more than a slight flesh wound. There appears to be no doubt, though another motive has been assigned for the act, that the attempt was connected with Akbar's designs on the honour and happiness of his subjects. He, at any rate, so regarded it and caused the assassin to be put to death on the spot, without inquiring, as his advisers urged, what had been his motive and who were his instigators. He abandoned his disgraceful search, and no more is heard throughout his reign of his molesting the wives and daughters of his subjects.

In this year he made another appointment which indicated his intention of bringing the whole of the administration of the empire under his personal control. Muzaffar 'Alī of Turbat, who had been in Bairam Khān's service and whose life had been spared in spite of the efforts of the harem party to procure his condemnation, had since done good service as collector of a sub-district and superintendent of the imperial stores. He was now entitled Muzaffar Khān and appointed *Dīwān*, or revenue minister, of the empire.

From Delhi Akbar returned, on 10 February, to Āgra, where he was on 11 March, the beginning of the ninth regnal year, which was signalised by the abolition of the *jizya*, or poll-tax, on Hindus and other non-Muslims. Badāūnī places this event in the year 1579 and, strange to say, does not condemn it.[1]

This year was marred by another domestic tragedy. Akbar's maternal uncle Khvāja Mu'azzam, a violent and irresponsible man, had threatened to murder his wife, and Akbar rode to his house to the east of the Jumna to forestall the crime, only to find that it had already been committed. The murderer was seized, roughly handled, and ducked in the river in the hope that he would drown, but came out alive and was sent to Gwalior, where he presently died insane.

This event marks Akbar's final emancipation from family influence, or rather from that of blood relations, for there is no doubt that in later years he was influenced, like Solomon, by his wives, who familiarised him with Hindu doctrines and practices.

Āsaf Khān, the governor of Karā, who had recently reduced to obedience Rām Chand Bāghel, Rājā of Bhath,[2] was now ordered to subdue the Gond kingdom of Garha-Katanga, known to English historians as Garha-Mandla, which had existed for nearly ten centuries and extended from Ratanpur on the east to Rāisen in Mālwā

[1] II, 276.

[2] Sometimes wrongly transliterated as Panna. Now in Rewah state. See Hīrānanda Shāstrī, "The Bāghela dynasty of Rewah", Memoir no. 21, *Arch. Survey of India*. [Ed.]

on the west and from the southern border of the Bhath principality on the north to the frontier of the Deccan on the south. At this time the Rānī Durgāvatī, a princess of the Chandel dynasty of Mahobā, was regent of the kingdom for her son, Bīr Nārāyan, who, though he had attained manhood, left the management of affairs in her hands. She governed wisely and well, and had fought with unvarying success against both Bāz Bahādur and the Afghāns. Her army consisted of 20,000 horse and 1000 elephants, and besides being an intrepid warrior she was devoted to field sports.

Āsaf Khān advanced with 10,000 horse and a large force of foot to Damoh, where he halted and was joined by petty chiefs who brought his strength in horse up to 50,000. Durgāvatī and her son, with an army greatly inferior in numbers, advanced to meet him and chose a defensive position at Narhī to the east of Garha. Here, with her 5000 men, she stoutly withstood the invaders for two days, but on the second her son was wounded and she sent him from the field. The withdrawal of his escort so weakened her small army that it was almost immediately overpowered. She was wounded with two arrows and stabbed herself to avoid capture.

Āsaf Khān marched from Narhī to Chaurāgarh, the capital of the Gond kingdom, where Bīr Nārāyan, wounded as he was, came out to give him battle, but was defeated and slain, so that the fortress fell at once into the hands of the Mughuls. The raja's servants, obeying the orders which they had received from their master, burnt all the females of his house except two, who miraculously escaped and were saved and sent to Akbar. One of these was Kamlāvatī, sister of Durgāvatī.

The spoils taken by Āsaf Khān were immense, and comprised jewels and rich stuffs, gold and silver both coined and uncoined and in the form of idols, and a thousand elephants. Āsaf Khān remained at Chaurāgarh to administer his conquest and retained for himself all the jewels and stuffs and 800 of the 1000 elephants, but Akbar paid no heed to his contumacy at the time.

This act of aggression was entirely unprovoked and there was not the shadow of a pretext for it except Akbar's own frankly expressed view of a king's duties, "A monarch should be ever intent on conquest, otherwise his neighbours rise in arms against him." There is nothing surprising in the discovery that an eastern monarch of the sixteenth century was a mere annexationist requiring no excuse for attacking his neighbours beyond a desire to acquire their possessions, but Akbar has been so extravagantly lauded, not only by his own secretary but also by some modern writers, that it is necessary to remember that in this respect at least he was no better than other eastern rulers of his age.

It was now reported at court that 'Abdullah Khān the Uzbeg, who held the government of Mālwā, was preparing to rise in rebellion, and Akbar left Āgra on 1 July and marched to Narwar on the pretext of an elephant hunt. Heavy rains detained him for nearly a fortnight on the banks of the Chambal and it was with the utmost difficulty that the march was continued through Mālwā. 'Abdullah, although envoys were sent to reassure him, fled from Māndū as Akbar approached, but the emperor pursued him, came up with him at Lawānī, only seven miles from Māndū, and though the rapidity of Akbar's march had left him with no more than 300 men he attacked and defeated 'Abdullah, capturing not only his elephants but the women of his harem. 'Abdullah fled to Gujarāt; Akbar returned to Māndū and sent an emissary to Chingīz Khān, the regent of Gujarāt, to demand the surrender or dismissal of the fugitive. Chingīz Khān sent a conciliatory reply begging forgiveness for 'Abdullah and promising to dismiss him if he were not pardoned.

Akbar remained for nearly a month at Māndū, setting in order the affairs of Mālwā. He also sent a mission to Mubārak Shah II of Khāndesh, demanding of him a daughter in marriage. Mubārak complied with the demand and Akbar's new bride was conducted from Burhānpur to Māndū by I'timād Khān the eunuch. Qarā Bahādur Khān, a cousin of Mīrzā Haidar the historian and conqueror of Kashmīr, was appointed to the government of Mālwā, and Akbar, after an unsuccessful attempt to induce Bāz Bahādur to leave Dungarpur and make his submission, returned to Āgra, arriving there on 9 October.

He now had some leisure which he employed in indulging his passion for building. He had been attracted by the situation of the village of Kakrālī, seven miles to the south of Āgra, and there built himself a palace, to serve as a hunting lodge and pleasure house. The courtiers were encouraged to build houses for themselves, gardens were laid out, and a small town sprang up round the palace. To this Akbar gave the name of Nagarchain, or "abode of ease", and here he amused himself with coursing, pigeon-flying, and polo, which he played at night with balls made of the wood of the *dhāk* or *palās* tree (*Butea frondosa*) which smoulders when ignited.

Nagarchain was deserted when Fathpur Sīkrī became, some years later, Akbar's favourite abode, and by the end of the reign scarcely a trace remained of it. Dr Vincent Smith says that there still exist trifling remains of mosques and a well.

At the same time Akbar undertook the restoration of Āgra, the old brick fort of which had become ruinous. He had already adorned the city with two new buildings and he now gave orders for the construction of the fort of stone, which still stands, to replace the old fort. The new fort was fifteen years in building and cost three million and a half rupees, equivalent to nearly £400,000 sterling. According to Abu-'l-Fazl Akbar erected at Āgra "more than five hundred buildings of masonry, after the beautiful designs of Bengal and Gujarāt, which masterly sculptors and cunning artists of form have fashioned as architectural models". The old Āgra of the Lodī dynasty, a comparatively mean town, lay on the left bank of the river and was replaced by Akbar's magnificent city on the right bank, the name of which was altered by his grandson Shāh Jahān to Akbarābād and fittingly commemorates its great builder.

While Akbar was thus employed in restoring order in Mālwā and in building, Khān Zamān brought a very doubtful campaign in Bihār to a successful conclusion, snatching victory from the very jaws of defeat. The Afghāns invaded Bihār in force and occupied the province, including some of Khān Zamān's assignments, which lay on its frontier. Khān Zamān marched to repel them but, finding them too strong to be attacked, entrenched himself at Andhyārī Bārī on the Son. While he was there he was visited by some emissaries from Akbar's court who had been sent to convey promises of favour and protection to Sulaimān Kararānī, king of Bengal, but had also been ordered to obtain satisfactory guarantees from Khān Zamān, who had long ceased to correspond with the central government and whose loyalty was suspected. They were still awaiting his answer when the Afghāns attacked the entrenched camp. Khān Zamān drew up his army to receive them but it was overpowered and put to flight, and the Afghāns began to plunder the camp. Khān Zamān, with a few attendants, withdrew to one of the bastions of the fortifications and thence fired a mortar or howitzer, killing the elephant ridden by Hasan Khān, brother of Fath Khān, the commander of the Afghān army. Hasan Khān's contingent at once took to flight and at the same time a vicious elephant from the Afghān camp broke its chains, slew another elephant in the field, and threw the whole Afghān force, who believed that they had fallen into an ambush, into confusion. They broke and fled and the Mughul troops, rallied by Khān Zamān, pursued them with great slaughter, taking much booty. Khān Zamān then returned to Jaunpur and on his way dismissed the emperor's envoys at Zamāniyā, without vouchsafing an answer to their proposals.

Akbar's next attempt at reforming the general administration was unfortunate. Khvāja Muhammad Sālih was removed from the post of *Sadr-us-Sudūr* and Shaikh 'Abdun-Nabī was appointed in his place, in the belief that he would be more likely than his predecessor to collaborate with Muzaffar Khān, the revenue minister, in limiting the expenditure on free grants of land or money to those who devoted their lives to scholarship or religion; but the selection was unfortunate, for 'Abdun-Nabī was a narrow-minded ecclesiastic who held that any pretensions to piety or learning entitled the pretender to live luxuriously at the public expense, and proved "a sair sanct for the Crown". Grants on a scale hitherto unheard of were assigned with a lavish hand and the Shaikh paid no heed to the revenue minister. He succeeded, however, in retaining his appointment until 1578 and when he ultimately fell into disfavour it was not for dishonesty or administrative incapacity.

The Uzbegs in Akbar's service formed a family party, the members of which were employed for the most part in the eastern province of the empire. Khān Zamān, their chief, held Jaunpur while his brother, Bahādur Khān, was in the same neighbourhood; Ibrāhīm Khān, their uncle, was at Surhurpur, north of Jaunpur, and Iskandar Khān, entitled Khān 'Ālam, another member of the family, held Oudh. They were proud of their descent from the royal line of Shaibān and it was to them, after Bairam Khān, that Akbar chiefly owed his throne. They had some reason for considering that their services had been ill rewarded. Their retention in the eastern provinces where what may be called active service conditions continually prevailed, amounted in effect to banishment from court, where they saw Persians and others advanced to the highest posts, and they resented their exclusion from favour. Akbar is said to have been so indiscreet as to attribute all his father's troubles to the Uzbegs and his promptitude in proceeding against 'Abdullah Khān in Mālwā, on what appeared to them to be mere suspicion, was regarded as proof positive of his hatred of all the tribe. Their isolation, while it aroused their resentment, was favourable to the growth of a spirit of independence, for the expenses of their military establishment furnished them with a pretext for not contributing to the imperial exchequer. Khān Zamān's unceremonious reception and dismissal of the imperial envoys had been sufficient to convince Akbar of his disaffection, and Ashraf Khān, who was usually employed on such missions, was sent early in 1565 to Iskandar Khān, who was believed to be more amenable, but the Uzbegs were resolved to stand or fall together and Iskandar would give Ashraf no answer until he had met his relatives at Jaunpur, where in a family conclave they resolved to take up arms and decided on a plan of campaign. Iskandar and Ibrāhīm were to march on Kanauj and raise the country in that direction and Khān Zamān and Bahādur were to attack Mānikpur, held for Akbar by Majnūn Khān Qāqshāl.

Ibrāhīm and Iskandar defeated on their way to Kanauj a small force of Akbar's troops and Khān Zamān and Bahādur besieged Majnūn Khān in Mānikpur. Āsaf Khān, whom he summoned to his aid from Chaurāgarh, relieved the pressure of the siege but their combined forces were not strong enough to attack the rebels.

When Akbar received reports of the situation he at once despatched Mun'im Khān, with such troops as were ready for the field, to Kanauj and on 24 May left Āgra, with a larger force, to join him, marching by night owing to the heat of the weather.

Ten days were spent at Kanauj in preparations for the passage of the Ganges but Akbar, on hearing that Iskandar was preparing to make a stand at Lucknow, crossed the river and, covering the 70 miles between Kanauj and Lucknow in two nights and a day, surprised Iskandar and forced him to flee. The horses of the cavalry were so spent that pursuit was impossible and Iskandar was thus able to join Khān Zamān before Mānikpur, but he, learning that Akbar had occupied Lucknow, raised the siege, retreated with all speed across the Ganges and took refuge in the rough and broken country to the north-east of the Gumti.

Akbar halted at Lucknow until the remainder of his army came up and then advanced, by easy stages, towards Jaunpur, which he reached on 13 July, having been joined on the way by Majnūn Khān and Āsaf Khān from Mānikpur. The latter took this opportunity of presenting to Akbar some of the spoils of Chaurāgarh, and of making his peace.

The rebels now retired to the neighbourhood of Hājīpur, whence they sent envoys to seek aid of Sulaimān Kararānī, the king of Bengal. An emissary sent by Akbar to deter Sulaimān from assisting them was intercepted and was detained in arrest in the rebel camp on his refusing to act as an intermediary between Khān Zamān and Akbar. The mission to Sulaimān having thus miscarried, Akbar sent a second, to Mukund Deo, Rājā of Orissa, requesting him to attack Sulaimān in the event of the latter's taking any steps to support the rebels. Mukund Deo promised to perform this service, and the envoys eventually returned to court after Akbar's return to Nagarchain, bringing with them several elephants and other valuable gifts.

Āsaf Khān, though he had made his peace with Akbar, had not propitiated Muzaffar Khān, the revenue minister, who accordingly reminded him that the spoils of Chaurāgarh had not been accounted for and that an investigation might be necessary. If his object was to obtain his fee he was disappointed, for the suggestion so alarmed Āsaf Khān that he fled, on 17 September, to his governorship, evading pursuit.

Khān Zamān was encamped at Narhan, on the Gogra, and Akbar's field force was on the south bank of the river watching him. To create a diversion he sent Bahādur Khān and Iskandar Khān into the country north of the Gogra, the present Bahraich and Gonda districts, but Akbar detached a second field force under Mīr Mu'izz-ul-Mulk the Sayyid to the Khairābād district to hold the Uzbegs in check and marched to Allahābād to await the result of the operations.

Khān Zamān, much disappointed by perceiving that Akbar's arrangements were in no way disturbed by the movements of Bahādur and Iskandar, sent a message to Mun'im Khān, who was favourably disposed towards him, opening negotiations for submission and a pardon. Akbar had little confidence in the genuineness of the rebel's repentance and not much more in the zeal and loyalty of Mun'im Khān, but sent Khvāja Jahān, in whom Khān Zamān had confidence, to arrange terms. It was agreed that Khān Zamān should send his mother and his uncle Ibrāhīm to court and that they should be followed, after he had been formally pardoned, by Bahādur and

Iskandar. Mun'im Khān accompanied Khān Zamān's mother and Ibrāhīm Khān to court, and Khān Zamān was pardoned on condition that he refrained from crossing the Gogra while the imperial troops were in the field.

Mīr Mu'izz-ul-Mulk had been joined in the Khairābād district by Rājā Todar Mal, and though both, as well as the two Uzbeg chiefs opposed to them, were well aware of the progress of negotiations for Khān Zamān's submission they ignored them and with the double object of frustrating Mun'im Khān's efforts and of distinguishing themselves in the field, deliberately provoked Bahādur and Iskandar to hostilities. The armies met and the imperial troops suffered a severe defeat and were forced to retreat on Kanauj, whence they reported the disaster.

Akbar well knew where to place the blame, for the battle of Khairābād was not allowed to affect the terms of the general pardon granted to the rebels, and Mu'izz-ul-Mulk and Todar Mal were reprimanded and for some time were not admitted to the imperial presence.

Akbar, who had returned to Jaunpur, marched in January, 1566, to Benares, inspecting on his way the fortress of Chunār, which he had not yet seen. His suspicions of Khān Zamān were soon justified, for the rebel violated the terms of his pardon by crossing the Gogra to Muhammadābād and sent detachments to Jaunpur and Ghāzīpur. Akbar reproached Mun'im Khān with his advocacy of a traitor so perfidious and marched to attack him, ordering Ashraf Khān to imprison his mother at Jaunpur. Khān Zamān fled across the Gogra and Akbar captured his tents and baggage and sent a force in pursuit of him, but it was ascertained that he had fled into the Himālaya and the pursuers returned. Akbar then learnt that Bahādur Khan had descended on Jaunpur, released his mother and imprisoned Ashraf Khān, laid waste the district, and marched on to Benares, which town and district also he plundered. He marched to Jaunpur and punished the sloth and incompetence of the officers who had permitted Bahādur to raid the town by declaring that it should be his capital until the rebels were captured, and the threat was taken so seriously that some began to build themselves houses. Khān Zamān, on learning Akbar's decision, once more approached Mun'im Khān with a view to a reconciliation, but Mun'im Khān dared not again broach the subject to the emperor and other intermediaries were employed. At their intercession Akbar, with an alacrity which showed that he was weary of the campaign and was desirous of peace at any price, pardoned the rebels and reinstated them in their positions. He reached Āgra on 29 March and enjoyed some well-earned leisure at Nagarchain.

Mahdī Qāsim Khān was sent into Gondwāna to seize the deserter Āsaf Khān, but the latter fled, and with his younger brother, Vazīr Khān, took refuge with Khān Zamān at Jaunpur.

Mahdī Qāsim Khān, disgusted with the wild and unsettled country which had fallen so easily into his hands, fled into the Deccan and thence travelled to Mecca without permission and it became necessary to send other officers to Gondwāna to restore order in the administration.

Āsaf Khān and his brother soon had cause to repent having placed themselves under the protection of Khān Zamān, who employed the former on arduous duties and detained the latter in prison as a hostage for his brother. With considerable difficulty, and not without having recourse to arms, they succeeded in effecting their escape and fled to Karā, where they were received by Majnūn Khān. From Karā, Vazīr Khān went to court, to seek the emperor's forgiveness for his brother. Akbar was now at Lahore, where Vazīr Khān made his submission and was graciously received. Āsaf Khān was instructed to remain with Majnūn Khān at Mānikpur or Karā and was informed that he would be received when the court returned to Āgra.

Akbar's leisure at Nagarchain had been interrupted and he had been summoned northwards by the news that his brother, Muhammad Hakīm, had invaded the Punjab and was besieging Lahore.

Muhammad Hakīm's invasion of the Punjab, a poor return for the assistance which Akbar had recently given him against Mīrzā Sulaimān of Badakhshān, who had invaded his territories, was instigated by some malcontents and mischief-makers at Kābul and encouraged by messages from the Uzbeg rebels, who had been in secret communication with him. Believing that the assignees in the Punjab would espouse his cause, he marched on Lahore by way of Bhera, on the Jhelum, but "the foster-father cohort", Khān Kalān, Qutb-ud-dīn Khān and Sharīf Khān, had assembled their troops and repaired the fortifications and Muhammad Hakīm, encamped in the gardens of Mahdī Qāsim Khān, kept at a respectful distance by the guns of the fortress.

Akbar set out from Āgra on 16 November, 1566, reaching Delhi ten days later, and Muhammad Hakīm, on receiving this news, beat a hasty retreat. Akbar did not hear of his flight until he reached the Sutlej and from that river continued his march to Lahore, which he reached at the end of January, 1567. A force sent in pursuit of the prince returned on learning that he had crossed the Indus.

At Lahore Akbar was again disturbed, this time by news of the rebellion of the princes known as "the Mīrzās", who were his distant relations, being descended from 'Umar Shaikh Mīrzā, the second son of Tīmūr, while Akbar himself was descended from Jalāl-ud-dīn Mīrān Shāh, the third. There were six brothers: (1) Ulugh Mīrzā, (2) Shāh Mīrzā, (3) Ibrāhīm Husain Mīrzā, (4) Muhammad Husain Mīrzā, (5) Mas'ūd Husain Mīrzā, and (6) 'Āqil Husain Mīrzā, of whom the last four rebelled, together with two sons of the eldest, Sikandar, also known as Ulugh Mīrzā, and Mahmūd Sultān, also known as Shāh Mīrzā. They had been provided with assignments in the Sambhal and A'zampur[1] districts and the nature of their grievance is not recorded. They may have considered that the provision made for them was insufficient for princes of the house of Tīmūr but, if so, they were hardly reasonable, for the degree of their relationship to Akbar was that of sixth cousins. They rose and occupied some crown lands not included in their estates; Mun'im Khān marched against them and they fled into Mālwā.

News yet more disquieting necessitated Akbar's return to his capital. The Uzbegs of Jaunpur were again in open rebellion, had proclaimed Muhammad Hakīm, had caused the *khutba* to be recited in his name at Jaunpur, and had invited him to make another attempt to oust his brother.

Before leaving Lahore Akbar organised an enormous *battue* of big game in the neighbourhood. Beaters, including the army, encircled an area of over 60 by 60 miles and, contracting the circle day by day, drove all living creatures towards the centre. About 15,000 wild animals of various kinds were counted, and the nobles, and afterwards the people generally, were permitted to join in the "sport". Akbar himself was employed for five consecutive days in slaughtering animals with sword, spear, musket and arrows. It may be conceived that the recollection of this slaughter troubled his conscience in later years, when he had adopted the Jain principle of the sanctity of animal life.

On returning from the hunt to Lahore he swam his horse across the Rāvī, and of the courtiers who followed him two were drowned.

He left Lahore on 23 March and at Thānesar enjoyed a spectacle even more exciting than his *battue* near Lahore, and equally repugnant to the opinions which he afterwards developed. Near the town is Kurukshetra, the legendary site of the great battle between the Pāndavas and the Kauravas, and here were assembled two bands of devotees, Sanyāsīs and Jogīs, who, it appears, were wont to celebrate the anniversary of the battle by a mock combat. On this occasion they had arranged that the combat should be fought in earnest, for there was a quarrel due to one band having occupied the site claimed by the other. Akbar sanctioned the proposal and ordered or permitted some of his own infantry to reinforce the Sanyāsīs, who could oppose only 300 men to the 500 mustered by the Jogīs. The miserable fanatics laid on and after a fierce contest in which, to Akbar's delight and amusement, many lives were lost, the Sanyāsīs were victorious.

When Akbar reached Āgra, Khān Zamān was besieging Mīrzā Yūsuf Khān in Shergarh, near Kanauj, and Bahādur Khān was besieging Majnūn Khān and Āsaf Khān in Mānikpur. Qiyā Khān Gung was sent to the relief of Shergarh and Akbar followed him on

[1] 29° N., 78° 10′ E.

6 May. Khān Zamān, on learning that Akbar was marching in person on Shergarh, raised the siege and marched to join Bahādur Khān before Mānikpur. Akbar accordingly detached a force to deal with Iskandar Khān in Oudh.

He now had trouble with his own troops, who had in the previous year carried on a tedious and laborious but fruitless campaign against the Uzbegs, and had since marched to Lahore and back. There was much sympathy with the rebels, and the troops disapproved of Akbar's restless activity and preferred a more leisurely system of warfare, but Akbar knew how to deal with discontent in his own army and was resolved on this occasion to finish with the Uzbegs. He marched from Rāe Barelī on 7 June and, learning that the rebels had bridged and crossed the Ganges at Singraur, sent the main body of his army under Rājā Bhagwān Dās and Khvāja Jahān to cross the river at Karā while he himself crossed it at Mānikpur, when it was already so swollen by the melting of the snows on the hills that only 1000 or 1500 men succeeded in crossing with him.

The rebels, meanwhile, were advancing towards Karā, between which place and them lay only the troops commanded by Majnūn Khān Qāqshāl and Āsaf Khān. They did not know that Akbar had reached the Ganges and did not believe that he would venture to cross it. A scout's report that he had crossed was regarded as a trick of Āsaf Khān and Majnūn Khān, and they spent the night in drinking and debauchery while Akbar was halted on the south-western bank of the Ganges within two miles of their camp. He marched to the camp at sunrise on 9 June, and finding that they had already moved towards Karā, sent his right wing under Majnūn Khān to cut them off, following him with his main body.

The imperial troops came up with the rebels at Fathpur Parsaki,[1] seven miles south-east of Karā, and the battle was fiercely contested for some time, but Bahādur Khān's horse reared and threw him and he was captured. The defeat of the rebels was completed by an attack of the imperial elephants on Khān Zamān's contingent, and they fled in confusion, one body of them being put to death by some villagers into whose hands it fell. Khān Zamān was trampled to death in the elephant charge and his head was severed from his body and laid before Akbar. Bahādur Khān was taken alive and executed on the spot, in spite of the intercession of many of the nobles, and

[1] This identification is not absolutely certain, but I believe it to be correct. Abu-'l-Fazl gives the name of the village as Sakrāval while Badāūnī and Nizām-ud-dīn Ahmad have Mangarwāl. Dr Vincent Smith (*Akbar, the Great Mogul*, p. 80, n. 1) identifies it with Mankuwār, "about ten miles south-south-west of Allahabad", but this cannot be accepted, for Akbar did not cross the Jumna and the battle was certainly fought in the lower Dūāb, not far from Karā. It may be admitted that Parsaki does not much resemble either Sakrāval or Mangarwāl, but they do not much resemble one another and all agree that the village received the name of Fathpur. The site of Parsaki exactly fits the description of the movements of the two forces, and it is the only village in the neighbourhood bearing the name of Fathpur.

Mīrzā Mīrak Rizavī, who had attached himself to the Uzbegs, was tortured by means of an elephant for five successive days, but his life was spared in consideration of his being a Sayyid, and he afterwards received the command of 900 horse and the title of Rizavī Khān, and held lucrative appointments.

The final suppression of this rebellion relieved Akbar's mind of a load of care. For the reasons already given the Uzbegs were completely alienated from him and irreconcilably disaffected. A party at court sympathised with them and they apparently never abandoned the hope of being able one day to overthrow Akbar and to establish a ruler more in sympathy with them. It is not impossible that Khān Zamān's descent from Shaibān of the Golden Horde, Khān of the Kirghiz Steppes, suggested to him his own fitness for empire.

Mun'im Khān received the assignments of the Uzbegs, which he ill deserved, and Akbar, after witnessing the execution of large numbers of rebels, returned to Āgra on 18 July.

On 31 August Akbar left Āgra for Dholpur and Gwalior, having two objects in view. The first was the suppression of the Mīrzās, who were still in Mālwā, where they had occupied some important towns and districts. He had no intention of compromising his dignity by marching against them in person but on reaching Gāgraun sent Shihāb-ud-dīn Ahmad Khān against them. They retired without fighting from Ujjain to Māndū and fled thence to Gujarāt, leaving Shihāb-ud-dīn Ahmad free to restore order in Mālwā.

Akbar's second object was the humbling of the pride of the Rānā of Chitor, the acknowledged chief of the great Rājput confederacy. Bihārī Mal of Amber had courted Akbar's favour and by offering him a daughter had made the most complete surrender possible to a Rājput. Uday Singh had stood aloof in sullen pride and it was known that he regarded Bihārī Mal as one who had disgraced his race. Akbar's own pride could not brook this attitude and he resolved to force the Rānā into submission.

While he was at Gāgraun, completing his plans for the subjugation of Uday Singh, Shaikh Faizī the poet, elder brother of Abu-'l-Fazl, made his first appearance before him, having been summoned to court owing to rumours of his learning which had reached the emperor.

Having completed his plans Akbar marched for Chitor and arrived, on 23 October, within sight of the fortress, with his first view of which he was deeply affected, as all must be who are sensible of the combined effects of nature, art and historical associations.

The fortress stands on a solitary hill three miles and a quarter long and about 1200 yards wide in the centre, rising to a height of 1889 feet above sea-level, but no more than four or five hundred above the plain. Chitor presents to the modern eye the appearance of a vast ironclad in a sea which is represented by the plain from which the fortified hill rises.

The fortress had already been twice taken and sacked by Muslim kings—by 'Alā-ud-dīn Khaljī of Delhi in 1303 and by Bahādur Shāh of Gujarāt in 1534—but never before had the race of Kusa been disgraced by an Uday Singh, who, to his eternal shame, abandoned his capital, leaving its defence to Jai Mal, who had defended Merta against Sharaf-ud-dīn Husain, and sought safety at Kumbhalgarh in the Arāvallī hills.

Akbar at once reconnoitred the fortress and assigned to each division of the army its sector of the lines of investment, so that each as it came up occupied without confusion the ground assigned to it, and the investment was complete and all batteries were constructed within a month of his arrival.

Husain Qulī Khān was sent in pursuit of the Rānā, and sacked Udaipur, slaying many of its inhabitants. Many isolated bands wandering in the hills were destroyed, but he failed to come up with the object of his search and returned to the imperial camp.

The siege promised to be protracted and laborious. Three batteries were constructed, the principal one being opposite the Lakholā gate on the north, on which side mining operations were conducted. Owing to the difficulty of dragging guns up the hill Akbar caused to be cast in his presence a large mortar capable of throwing a ball forty pounds in weight.

The imperial troops having suffered losses at the rate of about 200 daily, in direct assaults, Akbar resolved to rely chiefly upon mines and upon covered ways for the approaches. On 17 December two mines were fired, but the storming party rushed into the breach before the second exploded and lost 200 in killed, 100 of whom were officers. The garrison had lost no more than forty men and, as they repaired the breach, mocked the discomfiture of their assailants.

On the night of 23 February, 1568, while a body of the defenders was making a sortie a leader was observed at a loophole directing the operation. A marksman stationed in the covered way fired at him and as he appeared no more it was concluded that the shot had taken fatal effect. The marksman is said to have been Akbar, with his favourite musket "*Sangrām*", but the identity of his victim was not at once discovered. During the night, however, flames broke out at various places in the fortress, and it was observed that the defences were deserted. Rājā Bhagwān Dās informed Akbar that the rite of *jauhar* was being performed and when day broke it was discovered that he was not mistaken. Akbar's victim had been Jai Mal, whose death had so discouraged the garrison that they resolved to perform the rite with which the Rājput, despairing of success, ends his life.

One of the principal heroes of the siege was the young Sesodia Patta Singh of Kailwa, on whom the command devolved. He donned the yellow robe and with his wife and his mother was overpowered and slain by the victorious Mughuls.

The imperial troops entered the fortress immediately after dawn, and Akbar sullied his success by a ghastly massacre. The 8000 Rājputs who formed the garrison had received much assistance from the peasants, numbering 40,000, and a general massacre of both was ordered. Some, indeed, were spared and made prisoners, but the tale of the slain amounted to 30,000. Akbar's wrath was specially kindled against the musketeers of Kālpī, 1000 in number, who had done much execution among his troops, and it would have gone ill with them had they not escaped by a clever stratagem. Placing their wives and families in their midst they marched boldly from the fortress in the light of day, passing themselves off as a body of imperial troops escorting prisoners.

The massacre of Chitor, which has made the place unclean and accursed to its old royal house, has left an indelible blot on Akbar's name. No such horrors were perpetrated by the brutal 'Alā-ud-dīn, and Abu-'l-Fazl is at some pains to excuse the contrast by explaining that the civil population, which had been most active during Akbar's siege, had taken no part in the defence in 'Alā-ud-dīn's siege, but "the sin of the slaughter of Chitor" will ever sully the memory of Akbar. His commemoration of the heroism of Jai Mal and Patta by placing statues of them, mounted on elephants, at the gate of his imperial palace at Āgra was probably intended as a compliment, but it was open to misconstruction.

On 28 February Āsaf Khān was appointed governor of Mewār, the Rānā's state, and Akbar set out on his return to Āgra.

While the emperor was engaged in the siege of Chitor Mun'im Khān paid a visit to Sulaimān Kararānī at Patna. Sulaimān was the younger brother and successor of Tāj Khān Kararāni, who had risen to power on the ruins of the Sūr dynasty. The results of this interview were most satisfactory. Some outstanding frontier disputes were settled and Sulaimān caused the *khutba* to be recited and money coined in Akbar's name,[1] but Mun'im Khān ran considerable risk. Some of the more adventurous spirits among Sulaimān's Afghān officers were in favour of arresting and detaining the imperial governor, but the news of the fall of Chitor brought these short-sighted politicians to their senses and Mun'im Khān returned in safety to Jaunpur.

Akbar reached Āgra on 13 April, after a pilgrimage to Ajmer, and sent an expedition to besiege Ranthambhor, which Rājā Surjan Rāi held as a vassal of the Rānā, but before the force reached its destination news was received that the Mīrzās had invaded Mālwā and were besieging Ujjain. The design of besieging Ranthambhor was therefore abandoned for the time and the troops destined thither were reinforced and ordered to march into Mālwā and attack the Mīrzās. The latter, on hearing of their approach, raised the siege of Ujjain

[1] The coins are not known with certainty.

and fled towards Māndū, pursued by the forces of the local assignees. They were unable to make any stand and crossed the Narbadā, after losing many of their followers. Having thus placed themselves beyond the reach of the imperial troops they heard of the assassination of Chingīz Khān in Gujarāt by Jhajār Khān the African and, foreseeing rich opportunities in the disturbed condition of that state, returned thither without delay. Their anticipations were realised and for the next two years they were fully, and not unprofitably, employed in Gujarāt. The expeditionary force which had been sent against them returned to Āgra, where its leaders were, for a time, under a cloud on suspicion of their having been lukewarm in the pursuit of the Mīrzās.

"The foster-father cohort" had hitherto all held assignments in the Punjab under their chief, Khān Kalān, who was governor of the province. Akbar now decided to transfer them to other places, far removed from one another. They had bitterly resented the murder of Atga Khān and had been baulked of their vengeance by Akbar's decision to proceed against none but the actual murderer, but their loyalty was above suspicion and there seems to have been no reason for the measure beyond the observance of the general principles, sound in such an empire as that of the Mughuls, that nobles who were nearly related should be distributed in different provinces and that no great noble should be allowed to retain indefinitely the government of one particular province. It was the failure to observe these principles that eventually led to the dismemberment of the empire.

The family arrived at Āgra in September, and after a short stay received new assignments, far distant from one another. Khān Kalān was sent to Sambhal, his youngest brother, Qutb-ud-dīn Muhammad Khān, to Mālwā, and Sharīf Khān, the other surviving brother, to Kanauj. 'Azīz Kūka, the son of Khān Kalān, who bore the title of Khān A'zam, was permitted to retain his assignment at Dīpālpur in the Punjab. Husain Qulī Khān, afterwards entitled Khān Jahān, was promoted from the minor government of Nāgaur to that of the Punjab, but did not proceed to his new post until Ranthambhor had fallen, and Shihāb-ud-dīn Ahmad Khān was recalled from Mālwā, where Qutb-ud-dīn was to relieve him, and was placed in charge of the crown lands, the management of which was too heavy a burden for Muzaffar Khān, the revenue minister. He introduced some reforms in the direction of economy, but was hampered by the venality of subordinate officials.

Preparations for the reduction of Ranthambhor, which had been postponed by the activities of the Mīrzās in Mālwā, were now resumed, and Akbar, having decided to direct the siege in person, arrived before the fortress on 8 February, 1569, and at once opened the siege. A covered way was constructed and enormous mortars, similar to that used at Chitor, were dragged up to the eminence opposite to the *Ran* gate, where Akbar's own post was. The artillery of the fortress did some execution on the besiegers, but Akbar's mortar battery inflicted terrible damage on the buildings in the fort and caused much loss of life, and the fortress was surrendered on 18 March.

According to a Rājput legend preserved by Tod, Bhagwān Dās entered the fortress under a safe-conduct to induce Surjan Rāi to surrender and Akbar attended him, disguised as one of his companions and, having been recognised, conducted the negotiations in person, granting Surjan Rāi concessions and privileges most flattering to his pride of race.

Dr Vincent Smith is inclined to accept this story, which is mentioned by no Muhammadan historian, considering that the Muslim annals do not sufficiently explain the surrender and are not inconsistent with the Hindu story, but the legend must, we think, be discarded. Akbar's visit to Surjan Rāi, if it had ever been made, would have provided a panegyrist with a wonderful opportunity for extolling his courage, resource, romantic love of adventure and tenderness of human life, and we cannot conceive Abu-'l-Fazl missing such an opportunity. On the other hand the surrender is sufficiently explained by Badāūnī who, after relating the execution done by Akbar's mortars, adds, "Rāi Surjan, the governor of the fortress, when he contemplated the insufficiency of the fortress of Chitor and the misery which fell on its inhabitants, seemed to be contemplating his own fate, and sent his sons Dandā and Bhoj, by the mediation of some fief-holders [assignees], to wait on the emperor, and begged for quarter".

Anīs-ud-dīn Mihtar Khān, who had been Humāyūn's treasurer during his flight to Persia, was appointed to the command of the fortress and the government of the district and Akbar left Ranthambhor on his annual pilgrimage to Ajmer, returning to Āgra on 20 May.

Before the siege began news was received that the Mīrzās had again invaded Mālwā from Gujarāt, but Akbar did not on this occasion permit their movements to affect his settled plans.

Meanwhile the gradual consolidation of the empire proceeded, and in August Majnūn Khān Qāqshāl captured the fortress of Kālinjar, where Sher Shāh had lost his life and where his son Islām Shāh had been enthroned. It was in the possession of Rām Chand, Rājā of Bhath, or Rewah, who, having heard of the fate of Chitor and Ranthambhor, made no very strenuous resistance. Majnūn Khān's success was rewarded by the inclusion of Kālinjar and the district of which it was the centre in the government of the lower Dūāb, which he already held.

Akbar, though well provided with wives, had no children. Twin sons who had been born to him had died very shortly after their birth, and he had long been used to pray at the shrine of Shaikh Mu'īn-ud-dīn Chishtī at Ajmer and at those of saints at Delhi for the blessing of a son. There lived at Sīkrī, 23 miles to the west of Āgra, another Chishtī, Shaikh Salīm, to whom Akbar had had recourse, and who had promised him that his prayers would be answered. Shaikh Salīm, though described by Father Monserrate as "being stained with all the wickedness and disgraceful conduct of the Muslims"—a phrase of sinister import—had a great reputation for sanctity among his co-religionists, and when Akbar learnt, early in 1569, that his earliest Hindu consort, the daughter of Rājā Bihārī Mal of Amber, was with child she was sent to the Shaikh's hospice at Sīkrī, where, on 30 August, was born the prince who afterwards, under the title of Jahāngīr, succeeded his father. He received the name Salīm in honour of the saint. In November a daughter, Khānum Sultān, known as Shāhzāda Khānum, was born to Akbar, and on 7 July of the following year Salīma Begam gave birth to Sultān Murād. A third son, Dāniyāl, was born at Ajmer on 10 September, 1572, in the house of Shaikh Dāniyāl, one of the holy men whose prayers Akbar had sought. Two other children, both daughters, were born after Dāniyāl, Shukr-un-Nisa Begam, who was married to Shāhrukh Mīrzā, her fourth cousin, and Ārām Bānu Begam.

On 20 January, 1570, Akbar fulfilled a vow made by him on the occasion of the birth of Salīm by performing a pilgrimage on foot to Ajmer, where he reformed some abuses which had crept into the administration of the saint's shrine, and returned to Delhi, where he inspected the splendid tomb of his father. He reached Āgra on 2 May.

On 23 September he again set out on his annual pilgrimage to Ajmer, halting for twelve days at Fathpur Sīkrī, where he had resolved to found a city. On reaching Ajmer he improved and extended the fortifications of the city and had palaces built for himself and his leading courtiers, granting to others villages in the Ajmer district, the revenues of which would enable them to build themselves houses in the city. He left Ajmer on 3 November and on 5 November reached Nāgaur. Here he cleaned out and repaired one of the three great reservoirs on which the town had depended for its former prosperity and constructed a fountain with seventeen jets, which is still in existence.

At Nāgaur he received the submission of Chandra Sen, son of Māldeo, Rājā of Jodhpur, and of Rāi Kalyān Mal, Rājā of Bīkāner, and his son Rāi Singh, and married a relation of Kalyān Mal and also the daughter of Rāwal Har Rāi of Jaisalmer, who was conducted to his camp by Bhagwān Dās. Here also he received the tardy submission of Bāz Bahādur, who had abandoned all hope of recovering his kingdom of Mālwā and was fain to accept the nominal command of 1000 horse in the imperial service.

From Nāgaur Akbar made a pilgrimage to the shrine of Shaikh Farīd Shakarganj at Ajudhan, now known as Pāk Pattan, amusing himself on the way by hunting the wild ass in the desert, of which rare quarry he shot thirteen head.

From Pāk Pattan he marched by way of Dīpālpur to Lahore, and returned by way of Hissār to Ajmer, which he reached on 24 July. On 9 August he reached Fathpur Sīkrī, where he seriously prosecuted his design of building a city. His reasons for this step are thus recorded by Abu-'l-Fazl: "Inasmuch as his exalted sons [Salīm and Murād] had been born at Sīkrī, and the God-knowing spirit of Shaikh Salīm had taken possession thereof, his holy heart desired to give outward splendour to this spot which possessed spiritual grandeur. Now that his standards had arrived at this place his former design was pressed forward and an order was issued that the superintendents of affairs should erect lofty buildings for the use of the emperor."

Akbar had been kept regularly informed of events in Gujarāt, the condition of which kingdom was now deplorable. Its recent history had been the record of a series of bloody struggles for supremacy between ambitious and self-seeking nobles, and it was this state of affairs which had proved so attractive to the Mīrzās. Muzaffar III, the nominal king, whose claim to royal birth was extremely doubtful, was powerless to maintain even a semblance of order and was never more than a tool in the hands of others.

For the invasion of Gujarāt, on which he now decided, Akbar had a better excuse than for most of his attacks on his neighbours. A civil war was in progress, and one party, headed by I'timād Khān, invited his intervention. The country lay on the way to Mecca and all Muslims were interested in its tranquillity and good government. Its weakness invited the aggression of the Portuguese both on its coasts and on pilgrim ships sailing from its ports, and the emperor was powerless to punish their aggression while the independent kingdoms of Gujarāt and the Deccan separated their settlements from his dominions.

Before leaving Sīkrī he was obliged to make arrangements for dealing with a minor rebellion. Jay Chand, Rājā of Nagarkot (Kāngra), had visited his court, had offended him and had been imprisoned, and his son Bidai Chand, hearing of his father's imprisonment, concluded that he had been murdered and rebelled at Nagarkot. Husain Qulī Khān, governor of the Punjab, was ordered to capture Nagarkot and to hand it over, as a fief, to Rājā Bīrbal.

Having sent reinforcements to the Punjab lest Muhammad Hakīm should take advantage of his preoccupation in Gujarāt to invade India, Akbar marched for Ajmer, whence, on 12 August, he sent forward 10,000 horse under Khān Kalān as an advance guard and on 1 September followed with the main body of his army. Near Bāgor,[1]

[1] Dr Vincent Smith (*Akbar*, p. 110) has "Nāgaur", following the printed text of the *Akbar-nāma*. A glance at the map will show that Nāgaur is an impossible reading. Akbar, marching from Ajmer to Gujarāt, would not have been likely to march nearly 80 miles

where the court halted, he received news of the birth of his son Dāniyāl at Ajmer.

At the next stage he was informed of a mishap to Khān Kalān, who had been stabbed by a treacherous envoy at Sirohī. The wound was not serious and healed in a fortnight, and the Hindu who inflicted it was slain. It was probably to avenge his death that a number of desperate fanatics opposed Akbar when he entered Sirohī with his army. Eighty of these were slain in a temple and seventy in the raja's palace.

Rāi Singh of Bīkāner was sent to Jodhpur to watch the Rānā and keep the road open and Akbar marched to Pātan (Anhilwāra) sending Rājā Mān Singh in pursuit of the sons of Sher Khān Fulādī, who had fled from that town towards Junāgarh. He returned without the fugitives, but with much booty taken from them, and on 13 November Akbar left Pātan for Ahmadābād, where Sher Khān Fulādī, who had gained possession of the person of Muzaffar III, was besieging I'timād Khān. He raised the siege and fled on hearing of Akbar's approach, and Muzaffar, who had escaped from custody, was found lurking in a cornfield at Jotāna, two stages from Pātan, and on 15 November was brought into Akbar's camp. On the following day I'timād Khān and the leading members of his faction appeared in the camp and surrendered the keys of Ahmadābād.

Akbar appointed Khān A'zam governor of Gujarāt to the north-west of the river Māhī and wisely confided the government of the rest of the province, where the Mīrzās had established themselves, to I'timād Khān and his party, who were hostile to the Mīrzās.

He arrived at Ahmadābād on 20 November, and the *khutba* was recited in his name. He had reason to be satisfied with his conquest. Ahmadābād was one of the richest and greatest cities in India, and though it is not necessary to take too literally Abu-'l-Fazl's statement that it contained 380 quarters, each of which might be deemed a city, its commercial importance may be estimated from the fact that it was the emporium of the greater part of the Persian and of a very large part of the European trade.

At Ahmadābād Akbar discovered that it would be necessary for him personally to undertake the expulsion of the Mīrzās from the southern provinces of the kingdom, and, leaving Ahmadābād on 8 December he reached Cambay four days later. Here he enjoyed his first sight of the sea and received the merchants of Turkey, Syria, Persia, Transoxiana and Portugal. He left Cambay after a week's halt and arrived on 22 December at Baroda.

The Mīrzās had possessed themselves of the richest districts of

in a north-westerly direction when his objective lay directly to the south-west. The correct reading must be Bāgor (25° 22′ N., 74° 23′ E.) which is obtained by changing the position of one dot. That this is so is proved by the text of the *Akbar-nāma*, where it is stated that Akbar's next stage was "the neighbourhood of Amet". The distance from Bāgor to Amet is about 28 miles and that from Nāgaur to Amet about 140.

southern Gujarāt. Ibrāhīm Husain Mīrzā had occupied Baroda, Muhammad Husain Mīrzā Surat, and Shāh Mīrzā Chāmpāner. A large force under Sayyid Mahmūd Khān Bārha was detached to reduce Surat, and another, under Shāhbāz Khān, to reduce Chāmpāner, but had not reached their destinations when Akbar heard that Ibrāhīm Husain Mīrzā was about to leave Baroda with his troops and retire to some other district of Gujarāt. Akbar resolved to intercept him and set out at night with a small picked force. After marching the rest of the night and the whole of the following day he reached the Māhī river at sunset and discovered that Ibrāhīm Husain Mīrzā was at Sarnāl on the opposite bank, with a large force. Those with him advised postponing the attack until night had fallen but Akbar at once crossed the river with no more than 200 horse.

Ibrāhīm Husain marched forth from the town and drew up his forces while Akbar, having crossed the river, entered it by the river gate, after overcoming some slight resistance. He marched through the town and his small force deployed as it emerged from the streets. Ibrāhīm Husain attacked it and drove in the advance guard, and Akbar was in a position of great danger. He was attacked by three horsemen, one of whom was slain by Bhagwān Dās while he himself drove off the other two. His small force then charged the enemy and Ibrāhīm Husain turned and fled, followed by Akbar and his men until darkness ended the pursuit, when the Mīrzā succeeded in escaping by way of Ahmadnagar to Sirohī and Pātan.

The young Muzaffar Husain Mīrzā was carried off by his mother from Surat, on the approach of the imperial forces, to the Deccan, and the defence of the fort was left to Hamzabān, who had been page to Humāyūn, but had thrown in his lot with the Mīrzās. Akbar arrived before Surat on 11 January, 1573, and Hamzabān, after enduring a six weeks' siege, offered to surrender conditionally. Akbar granted him easy terms and the fortress was surrendered on 26 February. Hamzabān, "who was a foul-mouthed fellow", must have been guilty of insolence after the surrender, for his tongue was cut out.

The garrison had invited a force of Portuguese to assist in the defence of the town, but when they arrived and saw how matters stood they assumed the character of envoys, and offered gifts to Akbar, who questioned them about Portugal and the affairs of Europe. The fulsome Abu-'l-Fazl adds: "Although it is well known that the holy heart of the Lord of the World is the repository of all knowledge, both spiritual and worldly, his exemplary mind designed to make these inquiries a means of showing kindness to that crew of savages." This is a fair sample of Abu-'l-Fazl's style. The "crew of savages" could have told and probably did tell Akbar many things of which he had never even dreamed. For one thing they could tell him where Portugal was, and the names of the states of Europe.

The emperor, who was still an orthodox Muslim, had an interest in assuring the safety of the voyage to Mecca and was therefore dependent on the good will of the Portuguese. He sent an envoy to the viceroy, Dom Antonio de Noronha, who, after receiving him, sent back with him Antonio Cabral, who established a friendly understanding.

Mīrzā Sharaf-ud-dīn Husain, one of the members of the conspiracy which had compassed the death of Atga Khān, had fled from court in 1562 to his assignment at Nāgaur and thence to Gujarāt, where he had joined the Mīrzās. After their discomfiture he had gone towards the Deccan but had been captured by the Rājā of Bāglān, who was now called upon to surrender him. He complied and Akbar's envoys brought the fugitive, on 4 March, to the camp before Ṣurat. They were accompanied by Rājā 'Alī Khān, brother of Muhammad II of Khāndesh, who had been sent to do homage to Akbar. Sharaf-ud-dīn Husain was intimidated by being thrown before the feet of a harmless elephant, and was then imprisoned.

Muhammad Husain Mīrzā, Shāh Mīrzā and Sher Khān Fulādī now besieged Sayyid Ahmad Bārha in Pātan, and Khān A'zam and the army of Mālwā marched to his relief and defeated and dispersed the besiegers, Sher Khān fleeing to Junāgarh and the two Mīrzās to the Deccan.

Ibrāhīm Husain Mīrzā, after his escape from the field of Sarnāl, fled first towards Pātan and then towards Āgra, but Shāham Khān was ordered to raise the siege of Chāmpāner, which then engaged him, and intercept the fugitive, and the Mīrzā directed his flight towards the Punjab.

Akbar returned to Ahmadābād on 2 April and, having confirmed Khān A'zam as governor of the new province of the empire, allotted various grants to the leading officers who had accompanied him, and appointed Muzaffar Khān Turbatī to the government of Mālwā in the place of Qutb-ud-dīn Muhammad Khān, who had not shown sufficient promptitude in obeying his bidding to assist in establishing peace and order in Gujarāt. He left Ahmadābād on 13 April, and at Sirohī learnt that Husain Qulī Khān, governor of the Punjab, had captured both Ibrāhīm Husain Mīrzā and his brother Mas'ūd Husain Mīrzā. He arrived at Ajmer on 13 May, and, after performing his usual pilgrimage, continued his journey to Fathpur Sīkrī, which he reached on 3 June. Shaikh Mubārak, the father of Faizī and Abu-'l-Fazl, appeared before him on this occasion and welcomed him in a speech in which he congratulated him on his victories. In this speech he expressed the hope that the emperor might become the spiritual as well as the temporal head of his people. We may be sure that no such hope would have been expressed unless there had been some reason for supposing that it would be welcome, and the heterodox orator, a man who in religion was "everything by turns and nothing long", had probably heard that Akbar, while besieging Surat, had listened attentively to the famous *mūbid* or Zoroastrian theologian Dastūr Māhyārjī Rānā of Navsārī. It was not until nine years later that he promulgated his new religion, the Divine Faith, but he had always been given to religious discussions and it was certainly in 1573 that he began to feel misgivings as to the sufficiency of orthodox Islām. Henceforth he sought a more perfect way, but his spiritual pride misled him.

He was not left in peace to pursue his religious meditations, and in the course of his busy life he oscillated between various creeds before he collected his stock-in-trade as a prophet.

CHAPTER V

AKBAR, MYSTIC AND PROPHET

HUSAIN QULĪ KHĀN had been obliged by the flight of the two Mīrzās into the Punjab to raise the siege of Nagarkot, but had first exacted from Bidai Chand complete submission to Akbar. Having defeated the Mīrzās he carried his prisoners, 300 in number, to Fathpur Sīkrī where the head of Ibrāhīm Husain was laid before the throne, and Mas'ūd Husain, with his eyes sewn up, was delivered to Akbar, who, having caused the stitches to be cut, imprisoned the rebel in Gwalior. The other prisoners, clad in the skins of cows, asses, hogs and dogs, formed a grotesque pageant, after which some were released, others imprisoned, and others put to death with fantastic tortures. Husain Qulī Khān received the title of Khān Jahān.

Sulaimān Kararānī, king of Bengal, had died during Akbar's expedition to Gujarāt, and Akbar, on his return, was preparing for the conquest of Bengal when news arrived that Gujarāt was in revolt. Muhammad Husain Mīrzā, who had fled to Daulatābād, had returned to Gujarāt and joined a confederacy which the rebellious nobles of the old dynasty had formed with the Rājā of Īdar. They besieged Khān A'zam in Ahmadābād, and, on learning of the rebellion, Akbar left Fathpur Sīkrī on 23 August, and on 2 September arrived within four miles of Ahmadābād, having performed the march from Fathpur Sīkrī in eleven days.

Khān A'zam was apprised of Akbar's arrival, and the imperial troops, numbering no more than 3000, halted on the banks of the Sābarmatī. Akbar was advised to fall on the enemy at once, but his foolish punctilio restrained him from attacking even rebels unawares, and he caused the great kettle-drums to be beaten. Muhammad Husain Mīrzā, on being informed that the sound indicated that the emperor was present in person, refused to credit the account as his spies had reported that they had seen Akbar at Fathpur Sīkrī only a fortnight before, but he sent Ikhtiyār-ul-Mulk with 5000 horse to prevent Khān A'zam from issuing from Ahmadābād, and himself attacked Akbar's force. Akbar in person led a charge against the rebels, and the Mīrzā was wounded. His horse fell with him as he was fleeing, and he was captured and brought before Akbar, who delivered him into the custody of Rāi Singh. A fresh force advancing towards Akbar's troops was believed to be that commanded by Khān A'zam, but proved to be the 5000 horse led by Ikhtiyār-ul-Mulk. This force was likewise attacked and defeated by Akbar, and Ikhtiyār-ul-Mulk was captured and shared the fate of Muhammad Husain Mīrzā, who had been put to death by order of Rāi Singh. Late in the afternoon Khān A'zam issued from Ahmadābād and joined Akbar, who embraced him affectionately and greeted the officers with him. A column was sent to Broach and Chāmpāner in pursuit of the other rebel, Shāh Mīrzā, who had fled, but he escaped and is heard of no more.

Thus ended the most astonishing military exploit of Akbar's reign. In eleven days he had ridden, with 3000 horse, more than 450 miles; on arriving at his destination he had fought, in one day, two battles, each against a force superior in numbers to his own, and in each he had gained a decisive victory, and had completely crushed a dangerous rebellion.

He remained at Ahmadābād for no more than ten days after his success, but during that short period he made arrangements for the government of the province.

The finances of Gujarāt had fallen into the utmost confusion. The administration of the state had for years been lax to the verge of anarchy, and after a long period of internecine strife it had been the scene of almost uninterrupted warfare for a year. It had been impossible to collect any revenue, and it was probably difficult to ascertain on what principle and in what proportion the land rent should be collected. Rājā Todar Mal was appointed to revise the settlement and to restore order in the financial administration.

Akbar arrived at his capital on 5 October, and within a month Rājā Bhagwān Dās returned with the army and brought with him Umrāo Singh, son of Partāb Singh, Rānā of Chitor, sent by his father to court in order that he might enter the emperor's service.

A great measure of reform in the administration of the empire was now inaugurated by the promulgation of the "branding regulation", the conversion of all the assignments into crown lands, and the regulation of the grades of the officers of state.

The branding regulation applied to the horses which the nobles and lesser officers were obliged to maintain for their contingents, and was designed to prevent the fraudulent practice of producing at musters horses temporarily borrowed or hired. It was modelled on similar regulations issued by 'Alā-ud-dīn Khaljī and Sher Shāh, and was bitterly opposed by those whose opportunities for peculation it curtailed, one of its most obstinate opponents being Khān A'zam, the emperor's foster-brother.

The conversion of the whole of the imperial territories into crown lands was a root and branch measure, amounting to nothing less than the complete change of the administrative system. It was aimed against the corrupt practices of the officers of state who, while extracting the last penny of revenue from their assignments, failed to maintain at full strength or to pay at a just rate the contingents for the support of which the assignments had been made. Akbar's intention was that his territories should be administered by his own revenue officials, and that his troops should be a standing army regularly paid at uniform rates from the imperial treasury.

The regulation of the grades of the officers of state consisted in the establishment of a graded list of the *mansabdārs*, or officers of the army, whose rank ranged from that of commander of 5000 down to that of commander of ten horse. The measure affected civil as well as military officials, for the former held relative rank and were graded as commanders of horse even though they might never command troops. Akbar's intention was that all should, as a rule, enter in the lowest rank and rise by merit.

For the purpose of carrying out these reforms Muzaffar Khān Turbatī was appointed *vakīl*, or first minister of the empire, and Todar Mal on his return from Gujarāt was appointed his assistant, but Muzaffar Khān, who personally disapproved of the reforms, failed to enforce them and was consequently dismissed.

The reforms were, indeed, generally unpopular. Akbar succeeded in resuming the land in the more settled provinces of the empire, where the troops, from those in high command downwards, were paid from the treasury and the cavalry soldiers received branded horses from the state. Collectors of revenue were appointed, each to a tract estimated to yield a crore (*karor* = 10,000,000) of *dāms*, equivalent to Rs. 250,000, and were styled croris (*karorīs*). They were expected both to collect the revenue and to improve it by encouraging the extension of cultivation, but they proved to be both inefficient and extortionate, and many were severely punished. In 1582 Todar Mal was appointed *vakīl*, or prime minister of the empire, and was ordered to prepare a scheme for the improvement of the revenue administration.[1] The thirteen proposals which he submitted to Akbar were so elementary in their nature as to make it clear that the resumption of the land by the crown had in no way lightened the burden of the husbandman.

In the less settled and newly conquered provinces the old system remained undisturbed, but Akbar insisted on the enforcement of the branding regulation in all provinces. It is to the unpopularity of this measure that Abu-'l-Fazl attributes the rebellion which broke out in Bihār and Bengal in 1580, but though this may have been a contributory cause the rebellion was chiefly due to Akbar's religious innovations. In 1576, when Khān A'zam was summoned from Gujarāt to join a projected expedition to Badakhshān, it was discovered that he had made no attempt to enforce the obnoxious regulation in his province, and he so violently condemned it that he was deprived of office. Another might have lost his life, but Akbar could never cross the "river of milk".

Sulaimān Kararānī, who had been governor of Bihār under Sher Shāh, established his independence in Bengal when the power of the Sūr dynasty declined. He had placated Akbar by acknowledging his authority and occasionally sending him tribute, and had died in

[1] See also chap. XVI.

1572. His elder son, Bāyazīd, who succeeded him, had been put to death, after a reign of a few months, by his turbulent Afghān nobles, who raised to the throne his younger brother Dāūd.

This prince was intoxicated by his elevation to power and by the extent of his resources. He was the master of much treasure, of 40,000 cavalry, of 140,000 infantry, of 20,000 guns of sorts, of 3300 elephants, and of an enormous fleet of river boats. He defied Akbar by refusing to acknowledge his supremacy, and invaded his dominions and destroyed the fort of Zamāniyā, near Ghāzīpur. Mun'im Khān had been sent against him, and had compelled him to retire to Patna, where he besieged him. In the conduct of the siege he experienced considerable difficulties, less from the activity of the enemy than from the insubordination of Khān 'Ālam, who had been sent to assist him, and his reports caused Akbar to march in person to his assistance.

Before he left Fathpur Sīkrī his famous secretary, Abu-'l-Fazl, and the historian, 'Abdul-Qādir Badāūnī, were presented to him for the first time.

Abu-'l-Fazl was now a young man of twenty-three. As a boy he had studied assiduously under his father, Shaikh Mubārak, and had afterwards followed his own bent in reading and meditation, until he became, as he himself confesses, a prig of the first water. He meditated and speculated on the mysteries of all religions, and was so perplexed by the differences between the formalists of every faith that he had "neither strength to remain silent nor power to cry out". He was a mystic and a visionary, and was the worst possible adviser that one of Akbar's tendencies could have had in spiritual matters. It was probably not he who invented the "Divine Faith", for that seems to have been the bantling of Akbar's own brain, but both he and his father undoubtedly had a part in encouraging Akbar's extravagant view of his spiritual prerogative.

He was favourably received, and, though he did not at once enter the imperial service, he found, as he says, in Akbar his "true spiritual guide. His eyes were opened and he perceived the spiritual excellence of a sovereign who was the confluence of the oceans of religious and worldly duty, the dayspring of the lights of outward forms and inward graces", and much more to the same effect.

Abu-'l-Fazl undoubtedly had for Akbar an admiration none the less genuine for its coincidence with his interest, but few will agree with the late Mr Blochmann that the charge of flattery and wilful concealment of facts damaging to the reputation of his master is absolutely unfounded, or that he praises with much more grace and dignity than any other eastern writer. In gross flattery there can be neither grace nor dignity, and Abu-'l-Fazl's flattery is uncouth in form and style and differs from the formal and customary tribute of other panegyrists by verging on blasphemy.

Akbar left Āgra by boat on 20 June, his army marching by land,

and on 4 August reached Patna, where it was decided to capture Hājīpur on the north bank of the river, the dépôt whence the garrison of Patna drew its supplies, but Akbar first made a foolish proposal to Dāūd that the differences between them should be settled by single combat. Even Dāūd had the wit to understand that great armies are not maintained merely as spectators of tournaments, and rejected the proposal.

Hājīpur was taken on 7 August, and on 9 August the Afghāns evacuated Patna by night and fled. Akbar pursued them the next day as far as Daryāpur, near Bārh, and, though he failed to come up with them, took much plunder, including 265 elephants. The next day he was joined by Mun'im Khān who had followed him, and who was left to complete the conquest of Bengal, Akbar returning to Delhi, which he reached on 17 October. On his way he received two despatches from Mun'im Khān, the first announcing the bloodless capture of the fortified pass of Teliyāgarhī, the gate of lower Bengal, and the second the occupation of Dāūd's capital, Tāndā.

In 1575 the province of Gujarāt suffered severely from a pestilence, and from a famine which lasted for six months, a calamity rare in that fertile region and greatly aggravated by the wars and disorders which had devastated it.

Meanwhile the conquest of Bengal proceeded but slowly, owing to dissensions between the officers and the sloth and insubordination of the troops. Mun'im Khān made Tāndā his headquarters and left the direction of operations in the field chiefly to Todar Mal. Ghorāghāt,[1] Sātgāon[2] and Burdwān were occupied, but an imperial force was defeated in Chotā Nāgpur by Junaid Kararānī, Dāūd's cousin, against whom Todar Mal was obliged to advance in person. He defeated him, and occupied Midnapore, but Junaid soon recovered from his defeat, and marched into Bihār, which had been invaded by another Afghān force under Tāj Khān. The imperial governor, Muzaffar Khān Turbatī, was thus obliged to deal with two rebel forces and also to recover Hājīpur, which another body of Afghāns had recaptured, but after many vicissitudes he succeeded in expelling all the rebels and in restoring order in the province.

Todar Mal, still at Midnapore, was preparing to advance into Orissa, where Dāūd had taken refuge, but his troops insisted that their defeat of Junaid had earned them some repose and refused to embark on a fresh campaign. Mun'im Khān sent him a reinforcement which enabled him to prevent the malcontents from retreating, but not to induce them to advance.

Dāūd, hearing of these dissensions, assembled a considerable army and marched against Todar Mal, who advanced to Chitwa, but, mistrusting the spirit and the loyalty of his officers, again appealed to Mun'im Khān, who at length took the field in person and joined

[1] 25° 15′ N., 89° 18′ E. [2] 22° 58′ N., 88° 23′ E.

him. An attempt to turn Dāūd's flank and to cut his line of retreat compelled him to prepare for battle.

The battle is variously known as that of Bajhaura, Mughulmārī, and Tukaroī, and the researches of the late Mr Blochmann[1] have determined its site, which was on the road from Midnapore to Jaleswar, rather more than half-way from the former to the latter, and within three miles of the eastern bank of the Subarnarekha.

The result of the battle was for some time in doubt. Mun'im Khān was severely wounded, 'Ālam Khān was killed, and the centre broke and fled, throwing even the left wing, under Todar Mal, into some confusion. The centre was, however, rallied and drove back the vanguard of the Afghān centre. Todar Mal then pressed forward and drove the right wing of the Afghāns from the field. Their left wing also gave way, and Dāūd fled, and took refuge in Cuttack. Todar Mal pursued him vigorously as far as Bhadrakh, and after Mun'im Khān had joined him there envoys from Dāūd arrived, to sue for peace. Dāūd offered to appear before Mun'im Khān and swear allegiance to Akbar, to surrender his elephants and pay tribute, and to wait personally on the emperor when approved service should have ensured him a favourable reception. The troops had long been weary of field service in the unaccustomed climate of Bengal, so Mun'im Khān accepted these terms, and on 12 April received Dāūd on the bank of the Mahānadī. Dāūd made obeisance and delivered to Mun'im, besides many rich gifts, his nephew Muhammad, son of Bāyazīd, to be detained at the imperial court as a hostage, and in return received as a grant the greater part of Orissa. There was much rejoicing in the army at the termination of hostilities, but Todar Mal, the real hero of the campaign, stood aloof. He strongly disapproved of the treaty, and refused to affix his seal to it, but the news of peace was welcomed at court.

When Mun'im Khān, after returning to Tāndā, had expelled the local Afghāns who during his absence had occupied all the territory to the east of the Ganges, Bengal, though the seeds of future trouble remained, was at length quiet, and Akbar had leisure to turn his thoughts to other matters. For his favourite amusement he built at Fathpur Sīkrī his famous *'Ibādat-Khāna*, or "Hall of Worship", which would have been more accurately styled a hall of debate. Its exact design has never been ascertained, but it seems to have been cruciform in plan, the four arms of a Greek cross forming four halls for the accommodation of four classes of disputants and their supporters: (1) Shaikhs, or those who had acquired a reputation for sanctity or for the possession of peculiar spiritual gifts, (2) Sayyids, or descendants of Muhammad, (3) the *'Ulamā*, or jurists and doctors of the sacred law of Islām, and (4) nobles of the court interested in speculative theology. None but Muslims were at first admitted to the dis-

[1] *Āīn-i-Akbarī*, trans., I, 375.

cussions, for Akbar, though much attracted by the pantheistic mysticism of the Sūfīs, was still a professing Muslim, and even had he desired to admit professors of other faiths the strength of the orthodox party was then so strong that he could not have done so.

The orthodox, or Sunnī, party was led by Mullā 'Abdullah of Sultānpur, entitled Makhdūm-ul-Mulk, and by the *Sadr*, Shaikh 'Abdun-Nabī. Their orthodoxy was beyond question, but even the rigid Sunnī, Badāūnī, condemns the worldliness, avarice and duplicity of Makhdūm-ul-Mulk, but adds, with approval, "owing to his exertions many heretics and schismatics had gone to the places prepared for them". Shaikh 'Abdun-Nabī had put to death a Brāhman convicted of the offence of abusing the prophet of Islām, and had interpreted the marriage law with an exactitude which had given great offence to Akbar.

Shaikh Mubārak, the father of Faizī and Abu-'l-Fazl, had revelled in spiritual experiences. He had been in turn a Sunnī, a Shiah, a Sufī, a Mahdīist, and probably many other things besides. He had even professed to be the Mahdī, and for this offence had shortly before this time been obliged to go into hiding to save his life, for the jurists had decided to have him put to death for heresy. His position in the discussions was that of a free-lance. He had at first no system to offer as a substitute for orthodox Islām, and his object was purely destructive, the complete discomfiture of his enemies. His great learning fitted him for the task. He was versed in all contentious questions, and well knew how to set his persecutors by the ears, for even the orthodox had their differences. He soon had the doctors of the law cursing and reviling one another, and their vituperation and vulgar abuse at first diverted and afterwards disgusted Akbar. The introduction of Shiah disputants poured oil on the flames of strife, and the wrangles between the various sects and the intolerant violence of the orthodox gradually alienated Akbar from Islām, but he was still a professing Muslim, and in this year a party from his court, including his wife Salīma and his aunt Gulbadan, set out on the pilgrimage to Mecca.

Eastern Bengal was still unsettled, and Mun'im Khān transferred his headquarters from Tāndā to Gaur, further to the east. His officers knew if he did not why the old city had been abandoned, and protested, but in vain, against being compelled to inhabit so pestilential a spot. Their worst anticipations were soon realised. Fourteen officers of high rank fell victims to the climate, and the mortality among the troops was so great that the living were unable to bury the dead, and threw the corpses into the river. Mun'im Khān remained obstinate until he was recalled to Tāndā by the renewed activity of Junaid Kararānī in Chotā Nagpur, and there he fell sick and died after a short illness in October, 1575.

The officers elected Shāham Khān Jalāir as their leader, but could not agree among themselves, and Dāūd, profiting by their dissensions and by the broken spirit of their troops, took the field. He captured Bhadrakh and Jaleswar, and Shāham Khān, thoroughly disheartened, retired into Bihār, leaving the whole of Bengal in the hands of the Afghāns.

Earlier in the year Mīrzā Sulaimān of Badakhshān, having been expelled from his principality by his rebellious grandson, Shāh Rukh, had sought an asylum at the imperial court and Akbar had generously but thoughtlessly promised to recover his throne for him. The loss of Bengal postponed indefinitely the fulfilment of this rash promise, and Akbar attempted to console the disappointed exile with the chief command in Bengal, but the offer was rejected. In 1576 Sulaimān set out for Mecca, and the government of Bengal was bestowed upon Khān Jahān, governor of the Punjab, whose army had already been mobilised for the recovery of Badakhshān, and Todar Mal accompanied him. They found the officers of the Bengal army in an intractable mood. They trembled for the safety of the wealth which they had amassed in Bengal, they dreaded Akbar's wrath, and many, who were Sunnīs, resented their subordination to the Shiah, Khān Jahān, but he, with the assistance of Todar Mal, reduced them to obedience and established his authority. Dāūd, now re-established at Tāndā, had sent a force to occupy Teliyāgarhī, but Khān Jahān captured both the fortress and the pass and slew half of the force which garrisoned them.

Early in 1576 Akbar started on his annual pilgrimage to Ajmer, and while there opened hostilities against the Rānā, who had failed to appear at court and had fortified himself at Gogunda. Mān Singh was appointed to the command of the army sent against him, and with him were associated Ghiyās-ud-dīn, 'Alī Āsaf Khān, two of the Bārha Sayyids, and Rāi Lon Karan, a Rājput of the Kachhwāhā clan. The army marched from Māndalgarh towards Gogunda and halted in the plain of Haldīghāt, below the pass of that name. "At this pass Partāp was posted with the flower of Mewār, and glorious was the struggle for its maintenance. Clan after clan followed with desperate intrepidity, emulating the daring of their prince, who led the crimson banner into the hottest part of the field."

The battle was fought in the latter half of June, "when the air was like a furnace". A charge by Hakīm Sūr the Afghān, who was fighting for the Rānā, put Lon Karan's Rājputs to flight, and Āsaf Khān's contingent maintained a heavy fire of musketry and shot flights of arrows into the mingled mass. Badāūnī, who was present, asked Āsaf Khān how it was possible to distinguish friend from foe, and Āsaf Khān replied, "They will hear the whiz of the arrows, be they who they may, and on whichever side they fall the gain is Islām's".

For some hours the day appeared to be going in favour of the Rānā, but shortly after midday Mān Singh's rearguard arrived on the field, and it was believed that Akbar had marched to his assistance. The Muslims raised a shout, and the Rājputs lost heart and gave way, and "the best blood of Mewār irrigated the pass of Haldīghāt. Of the nearest kin of the prince five hundred were slain: the exiled prince of Gwalior, Rām Sāh, his son Khandīrāo, with three hundred and fifty of his brave Tuar clan, paid the debt of gratitude with their lives. Since the expulsion by Bābur they had found sanctuary in Mewār, whose princes diminished their feeble revenue to maintain inviolable the rites of hospitality. Māna, the devoted Jhāla, lost one hundred and fifty of his vassals, and every house of Mewār mourned its chief support." The loss to the imperial troops was not heavy, but they were too exhausted to pursue, and it was not until the following day that they occupied Gogunda.

The campaign in Bengal made little progress. Tāndā had been occupied, but Dāūd had retired into the fortress of Āk Mahall, now Rājmahāl, and Khān Jahān had reported that with the force at his disposal it was impossible to attack the fortress. News of the battle of Haldīghāt was sent to Bengal to encourage him, Muzaffar Khān Turbatī was ordered to march with the army of Bihār to his assistance, and he was informed that Akbar himself was about to start for Bengal.

The advent of the rainy season had made military operations almost impossible, but, after being joined by Muzaffar Khān, Khān Jahān attacked Dāūd. Progress over the flooded ground was toilsome and slow, and the advance was checked by a marshy stream, but fords were discovered and the troops crossed by degrees. Their left was checked by the enemy's right, but when Todar Mal was able to bring his whole force into action the Afghāns fled. Their left, which had been exposed all night to the fire of the imperial artillery, was already broken and their whole army was in retreat before Khān Jahān's centre was engaged. As he was advancing to the attack shouts of victory were heard, and two officers led Dāūd before him. His horse had stuck in the mud as he was attempting to flee, and he had been seized. He was at once executed and his head was sent to Āgra.

Akbar, perturbed by the absence of satisfactory news from Bengal, set out from Fathpur Sīkrī on 22 July, 1576. He had marched but one short stage when Sayyid 'Abdullah Khān arrived in his camp and threw down Dāūd's head before him. He returned to Fathpur Sīkrī and ordered public rejoicings for the victory.

The independence of Bengal was now finally extinguished. We may lament the defeat of the gallant Rānā and the misfortunes which befel his land of heroes, but no such sentiment is aroused by the extinction of Afghān dominion in Bengal, and the substitution of Akbar's milder and more sympathetic rule. The Afghāns were illiberal tyrants, either bigots or debauchees, without a spark of feeling for those subjected to their sway.

In September Akbar set out on his pilgrimage to Ajmer, where Mān Singh, who had been summoned from the Rānā's country in disgrace, joined the camp. He was a loyal servant of Akbar, and he had no reason to love Partāb Singh, who made no secret of his opinion of those Rājputs who had given daughters or sisters in marriage to Muslims, even of the imperial house, but he could hardly be expected to incur the infamy of delivering to disgrace, if not to death, the chief of his race, and he had undoubtedly let slip opportunities of taking the Rānā. Akbar should not have imposed such a task upon a Rājput, and he now seems to have understood that he had too severely tested a faithful servant, for after the lapse of a few days Mān Singh and his officers were pardoned and were admitted to his presence.

Akbar's zeal for the religion in which he had been bred now rose in a final flicker. A large number of pilgrims was about to start for Mecca, travelling by Gogunda and Īdar, a route selected with a view to giving the strong escort accompanying them an opportunity of attacking the Rānā in his mountain fastnesses. Akbar, in an access of religious frenzy, announced his intention of personally performing the pilgrimage. He was dissuaded from the insane project, but in token of his desire to fulfil one of the obligations of a good Muslim, donned the pilgrim's garb and accompanied the caravan for a few miles on its way to Gogunda. The troops accompanying the caravan had no success against the Rānā, but the Rājā of Īdar was reduced to obedience.

Akbar now perceived that he could not count on even the most loyal of his Hindu officers to aid him in humbling the chief of their race, and perforce contented himself for the time by reducing to obedience the minor chiefs of Rājāsthān. The Rāwals Partāb of Bānswārā and Askaran of Dūngarpur were constrained to pay him homage, and the latter to give him a daughter in marriage. In 1557 Zain Khān Kūka compelled the rebellious Rājā of Būndī to submit, and in 1578 the Bundelā, Madhukar Sāh of Orchha, who had been in arms for more than a year against an imperial force, surrendered to Sādiq Muhammad Khān, and was presented at court, where he swore allegiance to the emperor.

In the summer of 1577 Akbar sent to the Muslim state of Khāndesh an expedition which secured the submission of Rājā 'Alī Khān, who had lately succeeded his nephew as its ruler. The event is less trivial than it seems, for it was the first step in a great enterprise conceived by Akbar, but not finally accomplished until the reign of his great-grandson, Aurangzīb—the reconquest of the Deccan, which had been severed from the empire of Delhi for two hundred and thirty years. In the course of his rapid descent on Gujarāt in 1573 Akbar had learned that the small kingdom of Berār, the northernmost of the five independent states of the Deccan, which was annexed by Ahmadnagar in the following year, was in the last throes of its death struggle, that confusion and disorder reigned in Ahmadnagar, and that his movements had excited apprehension and alarm in that kingdom. This information suggested to him the reconquest of the Deccan between which and his dominions Khāndesh was the only political barrier.

Rājā 'Alī Khān was in a dilemma. His sympathy lay with the states of the Deccan, and he earnestly desired the maintenance of their independence, though he knew that their constant bickerings, their internecine strife, and their bitter and bloody domestic feuds, to which the continued independence of his own small kingdom was partly due, not only exposed them to the risk of imperial aggression, but deprived him of the hope of effectual assistance from any one of them should he venture to stand forth as their champion. He could not hope to withstand alone the might of Akbar, and he was thus obliged to belie his sympathies first by making formal submission to Akbar, and at a later period by aiding him with his forces against both Ahmadnagar and Bijāpur; but even when his troops were ranged in the field beside the imperial forces his influence was ever exerted to prevent the complete subjugation of Ahmadnagar.

Many years were to pass before Akbar found an opportunity of attacking Ahmadnagar, but it was with this end in view that he secured the allegiance of the ruler of Khāndesh.

The unfortunate province of Gujarāt, which had hardly begun to enjoy peace, was now the scene of another rebellion. The young Muzaffar Husain Mīrzā, son of Ibrāhīm Husain Mīrzā, who had been slain in 1573, had been carried off to Ahmadnagar by his mother, but was now persuaded by Mihr 'Alī, a turbulent and ambitious adherent, to attempt to wrest Gujarāt from Akbar. He was able, owing to the treachery or cowardice of the imperial officers, to occupy Nandurbār and Barodā without striking a blow, and on 25 May 1577 the expeditionary force in Khāndesh was ordered to march against him. He defeated one force, and compelled another to seek refuge behind the walls of Ahmadābād; but Todar Mal, who had been occupied at Pātan with financial affairs, hastened to Ahmadābād and drove the rebels towards Cambay. They were obliged to retire from Cambay and were defeated on 6 June near Dholka, whence the Mīrzā fled with a few followers to Junāgarh, but, after Todar Mal's departure, returned, plundered Cambay, defeated Vazīr Khān, the viceroy at Sarnāl, and drove him into Ahmadābād, where he besieged him. The rebels even effected an entrance into the city, and were engaged in plundering when a stray bullet killed Mihr 'Alī, their real leader, and the youthful Mīrzā and his followers fled in dismay to Nandurbār, whither Vazīr Khān, suspecting a trap, did not venture to follow them.

The gross inefficiency of Vazīr Khān compelled Akbar to recall him, and in September Shihāb-ud-dīn Ahmad Khān was transferred from the government of Mālwā to that of Gujarāt. Akbar was now at Ajmer, whence he marched, by Merta and Nārnaul, to the Punjab, occupied on the way by the issue of regulations for the reform of the administration of the imperial mints. At Nārnaul he lodged with the saintly Shaikh Nizām-ud-dīn, "a *Sūfī* who had attained the first stage of recognition of God, had overcome his desires, and had acquired complete hope in God's mercy",[1] but he was disappointed, when he attempted to lure the Shaikh into the paths of vague speculation in which he himself was wandering, to find that he was a staunch Muslim. Akbar had already assumed the character of a spiritual guide, for since leaving Ajmer he had rated Todar Mal for what Abu-'l-Fazl styles his "bigotry and prejudice". In the hurry of departure the images before which the Hindu was wont to perform his morning devotions had been mislaid, and he would neither eat, sleep nor work until he could perform his devotions after his rule. According to Abu-'l-Fazl Todar Mal's "good fortune" led him to give ear to his master's advice and he returned to his work.

Akbar was now meditating deeply on spiritual matters. At Shādīwāl,[2] which he reached on 30 January, 1578, he addressed his courtiers on his abhorrence of flesh as food, regretting that the demands which his duties made upon his strength compelled him to indulge in it, and assuring them that he proposed in future to abstain from it on Fridays. On 20 April he was at Bhera, on the bank of the Jhelum, where he organised a vast *battue* similar to the hunt of 1567 at Lahore. The barbarous sport had been in progress for four days, much game had already been killed, and the ring of beaters had almost closed in for the final slaughter when all engaged in it were surprised by a sudden order that the hunt was to cease, the beaters were to disperse, and no living creature was to be injured.

It is difficult to understand precisely what happened to Akbar, but he was evidently overcome by some form of religious ecstasy. He had for some time been working himself into a frame of mind susceptible of such a visitation. Badāūnī says: "A strange ecstasy and a strong sense of attraction to God came upon the emperor, and an unseemly change was exhibited in his manner, in such sort that it was impossible to explain it, and each attempted to explain it in his own way; but that which is secret is with God, and at once he ordered the hunt to be stopped."[3] Abu-'l-Fazl suggests that he was on the point of abdicating, or of dying. "He was near abandoning this state of struggle, and entirely gathering up the skirt of his genius from worldly pomp." The same author, naturally, represents him as having been singularly favoured, and of having communed with

[1] *Bad.* (trans. Haig), III, 44.
[2] 32° 31′ N., 74° 6′ E.
[3] Text II, 273, 274.

God face to face. "A sublime joy took possession of his bodily frame. The attraction of cognition of God cast its ray." He proceeds: "About this time the primacy of the spiritual world took possession of his holy form, and gave a new aspect to his world-adorning beauty.... What the chiefs of purity and deliverance (i.e. *Sūfī* seers) had searched for in vain, was revealed to him." The vision was perhaps preceded or followed by an epileptic fit, for Akbar was subject to that malady.

According to Dr Vincent Smith:

> Akbar was by nature a mystic who sought earnestly, like his Sūfī friends, to attain the ineffable bliss of direct contact with the Divine Reality, and now and again believed, or fancied, that he had succeeded. His temperament was profoundly melancholic, and there seems to be some reason to suspect that at times he was not far from the danger of falling into a state of religious mania. His ambition and intense interest in all the affairs of this world saved him from that fate, and brought him back from dreams to the actualities of human life. He was not an ordinary man, and his complex nature, like that of St Paul, Muhammad, Dante, and other great men with a tendency to mysticism, presents perplexing problems.[1]

On his way from Bhera to Fathpur Sīkrī Akbar sent a mission to his half-brother, Muhammad Hakīm, in Kābul urging him to make full submission to him, and another to 'Alī Shāh of Kashmīr demanding his allegiance, but neither was successful. Muhammad Hakīm continued to regard himself as a sovereign prince, and 'Alī Shāh, whose predecessors on the throne of Kashmīr had never owned the sovereignty of Delhi, saw no reason for acceding to an insolent demand.

After a rapid journey to the shrine at Ajmer, which proved that his physical endurance, despite his spiritual experiences, had in no way abated since the expedition of 1573, Akbar reached Fathpur Sīkrī on 12 September, and signalised his arrival at his capital by an act of profusion which may perhaps be connected with the vision at Bhera. He filled a dry cistern with coined money, to the value of four and a quarter million rupees, which was distributed in charity and in gifts to his courtiers and to learned men. Abu-'l-Fazl was not forgotten.

Another result of the Bhera vision was the revival of the discussions in the "Hall of Worship", and it was now that the Muslim dogmatists disgraced themselves. The orthodox party consisted of two factions, one headed by Makhdūm-ul-Mulk and the other by Shaikh 'Abdun-Nabī, whose differences were mainly personal, though Muslim theology presents difficulties sufficient to arouse strife even between the orthodox. Their recriminations either convinced Akbar that he could find no peace in Islām or furnished him with a pretext for abjuring a faith which claimed the obedience of one who was resolved to be supreme in spiritual as in temporal matters, and it was now that he first openly admitted to the discussions Christians, Hindus, Jains,

[1] *Akbar*, 160.

Zoroastrians and Sabaeans. 'Abdun-Nabī was dismissed, owing to his unseemly violence in dispute, from the office of *Sadr-us-Sudūr*, and his place was filled by Sultān Khvāja, who, although he had led the pilgrims of 1576 to Mecca, was a latitudinarian in religion and a self-seeker in politics and ultimately became a convert to the "Divine Faith".

Akbar suffered neither the death of Khān Jahān in Bengal nor the disturbances which followed it to interrupt his religious meditations and discussions. Muzaffar Khān Turbatī was appointed in 1579 to the government of the province, and peace was restored.

The Zoroastrian theologian Māhyārjī Rānā, who had been invited to court in 1578, had taken a prominent part in the conferences in the "Hall of Worship", and his influence was observed in Akbar's acts of reverence to the sun, and in rites ordained for the evening hour, when the lamps were lit, which led many to believe that the emperor had become a convert to the ancient religion of Persia; but no system could hold him, and he was really engaged in the compilation of a bewildering code of rites culled from all religions. In the same year a Portuguese mission arrived from Bengal, led by Antonio Cabral, a priest who aroused Akbar's curiosity, but was too diffident of his own learning and abilities to assume the post of a spiritual guide, and recommended the emperor to seek the advice of Jesuit missionaries of the College of St Paul at Goa. His advice was followed and Akbar sent an envoy to Goa, to beg for the services of "two Fathers well versed in letters" who should bring to his court the Gospels and other books on their faith. The Viceroy, Dom Luis de Athaide, was averse from complying with the request, fearing lest Akbar, despite his fair words, should detain the priests as hostages, but the zeal of the Jesuits overcame his scruples, and on 17 November Father Antonio Monserrate, Father Rodolfo Acquaviva and Father Francisco Enriques, a Persian convert from Islām, left Goa by sea.

Akbar was now, at the instigation and with the assistance of Shaikh Mubārak and his sons, Faizī and Abu-'l-Fazl, preparing to assume spiritual as well as temporal authority over his subjects. As a first step he decided personally to recite the *khutba*, following the example of Muhammad and his successors, the Caliphs. Faizī composed for him a *khutba* in verse, followed by selected texts and the opening chapter of the Korān; and on 26 June, 1579, the anniversary of Muhammad's birth, he ascended the pulpit of the principal mosque of Fathpur Sīkrī and recited Faizī's effusion and the rest of the *khutba*:

> In the name of Him who gave to us the empire,
> Who endowed us with a wise heart and a strong arm,
> Who guided us in the path of equity and justice,
> Putting away from our heart aught but equity—
> His attributes transcend man's understanding,
> Exalted be His majesty! God is most great!

The orthodox Badāūnī says that Akbar stammered and trembled, and had to be helped out by others in the recitation of the verses, and that he then descended from the pulpit and left the regular reciter of the *khutba* to complete the office; but other authors say that he acquitted himself of his task and then, descending from the pulpit, led the prayers. The innovation was generally unpopular. Many suspected that Akbar claimed to be prophet as well as king, and some even scented in the closing words (*Allahu Akbar*[1]) of Faizī's verses a pretension to divinity.

The notion of infallible human guidance is not entirely foreign to Islām. Each of the four orthodox schools of law of the Sunnīs virtually attributes infallibility to its founder, and the Shiah sect bestows the title "infallible" on its *Imāms*, 'Ālī, the cousin and son-in-law of the prophet, and his eleven successors. Since the disappearance of the twelfth *Imām* the *mujtahid*, who holds, in Shiah communities, the highest rank among divines and jurists is regarded as infallible in questions of faith and morals. But a text of the Korān and a traditional saying of Muhammad place the authority of the lawful and just ruler above that of divines and jurists, and the leading ecclesiastics of the court were so discredited by their dissensions, and by their unseemly wrangles in debates arranged by Shaikh Mubārak and his two sons in the "Hall of Worship", that their claim to religious leadership could be challenged without difficulty, and Shaikh Mubārak avenged himself on his former persecutors by preparing the famous Infallibility Decree. This was drawn up in the form of a petition beseeching the sovereign to assume the authority imposed upon him by the Korān and the Traditions, and was couched in the following terms:

Whereas Hindūstān is now become the centre of security and peace, and the land of justice and benevolence, so that numbers of the higher and lower orders of the people, and especially learned men possessed of divine knowledge, and subtle jurists who are guides to salvation and travellers in the path of the diffusion of learning have immigrated to this land from Arabia and Persia, and have domiciled themselves here; now we, the principal *'Ulamā*, who are not only well versed in the several departments of the law and the principles of jurisprudence, and well acquainted with the edicts based on reason and testimony, but are also known for our piety and honest intentions, have duly considered the deep meaning, first, of the verse of the Korān, "Obey God, and obey the Prophet, and those who are invested with authority among you"; and, secondly, of the genuine Tradition, "Surely the man who is dearest to God on the Day of Judgement is the just leader; whosoever obeys the *Amīr* obeys Me, and whosoever rebels against him rebels against Me"; and, thirdly, of several other proofs based on reason and testimony; and we have agreed that the rank of Just King is higher in the eyes of God than that of *Mujtahid*.

Further we declare that the King of Islām, the Asylum of Mankind, the Commander of the Faithful, Shadow of God in the world, Abu-'l-Fath Jalāl-ud-dīn Muhammad Akbar, *Pādishāh-i-Ghāzī* (whose kingdom God perpetuate!) is a most just, and wise King, with a knowledge of God.

[1] This phrase can be read as "God is great" or as "Akbar is God".

Should, therefore, in future, religious questions arise regarding which the opinions of the *mujtahids* are at variance, and His Majesty, in his penetrating understanding and clear wisdom, be inclined to adopt, for the benefit of the nation and in the interests of good order, any of the conflicting opinions which exist on that point, and should he issue a decree to that effect, we do hereby agree that such a decree shall be binding on all his people and all his subjects.

Should His Majesty see fit to issue a new order in conformity with some text of the Korān, and calculated to benefit the nation, all shall be bound by it, and opposition to it will involve damnation in the next world, and loss of religious privileges and property in this.

This document has been written with honest intentions and for the glory of God and the propagation of Islām, and has been signed by us, the principal *'Ulamā* of the Faith, and leading Theologians, in the month of Rajab, A.H. 987 (August–September, 1579).

This document, which, when approved by Akbar, became an imperial decree, was signed by Makhdūm-ul-Mulk, Shaikh 'Abd-un-Nabī, Jalāl-ud-dīn the chief *Qāzī*, Sultān Khvāja the *Sadr*, the learned Ghāzī Khān of Badakhshān, and Shaikh Mubārak. Badāūnī says that all signed it unwillingly, without specifying the nature of the pressure brought to bear on them, except Shaikh Mubārak, who added after his signature, "This is an affair which I desired with all my heart and soul, and for the accomplishment of which I have been waiting for years".

The decree limited Akbar to the adoption of one of the conflicting opinions delivered by the jurists of Islām, or, in case there was no dispute, to the authority of a verse of the Korān, and one of its chief objects was, ostensibly, the propagation of Islām; but these conditions were ignored by Akbar. He was now pope as well as king, and so far was he from propagating Islām that he ridiculed and persecuted it, and shortly afterwards attempted to substitute for it a religion of his own invention; but he did not venture at once to violate the conditions of the decree, and immediately after its issue set out on his last annual pilgrimage to Ajmer, earning thereby the contempt of the orthodox. "The wonder of wonders was that he should have all this faith in the saint of Ajmer while he denied the foundation of everything, the prophet from each fold of whose skirt many millions of perfected saints like him of Ajmer had sprung."

Shaikh Mubārak was not slow to avenge himself on his persecutors, and at Ajmer Makhdūm-ul-Mulk and Shaikh 'Abdun-Nabī discovered that their complaisance in signing the decree was to avail them nothing, and that they were to be banished to Mecca. Notwithstanding their orthodoxy, neither had any taste for the pilgrimage, still less for the society of the other.

In order to allay the resentment aroused by his innovations Akbar was obliged to descend to more hypocrisy. On his return march from Ajmer he ostentatiously recited every day the ritual prayers, and after his arrival at Fathpur Sīkrī he received with an extravagant display of devotion a heavy stone brought from Mecca, which was said to bear the print of Muhammad's foot. He did not believe the relic to be genuine, and would have felt no reverence for it if he had, but he and his courtiers went out for six or seven miles to meet the stone, and bore it, in turn, to Fathpur Sīkrī. This act of hypocrisy, too gross to deceive even the simplest, was performed, according to Abu-'l-Fazl, lest the Sayyid who brought the stone should be put to shame, and in order to silence those who regarded Akbar's inquiries and discussions with suspicion. Of the latter object, at least, it failed.

An opportunity of interference in the domestic affairs of Kashmīr now presented itself. Yūsuf, who had succeeded his father, 'Alī Shāh, on the throne of that kingdom, had been expelled by a kinsman, Lohar Chakk, who had usurped his throne, arrived at court in January, 1580, and sought Akbar's aid.[1] A few months later Akbar despatched him into the Punjab and ordered his officers in that province to restore him, but the nobles of Kashmīr, dreading the invasion of their country by an imperial army, promised Yūsuf their support if he would return alone. He defeated and captured his cousin, and on 8 November, 1580, regained his throne without Akbar's assistance. Some years were to elapse before Akbar found another pretext for intervention in Kashmīr.

On 18 February, 1580, the first Jesuit mission, under Father Monserrate, reached Fathpur Sīkrī and was most cordially received. The priests in their cassocks and hats, unarmed and clean shaven, were objects of great curiosity to the people as they passed through the town. They were graciously received and Akbar was favourably impressed by their refusal of a gift of 800 gold pieces, which he offered them. His reverence for the gospels and the images and pictures which they had brought with them, his eager inquiries, and his genuflexions in the chapel which he permitted them to furnish and open encouraged them to hope that they might succeed in inducing him to become the Constantine of the East, but they were grievously mistaken, and soon discovered their error.

Akbar's attitude towards Christianity is an interesting study. He was most curious in his inquiry into its doctrines, and probably held a higher opinion of the faith than of any other single religion which he studied. He invited no fewer than three Jesuit missions to his court, he permitted the priests of each mission to propagate their faith, and even sent his sons to them to receive instruction in Christian doctrine, and he encouraged each mission to hope for his conversion, but disappointed each.

The priests, despite the temptation to which the hope of attaining so great an object exposed them, were uncompromising in their statement of what the Church required of a convert, and two, at least,

[1] Coins of the Kashmir type, but bearing the name of Akbar, were struck in A.H. 987 = March, 1579, to February, 1580. [Ed.]

of their demands Akbar could never be persuaded to admit. The first was submission and implicit obedience, and the second was the dismissal of all his wives save one. The priests of each mission, though at first encouraged by his bitter hostility to Islām, soon perceived that his ambition was to become the prophet of a creed of his own compilation, and that submission and obedience were not to be expected of him. His refusal to dismiss his wives they attributed to his incontinence, but here, perhaps, they judged him harshly. He was a man of strong passions, but he might possibly have been persuaded to subdue these. The difficulty in complying with the demand of the priests was rather political than personal. It was with a political end in view that Akbar had married Rājput princesses, and those Rājput chiefs who had been persuaded to bestow daughters or sisters on him in marriage, though they had become closely allied to the throne, which was Akbar's object, had violated their own social code and incurred the condemnation of their more exclusive brethren. The dismissal of their daughters and sisters from the palace as discarded concubines would have raised the whole of Rājāsthān against Akbar, his bitterest enemies would have been those whom he had doubly disgraced, and his highest political object, the fusion of the two great rival faiths and the establishment of a united empire, would have been irretrievably lost. Some of the doctrines of the Christian faith, above all the Incarnation, presented difficulties to Akbar, but the priests were probably unable to appreciate the gravity of his chief difficulty, the political effects of his acceptance of Christianity, for those of each mission accused him of having wilfully deceived them.

In 1580 his religious vagaries began to bear their fruit. He had not yet promulgated his new faith, but he had given grave offence to all Muslims, who were the dominant community in the empire. His discourse was ever of universal toleration, but in practice he excepted the faith in which he had been bred. Its leaders had been expelled from court and few opportunities were lost of holding its doctrines and observances up to scorn and ridicule. Muslims believed their faith to be in danger, and many conceived that the only means of saving it lay in deposing its enemy and placing on his throne an orthodox sovereign. Their choice fell on Akbar's half-brother, Muhammad Hakīm, the ruler of Kābul and nominally, though not in fact, a vassal of the empire. He was a drunkard, a poltroon, and in no way comparable with Akbar, but he was believed to be an orthodox Muslim and that sufficed. It was in Bihār and Bengal that the Muslim officers first rose in rebellion. In Bihār orders had been issued for the resumption of all grants; both there and in Bengal the branding regulation had been enforced, and the foreign, or field service allowance of the troops, which had been fixed for Bengal at 100 and in Bihār at 50 per cent. on their ordinary pay, was reduced to 50 and 20 per cent. The unpopularity of these measures was enhanced by the severity with which they were enforced and it needed but little to rouse the malcontents. The fire of rebellion was kindled by Mullā Muhammad of Yazd, the *qāẓī* of Jaunpur, who, as a jurist, promulgated an authoritative decree that rebellion against a sovereign who had apostatised from Islām was a religious duty.

It was in Bihār that the fire of rebellion first broke into flame. The caravan conveying to the capital Bengal's annual contribution to the imperial treasury was there attacked by rebels and plundered. The skilful dispositions of the officer commanding the escort saved all but a few elephants, but he was himself captured and put to death.

Todar Mal was summoned from Bengal to suppress this rebellion and on his departure a rebellion broke out there. It was led by members of the Qāqshāl tribe of Turks and rapidly spread over the whole province. The Qāqshāls proclaimed Muhammad Hakīm as their sovereign, and Muzaffar Khān attempted to conciliate them by promising that the unpopular reforms would not be enforced. He might have succeeded in restoring peace had they not discovered his design of putting them to death at a conference to which he had invited them. They slew his emissaries and besieged him in Tāndā, and when the rebels in Bihār defeated a force which he had sent to defend Teliyāgarhī they attacked Tāndā, captured him and put him to death.

The rebel forces of both provinces then concentrated near Teliyāgarhī and caused the *khutba* to be recited in the name of Muhammad Hakīm, but retired when Todar Mal advanced against them. He followed them but his own troops were so disaffected that he was obliged to take refuge in Monghyr, where the rebels besieged him. Akbar sent Khān A'zam, who had been pardoned, with an army into Bengal, and he compelled the rebels to raise the siege. Some retired into lower Bengal but a force under Ma'sūm Khān Kābulī returned to Bihār, occupied the town of Bihār, and besieged Patna. Ma'sūm Khān Farankhudī attacked them and compelled them to retire to Gayā, and at the end of September they were dispersed by Todar Mal. Other minor operations cleared Bihār of rebels for the time, but disaffection was everywhere rife, and Ma'sūm Khān Farankhudī, repenting of his activity in Akbar's cause, retired to Jaunpur and there began to assemble a force with which to support that of Muhammad Hakīm. He was joined by Niyābat Khān, an officer who had rebelled in the Allahābād district but had been defeated and driven into Oudh.

Akbar's position, even in his capital, was so precarious that he had been unable to take the field in person against the rebels. He had detected a conspiracy among his courtiers, headed by Shāh Mansūr, the revenue minister, to invite Muhammad Hakīm to India and raise him to the throne. Shāh Mansūr was suspended from office, and the other conspirators were dispersed and prevented from combining, but Akbar refrained, perhaps prudently, from proceeding to extremities against them. He attempted to conciliate Ma'sūm Khān Farankhudī by conferring on him the assignment of Ajodhyā, and his acceptance of it and his promptitude in withdrawing from Jaunpur deceived Akbar into the belief that he had returned to his allegiance, but at Ajodhyā he was joined by a number of rebels from Bihār and Bengal and openly declared for Muhammad Hakīm. A force under Shāhbāz Khān was sent against him and defeated him, thus relieving Akbar of immediate fear of an attack from the east. Rebels were still in arms in Bengal, but peace had been restored in Bihār; and early in February, 1581, Akbar was able to leave Fathpur Sīkrī in order to meet his brother, who, encouraged by the invitations which he had received, and by exaggerated reports of the extent of the discontent with Akbar's rule, had left Kābul with the intention of wresting the crown from his brother. Shāh Mansūr, who had been pardoned and restored to office, accompanied Akbar's army, but it was discovered that he was again in correspondence with Muhammad Hakīm. Some of his correspondence was produced, and he was condemned to death, and on 25 February was hanged near Thānesar. He was intensely unpopular, owing to his inquisitorial methods, and some historians have suggested that the evidence against him was fabricated by his enemies, but there appears to be no doubt of his guilt, for Akbar fully appreciated his past services and deeply regretted the necessity for his execution.

Muhammad Hakīm had meanwhile crossed the Indus and advanced as far as Lahore, before which city he encamped. He had been persuaded that all Muslims in India were eager to rise in defence of Islām, and was bitterly disappointed to find that not even the *mullās* of Lahore would join him, while the nobles were prepared to defend the city against him and even to meet him in the field. His dismay was increased by confirmation of the report that Akbar was marching against him, for he had believed that he would not dare to leave his capital, and by the news that his chief partisan at court had been detected and executed, and he retreated hurriedly towards Kābul, losing many of his men in the passage of the Chenāb and the Jhelum. His departure enabled the nobles of the Punjab to meet Akbar at Māchīwārā on 8 March.

After a visit to Nagarkot (Kāngra) Akbar continued his march, and, on reaching the Indus, laid the foundation stone of the fortress of Attock and wrote to his brother commanding him to receive him at Kābul as his sovereign. To this order Muhammad Hakīm returned no reply, and on 27 June a force nominally under the command of the youthful Sultān Murād, Akbar's second son, but in fact under that of Mān Singh, was sent towards Kābul with orders to move slowly, in order to give Muhammad Hakīm an opportunity of making his submission. Akbar followed this force on 12 July, and received later two unsatisfactory replies from his brother. His nobles, either from sloth or from disaffection, urged him to pardon his brother and retire, but the advance was continued. Muhammad Hakīm, still encouraged by his counsellors to believe that Akbar's Muslim officers were ready to turn against their master and that the Hindus would be an easy prey, wrote privately to many of the Muslims urging them to join him, but one of his messengers was put to death, and all who received letters immediately disclosed them to Akbar, and Muhammad Hakīm fled from Kābul to Ghūrband. The forces of Akbar and his son Murād met on the march, and on 10 August both reached Kābul and lodged in the citadel. Muhammad Hakīm sent messages expressing his contrition and tendering his submission. He was pardoned, but Akbar humiliated him by appointing his sister, Bakht-un-Nisā Begam, to the government of the province of Kābul. Muhammad Hakīm, after Akbar's departure, returned and resumed the functions of his former office, but all official orders were issued in his sister's name.

Akbar reached Fathpur Sīkrī, on his return from Kābul, on 1 December, 1581. At the intercession of his mother and his foster-brother, Khān A'zam, he granted a free pardon to Ma'sūm Khān Farankhudī, even though he had once again risen in rebellion during his absence in Kābul, but the pardon was nothing more than a formal expression of respect for the mediators, for a few months after it was granted Ma'sūm Khān was assassinated while returning from court at midnight.

In order to celebrate in a fitting manner his victory over his brother Akbar summoned to court for the *Naurūz* feast all provincial governors, and the absence of Khān A'zam and Shāham Khān from Bengal and Bihār provoked a recrudescence of rebellion in those provinces, placing the loyal officers in a position of some peril.

The position of the Jesuit mission was now most embarrassing. Akbar's intermittent interest in the Christian faith had no effect on his hostility to the Portuguese. A small town near Damān had been ceded to them in 1575 by Gulbadan Begam, in order to ensure their protection on her voyage to Mecca, but on her return Akbar ordered his officers in Gujarāt to recover the town, and they attacked the Portuguese in Damān, but were repulsed with considerable loss. Shortly afterwards a party of young men who had landed for purposes of sport from the Portuguese ships near Surat was attacked, and nine of them were captured and put to death on refusing to apostatise to Islām. Their heads were sent to Akbar, as the priests learned, and when the governor of Surat came to court for the *Naurūz* he told them the whole story. Father Monserrate remonstrated with Akbar, who falsely denied that he had seen the heads and hypocritically expressed his regret at the occurrences at Damān and Sūrat. He issued public orders to the governor of Broach to desist from attacking the Portuguese, but sent secret instructions for the capture of Diu. A quantity of arms was smuggled into the fortress in bales of cotton, and the imperial officers requested the governor, Pedro de Menezes, to allow their troops passage through Portuguese territory. He was aware of their design, but acceded to their request, and even allowed them to enter the fortress, where the sight of the Portuguese troops standing to arms and ready to resist any act of aggression so alarmed them that they hastily left and withdrew their troops from Portuguese territory. Akbar was bitterly disappointed by the failure of the scheme and repeatedly asked the priests who were in command at Diu, but they, at the time, suspected nothing. The authorities at Goa so resented Akbar's perfidy that the Provincial of the Society of Jesus recalled the mission from his court. Akbar divined the reason for its recall, and swore to Father Monserrate that he had not been implicated in the hostile acts on the western coast. The Provincial's letter had left the priests some discretion, and it was decided that Rodolfo Acquaviva should remain at court, while the other two returned to Goa with Sayyid Muzaffar, Akbar's envoy, who bore a letter to Philip II of Spain and Portugal. This letter, written by Abu-'l-Fazl, bears the date corresponding to 14 April, 1582, and the mission must have left the court about that time.

Life at the holy city of Mecca had so palled upon Makhdūm-ul-Mulk and Shaikh 'Abdun-Nabī that they had prevailed upon Gulbadan Begam to allow them to return to India in her train, and they were now lurking in Gujarāt, hoping for eventual forgiveness, but their enemies at court had not forgotten them, and so excited Akbar's wrath at their returning without leave that officers were sent to Gujarāt to arrest them. Makhdūm-ul-Mulk, as Abu-'l-Fazl writes with malicious exultation, died of fright and left much wealth which was confiscated. "The other malevolent fellow" could not excuse his disobedience, and Akbar, after striking him in the face, sent him to prison, "where counsel is received", and he was shortly afterwards strangled.

It was now, in the rainy season of 1582, that Akbar took advantage of the presence of the provincial governors at court to promulgate his new religion, the *Dīn-i-Ilāhī* or "Divine Faith". This step was perhaps accelerated by a wonderful escape which he and his courtiers had had. They had been playing draughts, chess and cards beside the great lake to the north of Fathpur Sīkrī when the dam burst, and it seemed that all must be overwhelmed by the torrent which it released, but all escaped except one menial servant who was drowned. Abu-'l-Fazl represents the escape of the courtiers as a miracle due to Akbar's presence, but Akbar himself regarded the accident as a sign of divine displeasure at the playing of frivolous games and ordered their discontinuance.

He had examined the doctrine and the practices of many religions, Islām, Hinduism, Jainism, Zoroastrianism, Buddhism and Christianity, and had meditated on them but was satisfied with none. The formalism and the intolerance of the orthodox professors of the faith in which he had been bred had disgusted him. Many of the doctrines of Hinduism, Jainism and Zoroastrianism appealed to him but he could not join the bodies professing them, as members of those religious and social systems are born, not made. He would have been welcomed into the Christian Church, but as a lay member, and Christianity was as uncompromising as Islām, and made demands to which he was neither inclined nor able, without arousing the implacable hostility of the two great religious bodies in his empire, to submit. He was much attracted by the mysticism of the *Sūfīs*, but theirs was too vague a creed, and too bare of ritual, to which he inclined, to command his allegiance. Less fortunate in his counsellors than his predecessor, 'Alā-ud-dīn Khaljī, who, when he conceived the idea of proclaiming himself the prophet of a new faith, had been dissuaded by a faithful and fearless servant from committing an act of such folly and presumption, Akbar had suffered himself for some years to be flattered by Shaikh Mubārak into the belief that he was something more than king, and that it was his duty to assume his place as the spiritual as well as the temporal sovereign of his peoples. With the aid of this adviser he had concocted an eclectic creed likely, as his vanity persuaded him, to command an assent from all men which neither Christianity nor Islām had been able to ensure.

He summoned a general council, composed of the high officials present at the capital but not including Father Rodolfo Acquaviva, and, after discoursing on the evils of religious discord and strife, declared that all religious bodies ought to be united, "in such fashion that they should be both 'one' and 'all', with the great advantage of not losing what is good in any religion, while gaining whatever is better in another. In that way honour would be rendered to God, peace would be given to the peoples, and security to the empire". He called upon all to express their opinion, and the officials, doubtless warned of what was expected of them, assented to his proposals, agreeing that "he who was nearer to heaven, both by reason of his office and by reason of his lofty intellect, should prescribe for the whole empire gods, ceremonies, sacrifices, mysteries, rules, solemnities, and whatever else was required to constitute one perfect and universal religion". There was but one dissentient voice, that of Bhagwān Dās, who, admitting that neither Hinduism nor Islām was perfect, desired to know what the new religion was, that he might decide whether to accept it or not. Akbar was unwilling or unable to formulate his faith, and ceased to press the raja. It was not, indeed, an easy matter to define the creed, for, as Dr Vincent Smith says:

> The organization of the adherents of the Dīn-i-Ilāhī was that of an Order rather than of a church. The creed, so far as there was one, inculcated monotheism with a tinge of pantheism, the practical deification of the emperor as the vicegerent of God, filled with a special grace; and the adoration of the sun, with subsidiary veneration of fire and artificial lights....The whole gist of the regulations was to further the adoption of Hindu, Jain, and Pārsī practices, while discouraging or positively prohibiting essential Muslim rites. The policy of insult to and persecution of Islām, which was carried to greater extremes subsequently, was actively pursued, even in the period from 1582 to 1585.

Islām was the one faith excluded from the benefits of *sulh-i-kull*, or "universal toleration", on which Akbar continually descanted. The names "Muhammad" and "Ahmad" were disused, and one foolish ordinance required that all words containing letters peculiar to Arabic, the sacred language of Islām, should be misspelt, the nearest equivalents of such letters being substituted. For the ordinary Muslim salutation, "Peace be on you", and the reply "And on you be peace", the disciples of the new faith were required to substitute *Allahu Akbar* ("God is most great") and *jalla jalāluhu* ("May His glory be extolled"), and cavillers were not slow to note that each formula embodied one of Akbar's names. It is but just to add that the new faith condemned the Hindu practices of *satī*, the burning of widows, and child marriage.

Abu-'l-Fath and some later writers, loth to deprive Islām of the adherence of so great a man as Akbar, are at pains to prove that he never ceased to be a Muslim, and that the Divine Faith was but Islām reformed; but the Portuguese priests reported more than once that he was not a Muslim, and the question is decided by one of his "Happy Sayings", recorded by Abu-'l-Fazl himself. "Formerly I persecuted men into conformity with my faith, and deemed it Islām. As I grew in knowledge I was overwhelmed with shame. Not being a Muslim myself it was unmeet to force others to become such." The *shast*, as the vow which his disciples were required to take was called, comprised a repudiation of Islām, and the acceptance of the four grades of entire devotion, namely sacrifice of Property, Life, Honour *and Religion*.

By means of bribery and pressure eighteen more or less prominent converts, including one Hindu, Rājā Bīrbal, were secured for the Divine Faith. Mān Singh, at a later period, bluntly replied to Akbar's overtures, "If discipleship means willingness to sacrifice one's life, I have already carried my life in my hand: what need is there of further proof? But if it has another meaning, and refers to faith, I am a Hindu. If you order me to do so I will become a Muslim, but I know not of the existence of any other religion than these two."

Khān A'zam, Akbar's foster-brother, long resisted his importunities, and in 1593 fled to Mecca. He returned from his pilgrimage so disgusted with the rapacity of the guardians and attendants of the sacred shrine of Islām that he accepted, at length, the Divine Faith, but its disciples seem never to have numbered more than a few thousands of all classes. It languished after the murder of Abu-'l-Fazl, its high priest, in 1602, and on Akbar's death in 1605 it ceased to exist.

Another foolish experiment now completed was also a failure. Four years before, Akbar had shut up a number of wretched infants, appointing dumb nurses to attend them, and taking other precautions against their ever hearing the sound of the human voice. His object was to discover "the divine language", for, as none of the children could have learned to speak by human agency, if any one of them spoke, the language which he spoke would be, Akbar believed, the divine language. Of course the unfortunate children emerged dumb from their confinement.

The recrudescence of rebellion in Bengal and Bihār has already been mentioned. No serious steps had been taken against the Bengal rebels since their flight from Monghyr, and during the absence of Khān A'zam they invaded Bihār. On his return from court he expelled them from Bihār, captured Teliyāgarhī at the end of March, 1583, and followed them to the bank of the Kālī Gang. Desultory operations followed, the rebels sometimes fighting each other, but operations were interrupted by the recall of Khān A'zam, who had grown weary of campaigning in Bengal and had begged to be relieved. His successor, Shāhbāz Khān, attacked and defeated Ma'sūm on 26 November, 1583, restored order in that part of Bengal which he had occupied and carried off all the movable property of the rebels. After some further fighting the officers of the army quarrelled with Shāhbāz Khān, compelled him to retire and refused to face the rebels in the field. Shāhbāz reported his difficulties to Akbar, and both he and his officers were severely reprimanded, he for his arrogance and overbearing conduct and they for their insubordination. Reinforcements were sent, but it was not until early in 1585 that any operations were undertaken, and even then the success attending them was slight. Relations between Shāhbāz and his officers again became so strained that he was at length obliged to allow them to pursue Ma'sūm independently of his control, but five years elapsed before Bengal was completely reduced to obedience.

Bengal had not been the only disturbed province of the empire. In 1583 I'timād Khān, a noble of the former kingdom of Gujarāt, who had raised Muzaffar III to the throne, was appointed to the government of that province. When employed there in 1572 his loyalty had been doubted, but he was now above suspicion in that respect, and Akbar believed that his local knowledge would be useful in Gujarāt and that those who accompanied him would supply his other defects, which were indecision and lack of firmness. Unfortunately for him an attempt by his predecessor to enforce the branding regulation had so enraged the local officers that many of them had repaired to Muzaffar III, who had been living in retirement at Junāgarh since his deposition. I'timād Khān thus found himself confronted with a serious rebellion, for the suppression of which he was obliged to seek the unwilling aid of his predecessor, Shihāb-ud-dīn Ahmad, and while they were arranging the terms on which they would co-operate Muzaffar III occupied Ahmadābād. Qutb-ud-dīn Muhammad Khān, of the "foster-father cohort", advanced from Broach to Barodā but was compelled to surrender and was murdered by the rebels, and his wealth, in addition to that which they had already acquired, enabled Muzaffar to raise an army of nearly 30,000 horse.

Mīrzā Khān, son of Bairam Khān, was now sent to Gujarāt. In January, 1584, he defeated Muzaffar at Sarkhej, occupied Ahmadābād and drove Muzaffar into the hills between Nāndod and Nandurbār, and thence into Kāthīāwār. He was rewarded for his services with his father's title of Khān Khānān; but Muzaffar continued to cause trouble in Gujarāt until 1593, when Khān A'zam, then governor of Gujarāt, having captured Junāgarh, where he had taken refuge, pursued him into Cutch and induced the Rāo to point out his hiding place, where he was taken, and on the day after his capture he committed suicide.

Akbar had been occupying himself in 1583, at Fathpur Sīkrī, with administrative reforms. Departments were created for the supervision and control of (1) criminal justice and the registration of marriages and births, (2) camping grounds and halting places, (3) religious affairs, including the suppression of "bigotry", (4) grants, allowances and alms, (5) the appointment and dismissal of officials employed on the crown lands, and the extension of cultivation, (6) the administration of the army, and its allowances, (7) the regulation of the prices of supplies and merchandise, (8) arms, and roads, (9) the decision of questions of inheritance, (10) the buying and selling of jewels and minerals, (11) public buildings, and (12) civil justice. Most of these affairs needed regulating; others might have been left to regulate themselves, but this was a distinction which Akbar seldom drew. His suppression of bigotry was not entirely confined to orthodox Islām, for he saved from *satī* the widow of Jai Mal, a cousin of Bhagwān Dās, and imprisoned her son who had tried to compel her to burn herself.

On the other hand Hindu ideals were encouraged by the translation into Persian of the great Hindu epic, the Mahābhārata. The orthodox Badāūnī was one of those employed on the translation, which was styled the *Razmnāma*, or "Book of the War", and he was deeply disgusted with his task.

In the same year Akbar conceived a vast and characteristically extravagant design of conquest which came to nought. His intention was first to subdue the independent kingdoms of the Deccan, then to wrest the province of Kābul from his brother, Muhammad Hakīm, to extend his authority over Badakhshān, still vexed by the disputes between Sulaimān and Shāh Rukh, and then to recover from 'Abdullah II the Shaibānid, Transoxiana, the early home of his race. With a view to prosecuting the first part of his scheme he proposed to build at Allahābād, at the confluence of the Ganges and the Jumna, a site hallowed by Hindu legend, a great fortified city, which should serve the double purpose of securing the road to Bengal, hitherto so disturbed, and of forming an advanced post for the invasion of the Deccan by the little known eastern route through Gondwāna. He reached Allahābād in November, 1583, designated the site of his city and of four forts, only one of which was completed, and yet remains, and in February, 1584, on learning of his officers' temporary successes against the rebels in Bengal, returned to Fathpur Sīkrī.

Here, on the *Naurūz* festival of 1584, he introduced his "Divine Era". Everything connected with him was divine. This was a solar era, in which the year was divided into the old Persian solar months, and it was reckoned from the first *Naurūz* festival after his accession, 11 March, 1556.[1] A brief and inconclusive campaign against the Rānā, Partāb Singh, was then undertaken, and in the following year his great scheme of northern conquest was frustrated by 'Abdullah II, to whom Sulaimān had foolishly appealed for aid. 'Abdullah expelled both Sulaimān and his grandson from Badakhshān and took possession of the country. Shāh Rukh took refuge at Akbar's court, while Sulaimān went to Muhammad Hakīm at Kābul; but shortly after the receipt of the news of the loss of Badakhshān Akbar learned that his brother had died of a malady caused by strong drink. Although his death was no cause of regret to Akbar, at the moment it exposed the Kābul province to the risk of invasion by 'Abdullah; and Bhagwān Dās, now governor of the Punjab, and Mān Singh were commanded to march on Kābul and occupy the city.

The state of affairs in the country between Kābul and the Indus was such as to demand the presence of Akbar himself. The neighbourhood of the Khyber Pass was occupied by the *Raushanāīs*, a community of fanatical heretics who had imbibed strange doctrines from a native of Hindūstān, who had settled among the tribes, and regarded brigandage as a religious duty. The road between the Indus and the pass was infested by the Yūsufzāīs of Swāt and Bājaur, and there was one other object which drew Akbar to the Indus, the resolve to annex the kingdom of Kashmīr.

Akbar left Fathpur Sīkrī on 22 August, 1585, but not before he had

[1] See Hodivala, *Historical Studies in Mughal Numismatics*, p. 11, for an explanation of the era. [Ed.]

received the first Englishmen who visited his court. These were Newbery, Fitch and Leedes, a jeweller, the first of whom bore a letter of recommendation from Elizabeth. We know nothing of the nature of their reception, but Akbar took Leedes into his service. From Kalānaur Akbar sent a mission to Yūsuf Shāh of Kashmīr, summoning him to his camp to do homage for his kingdom, and Ya'qūb, Yūsuf's son, who was in the imperial camp on a conciliatory mission, fled on learning of the demand. Akbar's envoys rejoined him when he reached Hasan Abdāl and reported that though Yūsuf had received them well he had refused to do homage in person. Akbar, therefore, resolved to enforce obedience, and on the last day of 1585 an army, nominally under the command of Shāh Rukh Mīrzā but in fact under that of Bhagwān Dās, marched from Attock into Kashmīr. At the same time an expedition under Zain Khān was sent into Swāt and Bājaur to subjugate the Yūsufzāis. Zain Khān reported that his force was not strong enough to humble the enemy, and Akbar sent him reinforcements under the command of Rājā Bīrbal, the court wit, and Hakīm Abu-'l-Fath, a physician. The amateur soldiers had plans of their own for the campaign, and Zain Khān, fearing Bīrbal's personal influence with Akbar, dared not oppose his insane project of a military promenade through the difficult passes of Swāt. The army, demoralised by earlier misadventures, was attacked by the Yūsufzāis in the Mālandarai Pass, and Zain Khān, after fighting a most difficult rearguard action, was defeated and narrowly escaped with his life. The Yūsufzāis fell on the rest of the disorganised host, each man of which fought where he stood. Of the twelve officers personally known to Akbar who fell, the most important was Bīrbal, "who, from fear for his life, took the road of flight, and was slain, and entered the ranks of the dogs of hell, where he received a part of what was due to him for his base actions".[1] Eight thousand men—about half of the army—perished, and on 24 February, 1586, Zain Khān and Abu-'l-Fath led the remnant into Akbar's camp. Akbar, overwhelmed with grief for the loss of his intimate friend and early disciple, refused to see them and severely blamed Abu-'l-Fath for his insubordination to Zain Khān, but of the two amateurs Bīrbal had been the more to blame. The responsibility for the mishap was Akbar's, who had appointed a jester and a physician to a military command. Todar Mal was sent to retrieve the disaster, and established fortified posts throughout the Yūsufzāi country.

Meanwhile Bhagwān Dās had advanced into Kashmīr, and Yūsuf Shāh, fearing lest he should succeed, in spite of cold, rain, snow and scarcity of provisions, in reaching Srīnagar, offered to do homage to Akbar, and on 22 February, 1586, was received by Bhagwān Dās, who welcomed his submission, for the army, which should never have

[1] *Bad.* II, 350.

been sent into the mountains at that season of the year, was suffering severely. It was understood by all that Akbar required only personal submission and a promise of tribute, and that Yūsuf would then be permitted to return to his kingdom as the emperor's vassal. It was on this understanding that Yūsuf surrendered, and these were the terms granted to him by Bhagwān Dās. Akbar was displeased with the treaty but, in order to secure Yūsuf's submission, ratified it, and, having ratified it, detained Yūsuf as a state prisoner and prepared to send another army into Kashmīr to complete the subjugation of the country. Bhagwān Dās, whose honour had been besmirched by his master, could not be expected to command a second expedition, and was ordered to Kābul, but on his way thither attempted to commit suicide. Abu-'l-Fazl attributes the act to a fit of temporary insanity, but there is no doubt that he was in his right mind, and that his act, characteristic of his caste, was an attempt to wipe out the stain on his honour.

Nearly all the counsellors of the emperor deprecated a second invasion of Kashmīr, but Akbar persisted and in July Muhammad Qāsim Khān invaded the country at the head of a large army. On 15 October he entered Srīnagar, the *khutba* was recited in the name of Akbar, and Kashmīr was formally annexed; but Yūsuf's son, Ya'qūb Khān, evaded capture and remained in arms for nearly three years longer, until he surrendered to Akbar in August, 1589.

'Abdullah II had been suspicious of Akbar's movements, fearing lest, after settling the affairs of Kābul, he should attack Balkh, and he had sent an envoy to ascertain his intentions and to inquire the meaning of his religious vagaries which had perplexed him for some time. The envoy was not dismissed until September, 1586, by which time 'Abdullah's anxiety had been allayed by Akbar's withdrawal from the Indus. To 'Abdullah's implied censure he replied in a quatrain:

> Of God people have said that He had a Son;
> Of the prophet some have said that he was a sorcerer;
> Neither God nor the prophet has escaped the slander of men,
> Then how should I?

Mān Singh, having been appointed governor of Kābul, had reached that city and had sent Muhammad Hakīm's two young sons to Akbar. He had inflicted more than one defeat on the Raushanāīs on his way to Kābul, but they were neither crushed nor humbled, and towards the end of 1586 closed both of the roads between Kābul and the Indus and besieged Peshāwar. Akbar was now at Lahore, and Zain Khān was sent against the rebels, and with the help of Mān Singh compelled them to raise the siege, but they succeeded in forming a confederacy with the Afrīdīs, the Orakzāīs and the Yūsufzāīs, and kept the imperial troops in the field throughout the year 1587. It was not until the following year that the Afrīdīs and the Orakzāis submitted and undertook to keep the Khyber Pass open. Jalāl-ud-dīn, the youthful leader of the Raushanāīs, lost his influence over his followers and fled to Balkh, and Zain Khān completed the subjugation of the Yūsufzāis.

Before leaving Fathpur Sīkrī Akbar had sent an expedition into the Deccan. Some of the nobles of Murtazā Nizām Shāh of Ahmadnagar had made an attempt to overthrow his minister, Salābat Khān, but, having been defeated, had fled to Akbar's court and begged him to reinstate them in Berār as his vassals. Khān A'zam, governor of Mālwā, was ordered to invade and annex Berār, but the invasion of that province was delayed by quarrels between Khān A'zam and his officers, and it was not until 1586 that he led a futile raid into Berār. An attack on the fortress of Kherlā failed, and though some districts of the province were ravaged and its capital, Ellichpur, was plundered, the allied armies of Ahmadnagar and Khāndesh cut the raiders off from their base and compelled Khān A'zam to carry his plunder off into Gujarāt, harassing him on his way. After reaching Nandurbār he attempted to arrange with Mīrzā Khān, Khān Khānān, a concerted invasion of Berār, but the rainy season made military operations impossible, and he returned to Mālwā having gained nothing but plunder.

The invasion of Berār was not the only attempt made at this time to extend the imperial dominions. Sādiq Muhammad Khān, governor of Multān, made an attempt to subdue Mīrzā Jānī Beg, the ruler of Sind, and, though he was unsuccessful, Jānī Beg prudently sent to Akbar's court at Lahore an envoy with tribute and an offer of submission. His allegiance was accepted but his submission was merely formal, and it was not until 1590 that Sind was incorporated in the empire. Akbar desired to possess it on sentimental grounds, as the land of his birth, but also for use as a base of operations against Qandahār, now in the hands of Shāh 'Abbās of Persia. The Khān Khānān was therefore transferred to the government of Multān and was ordered to annex Sind. He invaded the state, and, after twice defeating Mīrzā Jānī Beg, exacted from him a promise to make his submission to Akbar in person. He appeared at court in 1593, and at once gained favour by abjuring Islām and accepting the Divine Faith. He was rewarded with the command of 3000 horse, and after a short time was sent back to Sind as governor of the province. This is a fair example of Akbar's method of gaining disciples.

The appointment of Mān Singh to Kābul had been a mistake. It may be that Akbar had appointed him to that province in order to punish the Afghāns, the champions, under Muhammad Hakīm, of orthodox Islām, and it is certain that his presence in Kābul with a large force of Rājputs was most offensive to the Muslim population; but Akbar was not obliged to admit his error, and recalled Mān Singh late in 1587 on the ground that he had been dilatory in dealing with the Raushanāīs, and appointed him to the government of Bihār. With him was sent the unfortunate Yūsuf of Kashmīr, who received the command of 500 horse and a grant in Bihār, in order, says Abu-'l-Fazl, that his fitness for restoration to Kashmīr as imperial governor might be tested. The command of a small body of horse and the administration of a small district are no tests of fitness for the government of a great province. Yūsuf never gained any promotion and there is no evidence that Akbar ever proposed to make amends for the wrong which he had done him.

In May, 1589, Akbar paid his first visit to Kashmīr, but before leaving Lahore availed himself of an opportunity of interfering again in the affairs of the Deccan. Before he left Fathpur Sīkrī Burhān-ud-dīn, the younger brother of Murtazā Nizām Shāh of Ahmadnagar, having rebelled against his brother, had fled from that kingdom and had taken refuge with Akbar, who had received him into his service. Murtazā Nizām Shāh had since been murdered by his son Husain, who succeeded him, but in April, 1589, had been murdered by his nobles, who then raised to the throne Ismā'īl, the son of Burhān-ud-dīn. Burhān now sought and obtained Akbar's permission to make an attempt to gain the throne to which his son had been raised, and Akbar offered to aid him, but Burhān declined his assistance lest it should provoke the hostility of his subjects and of the kings of Bijāpur and Golconda. He failed in his first attempt, but a second attempt, in which he was assisted by Rājā 'Alī Khān of Khāndesh, was more successful. He deposed his son, and ascended the throne of Ahmadnagar as Burhān Nizām Shāh II.[1]

In his tour through Kashmīr Akbar inquired into the revenue administration of the province, and at the end of July left Srīnagar for Kābul. At Bāramūla he received the submission of Ya'qūb, who had been in rebellion ever since the death of his unfortunate father. Akbar, as he was returning from Kābul to Lahore, was deeply grieved by the news of the death of Todar Mal on 20 November, 1589. He was himself much to blame for the death of his loyal and faithful servant, for Todar Mal, who was old and worn out, had sought and obtained permission to retire to Hardwār, but Akbar had recalled him before he could even reach that town, and he had died eleven days after his return to Lahore. He had served his master with no less ability than zeal, and Abu-'l-Fazl remarks that if he had not been a bigot he would have been truly great. This means, of course, that he was a pious and orthodox Hindu, who refused to acknowledge Akbar either as his prophet or his god. Bhagwān Dās attended his funeral, and probably caught a chill, for he died four days later. Badāūnī records the two deaths in a characteristic manner. "In the year 998 Rājā Todar Mal and Rājā Bhagwān Dās, *Amīr-ul-Umarā*, who had remained behind at Lahore, hastened to their

[1] See vol. III, pp. 461, 462.

abode in hell, and to torment, and in the lowest pit became the food of beasts and scorpions. May God scorch them both!"[1] Mān Singh, the heir of Bhagwān Dās, received the title of raja, and was promoted to the command of 5000 horse.

During 1590 the rebellion in Bengal, Bihār and Orissa was finally crushed by Mān Singh and his son, Jagat Singh. The great Hindu landholders, encouraged by the many Muslim rebels who yet remained in arms, had ceased to pay revenue, or to admit imperial officials to their estates. Order was first restored in Bihār, and Mān Singh marched in the spring through Chotā Nāgpur to Orissa. He received some slight assistance from Sa'īd Khān, now governor of Bengal, and prepared to attack Qutlū Khān Lohānī, who advanced to meet him. Qutlū was a rebel who, by formally submitting, had been recognised as governor of Orissa, and, having been left in peace there, had ceased to remit revenue to the capital or to acknowledge Akbar as his sovereign. He was now in failing health, and died before he could meet Mān Singh in the field. The Afghān officers attempted to set up his young son, Nasīr Khān, as their leader, but they were neither sufficiently strong nor sufficiently united to withstand Mān Singh, and sought safety in submission, but the weakness of the imperial cause in this remote province was disclosed by the terms of peace. Nasīr Khān made his submission in person to Mān Singh, and undertook that the *khutba* should be recited and the currency issued in Akbar's name, in return for which, and for 150 elephants and other tribute, he was confirmed in the government of Orissa. Hindu sentiment was conciliated and imperial authority asserted by the classification of the sacred area of Purī and Jagannāth as crown land.

It was in 1591 that the second Christian mission arrived at Akbar's court. In 1590 a Greek sub-deacon named Leo Grimon, passing through India with the object of travelling to Europe by way of Goa, had reached Lahore, and had been entrusted with a letter to the Portuguese authorities, requesting that some priests might be sent to court. The letter seemed to indicate a desire on Akbar's part to embrace Christianity, and two Portuguese priests set out for Lahore with high hopes, only to discover on reaching court that the emperor was in his usual frame of mind. He dallied with the priests, discussed the doctrines of their faith, and expressed his approval of them, but continued to issue regulations for his disciples in the Divine Faith. The priests were well content to find that he had abjured Islām, but were soon obliged to abandon all hope of converting him to Christianity.

In March of this year Akbar had sent missions to the courts of the Sultāns of the Deccan. Faizī was accredited to Rājā 'Alī Khān of Khāndesh and to Burhān Nizām Shāh, and other envoys to Bijāpur

[1] II, 371.

and Golconda. A report from Faizī acquainted Akbar with the attitude of Burhān, who refused to acknowledge the emperor as his overlord or to accept the position of a vassal. Akbar was furious and sent his second son, Sultān Murād, with a large force into Mālwā with instructions to intervene in the affairs of the Deccan whenever an opportunity should arise. It was not until 1593 that the missions returned from the Deccan to court. The Sultāns of Bijāpur and Golconda flattered Akbar's vanity by sending gifts rich enough to pass as tribute, but Burhān's was paltry and his treatment of Faizī had not been such as the emperor's envoy considered his due.

Meanwhile rebellion had once more broken out in Orissa. The young Nasīr Khān had observed the terms of his treaty with Mān Singh so long as his guardian lived, but on his death he had repudiated it, had seized the crown lands of Purī and Jagannāth, and had plundered the estates of those who refused to join him in rebellion. Mān Singh, leaving Bihār in November, 1591, defeated the rebel forces at Mednipur (Midnapore) on 18 April, 1592, and followed them through Orissa. They evacuated Cuttack on his approach, and took refuge with Rājā Rām Chand of Serāen.[1] Mān Singh left a force under Yūsuf of Kashmīr to besiege that fortress; on 8 June the garrison surrendered and Orissa was at length completely subdued.

The inquiry into the sources and amount of the revenue of Kashmīr had caused deep discontent. Mīrzā Yūsuf Khān, the governor, had already reported to Akbar that the assesssment which he had proposed was too high, but Akbar had sent two officials to investigate the question, obviously with a view to justifying his demand, and his officers in the province, convinced that if he persisted in levying revenue at the enhanced rate little or nothing would be left for them and their troops, rose in arms and elected as their leader Yādgār, the governor's cousin. Yādgār assumed the royal title and caused the *khutba* to be recited in his own name. Akbar left Lahore for Kashmīr on 3 July, 1592, and halted at Bhimbar while a force which he had sent in advance dispersed the rebels. Yādgār was captured and put to death and his head was presented to the emperor, who advanced and, on 14 October, entered Srīnagar. Mīrzā Yūsuf Khān resigned the government of the province, professing himself unable to administer it under the enhanced assessment, and the whole province was therefore classed as crown land and was placed under the charge of Khvāja Shams-ud-dīn, who had charge of the finances of the Punjab, though it was assigned to the *sūba* of Kābul, as a *sarkār* of that great province. Akbar then left Kashmīr and returned to Lahore on 9 January, 1593.

He was now at the zenith of his power. In one year Kashmīr, Orissa, Sind and Kāthīāwār had been reduced to obedience, and the last vestiges of rebellion had been wiped out in Gujarāt. He was at

[1] 20° N., 85° 45′ E.

leisure to pursue fresh conquests, and it was to the Deccan, where Burhān of Ahmadnagar had defied his authority, that his thoughts first turned. Murād, first in Mālwā but now in Gujarāt, had been ordered to seize an opportunity of invading Ahmadnagar, and now more extensive preparations were made. The young prince Dāniyāl was appointed to the nominal command of a great army, with the Khān Khānān and Rāi Singh of Bīkāner as his tutors or advisers; the governors of Delhi and Ajmer were ordered to join him with their contingents, Shāh Rukh Mīrzā and Shāhbāz Khān were sent to raise troops for him in Mālwā, and Mān Singh was directed to invade the Deccan from the east; but the elaborate scheme came to nought. Dāniyāl left Lahore in November, but loitered at Sirhind. He was twenty-two years of age, far too young to command a great army, but old enough to have his own way; and Akbar, incensed by his dilatoriness, recalled him. It was as well that he did, for Murād, who had, not unreasonably, regarded his appointment first to Mālwā and afterwards to Gujarāt as an assurance that he was to receive the chief command of the army of the Deccan, bitterly resented his supersession by his younger brother, and had written to his father a letter in which he announced his intention of rebelling if Dāniyāl were allowed to retain the command.

Akbar now learned that his foster-brother, Khān A'zam, who had fled to Mecca in 1593 rather than embrace the Divine Faith, had returned to India, having landed at Verāval, in Kāthīāwār. Akbar sent him a robe of honour, and he reached Lahore in 1594. The holy men of Mecca had plundered him so shamelessly that he was disgusted with orthodoxy and very readily abjured Islām, shaved his beard, and became a disciple of the Divine Faith. For a convert so distinguished and so beloved nothing was too good. His rank and title were restored to him and he was offered his choice of the provinces of Gujarāt, the Punjab, and Bihār, and chose the last.

The year 1595 was one of the most eventful in Akbar's reign. The road to Qandahār had been opened by the capture of the fortress and district of Sibī, and the Safavid prince, Muzaffar Husain Mīrzā, who held Qandahār nominally as fief of the Persian empire but in fact as an independent ruler, having quarrelled with his royal kinsmen and being menaced by the Uzbegs, surrendered Qandahār to Shāh Beg Khān, who had been deputed by Akbar to receive it. On 27 August the Persian prince arrived at Lahore with his escort of 2000 *Qizilbāsh*, and received the command of 5000 horse and an assignment at Sambhal, "which was worth more than all Qandahār".

The third Jesuit mission had already arrived at Lahore. Of the second mission the Provincial of the Order of Jesus at Goa had reported, with reference to its failure to convert Akbar: "Venerunt filii usque ad partum, sed virtus non est pariendi". The new missionaries, Jerome Xavier, a grand-nephew of St Francis, Father

Pinheiro and Brother Benedict de Goes, had been sent in response to another appeal from Akbar, and though no prospect of his conversion remained they were permitted and even encouraged to preach the Gospel to the people.

Akbar's own fantastic sect now lost one of its leading adherents, for on 13 October Shaikh Faizī died of a complication of diseases. The bigoted Badāūnī, who was deeply indebted to him and had never permitted his orthodoxy to debar him from profiting by his aid, extols him for his learning, justly enough criticises his poetry and finds no language too strong for the condemnation of his heterodoxy.

> He was a master of malevolent activity, idle jests, conceit, pride, and malice, and an epitome of hypocrisy, baseness, dissimulation, love of pomp, arrogance, and ostentation. All Jews, Christians and Fireworshippers, not to speak of *Nizārīs and Sabāhīs*, held him in the very highest honour for his heresy, his enmity to the followers of Islām, his contemptuous abuse of the noble companions of the prophet, and of holy *shaikhs*, both dead and living, and of his unmannerly behaviour towards all learned, pious, and excellent men....He used to regard all forbidden things as lawful, and all the injunctions of the sacred law as unlawful.[1]

Badāūnī also describes with much gusto his death agonies, and thus excuses himself for his vilification of a deceased benefactor. "If any should ask in accordance with what rules of generosity and fidelity I arraign him so harshly...I reply, 'All this is true, but what can I do? For the claim of the faith and the safeguarding of its covenant are above all other claims; and love is of God and hatred is of God'."

It is probably from regard for his patron's reputation that the usually careful chronicler Abu-'l-Fazl refrains from noticing the terrible famine of four years' duration which began in 1595; but there is other unimpeachable evidence of the calamity, which was followed by a pestilence. Relief measures were confined to the distribution of alms, and failed lamentably to alleviate the sufferings of the people. "In consequence of the dearth of grain and the necessities of ravenous hunger men ate their own kind. The streets and roads were blocked with corpses, and no assistance could be given for their removal."[2] From the annual report of the Jesuit missions for 1597 we learn that the pestilence was raging at Lahore in that year, and that the Fathers baptized many children abandoned by their parents.

The final plans for the conquest of the Deccan had now been completed. The Khān Khānān, with whom were associated Shāh Rukh Mīrzā and Shāhbāz Khān, was to invade the kingdom of Ahmadnagar from Mālwā, while Sultān Murād and Sādiq Muhammad Khān were to invade it from Gujarāt, the two armies meeting at Ahmadnagar, where Rājā 'Alī Khān of Khāndesh was to join them.

[1] *Bad.* (trans. Haig), III, 413, 414.
[2] *Zubdat-ut-Tawārīkh*, E. and D. VI, 193.

The course of the siege of Ahmadnagar has been followed in vol. III.[1] Its result was the cession of the province of Berār by Chānd Sultān to Akbar, and during the negotiations which ended with the cession of the province the arrogance of Sādiq Muhammad Khān drew from Chingīz Khan of Ahmadnagar the biting taunt: "I have heard that the emperor Akbar claims to be a god. I now find that his nobles claim to be prophets."

The peace procured by the cession of Berār was of short duration, and in the war which broke out between the imperial troops and those of the kingdoms of the Deccan, a battle was fought in the neighbourhood of Sonpet on 8 and 9 February, 1597.[2] On the afternoon of the first day both wings of the imperial army were put to flight, and in the left wing Rājā 'Alī Khān of Khāndesh, who attempted to make a stand, was slain, with thirty of his officers and 500 of his men. The centre, under the Khān Khānān, stood fast and the wings rallied during the night, and, finding the Khāndesh camp empty, concluded that their ally had either fled or deserted to the enemy, and plundered his camp. After the battle, which was resumed on the following day and ended in a decisive victory for the imperial troops, the corpse of the valiant and unfortunate prince was discovered, and those who had plundered his camp were overcome with shame. It was the behaviour of the imperial troops on this occasion that embittered Qadr Khān, who succeeded his father on the throne of Khāndesh under the title of Bahādur Shāh, against Akbar.

Further successes in the Deccan were gained by Mīrzā 'Alī Beg in 1598, but the local victories of an enterprising subordinate officer failed to counterbalance the injury suffered by the imperial cause from the disputes between Sultān Murād and the Khān Khānān, which compelled the Khān Khānān to retire into Mālwā. Owing to these quarrels field operations were almost suspended, until Sayyid Murtazā Sabzavārī, by cutting off supplies, compelled the garrison of the great fortress of Gāwīl to surrender, and by causing the family of the officer commanding Narnāla to be seized and detained as hostages obliged him to surrender that fortress to Sultān Murād on 13 December, 1598.

Akbar spent the summer of 1597 in Kashmīr, where he introduced a lighter assessment of the revenue and opened public works, which alleviated the distress of the famine-stricken, but returned to Lahore in the early winter. During his long sojourn in the north peace had not reigned in all parts of his empire, and the rebellion of Rām Chandra, Rājā of Bhath (Rewah), in Baghelkhand, was not suppressed until Rai Patr Dās captured his stronghold, Bāndhogarh.[3] Mān Singh had been occupied in suppressing sporadic outbursts of rebellion in Bengal and Orissa, had destroyed a nest of rebels in

[1] pp. 464, 465.

[2] See vol. III, p. 465.

[3] 23° 41′ N., 81° 3′ E.

the Sunderbans, and had suppressed two attempts to place a pretender on the throne of Cooch Behār, the ruler of which, Lachmī Nārāyan, had submitted to Akbar.

Akbar, whose presence had been most necessary in the Deccan, had been detained in the north by the apprehension that 'Abdullah II, who had wrested Badakhshān from his cousins, intended to annex Kābul also. His apprehensions were allayed by the death, on 4 February, 1598, of 'Abdullah. From his son and successor, 'Abdul-Mūmin, Akbar had nothing to fear, and he was now free to turn towards the Deccan, but the desire of recovering his ancestral home was revived by the opportune death of 'Abdullah and was, not improbably, encouraged by Abu-'l-Fazl, who perceived an opportunity of attaining his own ends. He detested Akbar's eldest son, Salīm, and suggested that the task should be entrusted to him; but the prince detected the malice which prompted the proposal. Akbar was growing old, a campaign in Central Asia, against unknown powers and unknown interests, might last long, and he had no intention of jeopardising his chance of ascending the imperial throne. Abu-'l-Fazl naïvely records his disappointment by attributing Salīm's refusal to certain "worshippers of India", the writer's own native land, and Akbar, too, was disappointed. He proposed to entrust the task to one of his two younger sons, but honest and outspoken counsellors dissuaded him from pursuing the scheme, and he wisely resolved to march to the Deccan.

Akbar set out from Lahore on 20 November, and on 1 January, 1599, put to death Shaikh Sultān, the governor of Thānesar, an orthodox old officer who had expressed himself too freely on the subject of the Divine Faith. On 15 February Akbar dispatched Abu-'l-Fazl from Āgra to summon Sultān Murād to court, and to order the Khān Khānān to march, with all the force which he could muster, to the Deccan. Abu-'l-Fazl was received near Burhānpur by Bahādur of Khāndesh, but the meeting was not cordial. Bahādur offered Abu-'l-Fazl some gifts, which were not accepted, but refused to join the imperial army in person, offering a contingent of 2000 horse under the command of his son, Kabīr Khān.

Sultān Murād, whose health was completely shattered, left Shāhpur and marched towards the frontier of the Ahmadnagar kingdom in order to avoid meeting Abu-'l-Fazl and receiving the orders which he bore, but Abu-'l-Fazl followed him, and joined his camp near Tembhumi[1] early in May, 1599. He found the prince's army in a state of mutiny. Pay was in arrears, the country was unfamiliar, the strength of the enemy was unknown, and it was uncertain whether the prince were alive or dead. On 12 May he died of *delirium tremens*, and Abu-'l-Fazl, with the help of his own contingent of 3000 horse, succeeded in restoring some degree of discipline in the demoralised

[1] 20° 7′ N., 76° 4′ E.

army, and the order to advance towards Ahmadnagar restored confidence.

Salīm, loth to accept any employment at a distance from the capital, declined the command in the Deccan, and his younger brother Dāniyāl, who was appointed in his stead, left Āgra on 4 June, but moved slowly, and in the meantime Shāh Rukh Mīrzā joined the army on 18 August. His presence was necessary, for the enemy, encouraged by the death of Murād, was besieging an imperial garrison in Bīr. Abu-'l-Fazl sent reinforcements which compelled the enemy to raise the siege, and urged Sher Khvāja, who commanded in Bīr, to leave the isolated fortress, but the gallant officer refused to abandon his post.

The disorganisation of the army in the Deccan had almost destroyed its fighting value. It was without funds and for months neither officers nor men had received any pay. Akbar ordered the governor of Gujarāt to transmit to the Deccan all the surplus treasure of his province, and remitted 300,000 rupees from Āgra by means of bills of exchange. He then set out for Mālwā with the object of supervising personally the operations in the Deccan and hastening the movements of Dāniyāl, who was loitering by the way. Salīm was appointed to the government of Ajmer, but as his loyalty was doubtful his brother-in-law, Mān Singh, was associated with him, Mān Singh's son, Jagat Singh, holding the government of Bengal as his father's deputy. But Jagat Singh died on 19 October, and his place was taken by his young son, Mahā Singh. Akbar left Āgra on 29 September with 80,000 horse, and sent the Khān Khānān to join Dāniyāl in order that Abu-'l-Fazl might be free to return to court.

The situation of the army was now much improved. The fortress of Baitālwādī,[1] in southern Berār, had been surrendered in October, and dissensions at Ahmadnagar weakened both parties in the state and advanced the imperial cause. Chānd Sultān was in the fortress, with the young king, Bahādur Nizām Shāh, but the army was weary of female rule and only a minority supported her. Āhang Khān the African was encamped before the town with the object of gaining possession of the young king's person and excluding the "noble queen" from the management of affairs. She entered into correspondence with Abu-'l-Fazl, who plainly told her that mere professions would not serve her, and that the emperor would judge her by her deeds. Eventually it was agreed that the imperial troops should remove Āhang Khān, and that Chānd Sultān should then surrender Ahmadnagar and tender her own and the young king's submission. Āhang Khān, having learned of these negotiations, took the offensive and sent an army to invade Berār, whence the imperial troops drew all their supplies, and this force was able, owing to the

[1] 20° 34′ N., 75° 36′ E.

negligence of the imperial officers in Berār, to penetrate as far as Ellichpur. Here, however, it was defeated and dispersed, its leader being slain.

On the arrival of Dāniyāl at Burhānpur in January, 1600, a new complication arose. Bahādur Fārūqī of Khāndesh remained in the citadel and refused to come forth and welcome him or to see him. Dāniyāl was furious and summoned the officers in Berār to his assistance, and many of the officers with Abu-'l-Fazl left him for the prince, and the camp at Paithan was exposed to considerable danger of being attacked.

Akbar, who had intended to halt for some time in Mālwā, hastened to Burhānpur on hearing of the defiant attitude of Bahādur Fārūqī. Dāniyāl was ordered to continue his march to Ahmadnagar and to leave his father to deal with the rebel. It was believed that Bahādur might have been withheld by some scruples from making his submission to the prince before he had made it to the emperor, but envoys sent to him reported that this was not so and that his attitude was defiant.

Akbar arrived before Burhānpur on 8 April, and on the following day sent a force under Khān A'zam to open the siege of Asīrgarh. Abu-'l-Fazl was appointed governor of Khāndesh, and succeeded in establishing some degree of order in the province. On 24 May Partāb Baharjī, Rājā of Bāglān, made his obeisance to Akbar and was rewarded with the command of 3000 horse.

Bahādur Fārūqī now attempted to open negotiations with Akbar, but it soon became apparent that his only object was to gain time in the hope that the exhaustion of supplies in Khāndesh would oblige Akbar to raise the siege of Asīrgarh.

Rebellion now broke out again in Bengal. Although Mān Singh's young grandson was nominally governor of the province, the raja himself was understood to be responsible for its administration, which he carried on by means of agents. Abu-'l-Fazl unjustly blames him for this arrangement, which was approved if not originally suggested by Akbar, who insisted on Mān Singh's presence with Salīm. He may be more justly blamed for placing too much confidence in the turbulent and perfidious Afghāns of Bengal. Mahā Singh and his tutor, falling into the common error of despising their enemy, were defeated on 6 May, and, though the province was not lost, the rebels occupied many important military posts.

Salīm had done nothing in Mewār beyond compelling the Rānā to take to the hills, and his father's unconcealed displeasure and obvious preference for Dāniyāl and the influential Abu-'l-Fazl's bitter hostility fanned his smouldering disaffection into rebellion. He first proposed to march into the Punjab and raise the standard of revolt there, but his brother-in-law, Mān Singh, whose influence was great in Bengal, where he could count on the support of the now successful rebels in any movement directed against Akbar, persuaded him to select that province as the scene of his activities, and on 23 July he crossed the Jumna in the neighbourhood of Āgra on his way to Bengal. His grandmother, Akbar's aged mother, hastened after him to implore him to make his peace with his father, but he avoided her and travelled by boat to Allahābād, where he obtained possession of the treasure from Bihār, amounting to over three millions of rupees. Akbar feigned not to believe that Salīm was in open disobedience, and wrote to him warning him against the sin of rebellion. Salīm replied evasively, but persisted in his disobedience and appointed his own officials in the provinces of Allahābād, Bihār and Oudh, ousting those appointed by his father. His success was largely due to his being the avowed enemy of Abu-'l-Fazl, who had encouraged the emperor in his religious innovations.

Meanwhile affairs in the Deccan progressed favourably for Akbar. The siege of Ahmadnagar was opened on 21 April, and those who resented Chānd Sultān's agreement with Abu-'l-Fazl caused her to be assassinated, but there remained within the walls many partisans of the imperial cause. The siege was vigorously prosecuted, and after the destruction of a portion of the defences by mines the fortress was stormed on 28 August. Bahādur Nizām Shāh was captured, and the rich spoils which rewarded the victors included the royal jewels, a splendid library, twenty-five elephants, and a large quantity of guns and ammunition.[1] The fall of Ahmadnagar was an event of such sinister import to the Deccan that Ibrāhīm 'Ādil Shāh II of Bijāpur deemed it politic to conciliate the emperor by tendering his congratulations.

Akbar's schemes of conquest in the Deccan overshadow at this period the importance of events in other parts of the empire, but the death of Jalāl-ud-dīn, the leader of the Raushanāīs, which secured tranquillity between the Indus and Kābul, merits notice. He was attacked by a force of imperial troops, defeated, pursued and slain.

Owing to the sloth and venality of many of the imperial officers the siege of Asīrgarh was progressing languidly and Abu-'l-Fazl was sent to stimulate the activity of the besiegers. On 9 December an important outwork was carried, and on 21 December Bahādur Fārūqī appeared in Akbar's camp and made his submission.

Akbar has been charged with gross perfidy in inveigling Bahādur into his toils and in detaining him in spite of solemn engagements, but the perfidy was not all on one side, and each strove to outwit the other. Akbar's terms included personal submission but made no specific mention of the surrender of the fortress. Bahādur must, however, have known that the demand would be made and had taken precautions for evading it. He had instructed Yāqūt, the

[1] See vol. III, p. 466.

African commander of the fortress, to hold it to the last, disregarding any orders purporting to be his which he might receive from the imperial camp, his object being to represent the garrison as rebels who defied his authority and thus escape responsibility. Yāqūt had opposed his leaving the fortress for Akbar's camp and bitterly resented his meanness of spirit but faithfully obeyed his orders, and when his own son, Muqarrab Khān, arrived from the imperial camp with Bahādur's orders that the fortress was to be surrendered he refused to hear him, and Muqarrab, on his return, reported that his father would never surrender the fortress, and was shortly afterwards stabbed to death by Akbar's orders. This atrocious murder is one of the darkest blots on Akbar's name.

The jealousy of the Fārūqī kings confined in the fortress of Asīr all males of the royal house except the reigning monarch, and there were at this time nearly fifty princes so imprisoned, among them seven near in blood to Bahādur. Yāqūt released them and implored one of them to ascend and defend the throne, but none replied. "Would to God that ye were women!" ejaculated the brave old African, and, turning away, took poison and died. The fortress surrendered to Akbar on 6 January, 1601, and Khāndesh was annexed to the empire. On 7 March Dāniyāl arrived in his father's camp and was received with the honour due to the conqueror of Ahmadnagar. He was appointed to the government of Khāndesh, which was fancifully renamed Dāndesh after him, and before leaving the Deccan Akbar formed the provinces of Khāndesh and Berār, together with so much of the kingdom of Ahmadnagar as had been conquered, into the viceroyalty of the Deccan, to which the prince was appointed. In Daulatābād, now the capital of the remnant of the kingdom of Ahmadnagar, the son of Shāh 'Alī, third son of Burhān I, was raised to the throne as Murtazā Nizām Shāh II, and Malik 'Ambar the African, long the virtual ruler of the state, defeated the imperial troops in south-eastern Berār and rose into prominence. Both parties in the Deccan were now weary of the strife, and on 3 January, 1602, some months after Akbar's departure for Āgra, Abu-'l-Fazl made peace with Murtazā II.

Akbar's counsellors had for some time been urging him to return to Āgra, but he had at first refused to leave the Deccan until Ahmadnagar and Asīrgarh had fallen, and after their fall had dallied with the project of conquering the kingdoms of Bijāpur, Golconda and Bīdar. He was aroused from these dreams by the menace of Salīm's rebellion, which was assuming more serious proportions. Akbar had sent the prince's school companion, Sharīf, to Allahābād to recall him to a sense of his duty to his father, but Salīm had seduced him from his allegiance and appointed him his minister.

Salīm, hearing that his father was returning from the Deccan, raised additional troops and conferred titles and assignments on his principal followers. Akbar, who reached Āgra on 23 August, hesitated to take the field against his son, and negotiations were opened; but Salīm's demands were so extravagant that they could not be granted, and he advanced from Allahābād towards Āgra with thirty or forty thousand horse, plundering the country on his way. Akbar contented himself with conciliatory messages and mild remonstrances, and though his weakness was condemned by his courtiers, who trembled for their own safety, his policy was so far successful that Salīm retired to Allahābād, and was rewarded with a *farmān* appointing him viceroy of Bengal and Orissa, with almost independent powers, but Salīm persisted in refusing to leave the vicinity of the capital, and declined the appointment, at the same time insulting his father by sending to him specimens of the coins which he had struck in his own name at Allahābād.

Akbar now longed for the counsel of Abu-'l-Fazl, and summoned him from the Deccan. He replied by promising to bring the rebel bound to court, and at once set out.

It was to him that Salīm attributed the estrangement between himself and his father, and when he heard that his enemy was to be consulted he was convinced that Akbar would be urged to put forth all his strength to destroy him. He therefore sent for Bīr Singh, the Bundelā, of Orchha, who was in his service, and ordered him to intercept Abu-'l-Fazl before he could reach the capital, and to put him to death. Bīr Singh accepted the commission, and on 19 August, 1602, waylaid Abu-'l-Fazl between Barkī Sarāī (25° 58½′ N., 78° 10½′ E.) and Antrī (26° 3½′ N., 78° 3½′ E.). He was an easy victim, for, though he had been warned that mischief was afoot, he refused to travel more rapidly, to alter his route, or to provide himself with a sufficient escort. Bīr Singh severed his head from his body, and sent it to Salīm, who received it with joy and treated it with insult. In his memoirs he describes the murder with unblushing effrontery and attributes the assassin's success to God's grace.[1]

Akbar was engaged in his childish sport of pigeon-flying when he received the news of his favourite's death. He shrieked and was for a time beside himself with grief and rage, even abstaining for three days from appearing in public. He railed bitterly against his son and ordered that Bīr Singh should be hunted to death. Patr Das, Rāi Rāyān, drove the murderer into the fortress of Erachh (25° 48′ N., 79° 6′ E.) on the Betwa, and his death or capture seemed certain, when he broke out and made his escape. Akbar was furious, and ordered that the circumstances of his escape should be investigated, but the inquiry was inconclusive. Akbar was old and nobody was eager to incur the resentment of his natural heir.

Again, in 1604, Rāi Rāyān, then entitled Rājā Bikramājīt (Vikramāditya), was sent in pursuit of the murderer but the operations

[1] Trans., Rogers and Beveridge, I, 25.

were a pure formality. Except Akbar, and perhaps Shaikh 'Abdur-Rahmān, the son of the murdered man, nobody expected and nobody specially desired to catch the elusive Bīr Singh. Salīma Sultān Begam, Akbar's cousin and wife, interceded for her stepson, and she was permitted to visit him at Allahābād, with a view to recalling him to a sense of his duty. On her return, in February, 1603, she reported that Salīm was now well disposed, and wished to visit his father. The Khudā Bakhsh Library at Patna contains the copy of the *dīvān*, or collection of the odes of Hāfiz, the great lyrical poet of Persia, used in the East as the works of Virgil were used in the West, for the taking of omens, from which Salīm took an omen before setting out, and in a note it is recorded by him that the passage from which he took his omen was an ode beginning:

> Why should I not set out for my own country?
> Why not become the dust beneath the foot of my friend?
> Since I cannot endure the grief and the toil of exile
> I will go to my own city and become lord of myself.[1]

The omen was clear enough, and Salīm set out. At his own request he was met at a distance of one stage from the capital by his grandmother, who led him by the hand into his father's presence. He rubbed his forehead on his father's feet, and with tears confessed his guilt. Akbar, though he probably never in his heart forgave him the murder of Abu-'l-Fazl, raised him up and embraced him. His gifts, which included 12,000 gold mohurs and 770 elephants, probably bore their part in the reconciliation but Akbar found it difficult to contemplate the prospect of being succeeded by his drunken and brutal first-born. He had, however, little choice, for his only other son, his favourite, was rapidly drinking himself to death in the Deccan. It was an open secret that Khusrav, Salīm's eldest son, was preferred to his father, but to designate him as heir without putting Salīm to death would have been to devote him to destruction. Akbar was thus compelled to complete his reconciliation with Salīm by designating him heir apparent.

On 14 October, 1603, the Hindu festival of the Dasahra, Salīm was again ordered to lead an expedition against the Rānā, and did not now venture on open disobedience, but loitered at Fathpur Sīkrī and, after a time, wrote to Akbar, complaining that his force was both insufficient and ill-equipped with artillery, and begging for permission to return to Allahābād in order that he might supply its deficiencies. Akbar probably knew that he had never intended to accept banishment to Rājputāna with an arduous task to perform, but complied with his request rather than provoke him again to open rebellion, and he withdrew, well pleased, to Allahābād, drinking freely by the way. Reports of his behaviour at Allahābād gave Akbar much pain. He had become so hardened a toper that pure wine had

[1] *Catalogue of Persian Poetry*, 1908, p. 249.

lost its savour and efficacy for him, and required the addition of opium. His first wife, the sister of Mān Singh and mother of Khusrav, had earlier in the year committed suicide in consequence of his ill-treatment of her, and Mān Singh was for this reason completely alienated from him, and had been occupied since parting from him in restoring order in Bengal and Orissa in the interests of Khusrav, of whose claim to succeed his grandfather he had become a warm advocate.

Meanwhile Salīm continued his drinking bouts, and in his fits of intoxication committed the most revolting cruelties. The news-writer who reported his misdeeds was flayed alive in his presence; he emasculated one of his father's servants, and beat one of his own to death. These atrocities roused the wrath of Akbar, and he set out from Āgra to call his son to account, but was first delayed by the grounding of his boat, and then by heavy rain, and before he could proceed was recalled to Āgra by the illness of his mother who died on 10 September immediately after his arrival. He mourned her in Hindu fashion, shaving himself clean.

On 16 November Salīm arrived at court from Allahābād, ostensibly to offer his condolences to his father, but actually in order to be on the spot in case the shock of his mother's death should seriously affect his health. He brought valuable gifts and was well received at the public audience, but Akbar afterwards had him arrested, and, after upbraiding him with his crimes, struck him in the face and imprisoned him in a room in the inner apartments where he could obtain no wine. He was released after ten days' confinement, but would have been deprived of his command and his fiefs had not the reports of his brother Dāniyāl's health restrained Akbar from proceeding to extremities against him. On 28 April, 1605,[1] this wretched drunkard died of *delirium tremens* at Burhānpur. He had been placed under restraint, but some of his personal servants, moved by his distress, contrived to convey liquor to him in a gun-barrel, and he died raving. They were arrested by the Khān Khānān and were beaten and stoned to death. Akbar was deeply grieved by the death of his favourite son, but reports from the Deccan had prepared him for the news, which he received with resignation.

Three Englishmen, Newbery, Fitch and Leedes, had already visited Akbar's court, in 1585, and in 1603 a fourth arrived. This was John Mildenhall, a merchant, who had been sent out in 1600 to try to acquire from Akbar for the newly founded East India Company trading privileges equal to those enjoyed by the Portuguese, and he bore a letter to this effect from Queen Elizabeth but was in no sense an ambassador or an accredited envoy. He presented to Akbar twenty-nine good horses, and received from him in return gifts worth £500. Salīm supported him, but the Portuguese Jesuits, who

[1] More probably in 1604, *vide* V. A. Smith, *Akbar*, p. 331. [Ed.]

denounced the English as "thieves and spies", bribed the ministers and were so successful that he obtained no concession so long as Akbar lived, and did not receive the *farmān* which he sought until 1608, when Jahāngīr had been for three years on the throne. He died in 1614 and, being a Roman Catholic, was buried in the old Jesuit cemetery at Āgra. He is thus described by one writer:

> John Mildenhall was not an estimable character. In plain words he was a dishonest scoundrel. He cheated, or tried to cheat, Akbar with an assumption of ambassadorial dignity; he tried to cheat the Company with concessions that, in all probability, he had never received; he ended by cheating his own employers, the merchants in London....But he was of some note—of a kind—even in his own day. He was a pioneer of Anglo-Indian enterprise, not less enterprising than his many enterprising successors. He was one of four Englishmen who spoke with Akbar face to face, and much the greatest of the four.[1]

The partisans of Khusrav, who was now aged eighteen, were headed by two of the most influential courtiers, Khān A'zam and Mān Singh, and were using every endeavour to induce Akbar to set aside his son and designate the grandson as his heir. Unfortunately the young prince, conscious of this powerful support, began to bear himself haughtily, as though he were already secure of the crown.

On 3 October Akbar fell sick of dysentery. A violent quarrel between the servants of Salīm and those of Khusrav, connected with an elephant fight, further embittered the relations between father and son and aggravated the emperor's disorder, which did not yield to the treatment of Hakīm 'Alī, his physician. Khān A'zam and Mān Singh conspired to seize and imprison Salīm on a day on which it had been arranged that he should visit his father, but he was warned in time of their intentions and returned home without entering the palace. They then convened a meeting of the courtiers, and laid before them a proposal that Salīm should be set aside, but dissolved the meeting on discovering that they could not command a majority. Salīm's supporters now bestirred themselves; Rām Dās the Kachhwāhā placed a guard of his Rājputs over the treasury in his interest, and the valiant Sayyids of Bārha declared for him. Mān Singh, on his failure to secure his nephew's succession, prepared to carry him off to Bengal, but Salīm's party converted many trimmers and some opponents by exacting from him two oaths, the first that he would protect Islām, and the second that he would refrain from punishing his son and others who had sought to deprive him of his birthright.

Hakīm 'Alī checked Akbar's dysentery by administering a powerful astringent, but the result was an attack of fever and strangury, and when Salīm, on 21 October, visited the patient, his condition was so serious that he could no longer speak, though he retained consciousness. He made a sign to his son to put on the imperial turban, and

[1] E. A. H. Blunt, *J.R.A.S.* 1910, pp. 495–8.

to gird himself with the sword of Humāyūn, which hung at the foot of the bed, and Salīm went out acknowledged as emperor.

The administration of an aperient brought on a return of the dysentery, and at midnight on 25–26 October[1] Akbar died, a month before completing the sixty-third year of his age. According to some authorities he recanted his errors before his death and died professing the faith of Islām, but there is little doubt that he was past speech, and could make no response to the exhortations of those who surrounded his bed, though the Jesuits were informed that he died attempting to utter the name of God.

At dawn his body was washed in accordance with the rites of Islām, and was carried out by the courtiers to the garden five miles from the palace, then known as Bihishtābād and since as Sikandra.

The age of Akbar has been described as an age of great rulers, and some hold that of his contemporaries, Elizabeth of England, Henry IV of France, and 'Abbās the Great of Persia, he was not the least. Some have even written of him as though he were no less than what his enemies alleged he pretended to be. But with all his faults, and they were neither few nor venial, he was by far the greatest of all who ruled India during the era of the dominance of Islām in that land. A foreigner in blood, though he happened to have been born on Indian soil, he was the only one of the long line of rulers professing Islām who even conceived the idea of becoming the father of all his subjects, rather than the leader of a militant and dominant minority, alien in faith, and to a great extent in race, to the nations of India.

Difference of religion was the chief bar between the nations of India and the ruling class, and to remove this Akbar first announced his adherence to the principle of *sulh-i-kull*, universal peace or toleration. He was so far ahead of his age that it was not surprising that he was misunderstood, for in that age toleration, in the East as in the West, was the symbol not of an enlightened and humane mind but of laxity of principle, for if a man would tolerate error he could not love truth; but toleration would have served Akbar well had he remained content with it as a means to his end. Unfortunately he lost patience with the obstinacy of the orthodox and was persuaded by self-seekers to assume the spiritual as well as the temporal sovereignty over his peoples, and, ere long, to violate the conditions under which his spiritual sovereignty had been accepted, to abjure Islām, and to found a faith of his own. This was not, as one writer has described it, merely "an association of students and free-thinkers who had transcended the barriers of faith and creed, and shaken off the tyrannous yoke of age-long customs"; it was a new sect, with minute rules of ritual and belief, and the acceptance of it was urged on all the leading men in the state; but it was condemned by Hindus

[1] Hodivala, *op. cit.* p. 267.

and Muslims, Sunnī and Shiah alike. Akbar perceived that all his subjects would not accept Christianity, Islām or Zoroastrianism, and knew that they could not, even if they would, enter the fold of Hinduism. He believed that he could invent a faith better than any of these, a faith which would be accepted by all, except perhaps an obstinate minority of his subjects. This was certainly, as Dr Vincent Smith describes it, "the outcome of ridiculous vanity, a monstrous growth of unrestrained autocracy", and Akbar was bitterly disappointed. But we must not lose sight of his object, which was to make all his subjects one people. The object was noble; the means adopted for attaining it absurd.

Some light is thrown on the character of Akbar by his "Happy Sayings", recorded by Abu-'l-Fazl. Most of these are unexceptionable as religious or moral aphorisms; but some few display ignorance, and some are such as might be expected from one who could amuse himself to the end of his life with the childish pastime of pigeon-flying, and could immure wretched infants with dumb nurses in order to discover the "divine language". Occasional drinking bouts indicate that the vice which killed two of his sons, and would certainly, but for the blessing of a robust constitution, have killed the third, was to some extent inherited; but Akbar was never a slave to drink and in his later years was temperate.

His life's record is smirched with more than one dark blot, his "earth-hunger" was insatiable, and he sometimes displayed duplicity and, despite his tenderness for animal life, cruelty; but we must beware of judging him by moral standards. Conquest was regarded as the principal pursuit of an oriental ruler, and, as Akbar said, "a monarch should be ever intent on conquest, otherwise his neighbours rise in arms against him". He grossly deceived Yūsuf of Kashmīr, Bahādur Fārūqī and others, but in duplicity and mendacity he was far surpassed by Elizabeth of England.

Instances of his courage and address, of his bodily strength, and of his great power of endurance have been cited. In spite of his illiteracy he was far from being unlearned, nor was his intellect uncultivated, for he delighted in listening to the reading of works on history, theology, philosophy and other subjects, and of discussing afterwards what had been read, and his memory was such that he acquired through the ear a stock of learning as great as that which most of his associates could acquire through the eye. The Jesuits at his court were probably not biased in his favour, but one of them thus describes him:

> Indeed he was a great king; for he knew that the good ruler is he who can command, simultaneously, the obedience, the respect, the love, and the fear of his subjects. He was a prince beloved of all, firm with the great, kind to those of low estate, and just to all men, high and low, neighbour or stranger, Christian, Saracen, or Gentile; so that every man believed that the King was on his side. He lived in the fear of God, to whom he never failed to pray four times daily,

HINDU KUSH
TIBET
KASHMIR
Srinagar
Peshawar
KABUL
INDEPENDENT TRIBES
Jhelum R.
Chinab R.
LAHORE
Ravi R.
HIMALAYA MOUNTAINS
Qandahar
SULAIMAN RANGE
BALUCH and BRAHUI TRIBES
MULTAN
Sutlej R.
Panipat
DELHI
Indus R.
Jumna R.
OUDH
Gogra R.
Gumti R.
Ganges R.
TATTA
AJMER
ARAVALLI HILLS
AGRA
Gwalior
Ranthambhor
KUCH
BIHAR
ALLAHABAD
Benares
Patna
Chitor
Chambal R.
Kalanjar
Patan
MALWA
VINDHYA RANGE
Probably Tributary Frontier Chiefs
BENGAL
AHMADABAD
Cambay
Nerbudda R.
GONDWANA
SATPURA RANGE
(Portuguese) Diu
Surat
KHANDESH
Asirgarh
Burhanpur
Daman (Portuguese)
Tapti R.
BERAR
Mahanadi R.
ORISSA
Bassein (Portuguese)
AHMADNAGAR
Proclaimed a Province but never annexed
Godavari R.
BIDAR
GOLCONDA
WESTERN GHATS
Krishna R.
BIJAPUR
Masulipatam
Goa (Portuguese)
Tungabhadra R.
EASTERN GHATS
Nellore
Pulicat
Mangalore
Kaveri R.
Calicut
POLYGARS
Cochin
Madura
INDIA
AT THE DEATH OF
AKBAR (1605)
The Mughal Empire ....
Akbar's Provinces thus.. ...DELHI
Approximate Boundaries

at sunrise, at sunset, at midday, and at midnight, and, despite his many duties, his prayers on these four occasions, which were of considerable duration, were never curtailed. Towards his fellow-men he was kind and forbearing, averse from taking life, and quick to show mercy. Hence it was that he decreed that if he condemned anyone to death, the sentence was not to be carried into effect until the receipt of his third order. He was always glad to pardon an offender if just grounds for doing so could be shown.[1]

We have two good contemporary verbal portraits of him. The first is by his son, Salīm, or Jahāngīr, who in his memoirs thus describes him:

He was of the middle height, of a wheat-coloured complexion, with black eyes and eyebrows. His beauty was of form rather than of face, and he was powerfully built, with a broad chest and long arms. On his left nostril was a fleshy mole, very becoming, of the size of a split pea, which physiognomists understood to be an augury of great wealth and glory. His voice was extremely loud, and in discourse and narration he was witty and animated. His whole air and appearance had little of the worldly being, but exhibited rather divine majesty.

The second portrait is by Father Monserrate, who writes:

He was in face and stature fit for the dignity of King, so that anybody, even at the first glance, would easily recognise him as the King. His shoulders were broad, and his legs slightly bandy, and adapted to riding. His complexion was fair, but slightly suffused with a darker tint. He carried his head slightly inclined to one side, towards the right shoulders; his brow was broad and open, and his eyes sparkled as does the sea when lighted by the sun. His eyelids were heavy, as are those of the Sarmatians, the Chinese, the Niphonians, and nearly all Asiatics of the more northern regions. His eyebrows were narrow, and his nose was of the middle size and drooping, but had a high bridge. His nostrils were expanded as though he were enraged, and on the left one he had a wart, which met the upper lip. He shaved his beard, but not his moustache, following the custom of young Turks before they assume the full costume of manhood, who, after they have taken the virile toga, cherish and arrange their beards. Unlike his forefathers, he did not shave his head, nor did he wear a cap, but bound his hair with a turban, which, they say, he did in imitation of the Indian custom, in order to conciliate them. He dragged his left leg slightly, as though he were lame in it, though he had not been injured in the foot. He has in his body, which is very well made, and neither thin and meagre nor fat and gross, much courage and strength. When he laughs he is distorted, but when he is tranquil and serene he has a noble mien and great dignity. In his wrath he is majestic.[2]

[1] *Akbar and the Jesuits*, pp. 205, 206.

[2] A portrait coin, struck by Jahāngīr, is illustrated at p. 56, *British Museum Quarterly*, v, 1930.

CHAPTER VI

JAHĀNGĪR

EIGHT days after his father's death the new sovereign crowned himself in the fort of Āgra, on Thursday, 3 November, 1605, being then thirty-six years old. In his memoirs he explains that he assumed the new name of Jahāngīr (Holder of the world) because the business of kings is the controlling of the world, and the title of Nūr-ud-dīn (Light of the faith) because he took his seat on the throne shortly after sunrise, and also because this title had been foretold by sages.[1]

Following ancient custom he issued a liberal proclamation of policy defined in twelve rules, which was forgotten almost as soon as it was written.[2] Prisoners were released, and for the moment some of his old enemies were conciliated. Feelings of gratitude which were innate in his character led to the appointment to high office of several mediocrities who had aided or favoured his revolt, and of descendants of Shaikh Salīm Chishtī whom he regarded as his spiritual guide. While such acts were regarded as not unusual, resentment was felt at the promotion of Rājā Bīr Singh Bundelā, the murderer of Abu-'l-Fazl, which showed itself in a rising led by the raja's brother. In two cases a wiser choice was exercised. Ghiyās Beg, a Persian, who had served Akbar well, was appointed revenue minister with the title of I'timād-ud-daula, and Zamāna Beg, a capable soldier, was ennobled as Mahābat Khān; both of these men were to exercise great influence in the reign, though not without the vicissitudes to which service of a Mughul emperor was liable.

A few months after his accession Jahāngīr celebrated the new year (March, 1606) or vernal equinox with the gorgeous display that marked his reign. Roe has described[3] these ceremonies observed some years later when he was present at the festival; the emperor sitting in public received rich presents, delighting in those which were rare or curious, and critical of those which did not strike his fancy. Almost at once, however, occurred a sudden challenge to the new emperor. Rājā Mān Singh, who had begged and obtained assurances for the safety of prince Khusrav, his nephew, had left for his post of governor in Bengal, and Khusrav had been placed in semi-confinement in the fort at Āgra. On the pretext of a ride to visit the tomb of Akbar, a few miles distant, he escaped northwards with a small body of men, which grew rapidly as the flight continued

[1] *Tūzuk*, trans. I, 1–3. An undated coin, struck at Ahmadnagar, probably by an adherent during his rebellion, gives his title as Burhān-ud-dīn.

[2] See the analysis in E. and D. VI, 493.

[3] *Journal*, 125.

through the Punjab. Funds were obtained by the capture of a convoy with treasure intended for the court, and 'Abdur-Rahīm, the revenue minister of Lahore, was appointed prime minister; Gurū Arjan Singh, the spiritual leader of the Sikhs, gave a present, and the force, which now exceeded 12,000, laid siege to Lahore. Here, however, the stout resistance of the governor gave time for pursuers to arrive. The emperor himself was following with I'timād-ud-daula, and he sent ahead Shaikh Farīd, a brave soldier whom he had promoted for his support during Akbar's last months. Khusrav was now in danger both from the garrison at Lahore and from the relieving force. With most of his troops he turned to meet the latter. Jahāngīr was still willing to treat with his son, who was a favourite even in rebellion, but the negotiations failed and a battle was fought at Bhairowāl. Most of the rebel army consisted of untrained men, and it was defeated by the imperial troops in spite of the success of its cavalry under Husain Beg. After the battle Husain Beg suggested flight to the north, but the fords were guarded and the fugitives were arrested and taken to Lahore. Husain Beg was sewn up in a raw hide and paraded through the city on an ass, while the skin slowly dried and crushed him to death. Several hundred of the rebels were impaled on stakes by the roadside and Khusrav was taken past them in chains to receive the ironical homage of his would-be subjects. Gurū Arjan Singh was executed for aiding the rebel, and his death raised among his followers a mutinous spirit which under Aurangzīb and his successors led to open rebellion. Not long afterwards Rājā Mān Singh was removed from the governorship of Bengal where he had done such excellent service under Akbar.

The stability of an empire under personal rule is particularly dependent on the estimate held from time to time by its officials and its enemies of the capability of its head. Akbar had left a fairly compact territory extending from the confines of Persia to the Bay of Bengal, and from Kashmīr to Ahmadnagar. On the west Shāh 'Abbās of Persia, a ruler of equal ability, was watching for an opportunity of recovering Qandahār, the gate through which traffic passed between India and Persia. Along the southern border there were watchful foes from Malik 'Ambar who was consolidating the Muhammadan states, to Orissa which had not been perfectly subdued. Within the empire were many ambitious and unsettled chiefs who needed little inducement to rebel. Khusrav's revolt was followed by disturbances in Bihār which were soon quelled, and by a more dangerous attempt by Rāi Rāi Singh of Bīkāner who had been promoted by Jahāngīr and was actually conducting the imperial harem to Lahore when he broke away. Rājā Jagannāth of Amber, with the forces intended for Mewār, soon captured and brought him to court.

The Persian attack was more insidious owing to preoccupation with war against the Turks under Ahmad I, and at first showed itself merely in border incursions and a siege not strongly pressed. A relieving force arrived early in 1607, the garrison was strengthened, and Shah 'Abbās wrote letters describing the attacks as unauthorised raids by disobedient officers. His immediate anxieties being removed, Jahāngīr sought relaxation in a visit to Kābul during the hot summer months, thus early in his reign displaying the love of pomp and personal ease which distinguished him from his more austere and energetic father. Some action was taken to reduce the turbulence of the Afghān tribes, but the emperor's personal interest was chiefly evident in horticulture. The low esteem in which he was held was soon shown by a fresh plot on behalf of Khusrav. Some of the younger men about the court, relations of high officials, formed a plan to kill Jahāngīr while he was out hunting. Information leaked out and the scheme failed. The ringleaders were executed or disgraced and I'timād-ud-daula, whose son had been concerned, was put in prison, but afterwards released on payment of a heavy fine. The danger to the throne of the growing popularity of Khusrav led to his being blinded, though his sight was partially restored later.[1]

Before his accession Jahāngīr had been deputed by his father to complete the conquest of Mewār, but had proceeded no farther than Fathpur Sīkrī. Early in his reign he sent his son Parvīz with a large force commanded by Āsaf Khān and accompanied by Rājā Jagannāth of Amber or Jaipur. Their plan was to instal, as Rānā, Sāgar, an uncle of the real chief Amar Singh, and thus create internal feuds. Amar Singh, who had succeeded his father in 1597, had devoted himself to internal reforms but had to some extent lost the martial vigour which had marked the rulers of Chitor. Spurred by his nobles he roused himself, and though the forces sent against him were able to occupy several places and left Sāgar in possession of Chitor, they were withdrawn when Khusrav rebelled and Amar Singh still held most of his state. Jahāngīr on his return from Kābul to Āgra despatched a new force under Mahābat Khān, whose skill and bravery were effective so long as he could meet the Rājputs in pitched battles. In the wild and broken country of the interior, however, the enemy was able to avoid defeat. After a year, a fresh commander, 'Abdullah Khān, who like Mahābat Khān had risen from the lowest rank, was appointed and had more success, defeating Karan the son of Rānā Amar Singh in 1611.

While Jahāngīr was thus attempting the reduction of Mewār which he had neglected when it was committed to his charge, another portion of his empire also claimed his attention. Akbar's last campaign in the Deccan had been checked, after the fall of Asīrgarh, by his need to return to northern India caused by Salīm's revolt.

[1] See Benī Prasād, *Jahāngīr*, p. 166, n. 12, for a discussion of the various accounts of the blinding.

The kingdoms of the Deccan, torn by constant broils with no object but territorial expansion, and misruled by successions of licentious and drunken monarchs, were still able to command the services of a few able men. One of these named Malik 'Ambar was an Abyssinian slave who had been in the service of Chingīz Khān,[1] the faithful general of Murtaza Nizām Shāh I. Akbar's departure had left his army without direction or capable leadership. Though the city of Ahmadnagar was still held by the imperial forces Malik 'Ambar had set up a ruler named Murtaza Nizām Shāh II in the south of the kingdom, and had instituted valuable reforms in the administrative system. He also saw the military advantage to be gained in the rugged country of the Deccan by developing guerrilla tactics and using the Marāthās as predatory bands. In 1608 Rājā Mān Singh was first ordered to command the imperial army, but when he proceeded to his home to make preparations the Khān Khānān who had come north from Burhānpur persuaded Jahāngīr to allow him to undertake the conquest, promising to complete it within two years if adequate troops and funds were supplied. Within a year, however, it had become clear that success was still remote, and prince Parvīz took command with Āsaf Khān as his tutor. Khān Khānān attempted a campaign on the arrival of the prince but his forces were ill-supplied, the terrain was difficult, and the commanders quarrelled. Having thus failed he came to terms with Malik 'Ambar and withdrew to Burhānpur, which was the base for operations in the Deccan. Ahmadnagar itself, though bravely defended by Khvāja Beg Mīrzā, a Persian soldier who had been in charge of it since its first capture, was beset; a relieving force from Burhānpur failed to reach it through bad leading, and it was surrendered.

Affairs were going so badly that Jahāngīr contemplated taking command in person, but decided to adopt the simpler though less satisfactory plan of changing his generals. Pīr Khān Lodī, who belonged to an old ruling family, and had won the title of Khān Jahān, arrived with reinforcements soon after the disasters. Impressed by his reports and promises Jahāngīr gave him the command, in 1610, and also restored to active service Khān A'zam, who had been kept at court since the rebellion of Khusrav, and though nominally governor of Gujarāt, had administered that province through his son as deputy. Khān A'zam had previous experience of warfare in the Deccan during Akbar's reign, and a disloyal letter written by him at that time to the ruler of Khāndesh, but craftily produced soon after Khusrav's revolt had nearly led to his execution. Mahābat Khān, who was probably at this time and for many years the most trustworthy servant of the empire, was deputed to bring Khān Khānān back to court. There he was received by Jahāngīr with strong marks of disfavour in spite of the old bond of affection which

[1] See Vol. III, pp. 451–5.

had existed since he had been guardian and tutor to the emperor's youth.

These changes in the supreme command, though accompanied by reinforcements in men and money, were ineffectual against the difficulties of the country of which the defenders made the most by their strategy and tactics. Want of combination continued to mark the leadership on the imperial side. Affairs in Mewār had been sufficiently prosperous to justify the replacement of 'Abdullah Khān, who was also sent to the Deccan in 1611, though he had been appointed governor of Gujarāt. An enveloping movement was planned in which Khān Jahān and Rājā Mān Singh were to take the left or eastern side through Khāndesh and Berār while 'Abdullah Khān advanced on the west. Eager to obtain the whole credit for himself, 'Abdullah Khān rashly pressed on through Nāsik with inadequate scouting and failed to keep touch with the other army though pressed by Rājā Mān Singh to make a concerted plan. Marāthā skirmishers harassed his forces by day and night, acting as a screen to hide the concentration by Malik 'Ambar of a large force. Though he penetrated the Ahmadnagar country as far as Daulatābād, his forces had suffered so much that in the absence of reinforcements he was forced to retire, and withdrew to Gujarāt sustaining heavy losses so long as he was within hostile territory.

The Punjabi Rājā Basu, who had replaced 'Abdullah Khān in the Mewār campaign, had not been successful in it, as might have been anticipated from his previous history. He had several times revolted during Akbar's reign, and had supported Salīm in his attempt to seize the throne. Apart from the Mewār campaign and the unsatisfactory operations in the Deccan the country was generally quiet. In 1610 a man who pretended that he was Khusrav, and to support his claim pointed to certain marks round his eyes alleged to be the result of an attempt to blind him (see p. 158), had seized Patna during the absence of the governor, but the rebellion was soon quelled. The Afghāns of Bengal had also given trouble. A Persian adventurer called 'Alī Qulī, after rendering good military service, had been attracted to Salīm's staff, and was rewarded by the title of Sher Afgan (tiger-slayer) for his gallant conduct during a hunting expedition. Though he had resumed his allegiance to Akbar after first joining in Salīm's revolt he had been forgiven by Jahāngīr on his accession and appointed to an office in Bengal. In 1607 he was suspected of complicity with the Afghāns and Qutb-ud-dīn, the foster-brother of Jahāngīr who had been appointed successor to Rājā Mān Singh as governor of Bengal, was directed to send him to court. Sher Afgan appeared before the governor and was at once surrounded by guards. Impelled either by apprehension for his own life, or by the knowledge of his own guilt, he immediately attacked Qutb-ud-dīn, wounding him mortally, and was cut to pieces on the spot.

Another successor died and Islām Khān became governor with a mission to subdue the Afghāns. Chief among these was 'Usmān Khān, a fat heavy man who went to war on an elephant. In his memoirs Jahāngīr gives a spirited account of the fight in which Islām Khān's commander defeated and killed 'Usmān Khān and restored order (1612).

Jahāngīr now felt that he could leave the capital and be nearer the control of the campaign in Mewār. He also wished to visit the tomb of Khvāja Mu'īn-ud-dīn Chishtī at Ajmer, whom he regarded as a patron saint. Leaving Āgra in the autumn of 1613 he proceeded in a leisurely manner, hunting on the way. The ladies of the imperial zanana took advantage of a Hindu festival, the Dasahra, to reconcile him to Khusrav and it was arranged that father and son should meet daily. The Khān A'zam, who had seen no advantage to himself in the unsatisfactory position in the Deccan, had been transferred to Mewār, and at his request Jahāngīr also deputed his own son Khurram, Rājā Basu having died while the emperor was marching to Ajmer. This arrangement was not congenial to Khurram, who reported that Khān A'zam was unsatisfactory and was suspected of intrigues in favour of his son-in-law Khusrav. Jahāngīr was so impressed by these reports that he removed Khān A'zam from the command and made him over to the custody of Āsaf Khān with instructions that he should be kept in the fort of Gwalior, which had been the enforced residence of so many *détenus*. Jahāngīr also forbade Khusrav to come before him, as he had shown no signs of pleasure at seeing his father but preserved a sad attitude. Orders were issued that the Khān A'zam was to be treated well, but his children were kept under surveillance at the royal camp in Ajmer. Before long he was himself released and brought to court where he was allowed to stay on condition that he restrained his language.

Relieved of the presence of one whom he believed to be his enemy Khurram pressed on the occupation of Mewār, establishing posts in a number of places. And though losses were severe from the heat of the summer, the unhealthiness of the rainy season and even from dearth of supplies, the injury to the defenders was still greater. The families of many Rājput nobles were captured, and the fortitude of the Rānā himself, which had never been strong, was gradually sapped. He sent overtures to Khurram offering to recognise Mughul supremacy, but begging that he might be excused attendance at court owing to his age. Jahāngīr, delighted[1] by the success which had escaped his father, accepted the submission in a letter under his own seal, and invited the Rānā's son to visit him. It was decided that Chitor should never again be fortified, but no matrimonial alliance was enforced and the generally favourable nature of the terms allowed

[1] A coin struck at Ajmer about this time probably commemorates the victory. See Panna Lal, "A rare rupee of Jahāngīr", *J.A.S.B.* 1915, p. 483.

bound the Rājputs to a loyalty which was honourably observed. Before long the Rānā abdicated in favour of his son Karan Singh.

At this period (end of 1614) occurs the first mention of the English in the Mughul records. Hawkins had resided at Āgra as ambassador from the king of England during 1609–11 and had received a welcome, though he had been unable to negotiate a treaty.[1] The unruly behaviour of British shipwrecked sailors produced a bad impression, and trade facilities were denied. Sir Henry Middleton's action against the trading vessels from Gujarāt to the Red Sea (1612), however, created a spirit of respect, and the hope that the newcomers might be of assistance to check the claim of the Portuguese to command of the sea. The capture by the latter of four Indian ships with many Muslim passengers (1613) had been irritating as they were provided with a Portuguese pass, and Jahāngīr's mother had an interest in the cargo. A year later when Downton arrived off Surat he was pressed by Muqarrab Khān the governor, a Mughul officer who had been envoy to the Portuguese in 1607 and was in the close confidence of the emperor, to join against the Portuguese, who had been intriguing at court to get the English expelled from India. Though Muqarrab Khān promised concessions, Downton was not prepared to do more than defend himself, and Muqarrab Khān sent messages to the Dutch at Masulipatam. In January, 1615, the viceroy of Goa arrived with his fleet, having sent his smaller vessels ahead. Having no naval force, and no promise of help from the English or Dutch, the Mughul governor made overtures for peace, which were contemptuously rejected. The Portuguese, feeling sure of success in crushing the English, attacked Downton and were beaten off with great loss. They were afraid to land troops and attack Surat and withdrew to Goa. This action is mentioned with approval by Jahāngīr in his memoirs, though he passes over in silence the visit of Hawkins and his successor Sir Thomas Roe[2] who arrived in India in September, 1615. The effect of Downton's victory was by that time evaporating, and peace was being arranged between the Mughuls and the Portuguese. Prince Khurram, whose governorship included Surat, was in their favour and actually issued an order that the English should be allowed to trade for only a month and should have no residence, while the draft terms with the Portuguese stipulated that the English should be absolutely excluded. Roe's stout resistance to indignities and solicitations for bribes had some effect on the local authorities, and he proceeded to the royal court at Ajmer. For nearly three years he strove to obtain a trade treaty, following the court in its progress to Māndū and to Ahmadābād. By the emperor he was treated with the courtesy that was natural to him, but Jahāngīr

[1] See vol. v, chap. IV.

[2] He mentions the use of a carriage presented by Roe.

had no inclination to deal on terms of equality with a nation of which he knew nothing except that it desired Indian trade, and which was represented to him by the Portuguese in the worst possible light. Khurram was anxious that nothing should be done to detract from his authority over the port, and Āsaf Khān, who dealt with the draft treaties put forward by Roe, showed himself greedy for gifts and unreliable in every way. By September, 1618, Roe secured a *farmān* or grant from Khurram as viceroy of Gujarāt which, though not so complete as the draft treaty he had first tried to obtain from the emperor, gave reasonable facilities for trade, but it did not allow any building to be bought or built as a permanent residence. Beyond this Roe's stay at the court and behaviour there did much to enhance the respect with which the newcomers were regarded.

The chief power in the empire was now vested in the empress Nūr Jahān, who acted with her father I'timād-ud-daula, and brother Āsaf Khān. A legend grew up later that Jahāngīr had fallen in love with her in childhood, and had treated her husband as David dealt with Uriah. Contemporary history does not support this story,[1] which appears to have grown up long after her influence was established. When Sher Afgan was killed in 1607 his widow who was then styled Mihr-un-Nisa (Sun of womankind) was sent to court and became an attendant on Salīma Begam, the widow of Akbar. At the spring ceremony in March, 1611, Jahāngīr was attracted by her and married her two months later, changing her name to Nūr Mahall (Light of the palace). Her charm and beauty was equalled by her devotion to Jahāngīr and by her capability and tact, and her own influence over the emperor was immensely enhanced by the other members of her family. Rapid promotion was given to her father and brother, and her mother's discovery of the way to prepare attar of roses won the admiration of the aesthetically-minded emperor. A year after his own marriage Jahāngīr celebrated the wedding of his son Khurram with Arjumand Bānū, daughter of Āsaf Khān, thus cementing a link which bound Khurram to the leading spirits for many years. As the emperor's intellect deteriorated through his bodily indulgences and his concentration on pleasure, he was glad to leave to his wife and her advisers the task of deciding most affairs of state. His biographer records that he repeatedly said that he had bestowed the sovereignty on Nūr Jahān and for himself needed nothing but a quart of wine and a pound of flesh. Within a month of his arrival at the court at Ajmer, Roe discovered the power exercised by her and her clique. When his draft of a treaty was returned with alterations which he could not possibly accept he at first supposed that the lower officials were responsible. He soon found that Āsaf Khān was unreliable and had strong influence over Khurram. He writes bitterly:

[1] See Beni Prasād, *Jahāngīr*, chap. VIII.

The King was my only refuge, from whom I was sure of justice if I complayned, but I feard I should draw upon me the hate of Normall the beloved queene, ante to Sultan Corrons wife, sister of Asaph Chan, whose daughter the Prince married, and all that powerfull faction, against whom, though I might once prevayle, yet the advantage of tyme, language, and opportunitye, the power of a wife, sonne, and a favorite would produce revenge.

The power of the faction was not unchallenged, and its growth was extended over a long period by the gradual appointment of its nominees to offices of trust. Of the opponents Mahābat Khān was the most notable and he was left without promotion for twelve years, though he was one of the most capable men in the country. Persuasion rather than domination was the method first used with the emperor. One element in the policy was the support of Khurram as heir to the throne, and this led to opposition by those who preferred the elder son Khusrav. In spite of the two rebellions of which Khusrav was the nominal leader Jahāngīr never appears to have lost his affection for him, and popular sympathy was strong in his favour. Though his perpetual confinement gave him no opportunity of showing his capability in administration, his disposition was admired and his devotion to his only wife, the daughter of Khān A'zam, was well known. In October, 1616, an attempt was made to get the charge of Khusrav transferred from Ani Rāy, a brave and faithful Rājput attendant on the emperor, to Āsaf Khān, and Roe narrates that a verbal order was actually obtained late one night when Jahāngīr was intoxicated. Ani Rāy, who refused to comply, appeared at court the next day and was commended. A few days later when Khurram was about to proceed in person to conduct the Deccan campaign his fear for his interests during his absence led him to make another attempt which was successful, and caused great fears for Khusrav's own life. Roe gives a vivid report of the consternation in the women's quarters, where Khusrav's relations threatened to burn themselves if he were killed, and of the rumours that Khurram desired the death of his father as well as of his brother, and he compares the state of India to that of Rome during the contest between Otho and Vitellius related by Tacitus.[1] It appeared to Roe that the Company would do well to avoid siding in the quarrel, to make few debts and to limit their establishments in the country.

During his seven years' tenure of the office of governor of the Deccan prince Parvīz and the officers under him had made no progress in their campaigns. Like his father he was addicted to wine and he was fonder of pleasures than of his business. Jahāngīr, anxious to complete his conquest of the Deccan, transferred Parvīz to the easier charge of Allahābād in 1616 and sent in his place Khurram on whom he conferred the title of Shāh, while he himself moved his court to Māndū so as to be nearer the scene of operations. A graphic description of the luxury of his camp equipage, with the ladies of

[1] *Hist.* 1, 50.

the court riding in gold howdahs on 50 elephants, is given by Roe, whose meagre allowance from the Company did not permit him to buy or hire reasonable equipment. The route lay through difficult country where supplies were always, and water was sometimes, scarce, while the straggling cortège was often liable to be plundered by the inhabitants. In December, 1616, Roe saw a hundred corpses of people who had been executed for robbery, and in January he writes: "I am yet following this wandering King over mountaynes and through woods, so strange and unused wayes that his own people who almost know no other god, blaspheame his name and hers that (it is said) conducts all his actions." While he stayed at Ujjain the emperor took pleasure in a visit to a celebrated *faqīr* called Chid Rūp[1] who had met Akbar some 15 years earlier. In the sage's teaching of Vedānta philosophy Jahāngīr thought he recognised the germ of Sūfī mysticism. The slow march through country which presented many opportunities for the emperor's favourite pastime of hunting ended in March, 1617, when he arrived at Māndū, the old capital of the independent rulers of Mālwā.[2] The magnificent buildings of the Mālwā kings drew his admiration, while his disgust at the misdeeds of one of the most infamous led him to desecrate the tomb and have the remains cast in the Narbadā river which flows a few miles away. The difficulties of water supply on the rocky hill where the emperor resided were so great that it had to be purchased, and Roe considered himself lucky in finding a residence near an assured supply. Throughout the summer intrigues continued regarding the succession, and attempts were made to arrange a marriage between Khusrav and Nūr Jahān's daughter by her former husband Sher Afgan. The match would have been generally popular, and might have secured Khusrav's position, but he declined to accept it, through devotion to his only wife.

Meanwhile Khurram had succeeded in a few months by negotiation in settling the affairs of the Deccan more effectively than his brother had done in as many years. The degenerate rulers of the Deccan were weary of the struggle and some of their officials had been corrupted by bribes. Khurram's success in Mewār had enhanced his reputation. Ibrāhīm 'Ādil Shāh II the ruler of Bijāpur agreed to pay tribute and restore the conquered territory, including Ahmadnagar. Jahāngīr celebrated the peace by a magnificent reception in Māndū of the Bijāpur envoys and his son Khurram received the unique privilege of a seat in his father's presence. He also received the title of Shāh Jahān (Sovereign of the world) which he retained later when he succeeded his father on the throne. Roe, who was

[1] Sometimes incorrectly transliterated Jadrūp. For a contemporary picture see *J.R.A.S.* 1919, p. 389.

[2] See vol. III, chap. XIV, for a history of the dynasty, and G. Yazdani, *Mandu*, 1929, for a description of the place.

present, was rather contemptuous of the whole affair, and rightly guessed that the boasted victory was no more than the avoidance of future loss. Some element of personal disappointment tinges his comments, as he had hoped a few months earlier to sell Malik 'Ambar a quantity of the Company's cloth and swords which were not in demand elsewhere. But in fact the settlement advanced the Mughul power no further than it had stood when Akbar left the Deccan, and while the Muhammadan rulers were rapidly losing hold the Marāthās who formed the bulk of the population had begun to realise their own strength. There was no longer any need for the emperor to remain in the magnificent but uncomfortable surroundings of Māndū, and he decided to visit Gujarāt, where for the first time in his life he saw the sea. Throughout the journey Roe was endeavouring to negotiate with Āsaf Khān, thwarted perpetually by Shāh Jahān, who was against the English and constantly feared that any grant to them of rights of trade would derogate from his powers as viceroy. Roe also attempted to get the Portuguese expelled from Gujarāt, but the emperor told him that he proposed to maintain the arrangements with them that had been concluded by the former rulers of Gujarāt. A respect for the power of the Portuguese on the sea was still the deciding factor. It was not until the late autumn of 1618 that Roe finally concluded an agreement with Shāh Jahān, by which he obtained better terms than had first been offered, but not the complete freedom he desired. In particular the English were not allowed to purchase or construct their own residences,[1] though they were allowed to hire, and either the disorderly conduct of the sailors or fear of actual invasion led to restrictions on the carriage of arms. Jahāngīr with his zest for the amenities of life was disgusted with the climate and scenery of Ahmadābād. He records that he did not know whether to call it Samūmistān (the place of hot winds), Bīmāristān (the abode of sickness), Zaqqūm zār (the thorn or cactus bed) or Jahannumābād (the house of hell). His reference to disease is illustrated by the descriptions of a mysterious pestilence at Ahmadābād the exact nature of which cannot be identified. It was characterised by a very high temperature and the appearance on the body of large dark-coloured blisters the matter from which produced others. Death ensued in a few hours and even the small English community lost seven members. Both the emperor and Shāh Jahān were attacked but recovered after a lengthy convalescence. There was nothing to detain the court in western India. Two chiefs in Cutch, the Jām of Navānagar and a lesser chief on the borders of Sind, had been reduced by Rājā Bikramājīt in 1617. Jahāngīr therefore set out for Āgra in the rainy season, and during the leisurely march of the court, a son was born to Shāh Jahān's wife, who was named

[1] The landing of a few bricks for recasting the broken bell of a ship caused rumours that they had projected the building of a fort.

Aurangzīb and later became emperor. Another epidemic now threatened the court and prevented its entry into Delhi. This, from the description given by contemporary writers, was clearly bubonic plague, as they describe the characteristic mortality among rats and the appearance of swellings in the neck and groin. It had broken out in the Punjab in 1616 and had spread south and east as far as Āgra, where it was still causing 100 deaths a day early in 1619, so that Jahāngīr on arriving at Fathpur Sīkrī remained there till April.[1] During the halt at that place Nūr Jahān distinguished herself by killing a tiger with one shot.

Jahāngīr's intemperance had now begun to tell seriously on his health, which had also suffered from the climate of the districts in which he had spent the last five years. The advice of his physicians, supported by the influence of his wife, induced him to reduce his potations, but a permanent cure was not within his power. During his journey to Kābul in 1606 the crossing of the Jhelum river had reminded him of two visits he had paid to Kashmīr in his father's lifetime, and he had recorded a wish that he might visit that lovely tract in the spring. Hoping that he might recover his health in more pleasing conditions, he left Āgra at the end of 1619 and spent the whole of the following summer in the hills. The ascent by the rough tracks which had to be followed was difficult, and on one day, after a fall of snow, as many as twenty-five elephants were lost.

As the royal train penetrated higher into the mountains it had to divide into parties, because supplies could not be brought together for the whole retinue. Arrived in the vale of Kashmīr Jahāngīr was able to indulge his love of nature, and the journal is full of well-phrased descriptions of the meadows abounding in wild flowers, the stately trees, the springs, cascades and the brooks starting from these and swelling into majestic rivers, or expanding into picturesque lakes. On this and his many succeeding visits he planned and carried out the construction of houses and gardens, some of which still exist. While the emperor thus found new pleasures to distract his mind from his failing health his court, from the highest nobles to the meanest servant, suffered from bad lodging, from the inclemency of the weather to which they were not accustomed, and from the dearness and scarcity of food.

The emperor was met at Srīnagar by the governor of Kashmīr, who had just succeeded after prolonged efforts in taking a small tract in the south of Kashmīr, known as Kishtwār, and who brought the raja in chains. Misrule and oppression by the official in charge, however, led to a revolt by the high-spirited inhabitants, who were not finally subdued for a couple of years.

A greater triumph was the conquest of Kāngra, a state protected

[1] The disease, being carried as is now known by the flea which infests rats, usually decreases as the hot season advances, because the people sleep outside their houses.

by many strong forts and containing the ancient shrine of Jwālāmukhi with its natural fire. The temple, enriched by many precious gifts from its devotees, had been plundered by Mahmūd of Ghaznī in 1009, but in spite of many attempts by the later rulers of Delhi, including Akbar, the fort of Kāngra had still held out, though the hill-country round it had been largely subdued. Efforts made under the orders of Jahāngīr himself to subdue this stronghold had failed, in some cases owing to the omission to press an attack by the commander, who really sympathised with the holders and finally broke into rebellion. Rājā Bikramājīt, who was then sent to command, crushed the revolt and after a close siege for more than a year during which the garrison was nearly starved, the fort surrendered towards the end of 1620, just after the emperor had started for the plains. Apart from the booty secured the capture had no political value, but it gave Jahāngīr exquisite pleasure that his forces had succeeded where so many of his predecessors had failed.

The failing health of the emperor, while it added to the influence of Nūr Jahān over the affairs of state, also increased her apprehension of diminished power if he should die. Of all Jahāngīr's sons Shāh Jahān was most to be feared, as Khusrav though more popular was still a prisoner and untried in public affairs. She now decided to arrange a marriage between Lādlī Begam, her daughter by her former husband, Sher Afgan, and Jahāngīr's youngest surviving son, Shahryār, whose mother had been a concubine, and who was then an immature young man with dissolute inclinations. The formal betrothal took place at Lahore, to be followed by a wedding at Āgra.

While Jahāngīr had been seeking health in Kashmīr the position on the southern frontier had deteriorated. Malik 'Ambar, ever restless and intriguing on behalf of his master, had again reconciled the kings of Bijāpur and Golconda and pursued his recruiting among the Marāthās. The Mughul governor was besieged in Ahmadnagar and the high commanders were quarrelling. They might succeed in pitched battles but lost ground after each and were so harried by marauding bands that they were forced to fall back on Burhānpur, which was beset, and even Māndū was not safe. The emperor, in reply to the pressing demands for reinforcements, appointed Shāh Jahān to command them, but progress was delayed by the fact that so many troops had been sent on the futile expedition against Kāngra. Shāh Jahān, himself, realising the uncertainties of the position at court, insisted on having charge of his elder brother Khusrav, and when Jahāngīr had at last acceded to this the two brothers left their father at Lahore (1620) and never saw him again. The expedition was successful in its immediate objects. One division which was detached to relieve Māndū soon scattered the Marāthās who were laying waste the country round, while Shāh Jahān forced the armies round Burhānpur to withdraw, and thus relieved the garrison which had been practically beleaguered for two years and had been greatly straitened for food and supplies. Before long the imperial troops had penetrated as far south as Khirkī, where the Nizāmshāhī rulers had established their headquarters after Ahmadnagar had been incorporated in the imperial dominions. Here they demolished the new buildings of the capital and set out to raise the siege of Ahmadnagar. By this time Malik 'Ambar, who had removed his royal master and his family for safety to Daulatābād, realised that his position was insecure. He offered terms and Shāh Jahān, already anxious about arrangements for the supply of food for his large army in a tract which had been devastated and plundered, agreed to treat. Besides restoring the territory which had previously become Mughul, the insurgents agreed to give a strip fourteen *kos* (25 to 28 miles) wide, and a tribute of five million rupees from the three kingdoms of Bijāpur, Ahmadnagar and Golconda. The rainy season of 1621 being now over he returned to Burhānpur and occupied himself with reorganising the administration which had been dislocated by two years' warfare. The rejoicing over this victory which delighted the emperor, and prompted him to reward generously those who had taken part in it, was marred by his illness. As he frankly admits in his memoirs, he indulged more frequently in liquor, and suffered for it, till the empress gradually persuaded him to reduce his potations and adapt his diet to his condition. In October he travelled to the upper courses of the Ganges to seek a place with a suitable climate where he might build a new city and avoid the trying heat of Āgra. He found Hardwār not pleasant, and decided to visit Jammū and Kāngra. Leaving the bulk of his great camp in the plains he had started for the hills when he was recalled by grave news about the health of I'timād-ud-daula, who was advanced in years and had been left behind ill. Both the emperor and empress returned and were present when he died. In spite of their earlier disagreements reconciliation had been effected and Jahāngīr mourned the loss of an able and faithful minister, and a wise and kind friend. He was then free to visit Kāngra and rejoice over his capture of that ancient place. To celebrate the achievement he took with him persons learned in the law of Islām and after prayers formally desecrated the temple by sacrificing a cow.

Suddenly, however, great sorrow came upon him by receipt of the news that Khusrav, who in spite of his two rebellions was still his favourite son, had died at Burhānpur (January, 1622). The cause of his death has never been established beyond doubt.[1] Shāh Jahān, in reporting it, said his brother had died of colic. It is significant that the emperor, who usually added comments when recording deaths, passes over this almost in silence. Local rumour, as recorded by the

[1] H. Beveridge, *J.R.A.S.* 1907, p. 597, held that murder was not proved. Beni Prasād, *Jahāngīr*, p. 336, after fully reviewing the evidence, thought it certain.

English factors in the neighbourhood, definitely assigned the cause to murder and the probability of this is strengthened by Shāh Jahān's later action.

Overshadowed by this event, the new year of the reign brought news of trouble on the western frontier. Shāh 'Abbās, king of Persia, had from time to time sent ambassadors to Jahāngīr professing friendship. One of these arrived at Ajmer in 1616 when Roe was at the court. Although Roe thought this envoy's behaviour servile, and not becoming the representative of an independent monarch, he recognised the difference between the reception of the Persian and his own treatment, and regretted that he himself was unable to offer such magnificent gifts as had been sent from Isfahān. Jahāngīr's estimate of the relative importance of the two envoys appears from the elaborate account in the memoirs of the Persian and a full transcription of the message which he brought, while the English ambassador is not mentioned. Moreover, a Mughul representative was sent to Persia in return and there received a gracious welcome. This exchange of courtesies was a mere cloak to hide designs of aggression by Shāh 'Abbās, and after a fourth embassy arrived at the end of 1620 the garrison of Qandahār fell to a few hundred soldiers, the main forces of the empire being collected in the Deccan. The city was important owing to its command of the land route to Persia on which the bulk of the trade between that country and India was still carried, and its possession was also a matter of pride since its capture by Akbar. News of the collection of a Persian force had been received and Shāh Jahān, the only commander who had been successful in recent years, was directed to take an army to defend the frontier. Before anything could be done the fort was beleaguered and it was reported that another army was marching on Sind. Great preparations were made to collect troops and the vast quantity of supplies required for an army in a tract the products of which barely support a thin population. A proposal by the officer in immediate command to take what forces were ready was not accepted as the emperor hoped to collect an army which could advance as far as Isfahān, the capital of Persia. His hopes had been stimulated by the offer of help from Imām Qulī, the ruler of Samarqand, who sent an envoy suggesting the recapture of Qandahār and an expedition against Khurāsān. The project, however, was not immediately accepted by Shāh Jahān. He despatched part of his camp from Burhānpur at once, but did not advance beyond Māndū, where he proposed to stay during the rainy season, and he demanded that when he took over charge of the campaign he should be allowed to have the fort of Rantambhor[1] for the residence of his family and should be sole commander, and also governor of the Punjab. Jealousy of the power of his stepmother Nūr Jahān, and anticipations of her

[1] In Rājputāna, where Shāh Jahān could count on strong support.

probable support of Shahryār's claim to the throne if the emperor died, were no doubt the cause of these requests, which were not granted. Jahāngīr sent orders that as Shāh Jahān did not wish to move till after the rains he should at once despatch the principal officers and the best of the troops including the Sayyids of Bārha and Bukhārā, the Shaikhzādas, the Afghāns and the Rājputs.

Almost immediately a fresh cause of dissension occurred owing to a dispute about the grant of Dholpur as an assignment. It was claimed by both Shāh Jahān and Shahryār and a fight took place between the officers of the brothers over its possession. Though Jahāngīr with his usual patience again wrote to his son he was soon persuaded not to accept his excuses. Shahryār was appointed to command the Qandahār forces and a further indignity was inflicted on Shāh Jahān by the transfer of his *jāgīrs* in the Punjab to Shahryār. Shāh Jahān's humble submission, presented through his most trusted officer, was rejected and he openly rebelled and marched towards Āgra, where the governor held back the treasure collected for the expedition and prepared for a siege. Interest rather than loyalty seems to have guided the action of the generals; thus the empress' brother Āsaf Khān abandoned the cause of his son-in-law the rebel who was, however, supported by Khān Khānān just as he had once sided with Jahāngīr in the rebellion against Akbar, and by many of those who had held office in the Deccan and in Gujarāt.

Mahābat Khān, the most capable soldier in the imperial forces, had for some years been governor of Kābul and had kept order in that difficult province. He was now summoned to take command, and after some demur, owing to his suspicions of Āsaf Khān whom he rightly believed to be his enemy, was persuaded to accept the post by the formal appointment of Āsaf Khān to Bengal. Shāh Jahān was unable to capture the fort of Āgra with its treasure, but plundered the city which had no walls. He then marched north to meet his father's army, and though he was successful in detaching 'Abdullah Khān, who came over with a large force during the battle, he was decisively beaten at Bilochpur (March, 1623), and lost Rājā Bikramājīt, one of his best commanders.

Shāh Jahān then retreated to Māndū, and was followed by his brother Parvīz, who was in nominal command, while his nephew Dāwar Bakhsh, son of Khusrav, marched towards Ahmadābād, the capital of Gujarāt, which had been committed to his charge. The emperor himself proceeded to Ajmer to be nearer the operations. The hot weather was now advanced and rainy weather made fighting difficult. Shāh Jahān's attempts to use Marāthā horse were ineffective and Mahābat Khān successfully intrigued to detach support from him. In a battle near Kaliya Dih some of the prince's soldiers deserted him, and he withdrew south across the Narbadā. An intercepted letter from the Khān Khānān to Mahābat Khān showed that treachery was everywhere. Though the strong fortress of Asīr yielded to him, his trusted officers in Gujarāt failed him, and 'Abdullah Khān, who was sent to restore his power in Gujarāt, was defeated near Ahmadābād, and finally had to join Shāh Jahān at Burhānpur with the small amount of money he was able to raise at Surat. The rebel was now reduced to pitiable devices. Malik 'Ambar, whom he had twice defeated, refused aid as he was himself gathering forces to attack Bijāpur. An envoy sent to Golconda had no greater success. In despair Shāh Jahān decided to approach his father, and sent Khān Khānān to Mahābat Khān after taking from him the most solemn oath of faithfulness. A casual skirmish on the banks of the Narbadā led to further defections from the force guarding the crossing, and Khān Khānān when he arrived at the imperial camp, disregarding his solemn pledge, offered his own submission to Parvīz. Flight was inevitable and hotly pursued for some distance in spite of the rainy season Shāh Jahān escaped into the kingdom of Golconda losing adherents on almost every march. From the king he received no more help than was sufficient to enable him to traverse the kingdom under a promise to leave it. The passage of his force, though reduced in numbers, alarmed the people, and the English factors at Masulipatam tried to get away. Better hopes were held of success in Bengal and Shāh Jahān marched into Orissa, which was surrendered by the local authorities without a struggle. Burdwān was taken by siege, but Ibrāhīm Khān (a brother of Nūr Jahān) refused to surrender his fort near Akbarnagar, backed by the help of Portuguese gunners from Hūglī who had rejected overtures from the rebel after the fall of Burdwān as they had little hopes of his success. In a battle outside the fort Ibrāhīm Khān was defeated and killed and the fort was mined and stormed. Emboldened by this success Shāh Jahān advanced up the Ganges valley. Kunwar Bhīm Singh of Mewār, who had been his most faithful ally, entered Patna without opposition and thus secured Bihār. When Shāh Jahān arrived the principal landholders, including the chief of the Ujjainiya Rājputs,[1] submitted to him, and the strong fortress of Rohtās was surrendered. One division of the force now occupied Jaunpur and advanced to Mānikpur while 'Abdullah Khān laid siege to Allahābād which was bravely defended by Mīrzā Rustam Beg, a Persian of royal blood. Shāh Jahān entered Benares and crossed the Ganges to Kantit[2] on the south side. By this time, however, Parvīz and Mahābat Khān, after securing peace in the Deccan by an alliance with Bijāpur, had arrived in the Dūāb. They had difficulty in crossing the river as Shāh Jahān's forces had seized all boats, but were finally helped by the Bais Rājputs.[3] The rebels retreated and were defeated

[1] Now represented by the Mahārājā of Dumrāon.
[2] Sometimes wrongly transliterated as Kampat.
[3] In what are now the Unao and Rae Barelī districts.

in a fiercely contested battle at Damdama[1] (1624) which completely destroyed their hopes, though at one time Shāh Jahān had nearly won the day, when a wounded elephant threw his army into confusion. Bhīm Singh was slain and Shāh Jahān who was himself present would in his despair have fought till killed if his followers had not seized his bridle and turned his horse away. He rode hastily to Rohtās where his wife had just borne a son (Murād Bakhsh) and leaving her there retreated to Bengal. Dārāb Khān, son of Khān Khānān, who had been left in command there, now failed him as his father had done, but met the death his treachery had earned, on the arrival of Mahābat Khān, though Khān Khānān himself was forgiven by the emperor and restored to rank and office.

Shāh Jahān, at the beginning of his rebellion, had been stigmatised by Jāhangīr as *Be-daulat* (infelix) and as he made his toilsome journey back to the Deccan felt the truth of the epithet. On arriving there he found conditions slightly more favourable. The alliance between Bijāpur and the Mughuls, concluded before Parvīz proceeded north to meet Shāh Jahān, had stimulated Malik 'Ambar to fresh intrigues with Golconda. A division of Bijāpur troops had joined the imperial headquarters at Burhānpur during the absence of Parvīz and Mahābat Khān, and Malik 'Ambar invaded Bijāpur territory, defeated the forces that tried to stop him and invested Bijāpur itself. Reinforced by part of the imperial army the Bījāpur division returned and forced Malik 'Ambar back to his own country. His efforts to persuade the imperial troops to stand aside and leave him to settle his own quarrels failed. He then made an unexpected attack on the combined forces and scattering them completely laid siege at first to Ahmadnagar and then again to Bijāpur, overrunning the whole of the Bālāghāt.[2] A year before he had declined to help Shāh Jahān, but now he offered him assistance and was glad to use him as commander of a force to attack Burhānpur itself, with 'Abdullah Khān as one of his chief officers. The fort was actually penetrated but the defenders still held out till Parvīz and Mahābat Khān returned from the Dūāb, when the siege was raised. Shāh Jahān, sick in body and despairing of success after so many failures, withdrew towards Berār. 'Abdullah Khān, the chief of the captains who had survived the recent campaigns, became a religious recluse at Indūr (now Nizāmābād) but retained sufficient interest in worldly affairs to send his submission to court. His other allies being dead or deserters Shāh Jahān saw no alternative but to seek pardon from his father. Nūr Jahān, who had become practically supreme, exacted terms which though rigorous were not excessive either as a punishment for rebellion or to safeguard the emperor

[1] A village in the Allahābād district near the junction of the Tons and Ganges.

[2] A name given to several elevated tracts in central and southern India. Here it refers to the hilly country in the western part of the present Hyderābād state.

against further attempts. Shāh Jahān was to give up the two forts of Rohtās in Bihār and Asīr in Khāndesh, which were still held by his adherents, and to send to court two of his sons, Dārā and Aurangzīb, who were still boys. He accepted the terms and was formally appointed governor of the Bālāghāt, a tract at a safe distance from the capital, and one in which the proximity of dangerous enemies might tend to keep him occupied.

Qandahār had been lost after a short siege at the beginning of the rebellion (June, 1622) and there was no hope or even talk of regaining it. Jahāngīr had become incapable of any mental exertion and by the end of 1624 had even discontinued writing his memoirs. Most of the elder generals were dead or in disgrace, and the only capable member of the royal family was banished. No internal disturbances threatened the crown, but the question of succession which could not long be deferred was ever present in the mind of the empress. Mahābat Khān with Parvīz the eldest prince had established some prestige by his successes against Shāh Jahān, and the first desirable object appeared to be to separate them. Parvīz was destitute of either ability or character and was easily induced to accept the government of Gujarāt, with Khān Jahān as his commander. Āsaf Khān's old enmity with Mahābat Khān prompted the appointment of the latter to the undesirable post of governor in Bengal. To embarrass him still further demands were made that he should despatch to court the elephants and treasure which he had captured during the rebellion, and as he did not at once comply an envoy was sent to recover them and to summon him to court. Of his cruelty and excesses in that country there was much evidence and complainants flocking to court had excited the emperor's compassion.

Early in March, 1626, Jahāngīr started for Kābul and Mahābat Khān arrived when the royal camp was on the banks of the Jhelum river. He had come fully prepared to protect himself against hostile designs, bringing with him four or five thousand loyal Rājput soldiers, and to make even more certain of their allegiance he took their wives and families whose honour and life would be at stake if they failed him. A fresh charge was now brought that he had arranged for the marriage of his son without consulting the emperor, and Jahāngīr was easily induced to order the treatment of the son with gross indignity, while Mahābat Khān was directed to remain in the camp but not to show himself at court unless specially summoned. With incredible disregard of the consequences of such insults Āsaf Khān took across the river almost the whole camp, leaving the emperor and empress with only a few attendants. Mahābat Khān, feeling he had no ally in court, now made a desperate attempt to secure the person of the emperor. He collected his Rājput troops, and placed a couple of thousand at the head of the bridge of boats with orders to burn it rather than to allow any one to come back across it.

Proceeding with a small body-guard to the royal tents he forced his way into the state apartment and, brushing aside the chamberlain, tried to enter the private tent. As his men were tearing down the boards which protected it the emperor came out with a few servants, and as the chronicle relates "twice placed his hand on his sword to cleanse the world from the filthy existence of that foul dog". He was dissuaded from using force and at Mahābat Khān's suggestion mounted a horse, and later an elephant, as if to go hunting. Trusted Rājputs were placed in the howdah with him, and he was taken to Mahābat Khān's tents. The rebel had acted on sudden impulse and in his distracted haste forgot to secure the empress also. He had managed the abduction of the emperor so rapidly that Nūr Jahān crossed the river to the main camp believing that Jahāngīr had gone hunting as usual. There she discovered what had happened and reproached her brother Āsaf Khān and the other nobles. They decided to attack the traitor and release the emperor next day, though a message was received from him that they should not attempt it. Mahābat Khān, though he had missed seizing the empress, secured Shahryār, burned the bridge and posted his Rājputs along the bank. Next day, when the attack was launched it failed completely owing to the absence of leadership among the members of the queen's faction.

One small party did indeed succeed in crossing and reached the tents of Shahryār, where their arrows actually fell in the courtyard near the apartments of the emperor himself, but this was an isolated effort. Nūr Jahān crossed a branch of the river, urging on the laggards. Her elephant was wounded and an arrow pierced the arm of either Shahryār's infant daughter or the nurse who were with her in the howdah, and she was forced to withdraw. Āsaf Khān fled to his fort at Attock on the Indus and the other high officials either followed his example or made their peace with Mahābat Khān, who now became dictator. A short siege of Attock and the promise of his life effected the submission of Āsaf Khān, who became nominally reconciled, though many of his followers were executed.

In May, 1626, Kābul was reached, and Mahābat Khān's influence soon began to wane. His ability was that of a soldier rather than that of a statesman, and even during the excitement of his *coup d'état* he had shown weaknesses and lapses of judgement. None of the other officers of state really sided with him and he had neither friend nor counsellor at court. Trouble arose over a petty squabble in a royal game reserve where some of the Rājput soldiers had taken horses to graze. One of the guards was killed and the others were not satisfied by the action taken in consequence. An attack was organised on the Rājputs in which 800 or 900 of them were slain, and this was followed by a general rising of the Afghāns which seriously depleted Mahābat Khān's only reliable force. Nūr Jahān's intrigues against him increased though the emperor still continued, either through guile or the foolish loquacity of a drunkard, to express confidence in him.

In November, 1626, the court moved from Kābul and on the way plans were perfected to break the power of the dictator. Orders were still issued in the name of Jahāngīr, who sent word to Mahābat Khān, a day's march from Rohtās, that he was going to hold a review of the imperial troops and Mahābat Khān would be well advised to take his own forces a stage ahead to avoid the possibility of a collision. He had now realised that his influence had faded beyond the hope of revival, and he marched hurriedly towards Lahore, being careful to take with him as hostages Āsaf Khān with a son and two nephews of Jahāngīr. Under pressure from Nūr Jahān Mahābat sent back first the princes, then Āsaf Khān and later the son, and he marched east hoping to secure a large remittance of treasure which was on its way from Bengal.

The growth of the intrigue against Mahābat Khān had been fostered by news of the death of Malik 'Ambar about the time that Jahāngīr reached Kābul. He was the ablest man of the period, distinguished alike in the strategic conduct of a campaign, in the tactics of a battle, or during times of peace in the administration of a kingdom. His death appeared to free the emperor from menaces in the south. One of his officers who succeeded him as commander soon offered allegiance to the empire through Khān Jahān, the governor who was now in sole charge at Burhānpur, as Parvīz had died from the effects of constant intoxication (October, 1626). The titular king of Ahmadnagar had, however, come under the influence of a woman employed in his harem who pandered to his depraved passions, and obtained great influence over him. Her husband Hamīd Khān, like Malik 'Ambar, was a capable Abyssinian slave. When the king assumed a hostile attitude and drew the imperial forces to attack him, Hamīd Khān offered a large bribe which Khān Jahān accepted. The commandants in the territory of Bālāghāt (see p. 173) were ordered to evacuate their posts and most of them complied and withdrew to Burhānpur, but the garrison at Ahmadnagar still held out in the absence of orders from the emperor.

Shāh Jahān, after his submission, had remained in the Deccan[1] till he heard of Mahābat Khān's seizure of the emperor. He suggested to Khān Jahān his intention of proceeding to the assistance of his father, but received no support. Collecting a small force he marched north, avoiding Burhānpur where Parvīz still lay ill. When he reached

[1] According to Rājput tradition he was sheltered for a time at Udaipur, where the beautiful marble residence constructed for him still exists. The tradition is confirmed by an inscription dated A.D. 1675 (*Annual Report, Rājputānā Museum*, p. 2).

Ajmer Kishan Singh, son of his old ally Rājā Bhīm Singh, died and the small body of Rājput horse commanded by Kishan Singh fell back to their homes. As no reinforcements joined him he turned north-west through the desert country and made for Tatta in Sind.

In spite of the Persian capture of Qandahār, Shāh Jahān had retained friendly relations with the Shāh and he now hoped that if he could get to Persia he might be well received. His progress was delayed by the governor of Tatta, who was a partisan of Shahryār and collected a large force to resist him. Shāh Jahān's followers, however, attacked the fort against his orders and were easily repulsed. A letter from Nūr Jahān now warned him that Mahābat Khān's influence had been broken. He himself was in poor health, and the news of Parvīz's serious illness and his own want of troops induced him to fall back. Borne in a litter he withdrew through Gujarāt to Nāsik, hearing of his brother's death on the way. Mahābat Khān had, in fact, been ordered to proceed to Tatta to repel Shāh Jahān's designs on that place, and had omitted to comply as he wished to intercept the Bengal treasure. Failing in this design he took refuge in Mewār and offered his services to Shāh Jahān, whom he joined at Junnar with about 2000 troops. Though these two were the most competent commanders in the empire their resources were for the time being exhausted and during the few months that remained of the emperor's life they were content to await the course of events. Khān Jahān, who had already betrayed his trust, was not disposed to take any action against them, though warned by Nūr Jahān to be on his guard.

Early in the spring of 1627 Jahāngīr left Lahore to spend his last summer in Kashmīr, the part of India which was his favourite place of residence. This year its invigorating climate failed to restore him, and the rarefied atmosphere at a high altitude increased the sufferings of one affected by asthma. He grew weaker daily, and was unable to ride. As his infirmities increased he lost his appetite for food and even his taste for opium, in which he had indulged for many years. Instead of the heavy daily drinking which had been his practice he now took only a few cups of wine with no spirits. Shahryār also suffered from a disease which caused complete loss of hair, and his unsightly appearance was regarded as a mark of dishonour so that he took advantage of the physicians' suggestion that he might be better in the warmer climate of Lahore.

As autumn approached the sick emperor moved slowly down through the mountains. At one place his love of sport revived and he sat with his gun resting on a wall while the beaters drove the game up to him. He wounded a stag and a soldier who followed it slipped and was dashed to pieces at the foot of a precipice. This accident greatly shocked the dying ruler who felt that he had seen the angel of death. He could get no rest or ease and though he was carried two stages further the attempt to make a third march exhausted him and he died early next morning (7 November, 1627). His body was then taken to Lahore and buried in the garden outside the city where a noble tomb was built later by his widow.

During the first seventeen years of his reign Jahāngīr himself maintained a record of events, and when failing health prevented him from still writing this, it was carried on under his direct supervision. Although the memoirs are not a confidential record of human aspirations, fears and hopes, and are not remarkable for the shrewdness of their assessment of passing events, they are of great value in estimating the character of their author. Jahāngīr shows himself a man of wide interests, but these are devoted more to material objects and to the rare, novel or curious element, than to the intellectual. He thus presents a marked contrast to his father, who though entirely illiterate, and occupied throughout his reign with great enterprises and administrative reforms, was constantly engaged in discussing the basis of religion and took more pleasure in hearing the debates of learned men than in the beauties of nature or art.

Jahāngīr's love of natural beauty was genuine and his aesthetic sense sometimes widens and almost expands into a spirit of scientific enquiry, which was, however, cramped by the empirical doctrines of his time and country. He made an arduous journey through the mountain passes to Kashmīr to enjoy a view of the spring flowers there and during repeated visits recorded the names of the animals, birds and flowers he saw, distinguishing those which are not found in the plains of India. Occasionally he would have a bird or animal dissected and note the peculiarities observed. But when it was found that the gall bladder of a lion was enclosed in the liver his deduction was that the courage of the lion might be due to this cause. More wisdom appears in his suggestion that the sweetness of camel's milk might be due to the nature of its food, and he made experiments in breeding wild birds in captivity. In art his favourite branch was painting, which rose during his reign, owing to his patronage, to its highest state. Mughul pictures were developed from the Safavid type of Persian art, modified by Indian influence and to some extent by the study of European pictures.[1] Jahāngīr constantly notes that he had rare birds or animals painted, and his remarks about his own excellence as a connoisseur are valuable not only for the light they throw on his tastes and character, but also for their explanation of the composite work performed by Indian artists:

> As regards myself, my liking for painting and my practice in judging it have arrived at such a point that when any work is brought before me, either of deceased artists or of the present day, without the names being told me, I say on the spur of the moment that it is the work of such and such a man. And if there

[1] V. A. Smith, *History of Fine Art in India*, 1930, p. 215.

be a picture containing many portraits, and each face be the work of a different master, I can discover which face is the work of each. If any other person has put in the eye and eye-brow of a face I can perceive whose work the original face is and who has painted the eye and eyebrows.[1]

When Sir Thomas Roe presented to him an English miniature, the emperor offered to wager that a court painter would copy it so exactly that Roe would be unable to distinguish the original, and the ambassador had in fact to scrutinise the pictures carefully.[2]

Jahāngīr had less interest in architecture, and though he would admire a beautiful building he was usually content to order a construction and leave the execution to his architect, unlike his son who busied himself with every detail. He did, however, alter the design of Akbar's magnificent tomb at Sikandra, which he rebuilt after three years' work had already been done on it. This lofty building of red stone, composed of five square terraces relieved by cupolas, resembles a pavilion in Akbar's palace at Fathpur Sīkrī. While the stone of the fabric is varied only by coloured tiles and some marble inlay, the top story is an open court of white marble, in the centre of which is a cenotaph richly carved and bearing Akbar's religious formula and the ninety-nine attributes of God.

The tomb of I'timād-ud-daula near Āgra, built under the direction of his daughter the empress, is of a totally different style, being constructed entirely of white marble, adorned with mosaic work outside and richly painted inner walls and ceilings. At Lahore Jahāngīr directed the construction of a great mosque, which rivals that built by his son at Delhi, and he also adorned the fort with palace buildings which have recently been restored after suffering much dilapidation during Sikh and early British rule. The enamelled tile panelling on the walls of the fort which covers about 8000 square yards and on a mosque built by Vazīr Khān is very remarkable. While the memoirs indicate that Jahāngīr left others to plan the buildings he required, they show that he took great delight in the arrangement of gardens in Kashmīr and elsewhere.

His artistic tastes led him to adorn the currency with the finest calligraphic designs which have appeared on Indian coins. Akbar had introduced new denominations, and Jahāngīr went further and raised the standard weight of the gold and silver units immediately after his succession. This change, which had no economic basis, was no improvement and was cancelled after five years. The *ilāhī* system of reckoning which had been started by Akbar was maintained in the records of the reign, though the lunar system was partly restored in the coinage. In spite of the prohibitions of Islām against the representation of human or animal life the emperor was bold enough to

[1] *Memoirs*, translated by Rogers and Beveridge, II, 20.

[2] A beautiful copy by an Indian painter of a picture by Bihzād the celebrated Persian artist, certified by the autograph of Jahāngīr, was lent by the Gulistān Museum, Teheran, to the Persian exhibition in London, 1931. See Catalogue No. 498.

strike medals and coins on which his portrait was stamped. Roe tells us that one of these was presented to him and he was instructed by Āsaf Khān to wear it round his neck, while Austin of Bordeaux wore one on his hat. One type of this coin even shows the emperor with a drinking cup in his hand.[1] In 1618 Jahāngīr decided to substitute the figure of the zodiacal sign for the name of the month in which a coin was struck, and with his usual naïve conceit adds in his memoirs: "This usage is my own, and has never been practised until now."[2] A further innovation was the issue of coins bearing the name of the empress Nūr Jahān, and various legends grew up that she was responsible for the beautiful zodiacal issue. The coinage of Nūr Jahān is, however, limited to only a few years, during which she was at the zenith of her power, and it was struck only at places where her adherents in the struggle for power were in authority.[3] Jahāngīr had called his gold coins of the heavy standard *nūr-jahāni*, and this probably added to the confusion of thought.

Jahāngīr was well versed in Persian literature and occasionally composed himself. His memoirs contain many references to verses he admired for their beauty, wit or aptness to a special occasion. An attendant at court who discovered that the numerical values in Arabic notation of the letters in the name of the emperor and in the phrase *Allahu Akbar* were equal was rewarded and a couplet recording the fact was placed on the coins with a bacchanalian effigy. A poet, Nāsirī of Nīshāpur, "who excelled other men in the art of poetry", was attracted to the Indian court. Jahāngīr's love of nature led him to admire the description by Hindu poets of the bee as an attendant on flowers, and he calls their account of it sublime, as recalling the Persian poets on the subject of the nightingale. As in the case of architecture, however, Jahāngīr's taste for literature was dilettante and had less effect on the progress of culture than his successor's.

Fastidious in matters of art and literature he was also particular in his dress and critical of the pleasures of the table. He chose certain fashions and stuffs for his own clothing and forbade other people to use them. He records the number of the delicious cherries of Kābul he ate in one day, and recognises the excellence of figs picked and eaten at once, but notes a warning against too many at a time. Regarding his own intemperance he is entirely frank and relates that he began to drink wine at the age of 18 and increased his potations until wine ceased to intoxicate him, when he changed to spirits. The time came when his hand shook so much that he could not drink from his own cup; and then under the influence of Nūr

[1] R. B. Whitehead, "The portrait medals of the emperor Jahangir", *Numismatic Chronicle*, 1929, p. 1.

[2] *Memoirs*, translated by Rogers and Beveridge, II, 6. His congratulation of his own originality is misplaced, *vide* B. V. Head, *Historia Numorum*, p. 863. For the coins see R. B. Whitehead, *Numismatic Chronicle*, 1931, p. 91.

[3] S. H. Hodivala, "The coins bearing the name of Nūr Jahān", *J.A.S.B.* 1929, p. 59.

Jahān he recovered to some extent by diluting the spirits with wine. On Thursday evenings (the eve of the Muslim sabbath) he abstained from drinking and he ate no meat on Thursday, the day of his own accession or Sunday, the day on which his father was born. Intemperate himself, he recognised his own weakness and no courtier was admitted to audience whose breath was tainted with the smell of liquor. Though he was hospitable enough to bid them drink when he did himself, he sometimes forgot his own command and ordered savage punishments for their imagined disobedience.[1]

In political affairs Jahāngīr was simple and straightforward with no depth of insight and no cunning. His rebellion as prince was due to bad advisers rather than to ambition. He continued the operations against Mewār because his father had planned them, and perhaps because he had failed as prince to advance them. He even hoped when the first expedition was planned to follow it up by a conquest of Transoxiana, but was never able to venture on that project. When Shāh Jahān was sent on the Deccan campaign the emperor's hopes were that after his son had subdued the country and captured its forts "he will bring with the ambassadors such an offering from the Deccan as no other king of this age has received". To enlist the aid of the king of Bījāpur he offered to him any territory of the Golconda and Ahmadnagar rulers which he could conquer. Over the taking of Kāngra fort he rejoiced, not because of its value, but because no other invaders for centuries had been able to subdue it.

In the affairs of his own empire his disposition was rather to ease comparatively small distresses than to plan great reforms as Akbar had done, and his humanitarian changes had no lasting effect. Early in his reign he forbade the sale of hemp drugs and rice spirit and the practice of gambling. He directed the payment of compensation for crops damaged by troops on the march. In the foothills of the Himālayas he found that Muslim converts had retained the Hindu customs of *satī* and female infanticide and he made these practices a capital offence. Death was also the penalty for giving a Muslim girl in marriage to a Hindu, though Hindu girls could be taken by Muslim youths. The establishment of free kitchens for the poor, the abolition or reduction of customs dues and of a cess for police purposes complete the list of his administrative reforms. Towards his subordinates he was generous and he easily forgave faults. The memoirs open with lists of promotions, gifts and relaxation of punishments and of strictness in the collection of revenue, and are full of examples of clemency towards rebels and treacherous officials. In the early months of his reign he could write to the Amīr-ul-umarā when deputing him to pursue his rebellious son Khusrav: "If he will go in no way in the right road, do not consider a crime anything that results from your action. Kingship regards neither son nor son-in-law. No one is a

[1] Roe, p. 265.

relation to a king." But after the rebellion was crushed Khusrav's life was spared. Jahāngīr regarded the daily administration of justice in public as one of his most sacred duties, and in sickness or in the most trying conditions of climate was accessible to his people. When he found that a capital sentence had been carried out before his final order on the case had been received he directed that no execution should take place till sunset, to allow time for a possible reprieve. His conduct of the greater affairs of state which were decided in private council was, however, often delayed and hampered by the complete intoxication in which his evenings ended.

Religion was a subject on which he did not think deeply. Though outwardly a Muslim, his fondness for art made him disregard the strict prohibitions of Islām. While he observed many Hindu festivals and customs, he argued against idol worship, and after the capture of Kāngra sacrificed a cow in the temple. Towards Christians he was usually tolerant, and English visitors to his court record that he allowed two of his nephews to be educated by a Jesuit and actually to be baptised, though the conversion was only temporary.

He stands in the roll of Indian monarchs as a man with generous instincts, fond of sport, art and good living, aiming to do well to all, and failing by the lack of the finer intellectual qualities to attain the ranks of great administrators.

CHAPTER VII

SHĀH JAHĀN

ACCORDING to the rules of Muslim law Shāh Jahān was now the rightful heir to the throne, as both his elder brothers had died, and their sons had no claim. In dynastic successions this rule has often yielded to force. The position was, however, favourable to Shāh Jahān, who was openly supported by Mahābat Khān, the most eminent soldier of the day, and secretly by his father-in-law Āsaf Khān, who had the largest influence at court. In the country generally he had the favour of the Rājputs and some reputation in the Deccan. Elsewhere the people were indifferent, and officials and soldiers other than those who were personally related or otherwise attached to Nūr Jahān were inclined to side with any successful claimant. Āsaf Khān was not prepared to act on behalf of Shāh Jahān in an open manner. He placed his sister the empress under guard, removing Shāh Jahān's sons from her charge, and with the approval of officers at headquarters proclaimed Dāwar Bakhsh (also known as Bulāqī) the son of Khusrav as emperor. Prayers were read and coins were struck in his name, but the briefness of his rule and its scanty extent are shown by the rarity of the coins and the fact that they bear the name of only one mint town, Lahore.

Meanwhile messengers were despatched by Āsaf Khān to Shāh Jahān and by Nūr Jahān to Shahryār. The latter at once assumed the title of emperor and seized the treasure at Lahore, distributing large sums to gain support and to raise forces, which he placed under the command of a son of his uncle Dāniyāl. Āsaf Khān had little difficulty in defeating the hastily recruited troops who met him on his approach to Lahore, and Shahryār was given up by the guardians of the harem in which he took refuge on learning of the defeat of his army. He was made to do homage, and then cast into prison and blinded. The long journey to the Deccan was performed in twenty days by a fleet messenger, who carried Āsaf Khān's signet to Shāh Jahān and arrived in time to stop him from a project he was meditating of another expedition to Bengal. Khān Jahān was still opposed to him, so he made a *détour* through Gujarāt, where the Dutch and English both sent him presents and congratulations. He passed on through Mewār where he had always received support and hastened to Āgra. There he was welcomed and proclaimed emperor with suitable pomp. Determined to avoid the dynastic strife which had marked his father's accession he had sent orders to Āsaf Khān suggesting the murder of all possible claimants, which were carried out by the execution of Dāwar Bakhsh and another son of Khusrav, of Shahryār, and of two sons of Dāniyāl. Nūr Jahān alone was spared, perhaps in memory of the support she had given her stepson in early life, and certainly in the full conviction that a woman with no son or near male relative could not be dangerous to the new emperor. She received an adequate pension and was allowed to spend the rest of her life in or near Lahore, building and ornamenting the tomb for her husband at Shāhdara, a few miles from the city, and carrying on the works of charity for which she had been famed during her husband's lifetime.

At his accession Shāh Jahān had a stronger position than his father had held at the death of Akbar. He had ruthlessly disposed of a brother and nephews who might have continued, like Khusrav, to be a focus of intrigue. The more distinguished officers of the army were on his side, and Āsaf Khān, the most able statesman of the time, was his father-in-law and had been active in obtaining his succession to the throne. He himself was a capable leader, and in particular had won the support of the Rājputs, with whom he had close blood affinities through his mother and grandmother. With all these advantages he had to administer a state which had been shaken and impoverished by his own rebellious acts. No body politic convulsed as India had been during the last few years could settle down at once to a peaceful existence. Khān Jahān Lodī, headstrong and fickle, as many Pathāns were, believed that Shahryār or Dāwar Bakhsh was more likely to succeed, and while Shāh Jahān was on his way to Āgra, Khān Jahān left a small garrison in his headquarters at Burhānpur and marched himself to seize Māndū. When news came that Shāh Jahān had reached Ajmer he was abandoned by some of his Hindu supporters and sent in a humble submission, which was accepted. He was forgiven and confirmed in his governorship of the Deccan and ordered to return to Burhānpur.

Nearer the capital a fresh anxiety arose before a year had passed. Bīr Singh Deo, the Rājā of Bundelkhand who had ministered to the revenge of Jahāngīr by the murder of Abu-'l-Fazl, died a few months before his patron, and was succeeded by his son Jujhār Singh, who at first came to court leaving his son Bikramājīt Singh to administer the country. Bundelkhand was a wild tract, especially difficult of access in the rainy season, and its chiefs after centuries of obscurity were rising in importance. Bikramājīt Singh showed himself harsh and rapacious and his father was alarmed by the enquiries made into past collections of revenue. Jujhār Singh, therefore, left Āgra and proceeding to his fort at Orchha began to prepare for independence. For a time no action was taken, as a Jānid chief of Transoxiana had made a raid on Kābul territory. This was beaten off by the local governor and Mahābat Khan, who had been hastily despatched to defend the frontier, was recalled and took a large force to subdue the rebel in Bundelkhand. Another force under 'Abdullah Khān was to march from the east, and Khān Jahān was ordered to advance from the Deccan with Rājā Bharat who also aspired to the chieftainship of the Bundelas. Shāh Jahān himself left Āgra and arrived at Gwalior at the beginning of January, 1629. Abdullah Khān promptly attacked and took Erachh,[1] while Khān Jahān approached from the south and began to ravage the country. Jujhār Singh had also to face opposition among his own people. Suspecting his wife of an intrigue with his brother Hardaur Singh, he had poisoned the latter, who had a considerable following.[2] Opposition to the imperial forces being thus hopeless, he made his submission to Mahābat Khān and his offences were pardoned on condition that he gave up some of his assignments and proceeded on service to the Deccan.

Shāh Jahān was thus able to return to Āgra in a few weeks, and devoted his attention to the affairs of the Deccan. In restoring Khān Jahān to the governorship of that province he had directed him to recover the Bālāghāt which Khān Jahān had corruptly surrendered in the previous reign. As no effort had been made to carry out this instruction Khān Jahān was recalled to headquarters and Mahābat Khān replaced him as governor, being represented at first by his son Khān Zamān. Though he was subjected to no punishment beyond the loss of office Khān Jahān remained at Āgra, moody and discontented, and ready to listen to the mischievous remarks which were passed about at court. One evening his son heard a report that he and his father were to be imprisoned at once. Khān Jahān ceased to attend the daily court and kept in his own quarters with a guard of two thousand fellow Afghāns. The emperor, noticing his absence, sent to enquire the reason and hearing of his suspicions had a letter despatched to him forgiving his offences. On receipt of this Khān Jahān again began to visit the court, but consciousness of his own treachery and a suspicious nature prevented him from wholly trusting the emperor. In October, 1629, Āsaf Khān reported that he had received news that Khān Jahān was preparing to fly. Shāh Jahān, who was not inclined to go back on his promise of forgiveness, decided to wait on events. That same night Khān Jahān rode out with his followers and took the road to the south. He was immediately followed and overtaken near the Chambal river. His force was attacked and though he inflicted much loss on the imperial troops he thought it safe to escape, and with his sons and a few followers managed to cross the swollen stream, leaving his treasure and harem behind. While the pursuers were collecting boats he gained sufficient time to evade them, and being guided by Bikramājīt, son of Jujhār Singh, through the by-paths of Bundelkhand, he crossed Gondwāna and safely reached Ahmadnagar and Daulatābād. Here he was well

[1] Now in the north of Jhānsī district; sometimes transliterated as Irij or Irichh.

[2] Popular tradition still keeps the memory of Hardaur Singh, who is regarded as a martyr and demi-god, while Jujhār Singh is an object of execration.

received by the king, who placed him in charge of Bīr and nominally assigned to his friends tracts which were actually held by the Mughuls, with instructions to conquer them.

Shāh Jahān, with the energy which marked the early days of his rule, left Āgra for the Deccan in December, 1629. Early in the following year the Mughul forces invaded the Bālāghāt but were not well organised and after gaining one success suffered a defeat by Khān Jahān. The emperor therefore laid his plans for a concentrated attack after the rains. In dealing with the rebel Khān Jahān he also had to take account of the three kingdoms of the south, Ahmadnagar, Bijāpur and Golconda, which though jealous of each other could on occasion form alliances to repel the Mughuls. Experience had also shown that the Marāthās could not safely be neglected. One force under Khvāja Abu-'l-Hasan was sent west to Dhūlia to command the route for supplies from Gujarāt and to threaten Ahmadnagar from the north-west, while the main army was concentrated at Dewalgāon in the south of Berār ready when the time came to attack from the north-east. A third force was sent towards Telingāna (north of Hyderābād state). At the beginning of the reign the Marāthās had accepted posts under the Mughuls, but their leader Jadu Rāi, desiring to keep on terms with the ruler of Ahmadnagar, had sent sons and relations to take service with him. The king, knowing his duplicity, resolved to arrest Jadu Rāi and summoning him to court had him murdered, thereby driving the Marāthās for the time being into the Mughul camp.

The rains of 1630 failed completely in Gujarāt, the Deccan and the country extending across India to the east coast. For three previous years the seasons had been unfavourable and the result was a terrible famine, aggravated by a campaign in part of the territory affected.[1] Muqarrab Khān, commander of the Ahmadnagar forces, had been holding Jālna a few miles south-west of the main Mughul army. When in the autumn A'zam Khān moved out of Dewalgāon, Muqarrab Khān withdrew to the south, closely followed by the Mughuls. Khān Jahān remained at his headquarters at Bīr, awaiting the scattered parties he had sent out to collect revenue, a difficult task in time of famine, and hoping to receive reinforcements from Muqarrab Khān. Hearing of A'zam Khān's approach he decided to move, but before he started A'zam Khān made a night march and drew an attack by sending a small force while holding his main body in reserve. The attacking force withdrew in disorder when it found the whole of the imperial army was coming against it. Khān Jahān, finding that his retreat was cut off, determined to make a stand. He sent away his women towards the north-west and rallied his troops, sending a nephew against one of the smaller detachments of the Mughuls, with some preliminary success. A fierce battle raged and

[1] W. H. Moreland, *From Akbar to Aurangzeb*, pp. 210 *sqq.*

though the rebels fought bravely they were defeated and pursued till the tired horses of the Mughuls, who had traversed sixty miles in twenty hours, could go no farther. Khān Jahān with a few followers, who were mostly wounded, escaped on fresh horses with his ladies, who had to abandon their elephants and also ride on horseback.

They hastened north to Vaijāpur hoping to find refuge in Daulatābād. A'zam Khān after giving his troops time to rest again advanced north, and Khān Jahān with another Afghān leader named Daryā Khān moved restlessly from place to place round Daulatābād where the king of Ahmadnagar had shut himself up in the fort. Shāhjī Bhonsle, son-in-law of Jadu Rāi, who had withdrawn Marāthā support from Ahmadnagar after the murder of Jadu Rāi, now offered his services to Shāh Jahān, who accepted them gladly. The rebels attempted a diversion by sending Daryā Khān with a force of Afghāns north-west between Chāndor[1] and Chālīsgāon,[2] where they raided the country for provisions, as scarcity round Daulatābād had been intensified by the presence of troops, but they returned on the news that Abdullah Khān had been ordered to follow them. Owing to the desolation of the country A'zam Khān thought it wiser not to besiege the king but to turn back upon the forces under Muqarrab Khān, so he marched south to Jāmkhed,[3] intending to attack Muqarrab Khān who was still on the northern edge of the Bālāghāt. As the imperial forces approached them the Ahmadnagar troops withdrew towards Bīr, and when followed up by A'zam Khān they fled towards Daulatābād, but were unable to stay owing to the failure of supplies and again went south. Meanwhile, A'zam Khān despatched Shāhjī Bhonsle to secure the country west and north of Ahmadnagar.

With his country stripped bare of the necessities of life, and almost completely surrounded by hostile forces, the king of Ahmadnagar repented of his support to the rebel Khān Jahān, whose help against the Mughuls during the last year had been almost negligible. Khān Jahān and Daryā Khān with their followers were turned out and decided to pass through Mālwā to the Punjab, hoping to find allies among the disaffected Afghāns on the frontier who would support their insurrection. Shāh Jahān, who was at Burhānpur in close touch with the operations, and able to draw supplies from tracts in northern India untouched by the famine, had foreseen this and detached forces to catch them. The fugitives arrived in central India hotly pursued and resisted by the local garrisons. They hoped to find aid and refuge in Bundelkhand where they had been assisted on their flight from Āgra. Bikramājīt Singh had, however, learned that his previous assistance to them had brought the royal censure on his father

[1] 20° 21′ N., 74° 15′ E.
[2] 20° 27′ N., 75° 1′ E.
[3] 18° 49′ N., 75° 23′ E.

Jujhār Singh. To atone for this, he attacked the rear-guard and killed Daryā Khān and his son with many of their followers early in January, 1631. Khān Jahān escaped but was again worsted in a sharp fight and finally brought to bay and killed at Sihonda.[1]

Meanwhile, A'zam Khān had again opened the campaign against the army of Ahmadnagar. The strong fort of Dharūr, full of treasure and munitions, was taken without an assault, after the town and market below it had been plundered, and Parenda[2] was invested. Attempts were also made to take advantage of the dissension which usually existed between the kingdoms of Ahmadnagar and Bijāpur.[3] During the later years of Jahāngīr's reign when Mughul pressure was slight Malik 'Ambar, the capable Ahmadnagar general, had invaded Bijāpur and plundered Nauraspur, the new capital which the king was building. Ibrāhīm 'Ādil Shah II of Bijāpur died in 1627, shortly before Jahāngīr, and his eldest son Darvesh was blinded and set aside in favour of Muhammad 'Ādil, a younger son aged only fifteen, through the influence of a clique headed by Mustafa Khān, a capable minister, and Daulat (or Khavāss) Khān, a man who had risen from a low origin. The succession was recognised by Shāh Jahān but not by the king of Ahmadnagar, who favoured Darvesh, and invaded Bijāpur to support his claim. Shāh Jahān, busy with consolidating his own position, tried to make peace, but the quarrel was embittered by a dispute about Sholāpur which Malik 'Ambar had taken from Bijāpur. When Shāh Jahān came to the Deccan to suppress Khān Jahān's rebellion, and if possible to crush Ahmadnagar, the rival ministers of Bijāpur were still divided over the attitude which the kingdom should assume. Mustafā Khān, whose father-in-law had been executed by Malik 'Ambar, was in favour of supporting the Mughuls, but Randola Khān, the commander-in-chief, felt that the Mughuls were the enemy most to be feared. A'zam Khān's reduction of Dharūr increased the hope that Bijāpur might regain some of the territory taken by Malik 'Ambar and terms were considered. But Randola Khān demanded an excessive area including Dharūr, and refused to furnish troops in aid of A'zam Khān when he was pursuing Muqarrab Khān and the army of Ahmadnagar. Being in great straits Muqarrab Khān offered to restore Sholāpur to Bijāpur, and A'zam Khān feared an alliance between the two kingdoms. His assaults on Parenda had failed, and the drought had so parched the country that even grass for horses could not be found within a range of forty miles. He therefore withdrew to Dharūr, losing rear-guard actions on the way. More success attended the other divisions of the Mughul troops, as Nasīrī Khān, though resisted by combined forces of Bijāpur and Ahmadnagar, took the strong fortress of Kandhār on the eastern edge of Bālāghāt, Berār was cleared, and Khvāja

[1] Now in the Bānda district, U.P., 25° 27′ N., 83° 24′ E.
[2] 18° 16′ N., 75° 27′ E.
[3] See chap. IX.

Abu-'l-Hasan, though with great difficulty, had reduced Nāsik and Sangamner on the north-west of Ahmadnagar. In the midst of these successes the emperor sustained a blow which left an impression never effaced in the death of his favourite wife, Mumtāz Mahall, on 17 June, 1631.[1] She was buried at first in a garden called Zaināběd near Burhānpur, and afterwards her remains were removed to Āgra, where they lie with those of Shāh Jahān in a beautiful tomb.

The kingdom of Ahmadnagar, like that of Bijāpur, was under a nominal ruler, swayed against his will by factions among the nobles. Muqarrab Khān had superseded and strictly confined his brother-in-law, Fath Khān, who was a son of Malik 'Ambar. While Muqarrab Khān was attempting to resist the Mughul forces, the king of Ahmadnagar asserted himself for a brief space and released Fath Khān. Feeling that resistance was useless, Muqarrab Khān, who was of Persian origin and had no hereditary connection with the kingdom, changed sides and offered his services to the emperor, which were accepted, and he was shortly afterwards transferred to Katehr (now Rohilkhand) in northern India. Fath Khān himself, knowing his master's changeable mood, placed the king in confinement, as his father had done, and reported this to Āsaf Khān, expecting some mark of favour. Āsaf Khān, who was ruthless in such matters, suggested that his sincerity would be best proved by murder, and Fath Khān poisoned the king and replaced him by Husain, a boy of ten. With the hesitation usually found in traitors he delayed the surrender of treasure and elephants he had agreed to give up, and Shāh Jahān despatched Muqarrab Khān, now dignified by the title of Rustam Khān, to reduce Daulatābād which had become the actual headquarters of the Ahmadnagar kingdom. This fresh danger alarmed Fath Khān, who submitted.[2] Randola Khān, the Bijāpur general, had still shown opposition to the Mughuls and had detained an envoy who was carrying presents to the emperor. Hearing of the collapse of resistance in Ahmadnagar, he also offered peace and promised allegiance to the emperor and that he would let the envoy pass. A'zam Khān, however, rejected the terms and marched south but suffered losses and fell back. In December, 1631, the emperor deputed Āsaf Khān to invade Bijāpūr. Taking a route farther east than that followed by A'zam Khān in the earlier campaign, Āsaf Khān reached Bhālkī[3] and took it. A message of submission from Bijāpur was rejected and the Mughuls marched on, sacking Gulbarga

[1] The chronogram recording the date in the Hijrī era is the single word *Gham*, meaning sorrow, the numerical value of the two Arabic letters used in writing it being equal to 1040.

[2] The histories record that he struck coin in the name of Shāh Jahān, but the issue seems to have been confined to Ahmadnagar dated about October, 1631. Shāh Jahān's suzerainty at his accession had been recognised by striking coins at Daulatābād in his name, dated 1037 Hijrī, though the issue was not continued.

[3] 18° 3′ N., 77° 12′ E.

and massacring the population. The army camped between Naurаspur and Shāhpur, a few miles north-west of Bijāpur, and opened the siege. Fresh negotiations were set on foot and Mustafā Khān, who headed the party favourable to the Mughuls, came into the camp of the besiegers to discuss terms. His offer seemed favourable, but his colleague, Khavāss Khān, declined to concur in them, and made a fresh suggestion, which Āsaf Khān was disposed to accept, owing to his difficulties in obtaining supplies, as the Bijāpur army, while falling back, had destroyed whatever the famine had left. During the truce and parley, however, the straitened circumstances of the besiegers had become known to the garrison, and a letter dropped in the Mughul camp by an adherent of Mustafā Khān warned Āsaf Khān that he was merely being played with till exhaustion should overcome his force. During the short siege of twenty days no grain had been brought in and the provisions which had been carried with the army were almost finished. Āsaf Khān therefore retreated west to Mirāj,[1] seeking supplies, plundering the country and killing or enslaving the population. He then struck north past Sholāpur, where the pursuing army of Bijāpur turned back, and he returned to the Mughul territories. The emperor was by this time disgusted with the Deccan where his wife had died, his plans had not succeeded and the desolation of famine still continued. He was persuaded by Mahābat Khān that the conquest of Bijāpur was not impossible, and entrusted to him the command in the Deccan, recalling to court Āsaf Khān, who was more distinguished in political craft than as a general in the field.

Although the Deccan had hitherto been the scene of the most important events affecting the empire military operations had been undertaken elsewhere, especially in Bengal. Nearly a century earlier the Portuguese had obtained a footing at Hooghly, whence they traded to other parts of India, to China, the Moluccas and Manilla. They had a monopoly of the manufacture of salt and practically exercised their own administration in the settlement. Converts and half-castes were numerous, and the new port gained at the expense of Sātgāon a little higher up the river and Sonārgāon in eastern Bengal. Some of the inhabitants joined the half-castes of Chittagong, descended from Portuguese refugees from Goa, who were notorious pirates and ravaged the rich districts of eastern Bengal. During the reign of Jahāngīr the Portuguese had been left very much to themselves by the Mughul governors, who moved their headquarters from Sonārgāon in 1608 to Dacca, calling it Jahāngīrnagar, after the emperor. Qāsim Khān, who became governor soon after the accession of Shāh Jahān, reported to the emperor that the Portuguese were a danger as they had fortified their settlement, levied tolls on ships that passed it, and had ruined Sātgāon. He also called attention to their

[1] 16° 49′ N., 74° 41′ E.

complicity in piracy[1] and their practice of kidnapping or purchasing children and disposing of them as slaves. These statements reminded the emperor of his own personal reasons for disliking the foreigners. During the first successes of Shāh Jahān's rebellion against his father the governor of Hooghly, who was afraid of an attack on that place after Burdwān had fallen, visited the prince. Shāh Jahān had a high opinion of the value of the European gunners employed by the Portuguese and offered great rewards for their services. The governor, while sensible of the immediate danger to his settlement during the temporary collapse of imperial power in Bengal, did not believe in the possibility of the ultimate success of the rebel. Unfortunately for the Portuguese the language of his refusal to help was reported to have been very insulting. At a later stage the Portuguese gave some assistance to Parvīz. When Shāh Jahān succeeded to the throne the foreigners omitted to recognise the accession by the usual presents. The late empress had also had a personal grievance during the flight, as one of the Portuguese had first given some help and had then deserted, carrying off boats one of which contained two slave girls who belonged to her. A striking example of the lawlessness of the time occurred in 1629, when a Portuguese from the Magh territory in eastern Bengal plundered a village near Dacca and violently assaulted a Mughul lady.[2] Shāh Jahān thus welcomed the proposal of Qāsim Khān that these troublesome aliens who did not conform to Islām and who were actively injurious to the realm should be suppressed.

An opportunity for action soon presented itself. A Portuguese merchant at Sātgāon named Afonso, who had made a claim to certain land in Hooghly, applied to Qāsim Khān in 1632 and held out the promise of rich booty if the settlement were taken, which would be an easy task. The governor acted cautiously, as the Portuguese were known to be capable soldiers, and he feared that if he became involved in a long struggle the Magh king would take advantage of his concentration of forces at Hooghly to attack and plunder Dacca. He therefore assembled a considerable force under the pretext of coercing refractory landholders near Murshidābād north of Hooghly and Hijilī to the south, and he also collected boats, as the Portuguese were particularly redoubtable on the water. Warnings had been received from priests at Dacca and Āgra, but were disregarded, and when the large Mughul army approached Hooghly at the end of June, and it was known that the fleet was not far away, barricades and palisades had to be improvised, and a Jesuit was sent to parley. Bahādur Khān, who was in command, detailed the offences described above and proposed to search for Bengali slaves and punish those who had purchased them. The Portu-

[1] For the damage done by the pirates of eastern Bengal see *J.A.S.B.* 1907, p. 422.
[2] See Manrique, II, 318. She was subsequently baptised and married a Portuguese.

guese declined to allow a search, and after some preliminary skirmishing an attack was launched by both land and the river, which was repulsed. A few days later the besieged sent out fresh envoys to sue for peace, and were bidden to despatch four of the principal residents with power to make terms. These agreed to give up the slaves, but surrendered only a small number. Further hostages were obtained and a large ransom demanded from the church with half the property of the inhabitants, and the hostages were fettered and threatened with death. The negotiations were being prolonged as reinforcements were expected by the Mughuls, who soon attacked again and obtained a footing in part of the settlement. For about five weeks the siege continued till artillery was brought up and trenches were dug. During a fresh armistice the Portuguese gave up 200,000 rupees with which the Mughuls paid their troops, Afonso tried to block the river with a bridge of boats and a chain, and prepared a number of fire-boats to burn the Portuguese ships. Finally the Portuguese decided to evacuate the town in their boats, but delayed and were attacked before the boats cast loose. A running fight ensued, and about 3000 refugees escaped down the river, while 400 Christian prisoners were taken the long slow journey to Āgra.[1] Most of them refused to apostasise and were imprisoned. While the emperor had substantial reasons for coercing the Portuguese, evidence of his religious intolerance at this period exists in orders issued for the demolition of newly built Hindu temples, particularly in and near the sacred city of Benares, where seventy-six were said to have been destroyed.

Apart from a slight insurrection among the Bhīls of Mālwā, which was easily suppressed, the internal peace of the empire was unbroken at the end of 1632. The southern border was, however, far from quiet. Shāhjī the Marāthā chief, when he first made his submission to the Mughuls, had been rewarded with grants of land which had been held by Fath Khān of Ahmadnagar. These grants were restored to Fath Khān as a reward for his murder of the king. Enraged by this alienation Shāhjī offered his services to the king of Bijāpur, promising to take Daulatābād from Fath Khān if an army from Bijāpur would help him. Daulatābād was not ready to stand a siege and Fath Khān addressed Mahābat Khān, offering to make it over to the imperial forces, and to proceed himself for service at the court. A force under Khān Zamān, son of Mahābat Khān, defeated the troops from Bijāpur, and their general Randola Khān, having lost in the field, had resort to intrigue. He offered Fath Khān a considerable sum of money and supplies, and was successful in getting him to break his pledge to the Mughuls. On hearing of this treachery Mahābat Khān decided to take Daulatābād by storm, a task which had never been accomplished since the construction of the central fortress by

[1] For a contemporary Portuguese account of the siege see Manrique, II, App. 392.

Muhammad bin Tughluq three centuries earlier.[1] It was protected by a number of later fortifications, especially the works known as 'Ambar Kot, which had been built by Malik 'Ambar. The place was invested under the direct supervision of Mahābat Khān who proceeded by sapping and mining. At the same time, having an army of about 20,000 cavalry in the field against him, he maintained a large mobile force to prevent the reinforcement of the garrison and the entry of supplies which were badly needed. Within six weeks a large mine was exploded which tore down a long stretch of the outer wall and part of a bastion. As the explosion had been premature the storming troops were not ready and a fierce struggle ensued before the defences made by Malik 'Ambar were taken. Diversions made in Berār, and attempts by Randola Khān and Shāhjī to relieve the garrison, all failed. The small contingent of Bijāpur troops within the fortress, dispirited alike by the straits to which they had been reduced, and by the success and vigour of the besiegers, asked to be allowed to escape secretly. Mahābat Khān sent a written consent and received them kindly when they made their way down a ladder and gave them presents. In less than two months after the penetration of the outworks, a mine was ready for exploding under the next line of defences. Communications between opposing forces were more frequent than in modern warfare, and Fath Khān, aware of the instant danger, asked for a day to arrange for terms with his Bijāpur allies. His treachery had been exposed so often that Mahābat Khān declined to allow any terms unless Fath Khān would send his son as a hostage. The son did not appear and the mine was sprung, tearing down a bastion and part of the wall. Fresh trenches were started within the wall, and renewed attempts by the Bijāpur army were defeated. An epidemic had broken out in the fortress, and Fath Khān was now alarmed for the safety and honour of his own ladies and the harem of the king. To save them he sent his son with a prayer for forgiveness and help to remove the women. Exulting in his victory Mahābat Khān was generous, and not only provided his own elephants and camels with several litters for the women, but also restored some of the treasure already taken. At the end of June, 1633, after a siege of three and a half months, Fath Khān yielded up the stronghold with all the guns and munitions of war, and Mahābat Khān, entering, had prayers read in the name of the emperor. Fath Khān and Husain Nizām Shāh, the boy king, were sent to court; their lives were spared but Husain was committed to the state prison in the Gwalior fort for life, while Fath Khān was allowed to live at Lahore with an ample pension.

Mahābat Khān's brilliant conduct of the siege was the last success of a great soldier who, throughout his career, had excelled as tactician rather than strategist. The capture of Daulatābād by no means won

[1] See vol. III, p. 141.

the whole territory of Ahmadnagar for the Mughuls. In the west the Marāthās had a firm hold over the northern half of the present Poona district and the Konkan. Parts of the Bālāghāt were still in the hands of Ahmadnagar officers who maintained their loyalty to a phantom ruler or denied allegiance to the Mughuls for their own benefit. Parenda, which A'zam Khān had failed to take two years before, had been made over to Bijāpur by its commander, and Mahābat Khān now proposed to the prince Shāh Shujā' that the Mughul forces should take it in order to subdue the outlying portions of Ahmadnagar and to establish a base for the reduction of Bijāpur. He detached his son Khān Zamān to ravage the frontier districts of Bijāpur and he established outposts along the line from Daulatābād towards Parenda so as to shut off the Marāthās. Shāhjī, however, announced the succession of another member of the Nizāmshāhī dynasty of Ahmadnagar and by raiding continually tried to break the Mughul line and thus relieve the pressure on Parenda. To counteract these movements a Mughul force was sent to force Shāhjī back to Junnar and to sack or capture some of his strongholds.

As Khān Zamān's attempt to take Parenda was not successful, Mahābat Khān himself with Shāh Shujā' left the Mughul headquarters established at Malkāpur. The effects of the great famine had not yet passed away. Thousands of cultivators had perished, and many of the survivors had moved to districts which had suffered less. In the absence of proper organisation supplies for the army in the field were lacking, and foraging parties had to go to distant places where they were subject to attack. Mahābat Khān himself narrowly escaped capture, being rescued by Nasīrī Khān who had now received the title of Khān Daurān for his services in the capture of Daulatābād. The incident caused jealousy, as Khān Daurān continued to boast of his exploit. The hot weather was well advanced, and as the rains were due Mahābat Khān advised Shāh Shujā', who was unable to control his generals, to raise the siege and retire to Burhānpur. The failure vexed the emperor, who recalled Shāh Shujā' and Khān Zamān to court and censured Mahābat Khān. The old general was suffering from fistula, and distracted by his sufferings and the failure of his enterprise behaved madly till his death in October, 1634.

While affairs had been progressing so badly in the Deccan the emperor had been making his first visit to Lahore since his accession. On his return to Āgra he conferred on Āsaf Khān the title of Khān Khānān which had been held by Mahābat Khān. A fresh insurrection now broke out in Bundelkhand. For five years Jujhār Singh had served in the Deccan and had assisted in the capture of Daulatābād. He then returned to Orchha, leaving his son and the Bundelā contingent with Mahābat Khān. Reviving his old ambition he sought to extend his authority over Gondwāna, the hilly tract lying south of Bundelkhand, which had never been brought under direct Mughul rule, though one of Akbar's generals had raided it and stormed the extensive fortress of Chaurāgarh. Jujhār Singh laid siege to this place and, though he received warnings from the emperor not to persist, he took it and treacherously put to death the Gond Rājā Prem Nārāyan. The son of the dead raja appealed to Shāh Jahān, who called on Jujhār Singh to surrender the conquered territory to the imperial officers, or to give up his own lands, and also to pay a fine of a million rupees. Jujhār Singh refused to obey and sent a message to his son to bring back his troops from the Bālāghāt. On their way back they were attacked by imperial forces and lost heavily, but the son escaped, though wounded, and joined his father. Prince Aurangzīb was now deputed with an army to suppress the rebellion. The force concentrated at Bhānder and marched south on Orchha, which was surrounded by thick jungle not traversed by open roads. Making slow progress through this, the troops were subject to constant attacks by the Bundelās, but still pressed on. Alarmed by their progress, Jujhār Singh left Orchha in charge of a garrison and with his son, their families and valuables retreated south to Dhāmonī.[1] Orchha was stormed and the prince drew near Dhāmonī, when news was received that Jujhār Singh had left for Chaurāgarh which he hoped to be able to hold against all attacks, if the Mughuls pursued him into such difficult country. Dhāmonī was stormed and the imperial army still advanced. Dismayed at last, Jujhār Singh abandoned Chaurāgarh and hastened towards the Deccan with a force about 6000 strong, and sixty elephants carrying his family and valuables. The rebels had a fortnight's start and travelled speedily, but were pursued and pressed. Jujhār Singh put to death several of his women whose horses had foundered and turned on the Mughuls, but was beaten and his men scattered in the jungles. The remnants made for Golconda and were again taken by surprise. They had not time to perform the full rites of *jauhar* (the Rājput sacrifice of women in such an emergency) but stabbed a number, and were about to fly when they were forced to fight. The Mughuls took several male relatives of Jujhār Singh prisoners, and picked up the wounded women. While they rested after their long marches news came that Jujhār Singh and one of his sons had been murdered by the Gonds in the jungles where they had sought to hide. Shāh Jahān himself had proceeded towards Orchha and just before Christmas, 1634, came news of the capture of the strong fort of Jhānsī, a few miles away. For several years following these defeats the Orchha branch of Bundelās had no chief recognised by the emperor.

The death of Mahābat Khān and the removal of Mughul forces from the Deccan had the usual result of causing the rival factions in the Bijāpur state to renew their bickering. For a time, Khavāss Khān obtained the upper hand and imprisoned Mustafā Khān in

[1] 24° 14′ N., 78° 45′ E.

the fort of Belgaum, as he had refused to give up the royal seals when ordered by the king. An intrigue was started which ended in the murder of Khavāss Khān and his right-hand man Murārī Pandit. Mustafā Khān obtained his release and was restored to the position of Peshwā or chief minister. The emperor now took the opportunity of obtaining renewed pledges of allegiance from Bijāpur and Golconda, and himself came south to direct what operations might be necessary, crossing the Narbadā early in 1636, and proceeding to Daulatābād. He called on the king of Bijāpur to be regular in payment of tribute and to make over to imperial officers the Ahmadnagar territories which Bijāpur had seized. In particular he demanded that the Marāthās and other supporters of the evicted Ahmadnagar dynasty should be turned out of Bijāpur. To strengthen his demands he detached a force towards the Bālāghāt with instructions to take the forts of Udgīr and Ausā, which had belonged to Ahmadnagar. Mustafā Khān, who had always favoured the Mughuls, agreed to the terms, and sent apologies for recent contumacious behaviour for which he had not been responsible. The envoy who returned to the imperial camp reported that there were still dissensions among the leading nobles and, as it was discovered that money had been sent to the commandants of Udgīr and Ausā, Shāh Jahān decided to invade Bijāpur. This danger induced the general Randola to unite with Mustafā Khān in suing for peace. Delay and secret contumacy had made the emperor inclined to greater severity and his first impulse was to execute the envoys to prove the reality of his intentions. Āsaf Khān, however, succeeded in dissuading him and the entreaties of Mustafā Khān's son, who had come to court, appeased his anger. The terms were, however, severe. Bijāpur was to acknowledge Mughul supremacy, to pay an annual tribute of two million rupees, and to keep the peace with Golconda, submitting to the emperor's arbitration any dispute with that kingdom. The boundary of the old Ahmadnagar state, now Mughul, was settled, and Bijāpur was confirmed in the possession of Parenda, and of the Konkan, while that state agreed to assist the Mughuls if Shāhjī did not surrender his chief possessions near Junnar and Trimbak. The peace thus concluded (May, 1636) continued till the death of Muhammad 'Ādil Shāh of Bijāpur in November, 1656, though Mughul authority had to be asserted on one or two occasions.

The settlement of affairs with Golconda was an easier task as the king had usually been more complaisant than the rulers of other Deccan states. Friendship with Shāh Jahān had been shown by help given to him during his rebellion against his father, and his gratitude was expressed in 1626 when 'Abdullah Qutb Shāh succeeded his father. The emperor on his arrival in the Deccan to crush the rebel Khān Jahān sent an envoy to the Golconda court who returned with presents early in 1631. Some alarm was, however, felt at Golconda when in the operations which ensued one of the Mughul divisions took the fort of Kandhār, and troops were sent to patrol the frontier in that direction. Further mistrust of the imperial designs was caused by the governor of Orissa, who took a fort on the northern borders, but the emperor stayed a further advance by him. When another envoy was sent at the end of 1631 Āsaf Khān was starting on his unsuccessful expedition against Bijāpur and the envoy was detained in Golconda and finally dismissed without the usual presents on the receipt of news of Āsaf Khān's failure and return to the north. Either the old friendship or fear of Mughul prowess held back the king two years later from joining the Bijāpur forces which tried to relieve the Daulatābād garrison during the siege by Mahābat Khān. Fugitive relatives of Jujhār Singh who succeeded in reaching Golconda when he met his death in the jungles were made over to the Mughul commander.

These bonds of friendship and complaisance were, however, strained by the force of religious difference. While Shāh Jahān was a strict Sunnī the kings of Golconda belonged to the Shiah sect and for more than thirty years had included the name of the reigning Shāh of Persia in the weekly Friday prayers, as a recognition of his authority. The demands on Golconda thus included the abolition of Shiah practices and an explanation why the authority of the Shāh was respected, besides the usual request for presents. Some show of resistance was made as had been the case with Bijāpur. Judges of the Islamic law and divines were assembled at Golconda and they advised compliance. Shāh Jahān's name was inserted in the Friday prayers, and the Mughul troops were withdrawn from the frontiers, without having to make the show of force which had been necessary at Bijāpur. As the Golconda kingdom was weaker than Bijāpur the terms imposed on it were harder. They included the abolition of the Shiah formula and the use of the emperor's name on coins,[1] payment of an annual tribute of 200,000 *hūns*,[2] with arrears then due, continued loyalty, and the promise of help if Bijāpur attacked the imperial forces. Among the presents taken to the emperor with the written treaty (May, 1636) were included coins of Mughul type bearing his name for the first time. His return presents included his portrait and a gold tablet on which the details of the treaty were engraved.

While these arrangements were being concluded with the feeble kings of Golconda and Bijāpur, more trouble was being experienced in subduing the hardy Marāthās. As he approached Daulatābād the emperor despatched one force under Khān Zamān to occupy

[1] Golconda, unlike Bijāpur, had very little distinctive coinage of Muhammadan style, but appears to have used coins of the southern Indian Hindu types as did the Dutch, the Danes and the English. Cf. W. H. Moreland, *Relations of Golconda*, p. 91 *sq*.

[2] A well known gold coin in South India, worth at this period about 7*s*. to 7*s*. 6*d*. or three rupees.

the home land of Shāhjī south and south-east of Ahmadnagar and afterwards to clear the Konkan of Marāthās. Another division under Shāyista Khān invaded the districts north and west of Ahmadnagar. Shāyista Khān's enterprise was successful and he rapidly won over a Marāthā leader and a Muslim commandant serving under the nominal Ahmadnagar ruler, and his troops stormed or compelled the surrender of a number of forts. Khān Zamān found himself opposed to Shāhjī, who had crossed the line of his advance and was making for Parenda to join the Bijāpur forces, followed by Khān Zamān. When Shāhjī passed over the Bhīmā and entered Bijāpur territory where Khān Zamān had been ordered not to follow him, the latter halted. Receiving permission later, he took Kolhāpur and plundered Mirāj and Rāybāg though constantly harassed by the Bijāpur troops. While he halted on his return journey northwards he received news that Bijāpur had submitted to terms and he was ordered to take Junnar from Shāhjī, to whom an offer of service was made by Bijāpur if he would peacefully surrender his fortresses. Shāhjī, however, continued to hold out after the treaty with Bijāpur had been concluded and a further campaign was necessary to reduce him, which was prolonged by the setting in of the rainy season. Khān Zamān invested Junnar, but Shāhjī made rapid marches and counter-marches, evading both the Mughul troops and the Bijāpur forces which were now co-operating with them. Finally Shāhjī took refuge in a small fort, and after sustaining a siege by the combined armies, and haggling long over terms, he surrendered all his strongholds and agreed to enter the service of Bijāpur. Early in 1637 when Aurangzīb returned to court to be married, he brought with him the boy whom Shāhjī had set up as ruler of Ahmadnagar and had made over to the Mughul general when he surrendered. The boy was imprisoned in Gwalior, where there were already two of his predecessors.

While affairs in the Deccan had been the chief preoccupation of the Mughuls other projects for extension of territory had also been launched. For a hundred years they had coveted the barren and inhospitable country of Tibet, and in spite of the record of constant disaster renewed their attempts from time to time. An expedition under the governor of Kashmīr failed in the preceding reign and was obliged to retreat with great loss and much difficulty. Shāh Jahān's expedition was less ambitious and was directed against Abdāl the ruler of Bāltistān or little Tibet, who had offended him by giving refuge to the turbulent Chakks.[1] Abdāl had submitted in 1634 but again showed a recalcitrant spirit and the governor of Kashmīr was directed to enforce his obedience. Bāltistān lies among massive ranges with lofty peaks and vast glaciers and a campaign is possible only during two months of the year. A fort held by a young son of Abdāl

[1] For the earlier activities of this tribe see vol. III, chap. XII.

capitulated after a short siege and the failure of a sortie to drive off the besiegers. The surrender of a second fort and the knowledge that his people were not prepared to support him compelled Abdāl to yield and he agreed to pay an indemnity, while the leader of the Chakks was also secured. A new governor was appointed, and a year later sent news that Tibet proper was aggressive. In a short campaign, however, the Tibetan forces were routed and peace was restored.

An event of greater importance was the recovery of Qandahār, the possession of which was so long disputed by the rulers of Persia and India, even after its importance on a trade route had diminished. During the first ten years of Shāh Jahān's reign he lost no opportunity of trying to impress the Shāh of Persia with his own prowess. Persian envoys were received with great pomp and costly gifts were made to them. After each success in putting down rebellions or coercing the kings in the Deccan an Indian ambassador was sent to the Shāh to magnify the achievement. Shāh 'Abbās, the great Persian monarch, died a year after Shāh Jahān ascended the throne. His young successor was occupied for a number of years in contests with the Turks, and in suppressing the revolts which inevitably followed the death of a strong and merciless ruler. On the Indian border 'Alī Mardān Khān upheld Persian interests as governor of Qandahār, and was successful in subduing Sher Khān Tārīn of Qoshanj who had been oppressing travellers on the trade route. In 1632 Sher Khān appealed to Shāh Jahān, who granted him an interview and gave him a post in the Punjab. Though the Persian monarch was gradually improving his position, the Turks on the west and the Uzbegs on the north-east were still troublesome, and the Mughuls followed up their Indian successes by intrigues with 'Alī Mardān. He had a personal grievance against Sārū Taqī, the minister of the Shāh, who had called him to account for his governorship and when met by prevarication despatched a force to ensure compliance. Alarmed by this insistence 'Alī Mardān Khān asked help from the Mughul officers at Ghaznī and Kābul, and impressed by Shāh Jahān's recent successes offered to surrender Qandahār to him. Early in 1638 the commandant of Ghaznī arrived and was allowed to enter the fortress. He was followed in a few days by the governor of Kābul and 'Alī Mardān Khān publicly acknowledged his change of allegiance by having the name of Shāh Jahān recited in the Friday prayers and stamped on the coinage of the city, while the fortress was formally handed over to the Mughuls, though a party within it was still in favour of the Persians and corresponded with the leader of the force which had been sent to secure it. In a short campaign the surrounding district was again brought under Mughul sway. 'Alī Mardān Khān was handsomely rewarded and later in the year was made governor of Kashmīr, and honoured by a visit from the emperor.

About the same time peace was effected on the north-eastern frontier in Assam, where constant bickering and incursions had taken place during the previous century. The north of Assam was occupied by two groups of Mongoloid origin calling themselves respectively Koch and Āhom. Intervention by the Muslims in Bengal had taken place sometimes merely by way of aggression and sometimes when invited by the Koch either through internal faction or as helpers against the Āhom. During Jahāngīr's reign the Mughuls had obtained a footing as far east as the Bar Nadī on the border between the present districts of Darrang and Kāmrūp. The Āhoms were embroiled by a cousin of the Koch ruler who had taken refuge with them, and foray and counter-raid continued for some years. In 1635 the Mughuls after several defeats made a last stand at Hājo, which fell, and the Āhoms took the country west of the Bar Nadī. A fresh Mughul expedition in 1637 was successful and the rebel Koch was killed. By the peace established in the following year the imperial boundary on the Bar Nadī was again restored.

This campaign, like others which occupied the forces in various parts of the empire during the next few years, was of slight importance. The ruler of Bāglān, a fertile tract now in the Nāsik district, which lay on the route between Surat and Burhānpur, and was thus familiar to the earlier European travellers, had successfully resisted Akbar, but acknowledged the supremacy of Jahāngīr. Aurangzīb, when appointed governor of the Deccan, was directed to subdue it completely and was successful at the end of 1637. Further west the Mughuls besieged the Portuguese in Damān and Diu, but peace was made through the mediation of Fremlin, the British chief at Surat. In the north the affairs of Kāngra were troublesome. The nominal governor was Jagat Singh, who had given valuable assistance in the reduction of the fortress. He had been sent in 1634 to coerce the refractory Khattaks in the hilly country between Kābul and Peshāwar, and during his absence his son, Rājrūp, was in charge of the Kāngra valley. The revenue due from the tract was not paid and the Mughul officers failed to restore the administration. At his own request Jagat Singh was deputed to bring the tract into order in 1640, but for a year he did nothing and was deprived of his office as he had encroached on a neighbouring jurisdiction and had built a fortress. He disobeyed a summons to return to court and prince Murād Bakhsh was sent against him with three generals in the autumn of 1641. Murād's fiery advance soon caused Jagat Singh to offer terms which were refused, and the Mughul forces captured Nūrpur and besieged the new fortress of Tārāgarh. The demolition of the outer walls soon brought about a final submission early in 1642.

In Bundelkhand Champat Rāi, a new chief, had asserted his leadership. He had been a friend of Bīr Singh, had assisted Jujhār Singh in his rebellion and after Jujhār Singh's death adopted one of his sons named Prithvī Rāj. When Shāh Jahān travelled to Lahore early in 1639 Champat Rāi became more daring, and though 'Abdullah Khān was deputed to bring Bundelkhand into order his efforts were not successful. One of his officers surprised the Bundelā forces between Orchha and Jhānsī and took Prithvī Rāj, who was sent to be confined in the state prison of the Gwalior fort, but Champat Rāi escaped. Changes in the command produced no improvement till in May, 1642, Pahār Singh, son of Bīr Singh, secured the submission of Champat Rāi, who entered the Mughul service. Jealousy between these two rivals for chieftainship induced Champat Rāi to join prince Dārā, though even there he was pursued by the machinations of Pahār Singh.

The wild hilly country lying south of the Ganges and east of Bundelkhand also came under closer rule. Rājā Rudra Pratāp, brother of, and successor to, the Ujjainiya chief who had assisted Shāh Jahān in his rebellion against Jahāngīr, had been less subservient than his predecessor and was reduced to order by 'Abdullah Khān, the governor of Bihār. 'Abdullah Khān then attacked Lachman Singh, the Baghel chief of Ratanpur,[1] and with the assistance of the chief of Bāndho[1] soon obtained his submission. The Cheros, an aboriginal tribe in Palāmau, whose recorded history dates only from this period, were also troublesome and in 1641 the governor of Bihār was ordered to invade their country. Passing south through Gāyā he invested Palāmau and Pratāp Rāi, the Chero rājā, offered terms, which were accepted as the rainy season was approaching and further campaigns would be arduous and dangerous. Other chiefs who were dissatisfied with Pratāp Rāi arrested him, but failed to hold their tribesmen and after several changes in the leadership Pratāp Rāi was released and finally submitted to the Mughuls in 1643.

A minor insurrection in Mālwā, where the Gonds and Bhīls were frequently unruly, required the concentration of considerable forces. In April, 1643, the governor met the Gonds and scattered them, but further operations were delayed by the rainy season and the need for reinforcements. Early in the following year the stronghold held by the rebels was besieged and occupied.

During this period of his reign Shāh Jahān revived and extended the irrigation works in northern India, which had been first constructed towards the end of the fourteenth century by Fīrūz Shāh.[2] When the emperor arrived at Lahore towards the close of 1639 he was visited by 'Alī Mardān Khān, who had been familiar with canal systems at Qandahār and suggested tapping the Rāvī where it emerged from the hills to water the country as far as Lahore. 'Alī Mardān Khān's works have been incorporated in the modern systems known as the Bārī Duāb, the Rohtak and the western Jumna canals.

In 1641 the emperor lost his father-in-law, Āsaf Khān, whose death

[1] Now in the Rewa state. [2] Vol. III, p. 587.

greatly affected him. Kinship and loyalty of service had bound ruler and minister with ties that never weakened. A tomb was built for Āsaf Khān by that of Jahāngīr near Lahore, and his son succeeded him as chief minister just as he had followed his own father. The annalist of the time records that he had amassed great wealth, most of which, as was the custom, reverted to the crown.[1] A few years later (1645) the dowager empress, Nūr Jahān, his sister, died and was also buried in the garden close to the tombs of her husband and brother. Since the death of Jahāngīr she had abstained from politics and lived a retired life, dressing plainly and spending on charitable objects the ample income assigned by Shāh Jahān.

Since his accession Shāh Jahān had always cherished a desire to win back for his house Samarqand, the home and first capital of Tīmūr, which had been taken from Tīmūr's descendants by the Uzbegs under Muhammad Shaibānī. Since then another dynasty had sprung up known as the Jānids of Astrakhan, from which the founders had been expelled by the Russians. One of these married a daughter of the Shaibānid ruler and their son Bāqī Muhammad became chief of the Uzbegs. The offer of help by Imām Qulī, who was chief when Shāh 'Abbās took Qandahār in 1622, has been mentioned in the previous chapter. Uzbeg cupidity was aroused by the confusion in India during Jahāngīr's last years and shortly after the accession of Shāh Jahān Nazr Muhammad, brother of Imām Qulī, undertook the conquest of Kābul. He met with some success, but as the summer advanced his troops melted and he withdrew. There was still no breach between the Mughuls and Imām Qulī, and a second raid by Nazr Muhammad in May, 1629, ceased after his capture of Bāmiān. A few years later Nazr Muhammad himself sent apologies which were accepted and a return envoy carried the usual vainglorious accounts of Shāh Jahān's achievements.

By 1639 Shāh Jahān felt that he was strong enough to pursue his own aims and with his usual thoroughness went himself to Kābul to enquire into the routes to Transoxiana. A small campaign against the tribes who supported the nearest Uzbeg governor alarmed both Imām Qulī and Nazr Muhammad. Confusion among the Uzbegs was increased by Nazr Muhammad deposing his brother, who had lost his sight. The new ruler, less popular with his people than his predecessor, weakened his position by sudden changes in the administration, some of which affected the religious leaders. An attempt to annex Khwārizm or Khiva on the death of its ruler led to a general insurrection early in 1645, and 'Abdul-'Azīz, son of Nazr Muhammad, who was sent to quell it was induced to proclaim himself Khān of Bukhārā, his father taking refuge in Balkh. Shāh Jahān felt that his

[1] Manrique's return journey to Europe at this time was delayed at Multān and Qandahār because the Mughul officials suspected that some of Āsaf Khān's wealth was being surreptitiously removed to Persia, II, 249, 265.

opportunity had arrived and at once began to concert his plans. A Mughul commandant north of Kābul took the fort of Kahmard but lost it and winter closed the operations, though troops from India were collected. Nazr Muhammad and his son were contending for the possession of Bukhārā and agreed that the former should hold Balkh and the latter Bukhārā. An appeal by Nazr Muhammad to Shāh Jahān was met by an offer of help in dubious terms. The emperor himself again visited Kābul. Free from anxiety elsewhere he was able to collect a large force,[1] to staff it with his best officers, and to plan detailed instructions. His son, Murād, who was placed in command, though brave and dashing, was not enthusiastic about his mission. His first objective was the reduction of Badakhshān, and his entry into that tract was delayed by snow on the passes till the middle of June. He advanced into Narin and Qunduz was taken. His instructions were to be generous to Nazr Muhammad and to assist him to recapture Bukhārā with Samarqand, the real intention being to add them to the Mughul dominions. Nazr Muhammad did not fail to see through this thinly veiled design, and tried to stop the advance of the Mughul army, which was now rapid, by asking for time to prepare for a contemplated pilgrimage to Mecca. Murād, however, advanced and early in July, 1646, began his last march into Balkh. As he approached the city Nazr Muhammad fled west and Murād's army was free to enter and plunder the city, where a large treasure was secured. Tirmiz, on the Oxus, was captured and Nazr Muhammad after sustaining a defeat at Shibarghān escaped to Marv and then to Persia. The rapid success of the expedition caused great delight to Shāh Jahān, who marked the conquest by striking money at Balkh.[2] Murād, however, was already disgusted with his position in a country the climate of which was rigorous, while it offered none of the pleasures which he was accustomed to enjoy. He asked to be recalled, and when the offered post of governor of Transoxiana (which had still to be conquered) and the arguments of the able minister sent to advise him failed to alter his views, he was recalled.

Light is thrown on Shāh Jahān's diplomatic methods by his letter to Shāh 'Abbās II of Persia, which ostensibly was to congratulate him on his accession but was meant to secure his neutrality. And he wrote to Nazr Muhammad asserting that Murād had acted impetuously through youth and inexperience and his own object was merely to clear Balkh of dangerous people and hand it over to Nazr Muhammad. If this had indeed been his object he failed to secure it. The local Uzbegs were turbulent and the omission to guard the

[1] He took this opportunity to reorganise the army of the empire, reducing the nominal strength and the emoluments of the commanders.

[2] The short duration of his triumph is attested by the fact that only a single specimen is now known.

line of the Oxus left the north of Balkh and Badakhshān open to raids. No commander-in-chief had been appointed and the four generals could neither combine nor agree. In the spring of 1647 the prince Aurangzīb, who was summoned from Gujarāt to govern Balkh, found his march impeded by tribesmen. 'Abdul-'Azīz had consolidated his position and collected an army on the Oxus. He despatched a force across it to hold the country west of Balkh, and when Aurangzīb shortly after his arrival at the city marched out to meet it, news came of another force advancing direct on Balkh. Aurangzīb returned to meet this and defeated it in a pitched battle where 'Abdul-'Azīz was present. The Uzbeg forces, largely consisting of nomads, fierce in predatory attacks, but with little cohesion in face of a reverse, scattered after the losses of the day. They had been impressed by the calm bravery of Aurangzīb, who dismounted from his horse at sunset to repeat the obligatory prayer. 'Abdul-'Azīz offered to place his brother in charge of Bukhārā, while Nazr Muhammad, who had fled to Persia, offered to abdicate.

Successful as the Mughul enterprise had appeared it had no stability, and it was never pushed beyond the Oxus as Shāh Jahān had hoped and intended. Murād's distaste for service in a more rigorous climate than that of the plains of India was shared by all other officers.[1] Balkh itself, a city with ancient glories, had never recovered from its destruction by Tīmūr and could not be attractive even to a prince like Aurangzīb whose asceticism was coupled with strong ambitions. War had desolated the country and nomads raided it and prevented the revival of cultivation. Moreover, Nazr Muhammad had received help and encouragement from the Shāh of Persia, who was attaining manhood and desired to weaken Mughul authority. Nazr Muhammad was too wary to venture on an attempt to recover Bukhārā, but he advanced into what is now Afghānistān and even attacked the Mughul outposts. Aurangzīb marched out to repel these but was directed by the emperor to accept an apology if one was offered. The close of the short summer made it necessary to be content with a message carried by a grandson instead of the personal submission of Nazr Muhammad. Officers from the outlying garrisons were abandoning their posts in the belief that Nazr Muhammad was to be restored and Aurangzīb returned to Kābul, harassed throughout the march by bands of Uzbegs, who cut off stragglers.

In the following year (1648) Shāh 'Abbās II assumed full powers and at once prepared to recover Qandahār, to the loss of which the Persians had never been resigned.[2] His reply to Shāh Jahān's crafty messages was a summons to give up that city and to restore Balkh to Nazr Muhammad. Balkh had been abandoned, but Qandahār

[1] "For the Mogors were weaklings and luxurious and enervated rather than fighters or warlike soldiers", Manrique, II, 266.

[2] Early in 1642 Manrique heard of attempts to retake it, II, 266.

might still be saved. When news arrived that the Shāh himself had marched into Khurāsān with an army it was too late to send reinforcements from Kābul and Multān across the mountains. By Christmas the Shāh had invested the city and Aurangzīb, who on his return from Balkh had been made governor of Multān, was appointed to command a large army. Extra allowances were sanctioned to encourage the troops in a campaign which would be fiercely contested and would extend to an inhospitable terrain. All these efforts failed, however, to save Qandahār. A detachment of the Persian army invested the fortress of Bist while the main body commanded by the Shāh marched on to Qandahār. Bist surrendered after a siege of two months and some of its garrison were treacherously murdered. Daulat Khān, the governor of Qandahār, when making his dispositions to guard the citadel overlooked a vital point, which was soon occupied by the Persians. Dispirited by the belief that reinforcements could not arrive, and by the energy of the invaders, the garrison soon lost heart. An Uzbeg captain began to correspond with the Persians and the Mughul officials began to think that their own lives and the safety of their families from enslavement might best be ensured by surrender. Daulat Khān tried to suppress the weakness by mere advice instead of the use of strong measures. The traitors received letters from the Shāh which were accepted also by Daulat Khān. They were followed by an envoy, who was also admitted and promised a safe conduct. The Uzbeg hastened to give up the gate in his charge and Daulat Khān soon marched out of the citadel in February, 1649, a month before Aurangzīb, who had been unable to cross the mountains by the shorter route from Kohāt, was able to reach Kābul through Peshāwar.

Qandahār, which had fallen into Shāh Jahān's hands by the defection of its Persian commandant, was thus lost by the failure of a Mughul successor. Hopes of its recovery were still cherished. Advancing through Ghaznī and Kelāt-i-Ghilzāī the Mughul army was near Qandahār in May, and Shāh Jahān himself came as far as Kābul. Throughout the summer raids and fighting continued, but in the autumn the forces were withdrawn as in the haste of advance the organisation of supplies and ammunition had broken down, and the ordnance with the force was considered too light for battering the fortress.

Returning to Delhi, Shāh Jahān consoled himself for the loss of this prized outpost of his empire by rejoicings over the completion of his new capital. His grandfather had refounded the ancient city of Āgra and given it the name of Akbarābād. After long search for a site with amenities of landscape and climate, in 1639 he began to lay the foundations of a great fortress to contain the royal palace and of a city round it. The site chosen was on the bank of the Jumna, north of the older cities of Delhi, close to a small fort of the Sūr kings. For ten years work was concentrated on it, artificers and labourers being collected from all parts of the empire. Transport of stone from near Āgra, 150 miles away, by impressing carts, dislocated the ordinary trade of that neighbourhood so much that the English factors at Āgra could not move their goods to the coast. In nine years the fort and palace had been completed at a cost of six million rupees (£750,000), and to celebrate its occupation the peacock throne which had been set in hand at Shāh Jahān's accession and had taken seven years to complete was brought from Āgra, and great rejoicings took place. The new city was called Shāhjahānābād.

Early in 1651 the emperor set out on his last visit to Kashmīr. Skārdo, the principal fort in Bāltistān, had been taken by a rebel and a short campaign was authorised in which it was easily recovered. The court's stay in Kashmīr was, however, cut short by floods and storms which desolated the beautiful surroundings of the capital, and Shāh Jahān left for Lahore. He had now decided to renew his attempt to win back Qandahār, and warned by the previous failure began to make more complete preparations. Aurangzīb marched from Multān in the spring of 1652 with a large force, and Sa'd-ullah, the chief minister who had accompanied the emperor to Kābul, proceeded to join him with other troops and ample stores of munitions. Immediately after his arrival before the fortress Aurangzīb began the investment. In spite of the fierce bombardment by the Mughul artillery and the repulse of sorties the siege made little progress. The Persian guns were better served and the besiegers wore out some of their largest cannon. From the north the Uzbegs were already threatening Ghaznī, which lay on the route between Qandahār and Kābul, and Aurangzīb was recalled to Kābul after a siege of less than three months.

Another prince now asked for permission to take the city. Dārā Shukoh was appointed governor of Multān and Kābul and spent the winter at Lahore constructing large cannon, providing munitions, and arranging columns of supply. In February, 1653, he set out from Multān, and instead of confining his efforts to direct assaults he also attempted to occupy the surrounding country so as to prevent relief coming from Persia. Bist and Girishk, which lay to the west, were recaptured and the district round was laid waste. As usual endeavours were made to win over the garrison, but they were no more successful than the bombardment. The outlying posts were abandoned to favour concentrated attack. New cannon brought up destroyed a long stretch of the walls, but the attackers were unable to force an entry. The approach of autumn favoured the besieged and the exhaustion of munitions and supplies made it necessary to withdraw the Mughul army if it was to escape destruction by the rigours of winter in Afghānistān. Early in October Dārā Shukoh began his retreat to India.

His failure in these border affairs had perhaps made Shāh Jahān more watchful over dependent states within the empire. Shāh Jahān, while setting out for Ajmer, in 1654, sent Sa'd-ullah the chief minister with a considerable force to destroy some new fortifications which the Rānā of Udaipur had constructed at Chitor in contravention of the agreement made with Jahāngīr. The show of force was enough and the Rānā sought the intercession of Dārā, who was in favour with the emperor in spite of his failure to recover Qandahār. Sa'd-ullah was able to demolish the new works and even to obliterate what remained of the old, and the Rānā's submission was marked by sending his eldest son to carry his apologies to court. Dārā was received with costly presents and a high title and was allowed the privilege of a chair in the royal presence.

A small force was also detached during the return march from Ajmer against the Rājā of Garhwāl, whose country produced gold and the musk deer. An earlier attempt in 1635 under the governor of Kāngra had ended in disaster. That force had passed through Sirmūr, occupying the Dūn or valley between the Siwālik hills and the Himālayas, and marched up the hills to within a few miles of Srīnagar, the capital of Garhwāl. A nominal submission and promise of tribute were obtained, but the force was then surrounded and cut to pieces. This second expedition, conducted with more discretion, also overran the Dūn, hunting down the peasants who fled from their homes and massacring them. Though it was joined by the Rājā of Kumāūn, a jealous enemy of Garhwāl, the commander after crossing the Ganges and entering the enemy country was deterred by the approach of the rainy season and withdrew after making provision for the administration of the small tract he had occupied. A third expedition early in 1656 caused the raja to send his son to court to offer submission.

The king of Golconda, who remained submissive during the earlier wars in the Deccan, was now the cause of fresh warfare. His minister Mīr Muhammad Sa'īd, better known by the title of Mīr Jumla, had extended the authority of Golconda over a tract of country in the Carnatic where diamonds were found. For these services he received no reward owing to the jealous intrigues of other courtiers and he offered himself to the Mughuls. Aurangzīb, who had maintained touch with affairs in Golconda, and had been reappointed governor of the Deccan on his return from Qandahār, had had to press for arrears of payment under the existing treaty.[1] He recommended the acceptance of Mīr Jumla's offer and when the king, towards the close of 1655, imprisoned the minister and his son Aurangzīb claimed his release on the ground that he had been appointed to office under the emperor. To enforce this demand, and also with a view to recovering

[1] The amounts had been fixed in *hūns*, a currency of southern India, and exchange controversies added to the dispute. Cf. note 2, p. 197.

the arrears and securing the marriage of his own son Muhammad with the king's daughter, Aurangzīb assembled a force. For a time the king remained obdurate, but when Aurangzīb's army advanced within his territory he made professions of obedience and released Mīr Jumla's son and mother. As he still retained their property the Mughuls marched on Hyderābād. In alarm the king removed his treasures to the strong fortress of Golconda a few miles away and attempted to bribe Muhammad while allowing his own troops to oppose the Mughuls. Muhammad's forces quickly put the men of Golconda to flight and pursued them up to the walls of the city, while he executed the bearer of the bribe for his treachery. Hyderābād was taken and the king renewed his attempts to buy off the invaders. Grudgingly he parted with some of Mīr Jumla's property and while making protestations of his loyalty continued to strengthen the fortress of Golconda and to seek aid from the king of Bijāpur.

By the middle of February, 1656, Aurangzīb himself arrived in front of Golconda. An attack by the king's troops was repulsed, and he again sent presents and offered to despatch his own mother to ask pardon for his offences. Two further attempts to drive off the Mughuls failed, and reinforced by Shāyista Khān and troops from Mālwā, Aurangzīb was about to press the siege when he received orders from Shāh Jahān to pardon the king. These commands were for the present kept secret, as though the king had promised to pay arrears of tribute the negotiations about marriage were not complete. The payments and restoration of Mīr Jumla's property continued in instalments, and to hasten full compliance Aurangzīb mounted large guns. Finally, the king's mother was received and agreed to pay ten million rupees. Mīr Jumla now arrived in the camp and was formally invested with a robe of honour, and a month later the marriage was celebrated. Though the Qutb Shāhī dynasty lingered on for some years its independence was now thoroughly sapped and its decline is marked by the issue of coin shortly after this time with the touching legend "It has come to an end, well and auspiciously".[1] Mīr Jumla received the title of Mu'azzam Khān and Shāyista Khān that of Khān Jahān. After the death of Sa'd-ullah, the learned and capable minister of Shāh Jahān, Mīr Jumla was appointed to succeed him and exercised great influence.

The kingdom of Bijāpur, unlike that of Golconda, had emerged from the contests of twenty years before with independence, and had not become a tributary of the empire. During this period it had been well governed by Muhammad 'Ādil Shāh, who had maintained friendly relations with Shāh Jahān and in 1648 had been formally recognised by the emperor as entitled to be known as "Shāh" instead of "Khān". While busying himself with improving the internal administration of his government he had also extended his

[1] *J.A.S.B.* 1909, p. 317.

authority right across India from sea to sea, coming into conflict with the Portuguese in the west and with Golconda in the east. These successes led him to assume a splendour of display which annoyed Shāh Jahān and led to reproofs that were meekly accepted.

With Mīr Jumla in high favour at the court and entirely devoted to his interests Aurangzīb now began to plan aggressive measures against Bijāpur. These were already in train when the death of Muhammad 'Ādil Shāh in November, 1656, provided a plausible excuse for interference. A youth named 'Alī 'Ādil Shāh was placed on the throne, and some people doubted his right to succeed though the matter was uncertain. 'Alī 'Ādil Shāh was too young to control the factions at his court and rebellion broke out in the newly conquered territory to the east. Aurangzīb's intrigues won secret promises of allegiance from some of the nobles, and money was lavished to attract deserters. Sanction was received from the emperor, who gave clear definitions of the objectives, the complete subjection of Bijāpur if possible, and failing that the reconquest of those portions of the old Ahmadnagar kingdom which had been retained by Bijāpur. If this predatory campaign were successful the army was in the next place to make an end of even the nominal power of Golconda. Troops to aid these enterprises were sent from Mālwā and Mīr Jumla himself, who knew the Deccan better than any other officer, was in command. As soon as he arrived at Aurangzīb's headquarters the expedition started, but its progress was slow as ample provision had been made of heavy guns which could not be moved rapidly. The first serious operation was the siege of Bīdar, a strongly fortified town on a rocky plateau with an inner castle protected by moats deep in the living rock. In spite of a fierce defence and daring sorties the besiegers were able to fill the moats and damage the walls. A chance rocket caused an explosion by which the commandant was mortally wounded. An assault gave the city to Aurangzīb, and the dying commandant yielded up the citadel.

Aurangzīb now sent forward troops to disperse the Bijāpur army which had advanced to meet him, and an indecisive engagement took place. He was, however, able to advance to Kalyānī and laid siege to it. Here he was again stoutly opposed and his long lines of communication were persistently harassed by large mobile forces of the enemy. Feigning a retreat he attacked them and after handling them severely seized their camp. The siege was renewed and for two months the Mughuls were free to pursue it. When the Bijāpur forces again gathered they were attacked and dispersed before they could approach the beleaguered city, which was assaulted and capitulated.

Further operations were, however, stopped by orders from the emperor. His health was failing and he was more ready to listen to the envious suggestions of Dārā, who was approached by emissaries from Bijāpur. The advance of the monsoon, during which military operations are difficult, was made the pretext for instructions that peace must be arranged and the army should disperse. Negotiations were quickly settled. An indemnity was fixed, and Bijāpur agreed to cede besides the two captured fortresses the fort of Parenda, which had long eluded the Mughul grasp, forts in the Konkan, and Vangī. Even these meagre promises were not fulfilled as the Bijāpur officials, seeing the Mughul forces dwindle, refused to surrender their strongholds.

For many years the Marāthās had not been dangerous to the Mughul administration, but while Aurangzīb had been occupied with Golconda and Bijāpur Shivājī the son of Shāhjī had begun a career which was before long to shake the Muslim power and finally exhaust it. His father had been forced to enter the service of Bijāpur, and he himself offered to assist the Mughuls in their enterprise against that kingdom in return for part of the territory to be wrested from it, but he was put off with vague replies. When Aurangzīb was fully occupied with his invasion Shivājī surprised Junnar and organised raids through Mughul territory west of Ahmadnagar. Memories of the difficulties forced on the imperial arms by Shāhjī impelled Aurangzīb to make careful plans to ward off these dangers on his western flank. While he was occupied in the siege of Kalyānī one of his officers defeated Shivājī and nearly captured him. The rainy season, however, made campaigning more difficult in the Konkan than on the plateau and operations had to cease, and when the treaty with Bijāpur was made Shivājī thought it wise to submit also.

Aurangzīb's interests now pointed away from the Deccan to the capital of the empire. By far the most capable of Shāh Jahān's sons and the most ambitious, he had found his enterprises thwarted by the intrigues of his eldest brother, Dārā Shukoh. Succession by primogeniture is a dangerous rule in kingdoms beset by enemies and full of elements only partly subdued. Shāh Jahān, like his own father, was prematurely aged, though his weakness was due to indulgence in the pleasures of the harem rather than to wine, and as Jahāngīr had resigned his authority to his wife, so did Shāh Jahān place excessive reliance in Dārā Shukoh, and openly designated him as heir. While Aurangzīb was occupying the onerous post of viceroy of the Deccan his conduct of affairs was subject to irritating direction. His successes were not rewarded and his emoluments were in fact reduced. He saw that Dārā was allowed to govern rich tracts by deputy and had rank and honour heaped upon him. Even the bitterness of sectarian hatred was infused into the relations between the brothers, for while Aurangzīb was rigidly orthodox Dārā was an amateur of Hindu mysticism like many Muslims who adopt the creed of the Sūfīs. Shāh Jahān in the last few years had lost all his best counsellors by death, and affection for his eldest son had blinded his judgement, when he entrusted control to one who was lacking in experience of the affairs of either peace or war.

In September, 1657, Shāh Jahān fell ill, and for nearly a week his life was despaired of. His absence from the daily public receptions led to the belief that he was dying, or even dead. Believing his end was near Shāh Jahān had himself carried as soon as he was able to move to Āgra. News from their agents at court was carried to the three sons in their distant posts and was followed by wild rumours. Each of them was determined not to be supplanted by Dārā, but their actions were dictated by their varying characters and circumstances. Impetuous and daring, Murād Bakhsh, who was governor of Gujarāt, murdered his capable minister 'Alī Naqī and attacked and plundered Surat. He then proclaimed himself emperor and struck coin in his own name at Ahmadābād, Surat and Cambay. Shāh Shujā', a more capable person who had for many years administered Bengal with skill in both civil and military affairs, took the field and advanced with his forces to seize the crown. Both of them were in correspondence with Aurangzīb, whose object was to use them to further his own advantage. He wrote frequently to restrain Murād Bakhsh till his own plans were complete, devising a cipher to avoid discovery if his letters were captured, and he organised a relay of messengers through the wild country that lay between the Deccan and Bengal. Nor did he omit to set on foot intrigues with officers at the court. His own movements were hampered by uncertainty about the position at court and the exhaustion of his resources. At the first rumours of Shāh Jahān's precarious state the Bijāpur officers had completely suspended the fulfilment of the treaty and Aurangzīb was being pressed to enforce it.

Dārā's plan was to crush Murād Bakhsh and Shāh Shujā' first and then to march against Aurangzīb. Recognising the greater danger to be feared from the last he had spared no pains to weaken him. While Shāh Jahān was still dangerously ill, Dārā issued orders which removed Mīr Jumla from his post as chief minister but directed him to secure the surrender of Parenda, while at the same time they recalled the troops sent from headquarters to aid in the Bijāpur campaign. He tried to sow dissension by transferring Berār from Aurangzīb to Murād Bakhsh, an offer which was at once rejected. Shāh Jahān's recovery to some degree of health was marked by the despatch of a force under Dārā's son Sulaimān Shukoh with a capable general Rājā Jay Singh of Amber to meet Shāh Shujā'. Two other armies were sent west shortly afterwards to recover Gujarāt from Murād Bakhsh and to hold Aurangzīb in check. It was difficult to find commanders for these, so great was the respect in which Aurangzīb's generalship was held. Mīr Jumla was recalled to court, but was formally arrested and detained by Aurangzīb as a subterfuge, which was at once unveiled when his plans had succeeded.

The first army met Shāh Shujā' near Benares and an exchange of messages took place. Dārā's endeavours to stop news of affairs at the capital from reaching his brothers had given them the excuse that they were anxious to save their father from danger at his hands. In accordance with Shāh Jahān's instructions Rājā Jay Singh assured Shāh Shujā' that his father was alive and well and offered him forgiveness and the grant of Bihār if he would return to his post. Shāh Shujā' feigned compliance, intending to attack Rājā Jay Singh as he withdrew, but the raja, penetrating his design, attacked and scattered his forces, and pursued Shāh Shujā' to the borders of Bengal.

Before this battle took place Aurangzīb had matured his plans. To secure his rear he changed his attitude towards the kings of Golconda and Bijāpur, no longer holding them to the fulfilment of their engagements, but promising rewards when he should become emperor. He asked Bijāpur to employ Shivājī in the Carnatic while at the same time he was offering Shivājī permanent grants in the Deccan. Troops had been enlisted, European gunners employed and large stores of ammunition prepared. By February, 1658, he was ready to leave Aurangābād, and after a month's stay at Burhānpur set out on the march which was to conduct him to the throne. Omitting no precautions he even imprisoned his own father-in-law, who showed reluctance to join his rebellious enterprise. Near Dīpālpur he was joined by Murād Bakhsh and made a short march to Dharmat, fourteen miles from Ujjain.

The two imperial armies sent against the brothers, hampered by their instructions to fight only as a last resource, had wasted time and suffered from divided counsels and lack of intelligence. An attempt to stop Murād Bakhsh failed, and the earliest news of Aurangzīb's movements was that he had already crossed the Narbadā and was rapidly approaching. Aurangzīb sent messages to Rājā Jasvant Singh of Mārwār, who commanded the Rājput army, asking him to withdraw as Aurangzīb was merely going on a peaceful visit to his father. The raja's reply was to advance towards the prince's position. Then only he learnt that Murād had joined his brother; too late he offered his submission, and his honour prevented him from accepting the terms which were offered. In the battle which ensued the Rājputs attacked the rebel forces with great bravery, but the disposition of the imperial troops was bad, and they were unskilfully directed. Many of their chiefs lost their lives and Rājā Jasvant Singh, badly wounded, was forcibly led away as he advanced to sell his life for his master. Only one of the senior Muslim officers was killed and the following day four of them offered their services to Aurangzīb while the rest escaped. Shāh Jahān, who had left Āgra for the greater comfort of his new palace at Delhi, returned on hearing the news of this disastrous loss.

In the glow of his victory Aurangzīb ordered the foundation of a new town called Fathābād,[1] and after a short rest marched to Gwalior,

[1] "Fath" is Arabic for "Victory".

arriving there at the end of June in the height of the Indian hot season. Here he received news that Dārā had advanced from Āgra to meet him with a large army and was holding the fords of the Chambal river which lay between them. To a letter from his sister declaring that the emperor had quite recovered and that his revolt was impious, he recounted how Dārā had thwarted him and must be removed. The old jealousy between rival chiefs of the Bundelās led Champat Rāi, who had suffered at the hands of Dārā,[1] to lead a division of Aurangzīb's army to a little used ford far to the east of the main road which had escaped observation, and the main force also crossed by this, enduring great hardships from the roughness of the track and the intense heat.

By this détour and rapid march Aurangzīb forced Dārā to abandon his elaborately prepared position on the main road and, leaving behind much of his heavy artillery, to retreat towards Āgra. Near Sāmogarh, about ten miles east of the city, the two armies met. Dārā's army, though superior in numbers and containing many reliable Rājputs and Sayyids of Bārha, included masses of untrained men and foreign mercenaries whose loyalty could not be relied on. Unskilled in the conduct of a battle, he had few able leaders and in particular was unable to make the best use of his bravest men. His first error was to fail to attack Aurangzīb on his arrival at Sāmogarh with troops exhausted by the heat, and to allow them to rest for the night. Next morning when the battle began his guns opened before the enemy were in range, and his first attack on the left was launched on unscathed opponents who had reserved their fire and repulsed it. Changing front to the centre this force was rapidly met by Aurangzīb's reserves and cut to pieces, its leader, Rustam Khān,[2] being killed. On the right Khalīl-ullah made a half-hearted attack on Murād Bakhsh which was not pressed, but a reserve from the centre, largely composed of Rājputs, followed it up and penetrated the rebel forces, even attacking the elephant on which Murād Bakhsh was seated. He himself received three arrow wounds in the face and his driver was killed before him. In spite of his personal bravery he was forced back and the Rājputs attacked the fresh forces which Aurangzīb led against them in person. Their bravery and devotion to leaders won the admiration of Aurangzīb, who tried to restrain his bodyguard from striking down beaten foes.

Dārā's conduct of the battle was as inept as his character and training would suggest. At an early stage he left the centre and moved to the support of Rustam Khān, thus masking his own artillery, and losing control of other parts of the field. He was met by the fire of Aurangzīb's guns, which had been reserved till then. Attempting

[1] See p. 201.

[2] The later title of the general Muqarrab Khān (see p. 189), who had served Shāh Jahān well in Rohilkhand and in the Balkh campaign.

a fresh attack to the right he found his heavily armoured troops exhausted by the heat and met by fresh reserves, while the enemy's guns were moving to encircle him. His officers pressed him to dismount from his elephant on which he offered too conspicuous a mark. The empty howdah, seen from a distance, made his troops believe he was dead, and the shattered units broke and dispersed for safety. Dārā escaped on horseback, barely able to cover the short distance to Āgra without a halt, having lost 10,000 men in the battle, while many others perished from heat or exhaustion. Ashamed to meet his father after defeat when he had sallied forth boasting of the victory he expected, he fled in a few hours towards Delhi, accompanied only by a handful of servants, and leaving the emperor in despair.

The victor, after prayer, received his wounded brother, ascribing the victory to Murād Bakhsh's bravery and declaring that Murād's reign should begin at once. Then moving slowly towards Āgra he camped outside the city and received offers of service from the nobles, who easily abandoned the losing side. Shāh Jahān invited him to a meeting, to which he first agreed, but later withdrew his acceptance. Crafty himself, he feared an ambush. The emperor, finding his overtures rejected, and seeing the city occupied by his son's rebellious forces, was apprehensive for his own life, and closing the gates prepared to defend the fort, which contained a strong garrison of slaves and was almost impregnable by assault. Aurangzīb opened fire with his guns, but it was ineffective and time pressed. He therefore cut off the supply of water from the Jumna, and as the wells in the fort were brackish distress was quickly felt. After three days the emperor again appealed to the filial duties of his son and was met by renewed assertions that Aurangzīb was faithful to him while Dārā was the traitor. The gates were opened and the fort was cleared of Shāh Jahān's adherents, under the supervision of a grandson. Aurangzīb was again pressed to visit his father, who sent his daughter Jahānārā Begam with a proposal that the empire should be divided between the four brothers. Aurangzīb even set out in a gorgeous procession to enter the fort, but the dissuasions of his officers were reinforced by the delivery to him of a letter despatched by Shāh Jahān to Dārā assuring him that all would be well, and he passed by the gate.

After holding a darbar with great ceremony to receive his new officials he started in pursuit of Dārā, but his march was slow, as his ever suspicious mind was occupied with the possibility of danger from the ambition of Murād Bakhsh. Secluded owing to his wounds Murād felt that his brother's power was increasing while he himself was overshadowed, and he began to increase his own troops by offering liberal pay and titles. When so many captains were stark adventurers, more likely to gain profit by fighting than in a settled peace, it was easy to gain recruits. His clumsy designs were easily read by Aurangzīb, who met them by craft and ruthlessness. Having marched a short distance from Āgra he sent money and horses to Murād to aid his expenses in the pursuit of Dārā and invited him to a banquet. For some days the dissuasion of his more apprehensive officers kept Murād from accepting the invitation, but a personal attendant who had been corrupted by Aurangzīb induced him to enter his brother's camp after a heated day in the chase. The brothers ate together and Murād was invited to rest after the hunt. A female slave who was sent to his tent to shampoo his legs removed his weapons as he slept and he was easily made a prisoner, and carried off secretly and immediately to the fort at Delhi. Fickle troops at once joined Aurangzīb and their leaders accepted rich gifts.

Meanwhile Dārā, who had seized Delhi in his first flight and had begun to collect a fresh army, soon realised that he could not hope to resist Aurangzīb there. He therefore pressed on to Lahore, leaving guards on the Sutlej and striving to increase his own forces and to corrupt the generals of his brother. There was reason to hope that the fatigue of Aurangzīb's army would allow him time to organise a successful resistance.

By the confinement of Murād Bakhsh Aurangzīb was now relieved of immediate anxiety, and he marched on to Delhi, where he rapidly matured his plans. One force was sent at once after Dārā, and another was despatched east to capture Allahābād as a bulwark against Sulaimān Shukoh and the possibility of action by Shāh Shujā'. For three weeks he halted, busy with the details of civil administration. Here he finally achieved his original plan and assumed the imperial title, though with scanty pomp, taking the additional name of 'Ālamgīr (universe grasper). Thus ended the reign of Shāh Jahān, who spent the remaining years of his life a prisoner in the fort of Āgra. Here he was confined in the gilded marble palace he had built, from which he could gaze down the Jumna with its arid dusty banks to the magnificent tomb he was building for his wife—and himself.

By race Shāh Jahān was three-quarters Indian, both his mother and grandmother having been Rājput ladies of high birth, and the failure of his sons and army in the enterprise against Balkh showed that the Mughul line in India was no longer able to cope with the hardy and turbulent tribesmen beyond the Hindū Kush. Each of the Mughul emperors from Akbar to Aurangzīb seemed to realise and avoid the faults of his predecessor more diligently than to emulate any good qualities that existed. As a youth Shāh Jahān was accustomed to see his father indulging to excess in drink, and Jahāngīr himself records that he was unable to persuade his son even to taste liquor till he was twenty-four.[1] And throughout his life, while his

[1] While at this period Roe states that both father and son were fond of red wine it is clear that Shāh Jahān never became a drunkard.

marriage to Mumtaz Mahall proved a pleasing example of conjugal happiness for nearly twenty years, and later he became addicted to sensual pleasures, he never subordinated his own judgement to female influences as Jahāngīr did.

Even during boyhood the restless uncertainty as to their hopes of a crown that always obsessed the sons of an oriental ruler was forced upon him. The dispute with his elder brother Khusrav over the elephant fight which disturbed the last days of his grandfather Akbar occurred when he was not fourteen, and shortly afterwards he saw Khusrav try to wrest the throne from their father. During a stay of over three years (1615–19) in India Sir Thomas Roe was at the court for long periods and his business brought him into contact with Shāh Jahān, who was then governor of Gujarāt and thus of great importance to the British ambassador endeavouring to establish trade. The grievances of the English traders naturally prejudiced Roe against the man whom he believed to be responsible for not righting them. Moreover, the prince disliked Roe, who insisted on being treated with the dignity due to his office as ambassador and could not be cajoled or brow-beaten. Roe's allowances from the company did not permit him to offer presents so costly as those of the Portuguese who were his competitors for favour. Allowing for these sources of bias Roe's judgement of the prince is confirmed by other sources. He found Shāh Jahān at the age of twenty-four already mature, and writes:

> I never saw so settled a countenance, nor any man keepe so constant a gravety, never smiling, nor in face showing any respect or difference of men; but mingled with extreame pride and contempt of all. Yet I found some inward trouble now and then assayle him, and a kind of brokennes and distraction in his thoughts, unprovidedly and amasedly answering sutors, or not hearing.[1]

Elsewhere he describes the prince as "proud naturally" and as intolerant and more favourable to the Portuguese than to the English, which was natural, as the English were newcomers of whom nothing was known in India while the Portuguese had already established some dominion there.

When he came to the throne Shāh Jahān was nearly thirty-six, and his character had mellowed. He had disposed of all possible rivals of the blood royal and the people at large were prepared to welcome a ruler who had shown ability as general and administrator after the impotent government of his father. Nor were they disappointed, as Shāh Jahān, at last relieved from the long anxiety about his position, showed that he had unexpected geniality and moderation. His careful handling of the Afghān tribes round the Khyber pass who commanded the line of communications with Kābul and are even still a menace to civilised administration shows this.[2] These

[1] Shāh Jahān was just about to leave for the Deccan, having superseded his brother Parviz, of whom he was jealous.

[2] C. E. Biddulph, *Afghan Poetry* (1890), p. xiv.

qualities, however, did not permit toleration of abuses and negligence of their duties by the officials of the empire, and there were notable instances of local administrators being removed for such faults. Though in matters of religion his plain straightforward creed permitted no licence, he never degenerated into the bigot that his successor became. With the latitude of Akbar's religious beliefs and practices, and the looseness of Jahāngīr's court, he had no sympathy, and his objects were primarily to restore the strict profession of Islām rather than to persecute believers in other religions. Thus he soon abolished the ceremonial prostration before the throne which had been instituted by Akbar and maintained by Jahāngīr, and in its place prescribed forms which savoured less of divine worship. The ostentatious use of the divine era instituted by Akbar ceased so far as the record of months on the coinage was concerned a few years after Shāh Jahān's accession, except in one or two outlying places, though the practical value of a calendar of solar months led to their continued use (but not invariably) for fiscal purposes.

In 1633 Shāh Jahān ordered the demolition of Hindu temples which had been begun in the previous reign, especially at Benares, and many were demolished. These orders were followed by a prohibition of the erection of new shrines or the repair of older buildings. Intermarriage between Hindus and Muslims, which had been common in the Punjab and Kashmīr, was forbidden in 1634. Hindus were directed to keep to their own style of dress,[1] and to discontinue practices which were offensive to the tenets of Islām, such as cremation or the burning of widows near a Muslim cemetery, or the sale of intoxicating liquor. Mass conversions of Hindus to Islām were also encouraged, and in some cases were forcibly effected. All these acts, however, were dictated rather by the desire to maintain the strict tenets of Islām than to pursue the course of iconoclasm which was adopted by Aurangzīb. Thus the demolition of new temples was not followed by the erection of mosques on their sites. In his later years Shāh Jahān appears to have left Dārā unchecked in his studies of Hinduism, which led him to seek for common truths underlying two faiths differing so much in their external practices.[2]

For the expedition against the Portuguese at Hooghly there were grounds other than those of religious intolerance. But the small band of captives who eventually reached Āgra alive were severely treated in the hope of obtaining their conversion. Those who accepted Islām were more kindly dealt with, and employment was found for them. The buildings and land of the mission at Āgra were taken over, but

[1] A Hindu ordinarily fastens his upper garment on the left, and a Muslim on the right.

[2] "Les entretiens de Lahore" [entre le prince impérial Dara Shikuh et l'ascète Hindou Baba La'l Das] by Cl. Huart and L. Massignon, *Revue du monde musulman*, 1926, p. 285. Jahāngīr described the ascetic Chid Rūp as one who had thoroughly mastered the science of the Vedānta, which is the science of Sufism; *Memoirs*, I, 355. See also *J.A.S.B.* 1870, p. 273 and Sarkar, *History of Aurangzīb*, I, 296.

two years later were restored. Although it was ordered that the church should first be dismantled the materials were left with the priests, who were permitted to build a house and to baptize children of Christians, and perform marriages, to visit the sick, to hold services for their congregations, and to use the cemetery which had been granted by Jahāngīr and contains the oldest Christian tombs in northern India.[1] Churches in other parts of the Mughul dominions were also demolished, but in 1641 Manrique was successful in obtaining a grant for the restoration of the church in Sind, and also secured the release of one of the priests who had been taken prisoner at Hooghly.

The reign shows no new developments in administrative matters. Under Jahāngīr both finance and general administration had deteriorated and Shāh Jahān was largely occupied in restoring stability and efficiency. His chief measure was a reduction in the gross emoluments of the higher officials coupled with a clearer definition of the number of troops they were required to maintain, and its effect seems to have been to produce a real force instead of one merely on paper, while it left the officials with a better margin of pay.

Shāh Jahān's mind was orderly but not inventive. The court historians and foreign travellers praise his diligence in affairs of state, and the records of his military enterprises show the attention with which he controlled them. State revenues increased, in spite of the disastrous famine of 1630, owing to better supervision over officials and greater security of life. In Bengal Shāh Shujā' during his long term as governor made progress in the detailed assessments of land, which had been summary on the first conquest by Akbar. And in the Deccan a Persian named Murshid Qulī Khān, who had entered Mughul service with 'Alī Mardān Khān, performed a similar task after peace had been established. Trade, in spite of the edicts issued by Akbar and Jahāngīr, was subject to constant restrictions dictated by the theory that government should gain the highest possible revenue from it, rather than that it should foster its improvement. In 1633 Shāh Jahān declared a royal monopoly in indigo, and ordered that the sale of indigo throughout the Mughul dominions should be effected only through a certain Hindu merchant, who was to receive a loan from the treasury and share the profit.[2] The monopoly included the supplies in Gujarāt as well as those round Āgra, and it failed, though it had the support of Mīr Jumla, only because the Dutch and Portuguese, who were large buyers, combined to keep off the market. Commerce was much impeded by similar monopolies established by local governors, which were apparently unchecked by the central government.[3]

[1] For the grant of these privileges see *Journal, Punjab Historical Society*, VIII, 25.
[2] W. Foster, *The English Factories in India* (1630–33), p. xxxiv.
[3] W. H. Moreland, *From Akbar to Aurangzeb*, pp. 146 *sqq*.

In his relations with other powers Shāh Jahān's diplomacy usually consisted of attempts to dazzle by exaggerating his own prowess against the small kingdoms of the Deccan, and it was marked by no great statesmanship. Communications with Turkey were opened by the despatch of a horse dealer who also took presents, and for some years envoys were exchanged. A Turkish officer who arrived in 1653 brought a letter which mentioned the complaints made by Nazr Muhammad, and Shāh Jahān's reply, in which he taunted the Sultān with his youth and the incapacity of his councillors, closed the exchange of communication, which had been purely ceremonial. As a good Muslim Shāh Jahān frequently sent presents to the Sharīf of Mecca and gifts for the poor in the towns of Mecca and Medina.

With European nations the intercourse was less formal and embassies were not contemplated. Portuguese influence, in spite of the possession of territory, was waning, and that of the Dutch and English, though it increased, was still directed to mercantile affairs and had not achieved a political status. The Portuguese in 1630 attempted to get the English and Dutch ousted from Surat and offered to settle and trade there. They captured a Mughul ship to put pressure on the Mughuls, but an English fleet came to the governor's assistance, and later Shāh Jahān was able to induce Bijāpur to blockade Goa and the Portuguese were glad to restore the ship and waive their demands. In 1635 Methwold, the president at Surat, was able to arrange a convention with the viceroy at Goa with beneficial results. Rivalry between the Dutch and English continued, and Shāh Jahān offered concessions to the Dutch if they would expel the Portuguese from Damān and Diu, but the proposal was not accepted by the Dutch governor-general at Batavia. The persistence of the traders, both English and Dutch, and the profits arising from their operations gradually led to the grant of more privileges, though progress was chequered and factors were sometimes subjected to imprisonment.

Shāh Jahān had inherited some of the artistic taste of his father. His practical, more business-like nature, however, diverted this from the cultivation of painting and the accumulation of jewels and curiosities to bolder and more striking developments of art. On his accession he had taken from his treasury a large store of precious stones and gold and ordered the construction of the peacock throne with a canopy supported on twelve pillars adorned with enamel and jewels. Seven years later, at the celebration of the vernal equinox, he took his seat on it and the throne remained for a century one of the glories of the Mughul dynasty till Nādir Shāh after sacking Delhi took it away.[1]

It was, however, in the field of architecture that the reign was most distinguished. Indian art had still retained its faculty of learning

[1] For a picture of Shāh Jahān seated on the throne with Āsaf Khān presenting pearls see British Museum MS., Add. 20,734, folios 689, 690.

from foreign influence but making its own treatment and stamping its productions with the marks of an indigenous culture. Shāh Jahān had a strong interest in the designs and plans of buildings and personally discussed and revised them. When he ordered the construction of the peacock throne he also began to rebuild most of the existing palaces and apartments in the fort at Āgra to make a setting for it.[1] Of the most conspicuous erections of which he was the founder, the first to be begun (in 1632) was the Tāj at Āgra, to contain the tomb of his wife.[2]

While the Tāj is conspicuous, not only for its grandeur of conception and delicate profusions of detail, the pearl mosque in the fort at Delhi, constructed in 1646–53, delights the eye by its majestic simplicity. Of the splendours of the fort at Delhi and the new city founded there in 1639 much has been written.[3] The verse inscribed round the cornice of the hall of private audience declaring that if there is a heaven on earth it is here is less hyperbolical than the boasts of many great builders. In size alone the palace exceeds anything of the kind in Europe, covering an area more than double that of the Escurial. The main street of the city is nearly a mile long and very wide. The canals originally made for irrigation were extended to supply the city and palace with water, and the chronicle records that there was not a room in the palace nor a lane in the city to which the supply did not reach.

Shāh Jahān's activities in building were not confined to the centres of government alone. In 1644 he ordered the construction of a mosque at Tatta as a recognition of the welcome held out to him by the inhabitants during his rebellion against Jahāngīr, while a mosque near the tomb of Shaikh Salīm Chistī and a pavilion on the bank of the Ana Sāgar at Ajmer also date from this reign.

In literature the cultivation of the vernacular, with which Shāh Jahān was familiar, was notable. Persian naturally maintained the chief place and a court laureate named Abu-'l-Tālib, who came from Kāshān in Persia and took the pen-name Kalīm, versified the official chronicle in a simpler style than the ornate poetry of the Indian Muslims. Hājjī Muhammad Jān also wrote a chronicle in poetry and a description of the gardens of Kashmīr and the buildings for which Shāh Jahān was responsible. A Brāhman of the Punjab named Chandra Bhān, who was employed by prince Dārā Shukoh, also wrote Persian poetry and prose. Among the writers in vernacular Sundar Dās, a Brāhman of Gwalior, was especially honoured, and received the title of Mahā Kavi Rāi or great poet leader. Writing

[1] "The Āgra fort and its building", *Arch. Survey India* (1903–4), pp. 164 *sqq*.

[2] The first part of her title "Mumtāz Mahall" has been corrupted into Tāj. For a description see chap. XVIII, pp. 561 *sqq*.

[3] Fergusson, *History of Indian and Oriental Architecture* (1891), p. 591. For specimens of the coloured inlay work see *Preservation of National Monuments in India* (1896), plate 32, and of painting, plate 33. See also chap. XVIII, p. 564.

in the Braj dialect of Hindī he produced a great work on composition, besides a philosophical treatise and translations from the Sanskrit. Chintāmani of Cawnpore district, who composed a version of the Rāmāyana and a treatise on prosody, was also patronised by the emperor. An even more distinguished writer in Hindu estimation was Deb Dat, also a Brāhman, from the present Mainpurī district, who produced many works of religious poetry besides a treatise on prosody and rhetoric and a play.

While these Brāhmans under the influence of court patronage were producing works of literary merit, men of other castes were composing hymns which have done so much to deepen the spiritual life of the masses and to inculcate faith and devotion in place of philosophical abstraction. Prān Nāth, a Chhattrī of Pannā in Bundelkhand, wrote a number of poems which attempt to reconcile Hinduism and Islām, their language itself being marked by a grammatical basis of Hindī with a vocabulary of Persian and Arabic words. A cotton carder of Ahmadābād named Dādū, who lived most of his life in Rājputāna, was a prolific hymn writer and has many followers. These authors were the founders of sects which still exist, known as the Prānnāthīs and Dādūpanthīs. Still greater influence has been exerted by Tukārām, a grain seller of low caste born near Poona, whose hymns became so popular that he was persecuted by the Brāhmans as one who had no right to be a religious teacher.

CHAPTER VIII

AURANGZĪB (1658–1681)

AURANGZĪB'S conduct during the war of succession was marked by rapidity of movement, wise distribution and exact co-ordination of forces, and quick-eyed generalship in the field. When to these factors we add the previous war-experience of his troops and their training in concerted action under his eyes, as well as his royal gift of judging the character of men at sight and choosing worthy and faithful agents, we can easily understand his unbroken success in this war against three rivals of equal rank and resources, none of whom was a coward or imbecile. He had opened the campaign on 30 March, 1658, when he set out for Delhi from Burhānpur. In less than three months from that day, he had crossed two large rivers, won two severely contested battles, captured the capital, and imprisoned the sovereign (18 June). The administration of the empire now naturally passed into his strong and capable hands, and his supreme position was freed from all rivalry after his treacherous arrest of his discontented and jealous partner Murād Bakhsh (5 July). The cloak of legality was thrown over his usurped authority when he crowned himself emperor at Delhi on 31 July, 1658, with the title of Abu-'l-Muzaffar Muhiy-ud-dīn Muhammad Aurangzīb Bahādur 'Ālamgīr Pādishāh Ghāzī.

But he had two large enemy forces still to dispose of before his throne could be considered secure. Dārā Shukoh had escaped from the ruin of his hopes at Sāmogarh (8 June), first to Delhi and then to the Punjab, where he was raising an army, while Dārā's eldest son, Sulaimān Shukoh, after defeating his uncle Shujā' (at Bahādurpur on 24 February) and dictating peace to him (at Monghyr about 17 May), was advancing towards Āgra with his victorious troops. An eastward march of Dārā would have ensured the combination of the father and the son and created a serious danger for Aurangzīb. But the luckless Dārā had turned to the Punjab, as that province was held for him by trusty deputies, its people were mostly attached to him, and large numbers of recruits could be had at call among its martial population. This move ruined Dārā's cause. Aurangzīb inserted himself like a wedge between the father and the son and rendered the junction of their forces impossible except by following a wide loop to the north, of which he held the short chord in strength. On hearing of this blocking of their westward route, Sulaimān Shukoh's army rapidly melted away, his captains openly deserted him for their homes or for Aurangzīb's standard, and within two days of the arrival of the news of Sāmogarh and Dārā's flight to the north-west, Sulaimān's army shrank from 20,000 men to less than 6000. Aurangzīb, holding the inner line, moved his divisions with great ease and rapidity and blocked every ferry by which Sulaimān tried to reach the Punjab by skirting the foot of the central Himālayas, so that the young prince became in effect a hunted fugitive.

Thus, freed for the time being from all danger on the east, Aurangzīb turned his undivided attention to the pursuit of Dārā. That luckless aspirant to the throne was neither a general himself, nor had he the wisdom of being guided by veteran generals whose devotion to him was manifest. His sole strategy was to flee before Aurangzīb's forces, however small, without hazarding any action. His timid and contradictory orders took the heart out of such of his subordinates as were prepared to hold up the advancing vanguard of the pursuers at the rivers of the Punjab, which are so admirably situated to favour a defence by delaying tactics. The result was that Dārā, in spite of his getting possession of the imperial treasuries at Delhi and Lahore (the latter estimated to contain ten million rupees), besides the money and jewels that Shāh Jahān had sent to him from Āgra, could not get time enough to give cohesion and training to the 20,000 soldiers that he had gathered together at Lahore. He merely fled from town to town down the Punjab river at the first news of the arrival of Aurangzīb's troops behind him. The only difficulties of the pursuers came from the heat of the season, the rapidity of the marches they had to make (which led to large numbers of soldiers lagging behind), the exhaustion and death of their horses and camels, and their inability to overtake the enemy and bring him to a decisive action. Dārā had left Delhi on 22 June, 1658, and reached Lahore on 13 July. His rear-guard, holding the Sutlej at Talwandī and Rūpar, had its left turned by Bahādur Khān's crossing the river at Rūpar on 15 August and fell back on the Beās at Govindwāl and finally on Lahore. Once more Dārā's genius quailed before that of Aurangzīb; he despaired of success, and his despair infected his troops.

Leaving Lahore on 28 August, at the head of 14,000 men, the fugitive prince reached Multān on 15 September with his army reduced to one-half by desertion. Eight days afterwards he vacated this city and fled down the Indus towards the sea, finding rest nowhere and daily losing men. Finally, he left the province of Sind at Badīn (4 December) and entered the Rann of Cutch, at the news of which his pursuers turned back from Tatta on 15 December.

Meanwhile, Aurangzīb himself had given up the chase from Multān (10 October) and hastened to Delhi by rapid marches, because a new storm-cloud was reported to be gathering in the east. Shujā' was making preparations for a second advance on Āgra. The deposition of Shāh Jahān and the imprisonment of the once-beloved ally Murād Bakhsh had taught him the true value of Aurangzīb's solemn promise to let Shujā' enjoy Bengal and Bihār in full sovereignty unmolested. At Monghyr he heard of Aurangzīb's march in full force to the Punjab and imagined the road to Āgra to be open. Now was the opportunity to seize that capital and release his father.

So, early in November, 1658, Shujā' had advanced from Patna with 25,000 cavalry and a good train of artillery, got easy possession of the forts on the way up to Allahābād, and arrived at Khajuhā (in the Fatehpur district), ninety-five miles west of Allahābād, on 9 January, 1659. Here he was held up by an imperial army under Aurangzīb's eldest son, Muhammad Sultān.

That emperor had reached the environs of Delhi from Multān on 20 November and repeatedly sent detachments to strengthen his army near Allahābād so as to close Shujā''s path effectively. But as the latter had not given up his ambitious movement, Aurangzīb had made a rapid march from Soron and reached Korā, eight miles west of Shujā''s position, on 12 January, 1659. Here Mīr Jumla, released from his collusive imprisonment in Daulatābād fort, joined him on that day.

The decisive battle took place on the 14th. But the night before it, Mahārājā Jasvant Singh, who commanded Aurangzīb's right wing, made a treacherous and quite unexpected attack on his master, plundered the camp of prince Muhammad Sultān and also much of Aurangzīb's baggage, and then fled to his own country with his Rājput contingent (14,000 strong). Aurangzīb's cool courage and strict discipline in making the other divisions keep their own places during this night of alarm, prevented the confusion and panic from spreading and saved his army from further loss. With daylight many of his dispersed troops returned to his standard, and he advanced to the attack at the head of 50,000 to 55,000 men, as against Shujā''s 23,000.

With great judgement, Shujā' tried to make up for his hopeless inferiority in numbers by drawing up his troops not in the usual six divisions of Mughul battle-array but in one long line behind his artillery and taking the offensive himself. His right wing under Sayyid 'Ālam charged the imperial left and after scattering it fell upon the centre, driving in front three furious war elephants, each brandishing a heavy iron chain with its trunk, before which no man or horse could stand. At the same time the imperial right wing was assailed and partly dispersed by Shujā''s vanguard and left under prince Buland Akhtar. A false rumour spread through the field that Aurangzīb himself had been slain, and many of his followers fled away. One of these Bengal elephants, maddened by wounds, approached the emperor's elephant. If the latter had turned back, the entire imperial army would have broken and run away at the sight of it. But in the crisis, Aurangzīb's cool courage and power of quick decision saved the situation: he stood like a rock, chaining the legs of his elephant to prevent its flight, and soon the attacking beast's driver was shot down and it was brought under control by an imperial *mahout*. Sayyid ‘Ālam was at last repulsed with wofully thinned ranks. His centre thus saved, Aurangzīb turned to succour his hard-pressed right wing, which on being rallied and reinforced made a counter-charge and swept away the enemy divisions before it with great carnage. Meanwhile, the imperial vanguard had advanced, shaking the front line of Shujā‘. And now, emitting a thick shower of cannon-balls and bullets, Aurangzīb's entire army made a simultaneous advance and enveloped the centre, which alone remained of Shujā‘'s host. That prince saved his life only by dismounting from his elephant and galloping away on a fleet horse. His army at once broke and fled, giving up its entire camp and baggage, artillery (114 pieces) and elephants to the conqueror.

From the field of victory Aurangzīb sent a division, 30,000 strong, under his son Muhammad Sultān and Mīr Jumla in pursuit of Shujā‘, who fled eastwards, making a stand only at Monghyr and again at Sāhibganj (near the Sakrigalī or Teliyāgarhī pass) by blocking the narrow road there. But at each of these places Mīr Jumla turned his left by making a détour through the jungles under the guidance of the local *zamīndārs*. Finally, after a short halt at Rājmahāl, Shujā‘ evacuated the right bank of the Ganges and crossed over to the Mālda district. The imperialists immediately occupied Rājmahāl (23 April, 1659).

In the campaign that ensued, Shujā‘ was hopelessly inferior on land, his regular troops having shrunk to 5000 men, while Mīr Jumla's army was five times as large and man for man superior in fighting capacity. But the imperialists were a purely land force, with few pieces of cannon and not a single boat for operations in this land of waterways. On the other hand, Shujā‘ had an artillery of big guns admirably served by European and half-breed gunners, and the entire flotilla (*navvāra*) of Bengal was at his disposal, which gave wonderful mobility to his army and multiplied its striking force, while the lack of boats at first paralysed Mīr Jumla's efforts.

Shujā‘, making Tānda (four miles west of the old fort of Gaur) his base, entrenched various places on the eastern bank of the Ganges to prevent the enemy from crossing. But Mīr Jumla with great diligence procured a small number of boats from remote places, and making the best use of them twice surprised and defeated Shujā‘'s advanced outposts, but his third *coup* (13 May) failed with heavy loss, as the enemy had prepared an ambush for him. On 18 June, prince Muhammad Sultān, chafing under Mīr Jumla's tutelage, was lured by the offer of the hand of Shujā‘'s daughter and secretly went over to his uncle. But Mīr Jumla restored order and control among the prince's leaderless troops, and at a council of war all the other generals agreed to obey him as their leader. Next, during the torrential rains of Bengal, while the city of Rājmahāl was completely girt round by water, its grain supply was cut off by the Bengal flotilla and Shujā' by a sudden attack recovered it, the surprised imperial division of the city fleeing away (1 September).

In the following December Shujā' resumed operations on land and twice attacked Mīr Jumla, whose inferiority in artillery forced him to fall back from Belghāta towards Murshidābād. But Dāūd Khān, the governor of Patna, with a second army and plenty of boats and artillery, was advancing along the Ganges to co-operate with Mīr Jumla, and on hearing of this Shujā' evacuated Rājmahāl and fell back on Tānda. Thus, the whole country west of the Ganges was finally lost to Shujā' (21 January, 1660), who, however, held a line from opposite Rājmahāl to Tānda. Mīr Jumla easily crossed the Ganges with the help of the 160 boats received from Patna and then made a wide circuit round the north of Shujā''s position, reaching Mālda on 16 March. A month before this prince Muhammad Sultān had left Shujā' and returned to the imperial camp, but only to be sentenced to imprisonment for the rest of his life. On 15 April, Mīr Jumla crossed the Mahānandā and threatened to complete a circle round Shujā', who could no longer resist, but fled precipitately with his family to Dacca, abandoning all his soldiers, servants and property in Tānda to the imperialists. Only sixty boats accompanied him, while 402 became the victor's prize.

But even at Dacca Shujā' could make no stand. The *zamīndārs* rose against him, and Mīr Jumla arrived there hard on his heels. So, the prince finally abandoned Bengal on 22 May, 1660, and sailed for Chittagong to seek an asylum with the Magh Rājā of Arakan. Here his unquiet ambition brought him to a tragic end. With the help of the Musalman settlers in Arakan he planned to seize the throne of his protector and then advance once more for the recovery of Bengal. But the conspiracy was betrayed and the Mughul prince in trying to escape was pursued and cut down in the jungle (January, 1661).[1]

We now turn to the last days of Dārā Shukoh. After leaving Sind (early in December, 1658), with the small remnant of his army, he received help from the Rājās of Cutch and Navānagar, and reached Ahmadābād at the head of 3000 men. Here Shāh Navāz Khān, the governor of the province, joined him and opened the royal treasury to him (January, 1659). Dārā now raised his army to 22,000 men, took away the artillery of Surat castle, and, learning that Shujā' had advanced beyond Allahābād to attack Aurangzīb, he made a dash towards Āgra. On the way he turned towards Ajmer on receiving an invitation from Jasvant Singh, who promised

[1] See also chap. XVII, p. 480.

to join him with all the Rājputs. But in the meantime Aurangzīb had crushed Shujā', and he now won Jasvant over by mingled threats of invasion and promises of favour, and arrived near Ajmer with his victorious army. Thus, Dārā had no alternative but to fight. He entrenched the pass of Deorāi, four miles south of Ajmer, his flanks protected by the hills of Bithli and Gokla and his front by a low wall bristling with guns.

Aurangzīb attacked this formidable position from the south, suffering heavy losses on account of the low and exposed position of his troops. In the evening of the third day (24 March, 1659), under cover of a furious massed attack on Dārā's left wing and a general cannonade along his entire front, a body of hillmen belonging to Rājā Rājrūp of Jammū climbed the back of the Gokla hill unperceived and thus seized the rear of Dārā's left wing. Then these trenches were stormed, the general in command, Shāh Navāz Khān, was killed, and shortly after nightfall Dārā fled from the field. When these facts became known the rest of his troops submitted to Aurangzīb.

Dārā, accompanied by his family and only 2000 troops, moved towards Ahmadābād by rapid marches, undergoing extreme misery from the heat and dust and the death of transport animals. On the way he learnt that that city had turned against him and he would not find any safe refuge in Gujarāt. After a scene of unspeakable agony, so pathetically described by Bernier who was attending his sick wife, the prince, now "reduced to the poorest and sorriest dress, his retinue shrunk to a few men", fled to Kāthīāwār, crossed the terrible Rann again and entered Sind a second time (middle of May). A strong imperial detachment under Jay Singh and Bahādur Khān pursued him all the way with equal speed. In Sind Aurangzīb's local officers had closed Dārā's path to the north and the east. So he fled westwards, crossed the Indus and entered Sehwān, intending to flee to Persia by way of the Bolān pass and Qandahār. But his beloved wife Nādira Bānū died of illness and privations, and Dārā, now almost mad with grief and despair, sent away all his remaining troopers and his most devoted officer with her corpse to Lahore for burial in the graveyard of his patron saint Mīān Mīr. He then accepted the offered hospitality of Malik Jīvan, the chieftain of Dādar (nine miles east of the Bolān pass), and was seized by this Baloch traitor (19 June) and delivered to Aurangzīb's general.

Arrived at Delhi, Dārā and his second son Sipihr Shukoh were paraded through the streets with disgrace. He was put to death on the charge of apostasy from Islām by the sentence of Aurangzīb's court theologians (9 September). His remains were buried in a vault of Humāyūn's tomb.

Dārā's eldest son, Sulaimān Shukoh, on his way back from the war with Shujā', had heard of the disaster to his father at Sāmogarh, and on being deserted by most of his troops and headed off by Aurangzīb's forces from the west, he failed to reach his father in the Punjab. He therefore sought refuge with the Rājā of Srīnagar in the Garhwāl hills, who gave him a royal welcome. But a year later (July, 1659) Aurangzīb sent a force to coerce or bribe the raja into giving up the refugee. Sulaimān was delivered up by his host and brought to Delhi on 12 January, 1661. He was ordered to be confined in the fort of Gwālior and was there done to death (May, 1662) with overdoses of opium. In the same state prison, Murād Bakhsh was beheaded (14 December, 1661) under judicial sentence for the murder of 'Alī Naqī, his *dīvān* in Gujarāt, whose son, instigated by Aurangzīb, insisted on the retaliation of blood for blood allowed by Islamic law. The very young sons of Dārā and Murād were spared, only to be kept in prison for life. Thus, all possible rivals having been removed from his path, Aurangzīb became the indisputable lord and master of Mughul India.

In four severely contested battles for the throne, fought in the course of less than a year in widely separated provinces, Aurangzīb had marched rapidly and triumphed uniformly at the total cost of only two generals killed and one dead from sunstroke, while his opponents were crushed with terrible carnage among officers and privates alike. There could be no greater proof of his genius and efficiency than this.

The reign of Aurangzīb naturally falls into two equal divisions of about twenty-five years each, the first of which he passed in northern India and the second in the Deccan. During the earlier half of his reign the centre of interest lies unmistakably in the north, because the most important developments, civil and military, concerned this region. In the second half, the situation is reversed: all the resources of the empire are concentrated in the Deccan; the emperor, his court and family, the bulk of his army, and all his best officers live there, and Hindustān sinks back to a place of secondary importance; the administration in northern India grows weak and corrupt at the withdrawal of the master's eye and all the ablest officers; the upper classes decline in morals, culture, and useful activity; and finally lawlessness breaks out in most parts, dimly heralding the great anarchy which covered the eighteenth century.

After his final victory over Dārā, Aurangzīb celebrated his grand coronation on 15 June, 1659,[1] in the first month of his second regnal year, at Delhi, with prolonged rejoicings. Thereafter he lived for nearly twenty years at Delhi and Āgra, making only a trip to Kashmīr which kept him away for one year (1663) and an eighteen months' halt at Hasan Abdāl (1674–75) to direct operations against the frontier tribes. Early in 1679 he went to Ajmer to annex Mārwār, and thus became involved for the next two years and a half in the

[1] The official date was put twenty-three days earlier on the 1st Ramazān, A.H. 1068.

Rājput war, whose strange sequel drew him to the Deccan, there to pass the last quarter century of his life in strenuous but unavailing toil.

During the years 1661–67, Aurangzīb received complimentary embassies from many foreign Muslim powers, such as the Sharīf of Mecca, the kings of Persia, Balkh, Bukhārā, Kāshghar, Urganj (Khiva) and Shahr-i-nau, the Turkish governors of Basra, Hadramaut, Yaman and Mocha, the ruler of Barbary, and the king of Abyssinia. The only embassy from Constantinople in his reign arrived in 1690, charged with a letter for him. His policy was to dazzle the eyes of these princes by the lavish gift of presents to them and to their envoys, and thus induce the outer Muslim world to forget his treatment of his father and brothers. The fame of India as a soft milch cow spread throughout the middle and near East, and the minor embassies were merely begging expeditions, as Bernier shrewdly noted. The Sharīf of Mecca in particular used to send his agents to the Delhi court every year with the object of levying contributions in the name of the Prophet, till at last the emperor's patience was worn out and he refused to make the Sharīf his almoner at the holy city, but began to send his gifts to its scholars and mendicants through his own agents. On the embassies received and the return-embassies sent out Aurangzīb spent in presents nearly three million rupees in the course of seven years, besides the large sums which he annually distributed at Mecca and the gift of a million to 'Abdullah Khān, the deposed king of Kāshghar, who had taken refuge in India in 1668 and died at Delhi in 1675.

The grandest and most costly of these diplomatic intercourses was with Persia. But the overweening pride of Shāh 'Abbās II, who could not forget how the Mughul emperor Humāyūn had been a suppliant before his ancestor, how Shāh Jahān had thrice failed to recover Qandahār, and how a petty chief like Shivājī had sacked the greatest port of the Mughul empire with impunity, led to a rupture between the two sovereigns, which was aggravated by the Shāh's exaltation of the Shiah religion in his letters to an orthodox Sunnī like Aurangzīb. At last after sending two insulting letters to Aurangzīb and barbarously humiliating the Indian ambassador at the Persian court (Tarbiyat Khān), Shāh 'Abbās threatened an invasion of India, but his death (August, 1667) dispersed the war clouds, and the Persian monarchy soon afterwards sank into sloth and decay, to the immense relief of the Delhi court.

Many minor conquests were made in the outskirts of the empire during the first half of Aurangzīb's reign, the most valuable of which were the annexations of Palāmau (in south Bihār) by Dāūd Khān the governor of Patna in 1661 and of Chittagong by Shāyista Khān the governor of Bengal in 1666. A more romantic success was that of a mission from the province of Kashmīr (1665) which forced the ruler of Tibet (evidently little Tibet or Ladākh) to acknowledge the suzerainty of Aurangzīb, stamp coins in his name, and build a mosque at his capital where the Islamic call to prayer had never been heard before. The conquests in Assam made early in the reign were all lost by the year 1681.

The disturbances of internal peace during this earlier period were neither very important nor successful. The outbreaks which inevitably followed the collapse of civil authority during a war of succession subsided with Aurangzīb's assertion of his mastery. The Hindu risings against his policy of religious persecution will be described later. The vassal princes who revolted were all crushed like Champat Rāi Bundelā (1661) and Rāi Singh the usurper of Navānagar in Kāthīāwār (1663), or forced to sue for pardon like Rāo Karan of Bīkāner (1660). In fact, these few and strictly localised tumults hardly disturbed the profound internal peace which northern India enjoyed during the first half of this reign.

Aurangzīb had claimed the throne as the champion of pure Islām against the heretical practices and opinions of Dārā Shukoh. Soon after his grand coronation (June, 1659), he issued a number of ordinances for restoring the orthodox rules of conduct taught by the *Qurān*. He abolished his ancestors' practices of stamping the *kalima* (the Muslim *credo*) on their coins and of observing the *naurūz* or New Year's day of the pagan Persians; forbade the cultivation of *bhang* (*Cannabis indica*) throughout his realm; and appointed a censor of public morals (*Muhtasib*) in every large city to enforce the Prophet's laws and put down forbidden practices, such as drinking, gambling and the illicit commerce of the sexes. The punishment of heretical opinions, blasphemy and omission of the five daily prayers or of the Ramazān fast by Muslims lay within the province of this officer.

His puritanical rigour grew with age. In the eleventh year of his reign (1668) he forbade music at his court and pensioned off the state musicians and singers, many of whom had enjoyed honour and high rank under the preceding sovereigns. The royal band was, however, retained. The ceremony of weighing (*wazan*) the emperor's person on his birthday against gold and silver, which were then given away in charity, was discontinued; and so also the custom of the emperor applying a spot of sandal paste (*tīkā*) to the foreheads of the great rajas when newly investing them (1679), and the ceremony of the emperor showing himself every morning at an outer balcony of the palace for his subjects to look at him (*darshan*)—because all these were Hindu practices.

Gradually the festivities which used to be held on his birthday and the anniversary of his coronation were abolished (1677); only "betel leaves and scents were distributed among those present at court", and the grandees were forbidden to make the customary presents to the emperor. In many other minute points a literal compliance with the practice of early Islām was enjoined.

But this attempt to elevate mankind by one stroke of the official pen failed, as Akbar's social reforms had failed before. Aurangzīb's government made itself ridiculous by violently enforcing for a time, then relaxing, and finally abandoning a code of puritanical morals opposed to the feelings of the entire population, without first trying to educate them to a higher level of thought. As Manucci observed, there were few who did not drink secretly, and even the ministers and *qāzīs* loved to get drunk at home. Gambling continued to be practised in his camp, and his order to all the courtesans and dancing girls to marry or leave the realm remained a dead letter. In 1664 he issued an edict forbidding *satī* (the voluntary burning of Hindu widows), but his government was powerless to enforce the prohibition everywhere in the face of popular opposition. The castration of children for sale as eunuchs, though again and again denounced by him, continued in certain provinces.

Nevertheless much good was done in the economic sphere by the pious emperor's determined opposition to uncanonical taxes and illegal exactions (*abwāb*). Immediately after his second enthronement (1659) he gave prompt and much needed relief to his subjects in the scarcity which followed from the disturbances of the civil war by abolishing the inland transport duty (*rāhdārī*), amounting to 10 per cent. *ad valorem*, and the octroi (*pāndārī*) on all articles of food and drink brought from outside for sale in the larger cities. This was done in the crown lands by the emperor's order (at a loss of 2½ million rupees per annum under *rāhdārī* alone), while the *jāgīrdārs* (assignees) and *zamīndārs* (landholders) were requested to do the same in their estates.

The *abwāb* or exactions made under various pretexts, in addition to the regular land revenue or custom duty, were a prolific source of oppression to the people, and were more burdensome in their operation in proportion as their victims were poor and uninfluential and distant from the imperial headquarters. These imposts were again and again declared illegal and forbidden by Muslim sovereigns of Delhi like Fīrūz Shāh Tughluq (1375), Akbar (*c.* 1590) and Jahāngīr (1605), but they invariably managed to reappear after a short time. These *abwāb*[1] included duties on the local sale of produce (i.e. octroi), perquisites exacted by the officials for their own benefit, as well as fees and commissions levied on behalf of the state on almost every conceivable occasion, licence tax for plying certain trades, forced subscriptions, and gifts to officers, and special imposts on the Hindus. Among the last were taxes on bathing in the sacred waters (e.g. 6¼ rupees on every pilgrim at Allahābād) and a fee charged on the bones of dead Hindus carried for being thrown into the Ganges. As a tax was also levied on the father for the birth of a male child, we may say that under the Mughuls illegal

[1] The subject has been treated in full detail in my *Mughal Administration*, chap. v.

cesses pursued a man from birth to death. Aurangzīb's edicts for their abolition are dated 20 November, 1665, 29 April, 1673, and 1682. But the timidity of the common people, the weakness of the central government in the provinces and its lack of an adequate number of reliable agents left the Indian population helpless under official extortion, in spite of benevolent paper edicts from the court.

In the course of his enforcement of orthodoxy, Aurangzīb's hand did not spare the heretics of Islām. Even several Sūfī philosophers did not feel themselves safe, as their elastic pantheism was suspected to be a coquetry with Hinduism and a veiled abjuration of the pure dogmas of Islām. The emperor's accession was followed by the persecution of several holy men of liberal views but professed Muslims whom Dārā had favoured. The most notable victim of this class was Sarmad, a Jew of Kāshān (in Persia) converted to Islām, who composed many smooth-flowing verses breathing the ardent mystical fervour of the Sūfī and the spirit of lofty catholicity which recognised the truth inherent in all great creeds. Sarmad used to go about absolutely naked, because like an uncompromising monist he denied the existence of matter and felt no shame about anything pertaining to the material body. He is said to have blessed Dārā's banners in the civil war, and was beheaded on the charge of heresy soon after Aurangzīb's accession. We also read of the execution of Shiahs for cursing the first three Khalīfs, and of converts to Islām for returning to their old faith. The Isma'ilia (or Bohra) heretics of Gujarāt were subjected to bloody persecution by order of Aurangzīb.

So long as Shāh Jahān lived as a captive in Āgra, Aurangzīb never visited that capital, for his relations with his deposed father were extremely bitter and became the subject of public condemnation throughout India and even outside. The court theologians, particularly 'Abdul-Wahhāb (who was rewarded with the chief justiceship of the empire), justified his usurpation of a loving father's throne on the ground that the old emperor had grown infirm and intellectually unfit for governing the realm, and, therefore, the protection of the faithful required government by a pious and vigorous man like Aurangzīb. But the rest of the world denounced Aurangzīb's treatment of his father as an outrage on justice and decorum.

A very acrimonious correspondence that passed between father and son during the earlier days of Shāh Jahān's captive life can be still followed in Aurangzīb's replies, though Shāh Jahān's letters to him are lost. The ex-emperor's futile attempts to correspond with Dārā and Shujā' only led to an increase in the rigour of his captivity, under Mu'tamid, the harsh eunuch in charge, who "sometimes allowed it to be seen that he treated Shāh Jahān as a miserable captive" (Manucci). There were also disputes about the crown jewels and Dārā's property lodged in Āgra fort, which Shāh Jahān tried in vain to withhold from the victor. Then he wrote bitter letters charging Aurangzīb with being an unnatural son and a rebel subject, a robber of other people's property and a hypocrite. The latter replied in a lofty tone of self-righteousness, posing as the champion of pure Islām and of good government, and the humble but favourite instrument of God in the work of moral reform and popular beneficence, which had been endangered by his father's incompetence, sloth and unjust rule: "Kingship means the protection of the realm and the guardianship of the people....A king is merely God's elected custodian and the trustee of His money for the benefit of the subjects" (*Ādāb-i-'Ālamgīrī*). Worsted in this contest with the pen, Shāh Jahān resigned himself to his fate and prepared for the next world under the religious ministration of Sayyid Muhammad Qanaujī and the tender nursing of his eldest daughter Jahānārā, the Mughul Antigone. "All the ex-emperor's time was divided between professing obedience to God, prayer, performance of all the religious services, reading the *Qurān* and listening to the histories of the great men of the past." Seven and a half years passed in this way, and then he died on 1 February, 1666, aged seventy-four.

The first great war of Aurangzīb's reign was the invasion of Assam. Early in the sixteenth century a Mongoloid soldier of fortune had founded a kingdom in Cooch Behār, north of Bengal. Lakshmī Nārāyan, the third king of this dynasty (r. 1584–1622), had professed allegiance to Akbar. A younger branch of the family had been installed over its eastern districts or Kāmrūp, i.e. the country between the Sankosh and Bar Nadī rivers, which the Muslim writers called Kuch Hājo. In 1612, taking advantage of a contest between the two branches, the Mughuls conquered and annexed Kuch Hājo, but this brought them into collision with the Āhoms. These Āhoms were a branch of the Shān race, who had crossed the Pātkai range in the thirteenth century and established a kingdom of their own over eastern and central Assam. They were a hardy race of demon-worshippers, expert in building stockades, plying boats, and making night attacks. Their society was organised on a feudal basis, under a number of official nobles, who cultivated their estates by slave labour. Their army consisted entirely of infantry, stiffened with elephants; but during their wars with Bengal they had learnt the use of firearms. Their king was the patriarch of the clan and was venerated as a semi-divine being. After much desultory fighting with the Mughuls of Kuch Hājo, the Āhom king made peace in 1638, recognising the boundary line of the Bar Nadī.

During the war of succession, when Bengal was depleted of soldiers and left without a governor, the Rājās of Cooch Behār and Assam had sent troops from the west and the east respectively to seize the Mughul district of Kāmrūp lying between their realms. The Muslim local officers had fled away from their charge, and the Āhoms had occupied Gauhātī and plundered the whole district, driving out the Cooch Behār forces. When the civil war ended, Mīr Jumla was appointed viceroy of Bengal (June, 1660), with orders to punish these rebel rajas. Leaving Dacca on 11 November, 1661, with an army of 12,000 horse and 30,000 foot, and a flotilla of 323 vessels of different classes, Mīr Jumla captured the capital of Cooch Behār (29 December) without a blow, as the raja and his officers had vacated it in terror. The kingdom was annexed to the Mughul empire, and then the general set out (14 January, 1662) on the invasion of Assam. His men had to undergo unspeakable hardship in making their way through the dense jungle and across numberless streams, but all their sufferings were shared by their chief. The Āhom army offered a feeble resistance and kept retreating up the Brahmaputra, so that the imperialists captured the successive forts on the way—Jogīguphā, Gauhātī, Srīghāt, Pāndu, Beltalā, Kājali, Sāmdharā and Simlā-garh. In a naval battle fought on 13 March Mīr Jumla annihilated the enemy's naval power, and finally on 17 March entered their deserted capital Garhgāon. The spoils taken were immense: 82 elephants, three hundred thousand rupees, 675 pieces of artillery, 1345 *zambūraks* (swivels), 6750 matchlocks, and 1000 odd boats, besides much gunpowder and paddy.

The Rājā of Assam and his nobles having fled far away to the hills, Mīr Jumla could not conclude any treaty with them, but decided to hold the country during the coming rainy season. The Āhom capital, containing all the artillery, elephants, stores and property of the Mughul army, was occupied by a strong garrison, while the general himself went into quarters at Mathurāpur, a high-lying village, seven miles south-east of it. Many outposts were set up for guarding the routes. The fleet could not sail up to Garhgāon, on account of the shallowness of the river near that city; it, therefore, anchored at Lakhau, some eighteen miles north-west. This was the fatal weakness of the imperialists' position.

During the rainy season, from May to October, the country was flooded, the movement of troops by land became impossible, the imperial outposts were isolated, and the Mughul army in Assam had to live in a state of siege. No provisions or news could come from Bengal or from the fleet, as the gun-boats were too heavy to navigate the shallow river near Garhgāon and the roads were submerged. For lack of proper food, cavalry horses and draught cattle perished by the thousand. On 20 May the Āhoms captured the outposts at Gajpur and thus cut off communications between the Mughul army and navy. Around Garhgāon they concentrated and kept the garrison in perpetual alarm by attacks almost every night. Several assaults in force were delivered, and in one of them the bamboo fence of the fort was pierced and half the enclosure seized.

But all these attacks were finally defeated by the exertion of every man in the garrison.

In August a terrible epidemic broke out in Mīr Jumla's camp at Mathurāpur. Fever and flux carried off hundreds daily, reducing the army to nearly a quarter of its strength; no suitable diet or comfort was available for the sick. Coarse rice and the meat of commissariat bullocks were the food of all from the general down to the humblest soldier. Indeed, the whole of Assam was infected, and 230,000 of its people died of disease that year. At last the garrison of Mathurāpur fell back on Garhgāon (27 August), abandoning their numberless sick. But the refugees only infected the garrison of Garhgāon.

Through all these months, the fleet at Lakhau had maintained its ascendancy on water and kept up its touch with Bengal, and when, towards the close of October, the land became dry again, it pushed up large quantities of provisions, under escort, to Garhgāon. Mīr Jumla now resumed the offensive and marched eastwards by way of Solāguri to Tipām, the Āhom raja and his nobles having again fled to the hills of Nāmrūp. But the Mughul army to a man refused to enter these hills of pestilence and unknown magical terror. The general himself was seized with fainting fits. Fever and pleurisy supervened, which quickly turned into consumption, and he consented to make peace (December, 1662). The Āhom king agreed to pay an indemnity of 20,000 *tolas*[1] of gold, 420,000 *tolas*[1] of silver and 110 elephants, to send a daughter to the imperial harem, to cede to the Mughuls all the territory west of the Bharali river north of the Brahmaputra and west of the Kallang river on the south (i.e. more than half the province of Darrang, rich in elephants), and to give hostages. The princess, hostages and first instalment of the indemnity having reached his camp, Mīr Jumla set out on his return from Tipām on 20 January, 1663, a dying man, and died on 10 April before reaching Dacca. His genius had shone with supreme radiance during this campaign. No other general of that age conducted war with so much humanity and justice, or kept his soldiers under such discipline; no other general could have retained to the last the confidence and affection of his subordinates amidst such appalling sufferings and dangers. From the first day of the campaign he shared with the meanest soldier all the privations of the march and siege and brought premature death upon himself by incessant hard labour.

The Mughuls continued to hold his acquisitions in Assam for four years after his retreat. But in 1667, the vigorous Āhom king Chakradhvaj renewed the war and recovered all the lost territory, and even captured Gauhātī. Thus, the imperial frontier was pushed back to the Monās river. A desultory war continued for nine years; but the Mughul forces were hopelessly small, they had lost their supremacy on water, and their general Rām Singh (Rājā of Amber) had

[1] A *tola* weighs about 180 grains.

not his heart in the work, as he had been transferred to that pestilential province as a punishment for his connivance at the escape of Shivājī from Āgra in 1666. After staying for some years at Rāngāmātī doing nothing, he was recalled to court in 1676. In 1679, the Mughuls, taking advantage of the weakness of the Āhom kings and dissensions among their nobles, recovered Gauhātī by bribery, only to lose it two years afterwards to the new and war-like king Gadādhar Singh. Thus, Kāmrūp was finally lost to the empire. During Mīr Jumla's investment in Garhgāon, Cooch Behār had been recovered by its raja. But when Shāysta Khān came to Bengal as governor, the raja made his peace (1664) by offering submission and half a million rupees. Later in the century, the Mughuls annexed the southern and eastern portions of the kingdom, including the present districts of Rangpur and western Kāmrūp.

One of the tasks with which Mīr Jumla was charged by the emperor was the punishment of the pirates of Chittagong and the recovery of Shujā''s family. This work, which he did not live to attempt, fell to his successor in Bengal, Shāyista Khān. The Fenny river was the boundary between the Burmese (Magh) kingdom of Arakan and the Mughul empire, but during the reigns of Jahāngīr and Shāh Jahān the Magh pirates acquired complete domination over the rivers and creeks of East Bengal. Their naval power was strengthened by the settlement of Portuguese and half-caste (Feringi) adventurers in Chittagong, who acted as the agents of the local raja in these raids. "These pirates, both Magh and Feringi, used constantly to come and plunder Bengal, carrying off the Hindus and Muslims that they could seize, and employing some of the captives in degrading tasks and selling others as slaves at the Indian ports." Deltaic Bengal was so long and so thoroughly devastated by them that the riverside parts of the Backergunge and Dacca districts remained desolate and bare of inhabitants even at the time of Rennell's survey (1775).

> The sailors of the Bengal *nawara* felt such a terror of the pirates that whenever a hundred war-boats of the former sighted only four of the latter, the Bengal crews thought themselves lucky if they could save their lives by flight. Latterly the Rājā of Arakan had ceased to send his own fleet to plunder Mughul territory, as he considered the Feringi pirates in the light of his servants and shared the booty with them half and half.[1]

Bernier describes these Portuguese as "Christians only in name; the lives led by them were most detestable, massacring or poisoning one another without compunction or remorse". During their raids they practised fiendish cruelty on the people, men, women and children, whom they could catch, and their name *Harmād* (= Armada) is associated with horror and loathing in contemporary Bengali literature. Their ravages caused great loss to the imperial revenue and prestige in Bengal.

[1] Sarkar, J. N., in *Journal Asiatic Society of Bengal*, 1907, p. 423.

Shāyista Khān first set himself to create a navy anew, as the Bengal flotilla had practically ceased to exist during the Assam war and the subsequent confusion and maladministration, though there was an annual grant of 1½ million rupees for its maintenance. With great energy within one year he built and manned a fleet of 300 vessels, and protected Dacca by water on the south. Next, he conquered the island of Sandwīp, at the head of the Bay of Bengal, as it was a convenient half-way house between Dacca and Chittagong (November, 1665). He next bribed the Feringi colony of Chittagong, who were then quarrelling with the local raja, to migrate suddenly with their families and ships to Mughul territory (December, 1665)—the site of their new homes in Dacca town being still called Feringi-bāzār.

"The coming over of the Feringis gave composure to the minds of the people of Bengal", and on 24 December an expedition by land and sea left Dacca for Chittagong, under the governor's son Buzurg Ummed Khān and admiral Ibn Husain. The fleet moved close to the coast, while the army marched parallel to it, cutting a way through the jungle and naturally lagging some distance behind. The brunt of the fighting fell on the fleet (288 vessels) or rather on the forty ships of the Feringis which formed the imperial vanguard. Two battles were fought at sea (2 and 3 February, 1666) in which the Maghs were defeated and driven back upon Chittagong. A third battle, in the river below that town, resulted in the entire Magh squadron (135 vessels) of that region being captured. The fort of Chittagong capitulated to the fleet on 5 February, when the land force also arrived.

Chittagong was made the seat of a Mughul commandant and its name was changed to Islāmābād. Thousands of Bengal peasants, so long held there in serfdom by the pirates, were now released and restored to their homes. The Mughuls advanced up to the port of Rāmū, but soon abandoned it as too distant an outpost. Chittagong, however, has remained attached to Bengal ever since.

Aurangzīb was the champion of Muslim orthodoxy, and yet he had to wage many wars with his fanatical Muslim subjects of the north-western frontier. The causes were political and economic, not religious. The Afghān clans living in and around the passes leading out of India into Afghānistān have followed highway robbery as a hereditary profession from time immemorial. Their fields yield too scanty a sustenance for their fast growing numbers, and stout hearts, strong muscles and cunning brains do not remain satisfied with the poor and slow gains of agriculture, as compared with the plunder of industrious and tame plainsmen and of rich traders passing within easy reach. The Mughul emperors had learnt by bitter experience that it was cheaper to bribe these hillmen, as a means of keeping the passes open and the valleys at their foot safe, than to coerce the robbers. A sum of 600,000 rupees was annually allotted by Aurangzīb's government for paying subsidies to the various border chieftains and headmen of families. But even these political pensions did not always ensure peace on the frontier. In every generation some leader of ungratified ambition would gather together a band of fiery youths and raid the imperial territory or the villages of his rivals. The pressure of growing population made peace and a static condition impossible on this frontier.

Early in 1667 the Yūsufzāī clan, living in Swāt and Bājaur and the north Peshāwar plain, rose under Bhāgū, who crowned a pretended scion of their ancient kings under the title of Muhammad Shāh, and crossing the Indus above Attock invaded the Hazāra district, and attacked the imperial outposts there. Other Yūsufzāī bands plundered the western Peshāwar and Attock districts. Then they came over to the south side of the Indus at Hārūn, in order to prevent any Mughul force from crossing into their country at this ferry. But Kāmil Khān, the commandant of Attock, defeated and expelled them with heavy slaughter (11 April). Next month Shamsher Khān, with a larger army, crossed the Indus, entered the Yūsufzāī country, and leaving an entrenched camp at Und ravaged the cornfields in the level country of Mandrāwar. Then advancing farther he captured many of their villages, burning down the houses, looting the property and destroying all vestiges of cultivation, up to the Panjshīr river.

At the beginning of September the supreme command was assumed by Muhammad Amīn Khān at the head of a large force, and his hard blows quieted the rebel clansmen for some years.

In 1672 the tactless action of the commandant of Jalālābād caused another explosion among the Khyber clans. The Afrīdīs rose under their chieftain Akmal Khān, a born general, who crowned himself king and proclaimed a holy war against the Mughuls, summoning all the Pathāns to join the national movement. Muhammad Āmin Khān, now governor of Afghānistān, was enveloped and attacked by the Afrīdīs at 'Alī Masjid (1 May) and cut off from his water supply. Disorder seized the Mughul army; horses, elephants and men became mixed together in confusion. Then the Afghāns charged down the hillside, completing the ruin of the imperialists. Muhammad Āmin and some of his higher officers escaped, but everything else was lost: ten thousand men were slain, the entire camp property, valued at twenty million rupees, was plundered, and 20,000 men and women (including the viceroy's mother, wife and daughter) were dragged into captivity. This signal success lured more recruits to Akmal's banners, and the rising rapidly spread through the entire Pathān land "from Attock to Qandahār". Khūsh-hāl Khān, the poet and hero of the Khattak clan, now joining Akmal, became the leading spirit of the national rising and inspired the tribesmen with his pen and sword alike.

The emperor degraded Muhammad Āmin Khān, and recalling Mahābat Khān from the Deccan sent him to Kābul as viceroy for the fourth time. But this general made a secret pact with the Afghāns on condition of mutual forbearance, and so the Khyber route remained closed. Aurangzīb was displeased and sent Shujā'at Khān in independent command of a large force with abundant artillery (November, 1673). He was a man of humble birth who had risen to the emperor's favour by his ability, and therefore the high-born officers regarded him with jealousy, while he treated them with insolent contempt. This led to a lack of co-operation between them and a Mughul disaster on 3 March, 1674, when Shujā'at Khān was cut off in the Karāpā pass, but the remnant of his force was rescued by Jasvant Singh's Rājputs.

To restore imperial prestige in this quarter, Aurangzīb himself went to Hasan Abdāl (6 July, 1674) near Peshāwar, and stayed there for a year and a half directing the operations. Mahābat Khān was removed from the viceroyalty, and under the master's eyes imperial diplomacy and imperial arms alike succeeded. Many clans were bought over with pensions and posts for their headmen, while the lands of the refractory were ravaged by strong detachments operating from Peshāwar. Thus, in a short time the Ghorai, Ghilzāī, Shirānī and Yūsufzāī clans were crushed, and others peacefully submitted. Great deeds were done by the Turkī general Uighur Khān, who had often before distinguished himself in fighting the Afghāns. He first defeated a Mohmand attack and ravaged their homes; but his attempt to open the Khyber pass failed after heavy fighting near 'Alī Masjid. He next occupied Ningrahār and opened the Jagdalik pass, expelling the Ghilzāīs from it. Afghān mothers used to hush their babies to sleep with Uighur Khān's dreaded name.

In the spring of 1675, Fidāi Khān in coming back from Kābul was attacked at Jagdalik; his van was defeated and its baggage carried off by the enemy, but his courage and steadiness saved the rest of the army, while reinforcements under Uighur Khān turned the check into a victory. But in June next Mukarram Khān while operating near Khāpūsh in the Bājaur country was lured into an ambush and repulsed with heavy losses. At the end of August there were two local reverses; the *thānadār* of Jagdalik was slain and that of Barangāb and Surkhāb was driven out of his post with severe loss of men. But all the Mughul positions in Afghānistān were strengthened, and by December, 1675, the situation had sufficiently improved to enable the emperor to leave the Punjab for Delhi.

The good work done by his army under his eyes was confirmed by his happy choice of an extraordinarily capable governor for Afghānistān. Amīr Khān, the son of Khalīl-ullah, was appointed viceroy of Kābul in 1677 and continued to govern the province with signal ability and success till his death in 1698. He set himself to win the hearts of the Afghāns and enter into social relations with them with such success that the chiefs of the clans gave up their shy and unsocial manners and began to visit him without any suspicion. Every one of them looked up to him for advice in conducting his domestic affairs. Under his astute management, they ceased to trouble the imperial government and spent their energies in internecine quarrels. Once he broke up a confederacy under Akmal Afrīdī by secretly instigating that chieftain's followers to ask him to divide the conquered territory among them. When Akmal declined on the ground of the insufficiency of the land, the disappointed hillmen began to return home. And when at last he did make a division, his other followers left him because of his having shown greater favour to his own clansmen. Much of Amīr Khān's administrative success was due to the wise counsel, tact and energy of his wife Sāhibjī, a daughter of 'Alī Mardān Khān.

The emperor triumphed in Afghānistān by following the policy of paying subsidies and setting clan against clan. Amīr Khān's diplomacy broke up the confederacy under Akmal, and when that able leader died the Afrīdīs made terms with the empire. The Khyber was kept open. But Khūsh-hāl Khān Khattak continued the war single-handed for many years afterwards, till his own son betrayed him to the enemy. The fallen chieftain solaced his exile and captivity by composing stinging verses against Aurangzīb.

This Afghān war made the employment of Afghāns in the ensuing Rājput war impossible, though they were just the class of troops required in that field. Moreover, it relieved the pressure on Shivājī by draining the Deccan of the best Mughul soldiers and generals for service on the north-west frontier. The Marāthā king took advantage of this diversion of his enemy's strength to make his dazzling conquest of the Carnatic (1677) unchecked.

The most important feature of Aurangzīb's internal administration was his deliberate reversal of the policy of his predecessors towards his non-Muslim subjects and vassal princes, which change of policy is generally held to have caused the swift downfall of the empire after his death. But with him it was not a matter of personal caprice or earthly gain. According to the orthodox interpretation of the Qurānic law, it is the duty of every pious Muslim to "exert himself in the path of God", or, in other words, to wage holy wars (*jihād*) against non-Muslim countries (*dār-ul-harb*) till they are turned into realms of Islām (*dār-ul-Islām*). In theory the conquered infidel population is reduced to the status of slaves, but in practice even idol-worshippers were allowed to share in the modified form of protection which early Islām granted to the "People of the Book" (viz. Jews and Christians). A non-Muslim lived under a contract (*zimma*) with the state; life and property were spared to him by the Commander of the Faithful, but he had, in return, to undergo certain political and civil disabilities and pay a capitation tax; he was not allowed to wear fine dresses, ride on horseback, or carry arms; he must behave respectfully and submissively to every member of the dominant sect; and he could not be a citizen of the state. He was under certain legal disabilities with regard to testimony in law courts, protection under the criminal law, and in marriage. He must avoid any offensive publicity in the exercise of his faith and must not erect any new temple. For not embracing Islām, he had to pay commutation money (*jizya*) with marks of humility (*Qurān*, ix. 29). This tax has been called by some modern writers a fee for exemption from military service; but the analogy is entirely false, because the army of the Mughul empire was a purely mercenary body and in no sense a conscript force or a nation in arms. There was no compulsion on the Muslim population to enter the army in India, and no fine on those Muslims who did not enter it; every soldier, Muslim or Hindu, enlisted voluntarily, and every soldier, Muslim no less than Hindu, drew the regular salary.

Such was the legal position of the Hindus under Muhammadan rule. But in practice they enjoyed religious freedom in many periods through the moderation or indolence of their rulers. When an enemy capital or rebel stronghold was captured, the temples of the place were demolished or turned into mosques; but Hindu temples in general were left unmolested except by certain bigoted sultans like Fīrūz Tughluq or Sikandar Lodī.

In his Benares *farmān*, granted on 10 March, 1659, before his throne was secure, Aurangzīb had declared that his religion forbade the building of new temples but did not enjoin the demolition of long-standing ones. But his own action both before and after his accession had not respected this distinction. When acting as governor of Gujarāt (1645), he had not only demolished the new temple of Chintāman (at Sāraspur) but also several old ones. During his second viceroyalty of the Deccan he had pulled down the temple of Khānde Rāo on a hill south of Aurangābād. His first step after his accession was to forbid old temples to be repaired (1664). A little later his iconoclastic zeal burst forth in full force. On 19 April, 1669, he issued a general order to "the governors of all the provinces to demolish the schools and temples of the infidels and put down their teaching and religious practices strongly". Officers were sent to every *pargana* to demolish the local temples and the governor had to send the report of the execution of the order under the seal of the *qāzī* and attested by pious Shaikhs of the locality. The censors of public morals (*Muhtasibs*) appointed to every subdivision and city had it as their normal duty to go round and destroy Hindu places of worship within their jurisdiction. So large was the number of official temple-breakers that a *dārogha* (superintendent) had to be placed over them to guide and unite their activities. Besides numberless minor shrines throughout the empire, all the most famous Hindu places of worship now suffered destruction: the temples of Somnāth at Pātan, Vishvanāth at Benares and Keshav Dev at Muttra. Even the loyal state of Jaipur did not escape, sixty-six temples being demolished at Amber. During the Rājput war, in Udaipur and Chitor alone in two months 239 temples suffered ruin by his order.

The work of destruction was often accompanied by wanton desecration, such as the slaughtering of cows in the sanctuary and causing the idols to be trodden down in public squares.[1]

On 12 April, 1679, an edict was issued reimposing "the *jizya* tax on the unbelievers with the object of spreading Islām and overthrowing infidel practices". For the purpose of assessment the non-Muslim population was roughly divided into three classes, poor, middle class and rich, with incomes below 200 *dirhams*, 200–10,000 *dirhams*, and above 10,000 *dirhams* respectively, the rate of taxation being 12, 24, and 48 *dirhams* a year.[2] The professional classes, merchants and landowners were ranked as rich, and artisans as poor. The last class paid the tax only when their income exceeded the cost of maintaining their families. Women, children below fourteen years of age, slaves, beggars and paupers were exempt from the tax; blind men, cripples and lunatics paid only when they were "rich"; monks were untaxed, unless they belonged to wealthy monasteries, in which case the heads of these houses had to pay. All government officials were exempted from the tax. A crowd of Hindus that gathered in Delhi, blocking the road from the fort-gate to the Jāmiʿ mosque and appealing to the emperor to withdraw the tax, was trodden down by elephants when they did not disperse in spite of warning. A temperate and closely reasoned letter of protest from Shivājī had no better success. "Many Hindus who were unable to pay turned Muhammadans to obtain relief from the insults of the collectors... Aurangzīb rejoices" (Manucci). The heaviness of the tax interfered with the adequate flow of grain to the imperial camp bazaars in the Deccan later in the reign.

We have certain figures from which we can judge of the comparative burden of this religious impost. In Gujarāt the land revenue yielded 11 million rupees and the *jizya* 500,000. In the city of Burhānpur (1682) the total assessment under this head seems to have been over 850,000 rupees. The police were under orders to chastise those Hindus who delayed in making payment.

Similarly, the customs duty was regulated to put pressure on the Hindus. It was originally fixed at the uniform rate of 2½ per cent. *ad valorem* for all, but in 1665 it was doubled for the Hindu merchants,

[1] A list with dates and authorities is given in my *History of Aurangzīb*, vol. III, chap. XXXIV, Appendix V.

[2] A *dirham* weighed about 47 grains of silver or rather more than a quarter of a rupee, S. H. Hodivala, *J.A.S.B.* 1917, p. 45.

and two years later abolished altogether in the case of Muslims, with the result that the revenue suffered still more from many Hindu merchants collusively passing off their goods as the property of Muslims. A third instrument of the policy of luring his subjects to embrace Islām was the granting of stipends and gifts to converts, and the offering of posts in the public service, liberation from prison in the case of convicted criminals or captive rebels, or succession to disputed estates and principalities on condition of turning Muslim. Some Muhammadan families in the Punjab still hold letters patent by which their Hindu ancestors were expressly granted posts as *qānūngo* or revenue inspectors as a reward of apostasy, *qānūngoī ba shart-i-Islām.* In 1671 an order was issued that the revenue collectors of crown lands must all be Muslims and that the Hindu head-clerks and accountants in all provinces and *taluqs* (estates) should be dismissed in order to make room for Muhammadans. The enforcement of this order was found to be impossible on account of the lack of competent Muslims, and therefore the emperor had later to tolerate Hindus in half of these public posts. In 1668 Hindu religious fairs were forbidden throughout the empire, and in 1695 all Hindus, with the exception of Rājputs, were forbidden to ride in palanquins, on elephants or good horses, and to carry arms.

Forcible opposition to temple destruction was offered only in Rājputāna, Mālwā, Bundelkhand and Khāndesh, which were remote from the centre of the imperial authority, and even there only when the emperor was not present. But we read of reprisals in the second half of the reign by certain Rājput and Marāthā chiefs, who demolished converted mosques in retaliation or stopped the chanting of the call to prayer in their locality. In some places the *jizya* collector was expelled after plucking his beard out.

The first extensive outbreak of Hindu reaction against this policy of persecution took place among the sturdy Jāt peasantry of the Muttra district, where the local commandant 'Abdun-Nabī was a bigoted oppressor. In 1669 the Jāts rose under a leader named Gokla of Tilpat, killed 'Abdun-Nabī, and after keeping the whole region in turmoil for a year, were suppressed only after a bloody contest with a strong imperial force under Hasan 'Alī Khān. In 1672 came the Satnāmī rising, which, by disturbing the Nārnaul district close to Delhi and interrupting the grain supply of the capital, produced a much greater sensation than its importance justified. These people, popularly called *Mundiyās* or "shavelings" from their practice of shaving off all the hair, even the eyebrows, from their faces, were a unitarian sect forming a close brotherhood among themselves, honest, industrious and earnest like the Puritans. A petty wrangle between a Satnāmī peasant and a foot-soldier of the local collector at once swelled into a mass-conflict through the soldier's violence and the solidarity of the Satnāmīs. The quarrel soon took on the colour of a holy war against the destroyer of Hinduism. An old prophetess appeared among the sectaries and promised them invulnerability through her spells. The movement spread like wildfire. The local officers sent out troops in small parties, which were successively defeated, and these victories only raised the confidence of the rebels and confirmed the tale of their magical powers. Nārnaul was looted and a rebel administration set up in the district around it. The alarm even reached Delhi. Superstitious terror of the Satnāmīs' magical power demoralised the imperial troops. At last Aurangzīb was roused. He sent a large army under Ra'dandāz Khān with artillery and a detachment of the imperial guards. The emperor, who had the reputation of a saint working miracles (*'Alamgīr, zinda pīr*), wrote out prayers and magical figures with his own hand and ordered these papers to be sewed on to the banners of his army in order to counteract the enemy's spells! After a most obstinate battle, two thousand of the Satnāmīs fell on the field, many more were slain in the pursuit, and the country was pacified.

The Sikh sect which Bābā Nānak (1469–1538) had founded at the beginning of the sixteenth century was entirely transformed from a religious body into a military brotherhood in the course of the seventeenth century. Though Aurangzīb's policy and action completed this change, it had begun earlier than his reign and was in fact latent in the racial character of the main element of the Sikh population, namely the Jāts. Nānak had merely aimed at spiritual liberation by means of humility, prayer, self-restraint, searching of the heart and fixed gaze on the one God—"the True, the Immortal, the Self-existent, the Invisible, the Pure" (*alakh niranjan*). He rejected idols and incarnations as abominations and denounced set prayers and dead ritual. In fact, he made a surprising approach to the basic principles of Islām, though he denounced the Muslims of his age as base perverts and his modern followers are bitterly antagonistic to that sect. Nānak's successors in the leadership of the sect—or rather the largest branch of it—were called Gurūs, and the line ended with the tenth Gurū, Govind Singh (d. 1708).

The early Gurūs won the reverence of the Mughul emperors by their saintly peaceful lives. But their successors aspired to a temporal domination for themselves and made military discipline take the place of moral self-reform and spiritual growth. Under Arjan, the fifth Gurū (1581–1606), the number of Sikh converts greatly increased, and with them the Gurū's wealth. He organised a permanent source of income: his agents were stationed in every city from Kābul to Dacca where there was a Sikh to collect the tithes and offerings of the faithful and transmit this spiritual tribute to the central treasury at Amritsar. The Gurū lived like a king and was girt round by a body of courtiers called *masands* (a Hindī corruption of the Muhammadan title *masnad-i-a'la*). At the same time he completed the two sacred tanks at Amritsar, built the first temple for enshrining the Holy Book (*Ādi Granth*)—on the site where the Golden Temple now stands—and gave the final shape to their Scriptures by compiling a volume of hymns from the works of the principal Indian saints. But in the last year of his life he made the mistake of blessing the banners of Khusrav, the rival of Jahāngīr for the Mughul throne, and even gave him money help. On the defeat of the rebel, Jahāngīr fined the Gurū two lakhs of rupees for his collusion with treason. The Gurū refused to pay and died under torture, which was the usual punishment of revenue defaulters in those days (1606).

His son Har Govind (1606–45) "constantly trained himself in martial exercises and systematically turned his attention to the chase". He increased his bodyguard to a small army. He next provoked war with Shāh Jahān by encroaching on that emperor's game preserve and attacking the servants of the imperial hunt. The first few forces that were sent against him were defeated by his followers, and his fame spread far and wide, inducing many men to enlist under his banners, as they said that no one else had power to contend with the emperor. But finally his house and property at Amritsar were seized and he was forced to seek refuge at Kīratpur, in the Kashmīr hills, where he died in 1645. Then followed the peaceful pontificate of Har Rāi (1645–61), a disputed succession between his sons, and the early death of his chosen heir Har Kishan (1661–64). A wild scene of rapacity and disorder broke out among the Sikhs; "twenty-two men of Batālā claimed the right to succeed him; these self-made Gurūs forcibly took the offerings of the Sikhs". But after a time Tegh Bahādur, the youngest son of Har Govind, succeeded in being recognised as Gurū by most of the Sikhs. After fighting under Rām Singh (of Amber) in the Assam war he came back to the Punjab and took up his residence at Ānandpur.

While residing here, he was roused to action by Aurangzīb's acts of religious persecution. The emperor had ordered the temples of the Sikhs to be destroyed and the Gurū's agents (*masands*) to be expelled from the cities. Tegh Bahādur encouraged the resistance of the Hindus of Kashmīr and openly defied the emperor. Seized and taken to Delhi, he was called upon to embrace Islām, and on his refusal was tortured for five days and then beheaded on a warrant from the emperor (December, 1675).

Now at last an irreconcilable breach took place between the Sikhs and Islām. Govind Singh, the tenth and last of the Gurūs, was not a man to leave his father's death unavenged. He organised the sect into the most dangerous and implacable enemy of the Mughul empire and of the Muslim faith. All his thoughts were directed to turning the Sikhs into soldiers, to the exclusion of every other aim. He constantly drilled his followers, gave them a distinctive dress and a new oath of baptism, and began a course of open hostility to Islām.

He harangued the Hindus to rise against Muslim persecution and severely put down the adoration of Muhammadan saints to which Sikhs and many Hindus were addicted. As he told his mother, "I have been considering how I may confer empire upon the Khālsa", as the Sikh army was called.

This change he was able to effect because most of his converts were Jāts, the best raw materials for soldiers under proper training and leadership, naturally fearless, hardy, amenable to discipline, and ready to march anywhere and face any danger at the prospect of plunder. Already their religious teaching had knit the Sikhs together by an implicit faith in their spiritual head and a sense of the closest brotherhood. Caste distinctions among them were abolished under orders of Govind and all restrictions about food and drink discarded. The Sikhs felt themselves to be a chosen people, the Lord's elect, superior to every other sect. Everything was, therefore, ready for converting the sect into a military body obedient to the death to its chief and ever ready to surrender the individual conscience to that of the Gurū. It was as if Cromwell's Ironsides were inspired by the Jesuits' unquestioning submission to their Superior's decisions on moral problems.

In the hills of the northern Punjab Govind passed most of his days, constantly fighting with the hill-rajas from Jammū to Garhwāl or with Mughul officers and local Muslim chiefs who had entered the hills. Large imperial forces were sent from Sirhind to co-operate with the hill-rajas against him; but they were usually defeated. His army went on increasing, as recruits from the Punjab plains flocked to him for baptism; and he even enlisted Muhammadans. Ānandpur, his stronghold, was five times invested. In the last attack, after undergoing great hardship and loss, the Gurū evacuated the fort and then entered the Punjab plains, closely pursued by the Mughuls. At Chamkaur, with only forty followers, he was besieged in a Jāt cultivator's house; but two of his sons were slain and he fled again, from place to place like a hunted animal, undergoing many adventures and hairbreadth escapes. His two remaining sons were put to death by the governor of Sirhind (1705). Then the baffled Gurū with a few faithful guards made his way to the Deccan by way of Bīkāner, but returned to northern India on hearing of Aurangzīb's death. In the war of succession among that emperor's sons, he took the side of Bahādur Shāh, and accompanied that monarch when he marched to Golconda against Kām Bakhsh (1707). Here the Gurū took up his residence at Nānder on the Godāvarī, 150 miles north-west of Hyderābād, and here he was stabbed to death by an Afghān follower in 1708.

With him the line of Gurūs ended no doubt, but his parting instructions to his followers had been to make the Sikhs independent of a supreme leader and to turn them into a military democracy:

"I shall always be present wherever five Sikhs are assembled". Hence, isolated bands of Sikhs, each acting under an independent *sardār*, continued to harass the Mughul officers and raid the Punjab and the upper Gangetic Dūāb almost to the end of the eighteenth century.

Mārwār was the foremost Hindu state in Aurangzīb's empire. Its chieftain was Jasvant Singh Rāthor, who enjoyed the unique rank of Mahārājā and whom the death of Jay Singh Kachhwāha in 1667 had left without a rival as the foremost Hindu peer of the Mughul court. Jasvant's audacity in confronting Aurangzīb at Dharmat and treachery to him at Khajuhā had evidently been condoned by the emperor, who had afterwards given him high and responsible posts. When Jasvant died (20 December, 1678) in command of the outpost of Jamrūd, Aurangzīb at once seized his kingdom and placed it under direct Mughul rule, and himself moved to Ajmer in order to be close enough to Jodhpur to overawe Rāthor national opposition. The success of the emperor's plan for the forcible destruction of Hinduism required that Jasvant's state should sink into a tame dependency or a regular province of the empire, and Hindu resistance to the policy of religious persecution should be deprived of a possible head and rallying point.

The death of Jasvant while serving with his contingent and captains in far-off Afghānistān had left his state without a head, and no opposition was offered to the vast and well-directed imperial armies that poured upon the land. In February, 1679, the emperor learnt that two of Jasvant's wives had given birth to two posthumous sons, but he was not to be moved from his policy by any claims of legitimate succession. Mārwār having been brought under control, he returned in peace of mind to Delhi (12 April), and on that very day imposed the *jizya* on the Hindus after more than a century of abeyance. A little later the throne of Mārwār was sold to Indra Singh, the servile chieftain of Nāgaur and a hereditary partisan of the Mughuls, but the Mughul administrators and generals in occupation of the country were retained there, as Indra Singh enjoyed no local support.

In June Jasvant's family and retainers with his surviving infant Ajīt Singh reached Delhi, the other son having died in childbed. The rights of Ajīt were again pleaded before Aurangzīb, but he only ordered the child to be transferred to the imperial *harem* with a promise to give him a grant and investiture as raja when he came of age. According to one contemporary account, the throne of Jodhpur was offered to Ajīt on condition of his turning Muslim, and this we can believe from the authentic record of a similar offer made to the captive Shāhū in 1703. The loyal Rāthors determined to rescue their late chieftain's heir by sacrificing their lives. Their leader and guiding genius was Durgā Dās, the son of Jasvant's minister Askaran, whose character displayed a rare combination of the dash and reckless valour of a Rājput warrior with the tact, diplomatic cunning and organising power of the best Mughul ministers. But for his twenty-five years of unflagging exertion and skilful contrivance, Ajīt Singh could not have secured his father's throne. Fighting against terrible odds, he kept the cause of his nation triumphant, without ever looking to his own gain.

On 25 June Aurangzīb sent a strong force to seize the Rānīs and Ajīt and lodge them in the state prison of Nūrgarh. The Rāthor plan was to effect the escape of their prince by sacrificing their lives in a series of desperate rear-guard actions. First Raghunāth Bhatī with a hundred desperate troopers made a sortie from Jasvant's beleaguered mansion in Delhi and for a time drove back the imperialists, while Durgā Dās, seizing the momentary confusion, slipped out with the Rānīs dressed in male attire and rode away directly for Mārwār. By the time Raghunāth's party was killed to a man, Durgā Dās had covered nine miles. When he was overtaken, Ranchhor Dās Jodhā faced round and checked the pursuers with the lives of his band. This happened thrice. In the evening the weary Mughuls abandoned the murderous chase and Ajīt was safely conveyed to Mārwār and lodged in a secure place of hiding. Aurangzīb brought up a milkman's infant in his *harem* as the true Ajīt, gave him the significant name of Muhammadi Rāj and proclaimed Durgā Dās's *protégé* to be a bogus prince. At the same time Indra Singh was deposed for manifest incapacity to rule the Rāthors, and the whole of Mārwār was placed under a Mughul commandant, who was at first the governor of Ajmer and later of Gujarāt.

The emperor again went to Ajmer (5 October) and sent a strong force under his son prince Akbar to reconquer Mārwār. Its vanguard, led by Tahavvur Khān, after a three days' fight near Pushkar, destroyed the brave Rāthors of the Mairtia clan who barred his path. Thereafter the Rājputs always carried on a guerrilla warfare from their lurking places in the hills and deserts, without venturing on pitched battles. The whole country was soon occupied by the imperialists, anarchy and slaughter were let loose upon the doomed state; all the great towns in the plain were pillaged; the temples were thrown down.

Aurangzīb intended the annexation of Mārwār to be a preliminary step to the conquest of Mewār. He had already called upon the Mahārānā Rāj Singh to pay the poll tax for his entire state. The Mahārānā and his clansmen, the Sisodias, felt that if they did not stand by the Rāthors now both these first-rate Rājput clans would be crushed one by one and all Rājputāna would lie helpless at the emperor's feet. Moreover, Ajīt Singh's mother was a niece of the Mahārānā. While Rāj Singh was making his war preparations, Aurangzīb struck the first blow. Seven thousand picked troops under Hasan 'Alī Khān marched from Pur, ravaging Mewār and clearing a way for the main Mughul army. The Rājputs could make no stand against the excellent Mughul artillery served by Europeans. Rāj Singh abandoned the low country and retired with all his subjects to the hills. The Mughuls took possession of his capital Udaipur and the famous fort of Chitor, demolishing all the temples there. Hasan 'Alī entered the hills north-west of Udaipur and inflicted a defeat on the Mahārānā (1 February, 1680), capturing his camp and much property.

The emperor, deeming the power of Mewār crushed, returned from that kingdom to Ajmer in March, while one strong army (probably 12,000 men) under prince Akbar held the Chitor district and another occupied Mārwār. But the imperial outposts were too far scattered to be defended easily, and nearly the whole of Rājputāna was seething with hostility. The Mughul positions in Mewār and Mārwār were isolated from each other by the intervening Arāvallī range, whose crest Rāj Singh held in force and from which he could make sudden descents and surprise Mughul divisions on the east or the west as he pleased, while the Mughuls in transferring troops from Chitor to Mārwār had to make a long and toilsome détour.

Prince Akbar had been left in Chitor in charge of all the Mughul posts east of the Arāvallī and south of Ajmer. But his force was too small for the effective defence of this vast region. A marked increase of Rājput activity began with the emperor's retirement to Ajmer; they made raids, cut off supplies and stragglers, and rendered the Mughul outposts extremely unsafe. In terror of the enemy's prowess, the Mughul troops refused to enter any pass, detachments shrank from advancing far from their base, and the command of outposts went begging. About the end of May, Akbar's camp near Chitor was entered at night and some slaughter done in it by a Sisodia band. The Mahārānā descended to the Bednor district, threatening Akbar's communications with Ajmer, while another army under his son Bhīm Singh ranged the country, striking swift blows at weak points and cutting off grain supplies coming from Mālwā. A fortnight after the surprise of his camp, Akbar himself was defeated with severe loss. At these signal instances of Akbar's incapacity the emperor transferred him to Mārwār, and gave the Chitor command to Prince A'zam. The plan of war adopted now was to penetrate into the Mewār hills in three columns: from the eastern or Chitor side by way of the Deobārī pass and Udaipur under A'zam; from the north by way of lake Rājsamudra under Mu'azzam, and from the western or Mārwār side through the Deosurī pass under Akbar. The first two of these generals failed to achieve their tasks.

Prince Akbar took post at Sojāt in Mārwār on 28 July, but could not repress the Rāthor bands that spread over the country, closing the roads to trade and disturbing every weak post. His instructions were to occupy Nādol, the chief town of the Godwār district, and from this new base penetrate eastwards into Mewār by the Deosurī pass and invade the Kumbhalgarh region, where the Mahārānā and many Rāthors had taken refuge. Akbar reached Nādol at the end of September, but for nearly two months did nothing. At last the emperor in wrath sent the imperial paymaster to his camp to enforce a forward movement. It was only then that Akbar advanced to Deosurī and, sending his lieutenant Tahavvur Khān ahead, forced the Jhilwārā pass (2 December). The next step would have been to push on eight miles southwards to Kumbhalgarh and drive the Mahārānā out of his last refuge. But it was not done. There followed a lull of inactivity for five weeks, during which the prince's treasonable plot was fully hatched, and at last on 11 January, 1681, he united with the Rāthor and Sisodia contingents and proclaimed himself emperor of India!

Smarting under repeated censure from his father for his failure in war and seeing no means of defeating the Rājputs, Akbar had early lent a ready ear to the tempting invitation of the Rājputs to seize the Delhi throne with their help. Tahavvur Khān was the intermediary of these treasonable negotiations. The Mahārānā Rāj Singh and Durgā Dās told the prince how his father's bigoted attempt to "root the Rājputs out" was threatening the stability of the Mughul empire, and urged him to seize the throne and restore the wise policy of his forefathers if he wished to save his heritage from destruction. They promised to back him with the armed strength of the two greatest Rājput clans, the Sisodias and the Rāthors. The death of Rāj Singh (1 November) and the succession of his son Jay Singh interposed a month's delay in the execution of this plot. But when Tahavvur reached Jhilwārā, the negotiations were resumed and quickly concluded. The new Mahārānā promised to send half his army under his brother for the attack on Aurangzīb, and 12 January, 1681, was fixed for the march on Ajmer. Two days before that date Akbar wrote a deceptive letter to his father saying that two Mewār princes and the Rāthor leaders had come to him begging him to secure the emperor's pardon and peace for them, to present them to the emperor and personally to intercede with him for them, and that with this object he was marching on Ajmer. Then Akbar threw off his mask. Four theologians in his pay issued a decree under their seals, declaring that Aurangzīb had forfeited his throne by his violation of the Qurānic law! Akbar crowned himself emperor (11 January, 1681) and next day started for Ajmer with his new Mewār and Mārwār allies, dragging most of the imperial officers in his camp with him in this act of rebellion.

At this time Aurangzīb at Ajmer was very slenderly protected: his faithful sons were far away and even the imperial guard had been detached on a distant expedition. His immediate retinue consisted of a few thousands of unserviceable soldiers, personal attendants, clerks and eunuchs. He had loved Akbar above all his other sons, and now in the bitterness of disillusionment he cried out, "I am now defenceless. The young hero has got a splendid opportunity. Why, then, is he delaying his attack?" But Akbar was not the man to seize this opportunity by a rapid dash on the imperial camp; he began to spend his days in pleasure and took a fortnight to arrive near Ajmer. Every day told in Aurangzīb's favour. Loyal officers from far and near strained every nerve to reach him by forced marches, and on the day of Akbar's arrival in his neighbourhood, prince Mu'azzam joined the emperor, doubling his strength. In the meantime, Aurangzīb, with wise audacity, had refused to shut himself up within the walls of Ajmer, but advanced into the open, and taken up his position at Dorāhā, ten miles south of that city.

Despair and defection now reigned in the camp of Akbar. As he came nearer, increasing numbers of Mughul officers began to escape from his army to the imperial camp: only the 30,000 Rājputs remained true to him. Arrived within three miles of Dorāhā (25 January), he halted for the night, after fixing the next morning for the decisive battle. But during that night, Aurangzīb's cunning diplomacy secured the completest victory for him without any resort to arms. Tahavvur Khān was the *vazīr* and life and soul of Akbar's government, that prince being a vain sluggard. Tahavvur's father-in-law 'Ināyat Khān, then in the imperial camp, was made by Aurangzīb to write him a letter, urging him to come to the emperor, with a promise of pardon for the past, otherwise his wives and sons, held by Aurangzīb as hostages, would be ruined. In the darkness Tahavvur stole away alone from his tent without informing either Akbar or Durgā Dās, arrived at the imperial camp about midnight, and was killed by the emperor's attendants in a wrangle when he wanted to enter the presence without being disarmed.

Meantime, Aurangzīb had written a false letter to Akbar, praising him for having so successfully carried out the emperor's stratagem of luring all the Rājput fighters within his reach, and now instructing him to place these Rājputs in his van in next morning's battle so that they might be easily crushed between the imperial forces and Akbar's own troops. As contrived by the emperor, this letter fell into Durgā Dās's hands, who read it and in surprise went to Akbar's tent for an explanation. That prince was reported to be asleep and his eunuchs refused to wake him. Durgā Dās next sent some men to call Tahavvur, when it was discovered that the soul of the whole enterprise had secretly gone over to the emperor some hours before. The prince's sleep was taken to be a ruse. The intercepted letter was believed to have been verified by these facts. The Rājputs promptly arranged to save themselves. Three hours before dawn they took horse, robbed what they could of Akbar's property, and galloped off to Mewār. Profiting by this confusion, the remaining imperial troopers whom Akbar had forced to accompany him escaped towards Aurangzīb's camp. Tahavvur Khān was the connecting link between the Rājputs and Akbar; he had been the new emperor's commander-in-chief and prime minister in one, and his flight at once dissolved the confederacy. In the morning Akbar awoke to find himself deserted by all, save a faithful band of 350 horse. He hurriedly rode away for life in the track of his Rājput allies, taking only some of his wives and children and a little treasure with him. The rest of his property and his deserted family—one wife, two sons and three daughters—were seized by the emperor. Relentless punishment was meted out to his followers, especially the four Mullās; his ally, the princess Zīb-un-Nisā, was deprived of her property and confined in the Salīmgarh fortress.

During the second night after Akbar's flight, Durgā Dās, having discovered the fraud played by Aurangzīb, turned back and took the luckless prince under his protection. Rājput honour demanded that the refugee should be defended at all cost. After evading the pursuing Mughul columns and fleeing through Rājputāna and Khāndesh, Durgā Dās boldly and skilfully conducted Akbar to the court of Shambhūjī, the only power in India that could defy Aurangzīb (11 June, 1681).

Akbar's rebellion, however, had the effect of saving Mewār, by wrecking the Mughul plan of war at a time when the Mahārānā was about to be completely surrounded, and it also forced Aurangzīb to transfer himself and his best troops to the Deccan to watch the rebel and his new patron. Mewār was ravaged by war, so that the Mahārānā was as eager as Aurangzīb to make peace. He visited prince A'zam (24 June) and through his mediation was reconciled with the emperor on the following terms:

1. The Mahārānā ceded to the empire the parganas of Mandal, Pur and Bednor in lieu of the *jizya* demanded from his kingdom.

2. The Mughul army withdrew from Mewār, which was restored to Jay Singh with the title of Rānā and a command of 5000.

Thus Mewār regained peace and freedom, but Mārwār continued a scene of war and devastation for twenty-nine years more, which will be described in chapter x. In the height of political unwisdom, Aurangzīb wantonly provoked rebellion among the loyal Rājputs, while the frontier Afghāns were still far from being subdued. With the two leading Rājput clans openly hostile to him, his army lost its finest and most loyal native recruits. The trouble spread by contagion from the Rāthors and Sisodias to the Hārā and Gaur clans, and the lawlessness here set moving overflowed into Mālwā and heartened every opponent of the imperial government throughout India.

During the first half of Aurangzīb's reign affairs in the Deccan did not assume engrossing importance; the emperor's personal attention was engaged elsewhere and he felt that he could safely leave the south to his viceroys, because Bijāpur and Golconda were hopelessly decadent and the full significance of the rise of the Marāthā people under Shivājī was not realised till near the close of that hero's career (1680). Qutb Shāh remained throughout a quiescent vassal, except for armed assistance rendered to 'Ādil Shāh against Mughul attacks in 1666 and 1679; but these acts of disloyalty to his suzerain were compounded for by the payment of fines. A vigorous forward policy was pursued by the imperialists against Bijāpur only under Jay Singh (1666), Bahādur Khān (1676–77) and Dilīr Khān (1679–80). Military operations against Shivājī were actively carried on by Shāyista Khān (1660–62), Jay Singh (1665), Mahābat Khān (1671–72), Bahādur Khān (1673–75), and by Dilīr Khān for a short while in 1678–79, though a state of war continued languidly between the two powers for the entire period, except the four years of peace 1666–69.

Only a few clear successes but no decisive result was achieved by Mughul arms in the Deccan during the first twenty-four years of the reign, because Shāh 'Ālam, who was viceroy for nearly one-half of this period, was a timid and unenterprising prince, and was further thwarted by the open hostility of his chief officer, Dilīr Khān; the Hindu officers in the Mughul camp secretly fraternised with the Marāthā defender of their faith, while the Muslim generals were glad to bribe him to let them live in peace. The annexation of the Deccan was impossible except by a much more powerful army than any provincial viceroy's and a chief with the relentless vigour and determination of Aurangzīb.

Golconda may be left out of our account. 'Abdullah Qutb Shāh (reigned 1626–72) was throughout his life indolent and almost imbecile, and his narrow escape from assassination by Aurangzīb's son in 1656 gave him such a fright that he "lost all mental energy and ceased to hold the reins of government, or even to appear outside the walls of the fortress of Golconda" ever afterwards. All his time was given to ingenious forms of sensuality, while his mother and afterwards his son-in-law conducted the actual administration throughout his reign. His successor, Abu-'l-Hasan surnamed Tānā Shāh, was equally indolent and pleasure-loving, though possessed of a more delicate and artistic taste; under him his Brāhman ministers Mādanna and Ākkanna freely misgoverned the realm, following the traditional foreign policy of outward loyalty to the Mughuls with the addition of a secret defensive alliance with Shivājī in return for a subsidy of 500,000 rupees a year.

With Bijāpur Mughul relations were more complicated. Briefly put, the grouping of powers in the Deccan was this: the dread of imperial aggression drove the Sultān of Golconda whole-heartedly, and that of Bijāpur distrustfully and intermittently, into the arms of Shivājī. Bijāpur's leagues with Shivājī were formed only when Mughul invasion was an insistent fact and the situation of 'Ādil Shāh was hopeless, and these leagues were soon dissolved by the growing fear that the Marāthā coming in as a friend would treacherously seize 'Ādil Shāhī forts and lands. During Shāyista Khān's campaign against Shivājī (1660), the Bijāpurīs did, indeed, render useful co-operation to the Mughuls, but such aid to the imperial power ceased after the ministers of Bijāpur had formed a secret pact with Shivājī (about 1662) on condition of his sparing the heart of the kingdom, i.e. the royal territories proper, while he was left free to rob the semi-independent nobles whose grants lay in the outlying provinces.

Aurangzīb, when freed from the anxieties of the war of succession, determined to punish 'Ādil Shāh for his evasion of the promises made in the treaty of August, 1657, and his covert aid to Shivājī. He sent Jay Singh to the Deccan early in 1665 "to punish both these rebels". That general's first task was to humble Shivājī, which he effected in less than three months by his masterly campaign of Purandar (concluded in June, 1665). In the ensuing cold weather he set out for the invasion of Bijāpur, at the head of 40,000 imperial troops and 9000 Marāthā auxiliaries under Shivājī himself and his lieutenant Netājī Pālkar. The 'Ādil Shāhī forts on the way fell to him without a blow, and he had his first encounter with the Bijāpur army on 3 January, 1666, when a small detachment was cut off. The Deccani horsemen tried to envelop the Mughuls, evading their charges and breaking into several loose bodies which harassed the heavy cavalry of the north by practising their familiar "cossack" tactics. After a long contest the Mughuls, by repeated charges, drove the enemy back, but as soon as they began their return march the elusive Deccanis reappeared and galled them from both wings and the rear.

After two severe battles of this kind, he forced his way to within 12 miles of Bijāpur fort (7 January). But meantime the 'Ādil Shāhī capital had been rendered impregnable by strengthening its garrison, devastating the country around for 6 miles, draining all the tanks, filling up all the wells and cutting down every tree in its environs. At the same time a picked force under Sharza Khān and Sīdī Mas'ūd made a diversion by raiding the Mughul territories in the rear of the invaders. Jay Singh's sole chance of success lay in his taking Bijāpur by surprise, as he had bribed most of its nobles and his rapid march was expected to give the Bijāpurī forces no time to adopt measures of defence. He had, therefore, brought with him no heavy artillery or siege material. The hope of capturing Bijāpur by a *coup de main* having vanished, the baffled Mughul general decided on retreat (15 January), which he could do only after fighting two severe battles besides almost daily skirmishes. Netājī Pālkar deserted to 'Ādil Shāh; Shivājī failed with heavy loss in an assault on Panhālā and Qutb Shāh sent a large force to the rescue of his brother Sultān. After moving about in the Sultānpur-Dhārūr-Bhūm-Bhīr region, constantly harassed by the enemy and often suffering heavy losses to his detachments, without being able to effect anything decisive, Jay Singh returned to his headquarters (Aurangābād) on 6 December, after complete failure, incurring the severest financial loss. The Bijāpurīs now retired to their own country. The unlucky general was censured and recalled by his master and died, broken-hearted from disgrace and disappointment, on the way at Burhānpur (12 July, 1667).

After this war 'Alī 'Ādil Shāh II gave himself up to the pleasures of the harem and the wine-cup, which prostrated him by a stroke of paralysis. His able and experienced minister 'Abdul-Muhammad, however, continued to carry on the administration with honesty and success; but with the accession of Sikandar 'Ādil Shāh, a boy of four (4 December, 1672), and the seizure of the post of minister by Khavāss Khān, civil war broke out between the Afghān and Deccani *cum* Abyssinian factions among the nobles, and the rapid decline and dismemberment of the kingdom began. Henceforth the history of Bijāpur became the history of its successive ministers: Khavāss Khān the Abyssinian (1672–75), Buhlūl the Afghān (1675–77), Mas'ūd the Abyssinian (1678–83) and Āqā Khusrav (1684). The Sultān remained all his life a helpless prisoner; the provincial governors became independent of the central authority; and assassinations and faction fights destroyed the nobility in the capital itself.

Solicited by the Deccani party then out of power, the Mughul viceroy Bahādur Khān invaded Bijāpur in 1676, but met with a crushing defeat near Indī, Islām Khān Rūmī (the governor of Mālwā) being slain (23 June). But soon afterwards he cowed the minister into allowing the Mughuls to annex certain 'Ādil Shāhī forts, such as Naldrug and Gulbarga (1677). Aurangzīb, being dissatisfied with this result and suspecting Bahādur of collusion with the Deccani powers, recalled him. His successor Dilīr Khān, in alliance with Buhlūl the Afghān *vazīr* of Bijāpur, invaded Qutb Shāh's territory at Mālkhed in September, 1677. Here they fought for two months, being put to the severest distress by the cutting off of their provisions, and were finally forced to make a disastrous retreat to Gulbarga, abandoning all their baggage.

On the death of Buhlūl (2 January, 1678), Sīdī Mas'ūd made himself minister of Bijāpur with the support of Dilīr Khān, agreeing to make himself virtually a servant of the Mughuls and to send the Sultān's sister Shahr Bānū (Pādishāh Bībī) to the Delhi court for marriage with a son of Aurangzīb (A'zam). These humiliating terms made him universally unpopular. The treasury was empty, and the unpaid soldiery broke out in lawless fury, plundering and torturing the rich, while the minister hid himself in fear and impotence. Many people began to emigrate from the doomed capital. In the provinces the regent's authority was openly flouted.

Then Mas'ūd made a secret pact with Shivājī, on hearing of which Dilīr Khān marched out to Āklūj (October, 1678), threatening to invade Bijāpur. The Marāthā allies who came to Mas'ūd's aid began treacherously to plunder the realm and even plotted to seize the capital by surprise. Mas'ūd then sought the protection of Dilīr Khān, who sent a relieving force to Bijāpur and captured Bhūpālgarh (12 April, 1679), which was the most important Marāthā stronghold in that quarter.

But the 'Ādil Shāhī government was now practically dissolved, there was utter anarchy in the country and the capital in consequence of the feud between Mas'ūd and Sharza Khān, the only defenders of Bijāpur fort were some three thousand starving men, "and even these hankered for Mughul pay". The greed of the imperialists was insatiable. Dilīr Khān now demanded that Mas'ūd should resign his post as minister in favour of a creature of the Mughuls. On meeting with refusal he invaded the 'Ādil Shāhī kingdom (September, 1679). This campaign was a complete failure, because of Dilīr Khān's utter lack of money, the open opposition of his chief Shāh 'Ālam (newly returned to the Deccan as viceroy) and the very prompt and effective aid which Shivājī in person gave to Mas'ūd. Dilīr only bombarded Bijāpur fort fruitlessly for some days and then marched through the country around it like a mad dog, plundering and burning the villages, selling the harmless villagers into slavery with fiendish cruelty, and turning rich cities like Āthni and the fertile valley of the Don and the Krishnā into a desert. Finally, he invaded the Berad country (modern Shorāpur), east of Bijāpur, in the fork between the Krishnā and the Bhīmā. Here, his attack on Gōgi (1 March, 1680) failed with heavy loss, his soldiers refused to follow him, and he was recalled in disgrace.

The Marāthā people created an independent state and became an important element in the politics of the Mughul empire only under Shivājī, late in the seventeenth century. His father was Shāhjī Bhonsle, who rose from the position of a small assignee under the Sultāns of Ahmadnagar to that of a kingmaker, and finally, after his defeat by Shāh Jahān (1636) and forced migration from Mahārāshtra, became one of the leading Hindu generals of the 'Ādil Shāhī government. His petty holdings in the Poona district, with a rent-roll of only 40,000 *hūns*, were given by him to his son Shivājī (born in 1627), while his later acquisitions, in Mysore and the Arcot district, were inherited by Vyankājī (also called Ekojī), his son by another wife.

Shivājī and his mother were practically discarded by Shāhjī, with the result that Shivājī became his own master at the age of twenty when his guardian Dādājī Kond-dev died (1647). He gained many forts from their hereditary owners or the local officers of Bijāpur, sometimes by force but more often by treachery and sowing dissension; and he was able to do so the more easily because the Poona district, having originally belonged to the fallen Nizām-Shāhī dynasty, was a recent and imperfectly subdued acquisition of Bijāpur and that monarchy at this time entered on a rapid course of decline owing to the prolonged illness of Muhammad 'Ādil Shāh (1646–56), the succession of minor princes and the rule of selfish regents.

This was Shivājī's opportunity. By his conquest of forts and annexation of Jāvlī (25 January, 1656), he more than doubled the extent and revenue of his heritage. His first encounter with the Mughuls was in 1657, when, taking advantage of Aurangzīb's invasion of Bijāpur and the diversion of the Mughul forces to the Bīdar-Kaliānī region, he raided the Ahmadnagar and Junnar districts (April) and even looted the rich city of Junnar (10 May). But Aurangzīb promptly reinforced his local officers in that region and Nasīrī Khān by forced marches surprised and routed Shivājī (14 June). The imperialists then ravaged the Marāthā villages and guarded their own frontier watchfully by turns. When 'Ādil Shāh made peace with the Mughuls (September), Shivājī too submitted. But Aurangzīb, though pardoning him for the time being, never really trusted him and merely deferred his punishment till after the war of succession.

Shivājī next entered the north Konkan, seized Kalyān, Bhiwandī and Māhulī and advanced as far south as Māhad. A grand Bijāpur expedition against him led by 'Abdullah Bhatāri (entitled Afzal Khān) failed. Shivājī slew Afzal at an interview and surprised and plundered his army (20 November, 1659). He then penetrated into the south Konkan and the Kolhāpur district. Next year, in the south a Bijāpur force under Sīdī Jauhar invested Shivājī in Panhālā fort and forced him to evacuate it (23 July, 1660), and at the same time in the north a Mughul army under Shāyista Khān occupied Poona (19 May) and took Chākan fort by mining after a fifty-four days' siege (25 August). Thereafter the Mughul viceroy rested in Poona for many months. A force sent by him into the north Konkan was defeated, and Shivājī rapidly extended his conquests down the coast-strip up to Khārepatan, though he lost Kalyān to the Mughuls in May, 1661.

Some desultory fighting and fruitless chase of the Marāthā light raiders by the Mughuls occupied the next two years, and then on 15 April, 1663, Shivājī with masterly cunning and secrecy penetrated into Shāyista Khān's harem in Poona at midnight with a small band of followers and took him so completely by surprise that the Mughul viceroy was wounded, one of his sons, one captain, forty attendants and six women of his harem were killed and two other sons and eight other women were wounded, while the Marāthās lost only six men killed and forty wounded and escaped from the camp without the least hindrance. This result was due to the connivance, or at least the slothfulness, of Jasvant Singh, the first officer of Shāyista Khān.

Next, from 16 to 20 January, 1664, Shivājī sacked the rich city of Surat unchecked, its cowardly governor having fled away without any attempt at resistance, though the English, Dutch and French factories successfully defended themselves. Nearly two-thirds of the town were destroyed by fire and the plunder exceeded ten million rupees in value.

Aurangzīb removed Shāyista Khān from the viceroyalty and sent Jay Singh of Amber to the Deccan to punish Shivājī (1665). This raja by marvellously skilful diplomacy raised a complete ring of enemies round Shivājī and laid siege to the fort of Purandar, in which the families of the Marāthā officers had taken shelter. In two weeks he wrested the fortified hill of Vajragarh (Rudramāl) which commands the main terrace of Purandar, and advanced along the ridge connecting the two forts, while a strong flying column burnt and sacked the villages of Mahārāshtra. At last, finding the fort doomed, Shivājī personally visited Jay Singh and made with him the treaty of Purandar (22 June) by which he ceded to the emperor twenty-three forts (with lands yielding 400,000 *hūns*), and retained for himself only twelve forts (with territory worth 100,000 *hūns* a year), acknowledged himself a vassal of the emperor and promised to send a contingent of 5000 horse to serve in the Mughul ranks in the Deccan. In the invasion of Bijāpur that soon followed, he served the imperial cause with complete loyalty.

Shivājī next, under the persuasion of Jay Singh, paid a visit to Aurangzīb's court at Āgra (22 May, 1666). But this purely country-bred warrior felt humiliated at being ranked as a noble commanding 5000 men and left unnoticed after his presentation. He created a scene, accused the emperor of breach of faith, and swooned away in vexation of spirit. At this display of unfriendly feeling, he was ordered to be kept under police surveillance and forbidden the court. His appeals to the emperor and his ministers for leave to return home were fruitless, and after three months of captivity he slipped out of Āgra (29 August) with his son, deceiving his guards by lying concealed in two large baskets of sweetmeats which were preceded and followed by baskets of real sweets. Then, following a roundabout route, via Muttra, Allahābād, Benares, Gayā and Telingāna, he reached home on 30 November, 1666.

For three years after this, he left the Mughul government unmolested and even made peace with it through the mediation of Jasvant Singh and prince Shāh 'Ālam. The emperor recognised his title of *Rājā* and made a grant to his son Shambhūjī. In January, 1670, Shivājī broke with the Mughuls again, and by rapid strokes recovered nearly all the forts ceded by him in 1665. He plundered imperial territory in the Deccan right and left. A bitter quarrel between the viceroy Shāh 'Ālam and his lieutenant Dilīr Khān made it impossible for the imperialists to chastise or even to check the Marāthā chief, and he looted Surat a second time (13–15 October,

1670), carrying away large booty in cash and kind and thoroughly ruining the trade of the greatest port of India. Then followed a period of the most daring and far-ranging raids into Mughul provinces—Bāglān, Khāndesh and Berār besides Aurangābād—and the capture of hill forts in the Chāndor range as well as Sālher. Mughul generals were repeatedly defeated by him in open fights, especially at Dindorī (27 October, 1670) and below Sālher (February, 1671).

After the failure of Mahābat and Dilīr (1671–72) against the Marāthās, Aurangzīb sent Bahādur Khān[1] again as governor to the Deccan, which he ruled for the next five years but without being able to cope with Shivājī. This was the full tide of the Marāthā hero's power; he made annexations and levied blackmail (popularly called *chauth* or one-fourth of the land revenue, in Marāthī *khandanī*) in the east and west, north and south, and permanently occupied the Kolī country (Rāmnagar and Jāwhar) south of Surat. The death of 'Alī 'Ādil Shāh II (4 December, 1672) opened a wide door to Shivājī's acquisitions at the expense of Bijāpur,[2] while the rising of the Khyber Afghāns (1674) detained the main imperial forces on the north-western frontier. The desultory warfare carried on against him by Mughul captains from 1672 to 1678 was barren of result. Taking advantage of these circumstances, Shivājī crowned himself king of kings (*Chhatrapati*) at Rāigarh on 16 June, 1674, and spent one year (1677) in conquering a vast realm in the Madras Carnatic and the Mysore plateau, estimated to cover "sixty leagues by forty and to yield 20 lakhs of *hūns* a year, with a hundred forts".[3]

In 1678 the new Bijāpurī regent Sīdī Mas'ūd made a pact with Shivājī for armed assistance in the event of a Mughul attack, and such assistance was most effectively given during the campaign against Bijāpur opened by Dilīr Khān in October, 1679. Shivājī, with a view to causing a diversion in Dilīr Khān's rear, formed his men into two parallel divisions of nine to ten thousand horsemen each, and poured like a flood northwards from Selgūr through the districts of Mughul Deccan, burning and plundering. But between Jālna and Aurangābād he was attacked by an enterprising officer, Ranmast Khān, and forced to fight a rear-guard action, which detained him for three days, while reinforcements hastened up from Aurangābād to complete the circle round the Marāthās (*c.* 25 November). In the third night Shivājī, after losing 4000 men killed and abandoning all his booty and many horses, slipped out by an obscure path under the guidance of his head spy, and escaped to his own dominion by incessant marching for three more days and nights. Evidently these privations weakened his health, and on 2 April, 1680, he was seized with fever and blood dysentery, of which he died on the 14th, at the age of fifty-three.

[1] Known as Khān Jahān from about 1674.

[2] See chap. IX, p. 275.

[3] See chap. IX, p. 276.

CHAPTER IX

THE KINGDOMS OF THE DECCAN DURING THE REIGNS OF JAHĀNGĪR, SHĀH JAHĀN AND AURANGZĪB, AND THE RISE OF THE MARĀTHĀ POWER

To complete the history of Muhammadan India during the reigns of Jahāngīr, Shāh Jahān and Aurangzīb narrated in separate chapters it is necessary to consider briefly the relation of the southern kingdoms with each.

At Akbar's death the shrunken kingdom of Ahmadnagar remained nominally in the hands of Murtazā II, the representative of the Nizām Shāhs, and actually controlled by Malik 'Ambar the capable African minister. The two greater kingdoms of Bijāpur and Golconda and the small state of Bīdar remained intact, but Bīdar was annexed by Bijāpur in 1620.

In September, 1609, Parvīz, Jahāngīr's second son, who had been appointed to the viceroyalty of Khāndesh and the Deccan, left Āgra for Burhānpur; and expecting invasion Ibrāhīm 'Ādil Shāh asked that a resident envoy from the emperor might be accredited to his court.

Malik 'Ambar also sought alliance with Ibrāhīm 'Ādil Shāh and obtained from him the fortress of Kandhār as a base of operations situate at a safe distance from the frontier of the imperial province of Ahmadnagar.

In 1610 prince Parvīz, against the advice of the Khān Khānān, attempted to invade Murtazā's territories by the eastern route, which was little known and difficult. His supplies were cut off by Marāthā auxiliaries and he suffered a disastrous defeat. His enemies, judging it imprudent to proceed to extremities against the emperor's son, permitted a retreat to Burhānpur, but pursued the Mughul army through Berār, plundering its baggage and otherwise harassing it, while even Ahmadnagar fell into the hands of Malik 'Ambar's troops. Jahāngīr most unjustly blamed the Khān Khānān for these disasters and recalled him from the Deccan, but other generals had no better success.

In 1616 Parvīz, whose sloth and incompetence unfitted him for active employment on the frontier, was transferred from the Deccan to Allahābād and in the same year Khurram, the most active and capable of Jahāngīr's sons, was appointed viceroy of Khāndesh and the Deccan. On 11 November Jahāngīr himself set out from Ajmer for the Deccan in the English coach which had been presented to him by Sir Thomas Roe.

Khurram recovered Ahmadnagar and some other fortresses which had passed into the hands of Malik 'Ambar, and opening negotiations with Ibrāhīm 'Ādil Shāh accepted from him valuable gifts. The prince was received with high honours on his return, promoted to the command of 30,000 horse, and entitled Shāh Jahān. What he had in fact effected was the re-establishment of the arrangement originated by the Khān Khānān, which need never have been disturbed, and a delusive alliance with Ibrāhīm 'Ādil Shāh which was construed at the Mughul court into the acquisition of a new vassal. Ibrāhīm himself regarded his action as an adroit bargain which for the time averted danger both from himself and from his ally.

Muhammad Qulī Qutb Shāh of Golconda had died on 24 January, 1612, and had been succeeded by his nephew Muhammad Qutb Shāh, who had married his uncle's daughter, Hayāt Bakhsh Begam. Neither of these two monarchs concerned himself much with the important struggle in the north-west of the Deccan otherwise than by supporting Malik 'Ambar by pecuniary contributions. Muhammad Qulī Qutb Shāh was occupied with the Carnatic, with Orissa and Bastar, and with intrigues between the Foreigners[1] and the Deccanis, the latter of whom gained the upper hand in the closing years of his reign, and Muhammad Qutb Shāh continued the policy of interference in Bastar, occupied himself with building and had not sufficiently robust health to indulge in other pursuits. He died on 11 February, 1626, and was succeeded by his thirteen-year old son, 'Abdullah Qutb Shāh.

In 1620 Malik 'Ambar took advantage of the emperor's absence from the Deccan to attack imperial posts on his northern frontier. Ahmadnagar was besieged, and though the Mughul officer in command of the Deccan claimed a victory he found it necessary, owing to the scarcity of supplies, to withdraw his troops to Berār, followed by the enemy, who ventured to attack him even there, but were repulsed. The scarcity of supplies was again due to the tactics of the Marāthā auxiliaries of Malik 'Ambar, who was now in possession of the whole kingdom of Ahmadnagar and of the southern districts of Berār, with an army of 60,000 horse. Many of the imperial troops deserted, and their commander had to retreat to Burhānpur and was besieged there. Jahāngīr, infuriated by reports of this retirement, sent Shāh Jahān again to the Deccan with a large army, and himself returned to Āgra. Before Shāh Jahān reached Ujjain a force of Malik 'Ambar's troops had advanced and plundered villages under the walls of Māndū. The marauders fled across the Narbadā before his advanced guard but were pursued and many were slain.

Shāh Jahān then compelled Malik 'Ambar to raise the siege of Burhānpur but was obliged to halt there for nine days to refresh the exhausted garrison.

[1] See vol. III, pp. 403–4.

Malik 'Ambar had now established Khirkī (called later Aurangābād) as the capital of the Nizām Shāh's kingdom. To ensure his safety he carried Murtazā into the strong fortress of Daulatābād, only ten miles distant. Shāh Jahān marched to Khirkī and "so devastated a city which had taken twenty years in the building that it was doubtful whether another twenty years would suffice to restore it to its pristine splendour".

The beleaguered garrison of Ahmadnagar was relieved and Shāh Jahān reached Paithan on the Godāvarī, where he received emissaries from Malik 'Ambar, who expressed contrition.

Shāh Jahān now experienced a foretaste of the Marāthā warfare which brought his son to the grave. He had driven before him like chaff before the wind an enemy who dared not withstand him in the field; he had confined his principal antagonist within the walls of a fortress, but his own troops were starving. By all the rules of war he was the victor. In fact he was as helpless as his adversary, and was obliged to come to terms, which, however, were honourable to the empire.[1]

Malik 'Ambar was soon relieved of the anxiety which Shāh Jahān's propinquity caused him; for early in 1622 the prince was recalled to the capital to aid his father in meeting an attack on Qandahār by Shāh 'Abbās I of Persia, and his rebellion later in the year dissipated for a time all apprehensions of imperial aggression in the Deccan.

When Malik 'Ambar's apprehensions had been thus removed he marched to the frontiers of Golconda to demand payment of his subsidy, which was two years in arrears, and having received the sum due and a renewal of Muhammad Qutb Shāh's promise to pay it regularly in future, he attacked Bīdar, expelled Ibrāhīm 'Ādil Shāh's garrison, and plundered the town and district, the annexation of which by Bijāpur during his preoccupation with the imperial troops he regarded as an act of bad faith. He then retired to Daulatābād, but in the following year returned with fifty or sixty thousand men and besieged Bijāpur.

Ibrāhīm 'Ādil Shāh had continued to act with conciliation towards the empire and had attached a force to the Mughul garrison of Burhānpur. He recalled these troops in his extremity to Bijāpur and begged further assistance. His appeal met with a generous response. Burhānpur was nearly denuded of troops and the Mughul governors of Ahmadnagar and Bīr marched with many other officers to the relief of Bijāpur. Malik 'Ambar vehemently protested, claiming to be, equally with Ibrāhīm, the emperor's vassal, and that the quarrel between them related to part of the ancient territory of Ahmadnagar, wrongfully occupied by Bijāpur. His protests were unheeded, and he raised the siege of Bijāpur and retired towards his own dominions. Meeting the army which was marching to the relief of Bijāpur he

[1] See chap. VI, p. 169.

suddenly fell upon it, routed it and captured many imperial officers. He then attacked Ahmadnagar but, discovering that a protracted siege would be necessary, left a force to blockade it and marched to Sholāpur, the possession of which had been contested between Bijāpur and Ahmadnagar ever since the two kingdoms had been founded. Sholāpur fell and Malik 'Ambar sent a force to besiege Burhānpur.

This was joined by the rebel Shāh Jahān who, retreating before his father's troops, arrived at Burhānpur. The strangely assorted allies took the town and were engaged in the siege of the citadel when the news of the approach of Sultān Parvīz and the Khān Khānān, who were pursuing the rebel, put the prince to flight and compelled the troops to retire to Daulatābād.

In 1626 Malik 'Ambar died, in the eightieth year of his age. Jahāngīr, in his memoirs, seldom mentions him without abuse, but his secretary, Mīrzā Muhammad Hādī, who continued the memoirs, thus did justice to his memory. "'Ambar, whether as a commander or a strategist, was without an equal in the military art. He kept the rabble of that country (the Deccan) in perfect order and to the end of his days lived in honour. There is no record elsewhere in history of an African slave attaining to such a position as was held by him."

In the same year Fath Khān, Malik 'Ambar's son, submitted at Jālna to a Mughul commander. This accession to the imperial cause was welcomed and rewarded, but it was short-lived. Fath Khān invaded Berār with the troops of Murtazā Nizām Shāh II and Khān Jahān was sent by the emperor to defend Burhānpur.

Murtazā now appointed as his minister Hamīd Khān, another African, and fell completely under his influence. He served his master well by inducing Khān Jahān to surrender, in consideration of a large gift in money, Ahmadnagar and the southern table-land of Berār. The treachery of "that faithless Afghān", as his master termed him, was partly neutralised by the refusal of the commandant to surrender Ahmadnagar, which he held successfully against Murtazā's troops.

Hamīd Khān's wife, the daughter of a foreigner, was a woman of great ability and unbounded energy. She obtained access to the harem of Murtazā Nizām Shāh II and soon became the recognised means of communication between the effeminate and slothful king and his subjects.

The death of Malik 'Ambar induced Ibrāhīm 'Ādil Shāh to avenge aggressions, and he sent an army to invade Murtazā's kingdom. As it approached Daulatābād the wife of Hamīd Khān solicited and obtained for herself the command of the army, by suggesting that if she were victorious the enemy would hide his head for shame, while if she failed he could only boast that he had defeated a woman. She cajoled the officers and distributed largesse to the soldiers and in the end she drove away the army of Bijāpur and captured all its elephants and artillery.

Ibrāhīm 'Ādil Shāh II died in September, 1627, and was succeeded by his son Muhammad 'Ādil Shāh. Ibrāhīm, unlike most of his house, was a Sunnī but in the later years of his reign he associated much with Hindus, who gave him the title of *Jagad-Gurū*, or "Spiritual Guide of the World". His Muslim subjects murmured that their king had become an infidel, like Akbar, but a historian asserts that he never wavered in devotion to the orthodox faith and that the tendency to associate with Hindus was due only to love of music, admitting at the same time that he imitated some of the superstitious invocations of Sāraswatī employed by Hindu musicians.

Early in the reign of Muhammad 'Ādil Shāh, Hamīd Khān invaded his territories with an army, but was defeated near Bijāpur and compelled to retreat to Daulatābād.

On 7 November, 1627, Jahāngīr died, and was succeeded by his son Shāh Jahān, early in whose reign the whole of the southern table-land of Berār was recovered by the imperial officers.

Shāh Jahān had learnt something of strategy and politics in the Deccan and clearly perceived that the key to it was the possession of the strong fortress of Daulatābād. He had learnt also that the canker-worm of treason and corruption which eventually destroyed the efficiency of the imperial armies flourished in the Deccan, so that the capture of Daulatābād required the sovereign's personal attention. At the end of 1629 he set out for Burhānpur, and many of the officers of Murtazā's army, learning that the emperor proposed to command in person, ensured their future prosperity by deserting their master.

Early in 1630 Shāh Jahān sent an army to invade Murtazā's dominions and Fath Khān, doubtful of his influence over Murtazā Nizām Shāh II, put him to death and proclaimed his young son, Husain Nizām Shāh III. The imperial army drove Fath Khān and Husain III into Daulatābād but was, as often before, compelled by scarcity of provisions to retreat.

Early in 1632 Fath Khān purchased a respite for Daulatābād by sending his son, 'Abdur-Rasūl, to the imperial court with gifts.

Muhammad 'Ādil Shāh's failure on his accession to send a complimentary offering to Shāh Jahān induced the emperor to invade his dominions. The commander marched through Bīdar, captured the fortress of Bhālkī, and on reaching Gulbarga occupied the city but refrained from attacking the citadel. He continued his march, appeared before Bijāpur with 30,000 horse, and encamped by the Rāmling Tank.

The city was not regularly besieged, but combats between the two armies, in which victory according to the historian of Bijāpur rested with Muhammad Shāh's troops, were of frequent occurrence. The real policy of Muhammad was, however, not to defeat but to starve the enemy. Negotiations were prolonged, while supplies were intercepted and the Mughul army was reduced to such distress that it was compelled to retire. It moved first to the fertile districts of Mirāj and Rāybāg on the Krishnā, where it obtained supplies by plundering the country and thence retired, by way of Sholāpur, to the territory held by the imperial troops in the former kingdom of Ahmadnagar.

Muhammad 'Ādil Shāh, as a precaution against future attacks on Bijāpur, transported the great gun *Malik-i-Maidān*, or "Lord of the Plain", from Parenda to his capital, where, on 1 September 1632, it was placed in the position which it still occupies.

Shāh Jahān professed to be satisfied with this expedition, the first to advance so far south as Bijāpur, but there can be little doubt that he was in fact disappointed by his discomfiture. Mahābat Khān, the Khān Khānān, governor of the Punjab, was therefore appointed viceroy of Khāndesh and the Deccan.

Shāhjī, the father of Shivājī, who had been annoyed by Shāh Jahān's action in transferring to Fath Khān, in return for the gifts which he had sent to court by his son 'Abdur-Rasūl, some assignments which Shāhjī had held in the former kingdom of Ahmadnagar, had fled to Bijāpur and persuaded Muhammad 'Ādil Shāh to send an army to recover his lands and to capture Daulatābād. Khān Jahān found this army in the neighbourhood of Khirkī on his arrival at that town and at once attacked and defeated it. He anticipated no difficulty in occupying Daulatābād, for Fath Khān had promised to surrender the fortress to him, but a common danger once more united the southerners. The officers of Bijāpur suggested that Fath Khān should join them against the imperial troops and promised to provide supplies for Daulatābād. A force from Bijāpur which attempted to bring up food and forage was driven off, but Fath Khān refused to fulfil his promise to surrender the fortress. Mahābat Khān now arrived and opened the siege, which lasted for more than four months. The imperial troops were much hampered by the army of Bijāpur, under Randola Khān an African and Shāhjī the Marāthā, which, though unable to convey supplies to the garrison, succeeded in cutting off those of the besiegers.

Mahābat Khān carried the outer defences of Daulatābād one by one until he reached Bālākot, the upper citadel, which was impregnable by assault and impervious to such artillery as then existed. Famine had, however, done its work, and on 28 June, 1633, Fath Khān, who had succeeded in obtaining most generous terms, led Husain Nizām Shāh III out, and the imperial troops occupied the citadel.

The Nizām Shāhī dynasty was at an end and its dominions were added to the empire, which now extended to the northern frontiers of the kingdoms of Bijāpur and Golconda.

Mahābat Khān, leaving Khān Daurān with a small force in Daulatābād, set out for Burhānpur, but the army of Bijāpur besieged Khān Daurān in the fortress and might have obliged him to surrender, as he was ill-supplied with provisions. They fled, however, on hearing that Mahābat Khān was returning and he, after victualling the fortress, resumed his march to Burhānpur.

At the end of August Shāh Jahān appointed his second son, Shāh Shujā', viceroy of the Deccan, and shortly afterwards addressed arrogant letters to Muhammad 'Ādil Shāh and 'Abdullah Qutb Shāh, criticising their use of the royal title, asserting a claim to sovereignty over them, and ordering them to cause the *khutba* to be recited and money to be coined in his name in their dominions. Muhammad replied in insolent terms, but concluded by saying that he would continue to pay the stipulated tribute.

The use of the royal title by the kings of the Deccan was always resented by the Mughul emperors, who wrote of them usually as "rulers" or "governors" of their diminions and addressed them as "'Ādil Khān" and "Qutb-ul-Mulk". A skilful retort was made by Abu-'l-Hasan Qutb Shāh to Aurangzīb's envoy to Golconda in 1685, who rudely told Abu-'l-Hasan that he had no right to the royal title. "You are wrong," replied the king, "for if I am not a king how can your master call himself the king of kings?"

'Abdullah Qutb Shāh took no overt action to relieve Daulatābād, but he and Muhammad 'Ādil Shāh entered into an alliance against the emperor.

Although Daulatābād had fallen, much remained to be done towards the complete establishment of imperial rule in the dominions of Ahmadnagar. In the west, towards the Konkan, Shāhjī Bhonsle held much territory and resided at the fort of Pemgarh. In the fortress of Jalodhan, sixteen miles from Junnar, some scions of the Nizām Shāhī line still remained imprisoned. Shāhjī obtained possession of the person of one of these, a child, and entitled him Murtazā Nizām Shāh III.

The commander of the strong fortress of Parenda, formerly included in the Nizām Shāhī dominions, had some time before this made his submission to Muhammad 'Ādil Shāh, on whose behalf the fortress was now held. Shāh Shujā' and Mahābat Khān were ordered to capture it and unsuccessfully besieged it for some months in 1634 owing to the activity of the army of Bijāpur, and they retired to Burhānpur. Mahābat Khān was blamed for the failure of the enterprise and both he and the prince were recalled to court.

The viceroyalty of the Deccan was now divided into two governments, the Bālāghāt, comprising the former dominions of Ahmadnagar and the southern table-land of Berār, and the Pāyānghāt, consisting of the rest of Berār and Khāndesh; and Khān Zamān was appointed to the government of the former and Khān Daurān to that of the latter. Of the rebels the most formidable was Shāhjī Bhonsle, who held the forts of Trimbak, Kondhānā[1] and Shivner above the Ghāts, besides many in the Konkan, and enjoyed the support and protection of Muhammad 'Ādil Shāh.

Khān Zamān and Khān Daurān vigorously prosecuted hostilities. The former pursued the Marāthā into the rich districts of the Bijāpur kingdom on the banks of the upper Krishnā, captured Kolhāpur, Mirāj and Rāybāg, carried off their inhabitants into slavery and devastated the country, and the latter captured Parenda, Bīdar, Gulbarga and Sholāpur, and marched to the gates of Bijāpur devastating the country in all directions.

Shāh Jahān visited Daulatābād in 1636 and Muhammad 'Ādil Shāh was compelled to sue for peace. The emperor, who had no designs against the two remaining kingdoms of the Deccan and sincerely desired peace, granted him terms more favourable than he had a right to expect. Parenda, Bīdar, Gulbarga and Sholāpur were restored to him, he was allowed to retain possession of Naldrug and eastern Kalyānī, and the Konkan, as far north as Kalyān, and the tract between the Nīrā and Bhīmā rivers, as far north as Chākan, which had formerly belonged to Ahmadnagar, were ceded to him. In return for these concessions he promised to pay an annual tribute of two millions of *hūns*, equivalent to eight millions of rupees.

Shāhjī's remaining forts were now reduced by Khān Zamān, who captured and sent to Gwalior Murtazā Nizām Shāh III, and the Marāthā tendered his submission and begged that he might be received into the imperial service, but was informed that he might enter that of Bijāpur, and he was received by Muhammad 'Ādil Shāh.

Golconda had suffered in no way from the hostilities between the imperial troops and Bijāpur, and had been free to wage "holy wars" against the Hindus of Orissa, Bastar and the Carnatic—chiefly against those of the last-named region, in which 'Abdullah Qutb Shāh now held much territory.

Muhammad 'Ādil Shāh, though not personally warlike, now imitated his neighbour and for some years despatched expeditions into the Carnatic. These undertakings, usually successful owing to the dissensions between the petty rajas of the peninsula, were dignified with the name of holy wars, but Shāhjī and other Hindu officers and troops were freely employed in them and they were in fact plundering excursions. Shāhjī, who was second in command under Randola Khān, obtained extensive and valuable assignments in the Carnatic.

In 1637 the two governments were again amalgamated to form the viceroyalty of the Deccan, under Aurangzīb, Shāh Jahān's third son, who was only nineteen years of age. Aurangzīb's intentions and policy towards the two independent Muhammadan kingdoms differed widely, as his subsequent conduct showed, from his father's, but he

[1] Now Sinhgarh.

did not molest them during his first tenure of the viceroyalty. He had, however, succeeded in obtaining from his father permission to annex Bāglān, the principality of the Rāthor Bairam Baharjī. The attack on Bairam was an act of purposeless aggression. Bairam received the command of 3000 horse in the imperial army and an assignment of the district of Sultānpur, adjoining his late principality.

The remaining period of Aurangzīb's first viceroyalty was uneventful until June, 1644, when in one of his real or feigned fits of religious enthusiasm he expressed his intention of retiring from the world and living a life of devotion, and Khān Daurān was appointed to succeed him.

Shivājī,[1] the son of Shāhjī Bhonsle who now began to rise into prominence, had hitherto lived at Poona. His first feat, in 1646, was to persuade the commander of the hill fort of Torna, probably by corrupt means, to surrender the fort to him. He sent agents to Muhammad 'Ādil Shāh to explain that he had taken this important stronghold in the interests of Bijāpur, but his overtures received no reply. A buried treasure discovered at Torna enabled him to build, in the following year, the fort of Rājgarh, 3 miles from Torna. The Bijāpur government called his father to account and he was censured, but merely temporised.

Shivājī then assumed the management of his father's estates, and retained the revenues, representing the expenses of their administration to be so high as to leave no margin of profit. He obtained possession of the fort and district of Chākan and of the stronger fort of Kondhānā, which he induced the Muslim commander to surrender to him in consideration of a bribe. He changed the name of Kondhānā to Sinhgarh, "the Lion's Fort", and made it his chief stronghold. He then expelled his father's agents from Sūpa, persuaded the revenue agents of Bārāmatī and Indāpur to recognise his authority, and possessed himself by treachery of the strong hill fort of Purandar.

> Thus did Shivājī obtain possession of the tract between Chākan and the Nīra: and the manner in which he established himself, watching and crouching like the wily tiger of his own mountain valleys, until he had stolen into a situation from whence he could spring on his prey, accounts for the difficulty found in tracing his early rise, and the astonishing rapidity with which he extended his power when his progress had attracted notice and longer concealment was impossible.[2]

Shivājī soon passed beyond the stage of concealment. The plunder of a convoy of government treasure destined to Bijāpur, the capture of ten more forts, and above all the arrest of the Muslim governor of Kalyān, the seizure of that place and of all forts in its neighbourhood, and the appointment of a Brāhman governor showed him in his true colours and involved his father in suffering and disgrace. Shāhjī, now governor of the Bijāpur Carnatic, was suspected of complicity in his son's rebellion. He was arrested by an artifice and conveyed to Bijāpur, where he was confined in a dungeon by Muhammad

[1] See chap. VIII, p. 256.

[2] Grant Duff, I, 114.

'Ādil Shāh, who refused to believe his protestations of innocence and threatened him with a lingering death. His peril suggested to Shivājī a device which he afterwards employed with great dexterity—the pitting of the northern against the southern Muslim—and he appealed to Shāh Jahān on behalf of his father. It was largely owing to the emperor's influence that Shāhjī was released from his dungeon, but he was detained at Bijāpur for four years as a prisoner at large.

Aurangzīb was reappointed in 1651 to the viceroyalty of the Deccan and selected as his residence Khirkī, which he extended, embellished and renamed Aurangābād. He had at first no dealings with Shivājī, who had hitherto studiously refrained from molesting the imperial dominions and whose depredations in Bijāpur territory were in no way opposed either to Aurangzīb's interests or inclinations.

During the period of his father's detention Shivājī had refrained almost entirely from acts of aggression, but on Shāhjī's return to the Carnatic, which had fallen, during his absence, into such disorder as to demand the whole attention of the government of Bijāpur, he renewed his activity, murdering Chandra Rāo, Rājā of Jāvlī, annexing his possessions, and building the strong fort of Partābgarh, near the source of the Krishnā.

In 1655 events in Golconda gave Aurangzīb an opportunity, which he eagerly welcomed, of interfering in the affairs of that kingdom.

The most powerful of the nobles of Golconda was a Sayyid of Ardistān, Mīr Muhammad Sa'īd, who had received the title of Mīr Jumla (prime minister) and very extensive assignments in the Golconda Carnatic. He had originally been a diamond merchant, and the experience which he had thus acquired enabled him to dispose, to the best advantage, of the produce of the diamond mines which his assignments contained. His wealth and his power were great, and he maintained at his own expense a force of 5000 horse. The dissolute and arrogant conduct of Muhammad Amīn, Mīr Jumla's son, who resided at court, produced the first open breach between the servant and his master. His offences culminated in his coming drunk to the royal palace, throwing himself down to sleep, in the king's absence, on the royal throne, and vomiting over its rich coverings. He was imprisoned and his father appealed to Shāh Jahān for protection. The appeal received the strongest support from Aurangzīb, and Shāh Jahān directed 'Abdullah Qutb Shāh to release Muhammad Amīn and to send both father and son to the imperial court. 'Abdullah resented this attempt to interfere between him and his servants and punished Mīr Jumla by the confiscation of his property.

Aurangzīb induced his father to sanction offensive action and sent his eldest son, Muhammad Sultān, at the head of a considerable force towards Golconda, announcing that the prince was on his way to Bengal to espouse his cousin, the daughter of Shujā'. The device succeeded, and the prince encamped within a few miles of Hyderābād, before 'Abdullah understood his hostile intent. Muhammad acting under his father's instructions neglected no means of provoking 'Abdullah to hostile action. The unfortified city of Hyderābād was sacked, some quarters were burnt, and neither the royal palace nor the dwellings of the nobles and the wealthier merchants escaped pillage. The king was in the fortress of Golconda and could not restrain his troops, some of whom slew some of the ruffians of the Mughul army. Aurangzīb was stealthily following Muhammad Sultān with the remainder of his army. Those who had attempted to stay the marauders were put to flight and Aurangzīb joined his son. 'Abdullah was now in an agony of terror. He had already promised to obey the imperial commands by surrendering Mīr Jumla and his son, and he sent one envoy after another, with gifts and promises, to Aurangzīb's camp, but it was discovered that he had, in this extremity, summoned to his aid the troops serving in other districts of his kingdom. This was made a pretext for opening the siege of Golconda, which was carried on though negotiations were also in train. Offerings tendered by 'Abdullah's envoys were insultingly rejected, but instead of being returned were thriftily retained pending the conclusion of a treaty.

Aurangzīb, to his intense chagrin, received a letter from his father directing him to inform 'Abdullah that his submission had been accepted and to retire to Aurangābād. He dishonestly concealed this order until he had compelled his victim to submit to his own terms. 'Abdullah, who had no son, was reduced to the necessity of sending his mother to Aurangzīb's camp to arrange for the marriage of his daughter to Muhammad Sultān, who was to receive, as her dowry, the district of Rāmgīr and his recognition as heir to the throne of Golconda. All arrears of the exorbitant tribute demanded by Shāh Jahān were to be paid and Mīr Jumla and his son were surrendered to Aurangzīb.

The prince contented himself with a substantial instalment on account of the tribute due to his father, but extorted many valuable gifts for both himself and his son, and on 27 May, 1656 retired, after the celebration of the marriage, to Aurangābād.

Few of Aurangzīb's many acts of duplicity, both before and after his ascent of the throne, are more deserving of reprobation than his treatment of 'Abdullah Qutb Shāh, but his behaviour on this occasion obtained for him the services of Mīr Jumla, a devoted adherent, who never grudged either wealth or abilities to the advancement of his cause.

Aurangzīb was soon again favoured by fortune. Muhammad 'Ādil Shāh of Bijāpur died on 16 November of this year, and was succeeded by his son 'Alī 'Ādil Shāh II, a youth of eighteen. Aurangzīb affected to regard the kings of Bijāpur and Golconda as mere assignees of the empire, whose succession to their assignments was a question to be decided by the emperor. They had, in fact, been independent kings for a century and a half, having acquired that status before Bābur invaded India, and the imperial prerogative had never been suggested, much less asserted, in the case of either kingdom. Aurangzīb, apparently conscious of the weakness of his case, invented another pretext for attacking Bijāpur and asserted that 'Alī II was not the son of Muhammad 'Ādil Shāh, and that the kingdom had lapsed to the empire.

For this slander, which is repeated, of course on Mughul authority, by Fryer, Tavernier, Bernier and Manucci, there is not a scrap of evidence. 'Alī II was accepted without hesitation in Bijāpur as the son of Muhammad and is so described both in the annals of the kingdom, where his birth, and the principal events of his childhood in the royal palace are circumstantially recorded, and in Marāthī manuscripts. Nor was there any necessity for raising to the throne a supposititious child of Muhammad, for Aurangzīb, when he captured Bijāpur in 1686, found there sixteen male scions of the house of Yūsuf 'Ādil Shāh. The fiction was invented to inflame the wrath of Shāh Jahān, who declared war on Bijāpur.

Dārā Shukoh, the eldest son of Shāh Jahān, dreading the unscrupulous ambition of his younger brother, had caused the issue of the orders for the conclusion of peace with Golconda, and attempted to frustrate his schemes by appointing Mīr Jumla to the chief command of the army sent to invade Bijāpur, but the device failed owing to the perfect understanding which existed between Aurangzīb and Mīr Jumla. The prince accompanied the expedition and Mīr Jumla, who by the emperor's orders held the chief command, was, in fact, subordinate to him.

Aurangzīb set out from Aurangābād in March, 1657, and on 12 April took Bīdar, one of 'Alī 'Ādil Shāh's strongest fortresses, after a siege of one day, the capture of the place being facilitated by the explosion of the principal powder magazine. Kalyānī, thirty-five miles west of Bīdar, was the next fortress attacked, but did not surrender until 10 August. Gulbarga was carried by assault and Aurangzīb marched on Bijāpur. He was much harassed at first by the army of 'Alī 'Ādil Shāh and might have been effectively held at one strong position which he had to pass had not 'Alī's prime minister and commander-in-chief treacherously allowed him to pass unmolested, though pressed by the other officers of the army to pursue the prince. When the commander-in-chief returned to the capital he was assassinated by his master's order.

The siege of Bijāpur was prosecuted with vigour, but Aurangzīb was once more disappointed, when success appeared to be within his grasp, by the receipt of an order recalling Mīr Jumla and all the officers, with their contingents, who had been appointed to the expeditionary force. He then determined to march to Āgra to secure his own pretensions as successor to Shāh Jahān, whose health was failing. Mīr Jumla, whose family was at Āgra and in Dārā Shukoh's power, could not join Aurangzīb in an act of open rebellion, but cheerfully submitted to imprisonment in Daulatābād in order to save appearances.

The question of peace with Bijāpur presented no difficulties. All that Aurangzīb required for the present was a sufficient contribution to the expenses of his march to the capital, with which 'Alī 'Ādil Shāh was not only willing, but anxious, to purchase peace. Aurangzīb, on his side, relinquished his conquests, returned to Aurangābād, and marched to Āgra. The story of his rebellion is told in chapter VII and its results are well known. He defeated his brothers, two of whom he murdered, deposed his father, and ascended the throne.

Shivājī had already, while Aurangzīb was engaged in hostilities against Bijāpur, in May, 1657, committed his first acts of aggression on the imperial dominions and been forgiven. Aurangzīb's preoccupation in the north left Shivājī and 'Alī 'Ādil Shāh free for some time, the one to pursue his ambitious schemes and the other to attempt to free his kingdom from incursions. Shivājī experienced his first serious reverse in an attempt to seize the territories of Sīdī Jauhar, an important assignee in the Konkan, but later in the same year, 1659, he obtained a signal success over the arms of Bijāpur.

'Alī 'Ādil Shāh perceived the necessity for subduing Shivājī and sent against him an army under the command of Afzal Khān, whose objective was the stronghold of Partābgarh, to which Shivājī had retired. The story of Shivājī's duplicity on this occasion is well known. Having secretly made arrangements to entrap the Muslim army, a measure perfectly justifiable in civilised warfare, he succeeded, by professions of submission and by promises, the fulfilment of which would have gained his victim great credit with his master, in enticing Afzal Khān to a private interview at which each was to appear armed only with a sword and attended by a single follower. Shivājī descended from the fortress armed, to all appearance, with only a dagger, but he wore armour beneath his clothes and held concealed in his left hand the weapon known as the *wāghnākh*, closely resembling the claws of the tiger, from which it is named, and consisting of four curved claws of steel, attached to the first and fourth fingers, beneath which they are hidden, by rings. When embracing Afzal Khān, who was clad only in muslin, Shivājī ripped open his belly with the claws and at once stabbed him with his dagger. His secret armour turned the sword cut which the wounded Muslim instinctively dealt him and Shivājī and his follower soon despatched Afzal Khān's gallant attendant. The Marāthā troops, obedient to a signal, sprang from their concealment on the unsuspecting army of Bijāpur, overpowered and dispersed it without difficulty, and enriched their master with its spoils, including horses, elephants, camels, treasure, arms and munitions of war.

Shivājī now obtained possession of the forts of Panhālā, Pavangarh and Vasantgarh and ravaged the country as far as the neighbourhood of Bijāpur, but in 1660 he was besieged in Panhālā by Sīdī Jauhar and compelled to seek safety in flight. 'Alī 'Ādil Shāh shortly afterwards entered the field in person and reduced Panhālā and Pavangarh, besides other forts already captured by Shivājī, who refrained from taking up arms against the king in person but continued his depredations in the Konkan and against Sīdī Jauhar.

In 1661 Shāhjī visited his son, by whom he was received with every circumstance of respect, and arranged between him and 'Alī 'Ādil Shāh an armistice which endured until its author's death in January, 1664.

This truce with Bijāpur set Shivājī free to renew his contest with the Mughuls (see chap. VIII, pp. 258 *sq.*). Shortly after the death of his father in 1664, he assumed at Rāigarh the title of raja and struck coins in his own name. He continued his depredations, both by land and by sea, until he learnt that a Mughul force was preparing to attack him, Aurangzīb's temper having at length been aroused by the plundering of pilgrim ships on their way to Mecca.

The imperial army attacked Purandar, and Shivājī surrendered. One of the terms of the treaty then arranged gave him permission to collect *chauth*, a fourth, and *sardeshmukhī*, a tenth of the revenue in the kingdom of Bijāpur. Aurangzīb probably did not understand the meaning of the claim to these exactions which he sanctioned for the purpose of weakening the government of Bijāpur, nor could he foresee that they would be levied at no very distant date in the imperial dominions, and that his feeble descendants would be constrained to acquiesce.

During Shivājī's absence at Delhi in 1666 Jay Singh had besieged Bijāpur, but the field army of that kingdom, assisted by a contingent from Golconda, had cut off his supplies, rendered his position before the city untenable and obliged him to retreat to Aurangābād. He was recalled to court, but died on the way thither, and Sultān Mu'azzam again returned to the Deccan with Jasvant Singh as his deputy.

In 1668 the court of Bijāpur purchased peace with the emperor by the cession of the fortress and district of Sholāpur, which yielded 180,000 *hūns* of annual revenue, and compounded with Shivājī for an annual payment of 300,000 rupees instead of permitting him to levy *chauth* and *sardeshmukhī* by his own agents, and the new king of Golconda undertook to pay him an annual sum of half a million rupees on the same account.

'Abdullah Qutb Shāh had died on 24 February, 1667. Aurangzīb's eldest son, Muhammad Sultān, whom he had, under compulsion, recognised as his heir, was a prisoner, and those whose business it was to regulate the succession ignored his claims. 'Abdullah left two other daughters besides the wife of Muhammad Sultān, one of whom was married to Nizām-ud-dīn Ahmad, a Sayyid of noble descent, and the other to Abu-'l-Hasan, a young man nearly related, through his mother, to the royal family. Nizām-ud-dīn Ahmad's pride and arrogance had rendered him obnoxious to the nobles and courtiers, and when 'Abdullah died Abu-'l-Hasan was raised to the throne, and Nizām-ud-dīn Ahmad died shortly afterwards.

Abu-'l-Hasan Qutb Shāh was indolent and luxurious, and immediately after his accession all power passed into the hands of his minister, Sayyid Muzaffar, to whom chiefly he owed his throne. The king had sufficient spirit to resent his minister's dominance and, taking into his confidence Mādanna, a Brāhman who was Sayyid Muzaffar's chief coadjutor in public affairs, conspired with him to overthrow the minister. The astute Brāhman succeeded and Sayyid Muzaffar was dismissed from his high place, but Abu-'l-Hasan gained little by the change, for Mādanna took his former master's place and appointed as his colleague his own brother Venkanna[1], and the two Brāhmans soon became more powerful than Sayyid Muzaffar had been. They supported the Deccanī party in the state, dismissed most of the Foreigners in the public service, and after a time even ventured to persecute Muslims.

During the years 1668 and 1669 Shivājī was apparently inactive, but he was in fact organising his government and his army, and building up an efficient civil administration. His rule was undoubtedly more popular than that of the Muslim powers with the Hindu peasantry of the Deccan. Shivājī's careful preparations bore fruit, and for some years the Mughul forces sent against him usually failed.

In 1672, however, his possessions on the coast suffered severely from a combined attack by the Mughul fleet of Surat and the fleet of Janjīra, but the loss which he thus sustained was more than compensated by a large contribution from Abu-'l-Hasan Qutb Shāh, which he obtained in the course of a secret visit to Golconda.

In June, 1672, 'Alī 'Ādil Shāh II was smitten with paralysis but lingered until 4 December, when he died and was succeeded by his son Sikandar 'Ādil Shāh, then in his fifth year. Before his death arrangements for the administration of his kingdom during his son's minority had been completed. Khavāss Khān, son of the traitor Khān Muhammad, was to hold the regency. 'Abdul-Muhammad Khān was to command at Gulbarga and in the districts contiguous with the imperial dominions, 'Abdul-Karīm Buhlūl Khān was to hold Mirāj, Panhālā, and the Konkan, and Muzaffar Khān was to command in the Carnatic. This arrangement came into force at Muhammad 'Ādil Shāh's death, but each of the four nobles who thus

[1] Or Ākkanna.

divided the management of affairs was more intent on his own aggrandisement and on the destruction of his rivals than on the protection of the interests of the kingdom, and Shivājī was not slow to take advantage of their dissensions. In March, 1673, he assembled a large force at Vishalgarh, recaptured Panhālā, and sacked the wealthy town of Hublī, where his troops took a greater amount of booty than they had ever before taken from a single town. The English factory was plundered with the rest of the town. The Marāthā fleet captured Kārwār and Ankola, and Shivājī, in order that he might be free to prosecute the war without interruption, made overtures to Bahādur Khān, governor of the Deccan, suggesting submission to and reconciliation with the emperor. Bahādur Khān was as amenable as his predecessors and readily undertook to refrain from molesting Shivājī provided that he, on his part, abstained from pillaging the imperial dominions.

Several places fell into his hands before the end of the rainy season, and he opened the siege of Ponda, near Goa. 'Abdul-Karīm Khān was sent from Bijāpur to recover Panhālā, but a Marāthā general, by plundering the neighbourhood of Bijāpur, compelled his government to recall him, intercepted him and on some ground which was regarded by Shivājī as insufficient granted an armistice and permitted him to return to Bijāpur. The general then, in fear of his indignant master, led an expedition into Berār. This operation greatly disconcerted Shivājī, who was concentrating his whole attention on the war against Bijāpur and was most anxious to avoid any acts of aggression in imperial territory. 'Abdul-Karīm Khān at once returned to Panhālā, but was eventually routed and driven back to Bijāpur.

Shivājī was unable to reduce Ponda, and raised the siege at the beginning of the rainy season, when he returned to Rāigarh, where on 6 June he was solemnly enthroned and performed other ceremonies which raised him to the dignity of a *Kshatriya* or Rājput.[1]

The Mughul troops absolved Shivājī, by some acts of aggression in his territories, from his compact with Bahādur Khān, and his troops raided Berār from Burhānpur to Māhūr. Shivājī, who had reopened the siege of Ponda, captured that fortress, penetrated the southern Konkan, and returned to Rāigarh with rich spoils.

Bahādur Khān was now engaged in negotiations with Khavāss Khān, the regent of Bijāpur, who, weary of the struggle against contending factions, agreed that Bijāpur should in future be held in subjection to the empire and promised to give Pādishāh Bībī, the only sister of Sikandar 'Ādil Shāh, in marriage to one of the imperial princes and his own daughter to Bahādur Khān's son.

The news of this compact aroused the liveliest indignation among the regent's enemies, led by 'Abdul-Karīm Khān, who first imprisoned him and shortly afterwards caused him to be put to death.

[1] Grant Duff, I, 225.

The success of 'Abdul-Karīm's faction produced an immediate rupture with Bahādur Khān, and the favour shown by 'Abdul-Karīm to his own countrymen, the Afghāns, bred fresh discord at Bijāpur. Afghāns are notoriously quarrelsome and have an unenviable reputation for treachery, and 'Abdul-Karīm's enemies contrived to enlist on their side the services of Sharza Khān, another Afghān noble, who had for years been the prisoner of Shivājī. Meanwhile the troops of Bijāpur acquitted themselves well against the Mughuls, and Bahādur Khān was persuaded to make peace with Bijāpur.

Shivājī had taken advantage of the embroilment of Bijāpur with the empire to recover the country between Panhālā and Tattora, and to connect those two strongholds with a chain of forts. In the latter part of 1676 he was detained at Sātārā by sickness, but during this period he was revolving a great scheme for the extension of his power, wealth and resources, and for the formation of an effective confederacy against the empire. This scheme was the invasion of the Carnatic with the sanction of the king of Golconda, whom Shivājī now took in preference to the king of Bijāpur as his ally against imperial aggression. The function of the Carnatic was to supply the sinews of war: the preference for Golconda was due to its being at the time less immediately exposed to imperial aggression and to its being ruled, in fact, by two Brāhmans.

Early in 1677 Shivājī reached Golconda with 30,000 cavalry and 40,000 infantry. His intrigues there were successful. The two Brāhmans fell in with his scheme and Shivājī personally convinced Abu-'l-Hasan Qutb Shāh that Golconda's salvation lay in an alliance with the Marāthā power. In the secret treaty which was executed Bijāpur had a place. Her possessions in the Carnatic were indeed to be divided between the Marāthās and Golconda, but if she dismissed 'Abdul-Karīm Khān from the regency and appointed Venkanna, the brother of Mādanna, she was to be admitted as a member of the confederacy. It does not seem to have occurred to Abu-'l-Hasan that this confederacy was to be a purely Hindu alliance, in which two puppet Muslim kings were to count for naught. Shivājī left Golconda for the Carnatic, handsomely supplied with money and with a train of artillery, in March. After passing Madras he persuaded the brothers, who held Gingee, to surrender that strong fortress to him, appointed one of his own officers to command the fort, and established throughout the surrounding country his own system of administration. The Tiruvannamalai district, which was held for the king of Bijāpur, and Vellore and three other fortresses were captured. All Shāhjī's rich assignments in the Carnatic were occupied by Shivājī, and in the rest of the possessions of Bijāpur in the Carnatic he followed his usual system of demanding *chauth* and *sardeshmukhī* and plundering the country indiscriminately if they were withheld.

Bijāpur had recently suffered on her northern frontier as she was now suffering on the south. The truce with 'Abdul-Karīm Khān, who had risen to power avowedly as chief of the party opposed to the imperial pretensions, was not unnaturally disapproved by Aurangzīb, who recalled Bahādur Khān from the Deccan and instructed Dilīr Khān to attack the hostile kingdom. Gulbarga was captured on 18 July and Naldrug on 13 August, 1677.

It was now easy for the enemies of 'Abdul-Karīm Khān, who was notoriously on friendly terms with Dilīr Khān, to represent that he had betrayed the kingdom, and the governor of Adonī visited Golconda and begged Abu-'l-Hasan Qutb Shāh to intervene for the sake of saving Bijāpur from the Mughul. Abu-'l-Hasan summoned 'Abdul-Karīm to Golconda to confer with him on the measures to be taken for saving the two kingdoms, and when he obeyed the summons upbraided both parties at Bijāpur, but specially that of 'Abdul-Karīm, with betraying the kingdom by their dissensions. He convinced 'Abdul-Karīm Khān that he had lost the confidence of all the friends of the southern kingdoms and persuaded him to make way for Mas'ūd Khān. 'Abdul-Karīm Khān raised a difficulty regarding the payment of his troops, to whom he owed 500,000 rupees, but Abu-'l-Hasan made himself responsible for the sum. An agreement having been reached Mas'ūd Khān and 'Abdul-Karīm Khān were reconciled and returned together towards Bijāpur, visiting Dilīr Khān at Gulbarga on their way. Dilīr Khān accepted the arrangement with the addition of one condition, the marriage of Pādishāh Bībī to Sultān A'zam, the emperor's third son. To this stipulation Mas'ūd Khān perforce agreed and, peace having been concluded, Mas'ūd Khān and 'Abdul-Karīm Khān continued their march towards Bijāpur, but 'Abdul-Karīm Khān fell sick and died, on 2 January, 1678, at Hīrāpur, and Mas'ūd Khān returned alone to the capital. He paid 'Abdul-Karīm Khān's infantry, but either would not or could not pay the cavalry, who dispersed, some joining Shivājī and some the Mughuls. The betrothal of Pādishāh Bībī was so unpopular at Bijāpur that it was only by promising that this condition should not be observed that Mas'ūd Khān could restore tranquillity.

Shivājī, having made arrangements for the administration of the Carnatic, set out, late in 1678, on his return to his own country. He ceded nothing to Abu-'l-Hasan Qutb Shāh, who dared not openly resent Shivājī's breach of faith. On his return march Shivājī and his officers made further annexations.

Mas'ūd Khān was not permitted to evade his promise to send Pādishāh Bībī to Delhi and Dilīr Khān was ordered to march on Bijāpur to enforce the fulfilment of this condition. A mob assembled in the streets of Bijāpur to oppose the surrender of the popular princess, but she herself, believing that she could yet save her brother and his kingdom, insisted on leaving for Dilīr Khān's camp. Her sacrifice came too late. Dilīr Khān sent an escort with her to

Aurangābād, but continued his march on Bijāpur. Mas'ūd Khān implored Shivājī's aid, and the Marāthā, while he hesitated to attack the imperial army in the field, attempted to create a diversion by harrying with fire and sword the imperial domains in the Deccan, from the Bhīmā to the Godāvarī, leaving the inhabitants homeless and the villages in ashes, and plundering even Jālna and Aurangābād, where the prince was residing.

These operations failed of their principal object, and Dilīr Khān maintained the siege of Bijāpur with vigour. Mas'ūd Khān begged Shivājī to relieve the city and he set out for Bijāpur, but on the way learnt that his son Shambhūjī had fled from Panhālā, where he was under restraint owing to his dissolute conduct which had culminated in an attempt to violate the wife of a Brāhman. He escaped to Dilīr Khān, who welcomed him with honour, his object being to widen the breach between father and son and to divide the Marāthās. The Marāthā army continued its march to Bijāpur, while Shivājī himself returned to devise a scheme for recalling his son. This, however, was no easy task, for Dilīr Khān flattered the youth's vanity by recognising him as Rājā of the Marāthās and captured for him one of his father's fortresses; and the Marāthā army sustained a severe defeat near Bijāpur. In the north, however, Moro Pant Peshwā overran and ravaged Khāndesh, and cut off Dilīr Khān's supplies, so that he was obliged, at the end of the rainy season, to raise the siege of the city. He was resolved, however, to chastise the kingdom, and plundered and ravaged it till the Marāthā troops in the northern Carnatic attacked and drove him northwards. Aurangzīb, disapproving of Dilīr Khān's Marāthā policy, ordered him to send Shambhūjī as a prisoner to Delhi, but he connived at the young man's escape and Shambhūjī rejoined and was reconciled to his father, who however confined him to Panhālā. At the same time Sultān Mu'azzam was recalled from the Deccan and Bahādur Khān was reinstated as viceroy.

For the assistance which he had rendered to Bijāpur Shivājī demanded the recognition by that state of his sovereignty in the districts of Koppal and Bellary and in all the territory which he had conquered in the Carnatic, and when Mas'ūd Khān had complied with his demand he secretly visited him in the neighbourhood of Bijāpur and took counsel with him on the subject of the further resistance to be offered to the imperial troops. In April Shivājī fell sick at Rāigarh, and died on 2 April, 1680. He was in his fifty-third year.

A slight sketch of Shivājī's character has already been given, and is supplemented by the chronicle of his life. It is difficult to decide whether to admire more the courage and high resolve which proposed an object so lofty as the restoration of a Hindu empire in India or the singleness of purpose with which that object was pursued. He had to contend with a mighty empire and two kingdoms, but he took the fullest advantage of the narrow and purblind policy of Aurangzīb, which divided the Muslims. The emperor learnt too late to appreciate his antagonist. For years he despised "the Mountain Rat" as the chief of a gang of mere brigands, but after Shivājī's death he conceived a juster opinion of his genius and admitted that he was a great captain. "My armies", he said, "were employed against him for nineteen years, but nevertheless his State has always been increasing." A Muslim historian thus does justice to his memory. "He persisted in rebelling, plundering caravans, and troubling mankind; but he was entirely guiltless of baser sins, and was scrupulous of the honour of the women and children of the Muslims when they fell into his hands." This is high praise from one whose religion made matrons, virgins and children taken in war the legitimate prey of their captors.

Shivājī's object was never attained, for his line produced no second Shivājī, but his nation overflowed the Deccan and overran the whole of the empire. His dominions at his death were extensive. They comprised the Konkan, a tract between the sea and the crest of the Western Ghāts, from the fifteenth to the twenty-first parallel of north latitude, excluding the Portuguese, African and English settlements of Goa, Janjīra, Chaul, Bombay, Salsette, Bassein and Damān, and southward of the Konkan the two isolated settlements of Kārwār and Ankola were included. Above the Ghāts, between Chākan and Kolhāpur, his territories extended eastward into the tableland of the Deccan to the confluence of the Bhīmā and the Nīrā and nearly to the confluence of the Krishnā and the Vārnā. On either side of the Tungabhadrā they included the districts of Koppal and Bellary, and, farther south, Sīra, Dod-Ballāpur, Kolār, Bangalore and Hoskote: the north-eastern districts of the modern Mysore state. Eastward of this tract the fortresses of Vellore, Ārnī and Gingee with the districts surrounding them, and southward of these again the whole of the present district of Tanjore, formed part of his domains. "The territories and treasures, however, which Shivājī acquired, were not so formidable to the Muhammadans as the example he had set, the system and habits he introduced, and the spirit he had infused into a large proportion of the Marāthā people."[1]

On Shivājī's death his widow, taking advantage of her husband's mistrust of his elder son, who was still imprisoned at Panhālā, exerted herself to secure the succession for her son Rājā Rām, Shambhūjī's half-brother, and enthroned him, but a strong party in the state favoured the claims of the legitimate heir and Shambhūjī, who inherited a portion of his father's energy, succeeded, after some vicissitudes, in securing the throne and put his stepmother and her leading partisans to death in circumstances of great cruelty. In 1680

[1] Grant Duff, I, 254.

he received the fugitive prince Muhammad Akbar, who was in rebellion against his father, the emperor, and Aurangzīb, after concluding an undignified peace with the Rānā of Udaipur, with whom he was then engaged in hostilities, marched southwards for the accomplishment of a task which he had set himself before his accession —the subjugation of the Deccan.

The history of the Deccan during the next twenty-six years is that of the later years of the reign of Aurangzīb, and will be related in the next chapter.

CHAPTER X

AURANGZĪB (1681–1707)

THE flight of his rebel son Akbar to the Marāthā king forced a complete change on the policy of Aurangzīb and hastened the fate of his empire as well. It became necessary for the emperor to go to the Deccan in person and to assemble there his best troops and generals and practically all the resources of his realm. The centre of gravity of the Delhi empire was shifted to southern India for the next twenty-six years, while north India, its real seat of strength, fell into neglect and decay. In Hindustān the administration rapidly deteriorated, peace, prosperity and the arts decreased, and the entire Indian civilisation fell backwards. The defence of the north-western frontier was neglected, and the material resources of the empire dwindled till they ceased to suffice for its needs. The vast annexations effected by Aurangzīb in the Deccan—Bijāpur, Golconda, eastern Carnatic and Mahārāshtra—were all illusive. Instead of adding to the strength and wealth of the empire, they brought down economic ruin upon it and destroyed its army as an instrument of power. In fact, the Mughul empire now became too large to be administered by one man or from one centre, and its disruption began which was to make the history of India in the eighteenth century one "great anarchy".

After patching up a peace with Mewār (June, 1681), Aurangzīb despatched his son A'zam with a large army to the Deccan (31 July), and soon afterwards he himself hastened there, arriving at Burhānpur on 23 November and at Aurangābād on 1 April, 1682. His main occupation now was to watch and check Shambhūjī, the new Marāthā king, and his protégé the rebel prince Akbar.

Shambhūjī had gained his father's throne on 28 June, 1680, ten weeks after the death of the latter and in the teeth of strong opposition. His succession had been disputed, a hostile faction at the capital having crowned his step-brother Rājā Rām, a boy of ten, who was too weak to maintain himself when Shambhūjī appeared in force at the capital. But for more than a year afterwards Shambhūjī's position continued to be insecure and it was only in October, 1681, after ruthlessly crushing a second plot by Annājī Datto against his life and liberty, that he could gain undisputed supremacy in the state. Under him the Marāthā army continued Shivājī's policy of setting out on plundering expeditions every year on the Dasahra day (October) at the end of the rainy season. In the winter of 1680–81 they raided north Khāndesh, and then passing farther east looted the suburbs of Burhānpur for three days unmolested (9–11 February, 1681), taking an enormous amount of booty. The surprise was complete and none of the people could conceal or remove their property. Many respectable men slew their wives and children to save them from outrage and slavery; many houses were set on fire after being ransacked. The governor was powerless. In November, 1681, an attempt to surprise the fort of Ahmadnagar was defeated.

Prince Akbar, who had been sheltered by Shambhūjī in the village of Pāli (six miles east of Nāgothān), gathered a small force of 2000 men with the jewels he had brought away with himself, and kept up the pageant of an emperor, issuing letters in the royal style dated in his regnal years! Shambhūjī promised to support him with a Marāthā army in gaining the Delhi throne, but nothing came of these promises. Aurangzīb's wise strategy blocked all the paths out of Mahārāshtra. Early in 1682 he began a vigorous offensive against the Marāthās; one division under Sayyid Hasan 'Alī Khān descended into the north Konkan and occupied Kalyān (*c.* 9 February), withdrawing in May next to avoid the heavy monsoon. Another, under Shihāb-ud-dīn Khān, invaded the Nāsik district and besieged Rāmsej, but after a six months' siege and the failure of three assaults the attempt was abandoned in October. Rūh-ullah Khān and Shāh 'Ālam were sent to guard the Ahmadnagar district, while prince A'zam was despatched towards Bijāpur to prevent aid coming to the Marāthās from that state. In fact, the emperor's spirit was now up; as the Kārwār factors wrote: "He is so inveterate against the Rāja that he hath thrown off his *pagri* and sworn never to put it on again, till he hath either killed, taken, or routed him out of his country." Khān Jahān gave the Marāthās a long and hot chase from Nānder and Bīdar to Chāndā and the Qutb Shāhī frontier. A'zam campaigned for one year in the north Bijāpur territory, capturing Dhārūr. In his absence his camp was attacked by the Marāthās, but, inspired by his heroic wife Jahānzīb Bānū, the Hārā Rājput guards repulsed the enemy, though losing 900 of their own men.

But nothing decisive was achieved by the Mughuls in 1682, and all their detachments were recalled to the emperor's side in April, 1683. His distrust of his sons and generals led him to follow a barren policy of waiting and vacillation. "The king's mind...is continually wavering and he is extraordinarily peevish and uneasy because of Sultān Akbar. Sultān A'zam, (his) Begam, and Dilīr Khān degraded for even nothing but only suspected, without any grounds, of being kind to Akbar" (Surat Factory letter).

But just at this time came a happy diversion for the Mughuls. In April, 1683, Shambhūjī began an invasion of Portuguese territory which occupied all his forces till the next January, when he was glad to make peace by the mutual restitution of conquests. In the meantime prince Akbar had realised that the Marāthā king would do nothing for him; his heart grew sick of hope deferred, and he decided to leave Mahārāshtra, go to Portuguese territory and there charter a ship for conveying him to Persia for refuge. In January, 1683, he left Pāli and took up his residence at Bāndā, and then (in September) at Bicholim, very close to Goa. In November he bought a ship and embarked at Vingurlā, but Durgā Dās and Kavi-Kalash arrived there with fresh promises of armed support from Shambhūjī and induced him to give up this attempt to sail to Persia. Throughout 1684 Akbar lived in the Ratnāgiri district as Shambhūjī's unwilling guest, but unable to make any successful dash into his father's territory. In fact, Shambhūjī was now too deeply sunk in vice and his government was too disturbed by the jealousy of the local nobles against the raja's all-powerful "foreign" favourite Kavi-Kalash (a Kanaujiya Brāhman) and the frequent rebellions among his vassals and court conspiracies against his life, so that the Marāthā power ceased to count in Indian politics. There were many desertions of Marāthā officers and nobles to the Mughul side, and the whole west coast was up in arms against Shambhūjī.

A fresh Mughul offensive was launched at the end of September, 1683; Aurangzīb himself advanced from Aurangābād to Ahmadnagar, while strong divisions were posted at Poona, Nāsik and Akalkot, and the Sīdī cruised off Vingurlā to watch Akbar's movements. But the main attack was entrusted to a grand army led by Shāh 'Ālam into the south Konkan by the Rāmghāt pass (between Goa and Belgaum). After conquering many places in the Belgaum district, this prince crossed the pass and descended into Sāvantvādi. At Bicholim (15 January, 1684) he destroyed the mansions and gardens of Shambhūjī and Akbar and then moved to the neighbourhood of Goa, the invasion of which was immediately abandoned by the Marāthās. But the prince, coming as a deliverer, plotted to seize Goa by treachery; this fatal policy set the Portuguese against him and they stopped his grain supply by sea. The prince next marched northwards, sacking and burning Mālvan, Kudal, Bāndā and Vingurlā in this region, and then returned to the river bank north of Goa. Famine stopped his further progress. No corn could be procured locally and none was allowed to come to him by sea from Surat. So, the baffled prince returned to the Rāmghāt pass on 1 March. Here a pestilence of such virulence spread that in one week a third of his men died, besides an even larger proportion of transport animals. This failure of transport led to a second famine, and more men perished of heat and thirst. The miserable remnant of the army crossed the pass and reached Ahmadnagar (28 May) without having done anything except burning a few villages and robbing a few towns, at the expense of half its strength.

The Mughul campaign in the first half of 1684 was highly successful in other quarters; many Marāthā forts were taken, their field armies repeatedly defeated, and much of their territory annexed, while many of their captains came over to the imperial side. The sieges of Bijāpur and Golconda, however, relieved the pressure on the Marāthās during 1685–87. Prince Akbar, thoroughly despairing of any success or even safety in India, sailed from Rājapur in February, 1687, and reached the Persian court in January, 1688, after some months' detention by the Sultan of Muscat, who tried to sell him to Aurangzīb.

While Shambhūjī was absorbed in drinking and merry-making with a small escort and in utter carelessness at Sangameshwar, twenty-two miles from Ratnāgiri, he was surprised and captured by an energetic Mughul officer named Muqarrab Khān, who had made a forced march from Kolhāpur. With him were captured his minister Kavi-Kalash and twenty-five of his chief followers (11 February, 1689). At Bahādurgarh, the two chief captives were brought to the imperial camp and publicly paraded dressed as buffoons with drum and trumpet. Shambhūjī was offered his life if he would give up his forts and divulge the hiding-places of his treasures; but he loosened his tongue in scurrilous abuse of the emperor and his Prophet and asked for one of his daughters to be given to him. After being tortured and mutilated for twenty-four days, Shambhūjī and Kavi-Kalash were hacked to pieces limb by limb on 21 March.

After the capture of Shambhūjī his younger brother Rājā Rām was crowned by the ministers at Rāigarh (18 February). But, soon afterwards, an imperial army under I'tiqād Khān (afterwards Zu-'l-Fiqār Khān, Nusrat Jang) laid siege to this Marāthā capital, and Rājā Rām slipped out of it disguised as a religious mendicant (15 April), and finally, after many adventures, made his way to Gingee (11 November). In the meantime Rāigarh capitulated on 29 October, and the Mughuls seized there the surviving ladies of the Marāthā royal family and Shambhūjī's children, including Shāhū, a boy of seven. These were detained in Aurangzīb's camp with every respect and privacy. Thus by the end of 1689 Aurangzīb became the unrivalled lord paramount of northern India and the Deccan alike; but it was the beginning of his end.

For four years after Dilīr Khān's failure (February, 1680) nothing decisive was done by the Mughuls against Bijāpur, as they were busy opposing Shambhūjī and Akbar. Prince A'zam's campaign (1682–83) was languidly conducted in the region north of the Nīrā river; thereafter even these desultory attacks ceased. In the meantime the condition of the 'Ādil Shāhī government grew hopeless. Mas'ūd resigned his post as minister in despair and disgust early in 1684, and his successor Āqā Khusrav died after six months of office (21 October). The leadership of the state then fell to Sharza Khān (a Mahdavī Sayyid) and 'Abdur-Rauf (Afghān). The Mughuls then resumed the appropriation of bits of the 'Ādil Shāhī kingdom and established their own outposts in these; Mangalvide and Sāngola were gained in May, 1684. Although a rupture between the two powers now seemed imminent and some acrimonious letters were exchanged, war did not actually break out until some months afterwards, and Aurangzīb continued to send friendly letters and robes of honour to the 'Ādil Shāhī court. But both sides used the interval in preparing for war, and on 11 April, 1685, the last Mughul siege of Bijāpur began. Rūh-ullah Khān and Qāsim Khān opened their trenches on the Shāhpur or north-western side, half a mile from the fort wall, while Khān Jahān ran his approaches from the Rasūlpur or western suburb. Prince A'zam arrived on 24 June and took over the supreme command, encamping at the Begam Hauz, south of the city.

The Mughuls were slow and clumsy in conducting regular sieges; the soil round Bijāpur is extremely hard, and therefore the besiegers made no real progress even after fifteen months of labour. The fort was not fully invested; the soldiers sallied out and returned whenever they liked; and allies flocked to 'Ādil Shāh, from Mas'ūd (now semi-independent chief of Adonī), Qutb Shāh and Shambhūjī. A'zam had to fight three severe battles in less than a month; his grain supply was totally stopped and a famine raged in his camp. But as he refused to retire, even when commanded by Aurangzīb, the emperor sent him provisions, reinforcements and money under the escort of Ghāzī-ud-dīn (Fīrūz Jang), who ably fought his way to the famished army and "turned the scarcity into plenty" (end of October). Fīrūz Jang next intercepted and cut off a force of 6000 Berad infantry, each with a bag of provisions on his head, whom Pām Nāyak tried to smuggle into the fort. At this time the Mughul capture of Hyderābād and the flight of its king to Golconda cut off all hope of aid to Bijāpur being received from that side.

But discord and mutual jealousy among the Mughul commanders thwarted their efforts. So the emperor himself went to Bijāpur (13 July, 1686) and pressed the siege vigorously. The fort was completely invested and the friends of the garrison in his camp were crushed. The sufferings of the Bijāpurīs were aggravated by a famine which was then raging in the Deccan on account of the failure of the annual rains. Countless men and horses died within the fort, and from the lack of horses the Deccanis could not follow their favourite tactics of hovering round the invaders and cutting off their stragglers and transport. But even then the Mughuls could neither make any practicable breach in the walls nor fill up the broad and deep moat. On 14 September Aurangzīb advanced his tent from two miles in the rear to a place immediately behind the siege trenches, and next day rode to the edge of the moat to inspect his raised battery.

And now the garrison lost heart; the future looked absolutely dark to them, and their ranks had been thinned to 2000 men, while no help was to be expected from outside. Their two leading nobles arranged the terms of surrender, which Aurangzīb readily granted. On 22 September, 1686, Sikandar, the last of the 'Ādil Shāhs, left the capital of his ancestors and waited on Aurangzīb in his camp at Rasūlpur. He was very kindly received and enrolled among the Mughul peers with the lesser title of *Khān* (instead of *Shāh*), and an annual pension of 100,000 rupees was settled upon him. All the Bijāpurī officers were taken over into Mughul service. On the 29th, Aurangzīb entered the fallen city through the southern or Mangali gate (henceforth to be called the "Gate of Victory", *Fath Darwāza*). In the 'Ādil Shāhī palace and the "Relic Shrine" (*Āsār-i-sharīf*) he erased all pictures drawn in violation of the Qurānic law and all Shiah inscriptions. The kingdom was ordered to be styled *Dār-uz-Zafar*. Complete desolation settled upon the city of Bijāpur after the fall of its independent dynasty; from a proud capital it became merely the headquarters city of one of the numerous provinces of the Mughul empire; its nobility decayed and disappeared, and the multitude of artisans and labourers, poets and scholars, lost their bread. Two years after its conquest, a terrible bubonic plague swept away more than half its population, and even the abundant water supply in the city wells suddenly grew scanty. The city and its once populous suburbs were deserted and fell into ruin.

After being at first lodged in the state prison of Daulatābād and then carried about with Aurangzīb's camp, Sikandar died outside Sātārā fort on 13 April, 1700, not yet thirty-two years of age.

For nearly thirty years after Aurangzīb's accession the kingdom of Golconda enjoyed respite from Mughul attack, because of the preoccupation of the Mughuls with the Marāthās and 'Ādil Shāh and also because Qutb Shāh paid his tribute regularly. Abu-'l Hasan (accession 1672), the last Sultān of this line, resigned his royal functions to his Brahman minister Mādanna and shut himself up in his palace with a host of concubines and dancing-girls. All power in the state was monopolized by Mādanna, his brother Ākkanna and their nephew surnamed Rustam Rāo; the administration grew more and more inefficient and corrupt, and the Muslims complained of Hindu predominance and their own humiliation in the state. Above all, Mādanna was a staunch supporter of the defensive alliance with the Marāthās for an annual subsidy.

Soon after the Mughul siege of Bijāpur had commenced, a letter from Qutb Shāh to his agent in the emperor's camp was intercepted, in which he called Aurangzīb a mean-minded coward for attacking a helpless young orphan like Sikandar 'Ādil Shāh, and promised to send a large army in support of Bijāpur. At this Aurangzīb sent Shāh 'Ālam with a strong force to seize Hyderābād (July, 1685); but this division was effectively checked at Mālkhed and practically besieged by a Golconda army for more than two months. There were frequent fights, in which the Mughuls could make no advance, as the enemy greatly outnumbered them; their heavy losses took the heart out of the imperialists and the rains added to their hardships. But early in October, the Golconda commander-in-chief, Mīr Muhammad Ibrāhīm, was bribed to come over to the Mughuls, and his disheartened soldiers fled back to their capital.

The defection of the commander-in-chief paralysed the defence of Hyderābād. Qutb Shāh fled precipitately to the fort of Golconda, leaving all his property behind in Hyderābād. Before Shāh 'Ālam could arrive and restore order in the city (*c.* 18 October), it presented the spectacle of a sack after assault by an enemy; indiscriminate looting and confusion raged in it, and many women and children were kidnapped and outraged. Qutb Shāh then submitted, and at Shāh 'Ālam's recommendation the emperor granted him pardon on the following conditions: (i) the payment of twelve million rupees in settlement of all past dues and in addition a tribute of two hundred thousand *hūns* every year, (ii) the dismissal of Mādanna and Ākkanna, and (iii) the cession of Mālkhed and Seram to the emperor.

Shāh 'Ālam halted at Kuhir for some months for the collection of the war indemnity. Abu-'l Hasan put off the dismissal of Mādanna as long as he could. At this his Muslim nobles and the two dowager Sultānas formed a plot and caused Mādanna and Ākkanna to be murdered in the streets of Golconda (March, 1686). The ministers' residences were plundered and their families ruined by the Muslim mob, who next made a general attack on the Hindu quarter, killing and plundering the Brāhmans. Golconda territory was then completely evacuated by the Mughuls.

But the fall of Bijāpur (September, 1686) set the imperialists free to deal finally with the Qutb Shāhī government. On 7 February, 1687, the emperor arrived before Golconda, to which Abu-'l Hasan had again fled. The Mughuls occupied Hyderābād for the third and last time. On the first day the Mughuls charged and drove in the Qutb Shāhī soldiers who were assembled in the dry ditch under shelter of the fort walls. Qilīch Khān (the grandfather of the first Nizām), in trying to enter Golconda pell-mell with these fugitives, was fatally wounded, and regular siege operations began (17 February). Aurangzīb himself encamped north-west of the fort along the Sholāpur road; trenches were opened against the south-eastern and southern faces of the fort, the Mughul soldiers with the city behind them moving along both banks of the Mūsī river.

But the emperor's aims were paralysed by bitter personal jealousies in his camp. Shāh 'Ālam was soft-hearted and wished to save Abu-'l Hasan from destruction. He welcomed Qutb Shāh's agents, who visited him secretly and bribed him to use his influence with the emperor to get Abu-'l Hasan pardoned and thus rob his brother A'zam of the credit of capturing Golconda. The emperor, on learning of these secret negotiations with the enemy, at once put Shāh 'Ālam and his entire family in prison (3 March), confiscated his property, and even punished his servants. Every hardship and humiliation was inflicted upon the prince in his captivity and it was seven years before he could recover his liberty.

Another cause of discord in the imperial camp was that the many Shiahs in the imperial service heartily disliked the prospect of the extinction of the last Shiah kingdom in India, and even many orthodox Sunnīs, like the chief Qāzīs Shaikh-ul-Islām and 'Abdullah, condemned the attacks on Bijāpur and Golconda as "wars between Muslims" and therefore sinful. Fīrūz Jang, a Turk and Sunnī, was at first the leading officer at the siege, and therefore Saf Shikan Khān, the chief of artillery and a Persian Shiah, after working strenuously for some time, resigned "in order to spite Fīrūz Jang". The next two chiefs of artillery were utter failures, and then this post, the most important in a siege, went begging, till at last Saf Shikan Khān was reinstated (2 July); but by that time the field-works had been demolished by the enemy and the investment had to be begun anew. The fort had an inexhaustible supply of munitions and its walls bristled with guns of large calibre. Its incessant fire caused heavy losses to the Mughuls, but they carried the trenches to the edge of the ditch in six weeks. The ditch however could not be filled up.

At midnight, 26 May, Fīrūz Jang made an attempt to surprise the fort by scaling the wall with ladders. But a carrion dog of the fort, on seeing strangers, set up a loud bark which alarmed the garrison and the Mughul party had to return without success.

While the siege operations languished, the Mughul army fell into the grip of famine, as the enemy infested the roads and effectually stopped the transport of provisions. In June the rain descended in torrents, turning the roads into quagmires and the camp into a lake, and completely washing out the trenches and raised batteries. The enemy seized the opportunity. In the night of 15 June, amidst a deluge of rain, they raided the Mughul advanced batteries and trenches, slew the careless gunners, damaged the guns, destroyed the materials and munition, and carried off the chief of artillery (Ghairat Khān) and thirteen other high officers as prisoners. It was only after three days of struggle that the Mughuls were able to reoccupy the lost battery. Meantime, three mines had been carried under the bastions of the fort and each loaded with heavy charges of gunpowder. On 30 June, under the emperor's own eyes, the first of them was fired, but the force of the explosion was directed outwards and the scattered rock killed 1100 of the densely crowded imperialists. After this the garrison made a sortie, seized the Mughul trenches and outposts opposite, and were driven out only after a long contest and heavy slaughter. Then the second mine was fired with the same disastrous consequences, the Mughuls losing another thousand men. The enemy immediately made another sortie and took possession of the field-works and outposts. The Mughuls fought desperately to recover them, Fīrūz Jang and two other generals being wounded and large numbers of their men slain. Aurangzīb himself advanced into the field to aid his troops; cannon-balls began to fall near him, but he coolly kept his position and cheered his soldiers by his example. While this battle was raging a tempest burst on the plain with the tropical fury of wind, rain and thunder. The rising water forced the Mughuls back, and then the enemy made another charge, seizing the trenches further off and carrying away or damaging all their guns. At sunset the defeated Mughuls fell back on their rear lines. Next morning the third mine was fired, but having been discovered and flooded with water by the enemy, it did not explode. Thus the Mughuls failed with all their efforts and the siege dragged on.

The *morale* of the imperial army was utterly gone; the famine grew worse than before; and a pestilence broke out which nearly depopulated Hyderābād and caused havoc in the camp. "At night heaps of dead bodies used to accumulate. After some months, when the rains ceased, the white piles of skeletons looked from a distance like hillocks of snow." But Aurangzīb held on with grim tenacity and called up reinforcements. Golconda was completely enclosed by him with a wall of wood and earth and ingress and egress from the fort stopped. At the same time he annexed the Qutb Shāhī kingdom by proclamation and set up his own officers in all places in it, so as to stop supplies and succour from coming to the fort.

On 2 October, 1687, Golconda was captured, but by bribery. An Afghān soldier of fortune named 'Abdullah Pānī (surnamed Sardār Khān), who had deserted from Bijāpur service and then from the Mughul to join Qutb Shāh, now sold his master. He left the postern gate of the fort open, and at his invitation Rūh-ullah Khān with a small force entered by this gate unchallenged at 3 o'clock in the morning, and opened the main gate, by which the Mughul supporting columns poured into the fort like a flood. No resistance could be made to a surprise in such force; only one faithful captain, 'Abdur-Razzāq Lārī, opposed the assailants single-handed, but he was borne down covered with seventy wounds. The Mughuls nursed him back to recovery and the emperor gave him high rank.

Abu-'l-Hasan, the last of the Qutb Shāhs, left his throne with calmness and dignity. When Rūh-ullah Khān entered his palace to seize him, he bade his captors to breakfast with him, consoled his women and servants, and left for the Mughul camp. In the evening he was presented by A'zam to the emperor, who read him a long lecture "on his corrupt government, wherein he had been very unfaithful in the charge he had committed to him, in encouraging the Brāhmans and discouraging the Moors, to the dishonour of their religion and country, whereby he had justly brought these troubles upon himself". After a time he was sent off to the prison-fortress of Daulatābād with an allowance of 50,000 rupees a year.

The spoils taken at Golconda amounted to nearly seventy million rupees in cash, besides gold and silver plate, jewels and jewelled ware. The revenue of the kingdom was, on paper, nearly thirty million rupees.

The emperor set himself to take possession of the forts and districts of the fallen kingdoms of Bijāpur and Golconda. Sāgar (the Berad capital), Adonī (the seat of Sīdī Mas'ūd), Karnūl, Rāichūr, Serā and Bangalore in Mysore, and Bankāpur and Belgaum in Kanara, as well as Wandiwāsh and Conjeveram in the eastern or Madras Carnatic, were gained by his armies, in the course of a year from the fall of Golconda. After his return to Bijāpur, a deadly bubonic plague broke out in the city and camp (November, 1688), which killed about a hundred thousand people, including the emperor's wife Aurangābādī Mahall, Jasvant's alleged son Muhammadī Rāj, and many grandees. Fīrūz Jang escaped with the loss of his eyes.

After the fall of Shambhūjī, Aurangzīb mostly encamped in Bijāpur and at different places south of that city (especially Galgalā) for many years, and finally settled at Brahmapurī (on the Bhīmā river) to which he gave the name of *Islāmpurī*. After four years and a half (June, 1695–October, 1699) passed here, he set out on the campaign against Marāthā forts from which he returned a broken down old man to Ahmadnagar (31 January, 1706), only to die there (3 March, 1707). The flight of the new Marāthā king Rājā Rām to Gingee (end of 1689) made that fort a centre of Marāthā enterprise on the east coast, while his ministers left at home organised resistance in the west and thus doubled the task of the Mughuls. The difficulties of Aurangzīb were multiplied by this disappearance of a common head and a central government among the Marāthās, because every petty Marāthā captain now fought and plundered in a different quarter on his own account. The Marāthās were no longer a tribe of banditti or local rebels, but the one dominating factor of Deccan politics, and an enemy all-pervasive throughout the Indian peninsula, elusive as the wind, the ally and rallying point of all the enemies of the Delhi empire and all disturbers of public peace and regular administration throughout the Deccan and even in Mālwā, Gondwāna and Bundelkhand. The imperialists could not be present everywhere in full strength; hence, they suffered reverses in places.

In 1689 the Marāthās had been cowed by the fall of Shambhūjī, the siege of their capital and the perilous flight of their new king. Many of their forts easily fell into Aurangzīb's hands. Throughout 1690 and 1691 the emperor's chief concern was to take possession of the rich and boundless dominions of the fallen 'Ādil Shāhī and Qutb Shāhī kingdoms in the south and the east. At this stage, he underrated the Marāthā danger, being satisfied with the annihilation of their state. He was soon afterwards confronted by a *people's* war, and about the middle of 1690 the first signs of the Marāthā recovery appeared, which became triumphant in 1692. The leaders in the west or homeland were the *Amātya* (Rāmchandra N. Bāvdekar), the Sachiv (Shankarājī Malhār), and Parashurām Trimbak (who became *Pratinidhi* or regent in 1701), while in the eastern Carnatic the king's supreme director was Prahlād Nirājī (created *Pratinidhi*), who stood above the nominal prime minister or *Peshwā*. Two extraordinarily able and active generals, Dhana Jādav and Santājī Ghorpare (rivals for the post of commander-in-chief), frequently passed from one theatre of war to the other across the peninsula, and caused the greatest loss and confusion to the Mughuls. The Marāthā plan of operations was for Rāja Rām to take refuge in the far-off impregnable fort of Gingee (in the South Arcot district) and make a stand there, while in the homeland independent commandos would be organised and guided against the Mughuls by Rāmchandra Bāvdekar, on whom was conferred the new office of dictator (*Hukūmat-panāh*) with full regal authority over all the officials and captains in Mahārāshtra. He had an inborn genius for command and organisation, chose the ablest lieutenants, and managed to make the mutually jealous Marāthā guerrilla leaders act in concert.

We shall deal with the eastern front first. The eastern Carnatic extended from Chicacole to the mouth of the Cauvery on the seaboard and over all the inland country including the Mysore plateau and the modern Madras districts north of it. As the result of Muslim conquests effected about the middle of the seventeenth century, this vast country was divided into two parts, the Hyderābādī and the Bijāpurī, by an imaginary line from Vellore to Sadras, and each of these parts was further subdivided into uplands and lowlands. But the new rulers had not consolidated their conquests; much of the country was still in the hands of unsubdued *poligars* (local chiefs), or held by nobles who were independent of Bijāpur and Hyderābād in all but name. The situation was further complicated by Shivājī's invasion of 1677 and establishment of a new Marāthā government at Gingee. After his death, his son-in-law Harjī Mahādik became the local viceroy, but practically assumed independence of his distant master Shambhūjī. After the fall of Bijāpur and Golconda, Mughul sovereignty was proclaimed over all the Carnatic once belonging to them, but without any adequate force to make it effective.

During this eclipse of royalty, Harjī invaded the Hyderābād Carnatic north of the Palār river and took easy possession of several forts (including Arcot) and a hundred towns. The Marāthās plundered the country and even the sacred city of Conjeveram (January, 1688). On the arrival of Aurangzīb's officers, the raiders retreated, but took post a day's march south of the Mughul camp at Wandiwāsh (March). For a year the two armies remained there watching each other, but daily sending out detachments which plundered the country indiscriminately. The trade and industry of the district were ruined, food stuffs became very scarce, and all who could fled to the fortified European settlements on the coast for shelter.

Harjī died about 29 September, 1689; Rājā Rām arrived at Gingee on 11 November, took peaceful possession of it and established his court there. Zu-'l-Fiqār Khān, as the supreme Mughul commander, reached the environs of Gingee about the middle of September, 1690, with the object of besieging the fort, but the task was too great for his means. The rock-fortress of Gingee consists of three fortified hillocks connected together by strong walls and forming a rough triangle nearly 3 miles in circumference. These hills are steep, rocky and covered with such enormous boulders that they are almost unclimbable. Zu-'l-Fiqār could neither bombard it nor cut off the garrison's communication with the outside. The activity of the Marāthā roving bands stopped his grain supply, he abandoned the siege, and at his request reinforcements under the *vazīr* Asad Khān and the young prince Kām Bakhsh reached him at the end of December, 1691. He renewed the siege in 1692, ran trenches and bombarded two points without doing any damage. His object was only to make a show, prolong the siege and thereby escape from being sent on campaign elsewhere. Thus, he effected nothing during 1691 and 1692. At the end of 1692 two disasters befell the Mughuls. Two large Marāthā armies raised in western India arrived in the Carnatic under the famous generals Santā and Dhana. The first of these captured 'Alī Mardān Khān, the imperial commandant of Conjeveram, with all the horses, elephants and other property of his army, near Kāveripāk (23 December). The Khān ransomed himself for 100,000 *hūns*. The other Marāthā division attacked the siege camp round Gingee, and compelled Zu-'l-Fiqār Khān to draw his outposts in for safety, in which operation Isma'īl Khān Maka was captured with 500 horses and carried off to Gingee.

The Marāthā light horse now dominated the country and stopped the coming of provisions and letters to the Mughul camp, which lived in a state of siege. Alarming rumours spread that Aurangzīb was already dead and that Shāh 'Ālam had gained the throne. Kām Bakhsh in fear and despair opened a secret correspondence with Rājā Rām, and planned to escape to Gingee with his family and then make an attempt on the throne of Delhi with Marāthā aid. This foolish plot was betrayed to Zu-'l-Fiqār and Asad Khān. They consulted the leading officers, who urged that the safety of the army required that the prince should be kept under guard, the siege trenches abandoned and all the troops concentrated in the rear lines after bursting the big guns. The retreat was effected only after a severe fight with the surrounding enemy and heavy losses. The prince, who had conspired to arrest the two generals, was himself detained a prisoner in Asad Khān's tent and was later sent back to his father under escort.

One great danger was thus averted, but the difficulties of the Mughuls only thickened. Santā and Dhana by daily attacks wore down the outnumbered imperialists and reduced them to famine. Asad Khān then bribed Rājā Rām to let him retreat to Wandiwāsh unmolested, but his soldiers had lost all spirit through famine and the death of transport animals; the retreat became a rout in which the Mughul army was plundered of its property and stores (2 February, 1693). Supplies and reinforcements under Qāsim Khān soon arrived at Wandiwāsh, where the Mughuls halted for some months.

In February, 1694, Zu-'l-Fiqār Khān set out southwards along the coast, conquering many forts in the South Arcot district and threatening Tanjore, the raja of which, Shāhjī II, had to sign a treaty (1 June) promising to obey the emperor, give up Rājā Rām's cause, and pay an annual tribute of three million rupees. Then, after storming Pālamcottah, the Mughul general returned to Wandiwāsh, and near the end of the year made a show of renewing the siege of Gingee. But he had come to a secret understanding with Rājā Rām, in expectation of the death of the old emperor and civil wars among his sons, so that nothing was achieved by the Mughuls during 1695. The arrival of Dhana and Santā early in 1695 forced Zu-'l-Fiqār to raise the siege and confine himself to the defensive in Arcot fort throughout 1696; he was hopelessly outnumbered and without money or food.

Early in 1697 he collected tribute from Tanjore and other places in the south and then returned to Wandiwāsh for the rainy season. A bitter quarrel between Santā and Dhana weakened the Marāthās, and Zu-'l-Fiqār renewed the siege of Gingee in earnest, in November. Dāūd Khān Pānī, his lieutenant, captured Chikkali-drug (the detached southern fort) by assault in one day and then entrenched opposite the south face of Gingee itself, but his further efforts were thwarted by Zu-'l-Fiqār, who gave the Marāthās secret intelligence of his intended attacks. At last Zu-'l-Fiqār had to take Gingee in order to save his credit with the emperor. He sent timely warning to Rājā Rām, who escaped first to Vellore with his chief officers but left his family behind. The three forts within Gingee were successfully stormed in gallant style by the Rājputs and Afghāns (18 January, 1698). A vast amount of booty was captured, and among the prisoners were four wives and five children of Rājā Rām. But the raja succeeded in arriving at Vishālgarh; the work of the long siege of Gingee was undone; the war was merely transferred to the western theatre.

We shall now turn to the affairs of western India after Rājā Rām's accession. The first flush of Mughul success was over in a year and a half, the Marāthās recovered from the crushing blows of Shambhūjī's capture and Rājā Rām's flight to Madras, and they gained their first signal victory over the Mughuls on 4 June, 1690, when they captured Sharza Khān near Sātārā with his family, 4000 horses and the entire camp and baggage of his army, after slaying 1500 of his men. Then they recovered several forts from the imperialists, Partābgarh, Rohirā, Rājgarh and Tornā. In 1692 there was a renewal of Marāthā activity and their success was conspicuous in many quarters, such as the recovery of Panhālā. The siege of this fort, urged by Aurangzīb, failed after many years of desultory attack under Mu'izz-ud-dīn Bīdār Bakht and Fīrūz Jang. The disaster to Sharza Khān in 1690 compelled the emperor to occupy the north Sātārā district in force, which led to frequent but indecisive conflicts with Santā Ghorpare, who had made the Mahādev hill his base, and used to raid far to the south and the east. The Belgaum and Dhārwār districts were harried by Santā and Dhana, which necessitated the strengthening of the Mughul forces there; but when these generals went off to the eastern Carnatic (end of 1692), the Mughuls on the western front enjoyed a short respite. Late in 1693 they returned home and renewed their attacks. Dhana destroyed the siege-works before Panhālā, while Santā sent off Amrit Rāo Nimbālkar to raid Berār, and he himself levied *chauth* in the Mālkhed region. Throughout 1694 and 1695 the Marāthā bands were active and the Berads troublesome all over the western Deccan, but nothing decisive or noteworthy was done on either side but desultory fighting and futile marches, which wore the Mughuls down.

Then came two terrible disasters. In November, 1695, the emperor, learning that Santā was conveying his rich store of plunder to his own home in north-western Mysore, ordered Qāsim Khān to intercept him, and sent a picked force of his personal retinue and the contingents of the nobles, under some of his highest officers, to reinforce Qāsim Khān. The two divisions united near Chitaldroog, and Qāsim Khān entertained his noble guests with all the pomp and luxury of a Mughul grandee, discarding military precaution. Santā came up from a distance by swift and secret marches and formed his men in three divisions which were very ably handled and co-ordinated. The first surprised and plundered the advanced tents of Qāsim Khān and his heavy baggage, the second intercepted and enveloped the Khān, who was advancing to the rescue, while the third Marāthā division looted the camp and baggage left behind by Qāsim Khān in his advance. The Carnatic musketeers and Marāthā light horse completely overpowered the Mughuls and drove them in headlong rout to the small fort of Dodderi, which had neither space nor food sufficient for them. Fully one-third of the Mughul army fell in the battle and the retreat; the rest capitulated through hunger; Qāsim Khān committed suicide. The remnant of his army, after promising a ransom of two million rupees and giving up all its cash, horses and other property, was set free (December, 1695).

Another great Mughul general, Himmat Khān, was in Basavāpatan (forty miles west of Dodderi). Santā appeared before it on 30 January, 1696, and lured Himmat Khān out of his refuge, and shot him dead as he was leading a charge. His baggage was plundered, and his men fell back into the fort. Here they were relieved after more than a month. The emperor took prompt measures to strengthen the defence of this district. Prince Bīdār Bakht chastised Barmāppā Nāyak of Chitaldroog, who had disloyally sided with Santā. Prince A'zam was posted at Pedgāon.

But now a civil war weakened the Marāthā strength. Santājī Ghorpare was mortally jealous of Dhana Jādav, his favoured rival for the post of commander-in-chief (*Senāpati*). His vanity, imperious temper and insubordinate spirit gave great offence at Rājā Rām's court; Santā was attacked by Rājā Rām and Dhana near Conjeveram (May, 1696), but he defeated them. When he returned to Mahārāshtra in March, 1697, a civil war broke out between him and Dhana, all the Marāthā captains being ranged on the two sides. In another battle most of Santā's followers, disgusted with his severity and insolence, went over to Dhana. Santā, defeated and despoiled of all, fled from the field, but near the Mahādev hill he was murdered by order of Rādhikā Bāi Mane, whose brother he had slain (June, 1697). In force of genius he was the greatest Marāthā soldier after Shivājī, but his temper was unbearable.

Nothing remarkable happened in the second half of 1697, nor for some time after Rājā Rām's return from Gingee to Vishālgarh (February, 1698). Next year, after forming plans for an extensive raid through Khāndesh and Berār, he issued from Sātārā (5 November, 1699) and took the road with a large force. But he was intercepted near Parenda by Bīdār Bakht, broken and driven towards Ahmadnagar; his raid into Berār was nipped in the bud; but one division under Krishna Sāvant crossed the Narbadā for the first time and plundered some places near Dhāmoni. Battles, however, were fought with Dhana and other generals in the Sātārā district with various results (January, 1700).

On 12 March, 1700, Rājā Rām died at Sinhgarh. His senior widow Tārā Bāi placed her son Shivājī III on the throne, while another wife Rājas Bāi crowned her son as Shambhūjī II, and the Marāthā ministers and generals were again divided into two rival factions. But Tārā Bāi's ability and energy, seconded by the genius of Parashurām Trimbak (the new regent), gave her supreme power in the state.

During the past decade, the Mughul cause had achieved remarkable and unbroken success in the northern Konkan through the ability and enterprise of a local commandant named Mu'tabar Khān, a Sayyid of the Navāit clan. He first distinguished himself by capturing or buying many hill-forts in the Nāsik district, and then descended into the Konkan, where he took Kalyān (April, 1689) and several other places, occupying the country southwards to the latitude of Bombay, and even forced the Portuguese of "the North" (Bassein and Damān) to make peace by promising not to support the Marāthās. At Kalyān he lived for many years, adorning the city with his many buildings and gardens, and restoring peace and prosperity to the district.

By April, 1695, Aurangzīb came to realise that his work in the Deccan was not finished with the conquest of Bijāpur, Golconda and the Marāthā capital; it was only beginning; for him there was no going back to Delhi, as he could see no end to the people's war in which he was entangled. Therefore, in May, 1695, he sent his eldest surviving son Shāh 'Ālam to govern the Punjāb, Sind and afterwards Afghānistān and guard the north-western gateway of India, while he himself took post at Brahmapurī for the next four and a half years in the very heart of the enemy country. During this period (1695–99), the Marāthā danger came nearer home and drove the Mughuls into the defensive in Mahārāshtra and Kanara. The movements of their roving bands were bewilderingly rapid and unexpected, and the Mughul pursuing columns toiled in vain after them. Local representatives of the emperor were often driven to make unauthorised terms with the Marāthās by agreeing to pay *chauth*. Worse than that, some imperialists made a concert with the enemy for sharing the plunder of the emperor's own subjects. The Mughul administration had really dissolved and only the presence of the emperor held it together, but merely as a phantom rule.

The fall of Gingee enabled Aurangzīb to concentrate all his resources in the western theatre of war, and now began the last stage of his career, the siege of successive Marāthā forts by the emperor in person. The rest of his life is a repetition of the same sickening tale: a hill-fort captured by him in person after a vast expenditure of time, men and money, the fort recovered by the Marāthās from the weak Mughul garrison after a few months, and its siege begun again a year or two later. His soldiers and camp-followers suffered unspeakable hardship in marching over flooded rivers, muddy roads and broken hilly tracks; porters disappeared, transport beasts died of hunger and overwork, scarcity of grain was ever present in the camp and the Marāthā and Berad "thieves" (as he officially called them) not far off. The mutual jealousies of his generals ruined his cause or delayed his success. The siege of eight forts, Sātārā, Parlī, Panhālā, Khelnā (= Vishālgarh), Kondhānā (= Sinhgarh), Rājgarh, Tornā and Wāgingerā, besides five places of lesser note, occupied him for five years and a half (1699–1705), after which the broken down old man of eighty-eight retired to die.

Leaving his family, surplus baggage and unnecessary officials in the fortified camp of Brahmapurī in charge of the *vazīr*, and giving Zu-'l-Fiqār, surnamed Nusrat Jang, a roving commission to fight the

Marāthā field-armies that hovered round the emperor or threatened this base camp, Aurangzīb started from Brahmapurī on 29 October, 1699. Capturing Basantgarh on the way without a blow, he arrived before Sātārā on 18 December and took up his quarters at Kāranja, a mile and a half to the north of the fort. The entire siege-camp, five miles round, was enclosed with a wall to keep the Marāthā raiders out. The rocky soil made sapping a very slow and difficult work, and the fort was never completely invested. The garrison made frequent sorties, which were repulsed with more or less loss, while the Marāthā field-forces reduced the besiegers to the condition of a beleaguered city, cutting off outposts and closing the road to grain dealers.

On 23 April the Mughuls fired two mines. The first killed many of the garrison, but the commandant Prāgjī Prabhu was dug out alive from under the debris. The second exploded outwards, killing two thousand of the Mughul soldiers, but making a 20 yards breach in the wall. Bājī Chāvan Daphle, a Marāthā vassal, mounted the breach shouting to the Mughul soldiers to follow him and enter, but they were too dazed by the catastrophe to advance, and he was killed. But after the death of Rājā Rām, the Marāthā commandant Subhānjī lost heart and yielded the fort to the imperialists (1 May, 1700).

Aurangzīb next laid siege to Parlī, a fort six miles west of Sātārā and the headquarters of the Marāthā government. It resisted for some time, and the invaders suffered terribly from excessive rain and the scarcity of grain and fodder. But the emperor held grimly on, and at last the commandant evacuated the fort for a bribe (19 June). These two sieges caused an enormous waste of men and animals; the Mughul treasury was empty and the soldiers were starving as their pay for three years was in arrears. Excessive rain aggravated their sufferings. On the return march from Parlī to Bhūshangarh, transport utterly broke down, much property had to be abandoned, even nobles had to walk on foot through the mud, and only forty-five miles were covered in thirty-five days. While the emperor was encamped at Khavāsspur (on the Mān river), the river suddenly rose in flood at midnight (11 October) and swept through the camp, destroying many men and animals, and ruining the tents and baggage. The emperor himself stumbled and dislocated his knee in trying to escape. This left him a little lame for the rest of his life, which the court flatterers used to say was the heritage of his ancestor, the world-conqueror Tīmūr-Lang! But reinforcements were summoned from northern India and many thousands of fresh horses purchased to mount the army again. The Marāthās and Berads plundered and levied *chauth* far and wide during this eclipse of the Mughul power.

Panhālā was the next fort attacked (19 March, 1701). The emperor formed a complete circle of investment, fourteen miles in length, around it and its sister-height Pavangarh. A mobile force under Nusrat Jang was sent out to chastise the Marāthās wherever heard of. But in that stony region the progress of mining was very slow, while the mutual jealousies of his generals led them to thwart each other and thus prolonged the siege. The siege dragged on for two months, without success seeming any nearer. Then a heavy bribe was paid to the commandant Trimbak and he delivered the fort on 7 June. Wardhangarh, Chandan, Nandgir and Wandan were next captured with little or no opposition.

Aurangzīb marched against Khelnā next winter. This fort stands on the crest of the western Ghāts, 3350 feet above the sea and overlooking the Konkan plain, with dense forests and thick underwood below it. With great labour a road was made through the Ambāghāt pass by Fath-ullah Khān, but even then the emperor's followers suffered terrible hardship and loss in crossing it and bringing his camp and equipage to the foot of the fort. The siege dragged on for five months; the Mughul artillery beat in vain against the solid rock of the walls, while the missiles of the garrison did terrible havoc among the imperialists crowded below. Some success was gained at the western gate by Bīdār Bakht's follower Rājā Jay Singh (Sawāī, of Amber) and his Rājputs, who stormed the *fausse braye* of the gate (7 May, 1702). But the terrible monsoon of the Bombay coast now burst on the heads of the Mughul army. They then bribed the commandant Parashurām to evacuate it (17 June). The imperialists underwent unspeakable hardship in their return from Khelnā, in crossing the Ambāghāt and the swollen streams on the way which raged like torrents. Grain sold at a rupee a *seer*,[1] "fodder and firewood appeared in the isolated camp only by mistake"; no tent was available. In this condition, traversing 30 miles in thirty-eight days, the miserable army reached Panhālā on 27 July.

On 12 December, the indomitable old man set out to conquer Kondhānā (Sinhgarh). But there was no life in the work of the besiegers, and after wasting three months they secured the fort by profuse bribery (18 April, 1703). After spending seven months near Poona, the emperor besieged Rājgarh, and captured its first gate by assault after two months of bombardment. Then the garrison made terms but fled away from the fort at night (26 February, 1704). Tornā was next taken (20 March), the only fort that Aurangzīb captured by force without resort to bribery.

Next, after a six months' halt at Khed (7 miles north of Chākan), the emperor marched to attack Wāgingerā, the capital of the Berads[2], an aboriginal people expert in musketry, night attack and robbery, who lived in the fork between the Krishnā and the Bhīmā, east of Bijāpur. The siege began on 19 February, 1705, but for many weeks afterwards the Mughuls could make no progress; every day the

[1] Fifteen pence a pound. [2] Beydurs in Meadows Taylor's '*Story of my life*.'

enemy sallied out and attacked them, the bombardment from the numerous well-supplied guns in the fort made the advance of the siege-trenches or even their maintenance within range impossible. One morning the imperialists captured by surprise the hillock of Lāl Tikri, which commands a portion of Wāgingerā, but the Berads soon drove them out with heavy loss, as mutual jealousy among the Mughul generals prevented the timely reinforcement of the captors of this position.

On 6 April, a Marāthā force under Dhana Jādav and Hindu Rāo (brother of Santā Ghorpare) arrived to support the Berads, because the families of many Marāthā generals were sheltered in Wāgingerā. These were cleverly removed by the newcomers through the back-door, while they kept the Mughuls in play by a noisy feint in front. The Marāthās halted in the neighbourhood in consideration of a daily subsidy from Pidiā the Berad chief, and made frequent attacks on the Mughuls, who were now thrown into a state of siege and all their activity ceased, while famine raged in their camp. Then Pidiā gained some time by delusive peace negotiations.

Nusrat Jang, who had arrived to aid the emperor, made steady progress by capturing some of the outlying hillocks and the village of Talwārgerā, in the plain south of the fort gate, after days of gallant fight and heavy loss among his Bundelā soldiers, till Pidiā found further struggle hopeless and evacuated the fort secretly at night (8 May, 1705) with his Marāthā allies. The Mughul camp-followers who first entered it in search of plunder set fire to the grass huts which caused terrible gunpowder explosions. The bare fort was captured, but its chieftain and his clansmen remained free to give more trouble to the emperor.

After the fall of the fort, Aurangzīb encamped at Devāpur, a quiet village on the bank of the Krishnā, eight miles south of it. Here he fell very ill on account of his extreme old age (ninety lunar years) and incessant toil. His entire army was seized with consternation; if he died who would lead them safely out of that enemy country? His courageous struggling with disease and insistence on transacting business in spite of fever made him very weak and at times unconscious. But after ten or twelve days he began to rally, though slowly. On his complete recovery, he broke up his camp on 2 November and marched slowly to Ahmadnagar, which was reached on 31 January, 1706. This was destined to be his "journey's end", for here he died a year later.

When Aurangzīb set out on his retreat to Ahmadnagar, he left desolation and anarchy behind him. His march was molested by the exultant Marāthās under all their great generals, who followed his army a few miles in the rear, cutting off its grain supplies and stragglers and threatening to break into its camp. When attacked by the Mughuls in force, they would fall back a little, but like water parted by the oar would close again as soon as the attackers retired on their main body. As the eyewitness Bhīmsen wrote:

> The Marāthās became completely dominant over the whole kingdom and closed the roads. By means of robbery they escaped from poverty and rose to great wealth. I have heard that every week they distributed alms and sweetmeats in charity, praying for the long life of the emperor, who had proved (for them) the Feeder of the Universe! The price of grain grew higher and higher; in the imperial camp in particular vast numbers perished of hunger and many kinds of illegal exactions and practices appeared.

The Marāthās reduced spoliation to a system:

> Wherever these raiders arrived they engaged in collecting the revenue of the place and passed months and years there with their wives and children in composure of mind. They divided the *parganas* among themselves, and in imitation of the imperial government they appointed their own *sūbahdārs* (governors), *kamāvish-dārs* (*chauth*-collectors) and *rāhdārs* (road-patrol). When a *kamāvishdār* was opposed by a strong *zamīndār* or imperial *faujdār*, the Marāthā *sūbahdār* came to his aid (with his troops)....In each *sūbah* the Marāthās built one or two small forts, from which they issued to raid the country around (Khāfi Khān).
>
> When the Marāthās invade a province, they take from every *pargana* as much money as they desire and make their horses eat the standing crops or tread them down. The imperial army that comes in pursuit can subsist there only after the fields have been cultivated (anew). All administration has disappeared....The peasants have given up cultivation; the *jāgīrdārs* do not get a penny from their fiefs....The servants of the Marāthā state support themselves by plundering on all sides, and pay a small part of their booty to their king, getting no salary from him. The coming of rent from the Mughul officers' *jāgīrs* ceased....The condition of the imperial army grew worse from the high price of grain and the devastation of the *jāgīrs*, while the resources of the Marāthās increased through robbery. Thus, a vicious circle was formed which aggravated the evil. The *mansabdārs*, on account of the scanty forces under them, cannot gain control over their *jāgīrs*. The local *zamīndārs*, growing stronger, have joined the Marāthās, raised troops and stretched the hand of oppression over the realm. As the imperial dominions have been given out in fief to the *jāgīrdārs*, so too the Marāthās have made a distribution of the whole empire among their generals, and thus one kingdom has to support two sets of *jāgīrdārs*!...The peasants, subjected to this double exaction, have collected arms and horses and joined the Marāthās (Bhīmsen).

The economic ruin and destruction of order caused to the empire by the Marāthā ascendancy will be clear from these two contemporary accounts. Another eyewitness, Manucci, thus describes the frightful material waste caused by this quarter-century of futile warfare, and the complete desolation of the Deccan:

> Aurangzīb withdrew to Ahmadnagar, leaving behind him the fields of these provinces devoid of trees and bare of crops, their places being taken by the bones of men and beasts. Instead of verdure all is black and barren. There have died in his armies over a hundred thousand souls yearly, and of animals, pack-oxen, camels, elephants, etc., over three hundred thousand. In the Deccan provinces from 1702 to 1704 plague (and famine) prevailed. In these two years there expired over two millions of souls.

After 1705 the Marāthās became masters of the situation all over the Deccan and even in parts of central India. The Mughul officers were helplessly reduced to the defensive. A change came over the Marāthā tactics with this growth of power; they were no longer, as in Shivājī's and Shambhūjī's times, light horsemen who plundered and fled or merely looted defenceless traders and villagers, dispersing at the first report of the Mughul army's approach. On the contrary, as Manucci noticed in 1704,

> These Marāthā leaders and their troops move in these days with much confidence, because they have cowed the Mughul commanders and inspired them with fear. At the present time they possess artillery, musketry, . . . with elephants and camels for all their baggage and tents. In short, they are equipped and move about just like the armies of the Mughul.

Even at Ahmadnagar, Aurangzīb's camp was threatened by a vast horde of Marāthās in May, 1706, and it was only after a long and severe contest that they could be repulsed. In Gujarāt a terrible disaster befell the imperialists. Inū Mand, a former brewer of Khāndesh, who had taken to highway robbery, invited Dhana Jādav and his army and sacked the large and rich trading centre of Barodā (March, 1706), the imperial commandant of the place being captured with his men. Similarly, the province of Aurangābād was frequently ravaged by raiding bands under different leaders. In July Marāthā activity near Wāgingerā forced the emperor to detach a strong force there. Pidiā Berad, in alliance with Hindu Rāo, gained Penukondā by bribing its starving Mughul commandant. Then they turned to Serā, the capital of the Bijāpur Carnatic uplands, the district around which had been plundered once before (in 1704). Dāūd Khān recovered Penukondā; but Siādat Khān, a high officer of the court, was wounded and held to ransom by the enemy. They also recovered Basantgarh. When the rainy season of 1706 ended in September, Marāthā activity was renewed with tenfold intensity. Dhana Jādav made a dash for Berār and Khāndesh, but was headed off by Nusrat Jang into Bijāpur and beyond the Krishnā. A long train of caravans coming from Aurangābād to the imperial camp in Ahmadnagar was plundered of everything on the way.

In the midst of this chaos and darkness Aurangzīb closed his eyes. The internal troubles of his camp were even more alarming. Prince A'zam Shāh's inordinate vanity and ambition urged him to secure the succession for himself by removing all rivals from his path. So he poisoned the ears of the emperor against 'Azīm-ush-Shān, the able third son of Shāh 'Ālam, and had him recalled from the government of Patna. Then he looked out for an opportunity to make a sudden attack on Kām Bakhsh and kill him. Every day A'zam's hostile designs against Kām Bakhsh became more evident, and therefore the emperor charged the brave and faithful Sultān Husain (Mīr Malang) with that prince's defence, which threw A'zam into uncontrollable anger. Early in February, 1707, Aurangzīb had one more of the attacks of languor and illness which had become rather frequent of late. He recovered for a time, but feeling that the end could not be far off, he tried to secure peace in his camp by making civil war there immediately after his death impossible. So he appointed Kām Bakhsh as viceroy of Bijāpur and sent him away with his army on 20 February. Four days later A'zam was despatched to Mālwā as its governor; but that cunning prince marched slowly, halting every other day. On the 28th the aged and worn-out monarch was seized with a severe fever, but for three days he obstinately insisted on coming to the court-room and saying the five daily prayers there. During this period he dictated two pathetic letters to A'zam and Kām Bakhsh entreating them to avoid the slaughter of Muslims and the desolation of the realm by civil war, but to cultivate brotherly love, peace and moderation, and illustrating the vanity of all earthly things. In the morning of 3 March, 1707, he came out of his bedroom, offered the morning prayer, and repeating the Islamic *credo*, gradually sank into unconsciousness, which ended in his death about 8 o'clock.

Muhammad A'zam Shāh, who had marched only forty miles in ten days, returned to Ahmadnagar in the night of the 4th, and after mourning for his father and consoling his sister Zīnat-un-Nisā, who had superintended the emperor's household throughout the Deccan period of his reign, took part in carrying his coffin for a short distance, and then sent it away to the *rauza* or sepulchre of the saint Shaikh Zain-ul-Haqq, four miles west of Daulatābād, for burial. This place was named Khuldābād and Aurangzīb was described in official writings by the posthumous title of *Khuld-makān* ("He whose abode is in eternity").

Aurangzīb's last years were unspeakably sad. In the political sphere his lifelong endeavour to govern India justly and strongly ended in anarchy and disruption. A sense of unutterable loneliness haunted his heart in his old age: one by one all the older nobles, his personal friends and the survivors of his own generation, died, with the sole exception of Asad Khān, his minister and personal companion. In his court circle he now found only younger men, timid sycophants, afraid of responsibility and eternally intriguing in a mean spirit of greed and jealousy. His puritan austerity had, at all times, chilled the advances of other men towards him, as one who seemed to be above the joys and sorrows, weakness and pity of mortals. His domestic life was darkened as bereavements thickened round his closing eyes. His gifted daughter Zīb-un-Nisā died in 1702, his rebel son Akbar in exile on a foreign soil in 1704, his best beloved daughter-in-law Jahānzīb in 1705, and Gauharārā, his sole surviving sister, in 1706, besides one of his daughters and two nephews in this last year of his life.

After Aurangzīb had left Rājputāna for the Deccan (1681) his troops continued to hold the cities and strategic points of Mārwār; but the Rāthor patriots remained in a state of war for twenty-seven years more. They occupied the hills and deserts and every now and then swooped down upon the plains, cutting off convoys, capturing weakly held Mughul outposts, and rendering the cultivation of the fields and traffic on the roads wellnigh impossible, so that famine was constantly present in Mārwār, and in some years "the sword and pestilence united to clear the land". The Rāthor national opposition would have gradually died out through attrition, if the emperor had not been plunged into a more serious conflict in the Deccan, which drained all his resources and ensured the ultimate success of the Rāthor patriots. The history of these twenty-seven years (1681–1707) in Mārwār falls into three well-defined stages: from 1681 to 1687 there was a people's war, because the chief was a child and the national leader Durgā Dās was absent in the Deccan. The Rāthor people fought under different captains individually, with no central authority and no common plan of action. By adopting guerrilla tactics they wore the Mughuls out and minimised the disadvantages of their own inferior arms and numbers. The second stage of the war began in 1687, when Durgā Dās returned from the Deccan and Ajīt Singh came out of concealment and the two took the command of the national forces. The success of the Rāthors was at first brilliant; joined by the Hārā clan of Būndī they cleared the plains of Mārwār and advancing beyond their own land raided Mālpurā and Pur-Mandal and carried their ravages into Mewāt and the west of Delhi. But they could not recover their own country, because in this very year 1687 an exceptionally capable and energetic officer named Shujā'at Khān became the imperial governor of Jodhpur and held that office for fourteen years, during which he successfully maintained the Mughul hold on Mārwār. He always kept his retainers up to their full strength and was very quick in his movements. Thus, he succeeded in checking the Rāthors when it came to fighting, while he also made an understanding with them by paying them one-fourth (*chauth*) of the imperial custom-duties on all merchandise if they spared the traders on the roads. On Shujā'at Khān's death (in July, 1701), A'zam Shāh, who succeeded him as governor, renewed hostilities with Ajīt Singh and the third stage of the Rājput war began which ended in the complete recovery of Mārwār by Ajīt Singh in 1707.

In 1687, Durjan Sāl Hārā, the leading vassal of Būndī, being insulted by his chieftain Anurudh Singh, rose and seized the capital, and coming over to Mārwār joined the Rāthors with a thousand horsemen of his own. The two united clans drove away most of the Mughul outposts in Mārwār, and raided the imperial dominions in the north, causing alarm even in Delhi. In 1690 Durgā Dās routed the new governor of Ajmer and continued to plunder and disturb the parts of Mārwār in Mughul occupation. But Shujā'at Khān restored the situation by tactfully winning many of the Rājput headmen over. Aurangzīb was naturally anxious to get back his rebel son Akbar's daughter Safiyat-un-Nisā and son Buland Akhtar, who had been left in the hands of the Rāthors on the failure of his rebellion in 1681. The negotiations for this purpose were happily concluded by Shujā'at Khān in 1694, when Durgā Dās was induced by the historian Ishwar Dās Nāgar to make terms for his raja and himself by giving up Akbar's daughter to the emperor. Aurangzīb was highly pleased with Durgā Dās on learning from his grand-daughter that the Rāthor leader had carefully educated her in Islāmic theology by engaging a Muhammadan tutoress for her in the wilds of Mārwār. In 1698 Buland Akhtar, the last pawn in the hands of the Rāthors, was delivered to Aurangzīb. In return, the emperor pardoned Ajīt Singh and gave him rank and the *parganas* of Jhālor, Sānchod and Siwānā as his *jāgīr* but did not restore the kingdom of Mārwār. Durgā Dās was rewarded by being taken into imperial service with the command of 3000 and appointment as commandant of Pātan in Gujarāt.

In 1702 Durgā Dās was driven into rebellion a second time. Both he and Ajīt Singh had continued to distrust the Mughul government and kept themselves at a safe distance from the court, while the emperor regarded both with suspicious watchfulness. In 1702 he tried to get Durgā Dās arrested or killed by the governor of Gujarāt. The Rāthor hero immediately fled to Mārwār and there raised the standard of rebellion, in which he was joined by Ajīt Singh. But they could effect nothing, as the economic exhaustion of Mārwār was complete and war-weariness had seized the Rāthor clansmen. Disagreement also broke out between Ajīt Singh and Durgā Dās; the youthful raja was impatient of advice, imperious in temper and jealous of Durgā Dās's deserved influence in the royal council and the country. In 1704, Aurangzīb, at last admitting his growing helplessness against a sea of enemies, made peace with Ajīt Singh by giving him Merta as *jāgīr*, and next year Durgā Dās also made his submission to the emperor and was restored to his old rank and post in Gujarāt.

In 1706 a Marāthā incursion into Gujarāt was followed by a crushing disaster to the Mughul army at Ratanpur. Ajīt Singh and Durgā Dās again rebelled. Prince Bīdār Bakht, then deputy-governor of Gujarāt, defeated Durgā Dās and drove him into the Kolī country. But Ajīt Singh defeated Muhkam Singh of Nāgaur, a loyal vassal of the emperor, at Drunerā, and thus gained an increase of prestige and strength. When the news of Aurangzīb's death arrived, Ajīt Singh expelled the Mughul commandant and took possession of his father's capital. Sojāt, Pālī and Merta were recovered from the imperial agents, and the Rāthor war of liberation ended in complete success (1707).

The endless wars in which Aurangzīb became involved in the Deccan reacted on the political condition of northern India, which continued during the second half of his reign to be annually drained of its public money and youthful recruits. The rich old provinces of the empire north of the Narbadā were left in charge of second-rate nobles with insufficient troops and the trade routes unguarded. The great royal road leading from Delhi to Āgra and Dholpur, and thence through Mālwā to the Deccan, passed directly through the country of the Jāts, a brave, strong and hardy people, but habitually addicted to plundering. In 1685, these people raised their heads under two new leaders, Rājā Rām and Rām Chehrā, the petty chiefs of Sinsanī and Soghor, who were the first to train their clansmen in group organisation and open warfare. Every Jāt peasant was practised in wielding the staff and the sword; they had only to be embodied in regiments, taught to obey their captains and supplied with fire-arms to make them into an army. As bases for their operations, refuges for their chiefs in defeat, and storing places for their booty, they built several small forts amidst their almost trackless jungles and strengthened them with mud walls that could defy artillery. Then they began to raid the king's highway and carry their depredations even to the gates of Āgra.

Rājā Rām gained some striking victories; he killed near Dholpur the renowned Turānī warrior Uighur Khān when on his way from Kābul to the Deccan (1687), and next year plundered Mīr Ibrāhīm (a former Qutb Shāhī general, now created Mahābat Khān), who was marching to join his viceroyalty in the Punjab. Shortly afterwards, he looted Akbar's tomb at Sikandra, doing great damage to the building and, according to one account, digging out and burning that great emperor's bones. This sudden development of the Jāt power alarmed Aurangzīb, and he sent his favourite grandson Bīdār Bakht to assume the supreme command in the Jāt war (1688). Bishan Singh Kachhwāha, the new Rājā of Amber (Jaipur), was appointed as commandant of Muttra with a special charge to root out the Jāts. Bīdār Bakht infused greater vigour into the Mughul operations. In an internecine war raging between two Rājput clans, Rājā Rām who was fighting for one party was shot dead (14 July, 1688). Bīdār Bakht laid siege to Sinsanī; his troops underwent great hardship from the scarcity of provisions and water; at last they fired a mine, stormed the breach and captured the fort after three hours of obstinate fighting, the Mughuls losing 900 men and the Jāts 1500. Next year Bishan Singh surprised Soghor.

As the result of these operations, the Jāt leaders went into hiding and the district enjoyed peace for some years. The next rising of the clan was under Churāman, a nephew of Rājā Rām. He had a genius for organisation and using opportunities and succeeded in founding a dynasty which still rules over Bharatpur. "He not only increased the number of his soldiers, but also strengthened them by the addition of fusiliers (musketeers) and a troop of cavalry,...and having robbed many of the ministers of the (Mughul) court on the road, he attacked the royal wardrobe and the revenue sent from the provinces" (Xavier Wendel). But this full development of Churāman's power took place after the death of Aurangzīb. About 1704 he recovered

Sinsanī from the Mughuls, but lost it to Mukhtār Khān, the governor of Āgra, a year later.

There were some serious Hindu risings in Mālwā and Bihār late in this reign, but owing to different causes. Pahār Singh, a Gaur Rājput petty chief of Indrakhi in western Bundelkhand and an imperial commandant, took the side of Lāl Singh Khīchī against the latter's oppressive overlord Anurudh Singh Hārā of Būndī, a loyal general of the emperor, and defeated Anurudh and plundered his camp and baggage (1685). He then broke with the imperial government and took to plundering the villages of Mālwā. Rāi Mulūk Chand, the assistant of the governor of Mālwā, attacked and slew the rebel at the end of the year, but the rising continued under Pahār Singh's son, Bhagwant, who totally defeated Mulūk Chand near Āntrī but was himself killed (March, 1686). Devī Singh, another son of Pahār Singh, joined Chhatra Sāl in plundering imperial territory in Bundelkhand. We find more rebels of this Gaur family active and troublesome up to 1692, when they were pacified by receiving employment in the imperial army. Gangā Rām Nāgar, the revenue officer of Khān Jahān, managed his master's assignments in Allahābād and Bihār while the Khān was campaigning in the Deccan. The other servants of the Khān jealously poisoned his ears against his absent officer, and Gangā Rām, after clearing his reputation once or twice, flew to arms in disgust and in despair of his life and honour. Collecting some 4000 soldiers he plundered the city of Bihār, laid siege to Patna, and set up a bogus prince Akbar, calling upon the people to rally round his standard (April, 1681). The siege of Patna was raised by imperial reinforcements, but Gangā Rām, after looting some other places, went over to the Rājput rebels in Mālwā and plundered Sironj (October, 1684). Shortly afterwards he died. Rāo Gopāl Singh Chandrāwat, the chief of Rāmpura in Mālwā and an imperial captain, rebelled when the emperor gave that estate to his son Ratan Singh as the price of his conversion to Islām (1700). But he was defeated and forced to submit. In 1706 he joined the Marāthās for a living and accompanied them in the sack of Barodā.

The English East India Company had established its first trade factory in India at Surat in 1612 and exchanged goods with Āgra and Delhi by the long and costly land route; it also had an agency at Masulipatam, a port then belonging to Qutb Shāh. In 1633 an English factory was opened at Balasore and another at Hariharpur (twenty-five miles south-east of Cuttack). In 1640, the foundations of Fort St George at Madras were laid, this being the first independent station of the English in India, though outside the Mughul empire. In 1651 they opened their first commercial house in Bengal, at Hooghly (twenty-four miles north of Calcutta). Their chief exports were saltpetre (from Bihār), silk and sugar. Prince Shujā', then governor of Bengal, granted a *nishān* (or prince's order) by which the English were allowed to trade in Bengal on payment of 3000 rupees a year in lieu of all kinds of customs and dues (1652).

In 1661 the English establishments in India were reorganised with the result of two independent governments ("President and Council") being set up at Surat and Madras, all the Bengal establishments being made subordinate to the Presidency of Madras. The trade with Bengal was very prosperous about 1658; raw silk was abundant, the taffetas were various and fine, the saltpetre was cheap and of the best quality; all these exchanged for the gold and silver sent out from England. The Bengal trade continued to grow rapidly: the value of the Company's exports from this province rose from £34,000 in 1668 to £85,000 in 1675 and £150,000 in 1680. In addition to buying local manufactures the English sent out European dyers to Bengal to improve the colour of the silk cloth made locally and also inaugurated a pilot service for navigating the Ganges from Hooghly to the sea (1668). The first British ship sailed up the Ganges from the Bay of Bengal in 1679.

The complaints of the English traders against the local agents of the Mughul government were three: (i) The demand of an *ad valorem* duty on the actual merchandise imported, instead of the lump sum of 3000 rupees per annum into which it had been commuted during the viceroyalty of Shujā' in Bengal. The English also claimed that Aurangzīb's *farmān* of 25 March, 1680, entitled them, on the payment of a consolidated duty of 3½ per cent. at Surat, to trade absolutely free of customs at all other places in the Mughul empire. (ii) Exactions by local officers under the name of *rāhdārī* (internal transit duty), *peshkash* (presents), clerks' fee, and *farmāish* (supplying manufactures to order of the emperor free). (iii) The practice of high officials opening the packages of goods in transit and taking away articles at prices below the fair market value and then selling them in the open market. The two claims of the English under the first head cannot be defended on any reasoning. The custom duty was fixed throughout the empire at 2½ per cent. *ad valorem* for all except the Muslims, while in the case of the Europeans 1 per cent. was added to it (1679) in commutation of the *jizya*. As for the second and third grievances, such exactions had been declared illegal by Aurangzīb and were practised only in disregard of his orders. *Rāhdārī* had been abolished in the second year of his reign, while "benevolences" were condemned in the general order abolishing cesses (9 May, 1673). The "forcing of goods" by his grandson 'Azīm-ush-shān for his private trade called forth the emperor's sternest censures in 1703. But the traders thus wronged by the local officers had no real means of redress; purity of administration was impossible in a society devoid of public spirit and accustomed to submit helplessly to every man in power; the emperor could not look to everything nor be present everywhere.

At last the English traders, getting no redress from the emperor or the local viceroy, resolved to protect themselves by force. The war broke out in Bengal in November, 1686. The English under Job Charnock, in reprisal for the arrest of three disorderly English soldiers by the commandant of Hooghly, sacked and burnt that town, captured a Mughul ship and burnt a large number of barges and boats. The viceroy Shāyista Khān seized all the English factories within his reach. The English then sailed away down the river from Hooghly (30 December, 1686). In February next they burnt the imperial salt-warehouses near Matiāburuj and stormed the fort of Thāna (south of Calcutta), and sailing to the sea seized the island of Hijilī (on the coast of the Midnapore district) where all their land and sea forces in the Bay of Bengal were assembled. Then one of their detachments plundered and burnt the town of Balasore and seized or destroyed the Indian shipping there. In May, 1687, a Mughul force sent by Shāyista Khān arrived before Hijilī to expel the English, who had been reduced by disease from 300 to 100 men and from forty to five officers, and even these few survivors were weakened by fever. So, they evacuated Hijilī with all their artillery and munitions (21 June). At the end of August Shāyista Khān offered terms to the English, permitting them to renew their trade at Hooghly. Next year Captain Heath arrived from England as Agent in Bengal. He decided to withdraw from Bengal altogether, wrest Chittagong from the Mughul officers and make it a safe and independent base for the English trade in Bengal. On the way he stormed Balasore fort and committed frightful excesses on the people. But the council of war turned down the Chittagong project as mad, and in disgust Heath withdrew the English to Madras, abandoning Bengal altogether (February, 1689).

Aurangzīb, on hearing of the commencement of these hostilities, had ordered the arrest of all Englishmen and the total stoppage of trade with them throughout his empire. But he was compelled to make terms with them, as they were supreme at sea and he was anxious to ensure the safe voyage of Indian pilgrims to Mecca; the loss of his custom revenue was also serious. At last, in 1690, peace was finally concluded between the Mughul government and the English. Ībrāhīm Khān, the new viceroy of Bengal, was a mild and just man, very friendly to the English, and at his invitation Job Charnock, the new Agent, arrived from Madras and settled at what is now called Calcutta (3 September, 1690). This was the foundation of the British power in northern India. The arrangement made by prince Shujā‘ was restored.

Such was the war in the eastern side of India. On the western coast the rupture began in 1687. Sir Josia Child, the masterful chairman of the East India Company in London, decided on a policy of firmness and independence in respect of the Mughul empire. He ordered the English factory to be withdrawn from Surat, which "was really a fool's paradise", the Company's trade and officers to be concentrated at Bombay beyond the reach of the Mughul, and Indian shipping at sea to be seized in retaliation for the injury done to English trade in the Mughul dominions. But Sir John Child, the chief director[1] of all the Company's factories in India, was weak and incompetent. When he himself left Surat on 5 May, 1687, the Mughul governor immediately put a guard round the factory there, detaining the factors left behind.

In October, 1688, Child appeared with a fleet before Swally (the landing place for Surat) demanding compensation, but the governor suddenly put the English factors and their Indian brokers in prison, and invested their factory. Child went back after capturing the Indian shipping on the coast. The Mughul government in reply kept the captive Englishmen at Surat in chains for sixteen months (December 1688–April, 1690). At the same time, the Sīdī of Janjīra, as Mughul admiral, landed on Bombay island, occupied its outlying parts, and hemmed the English garrison within the fort. Child, therefore, made an abject submission. The emperor by an order dated 4 January, 1690, restored the English to their old position in the Indian trade on condition of paying a fine of 150,000 rupees and restoring the prizes taken by them at sea.

In the second half of the seventeenth century the Indian seas were infested by a most formidable breed of European pirates, chiefly English. One of them, Roberts, is said to have destroyed 400 trading vessels in three years.

> The chief cause of their immunity lay in the fact that it was the business of nobody in particular to act against them.... Their friends on shore gave them timely information.... Officials high in authority winked at their doings, from which they drew a profit.... The native officials, unable to distinguish the rogues from the honest traders, held the E.I. Co.'s servants responsible for their misdeeds. (Biddulph.)

They ranged over the sea from Mozambique to Sumatra. The most famous of these pirates was Henry Bridgman *alias* Evory, of the *Fancy*, forty guns. After many notable captures in the Gulf of Aden, he took the *Fath-Muhammadī*, a richly laden ship of 'Abdul-Ghafūr, the prince of Surat merchants, and then the *Ganj-i-savāī*, eighty guns, a ship belonging to Aurangzīb and the largest vessel of the port of Surat, being employed in conveying Indian pilgrims to and from Mecca. On its return voyage in September, 1695, between Bombay and Damān it was attacked by the *Fancy* and another pirate. The artillery of the Europeans was most effective; in a short time the Mughul vessel had lost forty-five in killed and wounded and was set on fire. Then the pirates boarded the ship; the crew made no resistance, the captain having hidden himself in a lower cabin. For three days the pirates looted the ship at leisure; the women on board (many of them belonging to the Sayyid and other respectable families) were outraged

[1] See vol. v, p. 102.

and several of them flung themselves into the sea. When the ship, left by the pirates, reached Surat, the people were furious, ascribing the attack to Englishmen closely connected with Bombay. But I'timād Khān, the governor of Surat, an upright man friendly to the English, saved them from being lynched, by occupying their factory in force. Their trade was totally stopped.

During this captivity, Annesley, the president of the Surat Council, and Sir John Gayer, the governor of Bombay, were tireless in petitioning the Mughul government and their friends at court, demanding their release and the restoration of their trade, and asserting "we are merchants, not pirates". Aurangzīb was too wise a man to be swayed by his passions. His chief concern was to secure a regular escort of European war-vessels for his pilgrim-ships to Mecca, and this embargo on European trade was only an instrument for putting pressure on the foreigners to gain that end cheaply. After much higgling by the emperor as to the cost of the escort, Annesley signed a bond for the purpose and the English prisoners were set free (7 July, 1696).

Then a most redoubtable pirate, William Kidd, of the *Adventure*, thirty guns, came to the east, and his success brought him many allies. With a fleet mounting 120 guns and manned by 300 Europeans (the great majority of them being English), he dominated the Indian Ocean, having his base for munitions and stores in Madagascar. In 1698 he captured the *Queda Merchant* with a rich cargo belonging to Mukhlis Khān (a high grandee), and Chivers (a Dutch pirate) captured a fine ship with a cargo worth a million and a half rupees belonging to Hasan Hamīdan of Surat. The English, French and Dutch factories in Surat were again beleaguered and their friends were punished by the governor. Finally an agreement was arrived at: Aurangzīb withdrew his embargo on European trade, while the Dutch agreed to convoy the Mecca pilgrims, patrol the entrance to the Red Sea and pay 70,000 rupees as compensation, and the English paid 30,000 rupees and patrolled the South Indian Seas, and the French paid a similar sum and policed the Persian Gulf.

In September, 1703, two ships of Surat were captured by the pirates when returning from Mocha. The new governor of Surat, I'tibār Khān, extorted 600,000 rupees from the Indian brokers of the English and the Dutch nations. Aurangzīb, on hearing of it, disapproved of this action. But the captivity of Sir John Gayer and his council, brought about by the machinations of the New English Company[1] in February, 1701, continued for six years, with only occasional intervals of liberty and varying in rigour according to the caprice of the governor. The Dutch made reprisals by capturing a pilgrim-ship from Mecca with two pious descendants of the late chief Qāzī on board (1704), at which Aurangzīb, realising his utter

[1] See vol. v, p. 105.

helplessness at sea, made an unconditional surrender to the Europeans and forbade any bond to be taken from them in future for indemnity for the loss caused by the pirates.

From this survey of the emperor's activities and the events centring round him, we turn to the history of certain provinces whose affairs assumed an imperial importance.

The anarchy and desolation which marked Bengal during the dissolution of the Pathān sultanate in the sixteenth century were ended by the Mughul conquest of the province. But during Akbar's reign imperial rule in Bengal was more like an armed occupation than a settled administration, because the power of the old independent Hindu chiefs and Afghān princelings still remained unbroken. It was Islām Khān, a most ambitious, active and high-spirited noble, who, during his viceroyalty of the province from 1608 to 1613, by a series of hard-fought campaigns crushed all the independent chiefs of Bengal, destroyed the last remnant of Afghān power (in Mymensingh, Sylhet and Orissa), and imposed full Mughul peace and direct imperial administration upon all parts of Bengal. Thereafter, Bengal enjoyed profound internal quiet for 130 years; her wealth, population and industry advanced by rapid strides. The Arakanese and Feringi pirates of Chittagong were put down in 1666; the trade of the English and the Dutch grew by leaps and bounds and their factories stimulated production and wealth in the country.

Shāyista Khān governed Bengal from 1664 to 1677, and again from 1680 to 1688, a total of twenty-three years. He ensured peace from foreign attack, while his internal administration, by its mildness, justice and consideration for the people, promoted the wealth and happiness of its teeming population. He adorned his capital, Dacca, with fine buildings, and in his term food crops became incredibly cheap.

His successor, Ibrāhīm Khān (1689–97), was an old man of mild disposition and sedentary habits, and a great lover of books; personally just and free from caprice, but without strength of purpose or capacity for action. He let matters drift till a serious rebellion broke out. Shovā Singh, the chief of Cheto-Bardā (Midnapore district), rebelled, and in alliance with Rahīm Khān, the chief of the Orissa Afghāns, defeated and slew Rājā Krishna Rām, the revenue-farmer of the Burdwān district, and captured its chief town with the family and property of the raja. Then they seized the fort and city of Hooghly. They next plundered the rich cities of Nadiā and Murshidābād, Māldā and Rājmahāl. Shovā Singh was stabbed to death by a daughter of the Burdwān raja, and the rebels then chose Rahīm Khān as their king with the title of Rahīm Shāh. The English, French and Dutch, on the outbreak of the rebellion, obtained the viceroy's permission to fortify their settlements at Calcutta, Chandernagore and Chinsura, and the Dutch afterwards helped to wrest Hooghly fort from the rebels. The emperor dismissed Ibrāhīm Khān and appointed his own grandson 'Azīm-ush-shān in his place, but before the arrival of this new viceroy, Zabardast Khān, the commandant of Burdwān, recovered Rājmahāl and Māldā, Murshidābād and Burdwān and captured the rebel encampment at Bhagwāngolā. After the prince's arrival at Burdwān, his minister Khvāja Anwār was treacherously slain at an interview by Rahīm Khān, but that rebel leader was killed and his army broken up.

Bengal entered on a long period of unbroken prosperity under Muhammad Hādī (surnamed Kār Talb Khān, Murshid Qulī Khān, and finally Ja'far Khān), who was appointed revenue minister of Bengal in 1701 and rose after Aurangzīb's death to be the viceroy of the province and the founder of its dynasty of ruling Nawābs which lasted till the British conquest. "The prudent management of the new *dīwān* soon raised Bengal to the highest degree of prosperity. He took the collection of revenue into his own hands, and by preventing the embezzlements of *zamīndārs* and *jāgīrdārs* augmented the annual revenue." He repeatedly sent to the emperor large sums as the surplus income of the province, and this money came most opportunely to Aurangzīb, whose other resources had been exhausted by the endless war with the Marāthās. The coming of the Bengal treasure was hungrily looked forward to by the entire imperial court in the Deccan. The emperor highly favoured this able and successful servant, made him independent of the viceroy of Bengal, who was ordered to Bihār after a plot against Murshid Qulī's life (1703), and allowed him to remove the revenue offices away from the provincial capital to a new place which was henceforth called Murshidābād and soon became the new capital of Bengal. Under Murshid Qulī all felt that a strong master had come to the province, his orders were universally obeyed, and his impartial justice and rigid execution of decisions put a stop to oppression on all sides.

The province of Mālwā, extending from the Jumna to the Narbadā, with Rājputāna on its west and Bundelkhand on its east, enjoyed very great importance in Mughul India, not only on account of this geographical position, but also because it was rich in agricultural wealth (producing many of the more valuable crops—such as opium, sugarcane, grapes, melons and betel leaf), its industries stood in the first rank after those of Gujarāt, and moreover all the great military roads from the northern capitals of the Mughul empire to the Deccan passed through it. A preponderantly Hindu province like this, with a sturdy Rājput population, was not likely to submit tamely to Aurangzīb's policy of temple destruction and poll-tax on the Hindus. The Mālwā people often fought the emperor's agents sent there to enforce his Islāmic decrees; but, on the whole, the disturbances in this province during the first half of his reign were all on a small scale and confined to a few localities.

At the end of the seventeenth century began the Marāthā penetration which finally ended in the loss of this province to the empire a generation later. The first Marāthā raid was in November, 1699, under Krishna Sāvant, who plundered the environs of Dhāmoni. In January, 1703, the Marāthās crossed the Narbadā again and disturbed the country up to Ujjain. In October that year Nimā Sindia burst into Berār, defeated and captured Sharza Khān (the deputy-governor of that province) and then advanced across the Narbadā into Mālwā at the invitation of Chhatra Sāl Bundelā. He was defeated near Sironj and expelled by Fīrūz Jang (November), and again surprised and routed in the jungle of Dhāmoni in February next. This Marāthā invasion had totally stopped communication and trade between northern and southern India for three months, by holding up the official letters and trade caravans on the bank of the Narbadā. Prince Bīdār Bakht governed this province (1704–6) with great ability and vigour, with the loyal support of Sawāī Jay Singh, the young Rājā of Jaipur. But the local disturbers of peace in Mālwā in the closing years of the reign were too many to be counted; "Marāthās, Bundelās, and Afghāns out of employment are creating disturbances. . . . The province of Khāndesh has been totally desolated. . . . Mālwā too is ruined."

The greatest, most persistent and most successful enemy of the empire in this region was Chhatra Sāl Bundelā, a son of that Champat Rāi who had been hunted down by Aurangzīb in 1661. Through Mīrzā Rājā Jay Singh's kindness the poor young orphan Chhatra Sāl had entered the Mughul army as a petty captain and fought well in the Purandar campaign and the invasion of Deogarh in 1667. But he decided to take to a life of adventure and independence in imitation of Shivāji, whose service he next sought. The Marāthā king, however, advised him to return to his own country and promote risings there so as to distract the Mughul forces. The policy of temple destruction launched by Aurangzīb in 1670 roused the Hindu population of Bundelkhand and Mālwā in defence of their altars; they longed for a bold leader, and just at this opportune moment Chhatra Sāl appeared in their midst and was hailed as the champion of the Hindu faith and Bundelā liberty, who promised to repeat Champat's spirited defiance of the Mughul emperor. The rebels elected Chhatra Sāl as their king; the hope of plunder drew to his side vast numbers of recruits from this martial tribe and discontented Afghāns settled in central India. His earlier raids were directed against the Dhāmoni district and the city of Sironj, the Mughul commandants of which could not cope with him. Many petty chiefs now joined him, and he began to collect *chauth* like the Marāthās. Later, as Aurangzīb became more and more deeply entangled in the Deccan, Chhatra Sāl achieved more brilliant triumphs; the range of his raids extended over the whole of Mālwā, and he captured Kālinjar and Dhāmoni.

The local Mughul officers fought him with indifferent success. In 1705 Fīrūz Jang induced the emperor to make terms with the irrepressible Bundelā chief, and Chhatra Sāl was enrolled as a commander of 4000 and appointed to a post in the Deccan; but after Aurangzīb's death he returned home to resume his career of independence.

Gondwāna, which covers much of the modern Central Provinces and stretches on both sides of the Vindhya range, was another storm-centre in Aurangzīb's reign on account of its vicinity to Mālwā and Berār. The great Gond kingdom of Garha had been dismembered and ruined by Akbar and its royal line sank into obscurity in the middle of the seventeenth century, when the predominance among the Gond people passed to the chiefs of Deogarh and Chāndā. Their accumulated treasure, herds of elephants and collections of gems locally quarried, made them objects of cupidity to the Mughul government. In 1637 the imperialists had invaded the land, stormed Nāgpur (the seat of the Deogarh raja) and exacted the promise of an annual tribute. Arrears in payment led to further invasions in 1655, 1667 and 1669, and the payment of large sums as the price of peace and the promise of heavier tributes from both Deogarh and Chāndā. The Deogarh royal family embraced Islām in order to retain their lands (1670). The Chāndā raja's tribute also fell into arrears. Bakht Buland, the converted Rājā of Deogarh, was deposed in 1691 and his throne given to another Muslim Gond named Dīndār. The latter proved refractory and was expelled by a Mughul force in 1696. A brother of the Chāndā raja now secured the throne of Deogarh by turning Muslim under the name of Neknām. As both these kingdoms were now under mere lads and their old ruling branches ousted, Bakht Buland seized this opportunity and escaped from the imperial army in the Deccan where he was serving as a captain. Returning to Deogarh he raised the standard of rebellion with remarkable tenacity, resourcefulness and success; Berār and Mālwā were his happy hunting grounds and he captured Deogarh and Garha (1699). He also invited the Marāthās and Chhatra Sāl Bundelā to his aid, and with the former as allies attacked 'Alī Mardān Khān, the governor of Berār, but was defeated (1701). His disturbances, however, continued. "During Bakht Buland's reign the rich lands to the south of Deogarh, between the Waingangā and Kānhan rivers, were steadily developed. Hindu and Muhammadan cultivators were encouraged to settle in them on equal terms with Gonds, until this region became most prosperous." Many towns and villages were founded; manufacture and commerce made advances. After the death of Aurangzīb, this chief extended his kingdom over the Seonī district and the old principality of Kherlā. But on the death of his successor, Chānd Sultān (1739), the Marāthā house of Nāgpur secured his kingdom.

Next to Bengal, Gujarāt was the richest province in the Mughul empire. Its wealth was due to its handicrafts, which had a world-wide celebrity, and its commerce, for which its geography gave it exceptional advantage. On its coast were the greatest ports of India, and in Mughul times it was pre-eminently the gateway of India for pilgrims, travellers, merchants, fortune-hunters, and political refugees from Persia, Arabia, Turkey, Zanzibar and even Khurāsān and Egypt. The province had a very composite population and a large foreign strain from very early times, and even its Hindu inhabitants belonged to an immense variety of tribes and degrees of civilisation, which gave an unparalleled diversity to the racial complexion of Gujarāt. Primitive and predatory races were scattered throughout the province, such as the Kolīs in the south, the Bhīls in Bāglān (south-east), the pseudo-Rājputs in the eastern frontier, the Kāthis in the west, and the Girāsiās in most of the districts. The province of Gujarāt was hard to control and in Mughul times it bore the epithet of *lashkar-khez* (bristling with soldiers). It had also an evil reputation for famines since the Middle Ages, and there were five or six terrible outbreaks of crop failure in Aurangzīb's reign. Wars in Rājputāna also used to overflow into Gujarāt by way of the Īdar frontier.

Early in 1706, during the interval between the departure of prince A'zam from Ahmadābād and the arrival of Bīdār Bakht there as governor, the Marāthās took advantage of the unguarded condition of the province. Dhana Jādav entered at the head of a vast force, and at Ratanpur (in Rājpīplā) signally defeated the two divisions of the imperial army, one after another (26 March, 1706). Two Mughul generals, Safdar Khān Bābī and Nazr 'Alī Khān, were captured and held to ransom; their camps were looted, and vast numbers of Musalmans perished or were taken captive. When 'Abdul-Hamīd Khān, the deputy-governor of the province, arrived with another army, he was hemmed round by the victorious enemy near the Bābā Piārā ford, and himself and his chief officers were made prisoners and all their camp and baggage plundered. Then the Marāthās levied *chauth* on the surrounding country and retired after plundering the places that failed to pay blackmail. During these disorders, the Kolīs rose and sacked Barodā. Aurangzīb tried to put down by violence the Isma'īlia heretics, called *Bohrās*, who flourished, and still continue to flourish by trade, in this province. Their teachers were arrested, their funds confiscated, and Sunnī teaching was enforced upon them. Another branch of these sectaries, called *Khojās* or *Mūmins*, consisting mostly of converts from Hinduism, were roused to frenzy by the arrest of their spiritual head, killed the commandant of Broach, captured that city (October, 1685), and held out for a time, until it was reconquered and the fanatics within it massacred.

At the death of Aurangzīb (1707) his empire consisted of twenty-one *sūbas* or separate provinces, of which fourteen were situated in Hindūstān (viz. Āgra, Ajmer, Allahābād, Bengal, Bihār, Delhi,

Gujarāt, Kashmīr, Lahore, Mālwā, Multān, Orissa, Oudh and Tatta or Sindh), and six in the Deccan (namely, Aurangābād, Berār, Bīdar or Telingāna, Bijāpur, Hyderābād and Khāndesh), while one, namely Kābul, lay in what now forms Afghānistān. Another *sūba*, Qandahār or south Afghānistān, had been long lost, and even Kābul was a barren possession, being assessed at a revenue of only four million rupees, little of which was ever realised. The empire embraced, in the north, Kashmīr and all Afghānistān from the Hindukush southwards to a line thirty-six miles south of Ghaznī; on the west coast it stretched in theory to the northern frontier of Goa and inland to Belgaum and the Tungabhadrā river. Thereafter, the boundary passed west to east in a disputed and ever shifting line through the centre of Mysore, dipping south-eastwards to the Coleroon river (north of Tanjore). In the north-east Chittagong and the Monās river (west of Gauhātī) divided it from Arakan and Assam. But throughout Mahārāshtra, Kanara, Mysore and the eastern Carnatic the emperor's rule was disputed and most places had to submit to a double set of masters.

Excluding Afghānistān, the empire of Aurangzīb, about 1690, had a revenue of 334,500,000 rupees on paper, the actual collection being less. This figure stood for the land-revenue alone, and did not include the proceeds of taxes like the *zakāt* (tithe) and *jizya* (poll-tax). The proportion between the lands held as military assignments (*jāgīr*) and crown land (*khālsa sharīfa*) can be judged from their respective revenue demands of 276,400,000 rupees and 58,100,000 rupees. The total armed force of the empire in 1647 was

200,000 troopers with horses brought to the muster and branding,
8000 *mansabdārs*,
7000 *ahadīs* and *barqandāzes*,
185,000 *tābīnān* or additional troopers of the princes, the *umarā* and the *mansabdārs*, and
40,000 foot-musketeers, gunners and rocket-men (i.e. the artillery branch).

These numbers underwent further increase with Aurangzīb's warfare and annexations in the Deccan, until his finances hopelessly broke down under the weight of his military expenditure. To take one illustration, the total number of officers (both *umarā* and *mansabdārs*) increased from 1803 in 1596 to 8000 in 1647 and 14,449 in 1690; so that we can say that Aurangzīb's army bill was roughly double that of Shāh Jahān.

Foreign trade occupied a negligible position in the economics of the Mughul empire on account of its small volume. The state gained from import duties probably less than three million rupees a year (out of which two-fifths came from Surat), so that customs yielded less than 1 per cent. of the total revenue of the state. The value of the

Indian products exported by the English East India Company during the first sixty years of its trade (1612–72) did not average more than 800,000 rupees per annum; in 1681 it had risen to 1,840,000 rupees for Bengal alone. What little India imported from foreign countries was in the main paid for by her export of cotton goods, supplemented by a small variety of raw produce such as pepper, indigo and saltpetre; so that India was economically almost self-supporting (C. J. Hamilton).

The English trade with the East during the first half of the seventeenth century was to a large extent confined to five classes of goods—spices (from the Archipelago and the Spice Islands), raw silk from Persia, saltpetre, indigo and cotton goods from India. A fair quantity of the finer cotton cloths was consumed in England; but for the most part the Company's purchases of cotton goods were made not for England but for the markets of the Further East and of Persia, while India's export trade in silk goods was insignificant, England taking her raw silk chiefly from Persia and China, and her manufactured silk articles from China.

The chief imports into India in Mughul times were silver and gold, copper and lead, high class woollen clothing (for which Europe, and notably France, was the chief supplier), horses (from the Persian Gulf and Khurāsān), spices (from the Dutch Indies), superior brands of tobacco (from America), glass-ware, wine and curiosities from Europe, and slaves from Abyssinia. But the total value of all these, with the exception of the precious metals and broadcloths and other costly woollen fabrics, was very small. Towards the end of the century silk taffetas and brocades began to be exported in larger quantities and a distinct improvement in the dyeing and weaving of silk was effected in Bengal by the experts brought out by the English East India Company from home. The whole Madras coast, from Masulipatam to Pondicherry, and next, but far behind it, Kanara (or the country from Hublī to Kārwār), were the seats of the most productive ordinary cotton industry in India; but the wars following the overthrow of the Qutb Shāhī sultanate and the rise of the Marāthās completely ruined these regions, and the primacy in cotton manufacture passed on to Bengal at the beginning of the eighteenth century.

Aurangzīb was brave in an unusual degree. In him personal courage was combined with a coldness of temperament and a calculating spirit which we have been taught to regard as the special heritage of the races of northern Europe. In addition, he had from early life prepared himself for the sovereign's duties by self-reverence, self-knowledge and self-control. He was a widely read and accurate scholar and kept up his love of books to his dying day. His extensive correspondence proves his mastery of Persian poetry and Arabic sacred literature. To his initiative and patronage we owe the greatest digest of Muslim law made in India, the *Fatāva-i-'Ālamgīrī*. As a prince, he made the highest nobles of his father's court his friends by his tact, sagacity and humility; his career in Shāh Jahān's reign clearly marked him out for pre-eminence in the future. His private life—dress, food and recreations—were all extremely simple but well-ordered. He was absolutely free from vice and even from the more innocent pleasures of the idle rich. The number of his wives fell far short even of the Qurānic allowance of four and he was scrupulously faithful to wedded love. His industry in administration was marvellous; in addition to holding daily courts regularly (sometimes twice a day) and Wednesday trials, he wrote orders on letters and petitions with his own hand and often dictated the very language of official replies. Dr Gemelli Careri, who saw him at Galgalā in 1695 (when the emperor was already seventy-seven years old), "admired to see him endorse the petitions with his own hand, without spectacles, and by his cheerful smiling countenance seem to be pleased with the employment". Though Aurangzīb died in his ninetieth year, he retained to the last all his faculties (except his hearing) unimpaired. His memory was wonderful: "he never forgot a face he had once seen or a word that he had once heard".

But all this long self-preparation and splendid vitality in one sense proved his undoing, as they naturally begot in him a self-confidence and distrust of others which urged him to order and supervise every minute detail of administration and warfare personally. This excessive interference of the head of the state kept "the men on the spot" in far-off districts in perpetual tutelage; their sense of responsibility was destroyed, initiative and rapid adaptability to a changing environment could not be developed in them, and they tended to sink into lifeless puppets. No surer means than this could have been devised for causing administrative degeneration in an extensive and diversified empire like India. Aurangzīb in his latter years, like Napoleon I after the climax of Tilsit, could bear no contradiction, and his ministers became mere clerks passively registering his edicts.

Such a king cannot be called a political genius. He had indeed honesty and plodding industry, but he was not a statesman who could initiate a new policy or legislate for moulding the life and thought of unborn generations. Such a genius, though unlettered and often hot blooded, was Akbar alone among the Timurids of India. Obsessed by his narrow ideal of duty, Aurangzīb practised saintly austerities and self-abasement almost with Pharisaical ostentation. He thus became an ideal character to the Muslim portion of his subjects; they called him *'Ālamgīr, zinda pīr* or a saint who wrought miracles! But the causes of the failure of his reign lay deeper than his personal character. Though it is not true that he alone caused the fall of the Mughul empire, yet he did nothing to avert it, but rather quickened the destructive forces already in operation in the land. He never realised that there cannot be a great empire without a great people.

HINDU KUSH
TIBET
HIMALAYA MOUNTAINS
Kabul
Peshawar
INDEPENDENT PATHAN TRIBES
SULAIMAN RANGE
Jhelum R.
Chinab R.
Ravi R.
Lahore
Qandahar (PERSIA)
Multan
Sutlej R.
Indus R.
Panipat
Delhi
Jumna R.
RAJPUTS
JATS
ARAVALLI HILLS
Agra
Ajmer
Gwalior
Lucknow
Gumti R.
Gogra R.
Ganges R.
Allahabad
Benares
Patna
Brahmaputra R.
Chambal R.
VINDHYA RANGE
Nerbudda R.
GONDWANA
Tributary Chiefs
Chandernagore (French)
Serampore (Danish)
Calcutta (British)
(Portuguese) Diu
SATPURA RANGE
Surat
Tapti R.
Daman (Portuguese)
Aurangabad
Basseini (Portuguese)
Bombay (British)
Chaul (Portuguese)
MARATHAS
KONKAN
Mahanadi R.
Godavari R.
Bimlipatam (Dutch)
Satara
Krishna R.
WESTERN GHATS
Tungabhadra R.
EASTERN GHATS
Masulipatam (French)
Goa (Portuguese)
Pulicat (Dutch)
Madras (British)
Sadras (Dutch)
Pondichery (French)
Fort St. David (British)
Tranquebar (Danish)
Negapatam (Dutch)
Calicut
Kaveri R.
POLYGARS
Cochin (Dutch)
Madura
INDIA
AT THE DEATH OF
AURANGZIB (1707)
Approximate Boundaries
European Settlements thus...Goa (Portuguese)
In Rebellion.........JATS

CHAPTER XI

BAHĀDUR SHĀH, JAHĀNDĀR SHĀH, FARRUKH-SIYAR, RAFĪ'-UD-DARAJĀT AND RAFĪ'-UD-DAULA

THE death of Aurangzīb was followed by a short and sharp contest for the throne which ended in the death of two of his sons and three of his grandsons in the field. His eldest surviving son, Mu'azzam (Shāh 'Ālam), was at Jamrūd when, on 22 March, 1707, he heard of his father's death and set out for Āgra, taking six and a half million rupees from the public treasuries on the way, crowning himself emperor with the title of Bahādur Shāh at the bridge of Shāh Daula, twenty-four miles north of Lahore, and arriving at Āgra on 12 June. He could march in full strength so rapidly because for some years before he had made secret preparations, through his able and energetic revenue minister Mun'im Khān, for the inevitable war of succession by keeping an army in the Jullundur Dūāb, collecting transport animals and boats for bridges on the way, and enlisting large numbers of Rājputs. In the meantime, Bahādur Shāh's second son 'Azīm-ush-shān, the viceroy of Bengal and Bihār, on recall to the Deccan by order of Aurangzīb, had heard of his grandfather's death in Korā, and after enlisting more troops had pushed on to Āgra, occupied that city and laid siege to its fort. With his Bengal treasure (reputed to exceed 100 million rupees) he quickly increased his army to 40,000 men. On the arrival of Bahādur Shāh, Bāqī Khān Qul, the commandant of Āgra fort, capitulated, and thus the new emperor gained possession of the accumulated treasures of the Delhi empire, valued by report at 240 million rupees.

Meantime, A'zam Shāh, after hastening to the dead Aurangzīb's camp at Ahmadnagar, had ascended the throne on 14 March. But his utter lack of money, added to his impatience of advice, uncontrollable temper and insane vanity, doomed his cause to failure from the outset. At the time of Aurangzīb's death his soldiers in the Deccan were starving from their salaries being three years in arrears, and A'zam could give them no relief when dragging them with him to northern India. His promotion of his personal favourites alienated the veterans of Aurangzīb's time. The Turānī party (called *Mughuls* in India), led by Fīrūz Jang, Chīn Qilīch Khān (afterwards Nizām-ul-Mulk) and Muhammad Amīn Khān (later imperial *vazīr* or revenue minister), held aloof from him. Asad Khān and his son Zu-'l-Fiqār (entitled Nusrat Jang), the leaders of the Īrānī party at court, no doubt joined him, but on account of A'zam's incurable defects of character and temper they could do him no good. Leaving

Ahmadnagar on 17 March, A'zam arrived at Gwālior on 11 June. His able son Bīdār Bakht could have forestalled the enemy in the capture of Āgra, the viceroy of which was his father-in-law; but A'zam with fatal jealousy feared that if Bīdār Bakht got possession of the treasures in Āgra fort, he would raise an army of his own and oust his father from the throne. So he had ordered Bīdār Bakht not to increase his army nor advance on Āgra, but wait for him at Gwalior. In this way fifty precious days were lost by the young prince in enforced inactivity in Mālwā, while his father delayed coming up from the south, and the quicker movements of Bahādur Shāh and 'Azīm-ush-shān gave them Delhi and Āgra.

Then Bīdār Bakht, leading his father's vanguard, crossed the Chambal, but was again ordered to wait for him at Dholpur, instead of pushing on to Āgra. An offer from Bahādur Shāh to partition the empire amicably was scornfully rejected by A'zam. The decisive battle took place on 18 June, some four miles north of Jājau and not far from Sāmogarh, and began with an accidental collision of the vanguards, neither side being at first aware of the position or intentions of the other. A'zam had under him 65,000 horse and 45,000 foot musketeers but no large cannon or mortars, and he made the fatal mistake of despising the enemy's large and powerful artillery. Bīdār Bakht was marching with the vanguard three miles ahead of his father, when he sighted Bahādur Shāh's vanguard (under 'Azīm-ush-shān) pitching their advanced tents; his men charged, drove out the guards, burnt the tents and scattered for plunder. But 'Azīm held his ground and was soon reinforced by his father, while aid from A'zam to his son arrived too late. The fierce fire of Bahādur Shāh's army caused terrible havoc among Bīdār Bakht's troops, who had no arms for reply. Hampered by a confused medley of baggage, transport, cattle and followers, blinded by dust, dying of heat, thirst and a sand-storm blowing in their faces, they dispersed without any order in their ranks. They were slaughtered helplessly; Khān 'Ālam, Rām Singh Hārā, Dalpat Rāo Bundelā and many other chiefs on A'zam's side fell. Then the Rājputs and Zu-'l-Fiqār Khān fled from the field, Jay Singh of Amber went over to Bahādur Shāh; many other officers gave up making any exertion. Bīdār Bakht himself was shot dead and his brother Wālā Jāh mortally wounded. When A'zam came up with the main army the battle had already been lost; he was killed with most of his officers, and the remnant of his army broke and fled. The loss on each side was about 10,000 men, but A'zam's army ceased to exist at the end of the day. Bahādur Shāh treated the vanquished most kindly.

Freed from his most formidable rival, Bahādur Shāh lived in peace at Āgra till 12 November, when he set out for Rājputāna. This province he was forced to leave for the Deccan at the end of April, 1708, by the news of Kām Bakhsh's mad acts in the south. That prince had heard of his father's death when on the way to his viceroyalty of Bījāpur and been immediately deserted by the Turānī nobles under Muhammad Amīn Khān. But in Bījāpur he crowned himself emperor and lived for two months settling his government and raising an army. Some conquests were made by his agents, namely the recovery of Wāgingerā, Gulbarga and Hyderābād, besides control over the Karnūl and Arcot districts. But the folly, violence and caprice of this prince, who at the age of forty-three acted like an undeveloped child, and the bitter jealousy between his minister Taqarrub Khān and his paymaster Ahsan Khān, soon ruined his affairs. The minister and his allies succeeded in making Kām Bakhsh believe that Ahsan Khān and his friends wanted to imprison him. So, the helpless deluded prince seized by treachery and tortured to death Rustam-dil Khān (the viceroy of Golconda), Ahsan Khān and many other officers who were suspected of being in the conspiracy; their properties were confiscated and their families ruined. Many other acts of insane cruelty were done by Kām Bakhsh, who now came to be dreaded as a bloodthirsty tyrant. Bahādur Shāh, after crossing the Narbadā on 17 May, 1708, slowly proceeded south and sent a most generous and conciliatory offer of peace to his brother, which was rejected. As he came nearer to Hyderābād, all who could deserted Kām Bakhsh and went over to Bahādur Shāh. On 13 January, 1709, Kām Bakhsh's small force of 350 men was attacked by 25,000 imperial troops under Mun'im Khān and Zu-'l-Fiqār, and the prince mortally wounded, some four miles outside Hyderābād. Shortly after this, because the situation in Rājputāna had grown serious, the emperor set out on his return, and reached Ajmer on 22 June, 1710.

The attack on the Rājputs begun by Aurangzīb inflicted on the Mughul empire a deep and draining wound which was never healed though superficially covered at times. On hearing of this emperor's death Ajīt Singh had recovered his ancestral capital Jodhpur and expelled its Mughul commandant Mihrāb Khān. Bahādur Shāh marched out for Rājputāna in November, 1707, and reached Amber in January, 1708. The dispute for the succession to this state was decided by giving it to Bijay Singh, and the imperialists then advanced towards Jodhpur. Mihrāb Khān defeated Ajīt Singh and occupied Merta (February). Ajīt Singh now made his submission, waited on the emperor like a penitent rebel, and received a command of 3500 and the title of Mahārājā. The emperor returned to Ajmer, but while he was on his way to the Deccan to punish Kām Bakhsh, Ajīt Singh, Durgā Dās and Rāja Jay Singh Kachhwāhā fled from his camp (30 April, 1708). These two rajas joined the Mahārānā Amar Singh of Mewār in a joint resistance to the Mughuls. The Rājputs expelled the commandant of Jodhpur, defeated the commandant of Hindaun-Bayāna, and recovered Amber by a night attack (August). They next killed Sayyid Husain Khān Bārha, the commandant of Mewāt, and many other officers (September, 1708). The emperor, then in the Deccan, had to patch up a truce by restoring Ajīt Singh and Jay Singh to the Mughul service.

After overthrowing Kām Bakhsh and settling the affairs of the Deccan, Bahādur Shah returned to Rājputāna in May, 1710. Negotiations were opened with the two rebel rajas there, and the Sikh rising forced on the emperor a speedy solution of the Rājput trouble. Pardons were granted to them; they waited on him on 21 June and were sent back to their states with presents.

The Sikh revolt now assumed such a character that it threatened to repeat in the north the disruptive work of the Marāthā rising of the south, and totally destroy Mughul peace. Govind Singh, the tenth and last of the Sikh *Gurūs*, had died in November, 1708, without leaving any son behind him. But his followers produced a man who exactly resembled him and secretly sent him to the Punjab, declaring that he was Gurū Govind, miraculously brought back to life for leading his followers in a war of independence against the Muslims. This man was known under the name of *Banda* (Slave) or the sham Gurū, though he took the title of *Sachā Pādishāh* or the genuine Lord. The impostor appeared in the country north-west of Delhi and, calling himself Govind Singh, summoned the Sikhs to join their returned Gurū. He routed the commandant of Sonpat, and soon gathered 40,000 armed men around him, sacked the town of Sadhaurā (twenty-six miles east of Ambāla), killing many of the people, and gained his crowning victory by defeating and slaying Vazīr Khān, the commandant of Sirhind (22 May, 1710), and plundering his entire camp. Then the town of Sirhind itself was taken, and pillaged for four days with ruthless cruelty; the mosques were defiled, the houses burnt, the women outraged and the Muslims slaughtered. Over twenty million rupees in cash and goods fell into Banda's hands here. From Sirhind as a centre Banda plundered and occupied the country around, but his progress southwards from Thānesar was checked by a local Muslim officer. Bands of Sikhs crossed into the Jullundur Dūāb. Shams Khān, the commandant of Sultānpur, gathered a large defence force and drove the Sikhs, with heavy slaughter, back into the fort of Rāhon, from which they fled away after some weeks. They recovered Rāhon, after the Khān's retreat, but the rest of the Dūāb was freed from them. Another Sikh band raided east across the Jumna, plundered Sahāranpur and occupied half of that district, all the people fleeing away at the news of the Sikhs coming. But their attacks on Jalālābād (thirty miles south of Sahāranpur) and two large villages near it were defeated through the desperate courage of the Afghāns and other local volunteers. In the meantime, emboldened by the defeat of Vazīr Khān, the Sikhs assembled at Amritsar resolved to attack Lahore. They ravaged many villages, and reached the suburbs of Lahore, though the city itself escaped. The Muslims of Lahore organised a private expedition by subscription and expelled the Sikhs. Desultory fighting continued, the Sikhs being predominant on the whole, and the north-western road from Delhi was effectively closed.

The crisis drew Bahādur Shāh to the scene. Leaving Ajmer on 27 June, 1710, he reached Sadhaurā on 4 December. Before this, some imperial officers had fought the Sikhs and cleared the road from Sonpat to Sirhind, and also the Jullundur Dūāb. At the approach of the emperor, Banda evacuated Sadhaurā and took post in the fort Lohgarh, at Mukhlispur or Dabar, a place twelve miles north-east of Sadhaurā. Here he had been living like a king and striking coins in his own name.

In the campaign against Lohgarh the imperialists suffered greatly from the broken jungly nature of the country, excessive rainfall, intense cold, scanty supplies and heavy losses among the horses and cattle, besides terror of the Gurū's magical powers. The vanguard was led by Rustam-dil Khān, who made an advance of eight miles to the bank of the Som, after a hard fight in which 1500 Sikhs fell. On 10 December, 1710, the Sikh entrenchments on the top of the Dabar hills were attacked by prince Rafī'-ush-shān, the minister Mun'im Khān, Zu-'l-Fiqār, Chhatra Sāl Bundelā and other generals. The Sikhs lost heavily from both artillery fire and close fighting. At midday the imperialists halted outside instead of pressing into the fort of Lohgarh. Soon afterwards the captured Sikh trenches were entered by plunderers from the Mughul army, who set fire to what they could not carry off; several powder magazines were thus blown up. Other hill tops were still occupied by the Sikhs and the fighting was still undecided in the passes. Taking advantage of this confusion, Banda escaped down the other side of the hill with his chief men. The Sikh opposition ceased by evening-time. Many women, children and horses were captured, besides three cannon and seventeen light pieces. The flight of Banda nullified the victory of the imperialists. The emperor then turned to punish the hill-Rājās of Garhwāl and Nāhan, for having assisted Banda to escape. Two million rupees in coins were dug out of Lohgarh.

Desultory fighting with the Sikhs continued for some years after. Sirhind was reoccupied by the imperialists in January, 1711. In March Banda descended from the hills and raised fresh disturbances in the north Punjab plains. Shams Khān, on his way to Kasūr, was attacked and slain by an overwhelming force of Sikhs under the Gurū himself. The Bārī Dūāb fell an easy prey to the Sikhs, many inhabitants having fled in terror, and even the Rechnā Dūāb was devastated. But in June the Gurū was defeated and driven into the hills of Jammū near Pasrūr by Muhammad Amīn Khān and Rustam-dil Khān. Quarrels between these two generals led to the pursuit being abandoned and the operations slackened. Later, on the death of Bahādur Shāh (27 February, 1712), Banda took advantage of the war of succession to recover Sadhaurā and restore the fortifications of Lohgarh, so that all the work of Bahādur Shāh was undone. The siege of Sadhaurā in the reign of Jahāndār Shāh was abandoned after a few months (December, 1712).

After the campaign against Banda, Bahādur Shāh halted for some time in the Sirhind district, and then started for Lahore, which was reached on 11 August, 1711. With his four sons he encamped outside the city. Here he spent the last six months of his life, avoiding all serious work and engaged only in gardening, as he was now seventy (lunar) years old and Aurangzīb's treatment of him had destroyed what little spirit and activity he may have once possessed. Early in his reign Bahādur Shāh had ordered the title *wasī* (executor, *sc.* of the Prophet's will) to be added after the name of 'Alī in the Friday prayer recited for the sovereign in every public mosque. This was a Shiah innovation and implied a reflection upon the first three Caliphs as usurpers, which the Sunnīs resented. The emperor's order had provoked opposition and riots in many places, as the Sunnīs form the immense majority of the Muslim population of India. Arrived at Lahore, Bahādur Shāh called his opponents to a debate in his court and warmly pressed his point. The Sunnīs of the city, with the support of the Afghān soldiers, formed a body of nearly a hundred thousand men to resist the change by force. The emperor at first ordered his chief of artillery to cause the new prayer to be read in the principal mosque of Lahore on 2 October, 1711; but on that day, while a vast crowd, ready for rioting, was gathered in the streets, the emperor gave way, the old form was recited and peace was preserved. After declining in health for some weeks, Bahādur Shāh fell ill on 24 February, 1712 and died on the 27th. He was buried in the courtyard of 'Ālamgīr's mosque near the shrine of Qutb-ud-dīn Kākī outside Delhi.

Bahādur Shāh had a mild and calm temper, great dignity of behaviour, and excessive and inconsiderate generosity of disposition. He was learned and pious, without any bigotry, and possessed a power of self-control and profound dissimulation which was styled personal cowardice by his rival A'zam Shāh. He was incapable of saying no to anybody, and his only idea of statesmanship was to let matters drift and patch up a temporary peace by humouring everybody, without facing issues and saving future trouble by making decisions promptly and courageously. Still, the traditions of the dignity of the empire and of good administration left by Aurangzīb continued through his short reign, as he inherited his father's able officers and treated them with confidence and respect. On his accession, his own weak position and softness of fibre, coupled with advanced age, prevented him from asserting his will in any matter. He had promised the post of minister to Mun'im Khān, his able deputy and most useful servant of the days of his princehood, and yet he could not resist the demand of Asad Khān (Aurangzīb's minister) to be the first officer of the state. In his usual spirit of compromise, Bahādur Shāh tried to please both by creating Mun'im Khān *Vazīr* or revenue minister and Asad Khān *Vakīl-i-mutlaq* or prime minister. But this division of authority pleased neither of them, while it complicated the administration. He conferred titles with a profusion which made them ridiculous. The Turānī nobles (their chiefs being of the family of the Nizām) were kept in the background during this reign.

At the time of Bahādur Shāh's death all his four sons were with him at Lahore. The eldest, Mu'izz-ud-dīn (surnamed Jahāndār Shāh), was slack and negligent and without money or troops; 'Azīm-ush-shān (the second and his father's favourite and most influential adviser) was the ablest and strongest in resources among the brothers; Rafī'-ush-shān (the third son) was very jealous of 'Azīm, while the youngest, Jahān Shāh, was an invalid. Zu-'l-Fiqār Khān had secretly brought the other three princes together for joint action against 'Azīm and they had made a solemn agreement for partitioning the empire among themselves, with Zu-'l-Fiqār as minister for all the three! The death of Bahādur Shāh was followed by the immediate seizure of his camp by 'Azīm-ush-shān; the nobles deserted their posts and hastened to join one or other of the princes, the ordinary people in the imperial camp fled to the city for shelter and their property was looted by the ruffians. Terrible noise and confusion raged everywhere; the soldiers ill-treated and plundered the paymasters for their arrears. But 'Azīm-ush-shān took up "the attitude of a helpless waiter on events"; instead of striking quickly while his forces were so superior and his rivals unprepared, he stood on the defensive and thus gave them time to enlist fresh troops and to strengthen their coalition and artillery through Zu-'l-Fiqār's exertions. 'Azīm-ush-shān despised his rivals with the insane pride of Muhammad A'zam on the eve of Jājau, and with the same result. The three other princes soon besieged 'Azīm's camp, commanding three sides of it with their artillery. Battles at close quarters took place on 15 March and the next day, both being very obstinate and bloody contests. 'Azīm's soldiers were cooped up within their camp and suffered heavily from an artillery fire to which they could give no adequate reply, while their enemies could freely retire and refresh themselves after every fight. Zu-'l-Fiqār's contrivance led to the desertion of most of 'Azīm-ush-shān's suffering troops. Finally, a general attack was delivered on 17 March, 'Azīm's chief adherents were killed, his trenches penetrated, and his followers reduced to 2000 men only. Then a shot from a heavy gun wounded the elephant on which he was seated and the maddened beast rushed into the Rāvī river, where it and its rider were both swallowed up by a quicksand.

Zu-'l-Fiqār Khān, who had thus alone brought about the fall of the most powerful of the claimants to the throne, now became supreme in the state. He threw aside the two youngest princes in favour of Jahāndār Shāh; a quarrel broke out among the three brothers for the division of the booty taken from 'Azīm-ush-shān. The contest between Jahāndār Shāh and his youngest brother Jahān Shāh was fought out on 26 and 27 March, artillery playing the decisive part in these encounters. Jahān Shāh at first defeated his rival and put him to flight, but in the confusion caused by the dust and lack of generalship his troops were scattered in small isolated groups, he was shot dead and his army melted away. Rafī'-ush-shān, who had stood aloof during this duel, attacked Jahāndār in the morning of the 28th, hoping to gain an easy victory over the latter's exhausted troops. But most of his Turānī officers deserted him in the field, his raw levies fled away, and he was shot dead when fighting on foot against desperate odds. Jahāndār Shāh thus became the undisputed master of the empire of Delhi.

On the accession of Jahāndār Shāh, Zu-'l-Fiqār Khān became minister. Severe vengeance was taken on the leading supporters of his defeated rivals; they were subjected to ruthless confiscation, imprisonment and even execution. New men were raised to power as partisans of the new emperor and useful tools of the all-powerful minister. Even Muhammad Karīm, the eldest son of 'Azīm, was put to death in cold blood by order of Zu-'l-Fiqār. Jahāndār Shāh arrived at Delhi from Lahore on 22 June, 1712, and learnt that Farrukh-siyar, the second son of 'Azīm-ush-shān and his deputy in the government of Bengal, had advanced to Patna to prepare for an attempt on the crown. So a large force was sent against him under prince 'Azz-ud-dīn (Jahāndār's eldest son), too young and inexperienced a youth for such a command, to wait and watch at Āgra. Arrived at Delhi Jahāndār Shāh spent his time entirely in pleasure and merry-making with his concubine La'l Kumārī. Under infatuation with her he indulged in every kind of mad freak and low amusement. All decency was abandoned; her kinsmen robbed and mismanaged the state, the highest dignitaries were insulted and thwarted by the favourite's low-born associates, the crown was stripped of dignity and prestige in the public eye, and the entire tone of society and administration was vulgarised. La'l Kumārī received an allowance of twenty million rupees a year, besides clothes and jewels, and imitated the style of Nūr Jahān, the famous queen of Jahāngīr, while the army and civil officers starved. The emperor spent every night in drunken frolics with boon companions of the lowest rank in society; religious practices were openly abandoned. Punishment was not slow in coming. Zu-'l-Fiqār was regarded with bitter jealousy by 'Alī Murād Khān Jahān, the emperor's foster-brother (created Amīr-ul-Umarā), who always tried to contradict and thwart him by influencing the emperor against his minister.

Muhammad Farrukh-siyar, now aged thirty (lunar) years, had heard of his father's downfall when at Patna and had proclaimed himself emperor there (April, 1712). His resources were very poor and none of the nobles supported him in his ambition for the throne. Even men who owed their promotion or life to 'Azīm-ush-shān either stood aloof from Farrukh-siyar or went over to his enemies. But the young prince was saved and raised to fortune by the Sayyid brothers Hasan 'Alī (afterwards created 'Abdullah Khān, Qutb-ul-Mulk) and Husain 'Alī (afterwards Amīr-ul-umarā, Fīrūz Jang), who were destined to be remembered in Indian history as the king-makers and the worst examples of royal ingratitude. Their family was settled at Bārha in the upper Ganges-Jumna Dūāb, between Meerut and Sahāranpur, and its members were known for their unshaken bravery and capacity for command, which gave them the right to the honour of leading the imperial vanguard in battles. These two had held important commands in Aurangzīb's reign and risen to the rank of 4000 for their service at Jājau. They had subsequently fallen under Bahādur Shāh's displeasure and lost their employment owing to a quarrel with his minister. But 'Azīm had taken them under his protection and made them his deputies in Allahābād and Bihār respectively. Appealed to by Farrukh-siyar's mother, Husain 'Alī at Patna undertook to support that prince's ambition. His elder brother, the deputy governor of Allahābād, was hesitating when he heard that he had been dismissed by Jahāndār Shāh; so he openly espoused Farrukh-siyar's cause (August, 1712), seized the large Bengal treasure then on the way to the capital, and with it raised an army for that prince. These examples tempted other nobles to join Farrukh-siyar's side; the Rājputs of Bhojpur in west Bihār brought in a large accession of strength, 40,000 good fighters. Money was secured by seizing the Bengal revenue at Patna and robbing the Dutch factory in that town and rich Indians.

Farrukh-siyar left Patna on 18 September, 1712, at the head of 25,000 men, and advanced to Khajuhā (where Shujā' had been defeated by Aurangzīb in 1659), his forces swelling on the way. Here he encountered (24 November) prince 'Azz-ud-dīn, who had arrived with 50,000 men to bar his path. Chhabelā Rām Nāgar, the commandant of Karā-Mānikpur, deserted to Farrukh-siyar, and his money loans most opportunely relieved the serious distress of that prince and his army.

After some days of distant firing, Farrukh-siyar decided that 'Azz-ud-dīn's entrenched position should be stormed on 28 November. But in the preceding night that prince took flight to Āgra, abandoning all his property, treasure and camp, which were next morning plundered by the victorious enemy. On hearing of his son's defeat, Jahāndār Shāh moved from Delhi to Āgra; but his whole government had fallen into confusion and bankruptcy and he could not raise a large army nor equip his soldiers. All the gold and silver in Delhi fort and the imperial workshops were taken away and even the gold coating of the palace ceiling was broken up and distributed to the soldiers, and finally all the store-houses of goods accumulated since the age of Bābur were emptied indiscriminately by the troops. Leaving Delhi on 9 December, the emperor reached Āgra on the 29th, where he was joined by 'Azz-ud-dīn and Churāman with his Jāt tribesmen, and then advanced to Sāmogarh. Farrukh-siyar arrived near the opposite bank of the Jumna on 2 January, 1713. Lack of boats forced him to halt for some days, and in the meantime treachery did its work in Jahāndār Shāh's army—the Turānī chiefs being bribed to stand by during the coming battle. Sayyid 'Abdullah crossed over by a shallow ford five miles up stream (6 January) and Farrukh-siyar on the 8th. The news spread consternation in Jahāndār's army, and it fell back on Āgra. The decisive battle was fought on 10 January outside that city. Jahāndār Shāh's cause was ruined by his character and the state of parties at his court. He was entirely guided by La'l Kumārī, a vulgar thoughtless dancing-girl from the streets, his army chiefs (with the exception of Zu-'l-Fiqār Khān) were worthless upstarts, the imperial commanders were fatally divided by bitter personal jealousies and quarrels, in addition to the cross-currents of antagonism between the Turānī and Īrānī nobles as a class, each trying to thwart all the acts of the other. Zu-'l-Fiqār, who had won the throne for Jahāndār almost single-handed, now showed nothing of his usual energy and sagacity. With no unity of command and no devotion to their master's cause, the imperial army was paralysed and helplessly left the initiative to its enemy.

The imperial vanguard was drawn up in two divisions of 15,000 men each, under Jānī Khān (right) and Kokaltāsh Khān (left), with 10,000 more men behind them as supports under Sabhā Chand, 'Abdus-Samad Khān and Muhammad Amīn Khān. Farrukh-siyar's front was led by Sayyid 'Abdullah (left) and Husain 'Alī (right). Shortly after 3 o'clock in the afternoon the rival vans engaged and the battle began. Jahāndār's artillery did great havoc among Sayyid Husain 'Alī's ranks, while his rear was assailed by the imperial supports under 'Abdus-Samad Khān. Husain 'Alī, fighting desperately on foot, was wounded, rendered senseless and left buried under a heap of the slain; many of his retainers and clansmen were wounded or killed by Kokaltāsh Khān's onslaught. Meantime, Farrukh-siyar's men under Chhabelā Rām and Muhammad Khān Bangash had attacked the imperial right (under Jānī Khān), but after severe losses on both sides a desperate charge by these two commanders ended in Jānī Khān being shot, at which his troops fled away, but the victors also fell back.

Next the imperial artillery was turned upon Sayyid 'Abdullah Khān (at the rebel left front), who maintained his ground though his followers were reduced to only 200 of his clansmen. During this confusion, Churāman the Jāt began to plunder the elephants and baggage in the rear of Jahāndār's army. But Zu-'l-Fiqār, who had 25,000 fresh troops under him, stood motionless without reinforcing his front division or completing the victory by a home charge into the enemy's centre where only 6000 disheartened men stood round Farrukh-siyar. He ordered a forward movement of his division when it was too late. For, in the meantime, a force detached by 'Abdullah had checked Kokaltāsh Khān's advance upon Farrukh-siyar and killed that general as well as the chief of the imperial artillery. Thus both the leaders of the imperial vanguard were killed and their men driven back upon their centre, which was thrown into confusion by such crowds of fugitives. Taking advantage of this change in the tide of battle, 'Abdullah Khān, with his vanguard raised to 4000 men, which rapidly increased during his advance, worked his way unopposed to the rear of Jahāndār Shāh. The treacherous Turānī nobles stood aloof throughout the contest, and the imperial rear was without any defender. 'Abdullah at once attacked the elephants carrying Jahāndār Shāh's harem, and next made a desperate charge on his centre from the rear. This unexpected attack on the women, the activity of the Jāt plunderers looting the baggage and the double fighting in Jahāndār's front and rear, caused indescribable uproar and confusion. The imperial bodyguard fled away and the emperor himself escaped towards Āgra concealed in La'l Kumārī's howdah without any of his commanders knowing of it; his army abandoned the field at the approach of night, amidst hopeless disorder and loss from the stampeding elephants and recklessly audacious plunderers. Zu-'l-Fiqār Khan, whose personal troops remained intact, withdrew in good order towards Āgra, unmolested by the victors, and next day took the route to his father (Asad Khān) at Delhi, where he arrived on 14 January.

From the field of battle Jahāndār Shāh fled on his concubine's elephant to a place of shelter outside Āgra, and there shaved off his beard and moustaches, put on the disguise of a poor man, and early in the morning set out for Delhi in a small covered two-wheeled bullock-cart in the company of La'l Kumārī. Living like the poorest people and undergoing unwonted privations on the way, they entered Delhi by stealth at night (15 January), and the emperor immediately went to Asad Khān and appealed to him for protection and armed assistance from Zu-'l-Fiqār. But the crafty old minister dissuaded his son Zu-'l-Fiqār from making any further effort on behalf of Jahāndār Shāh, and in violation of their oaths to him decided to imprison him and hand him over to Farrukh-siyar's vengeance as the best means of gaining the new emperor's favour and retaining their wealth, titles and influence in the state. Zu-'l-Fiqār, who distrusted Farrukh-siyar in view of the harm he had done to that prince's family, wished to strike out for independence, but Asad

Khān rejected Jahāndār's cause as hopeless. Then, they deceived the fallen emperor with false promises of support, lured him within their reach, made him a prisoner, confined him in the fort, and informed Farrukh-siyar of this act of devotion to him. On 11 February, when Farrukh-siyar arrived near Delhi, Jahāndār was murdered in prison by his order.

In the morning after the battle, Farrukh-siyar enthroned himself (11 January, 1713) and marched to Āgra. Large numbers of nobles and officers came over to him every day. Sayyid 'Abdullah was sent to Delhi in advance to take possession of the capital, and attach the property of all the partisans of Jahāndār Shāh. The poll-tax was abolished. A letter was received from Asad Khān offering submission on behalf of himself and his son Zu-'l-Fiqār and reporting that he had imprisoned Jahāndār. Being thus reassured, the new emperor left for Delhi, which he entered in triumph on 12 February. In the meantime 'Abdullah had occupied Delhi and been welcomed by its chief men. He promised Asad Khān and Zu-'l-Fiqār to present them to the emperor and use his influence to save them from his anger. Many partisans of the old *régime* were arrested and their property seized for the state. Even Sabhā Chand, the revenue minister in charge of reserved lands and Zu-'l-Fiqār's right-hand man, was cast into prison and his house confiscated, in spite of Zu-'l-Fiqār's exertions on his behalf. Kind messages were sent by the new emperor to Zu-'l-Fiqār and his father. These two nobles were men of exceptional capacity and experience in civil administration and war; they were the last prominent survivors of the great age of Aurangzīb; and therefore if they were allied with the Sayyid brothers their power would be perpetuated by their unrivalled ability and reputation. Hence, Mīr Jumla,[1] the chief of the new men and personal favourites of Farrukh-siyar, plotted to clear his own path to power by destroying the old nobility. This party of selfish courtiers consisted of the intimate friends and personal attendants of the new emperor and their policy was to create an opposition to the Sayyid brothers. Their leaders were Mīr Jumla, who had gained young Farrukh-siyar's confidence when judge of Dacca and Patna, and Khvāja 'Āsim (surnamed Samsām-ud-Daula, Khān Daurān), an intimate playfellow of that prince in his boyhood. They first interposed between Sayyid 'Abdullah and Asad Khān and persuaded the latter that it would be better for him to approach the emperor through his personal favourites than through the domineering minister. With false vows of safety and support, Taqarrub Khān, the emissary of this party, induced Asad and Zu-'l-Fiqār to go to the emperor's camp with him. Farrukh-siyar, after giving them a deceptive welcome and even presenting jewels and robes of honour, sent Asad Khān away and treacherously captured Zu-'l-Fiqār, taunted him with his hostile acts

[1] The title given to 'Ubaid-ullah, Shar'iyat-ullah Khān, Turānī.

towards 'Azīm-ush-shān and his family (especially the murder of Muhammad Karīm, his younger son) and then had him strangled by Qalmaq slaves (13 February). His body was left exposed for a day. All the houses and property of Zu-'l-Fiqār and Asad were confiscated, their families were stripped of all and kept under guard. In this unhonoured and forlorn condition, Asad Khān lingered till his death at the age of eighty-eight (15 June, 1716).

Farrukh-siyar had naturally to give the highest offices in the realm to the king-makers. Sayyid 'Abdullah was made minister with the titles of Qutb-ul-Mulk Zafar Jang Sipāh-sālār; Sayyid Husain 'Alī was appointed first paymaster with the titles of Amīr-ul-umarā Fīrūz Jang. The post of second paymaster was conferred upon Muhammad Amīn Khān Chīn (the Turānī leader) with the titles of I'timād-ud-Daula Nusrat Jang, while his son Qamar-ud-dīn became paymaster of the Ahadīs.[1] Several secondary posts at court were given to the new emperor's personal favourites, and by reason of their intimacy with him they exercised very much real power over the administration and often succeeded in thwarting the ostensible ministers by influencing the emperor behind their backs. The chief examples of these "king's friends" were Mīr Jumla, the superintendent of the pages, and Khvāja 'Āsim, the superintendent of the audience-hall. New viceroys were sent to many of the provinces with this change of sovereigns, notably 'Abdus-Samad Khān (Lahore), Rājā Jay Singh Sawāi (Mālwā) and Sayyid Khān Jahān Bārha (Ajmer). The viceroyalties of Multān and Bihār were conferred on the two Sayyid brothers, with permission to govern them by deputy. Shahāmat Khān (now created Mubāriz Khān) was confirmed in the government of Gujarāt. Bengal was nominally given to Mīr Jumla, but its former revenue minister Murshid Qulī Khān (now created Ja'far Khān Nasīrī) was ordered to govern it as his deputy in addition to being substantive viceroy of Orissa. The six provinces of the Deccan were conferred on Nizām-ul-Mulk (Chīn Qilīch Khān Bahādur, son of Ghāzī-ud-dīn Fīrūz Jang of Aurangzīb's time), with his head-quarters at Aurangābād and deputies in each of the component provinces. The Nizām was the ablest man in the empire and now rose to the foremost position, which he retained till his death in 1748. He was one of the leaders of the Turānī party, the other being his father's first cousin Muhammad Amīn Khān (now second paymaster). The Turānī soldiers who came from Central Asia (north of the Oxus) enjoyed high favour and influence in the Mughul empire, being fellow-countrymen of the Timurid dynasty. They formed a large proportion of the army, and their leaders were remarkable for military skill and capacity for civil government alike. The foreign Muslim immigrants whose home was Persia and Khurāsān, known as the Irānīs, were also singularly gifted, especially in revenue and secre-

[1] Gentlemen troopers, W. Irvine, *Army of the Indian Moghuls*, p. 43.

tariat work, but they were Shiahs, and being comparatively few in number exerted less influence in the state except when the very highest offices were filled by their members. These two groups of foreign adventurers in India were constantly at war with each other for power and position at the Delhi court, and though the earlier strong emperors kept them under control, their rivalry became the predominant characteristic of Indian history under the weak later Mughuls and one of the causes of the downfall of the empire. The India-born Muslims, conspicuously inferior in intellect and capacity, looked upon both with envy and half-veiled but futile hostility. The Afghāns, though enlisted in large numbers in the imperial army, did not count in Indian politics till after 1748.

After securing himself on the throne Farrukh-siyar by the advice of Mīr Jumla put many members of his rival's party to death and created a reign of terror. Among the chief victims were Sa'd-ullah Khān (the deputy minister), Hidāyat-kesh (the chief news-writer), Sīdī Qāsim (the police prefect of Delhi), Sabhā Chand (Zu-'l-Fiqār's all-powerful man of business) and Shāh Qudrat-ullah of Allahābād, a learned Sūfī, whose fault was that though highly trusted and favoured by 'Azīm-ush-shān he had not joined Farrukh-siyar in his march against Jahāndār. Sabhā Chand's tongue was cut out, all the others were put to death. Next, Farrukh-siyar, in order to make it impossible for the Sayyid brothers to displace him and set up some other prince of the house of Bābur, resolved to blind the more prominent and more energetic of the members of the imperial family held in captivity, and this cruel form of mutilation was inflicted upon 'Azz-ud-dīn (eldest son of Jahāndār), Wālā Tabār (son of Muhammad A'zam Shāh) and Humāyūn Bakht (Farrukh-siyar's younger brother, a boy of ten), on 21 January, 1714. A little later a heroic Qalmaq woman-servant named Shādmān (surnamed Razā Bahādur Rustam-i-Hind) and the witty but indelicate poet Ja'far Zatallī were put to death for disrespect to the new reign.

Farrukh-siyar was utterly thoughtless, fickle and weak, and devoid of constancy or fidelity to his own promises. Like all weak men he was swayed by the latest adviser, and having resolved to do a thing could never hold to it long but soon sank into despair and went back on his undertakings. Constitutionally incapable of governing by his own will and controlling others, he would not trust any able agent, but was easily inspired with a childish suspicion of his ministers and induced to enter into plots for their overthrow. But his cowardice and fickleness made it impossible for any plot to succeed under his leadership, and his instigators had to suffer from the vengeance of the fruitlessly offended ministers. From the very commencement of his reign a party hostile to the Sayyid brothers was formed at his court by his personal favourites and attendants and they did their best to clog the wheels of the administration by inducing him to interfere in the minister's department and to issue secret orders contradictory to those that he had publicly sanctioned in the presence of his minister. The distribution of offices of state and of the confiscated property of the defeated party led to frequent and bitter differences between the Sayyid brothers and Farrukh-siyar as instigated by his intimate circle (chiefly Mīr Jumla). Mīr Jumla easily poisoned his ears against the Sayyid brothers by suggesting that they were amassing fortunes and increasing their forces and adherents with a view to ousting Farrukh-siyar after a time and seizing the throne for themselves. As early as March, 1713, the quarrel between the emperor and his ministers had become so bitter and open that the latter ceased to attend at court. But in a few days, Farrukh-siyar's courage failed, he personally visited 'Abdullah in his house and patched up a truce by an effusive display of friendliness and trust.

The Sayyid brothers were first separated by the Rājput campaign. Ajīt Singh Rāthor had taken advantage of the wars of succession following the death of Bahādur Shāh to expel the imperial officers from Jodhpur, forbid cow-killing and the call to prayer in his territory, and even to capture Ajmer. Husain 'Alī Khān, the head paymaster, was appointed to chastise him. But Farrukh-siyar, with the low cunning of weak minds, while publicly issuing orders in support of the expedition, sent secret letters advising the enemy to oppose and thwart the imperial general and even to assassinate him, with promises of the emperor's favour if he was successful. Leaving Delhi early in January, 1714, Husain 'Alī marched to Ajmer and thence to Merta, the gateway of Mārwār. His army underwent great hardship from the sandy deserts they had to cross and the want of water on the way. Ajīt Singh, terrified by Husain 'Alī's military reputation (earned in Aurangzīb's days) and the vigorous advance of his army, fled further and further into the desert of Bīkāner. The country now occupied by the Mughuls was settled, the peasants conciliated, and outposts established, as Husain 'Alī advanced. In spite of the approach of the hot weather and scarcity in his camp, the Mughul general resolved to make a forced march on Jodhpur. But just then Ajīt Singh made an abject surrender. He promised to give one of his daughters in marriage to Farrukh-siyar, to send his son Abhay Singh to attend at court, and himself to serve in the emperor's army when called upon (May). Thus fully successful, Husain 'Alī returned to Delhi, after restoring order in the province of Ajmer. But during his absence from the capital, his enemies, led by Mīr Jumla, had obtained entire control over the emperor. Sayyid 'Abdullah was a rough soldier who now pursued pleasure only and left all the state affairs in the hands of his subordinates, particularly a *baniā* (grocer) named Ratan Chand who used to look after the Sayyid's private estates. This man, abusing his influence over the sleepy minister, used to extort large bribes from office-seekers, as the price of issuing letters of appointment under the imperial seal to them. But Mīr Jumla, in rivalry with the minister, used to affix the seal to letters of appointment, without passing them through the minister's office. Thus, the minister suffered in both influence and emoluments, and this circumstance further strengthened the ranks of his enemies. While Husain 'Alī was absent in Rājputāna, 'Abdullah felt that power was slipping out of his grasp at court and that Mīr Jumla was acting as *de facto* minister. Farrukh-siyar even went so far as to urge him to resign his office. On hearing of these things, Husain 'Alī hurried back to the capital (16 July, 1714).

Farrukh-siyar's personal favourites urged him to neutralise the Sayyid brothers' predominance in the state by bringing forward two nobles and placing them on an equality with the former, so that all malcontents would gather under the leadership of these two men. In pursuance of this policy, Mīr Jumla and Khān Daurān were promoted to the rank of 7000, and placed in charge of 5000 guardsmen each. Their relations also received commands, and thus their combined forces threatened to overshadow the armed strength of the minister and the paymaster. No order was issued by the emperor without the approval of these two favourites. Even plots against the Sayyids' lives were formed in the palace. Meantime, Husain 'Alī had got possession of the secret letters sent against him by Farrukh-siyar to Ajīt Singh, and also learnt of the plotting at court. The two brothers ceased to attend on the emperor, and stood on the defensive in their own houses. At last, in December, Husain 'Alī and his brother wrote to the emperor, offering to resign as they had lost his confidence and he was resolved on their destruction. Farrukh-siyar's spirit quailed at this threat, and he entered into negotiations for conciliating them; Mīr Jumla, his favourite selection for the post of minister, "was only a carpet-knight; he talked well, but evaded dealing with the kernel of the matter"; he shrank from undertaking the overthrow of the Sayyids by force. Muhammad Amīn Khān, sick of Farrukh-siyar's treachery and weakness, refused to stir unless the emperor personally headed the army against the Sayyid brothers. Farrukh-siyar now totally lost heart and made a complete surrender to the Sayyids. They spared Khān Daurān, who had made a secret pact to serve them faithfully, but secured from the emperor Mīr Jumla's removal from court to the viceroyalty of Bihār, and the dismissal of Mīr Jumla's chief agent Lutf-ullah Khān Sādiq. In return, Husain 'Alī agreed to leave the court as viceroy of the Deccan. This settlement was effected in December, 1714. Husain 'Alī marched for the south in April, 1715, with the power to appoint and remove all officials in the Deccan (including even the commandants of the important forts). But the treacherous Farrukh-siyar wrote secretly to Dāūd Khān, newly appointed governor of Burhānpur, to resist Husain 'Alī. The attempt ended in Dāūd Khān's defeat and death (September, 1715).

On 27 September, 1715, Farrukh-siyar was married to Ajīt Singh's daughter, who had been converted to Islam on that day. The celebrations were held on a most gorgeous scale a month and a half later, because at the time of the marriage the emperor was suffering from an internal disease and only the skill of Dr William Hamilton, the surgeon of the English embassy, succeeded in curing him early in December next.

The most important feat of arms of this reign was the extermination of Banda. This Gurū had built a large fort near Sadhaurā since his last defeat and from it dominated the neighbourhood. 'Abdus-Samad Khān (the new governor of Lahore) laid siege to this fort. The Sikh garrison offered a brave and obstinate defence, making almost daily sorties; but the lines of investment being completed, their provisions were exhausted and one night they escaped from it to Lohgarh, where Banda himself was residing. 'Abdus-Samad Khān immediately pushed on to that fort; a panic seized the Gurū and his men and they evacuated Lohgarh without firing a shot (October, 1713). Soon afterwards Banda issued from his refuge in the hills and began to ravage the north Punjab plains again, plundering the parganas of Rūpar, Kalānaur and Batālā. Their atrocities drove the population into wholesale flight from the raided country. But a strong combination of imperial officers forced the Gurū to fall back from Kot Mīrzā Jān to Gurdāspur (44 miles north-east of Amritsar). Here he was invested by a large Mughul force under 'Abdus-Samad Khān (April, 1715). After almost daily fighting with the garrison, the Mughul soldiers raised a high earthen wall with a trench behind it all round Gurdāspur, so as to enclose the fort completely on all sides. Next, a stockade was constructed nearer the walls with a deep and wide ditch at its foot, so as to prevent the escape of the garrison. The Sikhs fought most gallantly, inspiring the Mughul troops with a terror of their prowess; but all attempts to break through failed and the Mughuls captured some of the bastions and gates. After all their food had been exhausted and they had undergone unspeakable privations, the Sikhs surrendered unconditionally (17 December, 1715). The captive Gurū and his 740 followers were paraded through Delhi in a humiliating procession like that in which Shambhūjī had been conducted to Aurangzīb's camp, and then they were put to a cruel death at the police office of Delhi (15 March, 1716). The Sikhs showed wonderful patience and strength of mind, and welcomed death as a deliverance; not one of them accepted the offer of Islām to save his life. Banda himself and his little son of three years were brutally hacked to death on 19 June. After Gurū Govind's death, his widow Mātā Sundarī and his alleged adopted son Ajīt Singh had set up as the rival heads of the Sikh sect; only a few families followed either of them. On the death of the two their spiritual succession was claimed by Jāhī Singh the son of Ajīt (who lived at

Muttra) and Sāhib Dei (or Kumārī Dūlā), the betrothed of Govind Singh, who lived at Delhi, each getting only a few followers.

Towards the close of Aurangzīb's reign, the Jāt peasantry of the region round Bharatpur (west of Āgra) were organised into a predatory power by Rājā Rām and after the death of that chieftain by Churāman, who hovered about the contending armies and greatly increased his wealth and armed strength by plundering both sides during the campaign of Jājau and the civil war between Jahāndār Shāh and Farrukh-siyar. Bahādur Shāh had won him over by the grant of an office and employed him in his campaigns. His robberies on the highway and extortions in other people's assignments made it necessary for the Delhi government to subdue him. Rājā Jay Singh Sawāī begged the command and invested Churāman in his new fort of Thūn (November, 1716). The stronghold was well armed and provisioned and surrounded by a thick thorny jungle. But Jay Singh built guard-houses all around it and was heavily reinforced by the emperor. The Jāts outside it and their village allies continued their depredations, making the roads unsafe and capturing a rich caravan worth two million rupees. The siege dragged on for twenty months. Churāman then opened negotiations with the minister over the head of Jay Singh, agreeing to pay a tribute of five million rupees. Under orders from the court, Jay Singh had to raise the siege, and Churāman visited Delhi in April, 1718.

Farrukh-siyar was constantly plotting the overthrow of the Sayyid brothers, but his own character was extremely timid and fickle, and the successive agents chosen by him, after intriguing for some time and even making armed preparations, either gave up the attempt as hopeless or went over to the Sayyids as more capable of protecting their personal interests. This went on throughout the reign, with the result that the central administration of the empire became more and more confused and weak, while the provinces fell into greater neglect than before. The life of the state seemed to consist in alarms and excursions which all ended in smoke; the only form of activity was lying talk and court intrigue, while the work of the government stood still or inevitably drifted towards anarchy and bankruptcy. About the middle of June, 1714, it was hoped to use Nizām-ul-Mulk (who had been ousted from the viceroyalty of the Deccan by Sayyid Husain 'Alī) as a lever for overthrowing the two brothers, but in two years he left the court in disgust, without attempting or even agreeing to make any *coup*. Mīr Jumla, who had been packed off to Patna owing to an earlier conspiracy against the minister, returned to Delhi (January, 1716) by secretly travelling like a veiled woman. The emperor, admonished by the minister for this breach of promise, ordered Mīr Jumla to retire to Lahore. But Mīr Jumla's troops mutinied for their arrears of pay and threatened the capital with civil war. At last they were pacified by part payment and disbanded, while Mīr Jumla was compelled to go to Lahore.

Farrukh-siyar's next idea was to raise up some of the older nobles of Aurangzīb's time as a counterpoise to the Sayyid brothers. 'Ināyat-ullah Kashmīrī, who had been disgraced at the beginning of the reign, now received the rank of 4000 and was made imperial revenue minister (April, 1717). He tried to purge the administration of the abuses that had recently crept into it and to restore the regulations and discipline of Aurangzīb's time. He reimposed the poll-tax[1] and proposed to reduce or resume the assignments which officials had continued to secure in excess of their legal dues or by fraud. He thus raised a host of enemies in that corrupt court, especially in Ratan Chand, the trusted man of business of the minister, and his friends and underlings. Ratan Chand used to lease the collection of revenue to the highest bidder, instead of dealing with the cultivators directly by servants of the state, and the result of this vicious system was rack-renting and the ruin of agriculture. Sayyid 'Abdullah, instigated by his evil genius Ratan Chand, refused to give up the practice of leasing out the collection; he also shielded revenue officers who had misappropriated public money. These facts as well as Farrukh-siyar's policy of restoring the older men to office embittered the relations between the emperor and his minister. Muhammad Murād, a glib-tongued Kashmīrī officer of the court, wormed himself into the emperor's favour and secretly proposed many plans for destroying the Sayyids. The credulous Farrukh-siyar believed in this man's capacity and courage, gave him the rank of 7000, and appointed him superintendent of the imperial harem with the title of I'tiqād Khān (May, 1718), lavishing money and gifts on him. But the Kashmīrī braggart, knowing his own incapacity, suggested Sarbuland Khān as the instrument best fitted to overthrow the minister. This noble was summoned to court and promoted to the rank of 7000, with the title of Mubāriz-ul-Mulk (July, 1718), but learning that Farrukh-siyar intended to appoint Muhammad Murād as minister he drew back from the conspiracy and resigned his post.

Next a plot to surround and seize Sayyid 'Abdullah at the '*Īd* prayer of 27 August was anticipated and foiled by the minister appearing in full force. Then the foolish emperor sounded Mahārājā Ajīt Singh, but the latter, knowing the inconstancy and deceitfulness of Farrukh-siyar, thought it better to give his adhesion to the Sayyid brothers, and henceforth became very friendly with them. Nizām-ul-Mulk was approached with no better success.

At the end of September, 1718, Mīr Jumla, who had been recalled by Farrukh-siyar from Lahore, reached Delhi, but immediately went over to the minister's camp. Even Samsām-ud-Daula lost the confidence of the volatile emperor and made friends with Sayyid 'Abdullah. In short, all his hostile plots were immature and failed to produce anything except talk and excitement in Delhi. The

[1] A "legal dirham" was struck at Lahore to commemorate this. See *Punjab Catalogue of Mughul coins*, no. 2271.

excessive favour shown to Muhammad Murād (I'tiqād Khān) alienated most of the former adherents of the emperor.

On hearing of the recall of Mīr Jumla, the minister had written to his brother to come back from the Deccan. Husain 'Alī left Burhānpur on 14 December, 1718, pretending that he was escorting to the capital an alleged son of Muhammad Akbar (the fourth son of Aurangzīb) delivered to him by the Marāthā Rājā Shāhū. His army numbered 25,000 cavalry, besides 10,000 foot-musketeers and artillery. Some 11,000 Marāthās under the Peshwā Bālājī Vishvanāth and Khande Rāo Dābhāde accompanied him. Their help was secured by promising to Rājā Shāhū (*a*) the *chauth* or one-fourth of the revenue of the Deccan, (*b*) the *sardeshmukhī* or 10 per cent. on the collections, (*c*) the confirmation of Shivājī's hereditary dominions, and (*d*) the release of Shāhū's mother and half-brother from captivity in Delhi, besides a cash salary to each Marāthā soldier. The Sayyid marched rapidly on, the province of Mālwā, lying in his way, having been vacated by its viceroy, and he arrived outside Delhi on 16 February, 1719.

In the meantime, Sayyid 'Abdullah, the minister, had given up visiting the emperor in anger at his perfidy. But in December Farrukh-siyar made an abject surrender to him, even exchanging turbans with the minister. He next tried to conciliate, with his minister's mediation, Ajīt Singh, Sarbuland Khān, Jay Singh Sawāī and some other grandees. He lavished honours upon the Sayyid brothers, raising them to the command of 8000 each, and made new appointments at the minister's dictation. Muhammad Amīn Khān, who had come away from his province of Mālwā, was dismissed by the emperor (20 January, 1719), and then made terms with the minister in self-defence. On 7 February 'Abdullah visited Nizām-ul-Mulk and seemingly conciliated him. At the near approach of Sayyid Husain 'Alī, Farrukh-siyar was in mortal fear lest he should be deposed and the alleged grandson of Aurangzīb crowned in his stead. He humbled himself in every possible way and granted all the demands of the Sayyids. At their first interview (23 February) he placed his turban on Husain 'Alī's head. But spies reported conspiracies formed by the emperor and his personal attendants to attack Husain 'Alī when off his guard in the imperial presence, and he decided to end such manœuvres once for all.

In the morning of 27 February, 1719, Sayyid 'Abdullah entered the palace with Ajīt Singh and his own adherents and troops, occupied the gates, office rooms and bed-chambers, and placed his own guards on all sides of it. In the afternoon, Husain 'Alī marched into the city from the suburbs, at the head of thirty to forty thousand men and strong artillery, while his Marāthā auxiliaries were posted outside the palace gates. Inside the palace there was a stormy scene between the emperor and the minister, the latter taunting him with ingratitude and perfidy and the former abusing his minister in uncontrollable anger. The rumour arose that the emperor had been deposed, and the city lay motionless in terror of a deadly outbreak.

Next day (28 February), shortly after dawn, there was a brawl in the streets between the Mughul retainers of Muhammad Amīn Khān and the Marāthās crowding the streets, and the latter were assailed and driven back by the citizens. A panic seized the Marāthās, they could offer no defence, and lost some 1500 of their number besides all the property on their persons. The wildest rumours spread in the city and added to the confusion and unrest. Several nobles appeared in the streets with their contingents and tried to fight their way to the fort. But the Sayyids were firmly in possession of the palace and their well-planted artillery scattered their foremost enemies. In the afternoon the nobles, learning that all was over with Farrukh-siyar, withdrew to their homes.

After his interview with the minister on the 27th, Farrukh-siyar had hidden himself in the female apartments. Next morning, when the tumult and street fighting began, Husain 'Alī from his house in the city wrote to his brother within the fort to put an end to Farrukh-siyar by force, otherwise he would have to enter the palace for settling the business. The riot raging in the city showed that no time was to be lost. Sayyid 'Abdullah sent his men who broke open the door of the harem, entered and brought away Rafī'-ud-Darajāt (a son of Rafī'-ush-Shān), who was immediately seated on the Peacock Throne and proclaimed emperor. Then a party of Afghāns was sent into the harem; they pushed away the ladies and seizing Farrukh-siyar dragged him with blows and abuse to the minister, who had him immediately blinded. The fallen emperor was kept in prison for two months, and then strangled (27–28 April, 1719). He lies buried in Humāyūn's tomb.

Farrukh-siyar "was strong neither for evil nor for good.... He was for ever letting 'I dare not' wait upon 'I would'. For seven years the State was in a condition of unstable equilibrium, and it is not too much to say that Farrukh-siyar prepared for himself the fate which finally overtook him. Feeble, false, cowardly, contemptible, it is impossible either to admire or regret him" (Irvine). His deposition by the Sayyid brothers cannot, therefore, be called wrong. "But their way of doing what had become almost a necessity was unduly harsh. Blinding a deposed king was the fixed usage.... But the severity of the subsequent confinement was excessive; and the taking of the captive's life was an extremity entirely uncalled for.... The Sayyids were forced into action by a regard for their own lives and honour" (Irvine).

Rafī'-ud-Darajāt was a very intelligent youth of twenty, but already seized with consumption when placed on the throne. He lived and died as a captive of the Sayyid brothers. They restored peace to the realm and reassured the alarmed public by leaving most of the old arrangements and office distributions unchanged. The poll-tax was again abolished to appease the Hindus. Nizām-ul-Mulk, who still maintained obstinate neutrality, was sent to Mālwā as viceroy, to get his Mughul troops out of Delhi. The Marāthā contingent was sent back with royal orders (dated 13 and 24 March) confirming the promises made to them. The two brothers quarrelled over the distribution of the treasure seized in the palace and the forfeited assignments of Farrukh-siyar's partisans.

On 18 May the garrison of Āgra fort, instigated by Mitra Sen (a Nāgar Brāhman of local influence), refused to recognise Rafī'-ud-Darajāt and proclaimed Nīkū-siyar (son of Akbar), who was kept in prison there, as emperor, with Mitra Sen (now created Rājā Bīrbal with the rank of 7000) as his minister. The imperial treasure hoard in the fort was used to enlist troops for the new sovereign. But the rebellion did not spread beyond the fort walls; Nīkū-siyar's two great friends, Jay Singh Sawāī and Chhabelā Rām, held back, and he wrote to the Sayyid brothers inviting them to accept him as emperor, in return for the recognition of their rank and honours.

Rafī'-ud-Darajāt grew rapidly weaker from his disease, and was deposed on 4 June, 1719, dying of consumption a week afterwards. His elder brother, Rafī'-ud-Daula, was enthroned (6 June), with the title of Shāh Jahān the second. He too lived within the fort, a prisoner of his two ministers in all matters, even in his private life. Ināyat-ullah, the brother of Farrukh-siyar's mother, began to raise an army for overthrowing the Sayyids. But his plot was detected and he was seized at Delhi (10 June, 1719) and thrown into prison. Jay Singh Sawāī was the rallying point of the discontented nobles, several of whom fled to him.

Husain 'Alī marched to Āgra and pressed on its siege vigorously. The walls and even the pearl mosque were damaged by his fire, but no breach or mine was completed. After a month the garrison began to suffer from scarcity of provisions. Nīkū-siyar's brother, in trying to escape, was captured. At last, on 12 August, the fort was surrendered, Nīkū-siyar was sent to another state prison and Mitra Sen committed suicide.

Jay Singh having advanced from Amber with hostile intent, 'Abdullah marched out of Delhi with the new emperor on 15 July, and arrived at Vidyāpur near Fathpur-Sīkrī on 1 September. Here Husain 'Alī arrived in a few days, and the two brothers made a division of the spoils taken at Āgra. Rafī'-ud-Daula was a very sickly youth, and much addicted to opium. An attack of diarrhœa in such a constitution baffled all the royal physicians and he died in the camp on 17 September, but the fact was kept concealed for nine days. The Sayyids, who had been already looking out for his successor, crowned Raushan-Akhtar, the son of Jahān Shāh (the fourth son of Bahādur Shāh), under the title of Muhammad Shāh, on 28 September, 1719.

CHAPTER XII

MUHAMMAD SHĀH

THE new emperor, though weak and inexperienced, was not so feeble as his two predecessors, but the condition of the empire was now such that none but an Akbar could have restored the imperial authority.

The Sayyid brothers were still all powerful at court, but the antagonism of the Turanian nobles and their own dissensions and unfitness for their positions were undermining their power, and the great provinces of the empire were only nominally subordinate to the imperial authority.

Ja'far Khān, who had originally been 'Azīm-ush-Shān's lieutenant in the province of Bengal, now ruled as viceroy the provinces of Bengal, Bihār and Orissa. The viceroyalty of the six provinces of the Deccan was held by Sayyid Husain 'Alī Khān Amīr-ul-Umarā, who derived his wealth and power from this great charge and who was represented at Aurangābād, during his absence at court, by his nephew, 'Ālim 'Alī Khān. Ajīt Singh of Jodhpur, a fine ally of the Sayyids, held, besides his own state, the government of the great provinces of Gujarāt and Ajmer. The province of Mālwā was held by Nizām-ul-Mulk, the leader of the Turanian party among the nobles, who was bitterly hostile to the Sayyids. He had been induced by a promise of the viceroyalty of Bengal to acquiesce in their deposition of Farrukh-siyar and when the measure had been carried out had been forced to content himself with the provincial government of Mālwā. Considering himself deceived he departed for Mālwā with an ill grace on 3 March, 1719.

The Allahābād province was held by Chhabelā Rām, who had been devoted to Farrukh-siyar and so resented the treatment of that prince that he had only been restrained by a rebellion in his own province from taking up arms on behalf of Nīkū-siyar. Chhabelā Rām might now be said to be in rebellion and the Sayyids were meditating an attack on Allahābād.

Sayyid 'Abdullah Khān, with the emperor, marched, on 14 October, from Fathpur-Sīkrī to Āgra and was about to open negotiations with Chhabelā Rām when the latter suddenly died. His nephew Girdhar Bahādur opened negotiations for the surrender of the strong fortress of Allahābād in return for appointment as governor of Oudh. He accepted these terms but delayed so long, on flimsy pretexts, that a force was sent to besiege Allahābād.

Budh Singh of Būndī, chief of the Hārā clan of Rājputs, had opposed the Sayyids' treatment of Farrukh-siyar and his kinsman

Bhīm Singh of Kotah sought to obtain the support of the powerful brothers to oust Budh Singh from Būndī and to usurp the position of chief of the Hārās. The Sayyids sent a force to assist Bhīm Singh with instructions, after completing this task, to remain on the confines of Mālwā and observe the movements of Nizām-ul-Mulk, whose intention of establishing himself in the Deccan was already suspected.

Meanwhile the Sayyid brothers had quarrelled over the spoils of Āgra. The younger claimed the spoils as he had taken them, while the elder maintained that they should be divided. After an acrimonious dispute Sayyid Husain 'Alī Khān was obliged to surrender over two million rupees to his brother and the two were never again on their former terms of amity. At the same time Sayyid 'Abdullah Khān incurred much odium by leaving the management of all public affairs in the hands of Ratan Chand, whose interference with ecclesiastical appointments caused such scandal that even his master was provoked to utter a mild rebuke.

Girdhar Bahādur had strengthened the defences of Allahābād, which he still hesitated to surrender. At length he said he would deal with nobody but Ratan Chand, who was accordingly sent, on 10 March, 1720, to negotiate the surrender. A month later Girdhar, leaving the gates of the fort open, marched off to take over his province. The evacuation was celebrated at Āgra as a great victory won by the imperial arms.

Nizām-ul-Mulk had done his utmost to restore order in Mālwā and to strengthen himself for a conflict with the Sayyids. He increased their dislike of him by employing Marhamat Khān, who had been dismissed from the post of commandant of Māndū. Marhamat Khān justified the selection by capturing Sironj and Bhīlsa from some Rājput rebels whom the Sayyids had ordered Nizām-ul-Mulk to punish. This success was so distasteful to Husain 'Alī that his service was unrecognised, and Nizām-ul-Mulk was warned by his cousin that the Sayyids, as soon as they had finished with Nīkū-siyar and Girdhar Bahādur, intended to attack him. He accordingly began to enlist troops in large numbers and Husain 'Alī abused his agent at court. A protest from Nizām-ul-Mulk led to a decree recalling him from Mālwā on the ground that it was necessary to place Mālwā under the control of the viceroy of the Deccan. The offer of a choice of other provinces failed to allay the suspicion that his destruction was intended, the movements of troops on the borders of his province confirmed this, and private letters from the emperor and his mother complaining of the Sayyids' usurpation of all authority removed any scruples which may have oppressed him. There was no longer any question of rebellion against the emperor. Action taken against the Sayyids would be an attempt to release him from the hands of gaolers. Nizām-ul-Mulk heard that mace-bearers were on their way from Āgra to compel him to return to court and on 9 May he crossed the

Narbadā and invaded Khāndesh, the northernmost province of Husain 'Alī's viceroyalty.

The Sayyid brothers quarrelled again over the question of the manner in which he should be dealt with, but the more vigorous counsel of the younger prevailed, Dilāvar 'Alī Khān was sent in pursuit and steps were taken to pursue him and to bar his way to the south.

Meanwhile Nizām-ul-Mulk had been active. He gained possession of the strong fortress of Asīr by the bribing of its garrison, whose pay was two years in arrears, and imprisoning its aged and incompetent commander. A few days later Burhānpur was occupied. A step-mother of the Sayyids was in Burhānpur, and the men of her escort, in their terror, offered to surrender all valuables carried by the party on condition that the lives and honour of their charges were spared. Nizām-ul-Mulk behaved gallantly. He refused to accept anything, sent a present of fruit to the children, and provided an escort to conduct the whole party in safety to the Narbadā. Early in June he turned northwards to meet the pursuing force, which was composed of picked men, including a large number of Bārha Sayyids, but their valour was no match for the tactics of Nizām-ul-Mulk, who gained a complete victory near Khandwā. A forced march to Burhānpur of a detachment of the troops which had taken part in the battle of Khandwā arrested the further progress of an army which was advancing from the south.

These successes dismayed the Sayyid brothers and various plans of action were discussed. Conciliatory letters and an imperial rescript promising Nizām-ul-Mulk the viceroyalty of the Deccan were estimated at their true value, in view of the continued presence of the Deccan army in the field. The rainy season rendered any rapid military movement impossible, and after some futile negotiations and much tedious marching and counter-marching through the heavy soil of Berār the armies met between the towns of Bālāpūr[1] and Shevgāon[2] in Berār. On 10 August both armies advanced to the attack. One historian has asserted that Nizām-ul-Mulk's cause was desperate and that his defeat was averted only by the death of the opposing commander, 'Ālim 'Alī Khān, the nephew and deputy of Husain 'Alī Khān. Many of the troops on the losing side, with the facility of those who fight for gain alone, transferred their services to the victor. A few days after the battle the governor of Hyderābād and his brother, who had announced that they were marching to the aid of the Sayyids, made their submission to Nizām-ul-Mulk in his camp, his authority was established in the viceroyalty of the Deccan, and he sent the head of Sayyid 'Ālim 'Alī Khān to the emperor as that of a rebel.

Husain 'Alī was already preparing to march to the Deccan when

[1] 20° 40′ N., 76° 50′ E. [2] 20° 48′ N., 76° 45′ E.

camel-riders, on 27 August, brought to Āgra the news of 'Ālim 'Alī's defeat and death. The Sayyid brothers were overwhelmed with grief and consternation and could determine on no course of action. At length it was decided that the emperor should march with Sayyid Husain 'Alī Khān to the Deccan and that Sayyid 'Abdullah Khān should administer from Delhi the northern provinces of the empire.

The Mughul nobles, both of the Turanian and of the Iranian factions, were now weary of domination by the Sayyids and Muhammad Amīn Khān, the leader of the former, who occasionally spoke Turkī to the emperor, having ascertained his resentment of their actions, formed a conspiracy to remove Husain 'Alī. Among the conspirators was Mīr Muhammad Amīn, a Sayyid of Nīshāpur who had lately received the title of Sa'ādat Khān and had also as a Sayyid and a Shiah, been a client and favourite of Husain 'Alī. The assassin, Mīr Haidar Beg, another Sayyid, was found by Muhammad Amīn Khān from his own contingent.

On the morning of 9 October, when Husain 'Alī, having made his obeisance to the emperor at the camp a short distance to the east of Toda Bhīm[1] which the army had just reached, was being borne towards his own tents Mīr Haidar Beg and one or two other Mughuls approached his palanquin and complained loudly of their treatment by their master, Muhammad Amīn Khān, who, they said, embezzled their pay. Husain 'Alī, who had ridiculed a warning that a plot against his life was on foot, beckoned to Mīr Haidar Beg, whom he knew by sight, and as the latter approached as though to present his petition turned to take a pipe from a pipe-bearer who stood on the other side of the palanquin. Mīr Haidar Beg, seizing his opportunity, drew his long knife and plunged it into Husain 'Alī's side, and then, dragging his body from the palanquin, sat astride it and began to hack off the head. The murderer was slain by a young cousin of the murdered man, who was in his turn put to death by some Mughuls.

Muhammad Amīn Khān at once appeared on the scene and carried the Sayyid's severed head into the emperor's tents, but Muhammad Shāh shrank from them and retired into the women's apartments. A conspirator threw a shawl over his head and, rushing into the tent of the women, seized Muhammad and took him to the scene of the murder, the elephants were brought up, and the party mounted. The Sayyid's head was raised aloft on a bamboo, the drums were beaten and orders were given that his tents and treasure should be plundered. Ratan Chand, who was accompanying the army to the Deccan, was seized and imprisoned.

Sayyid 'Abdullah Khān received by a camel-rider a scrap of paper from Ratan Chand informing him of the assassination of his brother.

[1] 26° 55′ N., 76° 49′ E.

Sending on his son-in-law and a few others ahead to Delhi to proclaim one of the imprisoned princes of the house of Tīmūr as emperor, he continued his march.

On the day following the assassination Muhammad Shāh held a formal audience at which Muhammad Amīn Khān was appointed minister and promotion was freely showered on the conspirators. Muhammad Amīn Khān and the cowardly Khān Daurān were both promoted to the command of 8000 horse, a rank hitherto restricted to princes of the imperial family; the new minister's son, Qamar-ud-dīn Khān, received the command of 7000, and Sa'ādat Khān of 5000 horse.

It was decided to turn northward and deal with 'Abdullah Khān, and by 14 November the imperial army reached the neighbourhood of Hasanpur, on the Jumna, about fifty miles south of Delhi.

The prince selected by the Sayyids' party for the dangerous honour of the throne was Ibrāhīm,[1] a brother of the two puppet emperors, Rafī'-ud-Darajāt and Rafī'-ud-Daula. He was proclaimed at Delhi on 14 October, two days before the arrival of 'Abdullah Khān, who assembled troops—many of which were of very poor quality. His army marched out to the Qutb Minār on 2 November and on the 14th reached Bilochpur, a village on the Jumna about five miles north of Hasanpur.

The battle, which began on 15 November, was throughout the first day chiefly a duel of artillery. The impetuous valour of the Sayyids of Bārha, who had gathered round their leader, held the imperial troops in check but 'Abdullah Khān's artillery was hopelessly outclassed by the imperial guns, which were not only far superior in weight of metal but were admirably served. Many of his raw and undisciplined troops melted away before the fire of the imperial guns, so that of 40,000 horse and 18,000 foot with which he had taken the field in the morning no more than a few thousands remained with him in the evening. There was a bright moon and the slightest movement in his camp drew on it the fire of the artillery, which was not only active during the night but was advanced to within a short distance of his position. By morning only a few of his relations and a thousand veteran troops remained; though they charged the imperial army, valour was of no avail. Nearly all the leaders were slain, wounded, or captured, and Sayyid 'Abdullah Khān and his wounded brother were taken and 'Abdullah was led before the emperor. 'Abdullah and his brother were eventually placed in the custody of Haidar Qulī Khān. Ratan Chand had been beheaded before the emperor's elephant at the beginning of the battle.

Prince Ibrāhīm was arrested in a mango grove at Bagpur on the Jumna, sixteen miles north of Hasanpur, and carried before Muhammad Shāh, who, recognising that he had been merely a pawn in

[1] Coin was actually struck in his name [Ed.].

'Abdullah's game, received him kindly and inflicted no penalty. But he was sent back to his prison at Delhi.

On 23 November Muhammad Shāh entered his capital in triumph and received provincial governors from the Punjab, Oudh and Rājā Jay Singh of Amber. Nizām-ul-Mulk and the lieutenant-governor of Orissa, who could not reach Delhi so soon, sent expressions of their loyalty, congratulations on the emperor's victory, and contributions to his treasury. A proclamation at the beginning of the reign had decreed the levy of the *jizya* and the levy was now confirmed but was suddenly abandoned at the instance of Jay Singh of Amber and Girdhar Bahādur, whom it was not politic to offend.

On 9 January, 1721, Muhammad Shāh married the daughter of Farrukh-siyar, and on 30 January the minister, Muhammad Amīn Khān, died of colic. His death was attributed to the magical arts of a Persian adventurer named Mīr Muhammad Husain, who calling himself Namūd announced himself as the prophet of a new religion, described in a volume of scripture in a strange language of which he was the sole interpreter. He had acquired a considerable following, and Muhammad Amīn Khān, whose fierce bigotry was notorious, resolved to punish the heresiarch and sent soldiers to arrest him. When the colic which had already attacked the minister suddenly grew worse, Namūd was taxed with having cast a spell upon him and admitted that he had. He declined to remove it and predicted his oppressor's immediate death. The fulfilment of his prediction greatly increased his influence among the vulgar and secured him from the attacks of the powerful. Namūd died two or three years later and was succeeded by his son, who bore the fanciful name of Numā Namūd. This avaricious successor deprived his father's chief disciple Dūjī Bār of the share of the offerings which he had hitherto enjoyed and Dūjī Bār in his wrath exposed the fraud. When the fabrication of the creed and scriptures was known the sect lost all its followers save a few fools.

The duties of minister were entrusted as a temporary measure, and pending the arrival at court of Nizām-ul-Mulk, to 'Ināyat-ullah Khān the Kashmīrī, an old noble of Aurangzīb's reign, Qamar-ud-dīn Khān received his father's title of I'timād-ud-Daula, and Sa'ādat Khān was appointed to the government of Āgra.

Ajīt Singh of Jodhpur, who had been a partisan of the Sayyids and still held the government of Ajmer and Gujarāt, refused to recognise the new government and assumed the state of an independent sovereign. Complaints of his tyranny and, above all, of his bigotry and intolerance, reached the court and orders were issued dismissing him from the government of both provinces. So strong was the sentiment aroused in Gujarāt by the raja's misgovernment that his deputy was attacked and expelled from the province, and the Mughul deputy had no difficulty in taking his place. In the province of Ajmer, contiguous to the contumacious raja's own state, it was less easy to provide, as none of the nobles at court was willing to undertake the task. Ajīt Singh invaded Ajmer with 30,000 horse, and news of this checked a Mughul officer who started. Sa'ādat Khān was summoned from Āgra to punish the rebel, but when he reached Delhi he could find nobody to accompany him and the emperor either could not or would not supply him with the funds for his troops. Intelligence was now received that the officer who had first advanced had entered the province of Ajmer and had plundered some of its villages, but all the plunder had been retained by his starving troops, who were in arrears of pay, and he had fled to Amber, to Jay Singh, and returned his commission as governor of Ajmer. While the courtiers wavered as to the order to be taken with Ajīt Singh, Nizām-ul-Mulk started from the Deccan, and the news brought Ajīt Singh to his senses. On entering Ajmer he rebuilt mosques which had been destroyed by his orders, allowed the butchers to kill cattle for food, and withdrew his former prohibition of the Muslim call to prayer. He then wrote to court a humble petition promising that, if he were allowed to retain Ajmer, he would be loyal and submissive in future, and this was granted.

Nizām-ul-Mulk had started from Aurangābād for Delhi on hearing the result of the battle of Hasanpur, but at the news of Muhammad Amīn Khān's appointment as minister he returned immediately to his capital. His ambition was to establish virtual independence in the Deccan and to control at Delhi the affairs of the empire. The Marāthās were already the chief obstacle in the south, and when he failed to attain his object at Delhi he was mean enough to free himself in the south by encouraging them to extend their ravages to the northern provinces of the empire.

He was dealing with disturbances in Bijāpur and the Carnatic when the news of Muhammad Amīn Khān's death reached him. Regarding the emperor's refusal to fill the place at once as an indication that it was reserved for him, he marched northwards, and was presented to the emperor at Delhi on 29 January, 1722. The jealousy and the intrigues of the courtiers delayed for a short time his appointment as minister, but on 21 February the emperor presented him with the pen-case symbolical of the post and he entered upon his duties. Meeting with interference and opposition he ordered his chief opponent, Haidar Qulī Khān, to repair to his province. The order was obeyed, but Haidar Qulī Khān's conduct in Gujarāt was as embarrassing as his behaviour at court. His violence and eccentricity now developed into mania, and he boasted that he would overthrow Nizām-ul-Mulk.

The new minister's unpopularity increased daily. Courtiers were alienated by his arrogance and the emperor by the strictness of his discipline. Some even encouraged the maniac Haidar Qulī Khān, but his administration of Gujarāt became such a scandal that wiser counsels prevailed and he was dismissed. He had, however, grown so strong in Gujarāt that only one of the most powerful of the nobles could depose him. The choice naturally fell on the minister as the most capable and least desired at the capital, and Nizām-ul-Mulk was appointed to the government of Gujarāt, to be held in addition to his post of minister and the viceroyalty of the Deccan. He left Delhi on 12 November and marched for Gujarāt. Haidar Qulī Khān, who decided that it would be folly to oppose him and had no desire to encounter him, left Gujarāt for Delhi by another route, and Nizām-ul-Mulk, finding no resistance, sent his deputy into Gujarāt and set out on his return march to Delhi.

Sayyid 'Abdullah Khān had recently been the cause of dissensions between the courtiers, some of whom advocated his release. The majority, however, persuaded the emperor that his removal was necessary, and on 12 October, 1722, he was poisoned.

Before Nizām-ul-Mulk left Delhi for Gujarāt Sa'ādat Khān, who held the government of Āgra, received the title of Burhān-ul-Mulk, by which he will henceforth be known, and was appointed to the government of Oudh, in addition to that of Āgra. The Jāts to the west and north-west of Āgra had long been a source of trouble. Their chief, Churāman, though he had sworn allegiance to Muhammad Shāh and was ostensibly ranged on his side at the battle of Hasanpur, had plundered the camps of both armies indiscriminately, and now exhibited scarcely a pretence of subordination either to the governor of Āgra or to the emperor. The deputy at Āgra, while riding abroad, was shot dead by a Jāt. Burhān-ul-Mulk set out from Oudh to avenge the death of his lieutenant, but Khān Daurān, who had resented his appointment to two such important provinces as Āgra and Oudh, in the absence of Nizām-ul-Mulk made the outrage a pretext for transferring the government of Āgra to Rājā Jay Singh of Amber.

Jay Singh received an order to crush the Jāts. Their country lay between Jay Singh's capital and the seat of his new government, and he attacked them on his way to Āgra. A family quarrel gave him the help of Badan Singh, Churāman's nephew, in the siege of Thūn,[1] in the course of which Churāman quarrelled with his son Muhkam Singh and poisoned himself. Muhkam Singh fled from Thūn, which was occupied by Jay Singh's troops on 19 November, and Badan Singh, in exchange for an undertaking to pay tribute regularly to Delhi, was recognised as Rājā of Dīg, where he laid the foundations of the Jāt state of Bharatpur,[2] which has played a prominent part in the later history of India.

The confirmation of Ajīt Singh in the government of Ajmer had been due to weakness rather than to clemency, and his tenure of Ajmer, sanctified by the shrines of Mu'īn-ud-dīn Chishtī and several

[1] 27° 23′ N., 77° 7′ E.

[2] See vol. v, pp. 374–5 and 577.

lesser saints, was repugnant to Muslim sentiment. Haidar Qulī Khān's prompt obedience to the order recalling him from Gujarāt and his reckless audacity led to his appointment as governor of Ajmer, from which he expelled the raja's officers.

On 5 July, 1723, Nizām-ul-Mulk arrived at Delhi, but soon found his position at court insupportable. His gravity and austerity had unfitted him for intercourse with courtiers who were rather boon companions than statesmen. Muhammad Shāh now neglected public business entirely beyond passing orders on the petitions of suitors and place-seekers recommended by his intimate associates, who reaped a rich harvest from the fees which they levied from their clients. Those to whom the execution of the duties of minister had fallen during Nizām-ul-Mulk's absence in Gujarāt were loth to surrender their power and he enjoyed the title without the power of his place. He ventured to offer serious advice to his sovereign, entreating him to abandon the practice of letting the reserved lands in farm, to abolish the wholesale bribery which prevailed at court, to exact the levy of the *jizya*, as in the time of Aurangzīb, from unbelievers, and to requite the services rendered by Tahmāsp I of Persia to his ancestor, Humāyūn, by marching to relieve Tahmāsp II, now beset by Afghān invaders, who had sacked and occupied his capital. This advice was rejected; Nizām-ul-Mulk obtained permission to make a shooting tour in the Dūāb, and on 18 December left the court.

News of Marāthā inroads in Mālwā and Gujarāt now reached Delhi, and Nizām-ul-Mulk, who was at Soron, near the Ganges, informed the emperor that these required his immediate presence in his own provinces, and, without waiting for formal permission, marched at once into Mālwā. On his approach the Marāthās, who had only followed his own secret advice, retired across the Narbadā and Nizām-ul-Mulk encamped for some time at Sehore. Here he learnt of the existence at Delhi of an elaborate conspiracy to compass his overthrow.

His post of minister had been bestowed on his cousin Qamar-ud-dīn Khān, I'timād-ud-Daula, and now his enemies persuaded the weak emperor to send secret instructions to Mubāriz Khān to oppose his return to the Deccan, promising as a reward the viceroyalty of that region, the greatest place in the empire.

Mubāriz Khān had served Sayyid Husain 'Alī Khān before Nizām-ul-Mulk, who had indulgently treated him, and had left him at Hyderābād as governor, when the viceroy went to Delhi.

On reaching his capital at Aurangābād late in June, 1724, Nizām-ul-Mulk discovered that Mubāriz Khān's preparations for attack were far advanced and that the Marāthās had extended their operations in the Deccan. Remonstrances proved fruitless, and in August, hearing that Mubāriz Khān's army was already in motion, he left Aurangābād to meet him.

Mubāriz Khān attempted, by passing far to the east of Aurangābād, to draw him away from the city, hoping to be able to descend on Aurangābād from the north and occupy it before his intentions were ascertained. He evaded Nizām-ul-Mulk, but the viceroy turned northward to meet him. The two armies met at Shakarkhelda[1] in Berār on 11 October. The historians represent the battle as having been fiercely contested. Nizām-ul-Mulk's army was at one time thrown into some confusion by the unsuccessful attempt of a force of the enemy to plunder its camp and baggage, a stratagem usual in the Deccan. But the losses of Nizām-ul-Mulk, which amounted to only three officers and a few rank and file, indicate that he met no very desperate resistance. Mubāriz Khān and two of his sons were killed and two other sons taken prisoners, and the losses in killed amounted to three thousand, including many officers.

Nizām-ul-Mulk, to commemorate his victory, gave Shakarkhelda the name of Fathkhelda, or "village of victory", and it is still known indiscriminately by either name. He sent the severed head of his opponent, in bitter irony, to court, as that of a rebel, and tendered to the emperor his humble congratulations on the victory which had attended his arms.

The battle of Fathkhelda marks the establishment in the Deccan of Nizām-ul-Mulk's hereditary rule, though he had been virtually independent since the fall of the Sayyid brothers.

Nizām-ul-Mulk marched, after his victory, to Hyderābād, which he reached on 16 January, 1725, and which he now made his capital. The wretched emperor was constrained to conciliate him and to humiliate himself by rewarding him, in June, with the title of Āsaf Jāh. However, the court faction strove to diminish his influence by removing officers whom he had appointed and by preparing to deprive him of the government of Gujarāt.

Nizām-ul-Mulk, in reply to these attacks, enlisted the aid of the Marāthās, and attempted to restrict their forays in his provinces.[2] The two most prominent Marāthā officers in Gujarāt were Kanthājī Kadam Bhānde and Pīlājī Gāikwār, and Nizām-ul-Mulk urged his uncle, Hāmid Khān, who represented him in that province, to protect himself against any new governor whom the emperor might appoint. Sarbuland Khān, Mubāriz-ul-Mulk, was the governor chosen, and he begged for the aid of Sayyid Najm-ud-dīn 'Alī Khān, who had been in prison since the battle of Hasanpur, but was favoured by Muhammad Shāh, who had been led by the Sayyid from his prison to his throne.

Sarbuland Khān did not at once proceed to Gujarāt but appointed as his lieutenant Shujā'at Khān, who had acted in the same capacity before. Hāmid Khān withdrew from Ahmadābād to Dohad and there entered into negotiations with Kanthājī who, on being

[1] 20° 13′ N., 76° 27′ E.

[2] See chap. XIII.

promised the *chauth*, readily joined him. The allies encamped at Kapadvanj and seized an opportunity of attacking Shujā'at Khān near Ahmadābād. He was defeated and slain and Hāmid Khān's authority was again recognised in Gujarāt, but an attempt by a brother of Shujā'at Khān who was commandant of Surat to avenge Shujā'at Khān's death was also defeated.

Sarbuland Khān had been in no hurry to leave Delhi, as the emperor had promised to appoint him minister if it were possible. When news of Hāmid Khān's two victories arrived the emperor decided that the power of the Turanian faction was still too great and begged Sarbuland Khān to depart for his province. In the summer of 1725 he and Girdhar Bahādur, who was going to take charge of the government of Mālwā, left the capital together, followed closely by Sayyid Najm-ud-dīn 'Alī Khān, who had been appointed second in command of a large force.

Nizām-ul-Mulk, distrusting his uncle's ability to withstand such an invasion, advised him to retire, but the vain and obstinate old man made an attempt to oppose the advance of the new governor. It failed and Hāmid Khān was forced to take refuge with his nephew in the Deccan.

In the following year Hāmid Khān, accompanied by a large force of Marāthās, returned to Gujarāt and plundered the country. After many indecisive combats the Marāthās were completely defeated, and expelled for a time from Gujarāt. Sarbuland Khān's army was so numerous that the revenues of the disordered province of Gujarāt did not suffice for its maintenance and he received from the central treasury a monthly subvention of half a million rupees. Through Sarbuland Khān's enemies at court, the expulsion of the Marāthās from Gujarāt was made a pretext for orders directing the reduction of the army and the discontinuance of the subsidy. He was still further weakened by the withdrawal of the gallant Sayyid, Najm-ud-dīn 'Alī Khān, who was appointed, as a reward for his services in Gujarāt, to the government of the province of Ajmer, and when the Marāthās returned in force the governor was obliged to recognise their claim to *chauth* and *sardeshmukhī* in Gujarāt.

Corruption at court had reached a climax. Raushan-ud-Daula had been appointed minister on the dismissal of Qamar-ud-dīn Khān, as a measure to break the power of the Turanian faction. He was found to have been appropriating half of the sum of one million two hundred thousand rupees which the province of Kābul contributed annually to the imperial exchequer and to have dealt similarly with other large sums of money. He was dismissed from his post, his accounts were examined, and it was discovered that he was indebted to the state in twenty million rupees. The whole sum was recovered and Khān Daurān was appointed minister in his place. Shāh 'Abdul-Ghafūr, a warm partisan of the Turanian party, was found to have accumulated a fortune from the proceeds of bribery in the administration of crown lands. He was sent as a prisoner to Bengal, and his house was found to contain twenty million rupees in cash, besides much valuable property.

One of Khān Daurān's earliest acts as minister was to dismiss Sarbuland Khān from Gujarāt on a charge that he had recognised the claim of the Marāthās to *chauth* and *sardeshmukhī*. But the reduction of his army had forced him either to buy off the Marāthās or to see his fertile province annually laid waste by them, and Khān Daurān's personal enmity was the true cause of his dismissal. Abhay Singh, who, having (according to some accounts) murdered his father, Ajīt Singh, in June, 1724, had succeeded as Mahārājā of Jodhpur, was selected as viceroy of Gujarāt. Sarbuland Khān, smarting under the injustice of his treatment by the minister, attacked the lieutenant sent to take charge and drove him from the province. A second representative, at the head of a larger force, shared the fate of the first, and Abhay Singh was forced in 1730 to set out for Gujarāt in person. Though accompanied by a large army of forty or fifty thousand horse Sarbuland Khān inflicted a defeat on him, forcing him to retreat for a few miles. After this proof of his military qualities Sarbuland Khān's heart failed him. Such acts of rebellion had become almost matters of course in the condition of feebleness to which the central government had fallen, but his situation was more than usually unfavourable. Abhay Singh might be reinforced from the capital and Khān Daurān might even seek the powerful aid of Nizām-ul-Mulk, who still resented his uncle's expulsion from Gujarāt. Sarbuland Khān therefore visited Abhay Singh, recalled his close friendship with the raja's father, and said that his resistance had been merely a vindication of his own honour, and that he would gladly allow Abhay Singh to enter Ahmadābād. Sarbuland Khān then set out for Delhi, but his opposition to the new governor had enraged the minister, who was bent on punishing him. He travelled by way of Mālwā, and on his arrival at Āgra was arrested by mace-bearers, being deserted by his troops, and remained a state prisoner. This was his reward for important services rendered to the empire. He had been guilty of high treason, but so had Nizām-ul-Mulk, on three occasions, yet Nizām-ul-Mulk was viceroy of the Deccan, where he was even now plotting treason against his sovereign.

> Treason doth never prosper. What's the reason?
> That when it prospers none dare call it treason.

Shortly afterwards when Sarbuland Khān was pardoned and appointed governor of Allahābād, he was so broken in spirit and disgusted by his treatment that he remained at Āgra and sent his son as his deputy.

Muhammad Khān Bangash, a stout Afghān soldier of fortune who had established himself in the reign of Farrukh-siyar in the central

Dūāb where he had built for himself a stronghold named after his master, Farrukhābād, had distinguished himself. Rude and illiterate, but faithful to a party which he had adopted, he might, had fortune smiled, have established a state like Oudh or the Deccan, and he narrowly missed success. In 1725 when appointed governor of Allahābād he found a powerful confederacy of Bundelās with a force of 20,000 horse and more than 100,000 foot occupying the whole of Baghelkhand and other districts. The Bundelās, unlike most of the Rājputs, were suspected, with good reason, of sympathy with the Marāthās. Muhammad Khān undertook the task with little sympathy and less support from Delhi. Throughout 1727 and 1728 he was engaged in incessant hostilities. An enumeration of his battles and sieges would be tedious and, without full details, uninstructive.[1] Muhammad Khān had considerable successes against the Bundelās, but early in 1729 the Marāthā troops of Bājī Rāo Peshwā invaded Baghelkhand and Bundelkhand, and in May, 1729, Muhammad Khān was compelled to take refuge in the fort of Jaitpur, where he was besieged for three months. Finally, in August, 1729, he was relieved by his son Qāim Khān, but he was still at the mercy of his enemies who extorted from him a promise that he would never again enter Bundelkhand. This failure was followed by his dismissal from his government.

The sole object of all Nizām-ul-Mulk's dealings with the Marāthās was to free his dominions, as far as might be, of their influence and institutions and, if that should be possible, of their presence. His attempt to compromise for payments of *chauth* and *sardeshmukhī* and to support the pretender Shambhūjī led to war in 1727–28, which is described in the next chapter.

In the end Nizām-ul-Mulk was compelled to accept all Bājī Rāo's terms, except a demand for the surrender of Shambhūjī, who was permitted to retire to Panhālā. His efforts to prevent Bājī Rāo's advance into Gujarāt by inducing the Marāthā officers employed there to oppose it were foiled by Bājī Rāo's rapid movements and victory over his opponents in April, 1731. When the Peshwā returned at the end of the rainy season, intending to punish the duplicity which had so nearly frustrated his plans, Nizām-ul-Mulk averted his wrath by unfolding a scheme for the extension of the Marāthā power into northern India. The design accorded with Bājī Rāo's policy and ambitions and he welcomed the suggestion, and the Peshwā's brother was at once sent into Mālwā at the head of a Marāthā force.

Malhār Rāo Holkar had already been engaged in ravaging Mālwā and Girdhar Bahādur, the governor, who enjoyed a respectable military reputation, commanded neither the troops nor the resources

[1] For a full account of this campaign see *A History of the Bangash Nawābs of Farrukhābād* (Calcutta, 1879), by Wm. Irvine, pp. 288–302.

which would have enabled him to offer effective opposition to the raids of so mobile an enemy. Repeated appeals to the imperial court fell on deaf ears and Girdhar died in battle (December, 1728). A relative who succeeded him was left to his own resources and met the same fate three years later.

Muhammad Khān Bangash, who was at Delhi explaining his defeat in Bundelkhand, was appointed to Mālwā, and reached Sārangpur on 26 January, 1731. The state of the province was appalling. It was out of cultivation and most of the inhabitants left were in league with marauding parties of Marāthās, who numbered by the end of 1731 nearly 100,000. Against such forces Muhammad Khān could do nothing. His appeals for help and a prayer that the emperor should take the field in person merely drew a letter of reproaches from the minister, Khān Daurān, who accused the governor of apathy and his troops of treachery. Landholders in the province were informed that they need pay no heed to Muhammad Khān as a new governor was about to be appointed, and on 25 October, 1732, the governor was recalled to Āgra and Jay Singh of Amber was appointed to succeed him.

Rājā Jay Singh was no more able than Muhammad Khān to restrain the ravages of the Marāthās, who had now, under Bājī Rāo, overrun the whole of Mālwā. Though his sympathies with his co-religionists were to some extent modified by his honour as a Rājput he came to an understanding with the Peshwā, but even this method of conciliation was ineffectual. In February, 1734, the Marāthās captured and occupied Hindaun, only seventy miles south-west of Āgra. Muzaffar Khān, who had been recalled from Ajmer, was sent to chastise them, but the Marāthās, who had had no intention of occupying Hindaun permanently, retired as he advanced, cut off his supplies and reduced him to distress. The court of Delhi was now content with little in the way of military success and Muzaffar Khān, who was considered to have accomplished his task by driving the Marāthās from Hindaun, was recalled to Delhi, where he was received with rejoicings and honours out of all proportion to the scanty measure of his success.

Later in the year the pacific minister himself indulged in a similar military promenade and in November, 1734, marched to Mālwā and back. These expeditions were entirely futile. The Marāthās, avoiding a general engagement, harassed the imperial troops and never ceased to levy contributions from the people. In March, 1735, only a few months after the minister's triumphal return to Delhi, a force of Marāthās advanced, sacked the town of Sāmbhar on the high road from Delhi to Ajmer, drove out the commandant and slew the *qāzī* at the door of his own house. Further resistance was clearly useless and the emperor, on the recommendation of Rājā Jay Singh, tacitly recognised Bājī Rāo as governor of Mālwā. Later in the year Abhay Singh of Jodhpur, who had proved to be a most inefficient governor, was dismissed from Gujarāt, but his deputy would not evacuate Ahmadābād and the new governor was obliged to court an alliance with Dāmājī Gāikwār before he could gain possession of the city.

A rising at this time in the Allahābād province illustrates both the decay of respect for the imperial government and the ineptitude of the imperial officials. A landholder named Bhagwant Rāi (son of Arārū Singh) in the Korā district slew the commandant, who was a brother-in-law of Qamar-ud-dīn Khān, I'timād-ud-Daula, plundered all his property and took his wife to himself. Qamar-ud-dīn Khān sent a relation to punish the murderer and recover the widow and property. On his approach Bhagwant Rāi withdrew for a time into a remote part of the district but returned to Korā, slew the new commandant and established himself with impunity in Korā. Qamar-ud-dīn Khān, lacking the courage to avenge in person his outraged honour, begged Burhān-ul-Mulk, the governor of Oudh, to undertake the punishment of the rebel. Burhān-ul-Mulk, passing through the Korā district early in November, 1735, on his way to Delhi, called Bhagwant Rāi to account for his misdeeds and Bhagwant Rāi, when he found that Burhān-ul-Mulk declined to be put off with fair words, unexpectedly attacked him. Mistaking another man for Burhān-ul-Mulk he drove his spear through his breast and slew him. Burhān-ul-Mulk and Rājā Durjan Singh, who was related to the rebel, attacked him, and Bhagwant Rāi fell, cut down by the raja's sword and pierced by an arrow from Burhān-ul-Mulk's bow. His head was sent to the emperor, and his skin, stuffed with straw, to Qamar-ud-dīn Khān.

In November, 1735, Muhammad Khān Bangash was reappointed to the government of Allahābād, which he held for no more than six months, being again dismissed in May, 1736, when Sarbuland Khān was once more appointed.

Bājī Rāo was now in serious pecuniary difficulties, owing to the size of his army and the high pay necessary to outbid Nizām-ul-Mulk. His troops were in arrears and he was heavily indebted to moneylenders. The emperor and his minister desired peace, but the less mean-spirited Turanian nobles were opposed to any disgraceful compromise. Muhammad Shāh's conciliatory attitude encouraged the Peshwā to demand the cession of the whole of Mālwā and the tract south of the Chambal, Allahābād, Benares, Gayā, and Muttra, the recognition of his right as hereditary *Sardeshmukh* and *Sardeshpāndya* of the six provinces of the Deccan, and an annual assignment of five million rupees. His claims threw the emperor into the arms of Nizām-ul-Mulk, who was implored to forget the past and to save the empire from destruction. In March, 1737, Khān Daurān and Qamar-ud-dīn Khān, each at the head of a great army, advanced one towards

Ajmer and the other towards Muttra while Burhān-ul-Mulk crossed the Ganges to help the Rājā of Bhadāwar, whom Holkar was besieging in his stronghold. Burhān-ul-Mulk fell on Holkar and pursued him towards Gwalior, and then, hearing that the Peshwā was encamped at Dholpur, turned northward to attack him, when he received letters from Khān Daurān.

Once more public interests were sacrificed to personal jealousy. Burhān-ul-Mulk had gained credit for his suppression of the rebellion at Korā and now his success against Holkar induced Khān Daurān, as the historian says, "either to make a name for himself or, if that might not be, to reduce Burhān-ul-Mulk to his own level of infamy". He begged Burhān-ul-Mulk not to be so rash as to attack Bājī Rāo single-handed, as he was hastening to join him and together they would crush the enemy. Burhān-ul-Mulk hesitated and Khān Daurān moved at his leisure to join him. This operation occupied three or four days and a week was spent in reciprocal hospitality. Treachery and folly combined gave Bājī Rāo his opportunity, which he was not slow to seize. Eluding the roysterers he advanced, by forced marches, and encamped only nine miles from the walls of Shāhjahānābād. After some minor acts of spoliation and the total defeat of a force of 8000 horse led from the city, as Burhān-ul-Mulk, Qamar-ud-dīn Khān, and Khān Daurān were closing on him, Bājī Rāo retired towards Gwalior, plundering as he went, and unmolested by the imperial troops.

Meanwhile Nizām-ul-Mulk was advancing from the south and Khān Daurān, prompted again by a jealous fear lest he should claim a share in the credit, hastened to come to terms; and Bājī Rāo withdrew on receiving a commission appointing him to the government of Mālwā and the promise of an annual subvention of one million and three hundred thousand rupees. His presence was required in the Konkan, where a campaign against the Portuguese and Angria of Janjīra was in progress.

The languid movement of Nizām-ul-Mulk was stimulated by the issue of a commission appointing his eldest son, Ghāzī-ud-Dīn Khān, governor of Mālwā and Gujarāt, on the condition of his expelling the Marāthā. He marched through Āgra and then through Kālpī into Mālwā and halted at Sironj. Bājī Rāo's business in the Konkan did not occupy him for long, and he returned to Mālwā. Nizām-ul-Mulk advanced to Bhopāl, where the two armies met in January, 1738, and betrayed his weakness by entrenching himself in a strong position. A battle produced no decisive result and Nizām-ul-Mulk's camp was surrounded by predatory hordes who cut off his supplies and repelled forces sent to relieve him. At length, leaving his heavy baggage behind him, he forced his way through the screen of light horse surrounding him and began a laborious retreat. At every step he was harassed by the Marāthās and though these failed to capture his artillery, his troops progressed slowly, and on 17 January, 1738, near Sironj, he was obliged to sign a convention undertaking to obtain for Bājī Rāo the whole of Mālwā, with sovereignty in the territory between the Narbadā and the Chambal and a subsidy of five million rupees. These terms were sufficiently disgraceful. They included nothing that was the Nizām's, and the cession of sovereignty in the tract between the two rivers may have covered a design to protect his dominions in the south by establishing an independent state between them and the territories of the emperor.

A grave peril now threatened India. The condition of the Safavī dynasty of Persia during the first quarter of the eighteenth century may be compared with that of the House of Tīmūr in India. Power and authority had fallen from the grasp of a weak and worthless prince and the country, in the hands of a band of quarrelsome but unwarlike nobles, lay an easy prey to an aggressor. Mahmūd Khān the Ghilzāī, son of Mīr Vais who had freed Qandahār from the Persian yoke, had risen against the feeble Tahmāsp II, conquered Herāt, Khurāsān, and at length, in 1722, Isfahān itself, and had driven the Safavī into the forests of Māzandarān. Russian and Turkish invasions had increased Persia's misery and confusion and the whole country, except a narrow strip in the north, lay at the mercy of aliens in race and religion. A deliverer appeared in the person of Nādir Qulī, a Turk of the Afshār tribe of Khurāsān, who in 1729 expelled the Afghāns from Isfahān and Fārs and extended the Persian monarchy to its ancient limits. 'Abbās III, the last of the Safavīs, was permitted to ascend the throne in 1731, but all power in the state had been wielded since the expulsion of the Afghāns by Nādir Qulī, who in 1736 threw aside all disguise and ascended the throne of Persia as Nādir Shāh. After defeating the Russians and the Turks, who had taken advantage of Persia's distress, he turned his attention to northern Afghānistān and captured Herāt and Balkh, reserving Qandahār, the home of the Ghilzāīs who had ravaged Persia, until later. Two envoys had been sent to inform Muhammad Shāh that Nādir Shāh purposed to punish the Afghāns of Qandahār and to request him to order his governor of Kābul to close the frontiers of that province to fugitives. Each envoy returned with a favourable answer, but nothing was done.

On opening the siege of Qandahār towards the end of June, 1737, Nādir Shāh found that many fugitives were escaping towards Kābul, and a third envoy was sent to demand an explanation, with instructions to stay only forty days at the court of Delhi; but the envoy could obtain neither an audience nor leave to depart.

Qandahār fell on 24 March, 1738, and Nādir Shāh, whose envoy had been absent for a year, advanced towards Ghaznī, which he entered on 11 June. He reached Kābul on 21 June, and after a combat beneath the walls, the citadel was besieged and surrendered on 29 June. Nādir stayed for some months in Kābul and its neighbourhood, and wrote to Muhammad Shāh, complaining again of his breach of faith, but the messenger was waylaid and slain, and it is doubtful whether the despatch ever reached the emperor.

On 26 November Nādir defeated at Jamrūd the governor of Kābul who, with a force of 20,000 Afghāns, attempted to bar his exit from the Khyber pass. He then occupied Peshāwar, where he halted for some time. On 27 December he crossed the Indus at Attock and in January, 1739, meeting at Wazīrābād on the Chenāb with some slight resistance he "swept it away as a flood sweeps away a handful of chaff". The governor of Lahore met the invader at a distance of twelve miles from that city but was at once defeated and on the following day appeared before Nādir, made his obeisance and presented a peace offering.

From Lahore Nādir Shāh sent to Muhammad Shāh a courteous letter, reminding him that they were both of Turkish blood and expressing wonder that he had not received more assistance in chastising the Afghāns, who had done more harm in India than they had in Persia—an apposite reference to the expulsion of Humāyūn by Sher Shāh. He also complained again of the gross discourtesy with which he had been treated, but attributed this to evil counsellors rather than to any deliberate design on the part of Muhammad. He was coming, he added, to punish these counsellors, and if they survived an encounter with him their fate would depend on such intercession as Muhammad Shāh might see fit to make for them.

The news that Nādir intended to invade India was received at first with ridicule, but when it became known that he had taken Kābul incredulity gave way to panic, which increased with every stage of the invader's advance. Khān Daurān and Nizām-ul-Mulk were first nominated to the command of an army to oppose him, but declined the honour, and it soon became apparent that the occasion demanded the presence of the emperor and of all the troops which he could place in the field. Burhān-ul-Mulk of Oudh and all other nobles and assignees were summoned, with their contingents, and the same command went to the chiefs of Rājasthān, but all of these made their excuse. Akbar, similarly situated, could have commanded the service of many thousands of valiant Rājputs, but the descendant of Aurangzīb could not persuade one to strike a blow in defence of his throne.

Even at this moment of peril the great nobles of the empire could not lay aside their personal quarrels and with scarcely an exception entered, either to assure their fortunes or to steal a march on their fellows, into treasonable correspondence with the invader. "Brother", said Nādir Shāh to Muhammad Shāh, when Muhammad Khān Bangash was presented to him, "you have three faithful servants, and the rest are traitors; those three are Nāsir Khān, Khān Daurān, and Muhammad Khān; from these I received no letters; from all the rest I received invitations to invade your country."

Muhammad Shāh and his army marched out to Sonpat, and in the latter half of February reached Karnāl, where it had been decided to meet the invader. The position was better suited for defence than attack, being protected by nearly impenetrable jungle and by the canal of 'Alī Mardān Khān. The imperial guns were chained together, and it seems that entrenchments were thrown up. Muhammad Shāh's elaborate precautions for his safety nearly tempted Nādir Shāh to leave this fortified camp on his left and to pass on to Delhi, but an action was precipitated by the inconsiderate haste of one commander.

Nādir Shāh marched from Lahore on 6 February and reached Sirhind ten days later. Thence he marched to Tarāorī, 10 miles north of Karnāl, reaching that place on 22 February. The governor of Ambāla had fallen back on Tarāorī and attempted to hold the large *sarāi* in that town, but a very brief bombardment by the Persian guns induced him to surrender. Nādir Shāh's system of intelligence was excellent, while in the opposite camp no attempt was made to obtain information.

The Indian army was distracted with terror and fervent prayers went up for the speedy arrival of Burhān-ul-Mulk, who was leading his large contingent to the imperial camp. Nādir Shāh, finding that dense jungle would impede a direct advance from the north on Karnāl, inclined slightly to his right, and encamped, on 23 February, in the open plain two leagues to the west of the town. On the following morning he advanced to within a league of the town. His patrols and scouts had already searched the country to the south of Karnāl and he knew more of the movements of Burhān-ul-Mulk than was known in the Indian camp. On 23 February he had sent a force to cut him off, but Burhān-ul-Mulk, moving between the main road and the river Jumna, had passed unmolested, though his baggage train was captured.

Burhān-ul-Mulk arrived in the camp on 24 February and was waiting for his baggage when he learnt that it had fallen into the hands of the enemy. He ordered his troops to mount in an attempt to recover his baggage. Nizām-ul-Mulk hesitated to join Burhān-ul-Mulk's troops, who were still weary from their march, but Khān Daurān decided to go to his support and led his troops to the attack, coming up about a mile to the right of Burhān-ul-Mulk. The emperor and Nizām-ul-Mulk followed him and their advanced troops closed the interval between Khān Daurān and Burhān-ul-Mulk, but the emperor with the main body of his army remained just without the enceinte of the camp.

The battle began at noon, according to the Persian account, so that there was little force in Nizām-ul-Mulk's objection. The Indian troops[1], whose serried ranks extended over two miles of front and to the same depth from front to rear, were of very small fighting value compared with Nādir's hardy warriors, and the *mêlée* was rather a massacre than a battle. Burhān-ul-Mulk was recognised by a fellow-townsman from Nīshāpur, who sprang from his saddle, clambered by the ropes into the howdah of his elephant, and caused the animal, apparently without resistance, to be driven into the Persian camp. Khān Daurān was mortally wounded and died on the following day. "My own rashness", he said to the courtiers who had come to visit him, "has brought me to this. Now there is one thing for you to do. By any means possible keep Nādir Shāh out of Delhi. Buy him off here, and persuade him to return at once." This sound advice was frustrated by the jealousy and treachery of the courtiers. Muhammad Shāh and the survivors took refuge in their fortified camp, where provisions were already scarce and where they were besieged as in a fortress, and the emperor wrote a piteous appeal to the conqueror, based on the latter's own reference to their community of race.

Nādir Shāh was apparently ignorant of the wealth and resources of India, and Burhān-ul-Mulk, hearing of the death of Khān Daurān, coveted the rank and title of Amīr-ul-Umarā, which the deceased had borne, and resolved to earn it by a signal service to his master. In the course of a long interview with Nādir he persuaded him to agree to leave Muhammad Shāh on the throne of Delhi and to retire from India at once in consideration of an indemnity of twenty million rupees. Nizām-ul-Mulk was sent by Muhammad Shāh to Nādir Shāh's camp to confirm the offer of this indemnity. His mission was successful, and he had little difficulty, on his return, in persuading his master to confer on him, as a reward for his service, the title of Amīr-ul-Umarā. Burhān-ul-Mulk's rage on learning that his hopes were dashed led him to address Nādir in terms very different from those first employed. It was absurd, he said, that the victor should be content with a miserable twenty millions. He himself, a mere provincial governor, could produce such a sum from his own house. The instinct of the Turkmān robber was aroused. He was ready to keep his promise to maintain Muhammad Shāh on the throne, but the question of the indemnity could stand over until he arrived at Delhi.

Muhammad Shāh twice visited Nādir Shāh in his camp. On one occasion the monarchs had a private interview at which only one or two officials were present and Nādir Shāh rated Muhammad Shāh for his past conduct. After repeating his old causes of complaint he ridiculed the folly and indecision of Muhammad Shāh's recent policy. The fortified camp at Karnāl had failed to arrest his progress,

[1] 200,000 horse and foot and 5000 field guns, besides swivel guns. Nādir Shāh had 125,000 horse.

but it had exposed Muhammad Shāh's cowardice to the contempt of all.

On 12 March Nādir Shāh set out for Delhi and six days later encamped in the Shālamār garden[1] while he contemptuously allowed Muhammad Shāh to precede him into the city to make preparations for his reception. The Persian festival of the new year coincided in this year with the Muhammadan feast of the sacrifice and on 21 March, the day after Nādir Shāh's entry into Delhi, both festivals were celebrated by the recitation of the *khutba* in his name in all the mosques of Delhi, by which ceremony he was acknowledged as lord of all India. His troops were quartered in and around the city. On the following day a dispute regarding billets and the price of food and forage arose, and some Persians were attacked. Mischief-makers spread the rumour that Nādir Shāh was dead, and the rumour caused a rising. Persians strolling aimlessly about the city, either alone or in twos and threes, were massacred. The nobles who had been supplied, at their own request, with Persian guards, either delivered these guards to the fury of the populace or took no measures to save them. Nādir Shāh, on hearing of this outrage, at once issued orders directing his troops to stand fast and defend themselves in their quarters and billets while abstaining from reprisals.

During the tumult two Mughul officers, believing Nādir Shāh to be dead and desiring to be in a position to overawe the foreign troops in the capital, had gone with a force of four hundred and seventy men to the imperial elephant stables, slain the Persian in charge and possessed themselves of the elephants.

In the morning Nādir Shāh mounted and rode through the city to ascertain the result of the tumult. About nine hundred Persians had been slain and their corpses were yet lying about the streets. He returned to the beautiful "golden mosque" which had been built not long before, and here the inhabitants of the neighbouring houses threw stones at him from their roofs and one fired a musket, missing him but killing a Persian officer by his side. The sight of the bodies of his men had enraged him and at this last outrage his wrath flamed forth, and he ordered a general massacre of the guilty inhabitants. Two of Muhammad Shāh's officers were sent by Nādir Shāh to seize those who had taken the elephant stables, and the guilty leaders and their four hundred and seventy men were brought before Nādir and put to the sword. The work of blood continued from eight in the morning until the evening, and the tale of the slain was 30,000.[2] In the evening Nizām-ul-Mulk and Qamar-ud-dīn Khān appeared before Nādir Shāh with a message from Muhammad Shāh, who

[1] Six miles north of the city.

[2] The *Jahān-kushā-i-Nādirī* is followed here (pp. 358, 359). Fraser (p. 185) says that the slaughter lasted from 8 a.m. to 3 p.m. and that the number of the slain was 120,000, though placed by some as high as 150,000. Scott's estimate of 8000 (II, 207) is certainly too low and it is not improbable that Muhammad Mahdī errs in the same direction.

begged that the remnant of his guilty people might be spared. Nādir Shāh issued orders that the slaying and plundering should cease and to the credit of his discipline[1] his excited soldiery at once stayed their hands. The flames were extinguished, but a great part of the city was in ruins and the stench of the dead was soon intolerable. The corpses were piled in stacks and burnt, whether Hindus or Muslims, with the timber of the ruined houses. All captives, to the number of 50,000, were set free.

Muhammad had surrendered to Nādir at Karnāl the keys of his treasury and both the wealth and the jewels of the empire were at the conqueror's disposal, but there remained the levying of contributions from the great nobles, in accordance with the suggestion made by Burhān-ul-Mulk. The traitor was now dead, having succumbed a few days after his return to Delhi to a malignant tumour. He had paid before his death thirty-three million rupees and a force proceeded to Oudh to recover from his nephew and son-in-law, Abu-'l-Mansūr Khān, Safdar Jang, the promised contribution of twenty million rupees. Safdar Jang paid partly in cash and completed the sum due from him with elephants, jewels and vessels of gold and silver. The value of the pearls, diamonds and other jewels taken from the imperial treasury was described as being beyond computation. They included Shāh Jahān's wonderful Peacock Throne, the jewels alone of which, without reckoning the precious metal of which the throne was made, were valued at twenty million rupees.

Sarbuland Khān, excused by his poverty from contributing anything himself, was charged to collect from the nobles, the officers of the court and army, and the wealthy inhabitants, and his zeal and activity were stimulated from time to time by threats and rewards. The property of Khān Daurān and his brother was confiscated and yielded to Nādir's treasury fifty million rupees. Nizām-ul-Mulk and Qamar-ud-dīn Khān each contributed fifteen million in jewels, treasure and goods. Violence and torture were used in extorting contributions. A grand-daughter of Kām Bakhsh was married to Nādir's youngest son, Nasr-ullah Mīrzā. Before leaving Delhi Nādir Shāh formally annexed the province of Kābul and all territory west of the Indus, and gave Muhammad Shāh advice which that prince had neither the sense nor the moral courage to follow. He expressed his horror at the idea of the misbelievers levying taxes in the dominions of Islām, counselled him to resume all assignments and to pay his nobles and officers direct from the treasury, permitting none to maintain troops. At the charges of the state the emperor should have picked horsemen under officers appointed by himself. He warned the emperor particularly against Nizām-ul-Mulk, whom he had found to be cunning, self-seeking and more ambitious than became a subject.

[1] The most rigid discipline was maintained in the Persian army. "Eighty Kuzzlebash had their Bellies ript up at Cabul, for only being present when some of their own People forced one of the Country women" (Fraser, p. 151).

It is said that Nādir Shāh admitted to some of his own officers that he had acted indiscreetly in two matters, namely in permitting Muhammad Shāh to retain a throne of which he was not worthy and in sparing the life of a courtier so crafty and unscrupulous as Nizām-ul-Mulk.

On 16 May Nādir Shāh left Delhi carrying with him his immense booty. Different authorities estimate the cash alone at amounts varying from eight to more than thirty million sterling, besides jewels, plate, cash, stuffs and other valuable property. The emperor also took with him a thousand elephants, seven thousand horses, ten thousand camels, a hundred eunuchs, a hundred and thirty writers, two hundred builders, a hundred masons, and two hundred carpenters. By a decree issued from Delhi Nādir Shāh generously remitted all taxes throughout Persia for a period of three years.

His departure left Muhammad Shāh and his courtiers stupefied with the blow which had fallen on them. For two months nothing was done or proposed in regard to the state of affairs in the empire. Even this blow could not awaken from the heavy sleep of security, and the lethargy of indolence, people who were so intoxicated with the wine of pride and self-conceit. They agreed only in ill-will to each other. It was not until November that the emperor and his courtiers could summon up energy for active intrigue.

Nādir Shāh's warnings had had some effect on Muhammad Shāh, who was now suspicious of Nizām-ul-Mulk and all the Turanian nobles. After secret conversations with the object of undermining the power and influence of the Turanian party, he promised to appoint 'Umdat-ul-Mulk in place of Qamar-ud-dīn Khān, the minister, who was second in importance only to Nizām-ul-Mulk among the Turanians. The latter now prepared to set out for his viceroyalty in the Deccan. Qamar-ud-dīn Khān learnt what had passed and wrote to Nizām-ul-Mulk, by whose advice he resigned his post, left Delhi and joined the Nizām. Muhammad Shāh consulted others and was told that 'Umdat-ul-Mulk could never stand against the power of the Turanian party. The result was the complete collapse of the emperor's plot. 'Umdat-ul-Mulk was himself sent to the camp to make his peace with Qamar-ud-dīn Khān and Nizām-ul-Mulk, and did so with such openness and honesty as to win the latter's warm approval. As he could not remain in the capital after what had passed, he left Delhi for Allahābād, of which province he held the government. Nizām-ul-Mulk, in view of the necessity for frustrating the emperor's schemes for the oppression of the Turanian faction, deferred his departure for the Deccan.

At the same time Safdar Jang, the nephew and son-in-law of Burhān-ul-Mulk, was formally confirmed in the government of Oudh, in which he had been acting since his uncle's death, while Zakariyā Khān received the Punjab and Multān, in which, until the battle of Karnāl, he had been merely the deputy of his father, Khān Daurān.

The affairs of the provinces of Bengal, Bihār and Orissa now claim our attention. The pernicious practice of uniting several rich provinces under the government of a viceroy to whom, and not to the emperor, the actual governor of each province was immediately subordinate was now as firmly established in this region as in the Deccan. Prince ʻAzīm-ush-Shān had held these three provinces and that of Allahābād in addition, and when the Sayyid brothers, who had been his deputies in Allahābād, left their province with the object of placing Farrukhsiyar on the throne Ja'far Khān,[1] who had been the prince's deputy in Bengal, governed the three provinces, from which Allahābād was then separated, as viceroy. Ja'far Khān had died in 1726, when Khān Daurān, who never concerned himself with the affairs of these provinces, was formally appointed viceroy, while the government of the provinces was actually carried on by Shujāʻ-ud-dīn Muhammad Khān, Ja'far Khān's son-in-law, who had been his deputy in Orissa, and received, on his promotion, the title of Shujāʻ-ud-Daula. He ruled the provinces ably and well for thirteen years and died on 24 March, 1739, while Nādir Shāh was at Delhi. He was succeeded, as a matter of course, the hereditary principle being by now established in the great provincial governments, by his son Sarfarāz Khān, who bore the title of ʻAlā-ud-Daula. Sarfarāz Khān was pious and devout, but weak, and attempted to favour his own personal servants at the expense of his father's old advisers, who were too strong for him. He also attempted to interfere in the administration of Bihār, the governor of which, appointed by his father, was ʻAlī Vardī Khān, entitled Mahābat Jang. ʻAlī Vardī wrote to an old friend at court and offered, for a commission as viceroy of the three provinces and written permission to expel Sarfarāz Khān, a gift to the emperor of ten million rupees. He had also a private wrong to avenge. Sarfarāz Khān had attempted to take away the wife of his grandson, Sirāj-ud-Daula,[2] and to marry her to his own son. ʻAlī Vardī's prayer was supported by an accusation that Sarfarāz had obeyed the order in a letter sent by Nādir Shāh to his father, but received after his father's death, and had caused the *khutba* to be read in the invader's name.[3] It was also suggested that if Sarfarāz Khān were captured or slain his father's considerable wealth would escheat to the crown. Money was scarce at Delhi, and these offers were very welcome, but time was required for the completion of the transaction and it was not until March, 1740, that ʻAlī Vardī received his commission.

[1] Also known as Murshid Qulī Khān, the founder of Murshidābād.

[2] The "Surajah Dowlah" of Macaulay and "Sir Roger Dowler" of contemporary English prints, afterwards infamous as the author of the tragedy of the Black Hole of Calcutta. See chap. VII, vol. V.

[3] Coin was actually struck at ʻAzīmābād (Patna) and at Murshidābād in the name of Nādir Shāh (Whitehead, *Punjab Museum Catalogue*, III, pp. lii and lxv) [Ed.].

Early in April 'Alī Vardī Khān marched from Patna for Murshidābād. Sarfarāz Khān was surrounded by traitors who kept the news of his enemy's movements from him as long as they could, and it was not until he had reached Rājmahāl that Sarfarāz Khān heard of his advance. He marched from Murshidābād on 19 April, and two days later reached Giria, on the eastern bank of the Bhāgīrathī, about twenty-five miles north-west of his capital. 'Alī Vardī Khān encamped on the opposite bank of the river and succeeded by protestations of fidelity supported by a false oath sworn on a brick wrapped in a cloth, which was supposed to be a copy of the Korān, and by the treacherous assurances of false counsellors in persuading Sarfarāz Khān that he had come to do homage. The simple Sarfarāz paid no heed to warnings uttered by the very few servants who remained faithful to him and 'Alī Vardī was able to surprise him shortly before dawn. Notwithstanding the surprise and the treachery of many of the troops as well as the counsellors the battle was fiercely contested, but Sarfarāz Khān was ultimately shot in the forehead by one of his own men and killed, and 'Alī Vardī Khān entered Murshidābād on 12 May, 1740, as viceroy of Bengal, Bihār and Orissa.

On 28 April, 1740, Bājī Rāo, the Peshwā, died, and the Turanian party at court took advantage of his death to appoint one of their number, 'Azīm-ullah Khān, as his successor in the government of Mālwā. The administration of the Marāthā commonwealth now exhibited some of the signs of weakness which were more clearly perceptible in the Mughul empire. The expansion of their sphere of activity had been followed by the enfeeblement of the central authority and the introduction of the hereditary principle in the great offices of state and the government of those parts of their dominions which were at a distance from the royal residence. Dāmājī Gāikwar had succeeded his father Pīlājī in Gujarāt; Rānojī Sindia was established as collector of the Marāthās' share of the revenue in Mālwā; Malhār Rāo Holkar administered from Maheshwar territory corresponding nearly to the state over which his descendant still rules, and a disputed succession in the Gond kingdom of Deogarh had already given Raghūjī Bhonsle, who was governing Berār on behalf of the Peshwā, an opportunity of intervention, and three years later he established himself in its new capital, Nāgpur. He was at this time commanding a mixed force of 50,000 men drawn from the armies of Shāhū, the Peshwā, and other chiefs and operating in the Carnatic, where it had defeated and slain Dost 'Alī, the nephew and successor of Dāūd Khān Pānī in the eastern Carnatic,[1] and was busily intriguing to prevent the succession of Bālājī Rāo, son of Bājī Rāo, as Peshwā. His intrigues were fruitless and Bālājī Rāo succeeded.

The death of Bājī Rāo encouraged Nāsir Jang, the second son of

[1] See chap. xiv, p. 408.

Nizām-ul-Mulk, who had been left by his father as deputy in the viceroyalty when he went to Delhi in 1737, to assume the position of an independent ruler. Remonstrances went unheeded and on 7 August Nizām-ul-Mulk set out for the Deccan to reduce his refractory son to obedience, leaving his eldest son, Ghāzī-ud-dīn Khān, as his representative at the capital in the post of assistant minister. He reached Burhānpur on 19 November and halted there for some time while fruitlessly endeavouring to induce Nāsir Jang to submit without an appeal to arms. His arguments had no effect, and the rebel continued to hide or fight till August, 1741, when he was taken prisoner[1] and was confined for a time in the fort of Kandhār.

The appointment of 'Azīm-ullah Khān to Mālwā was merely an expression of the hopes which the death of an important Marāthā leader invariably raised in the breasts of the imperial statesmen and soldiers, and which were as invariably blasted. The death of Shivājī betokened to Aurangzīb the immediate dissolution of the Marāthā forces, but was followed by no diminution of activity even under the dissolute Shambhūjī. After the capture and execution of Shambhūjī and the detention of his son Shāhū, Rājā Rām had stepped into the breach. Now, too, Bājī Rāo was dead, but the Marāthā grip was closed on Mālwā, and Bālājī Rāo, the new Peshwā, considered that the appointment of a Muslim noble was an invasion of his rights.

'Azīm-ullah Khān had made a futile attempt to assert himself as governor by the despatch of a deputy whom his resources permitted him neither to equip adequately nor to support efficiently. His failure provided the emperor with a pretext for humiliating a Turanian noble by dismissal. 'Azīm-ullah Khān, smarting under his disgrace, temporarily left Delhi but soon wearied of being continually watched and returned to his house, dismissed his establishment and lived the life of a recluse. In December, 1742, he again fled from Delhi to Lahore, where he took refuge with the governor, Zakariyā Khān, with whom he was connected by marriage, but Zakariyā Khān surrendered him and he was carried back to Delhi and confined in the palace, where he died on 24 October, 1744.

'Alī Vardī Khān had established his authority in Bengal, and in Bihār where he appointed his son-in-law Haibat Jang as his deputy, but Orissa was still in the hands of Murshid Qulī Khān, who had been Shujā'-ud-Daula's deputy in that province. After lulling suspicions by messages which led Murshid to believe that he was to be retained as governor of Orissa 'Alī Vardī marched from Murshidābād on 20 December, 1740, at the head of a large force. Murshid Qulī Khān came from Cuttack to Balasore and encamped near the south bank of the Burabalang river. 'Alī Vardī Khān halted at Rāmchandrapur and nearly a month was spent in negotiations.

[1] See chap. XIII, p. 383.

Murshid Qulī's more impetuous son-in-law, Mīrzā Muhammad Bāqar Khān, descended of the royal house of Persia, lost patience and on 16 February, 1741, crossed the river to attack, compelling Murshid Qulī Khān to follow him. The issue was long doubtful, but Murshid Qulī Khān was at length defeated and escaped by sea to Masulipatam. His family was conveyed from Cuttack to Ichchāpuram, beyond the reach of 'Alī Vardī Khān, and the latter, leaving his nephew, Saulat Jang, in Cuttack as his deputy in Orissa, returned to Murshidābād. Saulat Jang disgusted both his army and his people by his parsimony and his unbridled passions, and within a year of his instalment Bāqar Khān returned from the Deccan and not only deposed and imprisoned him, but carried his arms to the extreme northern limits of the province and caused alarm and apprehension even at Murshidābād. 'Alī Vardī Khān marched once more from his capital, while Bāqar Khān awaited him at Balasore; but the latter's army lost heart, and he was compelled to retreat, carrying with him for a time his prisoner, Saulat Jang, whom at last he had to leave behind. Saulat Jang was rescued by his uncle's troops, and Bāqar Khān escaped once more into the Deccan.

Meanwhile a fresh calamity was impending over Bengal. The Marāthās had for some time past cast covetous eyes on the rich eastern provinces of the empire, and when Murshid Qulī Khān was defeated by 'Alī Vardī Khān his minister, Mīr Habīb, had suggested to Bhāskar Pant, Raghūjī Bhonsle's minister, who was governing Berār during his master's absence in the Carnatic, the invasion of Bengal.

Raghūjī Bhonsle, on hearing that 'Alī Vardī Khān was again engaged with Bāqar Khān, sent Bhāskar Pant to invade Bengal. 'Alī Vardī Khān was chastising the Rājā of Mayūrbhanj when he heard in April, 1742, that Bhāskar Pant had left Nāgpur, and at once marched towards Murshidābād; but Bhāskar Pant was before him and attacked him with 12,000 horse at Uchālan, sixteen miles south of Burdwān. He pushed on to Burdwān, but here he was surrounded by the Marāthās, who cut off all supplies. When with infinite difficulty he fought his way to Katwā, on the Bhāgīrathī, about forty miles south of Murshidābād, he found that the Marāthās had plundered the town. A supply of food had, however, been despatched from Murshidābād and his army was refreshed. After a short halt at Katwā he reached Murshidābād, but a party of Marāthās, led by Mīr Habīb, who had deserted to the enemy, had previously visited and plundered it.

Bhāskar Pant now wished to return to Nāgpur, fearing the approach of the rains, but was persuaded by Mīr Habīb to remain in Bengal. The Marāthās occupied Katwā and the country from Rājmahāl to Jaleswar was in their hands throughout the rainy season. Hooghly was also occupied in June.

'Alī Vardī Khān vainly sought aid from the emperor and from the

Peshwā, whose succession Raghūjī Bhonsle had attempted to prevent. Collecting boats and troops from parts of Bengal to the east of the Bhāgīrathī still in his possession he moved rapidly down the river and on a night in October, before the rivers had fallen, secretly threw a bridge of boats across the river to the camp of the Marāthās, whom impunity had rendered careless. The lashings of several boats in the bridge gave way and 1500 men were precipitated into the swollen river, but the damage was repaired and the rest of the army crossed. The Marāthās fled in confusion, and 'Alī Vardī Khān's unrelenting pursuit allowed them no opportunity of recovery. They were driven into Bihār but returned to the Midnapore district and after sustaining defeat at Jaleswar fled through western Orissa to Nāgpur.

The relief afforded by Bhāskar Pant's flight was not of long duration. His master, Raghūjī Bhonsle, came in person from Nāgpur to establish his claim to the *chauth* and *sardeshmukhī* of Bengal. Following the same route as Bhāskar Pant he arrived in the neighbourhood of Murshidābād in March, 1743. But Bālājī Rāo Peshwā, receiving from the emperor a promise of the arrears of *chauth* due from Bihār and the government of Mālwā, arrived at Murshidābād when Raghūjī Bhonsle was encamped between Katwā and Burdwān.

As soon as Raghūjī heard that an agreement about the *chauth* of Bihār had been reached he retreated rapidly westward. 'Alī Vardī Khān and Bālājī Rāo marched in pursuit, and the latter, pressing ahead, came up with Raghūjī Bhonsle, defeated him, and plundered his baggage. Though the government of Mālwā was then conferred on the Peshwā, imperial susceptibilities were indulged by appointing him as the deputy of the emperor's son, prince Ahmad. In the same year an attempt was made to assert the unity of the empire and the authority of the emperor over viceroys and governors who were independent in all but name. 'Alī Vardī Khān of Bengal was excepted owing to the danger of incursions of Marāthās into his province, but 'Umdat-ul-Mulk of Allahābād and Safdar Jang, the latter after some hesitation, obeyed the summons and appeared at court, while Zakariyā Khān of the Punjab sent his son as his representative. Bakht Singh, the rebellious brother of Abhay Singh of Jodhpur, seems to have taken no notice of the summons, and Sawāī Jay Singh of Amber, who held the government of Āgra, was prevented by death from obeying it. He had ruled Amber for forty-four years, and was a generous patron of science. Latterly his friendship with the Peshwā, Bālājī Rāo, had been of great service to the empire.

Nizām-ul-Mulk of the Deccan excused himself on the ground of age and of important affairs in the Carnatic from obeying the summons. There he had recovered Trichinopoly, which had been captured by Raghūjī Bhonsle during his absence at Delhi, and captured Arcot from Dost 'Alī the descendant of Aurangzīb's general

Sa'ādat-ullah Khān the Navāit,[1] in whose family the town and district had become a hereditary principality.[2]

Abhay Singh of Jodhpur had proved most inefficient in the government of Gujarāt, and since his dismissal none of the great nobles at court could be induced to accept the government of a province in a great part of which the Marāthās were permanently settled. Mūmin Khān, who had acted as governor since the raja's dismissal, could do nothing without the approval of Dāmājī Gāikwār. In January, 1744, he was succeeded by Fakhr-ud-Daula, who was encouraged to attempt the task by Muhammad Yār Khān. The latter, weary of Nādir Shāh's stern discipline, had deserted him and remained in India with Safdar Jang of Oudh, but his actions displeased and alarmed his new master who took advantage of the visit to Delhi to dispense with his services. Muhammad Yār Khān had, however, overestimated the fidelity of his troops, only a few of whom were willing to accompany him to Gujarāt. Here master and servant were mutually dissatisfied, the one with the other. The enterprise was a failure and the Marāthās remained dominant in Gujarāt. Muhammad Yār Khān left India and returned to his old master. "You feared the violence of my temper," said Nādir, "how is it that you have returned to me?" "To be slain by a man like you", replied Muhammad Yār, "is preferable to spending one's life among a pack of cowards."

For some time before this a new power had been growing up to the east of Delhi. 'Alī Muhammad Khān was according to some accounts by birth a Hindu,[3] who had been brought up by an Afghān officer in the imperial service and was accustomed to associate with Afghāns. He had entered the service of the governor of Katehr,[4] the chief towns of which, Budaun and Sambhal, had lately been eclipsed by Morādābād, which had become the governor's residence. When Nizām-ul-Mulk was replaced in the Deccan by Sayyid Husain 'Alī Khān he became governor of this tract and, as a sop to his wounded vanity, the appointment was to rank with the greater provincial governments. More recently it was held by the minister, Qamar-ud-dīn Khān, who governed by deputies. 'Alī Muhammad rapidly gained advancement and increased the number of his followers, who were always Afghāns. He increased his possessions by grants from landholders who were too idle or too careless to defend their own lands, and when the Sayyid brothers were overthrown he took an active part in the extinction of their influence in the province

[1] A tribe of Muslims in southern India, descended from Hāshim, many of whose descendants were driven in the eighth century by the cruelties of Hajjāj b. Yūsuf, governor of 'Irāq, to take refuge in India. Wilks, I, 150 n.; Grant Duff, I, 505 n. Also *Tārikh-un-Navāitah* by the Nawab 'Azīz Jang, Shams-ul-'Ulamā, Khān Bahādur, of Hyderābād.

[2] See chap. XIII, p. 384.

[3] His origin is doubtful. It has recently been asserted that he was by birth a Sayyid.

[4] Now Rohilkhand.

and in the murder of one of the younger brothers. For this he was rewarded with the title of Nawāb, a command of horse, some assignments, and the government of some *parganas*. Qamar-ud-dīn Khān's assignments had also been in his charge since the minister had held the appointment of governor. Nādir Shāh's advance on Qandahār had driven from that neighbourhood a large number of Afghāns or Rohillas[1] who feared his vengeance, and most of whom had taken refuge in India and had been attracted to 'Alī Muhammad by his reputation as a patron and protector of Afghāns. His power had increased enormously and, encouraged by the confusion prevailing throughout the empire, he had conceived the idea of establishing himself as the ruler of an independent principality, and retained, instead of remitting to Delhi, the rents of Qamar-ud-dīn Khān's assignments. The minister appointed as commandant of Morādābād, Rājā Har Nand, and ordered him to look into the accounts. Incensed by this, 'Alī Muhammad attacked and slew the raja and then possessed himself of a large tract and maintaining a considerable force of Afghān horse conducted himself as independent.

Qamar-ud-dīn Khān, sunk in sloth and debauchery, entered into a disgraceful compact by which the independence of the rebel was virtually recognised, but Safdar Jang and 'Umdat-ul-Mulk, who were 'Alī Muhammad Khān's neighbours on the east and the south, aroused the emperor to a sense of his humiliation and assured him of their support. Safdar Jang's motives were partly selfish, for he had no liking for such a neighbour, but his advice was sound, and it was followed.

On 18 March, 1745, Muhammad Shāh left Delhi to attack the rebel, but his movements were leisurely. 'Alī Muhammad Khān did not venture to meet the imperial army in the field, and withdrew to his fortress of Bangarh, 14 miles north-east of Budaun. Even here he could not hold out, for the emperor had been joined by Rājā Nawal Rāi with the contingent of Safdar Jang and by Qāim Khān, the son and successor of Muhammad Khān Bangash, with his contingent from Farrukhābād. On 3 June he submitted, using the services of Qamar-ud-dīn Khān as a mediator. His life was spared but Qamar-ud-dīn Khān was ordered to keep him in custody. The death of Zakariyā Khān, governor of the Punjab, furnishes an example of the emperor's impotence in administrative affairs. Zakariyā's eldest son was in the camp and the minister, Qamar-ud-dīn Khān, who was both his uncle and his father-in-law, sent him off post haste to Lahore to settle his father's affairs. After his arrival the minister for the first time announced his brother-in-law's death and later persuaded the emperor to confer the provinces of the Punjab and Multān on himself. Before long Shāh Nawāz Khān, a younger but more capable nephew, dispossessed his elder brother and became governor of the Punjab.

[1] Men of the *Roh*, or hill country.

Muhammad Shāh, contemptible as was his attitude to public affairs, demanded that deference which a stronger character would have commanded. 'Umdat-ul-Mulk, who had at one time been so high in his esteem that he had proposed to make him his minister and to employ him to break the power of the Turanian party, now acquired great influence at court. When Qamar-ud-dīn Khān incapacitated himself for appearance at court for a period of seven or eight months by a fall while intoxicated, he entrusted his official business with the emperor to 'Umdat-ul-Mulk rather than to any of his own worthless sons. 'Umdat-ul-Mulk, who was outspoken and unceremonious, was accustomed to use in his intercourse greater freedom than Muhammad Shāh considered becoming and on one occasion he indiscreetly visited the princes of the imperial family imprisoned in Salīmgarh. On another occasion he was discussing some tedious business with the emperor, who impatiently told him to postpone it. 'Umdat-ul-Mulk persisted and began to repeat the whole of his discourse from the beginning. The chief eunuch, who was present, said in a low but audible tone that the matter was as endless as the chatter of two old women. 'Umdat-ul-Mulk lost his temper and Muhammad Shāh was obliged to appease him by promising to dismiss the chief eunuch, but after he had left complained bitterly of the manner in which he was treated by 'Umdat-ul-Mulk. The eunuch replied that the matter could be arranged and, with his master's sanction, found a ruffian who had been dismissed from 'Umdat-ul-Mulk's service. On 6 January, 1747, 'Umdat-ul-Mulk was stabbed as he entered the hall of audience, and died on the spot.

A dark cloud descended on the intellect of Nādir Shāh of Persia towards the close of his reign. He had always been a hard taskmaster and a rigid though fair disciplinarian, but with advancing years he suspected all his subjects, and suspicion became a sufficient ground for punishment. He blinded his eldest and most promising son, and none knew when mad caprice might single him out for destruction. On 2 June, 1747, Nādir was stabbed to death in his own camp. His line did not at once die out, but his great empire dissolved. Among his chief commanders was Ahmad, of the Sadozāī section of the Abdālī or Durrānī tribe, an Afghān who had been captured when Nādir conquered Herāt. He afterwards gained his captor's favour and rose to high rank in his service. When Nādir was assassinated Ahmad returned to his own country and with the the help of his tribe and a force of Qizilbāsh horse who threw in their fortunes with him established himself in Herāt, captured Qandahār from the Ghilzāī who held it for Nādir Shāh, and expelled from Kābul Nāsir Khān, who having entered Nādir Shāh's service had been governor of that province for him as formerly for Muhammad Shah of Delhi, and, having thus reduced to obedience the whole of Afghānistān proper, assumed the royal title. He had hardly established his authority in Afghānistān when the treachery of Shah Nawāz Khān, governor of the Punjab, encouraged him to devise schemes of foreign conquest.

Among the advisers of Shāh Nawāz Khān was one Ādīna Beg Khān, "a devil in human form", who seems to have gone about deliberately to ruin him. He reminded him that his elder brother, whom he had ousted, was the minister's son-in-law as well as nephew, and advised him, therefore, to come to terms with the Abdālī. Shāh Nawāz Khān followed this advice and his unexpected advances were welcomed by Ahmad Shāh, who accepted his offers and concluded an alliance. Ādīna Beg Khān then informed the minister Qamar-ud-dīn Khān of this treasonable correspondence. The crafty minister misled his nephew by suggesting that the emperor wished him to conquer the provinces of Kābul, Kashmīr, Sind and Multān, and to confer the government of these provinces, as well as that of the Punjab, on him. Shāh Nawāz Khān now regretted his precipitancy and, acting still on the advice of Ādīna Beg Khān, resolved to repudiate his agreement. Ahmad Shāh advanced to Peshāwar and called on Shāh Nawāz Khān to permit him to pass freely through the Punjab and to join him with his troops. Receiving a flat refusal Ahmad Shāh crossed the Indus with 30,000 horse and invaded the Punjab. Shāh Nawāz Khān entrenched himself before Lahore. Superstitious faith in the warning of a *darvīsh* kept him inactive and his troops lost spirit. An indecisive movement from his tent towards the city, which he was persuaded might be a better defensive position than his entrenched camp, was construed as an attempt at flight. Soon the whole army was on its way to Delhi and Shāh Nawāz Khān had no choice but to accompany it. The Afghān and Qizilbāsh troops entered and sacked the undefended city.

The emperor and the courtiers, on learning that Ahmad Shāh Abdālī had crossed the Indus, made preparations to resist the invader. A large army was assembled under the nominal command of prince Ahmad, the emperor's son, who was placed under the tutelage of Sādāt Khān, Zu-'l-fiqār Jang, and the great *amīrs*. Safdar Jang, Qamar-ud-dīn Khān, and others joined it with their contingents. On this occasion many of the chiefs of Rājasthān assisted in the defence of the empire.

The army left Delhi on 19 January, 1748, and marched through Sirhind to Māchīwārā on the Sutlej. Meanwhile Ahmad Shāh Abdālī had left Lahore and, marching by Ludhiāna, avoided the imperial army and occupied Sirhind, between it and Delhi. Sirhind was plundered and all men bearing arms were put to the sword. Prince Ahmad was thus forced to retrace his steps and near Sirhind, as had now become usual with the demoralised forces of the emperor of Delhi, he entrenched himself before an army greatly inferior in numerical strength. Ahmad Shāh Abdālī's troops had captured part of the imperial train of artillery and had thus supplied themselves with arms and munitions of which they stood much in need. The imperial army, devoid of every military virtue, was besieged in its entrenched camp from 15 March to 28 March and on 22 March the death of Qamar-ud-dīn Khān, the minister, who was killed by a gunshot while he was sitting at prayers in his tent, still further discouraged the army and caused the desertion of all the Rājput chiefs.

There still remained some able and brave officers in the army, and Safdar Jang, with a useful force of Persian troops, and Mu'īn-ul-Mulk, son of the late minister, insisted on taking the field. After three or four days of this desultory and indecisive fighting, operations assumed a more serious character. Ahmad Shāh Abdālī led a determined attack on Mu'īn-ul-Mulk, who opposed to it a resistance as determined. Another attack was then led on the imperial centre, commanded by the prince, who was so hard pressed that Safdar Jang was obliged to send some of his troops to his assistance. Safdar Jang then advanced with his Persian troops on foot, preceded by his artillery which kept up a continuous fire on the enemy, and attacked Ahmad Shāh Abdālī. By great good fortune a rocket or some other missile ignited the waggon-loads of rockets which the invaders had captured and these exploded in all directions, causing many casualties among the Afghān troops and throwing them into confusion. Many fled, but Ahmad Shāh Abdālī contrived to hold his ground until the evening, and during the night began his retreat towards Afghānistān.

The news of the victory was received with great joy in Delhi and Mu'īn-ul-Mulk was rewarded for his services with the government of the Punjab and set out for Lahore, while the prince, Sādāt Khān, and Safdar Jang returned slowly towards Delhi.

Muhammad Shāh had now fallen sick of dropsy and grew rapidly worse. Feeling his end approaching he sent repeated messages to his son and Safdar Jang, begging them to hasten, that he might see his son once more. The army moved, therefore, with greater speed, but Ahmad failed to reach Delhi in time to see his father alive and was met at Pānīpat by the news that he had died on 26 April.

Safdar Jang at once raised an umbrella over Ahmad's head in the camp, the march to Delhi was continued and on 29 April, 1748, the prince was enthroned in the Shālamār garden as Ahmad Shāh.

Muhammad Shāh demands our pity if he may not command our respect. Placed in a position which called for a genius he was a very ordinary person. Historians blame him for his devotion to pleasure rather than to business, but the tragedy of his situation was that the most absolute devotion to business by a man of his mental calibre would in no way have altered the course of events. A mere sickly puppet like Rafī'-ud-Darajāt or Rafī'-ud-Daula was perhaps hardly conscious of humiliation, but Muhammad Shāh appears to have realised both the hopelessness of the situation and his own powerlessness to amend it. The seeds of decay had been sown by Aurangzīb and the process was now nearly complete. The bigotry which had alienated the Rājputs and exasperated the Marāthās, the leniency which regarded laxity and even treachery as venial faults in a military officer and ultimately dissolved the bonds of discipline throughout the army, the shortsightedness which permitted or rather encouraged the erection of principalities on agglomerations of provinces, had now caused a result which is clear from a survey of the condition of the empire at the time of Muhammad Shāh's death.

India south of the Narbadā and west of the Wāingangā and the Godāvarī was ruled by a prince independent in all but name. This prince's authority was, indeed, disputed not without success by a great Hindu power, but in this dispute the emperor had neither a share nor an interest. The three provinces of Bengal, Bihār and Orissa were ruled by another independent prince, whose authority, like that of his neighbour to the south-west, was contested by a Hindu power that at this time wrested one of the three provinces from him.

In the same region a power was rising which was destined, at no distant date, to overthrow both Muslim and Hindu rule. With all these disputes between the competitors the emperor had no concern, save when a prince who deigned to describe himself as lieutenant found it convenient to appeal for aid. The viceroyalty of Bengal contributed not an officer or a man to the defence of the empire during the invasions of Nādir Shāh and Ahmad Shāh Abdālī. West of this state lay the viceroyalty of Oudh, already virtually independent under a hereditary ruler and destined soon to absorb the provinces of Allahābād and Rohilkhand, as Katehr soon began to be called from its new masters. The rich province of Mālwā formed part of the dominions of that Hindu power which was contesting supremacy with Muslim princes in the Deccan and Bengal, and the same may be said of the still richer province of Gujarāt. Rājputāna stood sullenly aloof from the empire, ruled by the descendants of her princesses, and the Punjab, Multān and Sind lay at the feet of the Afghān king. All that remained to Delhi were the northern half of the Gangetic Dūāb, a region of about twice the area of that tract on the west of the Jumna, the southern portion of which, however, was occupied by the rebellious Jāts, and a strip of territory which only at one point attained a width of a hundred miles, extending eastward from about the seventieth degree of east longitude, along the southern banks of the Indus, Panjnad and Sutlej rivers. Within this limited area the emperor of India exercised such authority as his ministers were pleased to leave in his hands.

The demoralisation of the army was one of the principal factors in the disintegration of the empire. It cannot be attributed to the puppets who during the first half of the eighteenth century disgraced the throne of Bābur and of Akbar, or even to Aurangzīb. The source of the weakness was the composition of the army, which consisted chiefly of contingents maintained by the great nobles from the revenues of assignments held by them for the purpose. The defects of this system had been clearly perceived both by 'Alā-ud-Dīn Khaljī and by Akbar, as later by Nādir Shāh, but neither had succeeded in permanently abolishing it. They were less apparent in the reign of a monarch who could command the affections and the obedience of the nobles, but the system was radically unsound, as every system must be which depends upon such an uncertain factor as the personal character of a monarch, and as the authority of the sovereign relaxed the general tendency among the great nobles was naturally to hold as their own those assignments which maintained their troops. Thus, the later emperors had no personal body of troops with which to assert authority.

Two other grave defects appeared, as early as in 1595, at the first siege of Ahmadnagar. The first was the jealousy which afterwards became so prominent a characteristic of the imperial officers that a commander would sometimes deliberately refrain from bringing to a successful conclusion a battle already more than half won or a siege which had reduced the garrison of a fortress to extremities if he perceived that another would share the credit of his success. The second was the habit of treacherous correspondence with the enemy. The constant internecine wars between the five independent Muhammadan kingdoms of the Deccan had been conducted on a most pernicious system. A campaign was regarded by the commanders on either side as an occasion for the display of diplomatic as well as of military skill, and as an opportunity for enriching themselves. This spirit appears to have infected the imperial army in the Deccan and during Aurangzīb's quarter of a century of warfare in that region only one fortress was taken by storm. Conflicts in the field, as well as the attack and defence of fortified places, were decided by negotiations and money payments as often as by force of arms.

Finally, the general laxity of discipline converted the army into a mob. Drill was unknown and a soldier's training, which he might undergo or not, as he liked, consisted in muscular exercise and in individual practice in the use of the weapons with which he was armed. He mounted guard or not as he liked, the punishment for absence, not invariably inflicted, consisting in the loss of a day's pay. There was, indeed, no regular punishment for military crimes. An infuriated commander might occasionally expose officers and men guilty of cowardice to the ridicule of their comrades by mounting them on asses and parading them through the camp, but even this grave crime frequently went unpunished, and Aurangzīb himself habitually overlooked as matters of course acts of treason, cowardice and deliberate neglect of duty before the enemy.

In an army thus composed and thus commanded no military spirit was to be looked for, and the imperial troops, both officers and men, were characterised by a complete absence of the will to victory. "The Deccan is the bread of the soldier" ran the proverb, and probably nobody, except Aurangzīb, saw why the war should ever end. In such circumstances an army dissolved before the first foreign invader.

CHAPTER XIII

THE HYDERĀBĀD STATE (1724–1762)

NIZĀM-UL-MULK (Qamar-ud-dīn, Chīn Qilīch Khān, Khān Daurān) had held the viceroyalty of the Mughul Deccan once in 1713–14 and again from 1720 to 1722, and though in February, 1722, he migrated to Delhi to take up the post of chief minister of the empire, he retained his Deccan appointment by means of his agents. Early in 1724, in despair of reforming the government of Delhi, he set out for the Deccan, with the secret intention of resigning the more responsible office. The intrigue by which his enemies sought to destroy his position in the Deccan by urging his deputy Mubāriz Khān to usurp power there, and the failure of the plan and death of Mubāriz Khān in the battle of Shakarkhelda, have been related in chap. XII. This one blow was decisive, and its effect was completed by the Nizām's wise conciliation of his dead rival's son and his peaceful acquisition of Golconda by liberal gifts (early in 1725). In a short time the entire Mughul Deccan was brought under his control and the revenue began to be collected regularly. The emperor recognised the accomplished fact by "pardoning" the Nizām and confirming him in the viceroyalty of the Deccan, with the title of Āsaf Jāh (June, 1725). This was the foundation of the present state of Hyderābād.

When in 1724 Nizām-ul-Mulk went to the Deccan for the last time as its governor, he dropped the curtain on one act of his career and began a new one. All his aspirations for restoring the power and prestige of the Mughul empire and guiding the government from its centre, as its minister, were abandoned, for he felt that the mean and jealous favourites of the fickle emperor would not let him do anything, and he was not the man to agree to a passive sleepy existence like Muhammad Amīn Khān, his predecessor, or Muhammad Amīn's son, his successor. He thus set out for the Deccan, determined to make it a stage on which he could at least play a man's part and build up a political structure that would justify his title of "Regulator of the Realm".

In the history of the Mughul Deccan, too, a new scene opens with the battle of Shakarkhelda. The constant succession of short-term viceroys, the discord due to the six divisions being held by six different officers, and the civil strife between rivals for the viceroyalty, henceforth ceased. There was now one ruler over the whole tract; he made it his home and planted his dynasty there; and he had not to take his orders from a far-off master. His strong arm brought peace to that unhappy land harried by war for forty years since the invasion of Aurangzīb. Ambitious local officers, rebel chieftains and robber leaders thought twice before challenging the vanquisher of Dilāvar 'Alī, 'Ālim 'Alī and Mubāriz Khān. This enforcement of law and order, coupled with his moderate revenue assessment and strict prohibition of illegal cesses, gave security to the peasant and the trader, and the wealth of the country increased rapidly.

It was a splendid heritage into which Āsaf Jāh had entered. The six Deccan provinces had a standard revenue of 160 million rupees, against 170 million from the other twelve provinces of the Indian empire taken together; and though the actual collection here had now fallen to 130 million or even less, it was still larger than what came to the impoverished exchequer of Delhi, and was capable of rapid improvement under an orderly and beneficent administration. For the land in the old Qutb Shāhī kingdom was exceedingly fertile and its wealth had excited the cupidity of prince Aurangzīb in 1654, when he described it to his father as "a spacious kingdom, well cultivated, rich in mines of diamond, crystal etc.—a money-yielding country, unmatched by the imperial dominions". Its annexe of the eastern Carnatic was proverbially rich, "a kingdom by itself". Bijāpur, though less favoured by nature, was enriched by the tributes of a wide belt of vassal states on its south and west, which made it the richest among the six provinces, Hyderābād being a close second. The population in Hyderābād and Berār was dense and industrious. Such a soil required only peace to yield gold, and that peace Āsaf Jāh's long and uninterrupted rule for a quarter of a century assured to it.

After the victory of Shakarkhelda, the terror of Āsaf Jāh's arms and the high reputation for capacity and spirit which he had brought with him cowed his own refractory subjects. But the Marāthās were an ever present menace to his state and proved his chief preoccupation throughout his rule, and they succeeded in nibbling away his state when he was no more. And yet he was sincerely desirous of living at peace with them. He had seen with his own eyes how the whole force of the empire wielded by a sovereign of the stamp of Aurangzīb for twenty-five years had failed to crush the Marāthā people. Āsaf Jāh therefore recognised the basic truth that the Marāthās were the native landowners of the Deccan and that the Mughul governor of that country must cultivate their friendship if he was to live at all. On the other side, Rājā Shāhū too was eager to remain on good terms with the Mughul government and to avoid war at all costs. Completely enervated by his long captivity in Aurangzīb's harem, constitutionally weak and unenterprising, faced with disobedience and tumult by many of his own subjects, the Marāthā king was content with the *chauth* and *sardeshmukhī* which had been legally granted to him by the Delhi sovereign in 1718, so long as he could collect them in peace.[1] Thus, the principals on the two sides sincerely sought

[1] Chap. xi, p. 338.

peace and the maintenance of the *status quo* established in 1718, but their followers forced their hands.

The Nizām rightly claimed to enter into the full territorial legacy of Aurangzīb in the Deccan, modified only by the grant of 1718. This completely barred the expansion of the Marāthā race and threatened to coop them up for ever within the narrow limits of Shivājī's small possessions in their homeland. Then began the inevitable clash between a legitimate but static authority and the dynamic spirit of expansion of a new people trying to find its place in the sun, which was witnessed a century and a half earlier when the Elizabethan adventurers burst upon the lawful Spanish government of the New World. There were some distinct centres of friction. The Nizām's possession of Bāglān blocked the easiest path for Marāthā penetration into Gujarāt; similarly, his province of Khāndesh lay across their way to Mālwā. Much of the true home of the Marāthā race, like the districts of Junnar and Ahmadnagar, still owned Mughul sway. In the closing years of his life the triumphant Marāthās swept onwards to raid the eastern Carnatic and also penetrated into the Kanarese country southwards (Savanūr, Bednūr, etc.), and squeezed the Nizām's tribute-payers there, while in the north-east the Bhonsles of Nāgpur conquered the Gond rajas and encroached upon the Deccan province of Berār.

Shāhū's authority as king was so little backed by force and was recognised by so few of the Marāthās that it was beyond his power to control the actions of the free-lances and adventurers among his nominal subjects and effectively keep them out of the Mughul Deccan. Thus, the regular payment of the stipulated contribution (*chauth*) did not invariably safeguard the Nizām's dominions from Marāthā depredation.

One of Āsaf Jāh's earliest acts, after taking full possession of his charge (1725), was to make an agreement with the Marāthās. The *chauth* of the Deccan provinces having been granted by the emperor by a royal rescript, Āsaf Jāh had to recognise the settled fact. But he did what was possible in the circumstances to save his realm from ruinous occupation and unlimited extortion by a host of greedy Marāthā tribute-collectors and their troops. He settled with Rājā Shāhū that in respect of the province of Hyderābād he would himself pay the amount of the tribute in cash from his treasury, so that no Marāthā collector need enter his dominions for the money. Unauthorised extra taxes (like the *sardeshmukhī* and *rāhdārī*), which the Marāthās used to realise in the Mughul Deccan by sharing with the former governors, were definitely abolished. This arrangement was concluded on Shāhū's behalf by his minister, Shrīnivās Rāo, while the Peshwā Bājī Rāo advocated a more aggressive and ambitious policy. Its details had not been fully worked out and the agreement had not been put into actual operation before war broke out. The

Nizām encountered opposition in taking possession of the Mughul territories in the Kanarese districts (south-west), while Marāthā raiders disturbed the country west and south of Aurangābād.

Unable to keep the Marāthās within their own limits, Āsaf Jāh took refuge in diplomatic machination. Malcontents among Shāhū's subjects and those ministers of his government who were jealous of the Peshwā's ascendancy all found welcome at the Nizām's court. By their advice, he planned to create division and weakness in the Marāthā state by undertaking to instal Shambhūjī of Kolhāpur (the first cousin of Shāhū) as the head of the Marāthā royal family (*Chhatrapati*) and to make an equal partition of Shivājī's kingdom between the two cousins. He attached the ancestral estate (*watan*) of the house of Shivājī, which Shāhū had so long enjoyed and to which Shāhū like all other Marāthās felt an almost religious attachment. The attempt ultimately failed through the utter incapacity of the Nizām's puppet Chhatrapati and the unreliability of his Marāthā allies, but mainly because of the superior genius and energy of Bājī Rāo. It left behind it two results very harmful to the Nizām's interests: Shāhū was bitterly estranged from him, and Bājī Rāo's ascendancy in the council of his king became unrivalled.

Shambhūjī of Kolhāpur had gone to Āsaf Jāh in October, 1726, and kept claiming to be placed on Shivājī's throne. Two great Marāthā nobles, Rambhā Nimbālkar and Chandra Sen Jādav (the ex-commander-in-chief of Shāhū), were on the Nizām's side. Shāhū's officer (*Rājādnyā*) Chimnājī Dāmodar joined Shambhūjī in 1727 and became his prime minister. Several captains of lesser note like Thorat were also in the same camp. With their support, Āsaf Jāh assembled a large army for the invasion of Mahārāshtra in November, 1727, in the interests of Shambhūjī. But his plan leaked out, Shāhū learnt of it long in advance, warned all his fort garrisons to be carefully on the defensive, and struck the first blow by launching Bājī Rāo upon the Nizām's dominions. The Peshwā, passing west of Pārner, forded the Godāvarī at Puntambe, and skirting the larger cities like Baizāpur and Aurangābād some distance on their west and north, burst into the Jālna and Sindhkhed districts at the end of October and sacked the country right and left. But now at last the Nizām was on the move; his advanced division led by 'Iwaz Khān attacked the Marāthā bands dispersed for plunder (17 November) and beat them back. Bājī Rāo, avoiding pitched battles, began a series of bewilderingly rapid marches, which completely baffled and exhausted his enemy. In fact, in this cross-country race over a vast broken country, the Nizām, with his mail-clad heavy cavalry and cumbrous artillery, was completely out-manœuvred by the Marāthā light horse and toiled painfully behind it without being able to prevent its ravages or to bring it to an action. After a feint against Burhānpur, Bājī Rāo made a dash eastwards to Mangrūl, beyond Bāsim in the extreme east of Berār (20 December), and then turning sharply to the north-west, crossed the Tāptī some distance west of Chopra (30 December) and the Narbadā at the Bābā Piārā ford (14 January, 1728), and arrived within twenty-five miles of Broach. Then he swooped down due south, spending a fortnight near Songarh (forty-five miles east of Surat), and doubled back northwards across the Tāptī and the Narbadā to the 'Alī Mohan country (fifty miles east of Baroda city) on 11 February. From this point he was recalled by news of the danger to Poona and reached Betāvad (twenty miles north of Dhulia in west Khāndesh) on 24 February.

In the meantime the Nizām, worn out by his long and futile marches, had wisely changed his plan of war. Giving up the pursuit of the elusive Bājī Rāo, he in full force entered the Poona district now denuded of defenders, his vanguard under Turktāz Khān opening the way. Nothing could stand against him. Rājā Shāhū and Chimājī (the Peshwā's brother and agent at court) took refuge in Purandar fort; every military station and town in the Poona district submitted to the Nizām in terror and was placed in charge of some agent of Shambhūjī. One fort alone, Udāpur, made a bold defence and had to be taken by bombardment. Finally, the Nizām entered Poona city, proclaimed Shambhūjī's authority over the country, and celebrated that raja's marriage with a princess of Rāmnagar.

All this time, owing to Bājī Rāo's rapid marches, Shāhū had received little news of his position and success, and was frantically writing to him to come back for the defence of his home. From Betāvad, Bājī Rāo turned southwards, crossed the Ajanta range at Kāsār ghāt[1] about 28 February, and like a master strategist ensured the automatic relief of Poona by marching upon the Nizām's capital Aurangābād. While he was sacking the Gandāpur and Baizāpur districts west of that city, the Nizām evacuated the Poona district, deposited his camp and baggage at Ahmadnagar, and then on 4 March set out in light marching order to overtake Bājī Rāo. But the Peshwā, by his "Cossack-like tactics", plundered on both sides of the Nizām's line of advance, stopped his grain supply, and harassed his troops at every difficult place like a watercourse or ravine. At last the Nizām was manœuvred into a broken waterless ground near Palkhed (twelve miles east of Baizāpur and twenty miles west of Daulatābād) and completely hemmed in (11 March). However, after undergoing unspeakable hardship, he cut his way out, but in utter disgust at the worthlessness of his Marāthā allies, he gave up the plan of backing Shambhūjī. Negotiations were opened with Bājī Rāo and a treaty was made at Shevgāon (22 March) by which the Nizām abandoned Shambhūjī's cause, gave up several forts as security for the payment of the tribute (including all arrears), and made Rambhā Rāo Nim-

[1] Twenty miles due east of Manmād railway junction and the same distance north of Baizāpur.

bālkar transfer "the Twelve Māvals" (western Poona and Nāsik) to Bājī Rāo. Shāhū's collectors were restored to all their former places and the Nizām returned to Hyderābād. It was a complete triumph for Shāhū.

But this treaty did not bring peace, any more than the former settlement of the Hyderābād tribute had done. Though there were no more regular wars between the Nizām and Shāhū's government, the events of 1727 left behind them a spirit of mutual suspicion and alarm which continued for the next four years, with occasional conflicts between local officers and small invading bands of both sides. Shambhūjī having been cast off as a broken tool, the Nizām formed a plot with Trimbak Rāo Dābhāde (the Marāthā commander-in-chief, jealous of the Brāhman Peshwā) and many other malcontents to crush Bājī Rāo. But before the two allies could complete their musters and effect a junction, Bājī Rāo's alertness again triumphed. Hastening to Gujarāt he slew Dābhāde near Dabhoi (12 April, 1731) and broke up his party. In the preceding month the Nizām had gone to Burhānpur, suppressed a rebel, Mohan Singh, and held secret consultations with Muhammad Khān Bangash (the new viceroy of Mālwā) on the bank of the Narbadā, and now after a fruitless chase of Bājī Rāo through Khāndesh and Bāglān, he returned to Aurangābād. Unsuccessful in war, the Nizām at last entered into a secret compact with Bājī Rāo, by which the Marāthā government promised to leave the Deccan unmolested and to levy nothing beyond the stipulated *chauth* and *sardeshmukhī* from them, while the Nizām agreed to remain neutral during the projected Marāthā invasions of Hindustān, provided that they did not injure his province of Khāndesh in their northward march through it. This pact was confirmed during Bājī Rāo's visit to the Nizām in the Christmas week of 1732. Thus Marāthā ambition was diverted to the north, and the heart of the Mughul Deccan enjoyed comparative peace.

During the next four years, the government of the Deccan followed an even course, only disturbed by minor Marāthā raids here and there. The Nizām used to go out on tour every winter and return to Aurangābād or Burhānpur for cantoning during the rainy season. He collected tribute from his dependents, like the Rājās of (western) Kanara and the Pathān Nawābs, and attended to the normal administration, following his usual practice of changing the local officers every two years.

When in 1736–37 the Marāthās carried their depredations to the gates of Delhi, the emperor repeatedly wrote to Āsaf Jāh to come to his aid. The Nizām reached Delhi on 13 July, 1737. His defeat by Bājī Rāo at Bhopāl (December, 1737) and the humiliating treaty (16 January, 1738) by which he extricated himself, his passive participation in the battle of Karnāl with Nādir Shāh (24 February, 1739), and his quarrels with the emperor's new favourites after the departure of Nādir, do not belong to the history of the Deccan and have been dealt with elsewhere. A second time despairing of reforming his master's government or even of preserving his own honour in that worthless court, he finally left Delhi on 7 August, 1740, and returned to Burhānpur on 19 November.

Here he found a perilous situation created by the ambition of his second son Nāsir Jang, whom he had left in the Deccan as his deputy during his three and a half years' absence in northern India. This young noble was of a fiery impetuous nature, in contrast with his father's cool and far-sighted judgment and perfect self-control. Taking advantage of the shock given to the imperial power by Nādir's invasion and Āsaf Jāh's absence, the Marāthās achieved some conspicuous successes. Raghūjī Bhonsle of Nāgpur slew the Mughul governor of Berār (January, 1738) and exacted contribution from Ellichpur. Chimājī raided the environs of Burhānpur. Gopāl Rāo seized the fort of Māhur (in Berār). In April, 1739, Bājī Rāo began to confiscate grants near the capital of Khāndesh, but retired at the end of next month on hearing of Nādir's retreat. In the winter of 1739–40 he renewed his depredations south of Aurangābād, but Nāsir Jang sallied out and drove him beyond the Godāvarī. For one month (28 January–29 February, 1740) there was daily marching and fighting. At last a meeting was arranged between the two chiefs and peace was made by granting the districts of Khargon and Handiya to the Peshwā.

Shortly afterwards Bājī Rāo died. Nāsir Jang, now freed of all enemies at home, formed the plan of usurping the government of the Deccan from his aged and absent father. Evil counsellors gathered round the hot-headed youth, who began to act with unrestrained caprice and tyranny.

This news brought Āsaf Jāh to Burhānpur, where he halted for two months, trying to reason with his son. Many of the rebel's adherents took this opportunity to come over to the Nizām's side. Nāsir Jang, unable to face his father in the field, sought asylum at the tomb of Shāh Burhān-ud-dīn. The Nizām crossed the Tāptī on 16 January, 1741, and after a friendly meeting with the new Peshwā Bālājī Rāo on the bank of the Purnā (at 'Ādilābād), crossed the Kāsār pass, and reached Aurangābād in March. Nāsir Jang, in fear of his father, fled to Mulher fort (in Bāglān), but while the Nizām's forces were dispersed in cantonments for the rains, the rebel returned to Aurangābād at the head of 7000 horse, on 2 August, 1741. Āsaf Jāh boldly rode out of the city with his small escort but strong artillery and encamped at the 'Īdgāh outside. In the next day's battle, most of the rebel captains fled away, Nāsir Jang was taken prisoner, and his chief counsellor Shāh Nawāz Khān (the future author of *Maāsir-ul-umarā*) went into hiding for five years.

After suppressing his son's rebellion, Āsaf Jāh engaged himself for some time in exacting tribute from refractory dependents, and then his attention was drawn to the Carnatic. This rich province, with its capital at Arcot, was governed by an Arab family of the Navāit clan, which had offended the Marāthās and the Nizām alike by neglecting to pay to the former the annual compensation agreed upon for the relinquishment of Shivājī's forts and territories in that region, and to the latter the homage and surplus revenue (1,200,000 rupees a year) due to him as the supreme representative of the emperor in the south. Besides, in 1737 Chanda Sāhib, the son-in-law of the ruling Nawāb of Arcot, had seized Trichinopoly and many other places in the Marāthā kingdom of Tanjore by treachery, with the Nawāb's support. But a Marāthā army, 10,000 strong, led by Fath Singh and Raghūjī Bhonsle, started from Sātārā on 17 January, 1740, invaded Arcot, defeated and slew its Nawāb Dost 'Alī (31 May), and took from his successor Safdar 'Alī a promise of ten million rupees as indemnity. On 6 April, 1741, they captured Trichinopoly, made Chanda Sāhib prisoner, and left Murārī Rāo Ghorpare as their governor there. On 13 October, 1742, Safdar 'Alī was murdered by his cousin Murtazā 'Alī and the whole province fell into anarchy.

Āsaf Jāh set out from Hyderābād in January, 1743, with a vast force, and after establishing his authority at Arcot, laid siege to Trichinopoly in March. Murārī, at the head of 2000 horse and 4000 foot, held out for five months, but evacuated the fort on 25 August and left the province with all his Marāthās. Āsaf Jāh took from the Rājā of Tanjore a million rupees in cash and three and a half millions in promises, left Trichinopoly in October, and at Arcot deposed the family of Safdar 'Alī and installed his own agent Anvar-ud-dīn as its Nawāb. When, in January, 1744, he reached the bank of the Krishnā on his return journey, he found his passage threatened by a large Marāthā force on the opposite bank and fell back three marches. But their opposition was removed by "treaty, which was more agreeable (than war) to the Nizām's general method of proceeding",[1] and he reached Aurangābād in April. The other notable events of his last years were the capture of Bālkonda (sixteen miles south of Nirmal) from a rebel noble (1746) and a terrible famine which desolated Gujarāt and the Deccan (1747), grain selling at 1½ seers a rupee.[2] Since his return from the Carnatic, Āsaf Jāh's health had visibly declined, and at last he died at the Mohan Nālā, outside Burhānpur, on 1 June, 1748, at the age of seventy-nine lunar years. Besides liberally patronising Muslim theologians and holy men, scholars and poets, from all parts of India and the outer Islāmic world, he himself wrote Persian poetry, filling two volumes. Among his constructions are the new walls of Burhānpur city (replacing the dilapidated walls built by Aurangzīb to keep Marāthā raiders

[1] *Madras Consultations.*

[2] About 10*d.* a pound.

out), a new city named Nizāmābād above the ruined pass of Fardāpur, protective walls round Hyderābād city, and the Harsul canal running through Aurangābād.

For a quarter of a century Āsaf Jāh had been the most outstanding personality in the Mughul empire. He was universally regarded as the sole representative of the spacious times of Aurangzīb and of the policy and traditions of that strenuous monarch. The higher minds among the younger generation of the court nobility looked up to him with the respect due to a father, while fools and knaves hated him for his love of discipline and honesty of administration. He was undoubtedly the foremost general of his time in India. In statecraft and diplomacy he was no less eminent. He had the true statesman's length of vision and spirit of moderation, and of this we have many proofs. He won over the surviving partisans of Mubāriz Khān by liberal provision for their support. After crushing the rebellion of his son Nāsir Jang, he destroyed unread the rebel's despatch-box, which was reported to contain promises of adhesion from thirty-eight nobles of his own court. Still more strongly was his wisdom shown when in 1739, Nādir Shāh, disgusted with the imbecility of Muhammad Shāh, offered the throne of Delhi to Āsaf Jāh, but the latter refused to be disloyal to his master. On his deathbed he gave his son Nāsir Jang several pieces of very good counsel—telling him to live on good terms with the Marāthās, to abstain from putting men to death except by the judge's sentence, to scorn repose and frequently to go out on tours, to live laborious days in doing state business, to respect the rights of his servants and treat every man in a manner worthy of his position, to be loyal to his king, and not to provoke war by aggression. The only wrong policy that he followed and recommended to his son was that of removing his local officers after only a year or two of service and putting new men in their places, on the strange ground that thus "a large number of God's creatures would be fed".[1] In fact, in spite of his possessing exceptional military capacity, his conduct was throughout marked by prudence, the avoidance of waste or unnecessary expenditure, and simplicity of living, worthy of a pupil of Aurangzīb.

With the death of Āsaf Jāh a change came over the scene. The striking inferiority of his successors to him in ability and character was aggravated by the domination of Indian warfare by the European system which requires far larger and far more punctual expenditure on troops and munitions than was necessary in the middle ages. Now more than ever before the life of the state depended on the regular collection and wise expenditure of the revenue. But Āsaf Jāh's sons had not half his skill in war and diplomacy, nor even the wisdom to choose able instruments and confide in them. After his death we find frequent change of ministers and of the *fainéant* ruler's

[1] *Hadīqat*, ii, 179–180.

guiding genius, the *Vakīl-i-mutlaq* (corresponding to the Peshwā in the Marāthā kingdom), and consequent mismanagement of the finances and shrinkage of revenue.[1] The state, faced with constant deficit, could not pay its troops; hence arose mutinies, and finally the pernicious system of mortgaging the revenue and government of districts to the creditors of the state, which inflicted untold misery on the subject population and which in the nineteenth century required all the genius of Sālār Jang and the strong support of wise British Residents to root out. Under Āsaf Jāh's successors we have a repetition of the scene of the declining 'Abbāsid Caliphate: "A brilliant and extravagant Court, where the arts flourished and hospitality and charity were practised on an immense scale, was supported by a rapacious hierarchy of peculative officials, who were always striving to extort a fortune from their functions before the Court should pounce upon their corruption."

The indigenous troops of the Hyderābād government were ineffective when pitted against the native forces of the Peshwā or Tīpū Sultān, and its sole defenders were the French and then the English.

On the cultural side the picture was equally dark. Light came to Hyderābād under the Āsaf Jāhī dynasty, but not progress. Its rulers continued to dream the dreams of Aurangzīb's reign and to live in the seventeenth century. Titles of hyperbolical sound and fury but signifying no real worth were profusely showered among the officials, regardless of the great Āsaf Jāh's threat of flogging.

The modern spirit was shut out with the scorn bred of ignorance. The impact of the west, which was causing a marvellous renaissance in the British provinces and breathing a new life into the dry bones of Hindu society and thought, left Hyderābād untouched. Thus it happened that the intellectual leadership of Indian Islām eluded the grasp of the foremost Muhammadan state in India.

At the time of Āsaf Jāh's death, his eldest son Mīr Muhammad Panāh (Ghāzī-ud-dīn Khān) was living in Delhi as his father's deputy at court. The viceroyalty of the Deccan was seized by his second son Nāsir Jang, who had for some years past acted as his father's lieutenant and being present on the spot could easily get hold of his treasures and troops. At the secret invitation of the emperor he started for Delhi with the object of overthrowing the new minister Safdar Jang, but had to return from the bank of the Narbadā (5 June, 1749), as the emperor was cowed by his minister and ordered Nāsir Jang to go back, formally creating him viceroy of the Deccan with the title of Nizām-ud-Daula. At this time Āsaf Jāh's daughter's son, Muzaffar Jang, claiming the viceroyalty, went to the Carnatic in concert with Chanda Sāhib, an aspirant to the Nawābship of Arcot,

[1] For Berār, Khāndesh, Aurangābād and Bīdar, the revenue amounted to 37 million rupees in 1785, against nearly 79 million in 1725, a reduction to less than one-half (Jagjīvandās).

who had recently secured release from a Marāthā prison. The two allies bought the help of Dupleix (July)[1] and gained Arcot after killing its Nawāb. Nāsir Jang, with a vast army of 70,000 horse and 100,000 foot, marched to the Carnatic, came upon his enemies near Valudavūr (end of March, 1750), secured the abject surrender of Muzaffar Jang (5 April), and returned to Arcot. But on 16 December he was shot dead by Himmat Khān, the Pathān chief of Kurnool, during a treacherous attack on his camp by the French under Dupleix's orders, twenty miles north of Gingee.[2]

The French raised Muzaffar Jang to the viceroyalty and marched escorting him towards his capital; but on the way, at Lakkaredi-palli (thirty-five miles south of Cuddapah city), the new viceroy fought his Pathān dependent and was slain (13 February, 1751). Bussy, the commander of his French escort, was bribed by his revenue minister Rājā Raghunāth ("a black Brāhman of Chicacole, originally named Rāmdās") to transfer his support to Āsaf Jāh's third son, Salābat Jang, who was at once proclaimed his successor, and ultimately gained from Delhi the titles of Āsaf-ud-daula Zafar Jang and Amīr-ul-mamālik and recognition as viceroy of the Deccan. "Muzaffar Jang was the first to engage Europeans and bring them into the realm of Islām. After his death the French troops continued in the service of Salābat Jang and got (extensive) jagirs, so that they soon became all-in-all in the Deccan" (Āzād Bilgrāmī).

Bussy soon justified the high price paid for his support. The succession of Salābat Jang was opposed by the Peshwā, who wished the Deccan viceroyalty to be given to Āsaf Jāh's eldest son, Ghāzī-ud-dīn, a tame scholarly priest-ridden man, without any military capacity or ambition, under whom the Peshwā would practically govern the Deccan as his deputy. Bālājī intrigued at the imperial court in favour of Ghāzī-ud-dīn, and at the same time obstructed Salābat Jang's agents in taking possession of their territory. War resulted. But while the Peshwā was entangled in a civil war with his domestic enemies, the Marāthā governors of Gujarāt and Berār, Salābat Jang invaded Mahārāshtra with his French contingent and forced his way towards Poona. The rival forces came into contact on 1 December, 1751, and there was daily fighting, the Marāthās retreating and the Mughuls advancing. In the night of 3 December, the French surprised Bālājī between Arangāon and Sārolā[3] on the bank of the Sinā, put him to flight in his undress, slew many of his troops and plundered all their property, including the Peshwā's idols and gold ritual vessels. But Bālājī soon rallied his scattered forces and delivered a counter-attack only five days later, in which many were slain on both sides. Salābat advanced plundering up to Tālegāon Dhāmdhera, eighteen miles north-east of Poona. The campaign, however, ended

[1] See vol. v, p. 126. [2] See vol. v, p. 127.

[3] Two railway stations, respectively eight and twenty miles south of Ahmadnagar.

indecisively owing to scarcity of provisions and dissensions in the Muslim camp. A truce was patched up and Salābat started for his capital in the middle of April, 1752.

The danger which Salābat Jang dreaded most now approached him. His eldest brother Ghāzi-ud-dīn started (17 May) from Delhi with a strong Marāthā escort, in order to wrest the viceroyalty of the Deccan which had been conferred upon him by the emperor with the titles of Nizām-ul-Mulk, Āsaf Jāh. To meet this invasion, Bussy arranged for Salābat Jang a defensive subsidiary alliance with Bālājī (signed on 5 August), ceding to the Peshwā the province of Khāndesh (reserving only the imperial forts and the city of Burhānpur), the district of Bāglān, and lands yielding 200,000 rupees a year in the Sangamner and Jālna subdivisions, besides tribute for the Carnatic and Hyderābād. The Peshwā on his part promised to defend Salābat Jang against all "who might come to dispute the Deccan with him, even if it were the *vazīr* himself, furnished with the emperor's authority", to look after his interests at the imperial court against his enemies, and to keep the Marāthās out of the rest of Mughul Deccan. He also freed Salābat Jang from any liability to pay the six million rupees for which Ghāzī-ud-dīn had given a bond to the Peshwā.[1] But the storm unexpectedly blew over. Ghāzī-ud-dīn was poisoned by his stepmother on 16 October, only seventeen days after his arrival at Aurangābād.

Salābat Jang thus gained security, but he had neither civil or military capacity, nor character enough to act of his own will or trust able agents. Throughout his régime he was a mere puppet in the hands of his successive regents who ruled the state, while the intrigues of his courtiers and the mutinies of his unpaid soldiery paralysed the administration. The best of these regents was Samsām-ud-daula Shāh Nawāz Khān (in office, December 1753–July 1757), who succeeded in removing financial insolvency, restoring administrative efficiency, repressing foreign enemies and rebellious vassals, and giving some peace and happiness to the subject population.

Shāh Nawāz Khān was versed in many branches of knowledge, particularly in history (in which his enduring monument is his *Maāsir-ul-umarā*, or biographical dictionary of the Mughul peers, in three large volumes). High-minded, sympathetic to all, habitually charitable, a lover of justice, dealing directly with suitors in an open court without allowing intermediaries, an expert in financial management and diplomacy alike, "he wrought a magical change during his four years of Chancellorship by his wisdom and administrative genius, converted the insolvency of the State—when household goods had to be sold for feeding the Nizām—into a balanced budget at the end of the fourth year" (*Hadīqat*), and kept the Marāthās within their own limits. If he failed, in the end, to reform the government,

[1] *Lettres et Conventions*, 261–2.

HINDU KUSH
Kabul
Peshawar
KASHMIR
TIBET
AFGHAN SUPREMACY
Ahmad Shah Durrani
Qandahar
SULAIMAN RANGE
Multan
Jhelum R.
Chinab R.
Ravi R.
Sutlej R.
SIKHS
Lahore
HIMALAYA MOUNTAINS
MUGHAL TERRITORY
Panipat
1761
Delhi
ROHILLAS
Jumna R.
BAHAWALPUR
Indus R.
RAJPUTS
ARAVALLI HILLS
Ajmer
Agra
JATS
OUDH
Lucknow
Gumti R.
Gogra R.
Ganges R.
Kora
Allahabad
BIHAR
Brahmaputra R.
Chambal R.
MARATHA TERRITORY
Plassey
1757
BENGAL
Calcutta
Indore
VINDHYA RANGE
BHOPAL
Baroda
Nerbudda R.
SATPURA RANGE
Surat
Tapti R.
ORISSA
Mahanadi R.
Aurangabad
BERAR
Bombay
(British)
Poona
Godavari R.
NORTHERN SARKARS
occupied 1758-9
NIZAM'S TERRITORIES
Satara
Krishna R.
Guntur
WESTERN GHATS
Goa
(Portuguese)
Tungabhadra R.
EASTERN GHATS
MYSORE
CARNATIC
MADRAS
Kaveri R.
1760
Trichinopoly
TANJORE
TRAVANCORE
INDIA IN 1761
Approximate Boundaries
British
Hindu
Muhammadan

it was due to the selfishness and incurable love of intrigue of the entire official class and nobility, the imbecile character of his master, and the domination of the French praetorians. The proved worthlessness of his indigenous troops made Salābat Jang absolutely dependent on the French corps for protection. In his letters he represents himself as a helpless orphan who looked for the defence of his rights to his deceased father's brother, "mon oncle le Gouverneur Bahadour" Dupleix! (*Lettres et Conventions*, p. 267).

In 1754 Shāh Nawāz exacted 500,000 rupees as tribute from Raghūjī of Nāgpur, and arrested Surjā Rāo, the rebel officer of Nirmal. Next year he sent the Nizām to Mysore and levied over five million. Early in 1756, he repulsed Jānojī Bhonsle's officers who were raiding Bīdar, and by a friendly alliance with the Peshwā reduced the Pathān Nawābs of Bankāpur and Savanūr to obedience. A year later he subdued Rāmchandra Nimbālkar, the Marāthā grantee of Bhālkī. The imperial forts of Asīr and Daulatābād—the greatest in the Deccan—were gained for the Nizām by bribery. But his attempt to rid his master of French domination led to Shāh Nawāz Khān's fall. These foreign troops had been constantly troubling the Government for their pay of 2,900,000 rupees a year. They now demanded the great fort of Bīdar in addition to holding vast districts in Chicacole and Rājahmundry. Bussy's chief of artillery, Ibrāhīm Khān Gārdī, was seduced by Nizām 'Alī, and Shāh Nawāz induced Salābat Jang to dismiss the French corps. Bussy took leave to go to his grants in Chicacole, but on the way he seized the city of Hyderābād, and stood at bay in the Chaumahalla palace (14 June, 1756). Here he received from Pondicherry a reinforcement of 300 Europeans and 2000 Gārdī troops under M. Law. Salābat and Shāh Nawāz failed to dislodge Bussy after a two months' siege, and at last had to make peace with him (August).

Within a year of this, French intrigue succeeded in overthrowing the great minister. The pay of the army was due for two years, and "instigated by others" the soldiers caused a riot in the city and forced the Nizām to dismiss Shāh Nawāz (23 July, 1757) and appoint the pro-French Basālat Jang as regent. A terrible popular rising broke out that day; the ruffians and the mob of the city wanted to sack Shāh Nawāz's house; but two nights later he escaped to Daulatābād, abandoning his house to plunder. Profiting by this internal division, the Peshwā's son Vishvās Rāo invaded the country east of Aurangābād. So, Salābat made terms with Shāh Nawāz and induced him to return (13 November). But all power now passed into the hands of Nizām 'Alī, who was appointed heir and regent. The campaign of Nizām 'Alī against the Peshwā in the Sindkhed region ended in a peace by which the Marāthās gained two and a half million rupees worth of land in the Deccan and the fort of Naldrug (January, 1758).

All this time Bussy and his force had been absent on the east coast.

They now returned to Aurangābād, where Bussy's manager Haidar Jang completely deceived Shāh Nawāz, seduced Nizām 'Alī's army by paying 800,000 rupees, and at last, on 5 April, 1758, caused Shāh Nawāz to be arrested. Salābat Jang himself was placed under a French guard. Haidar was planning to imprison Nizām 'Alī and to seize the supreme power, when he himself was treacherously murdered by that prince (12 May), who escaped the vengeance of the French brigade by "marvellous skill and bravery". A riot raged through the city, in the course of which Shāh Nawāz and his son were murdered in prison by Lachhmanā, an officer of the French corps. The new regent Basālat Jang (the fifth son of Āsaf Jāh) proved a cypher. The French star waned as the English asserted their armed superiority in the Carnatic in the Seven Years' War. These disasters reacted on the French position at the Nizām's court. Bussy was recalled by Lally to the Madras coast (June, 1758). Nizām 'Alī came back to Hyderābād, and after some quarrel among the three brothers succeeded in being invested with all power *vice* Basālat Jang dismissed (June, 1759).

The Nizām's army, deprived of its French corps and Ibrāhīm Khān Gārdī's artillery (the latter having entered the Peshwā's service now), was reduced to helplessness. On the other hand, the strength and ambition of the Marāthās proportionately increased from the adhesion of Ibrāhīm Khān, which stiffened their "myriads of light horse" with French-drilled modern artillery. The Peshwā renewed war with the Nizām; his cousin Sadāshiv Bhāo gained the important fort of Ahmadnagar by terms (9 November, 1759). A vast Marāthā army under the Peshwā's brother Raghunāth and cousin Sadāshiv, with Ibrāhīm Gārdī's artillery, began the invasion in the beginning of January, 1760. Nizām 'Alī with Salābat Jang issued forth to oppose them and reached Udgīr on the 11th. Daily fighting began immediately. Hopelessly outnumbered, the Nizām planned to force his way to Dharūr and join a large body of his troops who were detained there. The Mughul force, only 7000 strong, was completely enveloped by 60,000 Marāthā horse, its progress impeded, and its supplies cut off. "This time the Cossack-tactics of the Marāthās were combined with the European mode of warfare (of Ibrāhīm Khān Gārdī) against the Nizām." The march from Udgīr to Ausā was a long drawn agony. The small Mughul army, slowly moving in the open field in close column, presented a sure target to the French-drilled artillery hovering round, while the dispersed and wheeling Marāthā horse were practically safe from their enemy's fire. It was the situation of Pānīpat inverted in favour of the Marāthās. When on 3 February the Nizām reached Ausā, forty miles south of Dharūr, 40,000 Marāthās attacked his rear-guard, which was straggling some miles behind, and a great disaster fell on it, all the commanders and most of the men being killed. The victorious

Marāthās then fell upon the Mughul centre and the battle raged till sunset. The Nizām's army was in no condition to fight any more. So, he made peace by ceding territory, yielding six million rupees in the province of Aurangābād, half of Bijāpur and Bīdar, the forts of Asīr, Daulatābād and Mulher, and the cities of Bijāpur and Burhānpur to the Peshwā (February, 1760). The descendants of Āsaf Jāh retained nothing more than Hyderābād, some parts of the province of Bijāpur, and a little of Bīdar, and that, too, on condition of paying the Marāthās one-fourth of the revenue.

This was the apogee of Marāthā success. Nemesis came at Pānīpat within one year, followed by the death of Bālājī Rāo, the succession of his minor son, and the internal dissensions caused by the guilty ambition of his brother Raghunāth Rāo, which paralysed the Marāthā power. Seizing this opportunity, Nizām 'Alī invaded Mahārāshtra in November, 1761, and made his way to within fourteen miles of Poona. The Peshwā made peace (2 January, 1762), relinquishing nearly half of his father's territorial gains in the Mughul Deccan. Nizām 'Alī returned to Bīdar, seized the government, and threw Salābat Jang into prison (6 July, 1762), where the latter died two years later. The shadowy emperor of Delhi sanctioned the usurpation by creating Nizām 'Alī viceroy with the titles of Nizām-ul-mulk Āsaf Jāh II.

With the accession of Nizām 'Alī (1762) a long period of stability begins in the affairs of the Mughul Deccan. We have at last one man ruling for forty-one years, and passing an undisputed succession on to his progeny. Family dissensions, except for a short and futile outbreak by his son, end. At the same time the centre of gravity of the Marāthā power slowly shifts from Poona to northern India. The Peshwā's family was stricken by disease, physical and moral. The ensuing peace could have been utilised for reforming the Hyderābād state and improving its people's lot, if only there had been wise rulers and honest ministers.

CHAPTER XIV

THE RISE OF THE MARĀTHĀ EMPIRE (1707–1761)

THE aged emperor Aurangzīb died in February, 1707, worn out by his long guerrilla campaign in the Deccan. His successor, Bahādur Shāh, decided, on the advice of Zu-'l-Fiqār Khān, the viceroy of the Deccan, to put into effect Aurangzīb's plan of restoring Shāhū, the grandson of Shivājī, who, after the capture and execution of his father Shambhūjī in 1689, had been brought up in the Mughul court. He was not twenty-six years old. Dāūd Khān, the deputy viceroy, who was stationed at Aurangābād, was directed to give him all possible assistance. After Shambhūjī's death, the direction of Marāthā affairs had fallen into the hands of his half-brother Rājā Rām. Rājā Rām died in 1700, whereupon his widow Tārā Bāī, a strong and masterful woman, declared herself regent for her infant son Shivājī, and profiting by the disorders at Delhi, reconquered Poona and Chākan from the Mughuls. The return of Shāhū, as was intended, threw an apple of discord into the Marāthā camp. Tārā Bāī refused to give up her son's claims. She declared that Shāhū was an impostor, assembled her ministers, and made them take an oath of fidelity to resist the pretender to the last gasp. Shāhū was granted the customary dues of *chauth* and *sardeshmukhī*[1] of the six Deccan provinces of Khāndesh, Berār, Aurangābād, Bīdar, Hyderābād and Bījāpur, and the governorship of Gondwāna, Gujarāt and Tanjore; all these, of course, he was to hold from the emperor. Starting from north of the Narbadā in May, 1707, he advanced slowly southwards during the rains, entered Sātārā, and was crowned in January, 1708. He made Gadādhar Prahlād his *Pratinidhi*,[2] Bahiro Pant Pingle his Peshwā, and Dhanājī Jādav his *Senāpati* or commander-in-chief. Tārā Bāī fell back upon Panhālā, the great stronghold twelve miles from Kolhāpur, which became the capital of the rival kingdom. As soon as the rains were over, Shāhū, after celebrating the Dasara, the festival which marks the opening of the campaigning season, marched against Tārā Bāī and took Panhālā. In 1712, Tārā Bāī was removed from the administration by a palace intrigue, and her place was taken by her co-wife Rājas Bāī, who claimed the throne for her son Shambhūjī;[3] but this did not help Shāhū, whose hold on his new

[1] For the meaning of the terms, see M. G. Ranade, *Rise of the Maratha Power*, chap. XI, and Sen, *Administrative System of the Marathas*, pp. 97, 243.

[2] The office of Pratinidhi or King's Representative was created by Rājā Rām in 1690 and was supernumerary to Shivājī's Council of Eight. The word Peshwā, or Prime Minister, is Persian, and dates from Muhammad I Bahmanī (1358–77). Shivājī preferred the Sanskrit title Mukhya Pradhān. Briggs, *Ferishta* III, 150 note; Grant Duff, I, 150.

[3] For details, see Kincaid and Parasnis (1931 edition), pp. 204–5.

kingdom became every day more precarious. Very few of the great Marāthā leaders had espoused his cause, and his rule was practically confined to his capital, and a few hill-forts garrisoned by his commanders. The Deccan was in a state of open anarchy. The Deshmukhs and petty chiefs had fortified themselves in the villages in which they resided, and plundered caravans, held up travellers to ransom, and made war on one another with impunity. The new viceroy of the Deccan, Chīn Qilīch Khān, who succeeded Dāūd Khān at Aurangābād in 1712 with the title of Nizām-ul-Mulk, was inclined to favour the Kolhāpur party, and Chandra Sen Jādav, the Senāpati, who had assumed that office on the death of his father Dhanājī in 1708, had gone over to Kolhāpur, owing to a disagreement with Shāhū. This disagreement led to the rise of a very remarkable man, who was destined to become the saviour of his country.

Bālājī Vishvānāth was a Chitpāvan or Konkanāstha Brāhman, whose ancestors were hereditary Deshmukhs or revenue officers of Shrīvardhan near Bānkot. His early history is obscure, but towards the end of the seventeenth century his father appears to have migrated to the Deccan and taken service at the Sātārā court.[1] For a time he served under Dhanājī Jādav, the Senāpati, who held him in high esteem and gave him several responsible posts. This aroused the jealousy of Dhanājī's son Chandra Sen, and shortly after the latter became Senāpati a quarrel broke out which caused Bālājī to flee for his life to Shāhū's protection. Chandra Sen insolently demanded his surrender from Shāhū, and being refused, proceeded to join the Kolhāpur faction. Bālājī Vishvānāth, in gratitude to Shāhū, made himself invaluable to the king, in whose favour he rose daily higher and higher. He enlisted fresh forces, for which he received the title of *Senākarta*, or "maker of armies", and came to terms with the Nizām. He next attacked a notorious robber-chief, Dāmājī Thorat of Hingangāon, who, however, defeated him and held him up to ransom. He had better luck in putting down another rebel, Krishna Rāo of Khātāv. Meanwhile, Shāhū had despatched an army under Bahiro Pant Pingle, the Peshwā, to protect the Konkan and overthrow Kānhojī Angria, the hereditary admiral of the Marāthā fleet, who had taken the opportunity afforded by these disorders to ally himself with Kolhāpur, advance up the Bhor Ghāt and seize the forts of Rājmāchī and Lohāgarh, commanding this important highway into the Deccan. But the Peshwā was a mediocre general, and he suffered himself to be defeated and captured. Angria now threatened to march on Sātārā. Shāhū was in despair, and "looked around him to discover a fit person to recover his conquered districts". He applied to the Pratinidhi, but that officer excused himself on the

[1] The story of his early years, told by Grant Duff (I, 316), has been modified by later researches. See Kincaid and Parasnis, 202 *sqq.* and Sardesai, *Main Currents of Maratha History*, p. 102.

ground that "the army was not at his devotion". Then, in the words of the Marāthā chronicler,

> he sent for the Eight Pradhāns, communicated to them the accounts he had received, and desired them to take the necessary measures for checking these depredations. They all remained silent. He then looked towards Bālājī, who got up and addressed the Rājā, saying, "If you will give me orders, through your good fortune they will be carried into effect." Upon this the Rājā placed his hand on Bālājī's head and desired him to take the troops. The Mahārājā gave him the entire administration of affairs with the robes of the Peshwāship. His fame and greatness were daily augmented; the Eight Pradhāns of the State became subject to him.

The new Peshwā set about his task with a will. Being himself a Konkanī and an old friend of Angria's, his task was a comparatively easy one. He arranged a meeting with the Marāthā admiral at a spot not far from the modern town of Lonāvlā, and soon came to terms with him. He persuaded him to release the unfortunate ex-Peshwā, Bahiro Pant Pingle, and to transfer his allegiance from Kolhāpur to Shāhū; in return, he undertook to get him confirmed in the title of *Sarkhel* (admiral) and to allow him to retain possession of Rājmāchī and other strongholds. At the same time, he joined him in attacking Angria's hereditary enemy, the Sīdī, who was deprived of many of his conquests in the Konkan. This was Bālājī's first great diplomatic triumph. Kānhojī Angria, however, until his death in 1729, remained an ally rather than a vassal of the Peshwās. The Angrias behaved like independent rulers, making war at will upon their neighbours, the Sīdīs, the Portuguese and the English, and levying what they chose to call "the *chauth* of the Sea" upon coastal traffic. Several expeditions sent against these pests from Bombay were repulsed with loss, until, in 1755, Clive and Watson, co-operating with the Peshwā's land forces, overthrew their stronghold at Gheria or Vijayadurg, and put an end to their power.[1]

Bālājī, on his return from the Konkan, determined to put a stop to anarchy in Shāhū's kingdom. Freebooters were suppressed with a strong hand, and an example was made of Dāmāji Thorat, whose stronghold was razed to the ground, while he himself was thrown into a dungeon. Civil government was restored, and the Pratinidhi and the *Ashtapradhān*, or Cabinet of Eight, were appointed. But the old system of government established by Shivājī was no longer workable. Conditions had changed, and at home the real power lay in the hands of the Peshwā, while in the more distant parts of the country the great Marāthā chiefs were virtually independent. Bālājī realised that the only possible working arrangement was a confederacy of the Marāthā leaders; but even then, the separatist tendencies were constantly at work, and the jealousy felt by the Marāthā

[1] See Ives, *A Voyage from England to India*, I, chap. VII. Clement Downing, *History of the Indian Wars* (ed. Foster, 1924), pp. 28 *sqq*.

chiefs for the power wielded at the court by the Brāhman Peshwā was a constant source of friction and danger.[1]

But Bālājī was by no means contented with merely keeping the peace: his ambitions and far-seeing mind had already conceived the plan of freeing his country entirely from foreign domination.[2] His master was still the vassal of Delhi, and the Peshwā's dream was to make Shāhū absolute sovereign over Shivājī's *Swarājya*, that is, all the districts ruled over by Shivājī at the time of his decease.[3] The hour was propitious. The once-mighty Mughul empire was fast breaking up. The throne of Delhi was occupied by a series of puppet-rulers, all the real power being concentrated in the hands of the so-called "King-Makers", the Sayyid brothers. One of these, Husain 'Alī Khān, became viceroy of the Deccan in 1715. He found, however, that he could make no headway against court-intrigues which went on during his absence, and the depredations of the local Marāthā chiefs. In 1716, he was severely defeated by Khande Rāo Dābhāde, the veteran Marāthā leader, who was levying *chauth* on the Gujarāt border. In desperation, therefore, he opened negotiations with Shāhū, through the good offices of one Shankarājī Malhār. This gave to Bālājī Vishvānāth a long-sought opportunity, and the terms which he proposed to the Sayyid were as follows:

(1) The emperor should confirm king Shāhū in the right of collecting the *chauth* and *sardeshmukhī* from the six provinces of the Deccan and Mysore, Trichinopoly and Tanjore: Shāhū was to exercise sovereign rights in all the territory composing Shivājī's *swarājya*, except certain portions of Khāndesh, in lieu of which, territories in the Pandharpur district should be ceded. The fortresses of Shivner and Trimbak should be restored, and recent Marāthā conquests in Gondwāna and Berār confirmed. Shāhū's mother and family should be allowed to return to the Deccan.

(2) Shāhū, on his side, was to pay a million rupees as tribute in return for the *swarājya*, and 10 per cent. of the annual income for the hereditary rights of *sardeshmukhī*: to maintain a body of 15,000 horse in the emperor's service in return for the *chauth*; and to protect the country from depredation and robbery.

The wretched emperor Farrukh-siyar protested in vain against this base surrender of his rights and territories: Husain 'Alī Khān, accompanied by Bālājī and 16,000 Marāthā horse under Khande Rāo Dābhāde, marched on Delhi, and after some fierce street-fighting Sayyid 'Abdullah seized the emperor, blinded him, threw him into a dungeon, and finally (1719) murdered him.[4] Bālājī

[1] M. G. Ranade, *op. cit.* pp. 208 *sqq.*
[2] In common parlance, his aim was to re-establish the *Hindu-pād-pādshāhī*, or Hindu Empire of India.
[3] For its extent, see P. V. Mavji, "Shivaji's Swarajya", in *JBBRAS*, xx, 30 *sqq.*
[4] See chap. xi, p. 339.

remained in Delhi until the new emperor, Muhammad Shāh, was forced to get rid of his unwelcome visitors by issuing three imperial rescripts for the *chauth*, *sardeshmukhī* and *swarājya* respectively.[1] Bālājī returned in triumph to Sātārā, where honours were showered upon him; but he was now nearing sixty, and the hardships of the campaign had proved too great for him. He retired to his country-house at Sāswād near Purandar, where he expired in April, 1720. His lifework had been completed.

Bālājī Vishvānāth may without exaggeration be termed the second founder of the Marāthā empire. Without his directing brain, Shāhū Rājā, enervated by his upbringing in the Mughul court, would not have survived for a year. His two great diplomatic triumphs were the conciliation of Angria and the treaty with Delhi, but scarcely less characteristic was his method of revenue collection, to which the Marāthās owed to a great extent their power. As Elphinstone points out,[2] he deliberately preferred assignments on other proprietors, like *chauth* or *sardeshmukhī*, to a solid territorial possession, or even a consolidated sum. Hence the net work of revenue-collectors was spread everywhere in the imperial domains, affording the Marāthās endless opportunities of spreading their influence. Pretexts for interference and encroachment in an extensive territory were better than clearly defined rights in a small one. Secondly, by insisting that the revenue should be calculated on the assessments of the time of Todar Mal or Malik 'Ambar, which, he knew well, a country ravaged by war could never pay, he could always have a bill for arrears in hand. Thirdly, by parcelling out the revenue among the chiefs, he ensured that, while each had an interest in increasing the contribution to the common stock, none had a compact property such as might render him independent of the government. Lastly, the system was purposely made so complicated as to throw all the power into the hands of Brāhman revenue-collectors and agents, who, being of the same caste as the Peshwā himself, naturally played into his hands. The scheme was typical in its ingenuity.

"Bālājī Vishvānāth", says Sir Richard Temple, "had a calm, comprehensive and commanding intellect, an imaginative and aspiring disposition, and an aptitude for ruling rude natures by moral force, a genius for diplomatic combinations, and a mastery of finance." It is impossible to dispute the justice of this estimate.

When Bālājī Vishvānāth died, he left two sons, Bājī Rāo, a young man of twenty-two, and Chimājī Appa, a boy of twelve. Both were destined to play a distinguished part in their country's destinies. At the time of his father's death, Bājī Rāo was on field-service; but on his return, two weeks later, he was invested by Shāhū with the Peshwā's robes of office: the Peshwāship, *more Indico*, was already

[1] The terms are given in detail in Grant Duff, I, 337 *sqq*.

[2] *History of India*, Book XII, chap. II.

becoming hereditary.[1] Bājī Rāo, though so young, was admirably suited for the post. Bālājī, according to some of his critics, was a statesman rather than a soldier; he was even said not to have been a skilled horseman, and a spiteful story was told that at one time he had required a man on each side to hold him on! None, even in jest, could say this of Bājī Rāo, who had been brought up in the saddle, and had led a cavalry charge at an age when other lads are still at school. A contemporary artist represented him in the dress of a common trooper, sitting with his reins on his horse's neck, while he rubbed between his hands ears of corn.[2] On this dry grain he would subsist for days, and at night he would sleep on the ground like an ordinary soldier, his bridle over his arm, and his lance stuck in the ground beside him. Such a man the Marāthās would follow, as they followed Shivājī in the old days, to the gates of Hell if need be. From the moment he took office, he set out to carry into effect his father's lofty designs for the extension of the *Hindu-pād-pādshāhī*. Bālājī's expedition to Delhi had revealed to him the weakness of the Mughuls, and Bājī Rāo conceived the bold plan of attacking and overrunning the rich and fertile plains of Mālwā, and extending Marāthā rule into the heart of Hindustān. With a foresight rare in one so young he saw that such a plan would, by giving occupation to the turbulent Marāthā chiefs, not only extend the boundaries of Shāhū's kingdom, but lead to peace nearer home. This ambitious policy was vehemently opposed by Shrīpat Rāo, the Pratinidhi. The Pratinidhi or viceroy was really the first, and the Peshwā the second, official in the court; and Shrīpat Rāo and the other Deccanis viewed with jealousy the meteoric rise of the young Chitpāvan from the Konkan. At the Council the Pratinidhi stigmatised an invasion of Hindūstān, before Shāhū's domestic dissensions were composed, as rash and imprudent, and he advised as an alternative the reduction of Kolhāpur and the reconquest of the Carnatic. But Bājī Rāo's eloquence swept aside all opposition. "Now is our time", said the gallant Peshwā, "to drive the strangers from the country of the Hindus, and acquire immortal renown. Let us strike at the trunk of the withering tree, and the branches will fall off themselves. By directing our efforts to Hindūstān, the Marāthā flag shall fly from the Krishnā to Attock." "You shall plant it beyond the Himālayas!"[3] exclaimed Shāhū, carried away by the Peshwā's eloquence. "You are, indeed, a noble son of a worthy father!" From this day onwards, the faces of the Marāthās were turned northwards: it is significant that the chief gateway of every Marāthā fortress is the Delhi Gate.

In 1724, Bājī Rāo crossed the Narbadā in force. Little resistance

[1] Sen, *op. cit.* pp. 151 *sqq.*   [2] Grant Duff, I, 419.

[3] In the *Kinnara Khanda*, is the expression in the Chitnīs Bakhar. The Kinnaras, or celestial musicians, dwelt in a fabled country beyond the Himālayas. Kincaid and Parasnis render the words as "the throne of the Almighty".

was met with, for some of the Rājputs were now beginning to side with the Marāthās, and Rājā Jay Singh of Amber actively assisted them. Mālwā was repeatedly overrun, and three Marāthā chiefs, Udājī Powār, Malhār Rāo Holkar, and Rānojī Sindia were left behind to collect the tribute. They were the founders of the princely houses of Dhār, Indore and Gwalior: the two latter were soldiers of fortune, who had won their spurs on the battle-field. Malhār Rāo Holkar was of the Dhangar or shepherd caste, and had started life as a trooper: Rānojī Sindia had originally been in the service of Shāhū.[1] Another family which arose into prominence at that time was that of the Gāikwārs of Baroda. Dāmājī Gāikwār won distinction at the battle of Bālāpur in 1720, when fighting against the Nizām under Khande Rāo Dābhāde, for which Shāhū conferred upon him the title of Shamsher Bahādur, or illustrious swordsman, which is still borne by his descendants.[2] About this time also arose the practice of assigning the attack on a particular province to a certain commander. To Khande Rāo Dābhāde (who had been made *Senāpati* for defeating the forces of Husain 'Alī Khān in 1716) was in this way assigned the collection of the dues in Bāglān and Gujarāt. In 1720, Pilājī Gāikwār, the nephew of Dāmājī, built himself a fortress at Songarh, fifty miles east of Surat, and proceeded to levy *chauth* and *sardeshmukhī* as Khande Rāo's lieutenant. Sarbuland Khān, the Mughul viceroy, was powerless to interfere, and presently Pilājī was joined by Kanthājī Kadam Bhānde, an officer of Shāhū. From this time onwards, the fair province of Gujarāt enjoyed no respite from the Marāthā stranglehold.

> When the Marāthās (says their historian) proceeded beyond their boundary, to collect revenue and make war were synonymous; whenever a village resisted, its officers were seized, and compelled by threats, and sometimes by torture, more or less severe, to come to a settlement; money was seldom obtainable, but securities from bankers, with whom all the villages had dealing, were preferable, as they were exchanged for bills payable in any part of India.[3]

The harvest season was, for obvious reasons, usually selected for these *mulukgiri*[4] operations; villages which resisted were plundered and fired, and the crops destroyed. Only when the monsoon made the movements of troops impossible did the wretched inhabitants obtain a temporary respite. Then

> A deceitful calm succeeded: the fall of the rain brought back the cheering green: the beautiful province of Gujarāt, which for hundreds of miles may vie with the finest parks of the nobles of England, was clothed, in all its natural beauties, by rapid verdure and luxuriant vegetation. Tranquillity seemed to reign, where a short time before, nothing was to be seen but perpetual skirmishing, murder and

[1] The popular story that Rānojī was the Peshwā's slipper-bearer does not appear to rest on good ground. In *Selections from Peshwā's Daftar*, vol. VII, No. 23, is a list of Shāhū's officers, with their ranks, in 1715.

[2] *Vide infra*, p. 402.

[3] Grant Duff, I, 464, and compare the passage quoted in the footnote.

[4] An expedition to enforce the payment of revenue (p. 412 *infra*).

robbery in open day: caravans pillaged even when strongly escorted, and villages burning or deserted.[1]

The scene now changes once more to Delhi. Chīn Qilīch Khān, the Nizām-ul-Mulk, finding it impossible to cope with the disorders and corruption of the Mughul court, determined to set up for himself in the Deccan. In 1720 he suddenly crossed the Narbadā and marched southwards. Asīrgarh and Burhānpur capitulated, and Chandra Sen Jādav and a number of disaffected Marāthās flocked to his standard. He routed Dilāvar and 'Ālim 'Alī Khān, the governor of the Deccan, who had been sent against him by the Sayyids, at the battles of Khandwa and Bālāpur (June–August, 1720). In the latter battle, a detachment of Marāthās under Khande Rāo Dābhāde and Dāmājī Gāikwār fought on the imperialist side with great gallantry. Further opposition was ended when Sayyid Husain 'Alī was murdered,[2] and his brother defeated and thrown into prison, thus putting an end to the power of the "king-makers" for ever. The Nizām now made his way to the Deccan unopposed. No sooner did he arrive than he began to renew his intrigues with Chandra Sen Jādav and other rebels and also with Kolhāpur, but he was everywhere foiled by the young Peshwā, who had stationed the head of the army with a considerable army of observation to watch him. In 1722, however, he was recalled by the emperor, and on 21 February, at Āgra, he was formally invested with the office of minister. He at once set himself to restore the empire to some sort of order, and to abolish revenue-farming, the grant of assignments and the innumerable other abuses which had arisen. But his efforts only excited the derision of the young emperor and his degenerate court, who were determined to thwart everything he attempted to do, and even ridiculed to his face the stern soldier, whose rough manners were better adapted to the camp than the palace. In December, 1723, the Nizām could tolerate this state of things no longer. He determined to shake the dust of Delhi from off his feet, and under the pretext of going on a hunting expedition to retire to the Deccan. Muhammad Shāh, however, knew that this practically amounted to a declaration of independence, and treacherously sent word to Mubāriz Khān, the governor of Hyderābād, to intercept and kill him if possible. Shāhū, who disliked Mubāriz Khān, decided to help the Nizām, and Bājī Rāo found himself, for the first and last time, fighting side by side with his rival. The decisive engagement took place at Shakarkhelda in Berār (11 October, 1724).[3] Mubāriz Khān was routed and killed, and the Nizām marched on to Hyderābād and took it. He determined to make the city his capital, for which it offered many advantages. Being further from Sātārā than Aurangābād, it enabled him to conceal his move-

[1] Grant Duff, I, 366. For the Marāthās in Gujarāt, see Irvine, *Later Mughuls*, II, chap. VIII, and Forbes, *Rās Mālā*, Book III (chaps. I and V).

[2] See chap. XII, p. 344. [3] See chap. XII, p. 350.

ments more effectually from the Marāthās; and it was better placed for operations against the Carnatic, upon which the Nizām had already designs. From this time dates the virtual independence of the Nizām, and a new factor is added to Deccan politics.[1] Having failed to put him out of the way, the emperor pardoned and confirmed him in the government of the Deccan, depriving him, however, of the post of minister and the provinces of Gujarāt and Mālwā.

The peace between the Nizām and the Mārāthās could not, in the nature of things, endure very long. The Nizām chafed at the presence of the Marāthā tax-gatherers in Hyderābād, and in 1726, while Bājī Rāo was away in the Carnatic, he pursued assiduously his favourite policy of fishing in troubled waters—always an easy matter, as the Marāthā chiefs cordially disliked the Chitpāvan domination at Shāhū's court. Once again he came to terms with prince Shambhūjī of Kolhāpur, who viewed with apprehension the Peshwā's growing interest in Carnatic affairs. In 1726, while Bājī Rāo was absent on a campaign, the two allies made a surprise attack on Shāhū, who was for a time in considerable danger.[2]

The return of Bājī Rāo, however, soon restored the situation, and after the Dasahra festival, on 13 September, 1727, the Peshwā advanced northwards, driving his enemy before him across the Godāvarī, and devastating the country all round him. By a series of masterly manœuvres he then proceeded to draw the Nizām into the waterless region between Aurangābād and Paithan. Here he surrounded and attacked him near the town of Pālkhed (11 March, 1728). The Nizām's artillery alone saved him from annihilation: retreat through the devastated area was impossible, and on 22 March he was compelled to sue for peace. Thus Bājī Rāo, unaided, had brought to his knees the foremost soldier of his time. It was a feat of arms of which any commander might well have been proud. The treaty was signed at Mungī Shevgāon. The Nizām agreed to reinstate the Marāthā tax-gatherers, to pay up all arrears of *chauth* and *sardeshmukhī*, and to recognise Shāhū as sole monarch of the Deccan; but like an honourable soldier, he refused to consent to a clause requiring him to surrender his ally Shambhūjī. The importance of this treaty can scarcely be overestimated. It was a diplomatic triumph of the first order, and a worthy sequel to the brilliant manœuvres in the field which had preceded it. It left Shāhū at last the undisputed ruler in his ancestor's *swarājya*, and it was a deadly blow to Bājī Rāo's rivals in the Marāthā court. Little wonder that, after this, Shāhū depended still more upon his young minister, who had once again saved him from virtual annihilation.

There still remained the smouldering embers of the war to be extinguished. In Gujarāt, Trimbak Rāo Dābhāde, who had suc-

[1] Irvine, *Later Mughuls*, II, 146, 154.

[2] See chap. XIII, p. 380.

ceeded to the title of *Senāpati* after the death of his father, the veteran Khande Rāo, in January, 1730,[1] was assembling troops and plotting with Pilājī Gāikwār and other chiefs, "to protect the Rājā's authority", by ridding him of his Peshwā. He had opened negotiations with the Nizām; but Bājī Rāo, by means of his excellent system of espionage, was well aware of all that was taking place. Meanwhile, in the south, prince Shambhūjī, who had been allowed to retire to Panhālā after the signing of the treaty, had allied himself to a free-booter named Udājī Chauhān, and had encamped in bravado on the north side of the Warnā, insolently demanding to be recognised as independent ruler of the southern half of the *swarājya*.

As Bājī Rāo was preoccupied with affairs in Gujarāt, Shāhū sent Shrīpat Rāo Pratinidhi to deal with his cousin. The Pratinidhi took the field in January, 1730, and surprised the Kolhāpur army while it was encamped. The rout was complete, and Shrīpat Rāo captured the royal camp with all its inmates, including Tārā Bāī, Rājas Bāī, Shambhūjī's wife Jijā Bāī, and many Marāthā chiefs of note. Shāhū behaved with his usual magnanimity. He released all his prisoners. His aunt Tārā Bāī, however, asked not to be sent back. The lot of the senior Mahārānī when the son of her co-wife reigns is never an enviable one. "Wherever I go", she said, "I shall have a prison as my lot: here or there is all one to me. Let me stay in peace." Her request was, unfortunately for the state, acceded to: and the old queen retired to Sātārā to bide her time for fresh plots. Meanwhile, Shambhūjī had surrendered unconditionally, and the two cousins met at a magnificent *darbār*, where they were formally reconciled. A treaty, commonly known as the treaty of Warnā (the river being the boundary between the territories of the combatants), was signed on 13 April, 1731, which left Shambhūjī with only a shadow of his former power, and after this he ceases to be an important factor in Marāthā history until his death in 1760. The long strife between the rival houses of Kolhāpur and Sātārā, which had gone on since 1708, was for the time being settled.

Meanwhile, important events were taking place in the north. Throughout the rainy season of 1730, Bājī Rāo had been making preparations for the invasion of Gujarāt, with the assistance of his brother Chimājī Appa. On 10 October the brothers celebrated the Dasara in great splendour at Poona, and took the field at once. In February, 1731, Bājī Rāo reached Ahmadābād, and concluded a treaty with the new viceroy, Abhay Singh of Mārwār, who had been sent to supersede Sarbuland Khān. On 1 April, twelve days before Shāhū and Shambhūjī signed the treaty of Warnā, the Peshwā moved out to meet the forces of Trimbak Rāo and his lieutenant the Gāik-

[1] The date of Khande Rāo's death is unknown. Grant Duff gives 1721, which must be wrong, as contemporary correspondence shows that he was still alive in June, 1729. He probably died in July or August of that year.

wār, on the broad plain of Bilhāpur, between Barodā and Dabhoi. The Senāpati's numerous levies proved no match for the small but compact army of the Peshwā: the famous *Khās Pāgā*, the household cavalry, carried all before it. But Trimbak Rāo, disdaining offers to surrender, chained together the legs of his war-elephant, and continued the fight single-handed, until a musket-ball (fired, it is now known, by a traitor's hand) brought him down, while he was drawing the bowstring to his ear. The pious Shāhū, deeply shocked by this fratricidal strife, behaved with the utmost chivalry towards the family of his late Senāpati, and bestowed the office upon his younger brother Yashwant Rāo. But the family of Dābhāde never recovered its prestige, and Bājī Rāo, his last and greatest rival removed, was now sovereign in all but name. In Gujarāt, the power once wielded by the Dābhādes passed to their erstwhile lieutenants, the Gāikwārs, the Mughul viceroy receding more and more into the background. Pilājī Gāikwār was assassinated by Abhay Singh, the Mughul viceroy, in 1732, and was succeeded by Dāmājī II, who was present at Pānīpat, and died in 1768.[1]

We must now turn our attention to Mālwā, where Udājī Powār, Malhār Rāo Holkar and Rānojī Sindia had been steadily undermining the Mughul power. On 8 December, 1728, at Sārangpur, they defeated and killed the governor, Rājā Girdhar Bahādur, who for ten years had struggled to prevent the Marāthās from getting a firm footing in his province. His successor, Dayā Bahādur, suffered a similar fate at Tālā near Dhār (12 October, 1731). In 1732, the Peshwā himself took command over the Marāthā forces, sending back his brother and Pilājī Jādav to watch over his interests at Sātārā. On his arrival there he found the new viceroy was Muhammad Khān Bangash, whom he had defeated in Bundelkhand in 1729.[2] Muhammad Khān, receiving no support from Delhi, was unable to stay the Marāthā incursion and was relieved by Rājā Jay Singh of Amber. In 1733 the Peshwā placed in charge of Bundelkhand a Brāhman officer named Govind Pant Kher who afterwards was known as Bundele and played a part in the Pānīpat campaign. The great Rājput barons, who had once been the guardians of the empire on its western borders, were now more and more openly throwing off their allegiance, and welcoming the Marāthās as the champions of the Hindu religion.[3] In 1736, Jay Singh came to terms with the Peshwā, appointing him as deputy-governor on condition that he did not plunder imperial territories. This amounted to the virtual cession of the province, and had not the smallest deterrent effect on Marāthā depredations: the following year saw

[1] For the early history of the Gāikwārs of Baroda, see *Bombay Gazetteer*, vol. VII, and Forbes, *op. cit.* Book III, chaps. I–III.

[2] See chap. XII, p. 353. W. Irvine, *The Bangash Nawābs of Farrukhābād*, p. 302, shows that the Bundelkhand campaign was before Muhammad Khān's appointment to Mālwā.

[3] Malcolm, *Central India*, chaps. IV and V.

their horsemen crossing the Jumna and plundering the Dūāb. It was now that Bājī Rāo planned one of his boldest strokes. In March, 1737, Sa'ādat Khān, the governor of Oudh, had defeated Malhār Rāo Holkar, and elated by his success wrote a vainglorious letter to Delhi, boasting that he had driven the Marāthās across the Chambal. "Hearing this", wrote Bājī Rāo to his brother, "I was resolved to let the emperor know the truth, to prove that I was still in Hindūstān, and to shew him flames and the Marāthās at the gate of the capital."[1] Gathering a picked body of horsemen and covering ten days' march in two, he swooped down upon Delhi. Fugitives, distraught with terror, poured into the city. The government, at first incredulous and then panic-stricken, gathered together all available forces and despatched them to chastise the invaders. Bājī Rāo, adopting the usual Marāthā tactics, skilfully fell back until he had drawn his opponents away from the walls and well out into the open. Then he turned, and in a moment, Malhār Rāo Holkar, with Rānojī Sindia hard at his heels, crashed into their ranks. That day the Marāthā sword and lance drank deep of the blood of the proudest of the Mughul nobles: over six hundred were slain, and the troopers helped themselves freely to riderless horses with their gorgeous equipments of cloth of gold. The terrified emperor awaited in fear and trembling the approach of the victors; but before dawn Bājī Rāo had vanished as swiftly as he came, cleverly outmanœuvring an imperial army under the minister which tried to cut off his retreat (April, 1737).

By this time the opinion began to prevail that only one person could save the empire, and stem the flood of Marāthā invasion. This was the Nizām, who, as we have seen, had shaken the dust of Delhi from off his feet fourteen years before. He was now at Burhānpur, closely watched by Chimājī Appa, who had received orders, if his opponent crossed the Narbadā, "to fall on his rear and put heel-ropes on him". The Nizām's change of front was no doubt inspired by the apprehensions he must have felt at the growing power of the Marāthās in Hindūstān.

In April, 1737, the Nizām set out for Delhi, by way of Gwalior and Āgra. The capital was reached in July, and his reception was one of the most amazing sights ever witnessed in that ancient city: the minister escorted him personally to the emperor's presence, amidst crowds which loudly welcomed him as their saviour.[2] After staying as the imperial guest until August, he took the field in order to drive the marauders out of Hindūstān. But he found Bājī Rāo awaiting him, and once more he proved no match for his nimble antagonist. He suffered himself to be shepherded into Bhopāl,

[1] W. Irvine, *Later Mughuls*, II, 287. The letter is quoted in full in Kincaid and Parasnis, *History of the Maratha People*, pp. 451–3.

[2] Irvine, *Later Mughuls*, II, 301.

where he was closely besieged, and, as at Pālkhed almost exactly ten years earlier, he was once more compelled by the Peshwā to sign a humiliating treaty. He agreed to grant to Bājī Rāo the whole of Mālwā, with the complete sovereignty of the territory between the Narbadā and the Chambal, and to obtain the emperor's confirmation for these terms. Hence the calling-in of the Nizām, instead of helping the emperor, merely led to the humiliation of both, and to the crowning triumph of Bājī Rāo. The Mughul empire was tottering to its fall: it only needed the invasion of Nādir Shāh, already looming on the horizon, to complete its destruction.

The sudden irruption of Nādir Shāh into Hindūstān, in 1739, caused a panic at Poona, and for a moment Bājī Rāo thought that he might continue his march southward into the Deccan. "Our domestic quarrels", he wrote, "are now insignificant: there is now but one enemy in Hindūstān. Hindu and Mussalman, the whole power of the Deccan, must assemble, and I shall spread our Marāthās from the Narbadā to the Chambal." Fortunately, the menaced invasion of the Deccan failed to materialise, and the Peshwā was able to continue his operations uninterrupted. Mālwā and Gujarāt had been virtually added to the Marāthā empire, but the Konkan, the fertile strip of country between the Ghāts and the sea, still remained unsubdued. Here were three rival powers, the Angrias of Kolāba, the Abyssinians of Janjīra, and the Portuguese. The Angrias, in spite of Kānhojī's agreement with Shāhū, defied the control of the Peshwās, and levied, on their own authority, the "*chauth* of the sea" on passing vessels. Equally powerful were their rivals the Sīdīs, the hereditary Mughul admirals. The Marāthā campaigns in the Konkan were, however, a failure,[1] and their chief result was to bring the Marāthās into contact with the Portuguese. The Portuguese had been old enemies of the Marāthās, on religious as well as political grounds, but during the Peshwā's preoccupations in the north, they had been left in peace. Their possessions on the Bombay coast were grouped together under the title of the "province of the north"; its governor, "the general of the north", had his capital at Bassein. The island of Salsette, which was in Portuguese hands, is separated from the mainland by a long, narrow creek or arm of the sea, Bassein at the northern and Thānā at the southern extremities of which guarded the two entrances. Along the coast were a number of fortified posts. But the Portuguese power was fast declining. They were a proud, indolent race, with little aptitude for commerce. The English and Dutch had driven their fleets off the sea, and in 1661, the Lisbon government, despite frantic protests from Goa, had suicidally ceded the island of Bombay, at the southern extremity of Salsette, with its excellent harbour, to the English.[2]

[1] See Kincaid and Parasnis, chap. XXXIII.
[2] See vol. V, p. 86.

Receiving little or no help from home, the Portuguese had allowed their fortresses to fall into a state of disrepair: the walls were ruinous and manned only by a handful of tattered soldiers with a few rusty cannon. Bājī Rāo cast covetous eyes on the fertile and almost defenceless island of Salsette with its green rice fields, groves and orchards. Here was a fruit ready to be plucked. The excuse, if one was needed, was afforded by the haughty Luis Botelho, the governor of Bassein, who grossly insulted the Peshwā's envoy by speaking of his master as a "nigger".[1]

Bājī Rāo concentrated a large force at Poona in the cold weather of 1736–37, and being himself fully occupied with events in Hindūstān, he entrusted it to his brother Chimājī Appa. The Marāthā army moved down the passes with great speed and secrecy, and on 6 April, 1737, captured Thānā, which, as we have seen, commanded the southern entrance of the Salsette channel. Until the break of the monsoon, the Marāthās occupied their time in overrunning Salsette and reducing the fortresses on the island. As soon as the rains were over, they made a general assault on Bassein itself, but the storming party, 9000 strong, was completely defeated by its gallant defenders, who manned the walls, sword in hand, threw down the scaling-ladders, and killed or captured every one who reached the ramparts. Meanwhile the government of Goa, at last awake to the situation, sent two shiploads of troops under Pedro de Mello to the relief of Bassein. De Mello at once realised that Thānā was the key to the position: could he retake it, the Marāthā forces in Salsette would be cut off. But in the meantime, the Marāthās also received large reinforcements: Bājī Rāo's campaign in Mālwā had come to a successful conclusion, and Holkar and other Marāthā leaders had hastened to the scene of operations. De Mello was killed in action, and his troops were driven back to their boats in disorder.

Bassein was now doomed. The Portuguese appealed for help to the English at Bombay, and it cannot be said that the latter behaved with credit in the matter. They had, indeed, little love for their rivals, and they were anxious to do nothing to offend the Marāthās. They accordingly temporised: to the Portuguese they merely tendered good advice, while to the Marāthās they supplied powder and shot: it was even asserted that the Portuguese commander was killed by a piece aimed by an English gunner. The letters of the Portuguese commandant are full of dignity and pathos. The garrison, he says, is starving, and worn out by constant fighting. There is no money to pay the soldiers. All the church plate has long ago been melted down. "The Marāthās have carried on mines, covered ways and other approaches to the very foundation of the wall, their batteries being very near the town: they throw large stones into the place from

[1] "Tratando o de Negro", Kincaid and Parasnis, 261 note, quoting a Portuguese authority.

mortars." A little moved by this touching appeal, the council sent them two hundred barrels of gunpowder, and four thousand rounds of cannon-shot. Later, with the quixotic gallantry of his nation, the commandant actually offered to pledge to the English some of his best cannon in return for further supplies, "having this consideration, that it is most becoming my nation that it should be known to the world how, for the preservation of their king's city, Bassein was stripped of its artillery, the principal instruments of its defence, whilst they put their trust more in their personal valour, in their constant fidelity and zeal, than on the extraordinary force or hardness of metal". But nothing could save the city. On 13 May, a mine was sprung under one of the principal bastions, and the Marāthā storming parties, led in person by their greatest captains, Malhār Rāo Holkar, Rānojī Sindia, Mānājī Angria and Chimājī Appa himself, swarmed up the walls, only to be driven back in disorder. Eleven times the columns moved to the assault, and eleven times they were repulsed with slaughter; and when the attack was renewed at daylight, it was found that the Portuguese had repaired the breaches. But on the next day another mine was exploded, and the Marāthās established themselves in a position among the ruins, from which they could enfilade the defences. All that day the Portuguese maintained an unequal combat with the courage of despair, and in the evening Chimājī sent an envoy to say that, unless the town surrendered, further mines would be exploded, and the whole population put to the sword. The governor then capitulated, after one of the most heroic defences in history. The severity of the fighting is indicated by the fact that the Marāthā losses were estimated at 5000 out of a total of 22,000. Chimājī chivalrously allowed the garrison to march out with the honours of war, and a safe-conduct to Goa or Damān, while those who preferred to remain were promised complete religious freedom. The English, be it said to their honour, did all in their power to help the refugees.[1]

The fall of Bassein warned the English in Bombay to prepare for a similar peril. A sum of 30,000 rupees was subscribed by the Indian merchants of the town for the purpose of putting the defences in order and two embassies were despatched, one under captain Inchbird to visit king Shāhū in the Deccan, and the other under captain Gordon to congratulate Chimājī Appa at Bassein. Both were entirely successful, and a treaty was drawn up, dated 12 July, 1739, giving the English the right of free trade in the Deccan.[2]

In the following year, an irreparable calamity overtook the Marāthās. Their guiding spirit, Bājī Rāo Peshwā, worn out by his hard life in the field, suddenly passed away, at the early age of forty-

[1] Forrest, *Selections*, Maratha Series, I, 25–66.

[2] Forrest, *op. cit.* pp. 66–84; Aitchison's Treaties, v. 14. "First wars and Treaties of the Bombay Presidency", *Bombay Quarterly Review*, 1855, Art. IV.

two, on the banks of the Narbadā, on 28 April, 1740. "He died as he had lived," says Sir Richard Temple, "in camp, under canvas among his men, and he is remembered to this day among Marāthās as the fighting Peshwā or the incarnation of Hindu energy." He was the most remarkable man, next to Shivājī himself, that his nation had produced. In the words of the historian of the Marāthās, his was "the head to plan and the heart to execute". Tall and commanding in appearance, he was, like all his family, famous for his good looks. He was equally great as a soldier and as a statesman. He understood to perfection the peculiar tactics of the Marāthā horse, and his campaigns against the Nizām were masterpieces of strategy. He was as chivalrous in the hour of victory as he was brave in the field. As a politician, he had the lofty and far-reaching ambitions of his father, and he lived to see the tiny Marāthā race, once "a cloud no bigger than a man's hand", spread all over India, from Delhi to Tanjore. He was an eloquent and inspiring orator, and if in private life he had something of the haughty and imperious reserve of the Chitpāvan, he was a generous master to those who served him faithfully. He made his home, during the short intervals of his campaigns, at Poona, which was fast becoming the rival of Sātārā, and here in 1732 he built the famous Shanwār Wādā, or "Saturday Palace", which he decorated with the spoils of Hindūstān.[1] Captain Inchbird, who visited Poona in 1739, describes it as well built and abounding with people, and the district in appearance more fertile and valuable than any other he had passed through. He especially noted the Peshwā's gun-foundry. Bājī Rāo left behind four children, two of whom, Bālājī and Raghunāth Rāo, familiarly known as Ragoba, rose to fame. Another son, Shamsher Bahādur, borne to him by his beautiful Muhammadan mistress Mastānī,[2] fell at Pānīpat. In January, 1741, he was followed to the funeral pyre by his brother Chimājī, the conqueror of Bassein, who, had he not been overshadowed by the Peshwā's transcendent genius, would have been recognised as one of the greatest names in Marāthā history: as an administrator, he was, perhaps, Bājī Rāo's superior, but he was loyally content to give his brother the credit for his achievements. His son, Sadāshiv Rāo (the Bhāo Sāhib), was destined to play a tragic part in his country's annals.

The death of Bājī Rāo was followed by the usual scramble for office, but Bālājī Bājī Rāo, the late Peshwā's eldest son, had already insinuated himself into the old king's favour, and Shāhū had no hesitation about bestowing upon him the robes of office, although he was only nineteen at the time. The investiture took place in August, 1740. Bālājī's chief rival was Raghūjī Bhonsle of Berār, a

[1] *Poona in Bygone days*, by R. B. Parasnis, chap. I.

[2] Bājī Rāo's relations with Mastānī caused much scandal: she is said to have taught him to eat meat and drink to excess. For her history, see Kincaid and Parasnis, 270 *sqq*.

kinsman of Shāhū and an inveterate enemy of the Peshwās, who was away at the time on an expedition to the Carnatic. This expedition had been sent at the request of the Hindu rajas of the south, and in particular of the Marāthā prince Pratāp Singh of Tanjore, the descendant of Vyankājī, the half-brother of the great Shivājī: they were threatened with extermination at the hands of Dost 'Alī, the Nawāb of the Carnatic.

The Marāthā armies marched from victory to victory. Dost 'Alī was defeated and killed (31 May, 1740) at the Damalcherry pass and in the following August Raghūjī patched up a truce with his son Safdar 'Alī, and proceeded to Sātārā to dispute the Peshwāship. Not succeeding, he returned to the Carnatic, and in December laid siege to Chanda Sāhib, Dost 'Alī's son-in-law, in Trichinopoly, which fell in March, 1741. Chanda Sāhib was sent to Sātārā as a state prisoner, and remained there for eight years. Trichinopoly was handed over to the charge of Murārī Rāo Ghorpare of Gooty. Raghūjī next proceeded to threaten Pondicherry, the headquarters of Chanda Sāhib's French allies: but the Marāthās were no match for European troops behind ramparts, and prudently retired. This expedition, which was warmly supported by the party in court and advocated expansion in the south rather than conquests in Hindūstān, was completely successful.

Raghūjī Bhonsle continued, after his return from the Carnatic, to oppose the Peshwā, who was at length (1744) forced to buy off his formidable rival by allowing him a free hand in Bengal, where 'Alī Vardī Khān (Mīrzā Muhammad 'Alī) had set himself up as an independent ruler.[1] 'Alī Vardī Khān treacherously massacred in cold blood Bhāskar Pant, Raghūjī's revenue minister, and a score of Marāthā officers whom he had invited to a conference, but he had to pay heavily for his perfidy.[2] In 1751 he was forced to surrender the province of Orissa (Cuttack) to the Marāthās, with 1,200,000 rupees annually as the *chauth* of Bengal. The Marāthās never attempted to establish any civil administration in the province, but left it to the local chiefs. The "Marāthā ditch", built round Calcutta in 1742, long bore witness to the terror aroused by the Bhonsle's far-flung horsemen.[3]

Meanwhile Shāhū was slowly dying. "Shāhū the good" was an amiable and religious man, whose piety is still remembered with affection by the Marāthās. He could be magnanimous to a fallen foe, and was by no means destitute of ability. But his upbringing in the Mughul court had made him ill-fitted to deal with the turbulent spirits of his age. His grandfather had been reared in the wilds of the mountain forest; Shāhū's boyhood was spent in the imperial seraglio. He was content to pass his time hunting, fishing

[1] See chap. XII, p. 366. [2] See chap. XV, p. 441.
[3] Grant Duff, I, chap. XVIII; V. A. Smith, *Oxford History of India*, pp. 487–8.

and hawking, and left the drudgery of state affairs more and more to his Peshwā, little realising that he was building up a power destined to supersede his house. But it is a mistake to suppose that he was a mere puppet, like his successors. He exacted the homage due to his person on every occasion. "He was not the mere titular head of the Marāthā government", says Ranade:

> He directed all the operations, ordered and recalled commanders, and he exercised a great controlling power on the chiefs, though he led no armies in the field...Shāhū was strong enough to enforce moderation even over the towering ambition of Bālājī, and forced him to leave the eastern provinces of India free for the development of the Bhonsle's power. Bājī Rāo was only a general under Shāhū: and the Pratinidhis, Bhonsles, Nimbālkars, Dābhādes, Gāikwārs, Kadam Bāndes, Āngres and Ghorpades all respected his power.[1]

His chief defect was his intense conservatism. "Do not break the old, or introduce the new", was his motto, and he confirmed incapable assignees and other useless officers in their holdings, much to the detriment of the state. To the day of his death, he was incapable of shaking off the belief that he was still the vassal of the Mughul empire, for which, and for the memory of the great emperor in whose household he was reared, he cherished the profoundest reverence. For this reason he never approved of the policy of the Peshwās in northern India, though he was unable to check their soaring ambitions. His last years were clouded by failing health[2] and the quarrels of his two Rānīs, Sakwar Bāī and Sagunā Bāī. The latter died in 1748, and Sakwar Bāī, the survivor, was a turbulent and ambitious woman. Lastly, he was deeply distressed at the lack of a legitimate heir. The Peshwā wished him to nominate Shambhūjī, and so unite the crowns of Sātārā and Kolhāpur, but Shāhū could never overcome his dislike of his cousin, who was, moreover, an elderly man without heirs, and disinherited him.[3] He contemplated adopting a boy of the Bhonsle family, when Tārā Bāī dramatically announced the existence of a posthumous son of Shivājī II named Rām Rājā, who, she asserted, had been smuggled out of the fort of Panhālā at birth, and brought up in concealment by a *gondhālī*, or wandering bard, at Tuljāpur.

Whether Tārā Bāī's story was true or not will never be known, but Shāhū, after due enquiry, accepted it. Sakwar Bāī, on the other hand, stigmatised it as a fresh plot on the part of the old dowager to regain her influence. Feeling his end to be near, Shāhū sent for the Peshwā, and in the presence of Govind Rāo Chitnīs handed him two wills or rescripts. The first of these states

> We order that you should command the forces....The government of the empire must be carried on. Appoint therefore a successor, but none from

[1] *Miscellaneous Writings*, p. 348.

[2] Shāhū was eccentric, but not, as Grant Duff says, in a state of "mental imbecility". His actions show that he was *compos mentis*.

[3] *Selections from Peshwā's Daftar*, vol. vi, No. 147.

Kolhāpur. We have given full instructions to the Chitnīs. Act accordingly. Whoever succeeds, obey him and uphold the dignity of the throne. The Chitnīs has always been loyal to us. You are jointly to take measures to preserve the Kingdom. Our successors will not interfere with your post.

The second document adds nothing material, except a solemn injunction to Shāhū's successors to maintain the Peshwā in office.[1]

Shāhū died on 15 December, 1749, aged sixty-seven, after a reign of over forty-one years. The Peshwā at once occupied Sātārā with his troops, arrested the Pratinidhi and other rivals, and calling a meeting of the council produced the papers. These, he asserted, gave him the right to administer the kingdom on behalf of Rām Rājā and his heirs. Sakwar Bāī was offered the alternative of coming in on the Peshwā's side or becoming *satī*. She chose the latter, and went to her doom with the traditional courage of a Marāthā lady: the place of her self-immolation is still regarded as holy ground. The young king was brought in triumph to Sātārā, and solemnly crowned by the Peshwā amid great public rejoicings (4 January, 1750). He was a feeble-minded youth, and an easy tool in the hands of his astute minister. Tārā Bāī, who had hoped to control him as she had done his father, retired to Sinhgarh, ostensibly to be near her husband's ashes, but in reality in order to start intriguing with the Pant Sachiv, who was the commandant of the fort. Bālājī, who was attending some wedding ceremonies in Poona, thereupon summoned Tārā Bāī and the Pant Sachiv into his presence. Tārā Bāī was treated with respect, but the Pant Sachiv was thrown into prison. Rām Rājā was then invited to leave Sātārā, where he was in charge of Raghūjī Bhonsle, and come to Poona. This marks the culminating point in the Peshwā's *coup d'état*. Never before had the Chhatrapati been brought from his capital by his minister. "From this point", says Grant Duff, "Poona may be considered the capital of the Peshwās." Under Bālājī's directions, Rām Rājā drew up a document known as the "Sangola agreement", by which all the chief offices in the state were handed over to the Peshwā's adherents.[2]

When the monsoon of 1750 was drawing to a close, and the Dasara festival ushered in the campaigning season, the Peshwā thought himself sufficiently secure to set out for Hyderābād. The old Nizām had died on 1 June, 1748, at Burhānpur, aged seventy-nine, and a war of succession had broken out among his sons. The Peshwā, in return for important concessions, had agreed to support the elder Ghāzī-ud-dīn against Salābat Jang.[3] His real aim, however, was no less than the annexation of Hyderābād to the Marāthā empire. But he had reckoned without Tārā Bāī. Scarcely had he turned his back, than that indefatigable old queen, upon whom years seemed only to confer

[1] These momentous documents are in the Parasnis Museum, Sātārā. A photostatic copy is in *Itihāsa Sangraha*, Nov.–Dec. 1915, and an English translation in Kincaid and Parasnis, p. 455.

[2] Rajwade, II, pp. 115.

[3] See chap. XIII, pp. 387–8.

fresh energy, organised a far-reaching conspiracy to throw off for ever the yoke of the hated Brāhman. She found no lack of support among the Marāthā chiefs, who were smarting under the Sangola agreement. Her first step, however, was to get into her power the miserable puppet who sat on the throne of the great Shivājī. Having seized the fort of Sātārā, she invited Rām Rājā to a banquet and cast him into prison (24 November, 1750). She then prevailed upon another Marāthā lady, Umā Bāī, the widow of Khande Rāo Dābhāde, to call in her late husband's old lieutenant, the Gāikwār, from Gujarāt. Dāmājī Gāikwār was nothing loath. He advanced upon Sātārā with 15,000 men in order to link up with the forces of Tārā Bāī.

But the Peshwā was too quick for him. Hearing of what had happened while near Raichūr, by forced marches in which he covered 400 miles in thirteen days he descended upon Dāmājī Gāikwār, who was being hotly engaged by Nānā Purandhare and others. The Gāikwār fell back before his new opponent, and retreated into a *cul-de-sac* in the Krishnā valley. The Gujarāt troops, unused to jungle-fighting, became disorganised, and Dāmājī had no option but to negotiate. The Peshwā pressed him to surrender half Gujarāt and pay an indemnity of two and a half million rupees. Finding him obdurate, he suddenly, in spite of the truce, attacked and captured Dāmājī, together with his son and Umā Bāī Dābhāde, and sent them as prisoners to Poona. So incensed was Dāmājī at this piece of treachery, that ever after he refused to salute the Peshwā except with his left hand. Bālājī's terms of ransom—half of Gujarāt, and a yearly tribute of 500,000 rupees, were severe, and for a long time Dāmājī resisted. After six months of rigorous confinement, however, he capitulated, and in the cold weather of 1752–53 he returned homewards, accompanied by Raghunāth Rāo and a considerable force, with the object of reinstating himself as sole ruler of Gujarāt and expelling the Mughul viceroy. After a desperate struggle, Ahmadābād was captured, and the last remains of Mughul rule in Gujarāt were obliterated.[1]

Tārā Bāī still held out defiantly in Sātārā fort, and refused to come to terms until the Peshwā guaranteed her liberty under the most solemn oaths. The unfortunate Rām Rājā remained in custody, and Tārā Bāī now shamelessly declared that he was an impostor, and the son of a *gondhālī*. Imprisonment told on his reason, and he died in obscurity in 1777. Shortly before his death, he adopted a son, who received the name of Shāhū the Younger, and reigned till 1810. But after the death of Shāhū I in 1749, the kings were mere *rois fainéants*, though the Peshwās, always strict constitutionalists, professed to the last to act as their viceroys, and sent all documents for

[1] In July, 1756, Mūmin Khān, Nawāb of Cambay, temporarily occupied the town, but was expelled in the following year.

their signature to their state prison in Sātārā fort. For this change in the government, Tārā Bāī and the Marāthā nobles, rather than the Peshwā, were to blame. They had no fixed policy, and little thought except for personal aggrandisement. Shāhū had deliberately allowed the executive power to lapse into the hands of his capable and patriotic minister, and preferred to leave the young heir to the throne under the tutelage of the Peshwā, rather than expose the country to the risks of civil war. "The usurpation of the Peshwās", Scott Waring justly remarks, "neither attracted observation nor excited surprise. Indeed, the transition was easy, natural and progressive."[1] Its greatest disadvantage was that it aggravated the centrifugal tendencies of the Marāthā state, and especially the enmity between Brāhman and Marāthā, which were at least kept in check while a member of the house of Bhonsle actually ruled; after the Peshwā's prestige was shaken by the defeat of Pānīpat, the disintegration became more and more evident.

Bālājī, having crushed his rivals, was now once more at liberty to turn his attention to foreign affairs. In the cold weather of 1751 the war with Hyderābād was renewed, but Bussy's trained infantry outmanœuvred the Peshwā and inflicted more than one defeat upon him. At one time he penetrated to within sixteen miles of Poona: but the troops mutinied for want of pay and the campaign collapsed with the poisoning, in 1752, of Ghāzī-ud-dīn, the Peshwā's candidate. In 1754, Bālājī organised a *mulukgiri* expedition on a stupendous scale to collect arrears of tribute from the Carnatic, exterminate the last remnants of Mughul rule, plunder Mysore, and replenish the Peshwā's exhausted coffers. From every village through which the Marāthās passed money was extorted and treasure chests rifled, till the countryside looked as though it had been devastated by a swarm of locusts. On their return, laden with booty, the Marāthās combined with the Nizām's forces in attacking the Nawāb of Savanūr, who had put himself at the head of a confederacy of Afghān Nawābs and southern Marāthā chiefs who refused to acknowledge the Peshwā: the tremendous effect of Muzaffar Khān's artillery trained by Bussy at the bombardment of Savanūr greatly impressed his allies.

In 1758 Bussy was recalled by Lally from the Nizām's service, and a quarrel broke out between Nizām 'Alī, the brother of Salābat Jang, and the Peshwā. Bālājī, knowing that without their famous French commandant the Hyderābād troops would be easy to deal with, determined to attack them. He first scored two bloodless triumphs. Ahmadnagar, the Nizām's great fortress and place of arms in the Deccan, was taken without a blow, the commandant, Kavi Jang, having been bribed to open the gates to the Marāthās. This deprived the Hyderābād army of its advanced base. Secondly,

[1] *History of the Marathas*, p. 169.

Ibrāhīm Khān Gārdī, the commandant of the Nizām's artillery, a soldier of fortune who had been trained by Bussy himself, was induced to enter the Peshwā's service. The two brothers, Salābat Jang and Nizām 'Alī, were in no condition to fight: their troops were in arrears and mutinous: but they could not afford to neglect the challenge, when they saw the ancient stronghold of the Nizām Shāhī kings, which had cost the Mughuls so much blood and treasure to capture, filched away in this treacherous manner. The Peshwā put the Marāthā army, 40,000 strong, under the command of his cousin, Sadāshiv Rāo, son of Chimājī Appa. With it marched Ibrāhīm Khān Gārdī, with 5000 regular sepoys and his famous French artillery. Battle was joined on 3 February, 1760, at Udgīr, 200 miles east of Poona. The Mughuls fought bravely; but their crowded ranks were decimated by the Gārdī's artillery, and a smashing cavalry charge decided the action.[1] The Mughul army fell back in disorder upon the fortress of Ausā, where, after a four days' siege, the two brothers sued for peace. Seldom had the Marāthās won a more spectacular victory, and Sadāshiv Rāo insisted on terms which were calculated to cripple the state of Hyderābād for ever. Territory round Bijāpur, Bīdar and Aurangābād, to the extent of an annual income of six million rupees, together with the key fortresses of Daulatābād, Asīrgarh, Bijāpur, Ahmadnagar and Burhānpur, were to be surrendered.

The Marāthās were now a very different people from the sturdy hillmen who had fought and conquered under the great Shivājī, "like our old Britons", as Fryer describes them, "half naked and as fierce". Contact with the Mughuls had introduced into the Deccan a love of refinement and culture before unknown. The nobles and their wives went about arrayed in silk and cloth of gold. Contemporary correspondence contains constant applications from writers in the Deccan to their friends in Hindūstān to procure for them old Sanskrit manuscripts, pictures and carvings, other articles of luxury, and dancing girls and musicians. The fine examples of Mughul and Rājput painting to be found to-day in places like Sātārā probably found their way to the south about this time. The Shanwār Wādā in Poona, the Peshwā's official residence, was six storeys high, and contained a series of sumptuous halls decorated with mirrors and carved ivory, and marble courtyards where innumerable fountains played incessantly.[2] In the Peshwā's court, the elaborate etiquette of the Mughul nobility was strictly followed. But all this imported luxury had a demoralising effect upon the hardy and simple character of the nation.

Bālājī, in the intervals of his campaigns, did a great deal to improve the administration of the Marāthā state. Regularly appointed officers

[1] See chap. XIII, p. 390.
[2] D. B. Parasnis, *Poona in Bygone Days*, chap. I.

were placed in charge of the several districts; and the territory round Sātārā, being the best protected and most productive, was entrusted to the Peshwā's favourites. They had absolute charge of the civil administration, but they were expected to furnish proper accounts: this, however, was very irregularly done, as the holders of these offices, being usually absent on campaign or in attendance on the Peshwā in Poona, left the work in the hands of dishonest and extortionate deputies. Bālājī, however, placed the civil administration in the hands of his great minister Rāmchandra Shenvi, and after his death in those of his cousin Sadāshiv Rāo. The latter appointed as chief of the revenue-collectors a very able man by name Balloba Manduvaguni, who introduced sweeping reforms, and forced the collectors to produce their accounts. At the same time, the administration of justice was reformed: a strong police force was organised in Poona city: and a famous jurist, Bāl Kishan Gādgil, was appointed as chief justice.[1] The *panchāyats* or courts of arbitration were improved, and altogether the administration was established upon a sound basis; abuses in revenue collection were checked, and the villages were encouraged to resist the exactions of every petty commander of horse who tried to levy blackmail on them. Each village was, of course, a tiny republic, administered by the headman, assisted by the accountant and other village officers: over the headman was the sub-collector, and over him the collector, who had armed irregulars to assist in keeping order.

Bālājī Bājī Rāo (or Nānā Sāhib, as he was familiarly called) had the handsome appearance and gracious manner, but not the lofty character, of his father and grandfather. His conduct towards Sakwar Bāī and Dāmājī Gāikwār has been stigmatised as unpardonably treacherous, and later in life he became indolent and sensual. But the Marāthā peasantry, remembering the all-round improvement which took place in local government under his regime, have ever since blessed the days of "Nānā Sāhib Peshwā".[2]

The chief objection to be urged against the Marāthā system of government is that, outside its own territory, it was almost purely predatory. The Marāthā was never a colonist. While away on his expeditions, his thoughts were always with his little holding in the Deccan hills, and he seldom intermarried with the people of the country.[3] Other Hindu states took a pride in improving the condition of the territory they conquered. They constructed temples, wells, canals, roads and other public works. The Marāthās did nothing of this kind. Their *mulukgiri* raids, by destroying the industries and wealth of the countries overrun, merely "killed the goose which

[1] Grant Duff, I, 29 *sqq.* and 579 *sqq.* with Edwardes' footnotes. Sen, *op. cit.* Book II, *passim*.

[2] Grant Duff, I, 531–2.

[3] Grant Duff dwells on the devotion of the Marāthā to his *watan* or hereditary holding, I, 340, 370, *passim*.

laid the golden eggs". The Marāthā state was a *Krieg Staat*, pure and simple: and it is the fate of the *Krieg Staat*, as Sarkar justly observes, to defeat its own ends.[1] The severity of the Marāthā raids, for the collection of *chauth* and other arrears, varied of course in intensity. In Gujarāt, and in the Carnatic in 1754–56, the plundering was as thorough as it was merciless: in Mālwā, on the other hand, war was waged against the government rather than the people, and though the bulk of the revenue was appropriated at each incursion, the sources from which it was drawn were crippled but not entirely ruined. But the principle was the same.[2]

Meanwhile, stirring events were happening in Hindūstān, but only a brief outline of the tangled skein of intrigue can be given here.[3] Nādir Shāh died in 1747, and Ahmad Shāh Abdālī, the founder of Afghānistān, continued his policy of raiding the declining empire, which he invaded in 1748 and 1749. In 1751 Safdar Jang, the Nawāb of Oudh, with the sanction of the young emperor, Ahmad Shāh, and heedless of the danger of drawing the Marāthās into disputes in the very heart of the empire, called in Malhār Rāo Holkar from Mālwā, Jayappa Sindia from Nārnaul, and Sūraj Mal the Jāt, to help him against the Bangash Afghāns, who had invaded Oudh and plundered Allahābād and Lucknow. The Marāthās drove the Afghāns into the hills with severe loss, and occupied Rohilkhand in 1751. They "sacked the whole country, not allowing a single man to escape, and every article they carried away as booty".[4] For their help, they were given half the Bangash territory in the Dūāb, which they held precariously till the Pānīpat disaster (1761). This was the first territorial acquisition of the Marāthās beyond the Jumna. In 1752 Ahmad Shāh Abdālī invaded the Punjab for a third time. There was a wild panic at Delhi, and the invader was bought off with promises of the cession of the Punjab and Multān.[5]

A new figure now appears upon the scene in the person of Ghāzī-ud-dīn the younger, who at the time of his father's murder in 1752 was in Delhi, and, with the help of Safdar Jang, became paymaster-general. Almost immediately, he turned against his patron, and called in the Marāthās under Raghunāth Rāo and Malhār Rāo Holkar, who were just then engaged in exacting money from the Jāts. With the help of Holkar, Ahmad Shāh was deposed and blinded, and 'Ālamgīr II installed as emperor. Anarchy prevailed in the unhappy capital, and the rival factions fought daily in the streets. The Marāthās bled the empire white with their insatiable demands, and this led to a mutiny among the imperial soldiers, who were months in arrears and starving. They then retired to Rājputāna,

[1] *Shivaji*, 3rd ed. chap. XVI, 4.
[2] Grant Duff, I, 464, 585; Malcolm, *op. cit.* chap. IV.
[3] See chap. XV, p. 429.
[4] See chap. XV, p. 431.
[5] See chap. XV, p. 434.

where they had for some time been engaged in taking part in dynastic disputes and collecting tribute. Here Jayappa Sindia was murdered in July, 1755.

In October, 1756, the Abdālī once more invaded the Punjab. In January of the following year he entered Delhi and plundered it, and two months later sacked the holy city of Muttra. He returned with booty reckoned at twelve million rupees, leaving Najīb Khān as his agent in Delhi, and his son, Tīmūr Shāh, as viceroy of Lahore. As soon as Ahmad Shāh's back was turned, Ghāzī-ud-dīn once more called in the Marāthās, and in February, 1758, a Marāthā force under Raghunāth Rāo invaded the Punjab, drove out Tīmūr Shāh, and occupied Lahore (April, 1758).[1] The Marāthā power was now at its zenith. "Their frontiers", says Elphinstone, "extended on the north to the Indus and the Himalya, and to the south nearly to the extremity of the peninsula: all the territory which was not their own paid tribute. The whole of this great power was wielded by one hand...and all pretensions of every description were concentrated on the Peshwa."[2] News of these successes were received with wild elation in the Poona court, where it was fondly believed that the Bhagwā Jhanda was "flying over the walls of Attock".[3] As a matter of fact, the wisdom of Raghunāth Rāo's ambitious policy was open to grave doubts. It did not bring an anna to the Peshwā's coffers, and the Marāthās were not in a position to hold the country, where both Sikhs and Muslims looked on them as hated intruders. Lastly, by provoking the retaliation of the Abdālī, it led to the downfall of the Marāthā power in Hindūstān.[4]

In 1758 the main Marāthā army retired, leaving a garrison at Lahore in charge of Sābājī Sindia. Meanwhile the Abdālī, who was furious at the expulsion of his son, and resolved "to bring to a decisive issue the quarrel with the Hindu power which had crossed his track of conquest, ill-treated his allies, and made war on true believers", had settled his internal dissensions and was preparing a fresh invasion. He crossed the Indus in August, 1759, and Sābājī was forced to evacuate Lahore and fall back on Delhi. Having been joined by the Rohilla chiefs, Ahmad Shāh advanced on the capital, driving the Marāthās before him. His movements were hastened by the news of the cruel murder of the emperor by Ghāzī-ud-dīn on 29 November. On 9 January, 1760, at the Barārī Ghāt ten miles north of Delhi, Ahmad Shāh defeated and slew Dattājī Sindia; his nephew Jānkojī fled with the remnants of his army to Rājputāna, where he managed to effect a junction with Malhār Rāo Holkar. Worse, however, was to follow. On 4 March Ahmad Shāh's general Jahān Khān, after a forced march, surprised and completely routed

[1] See chap. xv, p. 445.
[2] Cf. Grant Duff, I, 507.
[3] Actually, the Marāthās never crossed the Chenāb.
[4] Sarkar, *Fall of the Mughul Empire*, II, 159.

Malhār Rāo near Sikandarābād. In one short campaign the power of the Marāthās in Hindūstān was completely shattered.

The news of the defeat and death of Dattājī reached the Peshwā on 15 February, while the Marāthās in the Deccan were jubilantly celebrating the victory of Udgīr. It was at once decided that a force must be despatched under a member of the Peshwā's family to restore Marāthā influence in Hindūstān. Raghunāth Rāo applied for the command, and with his experience of fighting in northern India, undoubtedly the choice should have fallen upon him. But Raghunāth Rāo had incurred very heavy expenditure during his last campaign, which had brought no revenue to the exchequer, and for this reason he was under a cloud. Little love was lost between the two cousins, and on the strength of this Sadāshiv Rāo, the hero of Udgīr, claimed the command. The Peshwā, now too indolent to take the field himself, unwisely agreed: but with him, "according to the ancient custom of the Marāthās", he sent his young heir, Vishvās Rāo, a gallant and handsome lad of nineteen years, as nominal commander and the Peshwā's representative.[1] The army which set out from Patdur in the Deccan on 10 March, 1760, was the most magnificent that the Marāthās had ever sent forth to battle. There were twenty thousand of the famous Marāthā horse, including the *Khās Pāgā*, or household cavalry, commanded by chieftains of note who had fought from one end of India to the other—Balvant Rāo Mehendale, Shamsher Bahādur, Bājī Rāo's son by the notorious Mastānī, Nāro Shankar, Vithal Shivdeo Vinchurkar, Trimbak Sadāshiv Purandhare, Antājī Mānkeshwar, and a host of others. With them went Ibrāhīm Khān Gārdī's corps of 9000 sepoys, trained under Bussy on the French model, with forty pieces of cannon, which had done so well at Udgīr. But the experienced observer would have noted signs about this imposing array well calculated to make him uneasy. Shivājī's successes had been due to the fact that his men moved without transport, subsisting on a nose-bag of grain carried on the saddle and on food taken from the surrounding country. And that great commander had made it an offence punishable with death to bring a woman into the camp. But the Bhāo Sāhib moved with a vast amount of equipage and thousands of camp followers; behind followed numbers of elephants, loaded with lofty silken tents; the wives of the principal nobles accompanied their husbands with numerous retinues, and the officers were resplendent in cloth of gold. Lastly, the Marāthās were forsaking their traditional tactics for new methods, based on European models imperfectly assimilated.

But no thought of disaster troubled the mighty but unwieldy host, as it slowly made its way, through Aurangābād, Burhānpur and Gwalior, to the banks of the Chambal, which was reached on 4 June.

[1] The best account of the campaign of Pānīpat is in Sarkar's *Fall of the Mughal Empire*, vol. II, which is based on the most recent researches and supersedes earlier narratives.

As it moved northwards, reinforcements poured in. Malhār Rāo Holkar, Jānkojī Sindia, Dāmājī Gāikwār, Yashwant Rāo Powār, with other Marāthā chiefs and innumerable swarms of vagabond Pindāris, flocked to the royal standard, till the total exceeded 300,000, of whom about one-fourth were fighting men, with 200 cannon. It was not merely an army, but a crusade, united to drive the Afghān invaders from the sacred soil of India. But now rifts began to appear. The Rājputs, offended at the high-handed conduct of Sindia and Holkar, held aloof. At the Chambal, Sūraj Mal, the Jāt chief of Bharatpur, rode in with his force, and a council of war was held. Sūraj Mal, a veteran fighter, earnestly advised the Bhāo Sāhib to park his baggage and artillery at Bharatpur, and then to start guerrilla operations in the traditional Marāthā fashion against the Abdālī's flank and rear: by this means, he said, and by avoiding a pitched battle, they would compel him very quickly to retreat. Holkar and Sindia heartily concurred, but the Bhāo Sāhib contemptuously rejected the sage advice of these experienced warriors, as "the chatter of goatherds and zamindars".[1] The taunt deeply wounded the pride of the Marāthā generals, and the old jealousy of the rule of the Chitpāvan broke out afresh. "If this Brāhman wins", they said, "he will send his couriers to collect the revenues of Hindūstān, and we shall have to wash his loin-cloths. It is better that he should meet with a defeat, or else what consideration shall we be allowed?" Sūraj Mal determined to slip away from the doomed force at the first suitable opportunity.

The Marāthās were outside Delhi by the end of July, and the fort was captured without much difficulty on 2 August. Here also the Bhāo Sāhib's conduct gave great offence. In order to pay his troops, he stripped off the silver from the ceiling of the great hall of audience, and plundered tombs and shrines which Persian and Afghān had respected.[2] A rumour was even spread abroad that he intended to place Vishvās Rāo on the Mughul throne. Dismayed at this behaviour, Sūraj Mal and his Jāts quietly decamped: the loss of these seasoned troops was a serious matter, but the Bhāo Sāhib affected to make light of it, saying that nothing better could be expected of mere landholders. The Marāthās spent the rainy season encamped in and around Delhi, while the Abdālī was in quarters at Anūpshahr in the Bulandshahr district; both parties being busily engaged in intriguing, through their agents, for the support of Shujā'-ud-daula, the Nawāb Vazīr, who had succeeded his uncle Safdar Jang in 1754 and at first remained neutral. Proposals were also made by the Bhāo Sāhib that the Abdālī should be given large territories north of

[1] Sarkar, *op. cit.* pp. 258 *sqq.*, doubts the arrogance of the Bhāo Sāhib. But Nānā Farnavīs, who was present, says: "His Highness had latterly become proud and arrogant, and had lost his usual wisdom", to which he mainly attributes the disaster.

[2] *Siyar-ul-Mutaākhkhirīn*, III, 385.

the Sutlej on condition that he withdrew, but they fell through, chiefly on account of the opposition of Najīb Khān the Rohilla, who had good cause to hate the Marāthās for ravaging Rohilkhand and wanted them to retire for good and all behind the line of the Chambal. Shujā'-ud-daula reluctantly decided to join his co-religionists.

The rains were now over; the Dasara festival was at hand,[1] and both sides prepared to take the field. The Bhāo Sāhib moved upstream, leaving Nāro Shankar with about 7000 Marāthās to garrison Delhi. The Abdālī was on the other side of the river: his army was slightly superior in numbers to that of his opponents, and the Durrānīs were men of great bodily strength, mounted on swift Turkī horses.[2] About seventy-eight miles north of Delhi lay the fortified post of Kunjpura, well-stocked with money and provisions, of which the Marāthās were in sore need, and commanding an important ford over the Jumna. It was held by Nijābat Khān with 10,000 picked Rohillas, and on 17 October the Bhāo Sāhib determined to attack it. It was taken by storm after a fierce bombardment by Ibrāhīm Khān's heavy guns, and the garrison was put to the sword on the pretext that Nijābat Khān had been responsible for the death of Dattājī Sindia at Badāūn Ghāt. The Jumna was still in full flood and impassable, and Ahmad Shāh was forced to look on helplessly while his troops were cut to pieces. The bad discipline and the notorious love of plunder of the Marāthās now proved their undoing. While they were engaged in ransacking Kunjpura for treasure and celebrating the Dasara feast, they failed to keep the enemy on the further bank under observation. Ahmad Shāh cleverly slipped away and marched down stream. With the help of Shujā'-ud-daula, he found a ford at Bāghpat, about twenty-five miles north of Delhi, and in spite of the flood, in two days he pushed his whole army across at all costs, losing numbers of men in the process. By this masterly stroke he placed himself between his opponents and their base. This was on 25 October. The Marāthās came up soon after and were repulsed with loss: had they arrived a little while earlier, they would have had the Afghāns at their mercy. Now that it was too late, the Marāthās attacked, but were driven off with loss, and fell back fighting on the little town of Pānīpat, about sixty miles north of Delhi. Holkar once more begged the Bhāo Sāhib to resume the old guerrilla tactics of the Marāthās, but Ibrāhīm Khān Gārdī threatened to turn his guns upon his own side if they deserted him. The Bhāo Sāhib therefore threw himself into Pānīpat, where with

[1] In 1760 it fell on October 19th.

[2] Sarkar, *op. cit.* II, 289, gives the forces actually engaged as Afghāns, 60,000; Marāthās, 45,000, excluding irregular troops and followers. Kāsī Rāj gives the numbers as follows: Afghāns, 41,800 cavalry, 38,000 infantry: total 79,800. Marāthās, 55,000 cavalry, 15,000 infantry, 15,000 Pindārīs: total 85,000. Both sides had immense numbers of camp-followers.

the help of Ibrāhīm Khān he proceeded to "dig himself in" in approved European fashion, throwing up a broad rampart with a ditch in front of it and mounting his cannon at regular intervals. He hoped to provoke the Durrānī to attack him, by means of raids upon his lines of communications, but the Afghān artillery was inferior to that of the Marāthās, and Ahmad Shāh was too old a soldier to be drawn into a conflict except on his own terms. He therefore proceeded to entrench himself also in a fortified camp with an *abattis* of felled trees, about eight miles away, between the enemy and the Jumna. By this fatal move, the Marāthās permanently lost the initiative, sacrificing also their mobility, which was their most valuable asset. But the Bhāo Sāhib made a still graver blunder. He had taken into the field his own wife and the wives of his officers, instead of leaving them behind at Delhi. The vast crowd of retainers and camp followers were bound to eat up the provisions of Pānīpat in a short time. Meanwhile, negotiations were proceeding behind the scenes. Shujā'-ud-daula was still inclined towards peace, but Najīb Khān, the sworn enemy of the Marāthās, again dissuaded Ahmad Shāh. "The Marāthās", he said, "are the thorn of Hindūstān: if they were out of the way, this empire might be Your Majesty's whenever you should please." The Bhāo Sāhib would not have been averse from an arrangement by which he should fall back behind the Chambal leaving northern India in the hands of the Abdālī. But such an idea met with strong opposition in Poona from Raghunāth Rāo, who was not unnaturally reluctant to see the fruits of his conquests abandoned.[1]

The space between the lines was now the scene of almost daily skirmishes: horsemen rode out challenging their foes to single combat, and a number of fierce actions developed from chance encounters. Raids by the Gārdī infantry on 19 November and by Sindia on the 22nd were repulsed with loss, after some initial successes; and on 7 December a Rohilla attack was defeated in a spirited manner by Balvant Rāo Mehendale, who drove off the Afghāns with great slaughter, but was unfortunately killed in the hour of victory, when his men fled. The Afghāns pursued them and nearly stormed the Marāthā camp, which was only saved by the approach of night. The death of Mehendale, his brother-in-law and most trusted counsellor, was a serious loss to the Bhāo Sāhib, but about the same time he managed to get into touch with Govind Pant, the Peshwā's collector in Bundelkhand and the Dūāb. Govind Pant advanced rapidly with a swarm of light horsemen, and skirmishing in the traditional Marāthā manner, began to cut off the enemy's supplies and harass his foraging parties.

The tables were now turned. The Afghān camp was in a state of

[1] His despatches are translated in the Appendix to Kāsī Rāj, *Account of the Last Battle of Pānīpat* (Oxford, 1926).

siege, and there was a serious shortage of food. Many of the Afghān generals became seriously alarmed, and urged the Abdālī either to attack the Marāthās or to break camp and retreat. But here Ahmad Shāh showed himself a great captain. "This", he answered, "is a matter of war with which you are not acquainted. Military operations must not be precipitated. You shall see how I will manage this affair, and bring it to a successful conclusion." He then proceeded to tighten the blockade. He established an advanced post of 5000 men half-way between the lines; and there he pitched a little red tent, which he made his head-quarters from sunrise to nightfall, riding fifty or sixty miles a day to visit his outposts. After dark, the advanced post was pushed up to the very walls of the enemy's camp, and remained under arms all night, while other bodies went the rounds. "Ahmad Shāh's orders were obeyed like destiny," says Kāsī Rāj, "no man daring to hesitate or delay one moment in executing them."

The effect of this pressure soon began to tell. On 17 December a body of horse under 'Atā Khān, riding fifty miles in a day, surprised Govind Pant and his raiders and cut them to pieces. A few nights later, some twenty thousand camp followers, who had left the Marāthā camp to go foraging, were caught by the advanced post and all slaughtered; and to crown everything, on 6 January a convoy bringing specie from Delhi to pay the troops, together with its escort, was similarly cut up.

The state of things in the Marāthā camp was now indescribable. Grief and terror prevailed. Hundreds died every day of famine, and an epidemic, the result of starvation and absence of sanitation, broke out in the vast host cooped up in this narrow area. "We were surrounded," says Nānā Farnavīs in his autobiography, "and the enemy's shots fell thickly among our tents daily....There we remained in a state of siege for two months, during which most of the cattle of the army died, and the stench was dreadful." Attempts to open negotiations with the enemy were once more foiled by the implacable hatred of Najīb Khān.

On 13 January the Marāthā chiefs approached their leader. "It is now two days since we have had anything to eat", they said. "Do not let us perish in this misery: let us make one spirited effort against the enemy, and whatever is our destiny that will happen." Holkar and Sindia urged once more that the cavalry should abandon the camp, leaving the infantry and non-combatants to their fate, and cut their way through to Delhi. Ibrāhīm Khān not unnaturally refused to be sacrificed, and the Bhāo Sāhib rightly declined to abandon the women to the mercy of the Afghāns. It was determined to deliver a general assault on the enemy's lines on the following day. Whatever were the Bhāo's feelings, he was too brave a man to show them; and at the close of the council, he distributed *pān* and *supārī* to his officers with all the dignified ceremony of a *darbār*.

Shortly before dawn, Shujā'-ud-daula received a last despairing letter from the Bhāo Sāhib. "The cup is now full to the brim, and cannot hold another drop.[1] If anything can be done, do it or else inform me plainly at once: hereafter there will be no time for writing nor speaking." It was plain from this that the Marāthās were coming out. The Nawāb at once told his men to fall in, and galloped off to warn Ahmad Shāh. Ahmad Shāh, who was sleeping, was aroused, and was soon up and seated on his charger outside the little red tent, calmly smoking his hookah, and listening to the commotion in the enemy's camp. It was as yet uncertain whether the Marāthās were preparing to attack or to slip away, but at length the long lines of troops were seen deploying in the dim light. "Your servant's news is very true", said Ahmad Shāh, and at once issued the necessary instructions to his officers. The Marāthās advanced slowly, the ends of their turbans loose and their faces anointed with saffron—a sign that they had come out to conquer or to die on the field. On the left of the line was Ibrāhīm Khān with his regular battalions, with Dāmājī Gāikwār on his immediate right. On the right flank were Malhār Rāo Holkar and Jānkojī Sindia. The centre was composed of the household cavalry.[2] The Bhāo himself, seated beside Vishvās Rāo on a magnificent war-elephant, took station beneath a black mango-tree, and over him floated the famous Bhagwā Jhanda, the national standard of the Marāthās. Three *Jari Phatkas*, or grand ensigns of the Peshwās, were in the field. The Afghān centre was commanded by the chief minister, Shāh Walī Khān, with the pick of the Durrānī troops on their great Turkī mounts. On the left flank were Shāh Pasand Khān and Najīb-ud-daula, the latter facing his old enemies, Sindia and Holkar. Between these and the centre was Shujā'-ud-daula with the Oudh troops. On the right flank were Barkhurdār Khān and Amīr Beg with Rohilla and Mughul contingents.

The two lines advanced obliquely on a front of about 7½ miles, the Marāthā left under Ibrāhīm Khān making contact first. The battle began with a fierce discharge of artillery and rockets all along the line, but the Marāthā gunners, deceived probably by the light, fired high, and the shots flew harmlessly overhead. Thus the weapon on which the Bhāo Sāhib chiefly relied failed him at the critical moment. Ibrāhīm Khān, who had promised Sadāshiv Rāo that on this day he would justify the trust placed in him, thereupon ordered

[1] Another version is "the flood has risen above my head" (Sarkar, *op. cit.* p. 320).

[2] The Marāthā order of the battle from the left was: Ibrāhīm Khān; Dāmājī Gāikwār; Vithal Shivdeo; Sadāshiv Rāo and Vishvās Rāo (centre); Jaswant Rāo Powār; Shamsher Bahādur; Malhār Rāo Holkar; Jānkojī Sindia. The Durrānī order, facing the Marāthās, was: Barkhurdār Khān; Amīr Beg; Dūnde Khān; Hāfiz Rahmat Khān; Ahmad Khān Bangash; Grand Vazīr (centre); Shujā'-ud-daula; Najīb-ud-daula; Shāh Pasand Khān.

the guns to cease firing, and closed his opponents with the bayonet. After a fierce struggle, during which their commander was wounded, the regular sepoys pressed back the Rohillas. This exposed the Afghān centre under the chief minister, and at once the Bhāo Sāhib, seeing his opportunity, charged into the gap with the whole of the household cavalry at full gallop. The impact was incredibly violent; the Afghāns were surprised and met their enemies at the trot, and the Marāthās broke through three lines of their opponents. It was now impossible to see anything for the clouds of dust, and nothing could be heard but the opposing cries of *Har, Har, Mahādeo!* and *Dīn, Dīn!*, as the troopers, locked in a death grip, stabbed and struck with lance and battle-axe, and even with daggers. The Shāh Walī Khān, who commanded the centre, dismounted and in full armour, in a paroxysm of rage, was trying to rally his men in vain. "Our country is far off, my friends," he was crying, "whither do you fly?" But none heeded his orders or his exhortations.

It now looked as if the battle was going against the Afghāns. Their right flank was turned and their centre was broken: only on their left were they holding their own. Here Najīb-ud-daula was facing his old enemy, Jānkojī Sindia. Anticipating modern methods, he advanced by short rushes, his men halting to "dig themselves in", and the sappers throwing up field-breastworks, while the Marāthā formations were broken up by salvos of rockets. From dawn to midday the engagement raged with the utmost fury, and at any moment the line might give way. But the Abdālī knew that the commander who throws in his reserves last wins. The psychological moment had now come. He brought up his fresh reserves, and at the same time sent military police to whip up, on pain of death, the stragglers who were dribbling away to the rear, and to call up the troops left to guard the camp. He then posted 4000 men to cover his right, sent 10,000 to Shāh Walī Khān, with orders for him to charge with the sword in close order at full gallop, and issued directions to Pasand Khān and Najīb-ud-daula to take the Marāthā centre in flank, as soon as he saw the minister's troops on the move. Meanwhile, the mounted infantry galloped along the enemy's line, firing from their saddles into the close ranks of the enemy.

The simultaneous counter-attack was launched all along the line early in the afternoon. It was excellently timed, and its effect upon the exhausted Marāthās was terrible. Men and horses had been starved for weeks, and had had no food at all since dawn.[1] Still, however, they contested the ground, inch by inch. "A furious engagement ensued," says the author of the *Siyar-ul-Mutaākhkhirīn*, "and for full two hours there arose such a cloud of dust that none of the com-

[1] Sarkar points out that Hindu armies, for caste-reasons, took no food into the field, and were accustomed to break off action in order to prepare a meal about noon. Clive at Plassey, and General Harris at Seringapatam, took advantage of this fact.

batants could distinguish the earth from the heavens. From midday to four o'clock, nothing could be heard or seen, but a furious slaughter which was going on at an incredible rate." To the fire of the mounted infantry was added that of the camel-guns (*shutarnāl*), which caused many casualties. About 2.15 p.m., Vishvās Rāo was wounded and had to be taken to his elephant, but the Bhāo still fought on at the head of his men for an hour longer. Then with dramatic suddenness, resistance collapsed. "All at once, as if by enchantment, the whole Marāthā army turned their backs and fled at full speed, leaving the field of battle covered with heaps of dead."[1] In the dramatic words of an eyewitness, the Hindu host suddenly melted away "like camphor". The victors pursued them to their camp, giving no quarter, and the ditch was soon choked with bodies. "The field of battle looked like a tract sown with tulips, and as far as the sight could extend, nothing could be discovered but bodies stretched at the foot of bodies, as if they had been asleep, or marshalled by art."[2] It was a moonlight night, and the slaughter of fugitives went on till dawn. Next morning the camp was stormed, and a further massacre took place. Surrender availed nothing. The unhappy prisoners were paraded in long lines, given a little parched grain and a drink of water, and beheaded. Every Afghān tent had heads piled before its doors. The plunder of the camp was prodigious, and the women and children who survived were driven off as slaves.[3] The body of Vishvās Rāo was brought to the Shāh, and every one gazed in admiration of the beauty of the lad, who seemed to be only sleeping. The Durrānīs cried out: "This is the body of the king of the unbelievers: we will have it dried and stuffed to carry back to Kabul." But Shujā'-ud-daula, who did all he could to help the vanquished army, arranged to have him cremated according to Hindu rites. He was, however, unable to protect Jānkojī Sindia or Ibrāhīm Khān, who were both taken prisoners and sacrificed to the conqueror's rage. Ibrāhīm Khān was a renegade, who had fought on the side of the infidel against true believers: Jānkojī was hated by the Rohillas. The Bhāo Sāhib, when he saw that all was lost, had mounted his charger, and collecting a few men, galloped into the thick of the battle to find a soldier's death. When last seen, he was surrounded by Afghāns and fighting desperately. A headless corpse, identified as his, was recovered and cremated along with that of his nephew.[4]

Meanwhile, the Peshwā had been planning an expedition to northern India to extricate the Bhāo Sāhib, and he had, without success, endeavoured to enlist the co-operation of the Nizām. Bālājī

[1] Kāsī Rājā, pp. 39–40. [2] *Siyar-ul-Mutākhkhirīn*, *loc. cit.*

[3] Twenty-two thousand, many of them of the highest rank in the land, says the *Siyar-ul-Mutākhkhirīn*.

[4] There is no doubt about his fate, though two impostors, claiming to be the Bhāo, appeared in Poona and Benares and were thrown into prison.

was now in failing health, and incapable of acting with promptness. He was distracted by family dissensions, and haunted by the spectre of bankruptcy, the result of his far-flung ambitions in the north. But in any case, the Bhāo and his heroic comrades were beyond the reach of earthly help. On 24 January, at Bhīlsa, a banker's letter was intercepted, which announced in enigmatic language the tragedy of ten days previously. "Two pearls have been dissolved," it said, "twenty-seven gold mohurs have been lost, and of the silver and copper, the total cannot be cast up." Bālājī pressed on, hoping that some of his family might have survived, but fugitives now began to come in, who confirmed the completeness of the tragedy. Bālājī slowly fell back on Poona, which he reached in June. Here, on the 23rd, he passed away in the palace which he had erected on the Pārvatī hill, calling for his lost son. It is easy to be wise after the event, and innumerable criticisms have been passed upon the Bhāo for his arrogance and refusal to take advice from his captains. But Sadāshiv Rāo, with all his faults, atoned by death for any errors of which he may be adjudged guilty. Defeat is sometimes as honourable as victory, and at Pānīpat the Marāthās went down fighting.

Holkar and Dāmājī Gāikwār withdrew when they saw that all was lost. But there does not appear to be sufficient reason for accusing the former of deliberate treachery. According to his own account, the Bhāo Sāhib sent him a message, telling him to "do as he had directed"—perhaps to rescue the women and children in the camp, who had been committed to his charge, and escort them to Delhi. In this he was unsuccessful. Nāro Shankar and part of the Delhi garrison managed to get away. Mahādjī Sindia and Nānā Farnavīs were among the few fugitives who escaped almost miraculously from the field; the former received a wound in the leg from a gigantic Afghān which lamed him for life. About 100,000 Marāthās must have perished: and only one-fourth of the fighting men ever saw the Deccan again. Many fugitives were murdered by the peasants, who were only too eager to turn the tables upon their former oppressors.[1] Those who straggled into Dīg were, however, hospitably entertained by Sūraj Mal, and in this way about four thousand men reached home. Shamsher Bahādur and Antājī Mānkeshwar died of wounds at Dīg.

"Never was a defeat more complete", says Elphinstone, "and never was there a calamity that diffused so much consternation. Grief and despondency spread over the whole Marāthā people: most had to mourn relations, and all felt the destruction of the army as a death-blow to their national greatness." Most disastrous of all, perhaps, was the fact that it dealt a fatal blow to the one unifying influence in the Deccan, the prestige of the Peshwās. It is, of course, true that the Marāthās, with characteristic resiliency, recovered from

[1] *Siyar-ul-Mutaākhkhirīn*, III, 392.

what would have been a crushing disaster to a less hardy nation. In August, 1763, they won a brilliant victory over the Nizām at Rākshasbhavan. But their armies were never again the same. The Arab and Hindūstānī mercenary to an increasing degree replaced the free Marāthā trooper, and most important of all, the weakened power of the Peshwā paved the way to English interference in Marāthā affairs. Pānīpat, in other words, was the prelude to Assaye and Kirkee. To Ahmad Shāh also, the victory was a Pyrrhic one: on 22 March, after ransacking Delhi, he withdrew his army. His men, who hated the Indian hot weather, were on the verge of mutiny, and insisted on returning home with their plunder. Ahmad Shāh, accordingly, after having left Najīb Khān as regent of Delhi, retreated beyond the passes, and did not again invade India.

A NOTE ON MARĀTHĪ LITERATURE

The Marāthās are typical hillmen, independent and freedom-loving, and their language and literature reflect these characteristics. Marāthī is a rugged tongue, with none of the courtly refinements of northern India, and the early poetic literature is the simple, natural expression of religious emotion. The earliest Marāthī poetry is an offshoot of the *Bhakti* movement which swept over India from the twelfth century A.D., and gave such an impetus to the development of vernaculars. Its essential doctrine is that salvation may be attained, independently of priests, ritual and caste, by devotion to the Divine Name. The Deity, whether manifested as Shiva, or Vishnu in his various incarnations, is Bhagavān, the Adorable, and his devotees are the Bhāgavatas. It has been not inaptly compared to the Protestant Reformation in Europe.

In Mahārāshtra, the central object of devotion was Vithobā, a local form of Vishnu, who dwells at the famous shrine of Pandharpur. It was upon him that the worship of the poet-saints of the Deccan was focused. The earliest writers in Marāthī (as opposed to the Mahārāshtrī Prākrit) belong to the thirteenth and fourteenth centuries, and flourished under the Yādavas, the last Hindu dynasty of the Deccan. They are Mukundrāj, Nāmdev (A.D. 1270–1350) and Jnāneshvar. Their object was to bring the learning of the pundits down to the level of the common people. Jnāneshvar, who lived at Ālandī near Poona, is commonly believed to have made a buffalo recite the Veda! He wrote a paraphrase of the *Bhagavad Gītā*. Nāmdev, a devotee of Vithobā, was a tailor by caste. He wrote in Hindī as well as Marāthī; some of his poems found their way to northern India, and were incorporated in the *Ādi Granth* of the Sikhs.

For the next three centuries, with the Deccan under the heel of the Muhammadans, no writer of note appeared. Then in the seventeenth century, the national renaissance which culminated in Shivājī began to gather force. The earliest poet of this period was Eknāth of Paithan, who, though a Brāhman, denounced the caste-system, and went so far as to dine with a Mahār, an almost unheard-of action. He died in 1608. His grandson Mukteshvar, together with Tukārām and Rāmdās, was a contemporary of Shivājī. Shivājī, though formally illiterate, was a fervent admirer of his country's songs and legends, and it is said that more than once he risked capture when going to Poona in disguise to hear a religious recitation. He tried to persuade Tukārām to come to his court. But Tukārām, absorbed in his intense love of Vithobā, cared for none of these things. He was a poor trader by profession, knowing no Sanskrit, and his artless verses are sung in countless village homes all over the Deccan to-day. Rāmdās, on the other hand, was a Brāhman, and was Shivājī's *gurū* or spiritual preceptor. It is said that

Shivājī surrendered his kingdom to him, and received it back "in trust from God", and for this reason, the national standard of the Marāthās, the *Bhagwā Jhanda*, was the orange robe of the ascetic. The verses of Rāmdās, full of wise saws, remind us of the Proverbs of King Solomon, and his teaching undoubtedly had a formative effect upon Shivājī. He died in 1681.

The most interesting products of the period, however, are the *pawādās* or ballads. Their most singular characteristic is that they are unwritten, being handed down from generation to generation by the *gondhālīs*, a tribe or caste of wandering bards who composed and recited them. The *gondhālīs* are devotees of the goddess Ambā Bhavānī, and the recitations are accompanied by an elaborate ritual, in which the goddess herself is supposed to descend upon the reciter. The ballads deal with the deeds of the Marāthā heroes in their struggles against the Muhammadans, such as the slaying of Afzal Khān, the taking of Sinhgarh by Tānājī Mālusre, the battle of Khardā, and the tragedy of Pānīpat. These ballads were intensely popular with the unlettered peasantry, and played a great part in arousing them against their Muhammadan rulers.[1]

The period after the death of Shivājī witnessed a great outburst of Marāthī poetry, and it will here be possible only to mention a few leading names. Shrīdhar was the most beloved of the writers of this time, and shares with Tukārām the palm of popularity in the Deccan to-day. His mission was to make the heroic legends of Hinduism accessible to women and others who knew no Sanskrit. The titles of his works, the Triumph of Rāma (Rāma Vijaya) and the Exploits of the Pāndavas, speak for themselves. He was born at Pandharpur in 1670 and died in 1728. "In every town and village in the Deccan and Konkan, especially during the rains, the pious Marāthā will be found enjoying with his family and friends the Pothi of Shrīdhar." Moropant, admired by connoisseurs for his verbal ingenuity, does not appeal to western taste. Another writer of great interest is Mahīpati, whose *Bhakta Vijaya* and *Santa Vijaya*, Triumphs of the Devotees and Saints, are a mine of information about the picturesque legends which have grown up round the poet-saints of the Deccan.

During the eighteenth century, the Marāthā character started to change. Poona was filled with loot from Hindūstān, and the manners and ceremonial of the Mughul Court were introduced. Contact with the western nations, especially the English at Bombay and Surat, was beginning to have its effect. Erotic poetry became popular, and Rām Joshī (1762–1812) was the most celebrated of the writers of *Lavanis* or Love Songs. The conquest of an empire, and the appearance of state-papers and despatches, led to the development of Marāthī prose. *Bakhars* or historical chronicles were compiled, but their barbarous idiom, three-quarters Persian, bears little relation to the elegant, highly sanskritised prose style which arose in the nineteenth century, as a result of contact with western literature.

[1] About sixty were taken down by Acworth and Shaligram, and ten have been translated into verse by H. A. Acworth, *Ballads of the Marāthās*, Longmans, 1894.

CHAPTER XV

AHMAD SHĀH, 'ĀLAMGĪR II AND SHĀH 'ĀLAM

THE new emperor was a young man of twenty-one, vicious, dissipated, perfidious, pusillanimous, and utterly worthless. The weakness of his character left him, throughout his short reign, a tool in the hands of others, and his natural instinct led him to prefer, as advisers, those least worthy of being associated in the administration of such territories as were left to him. The great nobles were entirely selfish, devoid of patriotism and honour, and interested only in dividing among themselves the remnant of the dominions of the House of Tīmūr. In this ignoble competition they employed intrigue, assassination, and open violence.

After returning from the inglorious though successful campaign against Ahmad Shāh, they were employed in a redistribution of the great offices at the capital and in the provinces. Mu'īn-ul-Mulk, a son of the late minister, had already secured the Punjab and had been permitted to leave Sirhind for Lahore after promising to remit large sums to Delhi as tribute, a promise which he was never able to redeem. The vacant place of minister was filled by Safdar Jang, the viceroy of Oudh, who governed his province by deputy. Nizām-ul-Mulk, now an old man in a very feeble state of health, had at once marched northward, but had not passed Burhānpur when he heard first of the defeat of the invader at Sirhind and immediately afterwards of the death of Muhammad and the accession of Ahmad Shāh. Turning back, he died on 1 June 1748 close to Burhānpur. His eldest son being at court, he was succeeded in the Deccan, as a matter of course, by his second son, Nāsir Jang.[1] His title of Amīr-ul-Umarā, with its privileges, was bestowed by Ahmad Shāh on Sādāt Khān, entitled Zu-'l-Fiqār Jang, who had already held high office as governor of the capital.

These offices of state were apportioned by the great nobles without reference to the personal wishes of the emperor, who tried to retaliate by forming a court faction of personal adherents. His attempt to assert authority may be traced to his mother, a woman of humble origin but pernicious activity. At the head of the party was the chief eunuch, Jāvīd Khān, who received high titles and in return for these unmerited honours taught his master to destroy a naturally feeble intellect by drinking to excess. The court party was, in fact, nothing but a cabal of women and eunuchs who pitted themselves against the great officers of state and their armed forces.

[1] See chap. XIII, p. 386.

'Alī Muhammad Khān, the chief of the Rohillas of Katehr, had been a political prisoner, and in the confusion which ensued on Ahmad Shāh Abdālī's invasion returned to Morādābād, where he completely re-established his authority. Safdar Jang, a Persian Shiah, detested all Afghāns and viewed with alarm the establishment of an Afghān state on the north-western border of his province. 'Alī Muhammad Khān died shortly after his return, but Hāfiz Rahmat Khān, the father-in-law of his elder son, Sa'd-ullah Khān, became regent of his territories. An officer appointed from Delhi as governor of Morādābād, but ill supplied with troops and munitions, ventured to cross the Ganges with a small force. The Rohillas whom he first attacked feigned flight, and pursuing them with triumphant shouts, he and his men were drawn into an ambush, where nearly all were slain.

Safdar Jang now thought of a new device. During the reigns of Farrukh-siyar and Muhammad Shāh the Afghān soldier of fortune, Muhammad Khān Bangash, had gradually acquired the greater part of the southern portion of the Gangetic Dūāb, from Kol, the modern 'Alīgarh, nearly to the south-eastern boundary of the present district of Cawnpore. In Farrukhābād, the capital which he built for himself, he commemorated the name of his first patron. In this area he was virtually independent and the viceroys of Oudh resented the growth of this Afghān principality on their western border as much as that of the more recently established Rohilla state. Muhammad Khān had died in 1743, but his territories were now governed by his son Qāim Khān, who bore the title of Qāim Jang, and Safdar Jang issued in the emperor's name an order directing him to attack the rebels in Katehr. Qāim Jang crossed the Ganges and besieged the Rohillas in Budaun, where the impetuous Sa'd-ullah Khān, elder son of 'Alī Muhammad Khān, sallied forth to meet him. Qāim Jang's superior numbers forced the enemy to give way, but by a stratagem Qāim Jang was enticed into an ambush and slain, and his troops fled. The defeat of the Bangash Afghāns and the death of their leader left them a safe object of attack and on 10 December 1748 Safdar Jang, carrying the emperor with him, marched from Delhi for Farrukhābād with 40,000 horse, having also directed Rājā Naval Rāi, his deputy in Oudh, to join him from that direction. The Afghāns were too broken to offer any resistance. Six million rupees were extorted from the mother of Qāim Jang and five of Muhammad Khān's younger sons were carried off and imprisoned by Naval Rāi in the fortress of Allahābād.

In 1749 Ahmad Shāh Abdālī invaded India for the second time, but did not advance beyond Lahore, where the governor bought him off by the cession of the revenue of four sub-districts.

Safdar Jang had left to the Bangash Afghāns only those districts which Farrukh-siyar had assigned to Muhammad Khān, and the remainder were administered by Rājā Naval Rāi. Ahmad Khān, the brother of Qāim Jang, who had succeeded at the instigation of his mother, began to assemble troops in preparation for an attack on Naval Rāi, who warned his master of the preparations and, advancing from Kanauj, entrenched himself at Khudāganj about half-way between Kanauj and Farrukhābād. Safdar Jang left Delhi on 3 August with a large army and sent troops in advance to meet Naval Rāi. The Afghāns, however, on 13 August penetrated the camp of Naval Rāi by surprise, put him to death in his tent, and captured his artillery and the whole of his equipage.

Safdar Jang had reached Mārahra, about sixty-seven miles north-west of Farrukhābād, when he received the news. His difficulties were increased by the turbulence of his troops who, in consequence of a dispute between a camel driver and one of the leading inhabitants, sacked the town of Mārahra while he halted there. Ahmad Khān turned north. The armies met on 24 September between Sahāwar and Patiālī, and Safdar Jang was completely defeated and he was himself wounded by a musket ball. He retired with his beaten army to Delhi, where he learnt with indignation that his defeat had been received by the court party with joy. His death had been reported and the emperor and Jāvīd Khān had prepared to confiscate his property, as was usual, but had waited until the rumour should be confirmed. His wife had assembled such of his troops as remained in Delhi to defend his property. On his return the emperor and Jāvīd Khān attempted to excuse themselves but failed to satisfy Safdar Jang, who warned the queen-mother, as the prime mover in the plot, that he was still alive and that it would go ill with any who attempted to molest him.

Ahmad Khān, after his victory over the minister, sent his young son Mahmūd Khān into Oudh to plunder the country and marched in person on Allahābād, where his younger brothers were confined, and besieged the fort. Failing to take it, and learning that the minister had taken the field, he plundered and burnt the city and retired to Farrukhābād carrying with him 4000 women captured at Allahābād.

Meanwhile Mahmūd Khan had crossed the Ganges into Oudh and attacked Bilgrām, but the determined attitude of the Sayyids of that town, of the same stock as the Sayyids of Bārha, saved it. He sent detachments to occupy the *parganas* of Shāhābād and Khairābād and marched to Phāphāmaū, on the Ganges, near Allahābād, whence he despatched a force to capture Lucknow. The Afghāns entered Lucknow, but one of Safdar Jang's officers raised the citizens and drove them out of the city, while other troops from Oudh moved towards Phāphāmaū and Mahmūd Khān fled. The expulsion of the Afghāns from Oudh was now a simple matter, but they still remained dangerous. Safdar Jang now decided to summon to his aid Malhār Rāo Holkar from Mālwā, Jayappa Sindia from Nārnaul, and Sūraj Mal the Jāt. He did this, intent only on his own ends and negligent of the danger of bringing Marāthās into disputes in the neighbourhood of the capital. The Marāthā horse were first sent against Ahmad Khān's governor of Kol and Jalesar, who was suddenly attacked and completely defeated, and fled to Farrukhābād. Ahmad Khān, on hearing of this, withdrew at once from Allahābād, which he had been again besieging. His army, largely composed of adventurers, deserted him, and he reached Farrukhābād with but a few followers. Safdar Jang and the Marāthās and Jāts marched on Farrukhābād and on their approach Ahmad Khān withdrew from the city to a fort now called Fatehgarh, which he had built on the bank of the Ganges, and appealed to the Rohillas for aid. There was some hesitation on their part in responding. The elders had been on good terms with the minister, since they had defeated Qāim Jang, and even the impetuous Sa'd-ullah Khān hesitated to join Ahmad Khān, who had not yet avenged his brother's blood. Ahmad Khān assured him that help at such a time would be ample atonement and Sa'd-ullah Khān marched, too late, to his aid.

The Marāthās sacked Farrukhābād and had for some time been endeavouring to throw a bridge of boats across the Ganges, hoping to surround the position held by Ahmad Khān, which was open in all directions on the east of the Ganges. Mahmūd Khān was unsuccessful in preventing this, and on 28 April the Ganges was bridged under cover of the Marāthā guns. Sa'd-ullah Khān joined Ahmad Khān two days later, and the latter, unwilling to stand a siege in his camp, came forth, and gave battle. The Afghāns were defeated, with heavy loss, and the remnant fled by way of Aonla and Morādābād to Chilkia, at the foot of the Kumāūn hills. The Marāthās occupied Rohilkhand throughout the rainy season of 1751 and were rewarded for their services in this campaign with half the Bangash territory. The power of the Bangash Nawabs of Farrukhābād was now finally broken. Early in the reign Zu-'l-Fiqār Jang had held the provinces of Allahābād and Āgra, but the minister, Safdar Jang, coveted the former, which adjoined Oudh, and transferred to Zu-'l-Fiqār Jang Ajmer, which adjoined Āgra, and took Allahābād. The emperor was obliged to sanction this arrangement, though it was detrimental to his interests. Zu-'l-Fiqār Jang was foolish, irresolute, and a poltroon, but events in Rājputāna gave him an opportunity. Bakht Singh of Jodhpur was in rebellion against his nephew, Rām Singh, who had succeeded his father, Abhay Singh, and he appealed for imperial support against his nephew, making specious promises which offered a prospect of the re-establishment of the emperor's authority. Zu-'l-Fiqār Jang promised him aid and set out for Ajmer. The Jāts meanwhile had extended their dominion northwards and had occupied Nīmrāna, which lay in Zu-'l-Fiqār's way. Though they were not hostile to the emperor, the fortress was weakly held and a cheap victory appealed strongly to Zu-'l-Fiqār Jang. The garrison was expelled without difficulty, but the simple victor had but embroiled himself disastrously with the Jāts. His illusory success turned his head, and after some hesitation he recalled his advanced guard and marched southward into the Jāt country. Here an advanced guard found the Jāts in force, under Sūraj Mal. At a moment when a little resolution might have ensured the success of a mistaken enterprise his heart failed, and instead of advancing in person to the support of his advanced guard, he ordered it to retire. Its retreat demoralised the rest of his army, which was attacked and defeated by the Jāts. He then thought of fleeing to Delhi and leaving his army, but his officers would not permit this. Sūraj Mal, though prepared to defend his own possessions, was loth to detain the imperial officer, and he offered Zu-'l-Fiqār Jang easy terms and undertook to fulfil his obligations to Bakht Singh and to send tribute from Rājputāna. Zu-'l-Fiqār Jang continued his march to Nārnaul, where Bakht Singh resided, accompanied by his Jāt ally. Bakht Singh did not conceal his contempt for an ally of the Jāts and would not permit them to join in the settlement of disputes between Rājputs; and ordered Zu-'l-Fiqār Jang to proceed to Ajmer. Sūraj Mal returned home in disgust and the submissive Zu-'l-Fiqār Jang was joined by Bakht Singh at Ajmer and they marched towards Jodhpur. The combined troops of Rām Singh and Khande Rāo, son of Malhār Rāo Holkar, met them at Pīpār.[1] Bakht Singh warned Zu-'l-Fiqār Jang to beware of the Jodhpur artillery concealed in the centre of the army, but the latter disregarded the warning. Fire was reserved until his army, in close formation, was almost on the guns and was then delivered with terrible effect, causing the whole mass to recoil. The battle was not decided and Bakht Singh's troops were fresh, but Zu-'l-Fiqār Jang had had enough of fighting and announced his intention of coming to terms. Bakht Singh vainly urged the importance of establishing the imperial authority in Jodhpur, but Zu-'l-Fiqār Jang persisted in his resolve. On the one side Bakht Singh and on the other Khande Rāo Holkar withdrew, leaving Zu-'l-Fiqār Jang and Rām Singh to arrange their own terms. Zu-'l-Fiqār Jang accepted 300,000 rupees in ready money and a promise of supplies to be delivered at various stages of his retreat and set out at once for Delhi. The reason for his haste was the news of Safdar Jang's defeat by Ahmad Khān. He assumed that the minister would at once be dismissed and his folly and conceit encouraged him to hope that he might secure the place, but Safdar Jang had already recovered his position. After Zu-'l-Fiqār's return to Delhi his failure preyed upon his mind. He begged the emperor to help him to discharge his debt to his troops and, when his request was rejected, began to

[1] 26° 23′ N., 73° 33′ E.

talk treason among his companions. Finally, he attempted to enter the hall of audience fully armed, to intimidate the emperor. Forbidden to appear at court, he appeared no more in public. His property was confiscated and he was deprived of his rank and of the title of Amīr-ul-Umarā, which was conferred upon Ghāzī-ud-dīn Khān,[1] the eldest son of the late Nizām-ul-Mulk.

In the Deccan, Nizām-ul-Mulk had been succeeded in 1748 by his second son, Nāsir Jang. Ahmad Shāh and Jāvīd Khān had from the first disliked Safdar Jang and had intended to confer the post of minister on Nizām-ul-Mulk. They sought to attach the powerful viceroy of the Deccan to the court party and thus escape the domination of Safdar Jang, and accordingly wrote private letters to Nāsir Jang begging him to come to Delhi. He set out with a large army and arrived at Burhānpur in April, 1749, but received another order cancelling the summons. Safdar Jang had probably discovered the design of the court party and had compelled the emperor to abandon it.

Nāsir Jang was content to return, for his sister's son Muzaffar Jang, who enjoyed the support of the French, had taken advantage of his departure to rise in rebellion and at the instigation of Husain Dost Khān the Navāit, known as Chanda Sāhib, and with the help of a force of French troops supplied by M. Dupleix, had invaded the lower Carnatic. Nāsir Jang's campaign in the Carnatic and his murder in December, 1750, have been described elsewhere.[2] A few months later Muzaffar Jang, who was proclaimed by the French viceroy of the Deccan, shared the same fate, and Bussy recognised as his successor Salābat Jang, the third son of Nizām-ul-Mulk.

Nāsir Jang, Muzaffar Jang, and Salābat Jang, as well as their foreign supporters, had all assumed that Ghāzī-ud-dīn Khān, eldest son of the late Nizām-ul-Mulk, had foregone his claim. Ghāzī-ud-dīn, though he had hitherto taken no steps to dispute Nāsir Jang's accession, early in 1751 demanded of the emperor a commission as viceroy of the Deccan in succession to his father. The issue of orders was delayed by the courtiers' claim that he should purchase his office with the customary large payment in which they hoped to share and by Ghāzī-ud-dīn's demand that it should be free of cost.

This dispute was interrupted by the third[3] invasion of India by Ahmad Shāh Abdālī, who crossed the frontier at the end of 1751, and at the same time sent an envoy to Delhi, demanding the cession of the Punjab and Multān. Mu'īn-ul Mulk the governor withstood the invader for four months and would probably have compelled

[1] His other titles were Fīrūz Jang and 'Imād-ul-Mulk.

[2] See chap. XIII, p. 386, and vol. V, pp. 127 *sqq.*

[3] The author of the *Siyar-ul-Mutaākhkhirīn* misnumbers all Ahmad Shāh Abdālī's invasions, making the first the second, and so on. Ahmad Shāh, as one of Nādir Shāh's officers, accompanied him on his expedition to India and Sayyid Ghulām Husain Khān Tabātabāī apparently reckons this as the Abdālī's first invasion.

him to retire had it not been for the treachery of Ādīna Beg Khān, who suggested an ill-timed *sortie*, of which notice was given to the invaders, and which failed.

As usual the emperor and his courtiers were overcome with terror. Safdar Jang, who had not returned to the capital since his successes against the Bangash Afghāns and the Rohillas, received pressing messages asking him to bring to court Malhār Rāo Holkar and other allies. Before he could reach Delhi the pusillanimous Ahmad had purchased safety by a disgraceful treaty which ceded the Punjab and Multān to Afghānistān. Ahmad Shāh Abdālī thereupon appointed Mu'īn-ul-Mulk as his governor of the Punjab and returned to Kābul.

Safdar Jang arrived at Delhi in May, 1752, and was furious on discovering that this treaty had been concluded. He had purchased the support of Malhār Rāo Holkar by promises of large subsidies, which he called on the emperor and the eunuch to fulfil. They, however, could not if they would; and relations between the emperor and his minister were irrevocably embittered.

The crafty Ghāzī-ud-dīn offered a solution of the difficulty. He promised, in return for a free commission, to carry Holkar with him and to close his mouth. The commission was issued and in May, having appointed his son to represent him at the capital, he left Delhi for the Deccan, accompanied by Holkar. Ghāzī-ud-dīn had already secured a promise of the support of Bālājī Rāo Peshwā who was levying contributions from districts of the Deccan in which Salābat Jang's authority was acknowledged. But with help from the French the Marāthās were defeated and Salābat Jang came to terms with them in January, 1752 (see vol. v, p. 135). Two months later Ghāzī-ud-dīn and Malhār Rāo Holkar started from Delhi and were met at Burhānpur by the Peshwā. To secure the fidelity of his Marāthā allies, who were bound to him by no ties save that of interest and were quite ready to change sides, Ghāzī-ud-dīn pledged large concessions (see chap. XIII, p. 388).

Salābat Jang's position was now difficult. He retained the support of his French allies but financial difficulties embarrassed him and his brother was at the head of an immense army. Negotiations and preparations for taking the field were begun at the same time, but before either had advanced beyond their earliest stages Ghāzī-ud-dīn was poisoned at Aurangābād by his stepmother and Salābat Jang remained in undisputed possession of the viceroyalty of the Deccan.

At Delhi the quarrel between the emperor and his minister had reached an acute stage. Safdar Jang returned to the city, after the departure of Ghāzī-ud-dīn for the Deccan. He laid the blame for the disgraceful treaty with the Abdālī entirely on the eunuch Jāvīd Khān, but when the first storm of his rage was passed he dissembled, made overtures for a reconciliation, and in August invited the eunuch to a banquet, where he was stabbed to death. The murder deprived

Ahmad Shāh of the only adherent whom he could trust and alarmed him for his personal safety. After the death of Ghāzī-ud-dīn his son, Shihāb-ud-dīn Khān, an able, violent, unscrupulous, and utterly fearless youth of eighteen, became a person of importance, and the emperor and Safdar Jang vied for his support. The former conferred on him at once his father's titles of Ghāzī-ud-dīn Khān Bahādur and Fīrūz Jang, and the latter obtained for him the high title of Amīr-ul-Umarā, but both were destined to disappointment. Ghāzī-ud-dīn II, notwithstanding his learning, his skill in calligraphy, his knowledge of many languages, his poetic gifts and his valour, was utterly bad and specially forgot his patrons. He first allied himself to the emperor and the court party, and encouraged Ahmad Shāh to require of Safdar Jang the resignation of the command of some appointments which he held in conjunction with the great offices of minister of the empire and viceroy of Oudh.

The minister was now deterred from taking up arms against the emperor only by fear of incurring the suspicion of aspiring to the throne and thus alienating all. He ignored the demand for the resignation of his minor offices, but Ghāzī-ud-dīn discovered a plan to deprive him of the most dangerous of them. The imperial artillery was stationed in the fort, and by a stratagem Safdar Jang's officer in charge of it was removed. The guns were then loaded and trained on the palace which the minister occupied. Safdar Jang then begged for leave to depart to his province. In the emperor's refusal of this permission may be traced the hand of Ghāzī-ud-dīn, who was opposed to a peaceful solution of the difficulty and wished, by driving Safdar Jang into active hostility, to complete his ruin.

Safdar Jang now raised the standard of revolt and, to avert suspicion from himself, proclaimed as emperor a man of unknown origin, whom he represented to be a prince of the imperial house.

The civil war, which broke out on 4 May, 1753, and lasted for six months, took the form of incessant combats in the streets and neighbourhood of the capital. Safdar Jang sent his wife and family for safety into the Jāt country and enlisted the aid of Sūraj Mal, raja of the Jāts. Ghāzī-ud-dīn's principal commander was Najīb Khān the Rohilla, whose hostility to Safdar Jang could be relied upon, and who afterwards rose to the rank of Amīr-ul-Umarā. Zu-'l-Fiqār Jang emerged from his retirement and joined Safdar Jang. Both parties summoned to their aid all the turbulent elements in the capital and the surrounding districts and the Sunnī Ghāzī-ud-dīn imported an additional element of bitterness into the strife by proclaiming the Shiah Safdar Jang a heretic. By this means as well as by bribes he was able to detach from Safdar Jang most of the Sunnīs serving in his troops, and individual heretics were seized in the streets and robbed and beaten, or even murdered. Sūraj Mal plundered Old Delhi, then more populous than Shāh Jahān's city, and the latter was a scene of continual bloodshed, plunder and murder. Neither party obtained any decided advantage over the other and both at length grew weary of the fruitless and devastating strife. In November they came to terms. Safdar Jang was permitted to retain the provinces of Oudh and Allahābād, and departed for the seat of his government, and Intizām-ud-Daula, son of Qamar-ud-dīn and uncle of Ghāzī-ud-dīn, was confirmed as minister.

During the six months' fighting Ghāzī-ud-dīn had summoned to his aid Malhār Rāo Holkar from Mālwā and Jayappa Sindia from Nāgaur, but they did not reach Delhi until peace had been concluded and Ghāzī-ud-dīn now employed them for the punishment of Sūraj Mal. He was deficient in artillery, and discovering, on entering the Jāt country, that without it he could make no impression on the strong fortresses, he asked the emperor to supply him with guns. Intizām-ud-Daula, who knew his nephew's turbulent and ambitious disposition, warned Ahmad Shāh against the request, and Ghāzī-ud-dīn instigated an attack on the minister's house, which failed. The timid Ahmad Shāh was now apprehensive of Ghāzī-ud-dīn, and opened communications with Sūraj Mal, who suggested that Safdar Jang should be summoned from Oudh. This suggestion was not adopted, but the emperor and the minister marched from Delhi with the army in order that they might watch the movements of Ghāzī-ud-dīn and, if necessary, unite with Sūraj Mal against him.

Ghāzī-ud-dīn resented this movement and disliked the proximity of the imperial army. He tried to induce the emperor by intimidation to retire, warning him that a force of several thousand Marāthā horse, whose intentions were unknown, had been seen in the neighbourhood. It happened that Malhār Rāo Holkar, whose son Khande Rāo had been killed in action against the Jāts, bitterly resented the emperor's refusal to supply the army with artillery, and had secretly left the camp to force compliance or to punish him for refusal. His presence in the neighbourhood of the camp became known, and the emperor, his mother, and the minister, whose cowardice was notorious, without warning any of their intention, entered their litters and fled towards Delhi, leaving the army and the imperial harem to their fate. In the morning the army, without a leader, was helpless before Holkar, who stripped the men of their arms, took their horses, and plundered the camp, capturing the ladies of the imperial harem, whom, however, he treated with respect.

When the emperor's flight became known, the siege of Dīg was raised, Jayappa Sindia returned to Nāgaur, and Ghāzī-ud-dīn and Holkar marched to Delhi, where they compelled the emperor to dismiss Intizām-ud-Daula, Ghāzī-ud-dīn himself becoming minister. On 2 June, 1754, Ahmad Shāh was deposed and prince 'Azīz-ud-dīn, the second but eldest surviving son of Jahandār Shāh, was raised to the throne under the title of 'Ālamgīr II. A week later both Ahmad Shāh and his mother were blinded.

The condition of the Punjab now appeared to offer Ghāzī-ud-dīn an opportunity for its recovery. Its governor Mu'īn-ul-Mulk, whose appetite might have vied with that of Sultān Mahmūd Bīgara of Gujarāt and Shaikh Abu-'l-Fazl, died in November, 1753, from an internal injury caused by riding hard immediately after a surfeit. Ahmad Abdālī permitted an infant son to succeed, the management of affairs remaining in the hands of his mother. Though the son died, his mother made herself feared. She was, however, not fitted to govern a large and impoverished province, and the administration was left to underlings who, beside enriching themselves, levied cruel exactions from the people, thus driving many to join the warlike sect of the Sikhs, who were able to protect their adherents. Anarchy prevailed throughout the Punjab when Ghāzī-ud-dīn, taking with him his puppet emperor, marched from Delhi to regain the lost province.

This first expedition was a failure. Ghāzī-ud-dīn maintained in his troops a corps,[1] composed of troopers whom he had detached by appeals to cupidity and bigotry, from Safdar Jang, the late minister. When the army reached Pānīpat this corps, which was highly paid, clamoured for arrears due to the members. After much wrangling Ghāzī-ud-dīn agreed to pay them after inspection of the corps by an independent officer. The officer selected was Najīb Khān the Afghān, who was known to be fearless, and clamour was renewed. Ghāzī-ud-dīn left his quarters to quell the tumult and was seized by the excited soldiery and dragged through the streets of Pānīpat, with every circumstance of indignity. Though he was roughly handled, and threatened with death, his courage never left him. He turned on his captors with foul abuse and recommended them to slay him quickly, lest they should be slain themselves. The officers, now terrified, endeavoured to pacify him, but he was still further infuriated by a message from the emperor, delivered to them in his hearing, which promised the arrears of pay and extraordinary favours if they would hand their prisoner over as he was. The officers, hoping that they had succeeded in allaying his wrath, sent him back to his own quarters on an elephant, but he hardly gave himself time to rearrange his dress before he remounted the elephant and ordered Najīb Khān and his Afghāns, and the rest of his troops, to attack the corps, massacre the men, and plunder their tents. Ghāzī-ud-dīn then returned to Delhi. When his troops were ready for the field he left again for the Punjab, carrying with him on this occasion not the emperor, but his eldest son, Mīrzā 'Abdullah, 'Ālī Gauhar. 'Ālamgīr II was left in the custody of confidential agents.

Mu'īn-ul-Mulk had been the maternal uncle of Ghāzī-ud-dīn, who

[1] It was known as the *Sīn-dāgh* or "S brand" from the letter branded on the horses.

was betrothed to his daughter. Arriving at Ludhiāna he requested his aunt to fulfil the contract of marriage. The widow, suspecting nothing, sent her daughter to Ludhiāna, where Ghāzī-ud-dīn married her in due form. He had expected the mother to accompany the daughter, and he was resolved to seize her and thus gain the government of the Punjab. He was already in league with Ādīna Beg Khān, the traitor who had for many years past been at the bottom of every trouble in the Punjab. He sent a picked force under trustworthy officers, who by a forced march arrived at Lahore, more than a hundred miles away, in little more than twenty-four hours. Eunuchs arrested the lady before she was awake, and next day the troops conducted her to Ludhiāna. The government of the Punjab was then conferred on Ādīna Beg Khān, who paid three million rupees for the appointment. Ghāzī-ud-dīn was unable to pacify his infuriated mother-in-law, who heaped abuse on him, and predicted that the outrage would bring him calamity. This impudent aggression aroused the wrath of Ahmad Abdālī, who marched on Lahore. Ādīna Beg Khān fled in terror and hid in the waterless district of Hissār and Hānsī, whither, he hoped, no army could follow him. From Lahore the Afghān advanced by forced marches on Delhi. Even Ghāzī-ud-dīn was alarmed and prevailed on his mother-in-law to intercede for him. As a suppliant, forty miles from the city, he met Ahmad, who at first rated him, but afterwards pardoned and confirmed him as minister. So low was the empire fallen that the disposal of its great offices of state was in the hands of the Afghān. The real offender thus escaped unscathed, but Ahmad Abdālī demanded reparation for the insult to his authority, and an innocent people had to suffer for the fault of a headstrong youth.

Ahmad Abdālī entered the fort of Delhi on 28 January, 1757, and met 'Ālamgīr II, and on the same day the sack of the city began. The pillage was not accompanied, as during Nādir Shāh's invasion, by massacre, but the people suffered great misery and many of the more respectable killed themselves to escape dishonour. Ahmad stayed in the city for nearly a month, during which time the daughter of prince A'azz-ud-dīn, the emperor's deceased elder brother, was married to prince Tīmūr, eldest son of the invader.[1] After resting his troops in Delhi he sent a force under one of his officers, with Ghāzī-ud-dīn, to punish Sūraj Mal the Jāt for having allied himself with Safdar Jang, and himself followed the troops. Sūraj Mal's forts were not easily reduced and Ghāzī-ud-dīn begged that a force might be sent with him into the Dūāb and Oudh, to collect tribute for the Abdālī, and that two princes of the imperial house should accompany him to provide against any attempt to set up a pretender at Delhi.

His motive was partly to ingratiate himself with the invader and

[1] Coin was also struck at Shāhjahānābād (Delhi) in the name of Ahmad Shāh. [Ed.]

to get rid of him, but chiefly to secure revenge on the son of his old enemy. Safdar Jang had died on 5 October, 1754, and had been succeeded in Oudh by his son Shujā'-ud-Daula. The expedition was not a conspicuous success. The army reached Farrukhābād, where Ahmad Khān Bangash presented gifts to the princes and to Ghāzī-ud-dīn and sent a contingent with it into Oudh.

Shujā'-ud-Daula met the invaders of his province at Sāndī, near Bilgrām, and after two unimportant affairs of outposts was reinforced by Sa'd-ullah Khān of Rohilkhand, who had now become his friend. The arrival of this new force and Sa'd-ullah Khān's advocacy of Shujā'-ud-Daula's cause put an end to hostilities and the aggressors retired after receiving 500,000 rupees in cash from Shujā'-ud-Daula and vague promises of more. Ghāzī-ud-dīn retired to Farrukhābād, where he halted to await the departure of Ahmad Abdālī.

Ahmad had been conducting a campaign in his own manner. After a siege of three days he had taken the Jāt fort of Ballabhgarh, twenty-four miles south of Delhi, and had put the garrison to the sword. He had sent another force to Muttra, where the massacre of a large assembly of unarmed pilgrims showed his zeal for Islām. Further enterprises of a like nature were stopped by the fierce heat of the Indian summer, and a pestilence, accompanied by great mortality, which broke out in his army decided him to return. Near Delhi he was met by 'Ālamgīr II, who complained bitterly of his treatment by Ghāzī-ud-dīn. Ahmad Abdālī promoted Najīb Khān, who accompanied 'Ālamgīr, to the rank of Amīr-ul-Umarā, and committed the helpless puppet to his protection. Najīb Khān received at the same time the title of Najīb-ud-Daula.

Ahmad Abdālī received, before leaving India, a strange appeal. Two widows of Muhammad Shāh bitterly resented the turbulence of Ghāzī-ud-dīn and the cowardice of the courtiers, which had caused them to fall into the hands of Marāthās. Fearing worse consequences one of them begged Ahmad to marry her and to remove both from the danger of dishonour. In spite of their age, their high rank and their distress aroused the conqueror's compassion. He accordingly married one and took both ladies with him to Afghānistān.

On Ahmad Abdālī's departure from India, Ghāzī-ud-dīn threw down the gauntlet to his former servant, Najīb Khān, by appointing Ahmad Khān Bangash Amīr-ul-Umarā and, summoning to his aid Raghunāth Rāo, brother of the Peshwā, and Malhār Rāo Holkar, marched on Delhi and besieged the emperor and Najīb-ud-Daula in the fort.

This action had been expected and some time before the departure of Ahmad Abdālī, the emperor had granted assignments to his eldest son, 'Ālī Gauhar, to the west of Delhi, and had sent him into these districts with secret instructions to raise an army for opposing Ghāzī-ud-dīn if he marched on Delhi. The participation of the Marāthās had not been expected and 'Ālī Gauhar, who was not strong enough to attack the combined forces, did nothing.

When the siege had lasted forty-five days, Najīb-ud-Daula purchased the protection of Holkar, and retired to his estates north-west of Delhi. The emperor could no longer resist, and Ghāzī-ud-dīn, with Ahmad Khān Bangash, entered the fort and resumed control of the emperor and the administration. His first act was to compel 'Ālamgīr to send a force to recall his son to the capital. Vithal Rāo, a Marāthā officer who had remained near Delhi after the retirement of Raghunāth Rāo and Holkar, warned the prince that the order had been wrung from his father and advised him to disregard it, and 'Ālī Gauhar, on this advice, crossed the Jumna into the Dūāb and occupied several *parganas*, but Vithal Rāo was induced by a heavy bribe to advise the prince to return to the capital. 'Ālī Gauhar entered Delhi with his troops but refused to live in the fort, and lodged in a private house. He soon found himself unable to pay his troops and Ghāzī-ud-dīn advised him to send them to the districts allotted for their payment as revenue could not be collected without their assistance. The prince was once more compelled to comply, but retained at Delhi a bodyguard and some of his most trustworthy officers. Ghāzī-ud-dīn, assembling ten or twelve thousand troops on the pretext that he intended to make a pilgrimage to the shrine of Nizām-ud-dīn Auliyā, surrounded the house in which the prince lodged. Some of his men forced an entrance, but 'Ālī Gauhar, who possessed the courage of his race, caused the outer wall of the house nearest to the Jumna to be breached, and at the head of his men cut his way through the minister's troops and rode to Vithal Rāo's camp across the river. Vithal Rāo was now overcome with shame for having advised the prince to place himself in the power of Ghāzī-ud-dīn, and pitched tents for him near his own camp, but it was only with great difficulty that the prince reached them, for some of the minister's troops barred his way. He would have been slain or taken but for the devotion of a gallant Sayyid who kept the pursuers employed. The Sayyid fell but the prince reached his tents and Vithal Rāo escorted him to Farrukhābād, where he was well received and supplied with money. From Farrukhābād the prince marched to Sahāranpur and took refuge with Najīb-ud-Daula, who protected him for eight months and then, fearing complications with the minister, advised him to attempt the reconquest of Bengal, where the imperial authority had long been disregarded and British influence was paramount. 'Ālī Gauhar accepted this advice and marched first to Oudh, leaving his lieutenant to enlist troops and collect supplies. Shujā'-ud-Daula met the prince near Lucknow, on 19 January, 1758, and received him hospitably; but, anxious to rid himself of so inconvenient a guest, supported Najīb-ud-Daula's advice to attempt the recovery of Bengal, and was relieved when he marched on to Allahābād.

The relief afforded to Bengal by the expulsion of Raghūjī Bhonsle in 1743 had been ephemeral. Bālājī Rāo Peshwā, having obtained his reward, had immediately entered into an agreement acknowledging Raghūjī's right to collect *chauth* and *sardeshmukhī* in Bengal, Bihār and Orissa; and in 1744 an army of 20,000 Marāthā horse invaded Bengal. 'Alī Vardī Khān craftily invited all the principal officers to an entertainment, which they were induced to attend by a false oath sworn by Mustafā Khān, an Afghān officer, on a brick wrapped in a cloth which was supposed to contain a copy of the Korān. On 14 April the twenty-one who attended were treacherously murdered and the single superior officer who had been left in charge of the camp tried to lead the army back, but the peasantry, exasperated by recent depredations, allowed few stragglers to escape.

Mustafā Khān's reward was not, in his estimation, commensurate with his services and he rose in rebellion in Bihār, where he attacked Haibat, 'Alī Vardī Khān's lieutenant.

This atrocious crime greatly enraged Raghūjī Bhonsle, but he was detained at Nāgpur throughout the year 1744 by a disputed succession in a Gond principality. Next year, having ascertained that conditions were favourable, he invaded Orissa and without difficulty occupied Cuttack and captured the inefficient governor. From Cuttack Raghūjī sent a message to 'Alī Vardī, demanding thirty million rupees as the price of evacuating Orissa. 'Alī Vardī evaded answering until he heard that the rebel Mustafā Khān was dead, when he returned a provocative reply to which Raghūjī answered by overrunning the country as far as Burdwān. When the rainy season was over he marched into Bihār in response to an invitation from the remnant of the Afghān rebels, who had been driven into the Kaimūr hills on the north bank of the Son. They joined him near Arwal on the east bank of the Son, within forty-five miles of Patna. 'Alī Vardī advanced to Bankipore, and surprised the Marāthās at Muhibb'alīpur on the eastern bank of the Son, about eight miles above Arwal. The advantage lay, on the whole, with the Muslims, but the engagement was not decisive and for some days the armies engaged in purposeless skirmishes. Then Raghūjī suddenly marched off, intending to reach Murshidābād and sack the town before 'Alī Vardī Khān could return. 'Alī Vardī Khān turned back and marched rapidly, but the more mobile Marāthās were a day before him and, though they could not enter the town, plundered and burnt the neighbouring villages and marched on towards Katwa, still followed by 'Alī Vardī Khān, who defeated them in a battle a few miles to the south of that town.

Raghūjī now returned to his own country, but left at Midnapore, to guard the approaches to Orissa, a force of two or three thousand

Marāthās under Mīr Habīb, and six or seven thousand Afghāns under Murtazā Khān.

In 1746 Mīr Muhammad Ja'far Khān, known as Mīr Ja'far, was appointed governor of Orissa with an injunction to recover it from the Marāthās. He defeated and drove southwards the garrison of Midnapore, but refrained from pursuing them lest he should provoke Raghūjī Bhonsle to invade Bengal in force. Later, hearing that Jānojī, Raghūjī's son, was marching on Cuttack, he fled panic-stricken to Burdwān. Jānojī followed him northward, but Mīr Ja'far had been reinforced and the Marāthās were defeated. They returned in the following year and were again defeated near Burdwān by 'Alī Vardī Khān, who pursued them to Midnapore but failed to overtake them and retired to Murshidābād for the rainy season.

Early in 1748 Haibat Jang engaged in Bihār a force of Afghāns who had been dismissed by 'Alī Vardī Khān owing to suspicions of their loyalty. It was believed that they might safely be employed in Bihār, where their opportunities for communicating with the Marāthās would be fewer; but the officers, on the occasion of their first reception, assassinated the governor, in revenge for the treatment which they had received from his father-in-law, 'Alī Vardī Khān. They then plundered the town and seized the government of the province. A large force was soon collected and the leader, knowing that he could enjoy no safety so long as 'Alī Vardī Khān retained the government of Bengal, made preparations for conquering that province.

'Alī Vardī Khān was again engaged with the Marāthās south of Katwa when this alarming news reached him. On 1 March, 1748, he marched towards Patna, leaving a sufficient garrison to protect Murshidābād. The Marāthās followed him, hanging on his flanks and rear, and gave his army no rest. When he met the Afghān rebels about eight miles to the west of the town of Bārh, on the Ganges, he was obliged to attack them while the Marāthās were still threatening his rear. His small army seemed doomed to destruction, but a fortunate discharge of artillery and musketry killed or wounded the three Afghān leaders early in the day, and this produced its usual result. The great host, largely composed of raw levies, fled in all directions. The Marāthās, fearing lest the victorious army should turn on them, dispersed, and 'Alī Vardī Khān, entering Patna, appointed Sirāj-ud-Daula, his daughter's son by Haibat Jang, governor of Bihār with Rājā Jānkī Rām as his guardian and deputy, and followed the retreating Marāthās.

Jānojī Bhonsle had been recalled to Nāgpur by the news of his mother's death and 'Alī Vardī seized the opportunity. He marched to Cuttack, reoccupied the town, captured the citadel, put to death the officers who had held it for Raghūjī, and expelled the Marāthās.

Their expulsion was, however, temporary and they returned to the province almost immediately. Again, in 1750, they were defeated at Midnapore, but it was as useless to defeat them in the field as it was to expel them, in face of the mobility of irregular troops living on the country and independent either of a base or of lines of communication. The Muslims, after a victory in the field, often found the beaten enemy immediately laying waste the country in their rear, and were obliged to hasten to save their capital from pillage.

The Marāthās claimed the right to levy *chauth* and *sardeshmukhī* in the three provinces of Bengal, Bihār and Orissa, and they had for some time been anxious for a composition. They proposed that Orissa should be absolutely ceded to them in place of the rights claimed in all three. 'Alī Vardī Khān admitted no right, but he could not exclude the Marāthās, who treated the provinces as an enemy's country, and destroyed what they could not carry off. The viceroy's advisers had long urged him to purchase peace for his unfortunate people. He had hitherto scornfully rejected this advice, but he was now seventy-five years of age, his health was failing, he had for twelve years been engaged in ceaseless and fruitless warfare, and a great part of his territory lay waste. He gave way and in November, 1751, ceded Orissa, salving his pride by the fiction of appointing Mīr Habīb Raghūjī's agent, as *his* governor of the province. He also saved the district of Midnapore, which had hitherto been included in Orissa, and fixed the Subarnarekha river as the boundary of the Marāthā province. Orissa thus passed finally out of the hands of the viceroy of Bengal and the land had peace.

On 9 April, 1756, 'Alī Vardī Khān died and was succeeded by his grandson, Sirāj-ud-Daula, whose history will be found in chap. VII, vol. V. Clive's victory at Plassey, on 23 June, 1757, established the supremacy of the British in Bengal and thus furnished 'Ālī Gauhar with the pretext for his demonstration.

It is not quite correct to represent the prince as being in rebellion against his father.[1] He originally left the palace by his father's wish and raised troops for service against Ghāzī-ud-dīn. Subsequent orders recalling him were actually issued by the minister, and though they bore the emperor's seal there is every reason to believe that the prince's course of action accorded with his father's wishes. Many circumstances contributed to the choice of Bihār as a field for his activity. Both Najīb-ud-Daula and Shujā'-ud-Daula were anxious to be rid of him and the latter was ambitious of adding the viceroyalty of Bengal, Bihār and Orissa to that of Oudh and not unwilling to employ the prince as his instrument. Muhammad Qulī Khān, Shujā'-ud-Daula's governor of Allahābād, a brave but foolish man, was also ambitious of annexing the viceroyalty, for his master, as he was careful to explain, but in reality for himself. Shujā'-ud-Daula

[1] See *Oxford History of India*, p. 495.

suspected his servant's ambitions but was ready to permit him to embark on the enterprise.

'Ālī Gauhar and Muhammad Qulī crossed the Karamnāsā late in 1758 and shortly afterwards camped near Patna, the governor of which, Rājā Rām Nārayan, feigned to submit. Though the invading force was contemptible, Clive himself marched from Murshidābād with a small force. The raja then shut the city gates and repulsed an attack, and 'Ālī Gauhar fled to Rewah.

After the Marāthā conquest of the Punjab[1] Dattājī Sindia sought to crush Najīb-ud-Daula, and marched towards Sahāranpur. Najīb-ud-Daula, unable to meet his enemy in the field, entrenched himself at Shukartār, seventeen miles south-west of Sahāranpur, where Dattājī Sindia besieged him throughout the rainy season of 1759 while another force under Govind Pant Bundele crossed the Ganges and devastated northern Rohilkhand, driving the Afghāns into the hills and depriving Najīb-ud-Daula of hopes of relief from that quarter. At the end of the rainy season, however, Shujā'-ud-Daula marched to his assistance, defeated Govind Pant near Chāndpur,[2] and put him to flight. Further operations were unnecessary as Dattājī Sindia was obliged by the news of Ahmad Shāh Abdālī's fresh invasion of India to abandon the blockade of Shukartār and recross the Jumna; and in December, 1759, Shujā'-ud-Daula returned to Oudh.

The unfortunate emperor had incurred the resentment of his minister by lending what little support he could to Najīb-ud-Daula, whom, since the departure of Ahmad Shāh Abdālī, he regarded as his potential protector, and had further offended by maintaining a correspondence, which he believed to be secret, with the Afghān king. On 29 November, 1759, he was inveigled to Fīrūz Shāh's Kotla beyond the city walls, on the pretext that a *darvīsh* who was worth visiting lodged there, and was assassinated. The corpse of the murdered emperor was thrown out on the sands of the Jumna where it lay naked for several hours, having been stripped of its clothes, before it was buried in Humāyūn's tomb. Intizām-ud-Daula was strangled next day.

Ghāzī-ud-dīn now proclaimed as emperor, under the title of Shāh Jahān III, Muhiyy-ul-Millat, grandson of Kām Bakhsh, the youngest son of Aurangzīb, and marched towards Shukartār to assist Dattājī Sindia in crushing Najīb-ud-Daula, but heard on the way that an armistice had been arranged and that Dattājī had marched towards Lahore to oppose Ahmad Shāh Abdālī.

Not only the great Muslim nobles of northern India but also the Hindu chieftains of Rājasthān were weary of the aggressions of the Marāthās, who were credited with the design of overthrowing even the pageant of Mughul sovereignty. Many had on this account

[1] See chap. xiv, p. 416. [2] 29° 8′ N., 78° 16′ E.

entered into correspondence with the Abdālī and had begged him to free them from the burden of Marāthā oppression. The Abdālī himself had recently received from the Marāthās provocation so gross as to call for immediate and severe chastisement.

When, after the sack of Delhi and the massacre at Muttra, he returned in 1757 to Afghānistān, he left as his governor in the Punjab his son Tīmūr, with Jahān Khān as his guardian and adviser. Jahān Khān appointed as governor of the Jullundur Dūāb the restless plotter Ādīna Beg Khān, who had served many masters and betrayed all. Shortly after his appointment he was summoned to Lahore in the ordinary course of official business, but, fearing to trust himself within his master's reach, fled into the hills. Ādīna Beg Khān then entered into a conspiracy with the Sikhs who, with the help of a detachment of his troops, attacked Jullundur, and expelled the new governor. Raghunāth Rāo, the Peshwā's brother, who was now in the neighbourhood of Delhi, also came to his assistance and, undeterred by the punishment which had followed previous intervention in the Punjab, marched northward in April, 1758. He defeated and captured the governor of Sirhind and in May entered Lahore as a conqueror while Tīmūr and Jahān Khān fled across the Indus. The Punjab to the Chenāb and as far south as the confluence of the Indus and the Panjnad, with the transfluvial tract of Dera Ghāzī Khān, fell into the hands of the Marāthās. Ādīna Beg Khān was appointed governor on promising to pay an annual tribute of 7,500,000 rupees and Raghunāth Rāo retired, as the rainy season was approaching. Leaving Jānkojī Sindia, nephew of Dattājī, in the neighbourhood of Delhi with instructions to overrun Rājputāna and to control generally Marāthā interests in northern India, he returned to the Deccan, where his recent adventure was the subject of much unfavourable criticism. In September, 1758, Ādīna Beg Khān died and Jānkojī Sindia appointed Sābājī Bhonsle as governor of the Punjab.

In August, 1759, Ahmad Shāh Abdālī crossed the Indus, driving the Marāthā outposts before him, and Sābājī retreated rapidly towards Delhi. Ahmad marched to Jammū, where he levied tribute from the Rājā, Ranjīt Deo, and then continued his advance towards Delhi. As the country west of the Jumna had been denuded of supplies by the frequent passage of Marāthā armies, he crossed the Jumna into the northern Dūāb, but sent a force by the western route to deal with Dattājī Sindia who, having abandoned the siege of Shukartār, had crossed the Jumna and was marching towards Sirhind to oppose his advance.

Ghāzī-ud-dīn had two heavy crimes to answer for, the murders of 'Ālamgīr II and of his own uncle, Intizām-ud-Daula, and on hearing of the invader's advance he took refuge with Sūraj Mal the Jāt, who sheltered him in one of his forts.

Ahmad was joined, on entering the northern Dūāb, by the Rohilla chiefs Sa'd-ullah Khān, son of 'Alī Muhammad Khān, Hāfiz Rahmat Khān, and Dūnde Khān, and by Najīb-ud-Daula and Ahmad Khān Bangash.

Dattājī Sindia retired before the Afghān force as the latter advanced from Sirhind and in January, 1760, had reached Barārī, ten miles north of Delhi. The force before which he had been retreating faced him, and as the action began Ahmad Shāh Abdālī crossed the Jumna with his whole army and suddenly attacked him in flank. Dattājī perceived at once that defeat was inevitable and sent his nephew Jānkojī with a small force to the Deccan to raise the Marāthās. He then dismounted and died fighting bravely.

Ahmad Shāh without halting to rest his army continued the pursuit of Jānkojī as far as Nārnaul, and halted there.

Malhār Rāo Holkar had hastened to meet Jānkojī and planned with him a campaign to harass the Afghāns in the usual Marāthā style. He crossed into the Dūāb and there received information of a large convoy of supplies and treasure in the Farrukhābād district, which the troops of Ahmad Khān Bangash were escorting to Ahmad Shāh Abdālī's camp, and which he promptly attacked and plundered. Ahmad Shāh at once sent a force to punish Holkar's temerity. This force rode from Nārnaul to Delhi, a distance of over eighty miles, in a day and a night, rested for a day at Delhi and marched again in the evening, traversing thirty-three miles and reaching Holkar's camp at Sikandarābād at dawn. Holkar was completely surprised, and his troops were routed with great slaughter. He escaped with only about three hundred men, mounted on bare-backed horses.

The Peshwā was encamped on the Mānjrā river, in the Mughul dominions in the Deccan, when he heard of these disasters, and sent his eldest son, Vishvās Rāo, in nominal command of a large army with Sadāshiv Rāo, known as the Bhāo[1] or cousin of Bālājī Rāo, as real commander-in-chief. The Bhāo's claim to be the virtual leader of the expedition into Hindūstān was admitted in view of his recent victories in the Deccan.[2] Vishvās Rāo was understood to be destined for the throne of Delhi, and his position in the campaign was analogous to that of a Mughul prince of tender years appointed to the nominal command in an important enterprise, the direction of which was, in fact, in the hands of a great noble designated as his tutor or guardian.

The great force advanced northwards, joined as it passed along by Marāthās, by parties of horse sent by a few of the Rājput chief-

[1] *Bhāo* is the Marāthī for "brother". Among all Hindus relationship on the male side, however distant, is commonly described by the terms "brother", "uncle", and "nephew". Fifth or sixth cousins of the same generation are "brothers". A remove of a generation changes the relationship to "uncle" and "nephew".

[2] See chap. XIV, p. 413.

tains,[1] by vast numbers of Pindārīs and by irregulars of all descriptions. It seemed a national cause to Hindus, and Sūraj Mal the Jāt, through the agency of Holkar, was induced to meet the army with 30,000 men.

Ahmad Shāh Abdālī had returned from Nārnaul to Delhi and, as the country to the west of the Jumna was suffering from recent depredations of the Marāthās, he crossed that river and encamped for the rainy season within easy reach of the Afghāns in the Dūāb and Rohilkhand, at Sikandarābād, the scene of Holkar's recent defeat. Najīb-ud-Daula was sent to invite Shujā'-ud-Daula to join the Afghān army, and, meeting him near Kanauj, easily persuaded him that the cause of the Abdālī was that of Islam. On 18 July he joined Ahmad Shāh's camp with his forces.

In July the Marāthā army reached the neighbourhood of Delhi. The rainy season was at its height and, the Jumna not being fordable, Sadāshiv Bhāo decided to occupy the capital before attacking the enemy.

Sūraj Mal and Ghāzī-ud-dīn were not prepossessed by the appearance or the methods of the Marāthā army, or by the personality of its commander. They had taken no part in the operations which had led to the surrender of the fort, and they now definitely and finally deserted the Marāthā cause and retired to the Jāt fortress of Ballabhgarh.

Sadāshiv Bhāo made strenuous but fruitless efforts to detach Shujā'-ud-Daula from Ahmad Abdālī, and when these failed tried to arouse Ahmad's suspicion and to create discord. On 10 October he deposed and imprisoned the puppet Shāh Jahān III and enthroned Mīrzā Javān Bakht,[2] son of 'Ālī Gauhar, appointing Shujā'-ud-Daula as his minister. Ahmad Shāh refused to be hoodwinked and Shuja'-ud-Daula to be ensnared, but correspondence still continued, after the oriental fashion, between him and the Bhāo, and he was, throughout the campaign, the Bhāo's channel of communication with Ahmad Shāh.

In October, at the close of the rainy season, Sadāshiv marched from Delhi towards Sirhind, his object being, apparently, to raise and occupy the Punjab and thus cut off Ahmad Shāh's retreat. On 17 October he reached the fort of Kunjpura, six miles north-east of Karnāl, now held for Ahmad Shāh. He took and plundered the fort, and continued his march towards Sirhind.

Ahmad Shāh Abdālī, learning of his movements, left Sikandarābād, crossed the Jumna at Bāghpat, twenty-five miles north of Delhi, and marched in pursuit, and Sadāshiv Bhāo, turning back, halted at Pānīpat, at which place Ahmad Shāh arrived three days later.

[1] Some of these probably now repented of their appeal to the Afghān. The Marāthās undoubtedly posed as the champions of Hinduism against the unclean alien.

[2] The enthronement of Javān Bakht was purely nominal.

As Sadāshiv Rāo had violated Marāthā precedent in the equipment of his army, so he now violated their traditional rules of war and displayed a consciousness of his inferiority by strongly entrenching himself in the town of Pānīpat, though this plan was opposed by many of the leaders, who wished to fight in the old Marāthā manner.

For more than two months after the arrival of the Abdālī's army, skirmishes continued which culminated in a great battle on 14 January, 1761, already described in the last chapter. This, the most desperate of the three contests fought on the field of Pānīpat, destroyed the great Marāthā confederation and, for a time, the power of the Marāthā chiefs. On the eve of the battle India from the Indus and Himālaya almost to the extreme limits of the Peninsula was forced to own, however unwillingly, their sway, and those tracts not immediately administered by them paid them tribute, and their numerous chiefs all owned allegiance to one man, the Peshwā. Various chiefs, Mahādjī Sindia in Gwalior, Raghūjī Bhonsle in Nāgpur and Berār, Malhār Rāo Holkar in Mālwā, and Dāmājī Gāikwār in Gujarāt, recovered portions of the Marāthā empire, but the Peshwā's authority was broken and cohesion was lost. Marāthā alliances and confederacies again vexed India, but all hopes of a Marāthā empire were destroyed at Pānīpat.

The conqueror's design of seizing the empire of India for himself was frustrated by the clamours of his troops demanding arrears of pay and an immediate return to Kābul. Before leaving India he nominated 'Ālī Gauhar, son of the murdered 'Ālamgīr II, as emperor of Delhi, under the title of Shāh 'Ālam; Shujā'-ud-Daula was appointed minister, from which circumstance he and his successors in Oudh were known to the British as Nawāb Vazīr, or "Nabob Vizier", until permitted, in 1819, to assume the royal title; and Najīb-ud-Daula was confirmed in the rank and appointment of Amīr-ul-Umarā. Ghāzī-ud-dīn disappeared from political life and according to some accounts lingered in obscurity till 1800.

The third battle of Pānīpat closes the history of the Mughul Empire. The destruction of the Marāthā power did nothing to weld the various states into which it had been broken or to restore the power and authority of the emperor. Shah 'Ālam was brutally blinded in 1788 by a Rohilla ruffian, Ghulām Qādir, and in 1803 was formally taken under the protection of that power which the victory of Plassey had already designated as successor of the Great Mughuls. His son Akbar II (1806–37) lived and died a pensioner of the same power, whose outraged authority sent his grandson, Bahādur II, to end his days as an exile in Rangoon.

CHAPTER XVI

THE REVENUE SYSTEM OF THE MUGHUL EMPIRE

THE fiscal resources of the Mughul empire may be considered in two main divisions—central and local. The local revenue, which was apparently collected and disbursed without reference to the central finance authorities, was derived from a bewildering variety of petty taxes and duties levied on production and consumption, on trades and occupations, on various incidents of social life, and most of all on transport. There is nothing to be said for this mass of imposts except that the system was accepted by the people as traditional, that it prevailed outside the empire as well as within, and that it can be traced back at any rate to the days of the Maurya rulers. In the fourteenth century these imposts had been forbidden in the mass by Fīrūz Tughluq as being contrary to Islamic law. The prohibition was renewed on other grounds by Akbar, and it was repeated by Aurangzīb,[1] but the effect of these orders was transitory, and the system maintained itself up to the close of the Mughul period.

The central sources of revenue were by comparison few in number; they may be classed as Commerce, Mint, Presents, Inheritance, Salt, Customs, Poll-tax, and Land. From time to time the state took an active part in commerce, but its operations were fiscally important only when they involved a monopoly of particular commodities; these monopolies ordinarily concerned munitions, such as lead or saltpetre, but occasionally other articles were affected, the most noteworthy case being the general monopoly of indigo created by Shāh Jahān in 1633, which, however, was quickly broken by the opposition of the foreign buyers. The working of the mints was commonly farmed, so that they must be regarded as a source of revenue; the yield is not recorded, but it cannot have been large so long as the prescribed standards of the currency were maintained.

Court etiquette required that presents of substantial value should be offered to the emperor on various occasions, and ordinarily these were worth much more than the presents given in return; an idea of their fiscal importance can be formed from the fact that under Shāh Jahān, when the incidence was heaviest, the presents given at the new year, the chief ceremonial occasion, totalled from one to three million rupees in different years, from which must be deducted the value, whatever it was, of what was given by the emperor in return. As regards inheritance, the state claimed all the property left by its officers, and the claim was extended on occasion to the

[1] River tolls, and also exactions by assignees were prohibited by Jahāngīr.

estates of wealthy merchants; anything relinquished for the maintenance of families and dependants was a matter of favour. The whole claim was formally abandoned by Aurangzīb, but there are some indications that his orders were not carried out in their entirety. Income from this source necessarily fluctuated; a particular officer might leave a really large sum, such as Āsaf Khān's fortune of twenty-five millions of rupees in the reign of Shāh Jahān, but such great accumulations were necessarily rare, while many officers died in debt or left very little for the treasury.

There was no uniform system of taxing salt, and some important sources were controlled locally; the mines in the Punjab and the salt lake at Sāmbhar in Rājputāna were, however, administered by the state. The income from these sources was apparently brought to account as part of the land-revenue, and cannot be stated in precise figures, but on the basis of the available statistics it cannot have been more than about one million rupees. Compared with the present standards, customs duties were formally low, ranging from 5 per cent. downwards, but in practice their incidence was seriously increased by arbitrary over-valuation, and by extra charges for prompt clearance of goods. Some idea of the magnitude of the customs revenue can be formed from the fact that in the middle of the seventeenth century the port of Surat, at that time by far the most important source, was reckoned to yield half a million rupees a year, after the cost of its administration had been met.

The *jizya*, or poll-tax, which according to strict Islamic law was payable only by Jews and Christians, had been claimed by some earlier Muslim rulers from their Hindu subjects. The claim was formally abandoned by Akbar, and in the Mughul period it was first asserted by Aurangzīb. Under effective administration the yield might have been substantial, but this condition was not present, and probably was unattainable in the circumstances of the time; the amount actually realised is not recorded in the published authorities for the period.

All these sources of the central revenue, taken together, were quite small when compared with the land-revenue, which was reckoned at more than ninety millions of rupees in the latter part of Akbar's reign, and at 220 millions in the larger empire of Shāh Jahān. The disparity is indeed sufficient to justify the practice traditional in India, and adopted in the remainder of this chapter, of using the word "revenue" in the restricted sense of land-revenue. The burden on the land was increased further by the levy of cesses, proportionate to the revenue, or charged on the unit of cultivation, as the case might be, some of them general and permanent, others local and temporary; but the authorities say very little about these, and no estimate can be formed of the aggregate addition which they made to the burdens of the peasant. The remainder of this chapter is devoted to Revenue in the restricted sense, beginning with a general view of the agrarian system of the country, and then describing the course of events during the Mughul period.

The Mughuls did not, as has sometimes been suggested, introduce a new revenue system into northern India; they took over the system which they found in operation, a system which in its main lines was consistent with Islamic law, as well as with the sacred law of Hinduism on which it was ultimately based. Under the sacred law occupation of land for production involved a liability to pay a share of the produce to the state, which determined within certain limits the amount of the share, and regulated the methods of assessment and collection. Under Islamic law a conqueror was authorised to dispossess infidel occupants, and distribute their lands among his followers; but if he permitted the infidels to remain in possession, as was usually done in India, he was entitled to claim from them a share of the produce, to be assessed and collected as he thought best, and to be applied for the benefit of Muslims in general, or in practice as the revenue of the state which he established. Thus the ordinary Indian peasant was not necessarily affected by conquest; he remained on the land, but he came under a new master, who might possibly increase his burdens, or more probably fall in for the moment with the arrangements which he found in existence. Under this system there were three questions of immediate interest to both the parties—the amount of the share claimed by the state, the method of its assessment, and the arrangements for collecting the sums due; these three points will be noticed in order, but something must first be said of the position occupied by the peasant.

The face of the country was divided into villages in the Indian sense of the word, which is very nearly that of the English "civil parish", denoting a specific area of land, usually but not necessarily inhabited, originating probably more or less at haphazard, but defined and recognised for administrative purposes. Most villages, though not all, were occupied and managed by what appears to be a very old institution, a brotherhood or community of peasants, acknowledging, and united by, the tie of common ancestry. Each member of the brotherhood held in separate possession the land which he cultivated, and enjoyed the fruits of his labour; but in the management of the affairs of the village the members acted as a body, their agents being the headmen, chosen from among themselves according to the custom of the locality. The headmen could let to tenants the land not required by members of the brotherhood, and they represented the village in its dealings with the administration; the extent of their powers varied in different regions, but they were everywhere important; and in those villages where a brotherhood did not exist, headmen were usually appointed by external authority for the discharge of similar functions. Each village had a hereditary registrar or accountant,[1] who maintained records of cultivation, receipts, and payments, and assisted the headmen in the performance of the duties which have just been described.

The villages were grouped into larger units known as *parganas*, which were also recognised for administrative purposes. There was a headman (*chaudhrī*) in each *pargana*; his functions in the Muslim period are not described in the authorities, but he received orders from the administration, and exercised some sort of local jurisdiction. There was also a registrar or accountant (*qānūngo*) for the *pargana*; the post was ordinarily hereditary, and its holder was the repository of local agrarian knowledge, and, as the name implies, the interpreter of local customs on whom foreign administrators relied.

The nature of the peasants' tenure cannot be described accurately in the precise legal terms now in use. When a peasant not belonging to the brotherhood was allowed by the headmen to cultivate land in the village, the conditions of his tenure were primarily matters for agreement between the two parties, and anything like uniformity cannot be postulated; but it is probable that, while such agreements were ordinarily made for a single year, the terms tended to be repeated until they became customary in the eyes of both parties, so that arbitrary ejectment or enhancement would have been viewed with disfavour, provided always that the tenant paid the stipulated sums. The amount of a tenant's payment was not usually fixed in the lump, but was made up of the revenue due on his cultivation, together with a proportionate addition representing the profit of the brotherhood; and consequently it would vary with any alteration made in the assessment of the village.

As regards the members of the brotherhood, there is no doubt that, subject to due payment of the revenue, their connection with the village was regarded as a settled fact; and if a village was deserted owing to economic or administrative pressure, there was a general understanding that the brotherhood could return and occupy it if they chose to do so. Individual members of the brotherhood could transmit their land to their heirs, and could transfer it by sale or mortgage, but always subject to the fundamental condition that the revenue due was paid. Under Hindu law a peasant could be ejected for inefficiency, and possibly for other reasons also; no similar provision has been traced in the extant official documents of the Muslim period, but these establish the fact that peasants could be flogged for failure to produce adequate crops, while sale of a peasant's wife and children, although not of the peasant himself, was a recognised process for the recovery of arrears.

The explanation of this position, which appears so anomalous at the present day, is to be found in the fact that neither Hindu text-

[1] Known in northern India as *patwārī*, in Gujarāt as *talātī*, in the Bombay Deccan as *kulkarni*, and in Madras as *karnam*.

writers nor Muslim administrators were concerned primarily with peasants' rights. In Hindu law, the emphasis is on the peasant's duty to cultivate land and pay the revenue; and the same idea persisted throughout the Muslim period, when failure to cultivate, or to pay, was regarded as tantamount to rebellion. So long as a peasant performed his duty, there would be no reason for displacing him, while if he failed in his duty, his displacement would follow as a matter of course, provided that a more efficient successor was available. This proviso is, however, important. During the Muslim period competition for productive land was not general; in most places land was waiting for peasants with the material resources needed for its cultivation; and an inefficient peasant might be better than none at all. In such circumstances the essence of successful administration was to keep peasants on the land, not to turn them off it.

The operation of these ideas can be traced in documents issued in the Muslim period by the Revenue Ministry, an organisation which was, of course, controlled by the ruler of the time, but which appears to have preserved its continuity during periods of violent political change, and to have maintained a permanent departmental tradition of its own. To attract peasants to vacant land, to induce peasants to extend the area tilled, to secure improvement in the class of crops grown, these were the permanent ideals, though in practice they might often be masked by the need or the greed of the moment.

The texts are not absolutely in accordance regarding the share of produce which a Hindu king might claim from the peasants without sin, but the commonest figure is one-sixth, which might be increased in emergencies to one-fourth, or even one-third. How far practice conformed to theory in this matter is doubtful; some cases which have been studied in detail indicate that the share actually taken in particular Hindu kingdoms was nearer one-half than one-sixth, but they are too few to form the basis of a confident generalisation. There is no similar arithmetical limitation in Islamic law; the sovereign has a free hand, subject only to the warning emphasised in the early texts that he should avoid discouraging production by excessive burdens. In Muslim India it may be said in a general way that the claim usually varied from one-third to one-half; and, in the economic conditions which prevailed, it is probable that the lower proportion was not far short of the danger-point, where production would begin to be checked, while the higher proportion was almost certainly injurious. There is nothing in the contemporary authorities to show that any deductions were allowed before the produce was divided, but it is not improbable that some small customary provision was made in this way for charity and for the menial servants employed in the village.

As regards methods of assessment, the primitive plan of dividing the produce of each field at harvest is open to obvious practical objections, and for an indefinite period the usual practice of the country has been to estimate the yield of the growing crop, and charge the grower on the estimate, dividing the produce only in those cases—ordinarily very rare—where the accuracy of the estimate is disputed. Under these arrangements, which are conveniently described as Sharing, by division or by estimation as the case may be, the grower's liability varies from season to season both with the area sown and with the yield harvested. In the common alternative called Measurement, a fixed charge, either in cash or in produce, is made on each unit of area sown, and the grower takes the whole risk, being in theory liable for the full charge even when the crop has failed; but in practice it was usually necessary to remit a portion of the state's claim in unfavourable seasons. These two methods of assessment—Sharing and Measurement—persisted side by side throughout the Muslim period, but at some uncertain epoch there emerged a third, which may be called Contract; under it the individual peasant came to terms with the assessor, or with the headman, to pay a stated sum for his holding, independent of the area he might sow or the crop he might reap, so that his position was substantially that of a tenant at the present day. Finally, in some parts of the country there was a fourth method, the Plough-rent, which is not easy to reconcile with the terms of the sacred law, and is perhaps even older; under it, a stated charge was made on each plough and team, the unit of productive power, and the owner of the team was free to cultivate as much land as he could, and in whatever way he chose.

Under each of these methods the demand on the peasant might be made either in cash or in produce at the option of the state, the amount of produce due being valued at current prices when payment was required in cash. Collection in kind was doubtless the earlier practice, but throughout the Muslim period cash payment was the general rule, though produce continued to be paid in some backward areas, and in two recorded instances cash payments were suspended to meet financial emergencies.

The modern idea that collection of State dues should be made by salaried officials directly from the person liable is not generally applicable to India during the Muslim period. The practice existed, and on occasion was enforced over wide areas by individual administrators; but the general rule was to delegate the work of collection to one class or another of a heterogeneous group, whom it is convenient to describe collectively as Intermediaries, and who in practice frequently decided on the method of assessment to be applied within their charge. The main classes of Intermediaries were Chiefs, Headmen, Farmers, and Assignees.

Under Muslim rule large areas of the country were left in the possession of Hindu chiefs who had, at any rate, a claim to sovereignty, but had submitted to the Muslim rulers on terms which preserved to them internal jurisdiction; these terms might include the payment of a fixed tribute, or merely the personal service of the chief with his troops, but in either case the Muslim administration did not ordinarily interfere with assessment or collection of the revenue, so long as the terms were observed. If a chief defaulted, the result was ordinarily a punitive expedition, and either his displacement or a revision of the terms previously in force; but so long as he remained loyal, he enjoyed the revenue of his territories subject to the payment of the stipulated tribute, if any.

The position of a chief depended partly on the accessibility of his territory, and partly on the strength of his clan. In broken country, remote from an administrative centre, even a petty chief might maintain himself for an indefinite period merely or mainly because his possessions were not worth annexing; in the open plains a chief who was the head of a numerous and martial clan settled in a compact area might survive because his fighting strength made him a dangerous enemy but a valuable ally. The chronicles tell us little of such chiefs, but their importance in the Muslim period can be inferred from the number who survived into the nineteenth century, not only in Rājputāna and Central India, where many of them were accepted as princes, but also in large areas in Bihār and the United Provinces, where they usually became landholders.

It was a common practice for the revenue assessors to come to terms with the headmen year by year for the revenue to be paid by the village as a whole; the sum to be paid was fixed on a consideration of the productive resources of the village, but was not assessed directly on the separate portions of cultivated land, or on the individual peasants. When this arrangement was made, the headmen distributed the burden of the revenue according to the custom of the village, collected each peasant's quota, paid the authorities in lump sums, and bore the brunt of official severity in case of default.

The practice of farming the revenue of a village, or larger area, is of old standing in India; the farmer engaged to pay a lump sum, hoping to collect more from the peasants, and so make a profit for himself. Almost up to the end of the Muslim period the duration of such farms was very short, one year being an ordinary term; but in the eighteenth century the duration tended to become indefinite, and in practice the position might even become hereditary.

Assignment was, however, the most distinctive institution of the period. Every officer of the State was entitled to receive an income defined precisely in cash, out of which he had ordinarily to maintain a specified force of cavalry, available for the service of the ruler at any time; but for all the more important officers payment of this income in cash was the exception. Ordinarily an officer's claim was satisfied by assignment of the revenue of an area estimated to yield the income due to him, and the assignee thereupon assumed the administration of that area, assessing and collecting the revenue, and endeavouring to obtain from it at least the amount of his claim, and if possible something more. The assignee thus stood to the peasants in the position of the state, and, subject to any restrictions imposed on him by authority, he had a free hand in the administration; he could assess and collect the revenue of each peasant through his servants, or he could deal with the headmen of the villages, or he could hand them over to farmers. Throughout the Muslim period the great bulk of the cultivated land was ordinarily in the hands of assignees, but certain tracts, described as *khālisa*, were reserved to provide the treasury with cash, and were managed by the Revenue Ministry on one or other of the systems already described.

The foregoing analysis is necessary for descriptive purposes, but, taken by itself, it might give a misleading idea of rigidity in what was essentially a flexible structure. It was a simple and natural arrangement for a salaried staff working at a distance to undertake to supply a stated net income, instead of rendering complicated and detailed accounts of receipts and expenditure, and collectors could thus easily be transformed into farmers. A farmer holding for an indefinite term could assume a position not distinguishable in practice from that of a tribute-paying chief; a village headman might in favourable circumstances become a village autocrat, and, by taking farms of neighbouring villages, raise himself by degrees to a similar position; and in periods when the central authority was weak such tendencies might operate to transform the conditions prevailing over large areas.

From these preliminary explanations we may turn to the history of the subject during the Mughul period. There is no formal description of the revenue system in force in northern India at the opening of the sixteenth century; but incidental notices in the chronicles show that under the Lodī dynasty the great bulk of the kingdom was held in assignment by the Afghān leaders who constituted its effective strength. They show also that in practice the assignees enjoyed a free hand in regard to assessment, as well as in the treatment of any minor chiefs whose lands lay within their assignments; and the only record of interference by the king is an order issued by Ibrāhīm Lodī prohibiting the assignees from taking revenue in cash, an order which appears to have been justified by the prevailing scarcity of silver currency. In the absence of any record of a change, it may be assumed that these arrangements persisted in their main lines under Bābur and Humāyūn, and the basis of Akbar's distinctive system is to be found in the reorganisation effected by Sher Shāh.

As depicted in the chronicles Sher Shāh stands out as a masterful and tireless administrator of the Indian type, attending personally to every detail of the business of his kingdom, and introducing large changes of system in what would now be thought a very summary manner; but his reign was too short to furnish a final test of the suitability of the measures he introduced. He stands out also as the only ruler of northern India who is known to have acquired practical experience in the detailed work of assessing and collecting revenue, for as a young man he had brought into order the assignment held by his father from the Lodī dynasty. The chronicler's account of his activities at this time shows that he had already accepted the principles which later on he was to apply on a larger scale in northern India; he believed in maintaining direct relations with the individual peasants, he distrusted the village headmen, and he regarded equitable assessment and strict collection as the two essentials of revenue administration.

The share of the produce which he claimed at this time is not on record; but after his accession to the throne in the year 1540 the general proportion taken from the kingdom, apart from one favoured region, was one-third, and probably this was not an innovation, but was a standard already familiar in practice. The method of assessment adopted was measurement, the charge on each unit of area sown being a stated weight of produce. The authorities do not indicate clearly whether the peasants were now required to pay in cash or in grain; the former is more probable, because Ibrāhīm's order for grain-payments was the result of scarcity of currency, and this difficulty must have disappeared under Sher Shāh, who reorganised the currency and coined both silver and copper in large quantities. The distinctive feature of the new arrangements was the way in which the demand on the peasants was calculated. Standard yields of each staple crop were calculated or estimated—how this was done is not recorded—separately for three classes of land, described as "good", "middling", and "inferior"; the average of these figures was struck; and one-third of the average was claimed as revenue from each unit of area, whatever its actual yield might be. The effect was necessarily to overcharge the bad land, and to undercharge the good; in the case of wheat, for instance, the charge works out at about 24 per cent. of the estimated produce of "good" land, while on "inferior" land it was 48 per cent. The inequality would, however, naturally adjust itself by variations in the crops grown, so that excessive charges would tend to be eliminated.

On one point of great practical importance the authorities are ambiguous; it is uncertain whether these standard yields were calculated separately for each agricultural tract, or whether single standards were adopted for the kingdom as a whole. If the latter course was followed, over-pressure on the less productive regions must, in an extensive kingdom, have led to a complete breakdown on the occurrence of unfavourable seasons; if the former, the arrangements might have been reasonably successful; but, as has been said above, the reign was too short for them to be adequately tested, and the political instability of the years intervening between the death of Sher Shāh and the accession of Akbar was such as to mask the operation of economic factors.

As regards the method of collection, Sher Shāh granted assignments as his predecessors had done; there is nothing on record to indicate that he curtailed the freedom which assignees had previously enjoyed, though the general character of his administration renders this not improbable. We may be confident that his methods were followed closely in the tracts reserved for the treasury, and we may conjecture that, to a varying extent, they prevailed also in assignments.

The historical importance of Sher Shāh's methods lies in the fact that they formed the starting-point of the series of experiments in administration which marked the first half of Akbar's reign. Much information regarding these experiments is furnished by the authorities, but they are in some respects incomplete, while their language is highly technical; particular statements divorced from their context may easily be misunderstood; and the account which follows, based on study of the authorities as a whole, differs substantially from much which has been written on the subject in the past. It deals in order, first, with the experiments in assessment made in the heart of the empire, from the Punjab to Bihār; next, with the practice in regard to assignments; and then with the working of the arrangements finally adopted for the empire as a whole.

In the early years of Akbar's reign the revenue was assessed by measurement, and the demand made on the peasants was based on a schedule of assessment rates which had been prepared under Sher Shāh: as has been said above, it is uncertain whether Sher Shāh used one schedule or several, but under Akbar there is no doubt that only one was employed. From the outset the demand was made in cash, the produce due under the schedule being valued at prices fixed by order of the emperor. These arrangements could not be made to work satisfactorily: nor is it possible that they could have worked for long. Just at first, the prices fixed for valuing the produce were uniform for the whole empire, and were apparently based on those which ruled in the vicinity of the court. In the tenth year of the reign varying local prices were substituted for the uniform scale previously used; but this measure, though obviously an improvement, did not suffice to remove the difficulties, and three years later the use of Sher Shāh's schedule was abandoned so far as the reserved areas were concerned, though seasonal cash-rates continued to be calculated from it, presumably for the use of assignees. For the reserved areas a more summary procedure was introduced, which is not explained in detail; probably it was assessment through the headmen, though it is possible that in some cases farms were given.

These summary assessments must be regarded as a temporary

measure, intended merely to tide over the emergency, for in the fifteenth year of the reign (1570–71) new schedules of assessment rates, applicable to all land whether assigned or reserved, were brought into force throughout the country. According to my reading of the authorities, the new schedules were of precisely the same form as the old, showing the demand to be made on the peasant as one-third of the average estimated produce; the difference lay in the fact that the average produce was now estimated separately for each *pargana*, and not for the empire as a whole, thus eliminating the difficulties which had resulted from ignoring local differences in productivity. The demand was still stated in terms of produce, and the prices at which it was valued in each season required the emperor's sanction.

These new schedules were worked out by the *qānūngos*, each for his own *pargana*, under the supervision of Rājā Todar Mal, who was now associated with Muzaffar Khān in the charge of the Revenue Ministry, and was in practice its effective head. Todar Mal's early history is obscure. He has been identified by some modern writers with one Todar Khattrī, who was employed by Sher Shāh in building the fort of Rohtās, and it has been assumed that he was connected with the revenue administration from that time onward; but the identification is not supported by anything in the contemporary chronicles, and the mere name is scarcely an adequate basis for a confident conclusion. In Akbar's reign he emerges first in the year 1565, when he was performing military duties; and from 1570 to his death in 1589 he fills a conspicuous place in the chronicles, sometimes as a successful commander in the field, sometimes as the Revenue Minister, to which post he returned from successive military expeditions, always as a highly competent and exceptionally honest officer, who at the same time was not easy to work with owing to his ill-temper, obstinacy, and vindictiveness.

The assessment schedules which were introduced in 1570–71 remained in force for ten years, and apparently they were found suitable, so far as the claim, stated in produce, was concerned; but recurring difficulties in calculating the seasonal cash-demand eventually led to their abandonment. The prices at which the produce-claim should be valued had to be sanctioned by the emperor, separately for each region and for each season. The emperor was constantly on the move, the distances to be covered increased with the expansion of the empire, the issue of orders was delayed, and the whole business of assessment and collection was thereby hindered, to the inconvenience of everyone concerned; while, in addition, the reports of local prices, on which the emperor's orders were based, were suspected in some cases to be fraudulent. Akbar met the emergency by deciding to discard schedules stated in produce, and to fix assessment rates in cash, which could be applied, season by season, to the area actually cropped without the need for recurring references to the court.

For this purpose the *parganas* were grouped into what would now be called assessment circles on the basis of agricultural homogeneity, and for each circle a schedule of rates was framed showing the amount of money to be demanded on the unit area of each crop, known as *bīgha*; the size of this unit varied within wide limits, but the *bīgha* to which the schedules refer was probably a little less than five-eighths of an acre. The range of the rates was extensive; one schedule, which may be taken as a fair sample, shows that small millets were charged 11 *dām*, large millets from 25 to 30, barley 40, wheat 60, sugarcane and indigo 120, and betel 220 *dām*, the *dām* being approximately one-fortieth of a rupee. Such figures make it easy to understand why the Revenue Ministry consistently pressed for improvement in the class of crops; a change from cereals to sugarcane for instance would immediately double or treble the revenue due from the area affected.

Contemporary descriptions of this reform are incomplete, but apparently the method adopted was to strike an average for each circle of the cash-demand rates which had been used within that circle during the ten years for which Todar Mal's schedules had been in operation. It is uncertain whether these averages were adjusted, or were used as they worked out; but the schedules, in which the rates are given in thousandths of a rupee, show that no attempt was made to secure round or convenient figures for the recurring calculations, and it is probable that no formal adjustments were made.

With these schedules of rates stated in cash, the process of seasonal assessment was simple. When the crops were showing above ground, measuring parties were sent into the villages to record the areas which had been sown. From these field records the total area sown by each peasant was extracted, crop by crop, care being taken to exclude areas where sowings had failed; the sanctioned assessment rates were then used to calculate the total revenue due from that peasant; and the sums due from each peasant were brought together in an assessment statement for the village, on the basis of which collections were made at harvest, though the rules provided for adjustments required by injury to crops after the assessment had been made.

So far as the chronicles show, this method of assessment remained in force until the end of Akbar's reign, but its application was not absolutely rigid. One case is recorded where the sanctioned charges were temporarily raised. Akbar's prolonged residence in Lahore had resulted in a marked rise of local prices, and the revenue demand was increased by 20 per cent. in the area affected, but this temporary increase was discontinued when the emperor left the Punjab in the year 1598. No other increase of the same kind is recorded, but the silence of the chronicles is not conclusive in such matters. On the other hand, a series of exceptionally good seasons occurring in the country between Delhi and Allahābād from 1585 to 1590 led to such a fall of prices that the revenue could not be paid, and large remissions had to be granted—by assignees as well as in the lands reserved for the treasury. There is no record of remissions having been made in years when the crops were bad, and we may assume that this eventuality was considered to be met by the standing provisions mentioned above for the exclusion of areas where sowings had failed, and for adjusting the assessment to meet subsequent injuries.

We now pass from assessments to assignments. In the opening years of Akbar's reign, officers were ordinarily remunerated by assignment, and a difficulty emerged which must always have been latent in the system. An eastern autocrat was bound to be liberal, if he was to retain the services of an adequate and competent staff; and liberality was even more indispensable in the case of an autocracy in the making, the position which Bairam Khān as regent for Akbar had to face. It is no matter for surprise therefore that the cost of establishment should have grown more quickly than the resources of what was a relatively small empire, and that the Revenue Ministry should have found itself unable to make assignments sufficient to cover the salaries granted by the regent. The way in which the difficulty was met was characteristic of the times. For the purpose of allocating assignments the Ministry maintained registers, which may be called "the Valuation of the Empire", or more shortly, "the Valuation", showing the income which each local area might be expected to yield, one year with another, to the assignee. When orders for assignments could not be met in full, the figures in the valuation were arbitrarily raised, so that the orders could be carried out on paper, but the assignee would in fact be unable to realise the income to which he was entitled. The inevitable result was dissatisfaction throughout the staff of the empire, and corruption inside the Ministry.

The original record having thus become worthless, Akbar in the year 1566 ordered the preparation of a new valuation, which was duly effected, but it went the way of the first, being corruptly falsified; and by 1573 the dissatisfaction in the state service was such that the emperor decided, with the concurrence, or perhaps at the suggestion, of Rājā Todar Mal, to pay salaries in cash, and to bring practically the whole of northern India directly under the Revenue Ministry. For this purpose the country was divided into circles, each estimated to yield, when fully developed, a crore (*karor*) of *dām* (250,000 rupees), and a staff of officials was posted to each circle with instructions to press on agricultural development as quickly as possible; the officer in charge of the circle was officially designated *'Āmil*, or *'Amalguzār*, that is to say, Administrator, but popularly he became known as *Karorī*, a soubriquet derived from the nominal extent of his charge, and eventually this designation passed into the official language. These arrangements lasted for five years. In 1579–80 a new valuation was made, calculated on the precise data furnished by the ten years' operation of Todar Mal's assessment rates, and the practice of assignment again became general, though this fact is not formally recorded in the chronicles. The reasons for the change are matters for conjecture. The most probable view is that the introduction of cash salaries was intended from the first as a temporary measure, pending the time when data for a trustworthy valuation should become available; but in any case the reversion to the practice of assignment may have been hastened by the occurrence of grave scandals in the revenue administration.

The large and sudden extension of direct assessment and collection was obviously an enterprise requiring careful supervision. This requirement was provided at the outset, for the initial measures were planned by Rājā Todar Mal, and executed by the staff which he had chosen; but shortly afterwards he was called away for military duty, and the charge of the Revenue Ministry devolved on Khvāja Shāh Mansūr, who, it may be assumed, followed the usual practice of the period, and replaced the existing staff by his own nominees. A period of corruption and extortion ensued, which brought the revenue administration into disrepute, and operated to restrict cultivation, and thereby reduce the financial resources of the empire, which it had been hoped to increase. When, after the execution of Shāh Mansūr for treason in 1581, Rājā Todar Mal resumed effective charge of the Ministry, he issued orders for the prevention of such malpractices in future, and at the same time took drastic action against the officials suspected of misconduct, calling them to account for the sums they had embezzled or extorted, and employing the traditional procedure, under which a suspect was detained in prison, and flogged, or otherwise tortured, periodically, until a satisfactory settlement was reached.

These processes dragged on for some years, but were at last brought to a close by the intervention of Akbar, who appointed Amīr Fath-ullah Shīrāzī as an imperial commissioner (*Amīn-ul-mulk*) to dispose of the cases pending in the Revenue Ministry, and in effect to be at its head, though Todar Mal was not formally superseded. The commissioner performed his duties effectively, and drew up proposals, which were sanctioned by the emperor, for reforming the procedure of the Ministry in its relations with the local staff. This measure, introduced in 1585, practically completes the revenue history of the reign, so far as it finds a place in the chronicles. The only important change recorded in later years was the decision, taken in 1596, to bring the provincial revenue officers, now designated *Dīwān*, directly under the orders of the Ministry, thus relieving the viceroy of responsibility for revenue administration, and originating the administrative dyarchy which persisted until the collapse of the empire, with revenue business (*dīwānī*) conducted independently of the general administration (*faujdārī*).

The result of the period of experiment which covered the first half of Akbar's reign was to provide a workable revenue system for northern India; but the system was not applied to the outlying portions of the empire, each of which was treated as the local circumstances required. The standard, or "regulation", system may be described as follows. The basis of the state's claim on the peasant was still one-third of the produce, but the actual demand was made in the form of a sum of money, varying with the locality and with the crop, on each unit of area sown in each season. The bulk of northern India was assigned, and the detailed conduct of assessment and collection was in the hands of the assignees, who, however, were bound by the sanctioned schedules of assessment rates. The area reserved for the treasury was divided into circles, each in charge of a *karorī* or collector, who was under the orders of the provincial *dīwān*, himself responsible, at first to the viceroy, but afterwards directly to the Revenue Ministry. The collector was required to deal with established cultivation strictly in accordance with the regulation system; but he was under constant pressure to increase the revenue yielded by his circle by the two traditional processes, extension of cultivation and improvement in the class of crops; and, in order to attain these objects, he was allowed a considerable degree of latitude. Thus he was authorised to reduce the standard rates on the more remunerative crops, when this was necessary in order to secure an increase in the area under them; he could make temporary reductions in the schedules of rates in case of land which had gone out of cultivation, so as to stimulate its reclamation; for extension of tillage in waste land he could agree to almost whatever terms the peasants offered; and when the village headmen exerted themselves successfully with this object, he could allow them a substantial commission by way of reward. When the assessments fell due, the peasants were encouraged to bring their revenue personally to the local treasury, though collecting agents were also employed in the villages; and, speaking generally, it may be said that the distinctive feature of the system was the direct relationship which it established between the collector and the individual peasant, who was to be treated as an independent unit, encouraged to increase production, and assisted with loans for that purpose, but held firmly to the engagements into which he had entered.

It will be obvious that the success or failure of this system must have depended entirely on the quality of the administration. The amount of detailed work, to be accomplished season by season under the strict time limit imposed by agricultural conditions, was very great; opportunities for extortion and oppression of individuals were numerous; and if there was dishonesty or inefficiency at the centre, the system must soon have broken down. There is no record of a collapse, or of a recurrence of scandals like those which occurred before the year 1581; but it must be borne in mind that our information regarding the closing years of the reign is much less detailed than for the earlier period. The most probable view is that, while the system worked reasonably well under Akbar, it disappeared under his successor, but definite evidence on this question is wanting.

This regulation system extended, broadly speaking, to the plains of northern India, excluding the areas left in the hands of the Hindu chiefs, that is to say, to the provinces of Multān, Lahore, Delhi (excluding the Kumāūn hills), Āgra, Allahābād, and the bulk of Bihār; but the southern parts of the two last-named provinces, bordering on the unadministered region known as Gondwāna, were excluded from its operations, as was the hill-country lying between Bihār and Bengal. The system was in force also in those parts of Ajmer which were not left to the chiefs, and it is said to have been introduced in Mālwā, but the records regarding this province are obscure; the eastern portion, bordering on Gondwāna, and the western portion, bordering on Ajmer, were left to chiefs, while apparently some arrangements more simple than the regulation system were in force over a large part of the remainder of the province.

In the outlying provinces, local practices were ordinarily continued. In the northern mountains—Kashmīr, Kābul and Qandahār—these practices were diversified, and too complex to be summarised in a few words; here as elsewhere, the basic idea was to take a share of the produce, but the share was ordinarily calculated by methods which gave an approximation to the system of measurement. In Sind one-third of the produce was claimed, and the demand was assessed by sharing. The records regarding Gujarāt are conflicting, but can be interpreted on the hypothesis that measurement was practised for a time, and then superseded by assessment on the village as a unit made with the headmen, or possibly with farmers. In Berār and (probably) Khāndesh such village assessments were the rule, and the same statement holds good of Bengal (including Orissa); contemporary authorities lend no support to the legend which was current at the end of the eighteenth century that Todar Mal made a detailed assessment on the individual peasants of Bengal. In most of these provinces large areas were left in the hands of chiefs, and thus were not assessed by the Revenue Ministry, or available for assignment.

Precise information is wanting regarding the fiscal relations subsisting between Akbar and those chiefs who retained jurisdiction over their domains. It is possible that revenue was claimed, at least from some of them, in the form of a stipulated annual tribute, as had been the practice at earlier periods; but the obscure records which alone are available for the territories of the more important chiefs can also be interpreted on the theory that the emperor claimed nothing beyond loyal service, including of course the periodical presents which etiquette required, and that the Revenue Ministry recorded a chief's territory as his assignment, valued at some arbitrary figure for the formal completion of its records.

Before passing to the reign of Jahāngīr a few words may be said regarding the practice of alienating revenue in grants made by way of charity or favour. Such alienation was traditional. In Akbar's time grants were officially described by the Turkī name *suyūrghāl*, but in the ordinary literature they appear as *milk* (domain), or *madad-i-ma'āsh* (assistance to livelihood), terms which are not distinguishable in practice. The usual form of grant was an area of stated size, which at first seems to have consisted of land already cultivated. Akbar made it a rule that one-half of the grant should ordinarily be waste land, so that while the grantee could forthwith collect the revenue due from the peasants on the moiety under cultivation, he had to exert himself to bring the remainder of the land under the plough in order to obtain the full benefit of the emperor's liberality. The grants were professedly charitable, and, in some cases at least, the formal document recited that the recipient had no other means of livelihood, but in practice this limitation was not strictly observed; they were made sometimes for the life of the grantee, sometimes for two generations, and sometimes for an indefinite term; but the records show that they could be resumed or revised at any time at the discretion of the administration.

The business connected with these grants was transacted, not in the Revenue Ministry, but in a separate department, which was presided over by the *Sadr*, a high officer charged with supervision of the administration of Islamic law. The *Sadr* exercised very extensive powers, subject of course to the emperor's personal intervention; and in practice the history of the office is one of profuse and sometimes corrupt liberality, punctuated by spasms of vigorous retrenchment. The tenure of a grant was thus insecure. A grantee might find himself deprived of some or all the land he held as the result of a change of policy, or of personnel; and on occasion he might be affected by a general order like that which was issued shortly after the year 1595, summarily reducing by one-half all the grants existing in the province of Gujarāt. On the other hand, influence and bribery might secure undisturbed possession, or the retention of land in excess of what had been granted; and such accounts as have survived of the working of the department indicate a thoroughly inefficient and corrupt administration. Some idea of the importance of these grants can be formed from the fact that in the statistics included in the *Āīn-i-Akbarī* the grants in the five northern provinces, from Lahore to Allahābād, amount to about $3\frac{1}{2}$ per cent. of the total revenue.

Contemporary authorities furnish very little information regarding the revenue system which was in operation under Jahāngīr, but the general slackness and inefficiency which characterised the greater part of his reign may safely be assumed to have left their mark on a department which, as has been said above, depended for success entirely on the quality of the administration; and this inference is borne out by the fact that the income from the reserved areas fell off seriously and progressively, so that, towards the close of the reign, the accumulations in the treasury were being drawn on to meet current expenditure. The most probable view is that Akbar's regulation system was discarded during this reign, and replaced by village assessments, made with the headmen or with farmers as circumstances might permit; and the silence of the chronicles is consistent with the hypothesis that this change was not made formally or deliberately, but came about gradually as the vigour of the administration declined.

The great bulk of the revenue continued to be assigned to officers in the state service, and there are some indications that in practice assignees now enjoyed a free hand in the management of their holdings, so long at least as complaints did not attract the emperor's personal attention. The system of managing assignments was not uniform, for, while some officers assessed and collected the revenue through a salaried staff, others handed the business over to speculative farmers. The instability which characterised the administration in general was particularly noteworthy in this branch. Assignments were changed so frequently as to make it dangerous for ordinary holders to pursue a constructive policy of development, or do anything beyond extracting as much money as was possible; and there is evidence that in some parts of the country the practice had grown up of collecting one or more instalments of revenue in advance as a sort of insurance against loss in the probable event of a sudden transfer. Judging from the descriptions of foreign observers, among others William Hawkins, the first Englishman known to have held a Mughul assignment, the Revenue Ministry at this period must have been a hotbed of intrigue and corruption, with the staff disposed to reserve the most productive, or most easily managed, areas, but willing to assign them for sufficient consideration, and with actual or prospective assignees struggling to obtain, and to keep, whatever suited them best, and to get rid of, or avoid, assignments which had already been squeezed dry. The effect of these conditions must have been to nullify any impetus that may have existed towards agricultural development, and it is probable that the decline which occurred in the receipts of the treasury was not due solely to embezzlement or inefficiency, but resulted in part from an actual fall in agricultural production.

The only definite change in practice recorded in this reign was the introduction of the *āltamghā* grant, a form of tenure which was already known in Central Asia but had not previously existed in India. A deserving officer could hope to receive a grant under this tenure of the village or *pargana* in which he was born, with the promise that the grant, once made, should not be altered or resumed. During the seventeenth century such grants appear to have been made very rarely, but the institution is of historical interest for two reasons. In the first place, it is the nearest approach to landownership which has been traced during the Mughul period; ordinary grants were, as has been said above, liable to resumption or variation at any time in the ordinary course of administration, but an *āltamghā* could be annulled only by the final authority of the emperor, or, as modern jurists might say, by an Act of State. In the second place, during the eighteenth century the original limitations on the tenure came to be ignored, and the *āltamghā* grants which were then made profusely were subsequently recognised by the British government as conferring a perpetual and transferable right to hold the land free of revenue, the most complete form of landownership now existing in the country.

The lack of contemporary information regarding Jahāngīr's revenue administration continues during the reign of his successor. It is known that Shāh Jahān reorganised the finances of the empire, and provided that sufficient areas should be reserved for the treasury to yield a recurring surplus after ordinary expenditure had been covered. It is known also that he devoted his personal attention to finance, and that he gave liberal rewards to collectors who had been successful in working up the revenue of their circles. Further, it is recorded that he issued general orders on the revenue system, but the text of these has not been found, and the extant description of them is too vague and eulogistic to be of any value to the historian. The nature of the system favoured by him can, however, be inferred from documents of the early years of Aurangzīb, which will be noticed below; briefly, it may be said that the general rule was to assess the village through the headmen at a sum calculated to yield the equivalent of from one-third to one-half of the produce, and that this rule applied, at least formally, to assigned as well as reserved areas. Assignment continued to be the prevalent practice, and in 1647, the twentieth year of the reign, revenue aggregating 190 millions of rupees was assigned, while thirty millions were reserved for the treasury. No records have survived to show how these figures were calculated, but the most probable view is that the valuation of the empire had been kept up to date in the Ministry, so that general re-valuations, such as had been made under Akbar, were no longer required, the figures for each local area being revised from time to time in the light of recent experience.

In only one region of the empire do we know what was actually done in the course of this reign. The Deccan provinces which were organised after the conquest of Ahmadnagar were found to be in a deplorable condition. They had suffered heavily in the terrible famine of 1630–32, and the war of conquest had practically completed their economic ruin, so that twenty years later the revenue accruing from them was still insufficient to meet the expense of their administration. During prince Aurangzīb's second viceroyalty of the Deccan, which began in the year 1652, a complete reorganisation of the revenue system of these provinces was undertaken by an officer named Murshid Qulī Khān, who was appointed *dīwān* of Daulatābād and Telingāna, and subsequently placed in charge also of Berār and Khāndesh.

As the result of his work, three methods of assessment emerged in this region. For some areas, presumably the tracts where agriculture was in a primitive stage, he retained the plough-rents which were traditional in the locality, the peasant paying a fixed annual sum for each plough and team, and being free to cultivate as much land as he chose in whatever way he found convenient. Elsewhere the *dīwān* introduced the two familiar systems—sharing and measurement—side by side, and it is probable that the peasants were allowed the choice between them. The system of sharing adopted was of a type well known in other Islamic countries but hitherto unfamiliar in Muslim India. The share claimed was not uniform, but varied with the nature of the crop and with the source of water; thus half the produce was claimed for crops depending on the rains, one-third for grain irrigated from wells, and from one-fourth to one-ninth for the various high-grade crops such as sugarcane or poppy. Under measurement, on the other hand, the assessment rates, which were fixed in cash, were based on a uniform claim to one-fourth of the produce, a distinctly low figure when judged by the standard of the times. This lenient assessment was accompanied by active measures to re-people and reorganise the ruined villages, and capital was advanced when required, with the result that prosperity was for the time being restored.

It does not appear that Murshid Qulī Khān's achievements in the Deccan had any reaction on the revenue administration in the north. The system which prevailed there in the first few years of Aurangzīb's reign can be studied in the general orders issued under his authority between 1665 and 1669, which describe the current practice, and indicate that it was then no novelty, but had prevailed long enough for the development of serious abuses. In certain, unspecified, tracts where the peasants were exceptionally poor, assessment was made by sharing, at rates varying from one-third to one-half the produce, the standard recognised throughout the orders; but as a rule the assessment was made annually in cash on the village as a unit. At the beginning of each year the assessor estimated the productivity of the village, having regard to recent experience and to the standard figures recognised in the department, apparently the figures for some particular year which had been selected as being normal or typical. Using these data, the assessor proposed to the headmen a lump sum to be paid for the year in the instalments usual in the locality. The headmen could refuse the proposed assessment, in which case the revenue was determined, either by sharing or by measurement, on the season's crops; but it must be borne in mind that these latter processes involved the intrusion into the village of a measuring, or estimating, party, the expense of which fell on the peasants, and which could be used effectively to punish recalcitrants, so that in practice the assessor was in a very strong position in his dealings with the headmen, and refusal of his proposals was probably rare. The best safeguard for the village lay in secrecy, so that the assessor should not be in a position to make an accurate estimate of its production. Various methods of concealing the facts appear in the later records as old-established practices; and it may reasonably be said that the well-known reluctance of the northern peasants to disclose their affairs to revenue officials has its roots in the system of village assessments.

The duty of the revenue officials was not confined, however, to ascertaining the yield of a village: they were required to stimulate efforts for improving it. Peasants were to be urged and encouraged to work their hardest; advances of capital and other favours were to be given to those who did so; the recalcitrant were to be threatened and flogged. Comparing this system with that which had been employed under Akbar, three main differences emerge. In the first place, the standard of assessment had been raised; the former average of one-third had now become the minimum, while as much as one-half of the produce might be taken. In view of the financial position, it is probable that the maximum tended to become the standard, and that it was during this period that the rule of claiming one-half, which was familiar throughout the eighteenth century, became established over the greater part of northern India. In the second place, the individual peasant was relieved from the charges, and the possible exactions, incidental to the detailed measurements and assessments of Akbar's time, and was left almost entirely in the hands of the village headmen. In the third place, the pressure on the headmen, and through them on the peasants, to pay the highest possible revenue had undoubtedly increased; the standard of the demand had been raised, but the actual claim tended to be the utmost sum that the village could be made to pay. The traditional veneration of the name of Todar Mal must be explained, not merely by the fact that his administration was in itself equitable, but also by the period of increased severity which followed it, so that the reign of Akbar, viewed through the hardships of later times, came to bear the aspect of a golden age.

In the authorities relating to northern India, the practice of assessing villages as units first becomes prominent in the reign of Aurangzīb, but it would be a mistake to regard it as an innovation. The most probable view, based on stray hints and casual expressions in a literature which is far from complete, is that village assessment was already practised before the Muslim conquest, and that it never entirely disappeared. In the fourteenth century, and again in the sixteenth, the state for a time entered into direct relations with individual peasants, but probably village assessments were the rule in the thirteenth and fifteenth, as they certainly were in the seventeenth and eighteenth. In an extensive kingdom assessment on individuals could be carried out effectively only by a strong, wise, and vigorous administration: in times when these qualities were not available, the line of least resistance was to deal with villages as units.

It has been said above that Aurangzīb's orders indicate the existence of serious abuses. Apart from the ordinary incidents of unauthorised cesses, levies and other exactions by local officers, the chief abuses were two, one in the revenue offices, the other in the village. Under pressure to increase the revenue, the practice had grown up of making sanguine assessments, more than could in fact be realised; then, as the year progressed, reports would come in of injury to the crops from drought, frost, hail and other calamities, injuries which involved a reduction in the assessments originally made. The Revenue Ministry considered, not unreasonably, that many of the calamities reported were fictitious, devised in order to get the local officials out of the difficulty caused by the original over-assessment, and stringent orders were issued to ensure that the controlling officers should be supplied with adequate information, and should closely scrutinise all reports of the kind. The effect of these orders is matter for conjecture, but the necessity for their issue is significant of the pressure which had been exerted to bring assessments up to the highest possible figure.

The other abuse was oppression of the weaker peasants by the village headmen, who had to distribute the amount of the assessment over individuals. The method of distribution in each village was determined by local custom, but manipulation was always possible in practice, and the Ministry suspected, again not unreasonably, that headmen were favouring themselves and their friends, to the prejudice of the peasants outside their circle. Records of the early British period show that something of the sort was in fact an inevitable incident of the system, not in all villages, but in some: the extent of the evil at any particular period cannot be determined with precision; but its existence has to be borne in mind in any attempt to estimate the relative advantages of the different systems of assessment. In actual practice, direct dealing with individuals was probably on the whole favourable to the weaker peasants, and unpopular with the stronger, who could be made to pay their full share; village assessment was doubtless an equitable system where a village consisted of a homogeneous body of peasants, but where cliques or factions existed, the weak sometimes had to pay for the strong.

A distinctive feature of the orders issued by Aurangzīb's Ministry in 1668 was the stress laid on compliance with the principles and traditions of Islamic law. The same attitude had been adopted by Fīrūz Tughluq in the second half of the fourteenth century, but the general practice in India had been to treat the revenue administration as a secular matter, lying outside the province of ecclesiastical jurists. The practical effect of these orders was not, however, great. The fundamental features of the existing revenue system were, as has been said above, in accordance with the canons of Islamic law; and Aurangzīb's orders consist mainly of a digest of rulings on questions affecting individual peasants which might come before revenue officers for decision—questions relating to inheritance and transfer of holdings, and the like. Their interest at the present day lies in the formal recognition of the fact that a peasant had a claim to retain his holding, and transmit it to heirs, purchasers, or mortgagees, subject always to the primary condition that the revenue due from the holding was paid. The silence of these orders regarding ejectment is noteworthy, but can be explained by the fact that at this time the administration was not in a position to pick and choose the most efficient cultivators; the great need of the period was to keep peasants at work in sufficient numbers.

The detailed provisions in Aurangzīb's orders leave no room for doubt that in the opening decade of his reign the administration was already seriously concerned about the scarcity of peasants and their readiness to abscond, topics which do not emerge in the literature of Akbar's time. They thus confirm in the essential points the description of the agrarian situation given by the French physician, François Bernier, whose experience was gained during this period. His observations, made during eight years' residence at the Mughul court, led him to the conclusion that agriculture was declining in consequence of the "execrable tyranny" which the peasants were experiencing at the hands of officials, farmers, and assignees alike; and that many of them were either absconding to other regions, especially the domains of the chiefs, where conditions were more tolerable, or were abandoning the land in order to work as servants in the towns or with the army. It may be taken therefore as an established fact that by this time the danger foreseen by the early Islamic jurists had become a reality; that agricultural production was being diminished by the excessive burden laid upon the peasants' shoulders; and that the efforts of the administration to increase the revenue were in fact leading in the direction of a progressive decline.

The system of annual village assessments which has been described above persisted up to the end of the Muslim period, and was adopted just at first by the British administration in northern India. Nothing further need be said therefore regarding the assessment of the revenue: the historical interest of the remainder of the period lies in the changes which took place among the intermediaries, and the transformation of a heterogeneous mass of chiefs, farmers, and grantees into a class which in the British period was to become a homogeneous body of landholders. The main factors in this change were the decline in the practice of assignment, the extension of farming, and the strengthening of the position of the chiefs.

The practice of assignment continued in operation throughout the reign of Aurangzīb, but early in the eighteenth century it lost the popularity which it had hitherto enjoyed, and there are some indications that the officers of the empire preferred to be paid in cash by the treasury, depleted as it was, an arrangement which had formerly been regarded as implying something like a slur on the recipient. Three factors can be distinguished as contributing to this result, but they are in fact merely different aspects of the collapse of the Mughul empire. In the first place, the progressive decline in agriculture necessarily resulted in a progressive loss of revenue, so that it became increasingly difficult for an assignee to realise his promised and expected income. In the second place, as has been explained in an earlier chapter, the emperor had been forced to grant the Marāthās a share (known as *chauth*)[1] of the revenue of the Deccan provinces; and this first charge on the declining produce, extended as it was to other regions, left so much less for the assignee. In the third place, the emperor was no longer able to guarantee the peaceable enjoyment of an assignment, so that questions of possession had passed from the forum of administration, and had to be decided by force of arms. The decay of the system of assignment was therefore inevitable.

The change may be looked at in another light. From the time of Akbar onwards, the service of the state had been the only possible career for men of talent, energy and ambition; and to such men it offered ample or even extravagant rewards. It is true that they could not hope to found wealthy families, because on their death their accumulations ordinarily reverted to the state; but, if successful themselves, they could be sure of obtaining for their sons and grandsons a good start in the same career, and, given the necessary personal qualifications, one generation might follow another in positions of power and affluence. In the eighteenth century, the service of a decaying empire ceased to attract, while a new avenue was opened for ambition, an avenue which led in the direction of kingship, and the revenue farm was one of the first stages on the road; it was now better to be a farmer than an assignee.

[1] See pp. 273 and 392 n. 1.

It is uncertain when the Revenue Ministry adopted the practice of farming out the areas reserved for the treasury. Possibly this expedient dates in some regions from the closing years of Shāh Jahān, but in any case its main development must be attributed to the reigns of Aurangzīb and his successors. In Bengal, in particular, farms came into existence of a type hitherto unfamiliar in northern India. Assignments in this province were unpopular among the northern officers, so that an unusually large proportion of it was reserved for the treasury; and a practice grew up under which the collectors in the reserved areas undertook to pay a definite sum of revenue for their circles instead of accounting for the money actually received from the peasants. The sum to be paid for such a farm was not ordinarily varied from year to year, and came by degrees to be regarded as fixed; and the collector-farmers retained their circles indefinitely, and were allowed to transmit them to their heirs, so long of course as the revenue was duly paid. In this way, their position came to be indistinguishable from that of the existing chiefs, and the two classes were eventually described locally by a single name, that of landholder (*zamīndār*), a term which in the precise official language of the north had been applied to the latter only.

These Bengal landholders were not, however, allowed to retain the entire profit resulting from the economic recovery which followed on the establishment of Dutch and British trade in this region after the middle of the seventeenth century. The revenue due from them was not formally enhanced, but it was supplemented from time to time by the imposition of cesses and other additional demands, amounting in the aggregate to an enhancement not far short of the whole sum originally payable. It was in this way that the situation developed which was found by the first English administrators in Bengal—the bulk of the country held by a relatively small number of landholders, who enjoyed practical freedom in their relations with the peasants, and paid to the state dues which were in fact adjustable at its discretion, but by methods which are not known to have been practised elsewhere in Mughul India.

In the north large farms, held for an indefinite term, emerged during the eighteenth century; and perhaps no other arrangement was possible, when the revenue administration had ceased to be effective, and assignments had lost their attractions. As was the case in Bengal, these farms tended to be transmitted by inheritance, and the annual payments tended to be repeated from year to year; but the peculiar feature of Bengal—fixed basic payments, supplemented by adjustable cesses—is not disclosed in the northern records, and the most probable view is that in this region both parties regarded the amount to be paid as variable, to be increased or reduced as circumstances might permit, while the farmer looked forward to a time when he might be strong enough to refuse payment altogether, and thereby establish himself as in fact an independent ruler.

Meanwhile, other independent, or practically independent, rulers were emerging. As has been said above, the Hindu chiefs who were included in the empire were men with traditional claims to sovereignty; and their traditional policy was to assert those claims whenever a suitable opportunity offered. This condition was fulfilled in the eighteenth century; and while the old families were busily engaged in strengthening their position, and were seeking to enlarge their domains, sometimes by force, and sometimes by taking farms of adjoining territory, adventurers and soldiers of fortune were pursuing a similar course, using as a base of operations any local influence they might possess, as grantees or otherwise. We thus have various classes—chiefs and farmers, adventurers and grantees—all following the same road. For all classes alike the essential thing was to establish so much authority over a local area that the peasants should be willing to pay revenue in return for some measure of that protection which the empire could no longer provide. Authority could be established only with the aid of force, and successful force tended always to enlarge the area of its operation.

The result of these tendencies was to produce the conditions which prevailed when, at the opening of the nineteenth century, the country which now forms the bulk of the United Provinces came under British jurisdiction, and was found to be parcelled out in what were then called *taluqas* (Arabic, *ta'alluqa*), or "dependencies", claimed by various titles, if that term can be applied in such a situation, but all resting on the basis of possession, maintained in the last resort by force. Each holder of a dependency claimed to collect the revenue from the peasants under his power, and each admitted liability to pay a portion of his receipts to any superior authority strong enough to insist on payment, the amount being a matter either for negotiation or for determination by the will of the stronger party. The peasants, on their side, recognised liability to pay revenue, ordinarily at the rate of one-half of the produce, and were prepared to pay it to whoever was in a position to take it. The actual sum to be paid by the peasants was usually fixed year by year by what may be called a process of bargaining. The holder of a dependency could enforce his views by the threat of detailed assessment: the peasants could rarely adopt an attitude of frank opposition, but in the circumstances of the time they could hope to mitigate the burden by concealing the facts of productivity, and would go a long way to avoid such detailed assessments as might bring these facts to light. There was no scope for any constructive policy of development, nor was it possible to look ahead. In some cases, the payments made by villages tended to be repeated until they became customary, but the settlement was still annual; the idea of an assessment fixed beforehand for a term of years was quite unfamiliar, and the arrangement was at first unpopular when it was introduced by British administrators.

The final stages in the history of the Mughul revenue system have been sketched in the foregoing paragraphs for the main tracts of country where authority passed from what was left of the empire to the East India Company. The changes which took place in the tracts which passed from the Mughuls to other Indian rulers, Marāthās, Sikhs, or Rājputs, lie outside the scope of this chapter.

CHAPTER XVII

BURMA (1531–1782)

ARAKAN

SHUT off from Burma by a hill range, Arakan has a separate history, but it is the same in kind. She seldom had a strong central government, and until 1437 Sandoway was independent.

The ease of sea communications renders it possible that Buddhism reached Arakan earlier than the interior of Burma, and, although unproved, the tradition which assigns the Mahamuni image to the reign of one Sandathuriya A.D. 146–98 is not incredible. But accessibility from the sea brought other things than Buddhism. Thus Brahmanism is indicated by the word Sanda (Chandra), which ends the name of every traditional king from 783 to 957, and by the fact that medallions ascribed to these kings bear Shiva's trident and Nāgarī script.[1] After the tenth century the country was professedly Buddhist, notwithstanding the spread of Islam, which by the thirteenth century had dotted the coast from Assam to Malaya with the curious mosques known as Buddermokan.[2] Doubtless it is Muslim influence which led to women being more secluded in Arakan than in Burma.

The capital was successively Thabeiktaung, Dinnyawadi and Vesali down to the tenth century, Pyinsa (Sambawut) till 1118, Parin 1118–67, Hkrit 1167–80, Pyinsa 1180–1237, Launggyet 1237–1433 and Mrohaung (Mrauk-u) 1433–1785. All are in Akyab district, Thabeiktaung on the Yochaung river, the others on or near the Lemro river.

Like the rest of Indo-China, the country suffered chronically from raids. Akyab district was exposed to the hill tribes and in the tenth century Shans temporarily overran it. Settled government was the exception. In the middle of the twelfth century even the Mahamuni image could not be found, for it had been overgrown with jungle in the prevailing anarchy. The Burmese under the Pagan dynasty 1044–1287 successfully established their suzerainty over north Arakan but not over the south, and even in the north the kings merely sent propitiatory tribute and continued to be hereditary kings, not governors appointed by Pagan.

Between 1287 and 1785 there is not even the pretence of Burmese

[1] Phayre, "Coins of Arakan, Pegu and Burma", in *International Numismata Orientalia*; Vincent Smith, *Catalogue of Coins in the Indian Museum, Calcutta*; Duroiselle, *Catalogue of Coins in the Phayre Museum*.

[2] Temple, "Buddermokan", in *Journal Burma Research Society*, 1925.

BURMA UNDER THE TOUNGOO DYNASTY 1531-1752

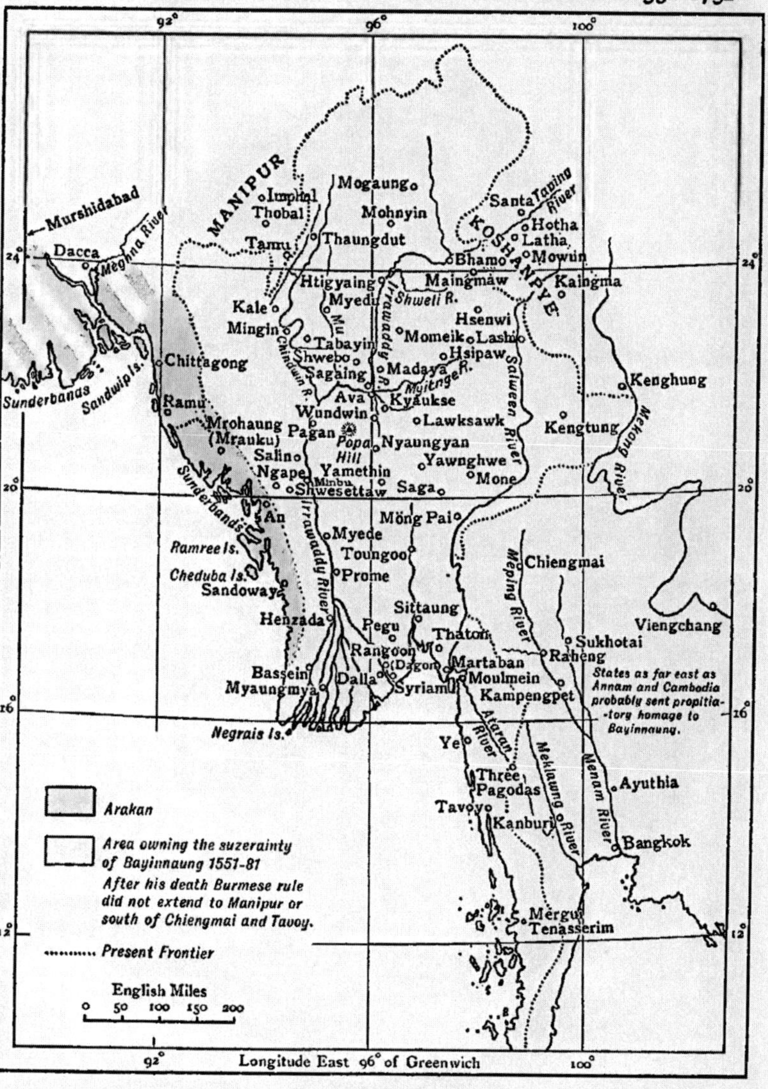

overlordship, save in the fourteenth century when some of the people, torn with dissension, asked the Āva court to nominate a king.[1] From 1374 to 1430 the country was subject first to Burmese and then to Talaing interference, and was raided by both on several occasions.

Narameikhla (1404–34), when ousted in 1404 by the Burmese,[1] fled to Bengal, was well received by the king of Gaur and served him with distinction in the field. After long years in exile he received a levy from Gaur to regain his throne, and although the Muslim commander at first betrayed and imprisoned him in Arakan, he was ultimately reinstated in 1430. His Muslim followers built the Sandihkan mosque at Mrohaung and it was under him that a court bard, Aduminnyo, wrote the historic song *Yahkaingminthami-egyin*. The turmoil of foreign inroads showed that Launggyet was ill-fated, and the omens indicated Mrohaung as a lucky site, so he decided to move there; the astrologers said that if he moved the capital he would die within the year, but he insisted, saying that the move would benefit his people and his own death would matter little. In 1433 he founded Mrohaung and in the next he died. A populous[2] seaport built on hillocks amid the rice plains, intersected by canals which served as streets, it remained the capital for the next four centuries.

Thereafter it is common for the kings, though Buddhists, to use Muslim designations in addition to their own names; and even to issue medallions bearing the *kalima*, or confession of faith, in Persian script; doubtless at first, about this time, the kings had these medallions struck for them in Bengal, but later they struck their own. Narameikhla's brother and successor 'Alī Khān (1434–59) occupied Rāmū. Basawpyu (Kalima Shāh) (1459–82) occupied Chittagong, and it was usually in Arakanese hands till 1666; indeed it had occasionally been subjected to Arakan since the tenth century, and according to the fluctuations of power in the Middle Ages, when Bengal was in the ascendant, the Arakanese sent tribute to Bengal and when they were in the ascendant they received tribute from the Ganges delta, "The Twelve Towns of Bengal".[3]

After 1532 the coast, though poor and largely uninhabited, was liable to pillage by Hpalaung (=feringhi=Portuguese). It would have been a bad age for Arakan, with the aggressive Tabinshwehti on the throne of Pegū, had not king Minbin (Zabauk Shāh) (1531–53) been capable. Foreseeing trouble, he put the defences of his capital, Mrohaung, into repair, with a deep moat filled with tidal water. When the Burmese invaders (p. 483) penetrated the eastern outworks of the city, he opened the sluice gates of his great reservoirs

[1] See vol. III, p. 544.

[2] Manrique in 1630 put the population at 160,000, excluding foreign merchants: *Itinerario de las Missiones del India Oriental*, Hakluyt edition, I, 216–17.

[3] For these, see Hosten, "The Twelve Bhuiyas or Landlords of Bengal", in *Journal Asiatic Society of Bengal*, 1913, p. 437.

and flooded them out. He retained Rāmū and Chittagong in spite of raids there by the Tippera tribes while he was engaged by Tabinshwehti, and coins bearing his name and styling him sultān were struck at Chittagong. He built at Mrohaung the Shwedaung pagoda, the Shitthaung, Dukkanthein, and Lemyethna temples, and the Andaw to enshrine a Ceylon tooth.

Unlike the other races of Burma, the Arakanese maintained sea-going craft, and Chittagong bred a race of capable seamen. For centuries they were the terror of the Ganges delta and at times they hampered even Portuguese shipping. Finally they united with Portuguese freebooters and thus brought about the greatest period in Arakanese history, *c.* 1550–1666. The Portuguese, subject to little control from Goa, had settled in numbers at Chittagong, making it a thriving port, since the middle of the sixteenth century. It was always held by a brother or faithful clansman of the king, with an Arakanese garrison; every year the king sent a hundred boats full of troops, powder and ball, and then the garrison and boats sent in the previous year returned home to Arakan.

Minrazagyi (Salīm Shāh) (1593–1612), the founder of the Parabaw pagoda at Mrohaung, employed De Brito in the expedition against Pegū (p. 494). It comprised land levies which went over the passes, as well as a flotilla from Chittagong and the Ganges delta. On the return journey the wise minister Mahapinnyakyaw, lord of Chittagong, died and was buried by the Hmawdin pagoda at Negrais; he had served the king from youth up, and his compilation of legal precedents, Mahapinnyakyaw *pyatton*, which placed the interpretation of Manu *dhammathat* lawbooks[1] on a definitely Buddhist basis, was thereafter among the most valuable works of its kind throughout Burma.

Minhkamaung (Husain Shāh) (1612–22), as crown prince, had been captured for a time by De Brito when trying to reduce him to obedience at Syriam (p. 494). His queen built the Ratanabon pagoda at Mrohaung. His great achievement was to overthrow the Portuguese pirates who had made Sandwīp island their stronghold. This island was a trade centre, it commanded the mouth of the Ganges delta, and its neighbourhood provided timber in abundance for shipbuilding. In 1608 the Arakanese had offered to let the Dutch trade and build fortifications in return for help in driving out the Portuguese, but their commitments elsewhere were too heavy to allow them to accept the offer.[2] Minhkamaung, aided by some Dutch ships, beat off repeated Portuguese attacks and finally in 1617 occupied Sandwīp.

After that the Portuguese ceased to be his enemies and became his

[1] See vol. III, p. 551.

[2] India Office Hague Transcripts, 1607–16, letter 62; De Jonge, *De Opkomst van het Nederlandsche Gezag in Oost-Indie*, III, 77.

tools. They centred at Chittagong and intermarried with the people there. They served the Arakanese in holding Sandwīp island, Noākhāli and Backergunge districts, and the Sunderbans delta south of Calcutta, and raiding up to Dacca and even Murshidābād, while Tippera sent propitiatory tribute. After they had sacked Dacca, his capital, in 1625, the Mughul governor felt so unsafe that for a time he lived farther inland. For generations an iron chain was stretched across the Hooghly river between Calcutta and Sibpur to prevent their entrance. In a single month, February 1727, they carried off 1800 captives from the southern parts of Bengal; the king chose the artisans, about one-fourth, to be his slaves, and the rest were sold at prices varying from 20 to 70 rupees a head and set to work on the land as slaves;[1] sometimes the sales were to Dutch, English and French merchants in the Indian ports. They would pierce the hands of their captives, pass a strip of cane through the hole, and fling them under the deck strung together like hens; a baby which cried would be decapitated under its mother's eyes, and its body flung overboard. A favourite formation was to sweep the sea in line, so as to cover a large area, but a hundred Bengal ships would flee at the sight of four Magh ships, and if they found they were being overtaken, the crews would fling themselves overboard and drown sooner than meet the Arakanese hand to hand.[2]

Sometimes the Maghs would sail back to the coast where they had captured their prisoners and wait till the villagers brought out sufficient presents to redeem their kinsmen from the ship. This they called collecting revenue, and the Portuguese among them kept regular account books. Their activity decreased when the English began to police the coast, but even in 1795 they were plundering the king of Burma's boats off Arakan, laden with his customs dues of 10 per cent. in kind.[3] They had forts at Jagdia and 'Ālamgīrnagar in the mouth of the Meghna river, and a little colony of 1500, speaking Arakanese and wearing Burmese dress, still survives on four or five islands in the extreme south-east of Backergunge.

Thirithudamma (1622–38) deferred his coronation twelve years because the wise assured him it would be followed by his death a year later. Finally he learnt to avert fate by sacrificing[4] the hearts of thousands of human beings, white cows and white pigeons, and was crowned in 1635, together with twelve vassal chiefs, amid the utmost splendour, his guards including Burmans, Talaings, Hindustanis, and even some Japanese Catholics. It was he who raided Pegū and brought back Anaukpetlun's bell (p. 495), which he set

[1] *Twenty-four Parganas Gazetteer*, p. 39.
[2] Jadunath Sarkar, "Feringhi Pirates of Chatgaon", in *Journal Asiatic Society of Bengal*, 1907, p. 422; and his *History of Aurangzīb*, vol. III.
[3] Symes, *Embassy to Āva*, p. 117.
[4] Manrique, *Itinerario de las Missiones del India Oriental*, ch. XXXI, Hakluyt ed. I, 357–8.

up at a pagoda near Mrohaung.[1] His queen had a royal kinsman as paramour, so he died suddenly, and his little son and heir soon followed him.

The queen thereupon placed her paramour on the throne as Narapatigyi (1638–45), and enforced the Massacre of the Kinsmen.[2] Narapatigyi built at Mrohaung the Mingalamanaung pagoda and, to house some scriptures from Ceylon, the Pitakataik.

Sandathudamma (1652–84), the builder of the Zinamanaung, Thekyamanaung, Ratanamanaung, Shwekyathein and Lokamu pagodas at Mrohaung, is revered as one of the best kings. In the last year of his reign some forty Arakanese monks went to Ceylon at the request of a mission sent by the aid of the Dutch.[3] The Dutch feared a revival of Portuguese influence in Ceylon and wished to strike at Catholicism by reviving Buddhist ordination, which was becoming extinct. They sent to Arakan, as they had a branch at Mrohaung from about 1626 to 1683; it was closed from time to time because the trade was not of great volume, and in 1670 the whole staff was massacred. But while it lasted they obtained more businesslike terms than in Burma, for under the articles[4] of 1653 they could claim their own interpreter at royal audiences and take away their children by women of the country (cf. p. 502).

Indeed, as might be expected of a maritime people, the Arakanese were in several respects less backward than the Burmese. Thus they permitted the export of rice (p. 501) under the control of an officer who regulated it so as to prevent a shortage. And about 1660 money began to be struck in Arakan; the Burmese struck some medallions for enshrinement in the Mingun pagoda in 1790,[5] having learnt the idea from Arakan; the Arakanese had used medallions since the tenth century for commemorative purposes, usually at a king's accession.

Shujā', brother to Aurangzīb, being defeated in his struggle for the throne, had to flee in 1660.[6] The people of Bengal regarded the Maghs as unclean savages, but Shujā' was in such straits that he asked the king of Arakan to shelter him and lend some of his famous ships to take him on the way to Mecca, where he wished to end his days. The king consented. Shujā' was brought to Mrohaung in Portuguese galeasses and greeted with courtesy. But with him were his family, including a beautiful eldest daughter, and half a dozen camel-loads of gold and jewels—wealth such as had never before been seen in Arakan. Shujā' kept away from the king, repelled by

[1] A Hindu officer of irregular horse in the 1824–26 war took it to 'Aligarh, U.P., see Wroughton, "Inscription of the large Arakan bell", in *Journal Asiatic Society Bengal*, 1838, p. 287.

[2] Dinnyawadi Yazawinthit, p. 219. See also vol. III, p. 556.

[3] Similarly in 1753 the Dutch obtained monks from Siam, Tennent, *Christianity in Ceylon*, p. 224; cf. Nga Me, *History of Arakan* (M.S.).

[4] Valentyn, *Oud en Nieuw Oost-Indiën*, vol. V, part I, pp. 140–6.

[5] Harvey, *History of Burma*, p. 275.

[6] See chap. VIII, p. 226.

his table manners. Eight months passed, and on one pretext or another the promised ships were never forthcoming. Finally the king demanded Shujā's daughter in marriage. A blue-blooded Mughul of the imperial house, Shujā' refused. The king told him to go within three days. Unable to move, and refused supplies in the bazar, he resolved to take his chance of overthrowing the king. He had two hundred faithful men, and many of the local Muslims supported him; thrones in Indo-China have been overthrown with fewer men, and good judges on the spot thought he had a reasonable chance. But there were too many in the plot, and the king heard of it in time. Shujā' was thus reduced to firing the city and cutting his way out in the confusion. Most of his party was taken, and though he himself succeeded in reaching the jungle he was ultimately traced and executed. For days it was a sight to see his treasure being melted down and conveyed to the palace strong-room. His daughters were taken into the harem, the marriage of the eldest to the king being celebrated in song and verse that are still greatly admired in Arakan. A year later the king, scenting a plot, starved them all to death, though the eldest was in an advanced stage of pregnancy by himself; and their brothers' heads were hacked off with dahs.[1]

Aurangzīb himself would have executed Shujā', but he did not like others doing it, and also it was necessary to curb the piracy of the Maghs. Shāyista Khān, the Mughul viceroy of Bengal, built a fleet, and in 1665 drove them out of their strong stockades on Sandwīp island. The news spread consternation, and the king in fear began to distrust the feringhis who, suspecting that he would exterminate their families, accepted the offers of Shāyista Khān and deserted to him with their families in forty-two galleys laden with munitions. In 1666 Shāyista Khān's force of 6500 men and 288 boats took Chittagong in a thirty-six hours' siege. They sold 2000 Arakanese into slavery, and captured 1026 cannon, mostly jingals throwing a one-pound ball. Many ships were sunk in action, 135 were captured, and two state elephants were burnt in the sack. Such of the Arakanese garrison as escaped tried to march home, but they were attacked by their former slaves, the kidnapped Muslims of Bengal, who had been settled on the land.[2]

The fall of Chittagong caused indescribable rejoicing in Bengal and ended Arakan's century of greatness. The trackless Ganges delta afforded scope not only to the Arakanese but also to nests of pirates recruited from the scum of every race, and so they continued their sea raids. But never again did they hold Chittagong or even Rāmū,

[1] Schouten, *Voyage aux Indes*, I, 228–37; Bernier, *Travels*, pp. 109–15; Manucci, *Storia do Mogor*, I, 369–76; Bowrey, *Geographical Account of the Countries round the Bay of Bengal*, pp. 139–42; Hamilton, *New Account of East Indies*, II, 27–9; Harvey, "Fate of Shah Shuja", in *Journal Burma Research Society*, 1922.

[2] Jadunath Sarkar, "Conquest of Chātgāon", in *Journal Asiatic Society of Bengal*, 1907, p. 405; and his *History of Aurangzīb*, III, 220–45; Bernier, *Travels*, pp. 174–82; *Chittagong Gazetteer*, p. 31.

and they lost their sword arm by the desertion of the feringhis. Sandathudamma's long reign saw the power of his race pass its zenith, and his death is followed by a century of chaos. There were twenty-five kings in the next hundred and nineteen years. The profits of piracy had gone but the piratical instinct remained, rendering government impossible.

Shujā's followers in 1661 were retained as Archers of the Guard who drew four rupees a month, equivalent to many times that amount of present currency. They murdered and set up kings at will and their numbers were recruited by fresh arrivals from upper India. In 1692 they burnt the palace and for twenty years roamed over the country, carrying fire and sword wherever they went. Finally they were suppressed by a lord who set up as king Sandawiziya (1710–31); he deported them to Ramree; there, and at Thinganet and Tharagon near Akyab, their descendants still exist, under the name Kaman (Persian *kamān* = a bow), speaking Arakanese but retaining their Islamic faith and Afghān features.

Sandawiziya was murdered and the country relapsed. King after king was murdered and village fought against village. Earthquakes are for centuries mentioned in the chronicles of the various states of Burma, but those of 1761–62 were particularly awesome in Arakan and the people felt that they were doomed. Sometimes the lords would induce a hardy spirit to take the throne, and as often others would combine to make his task impossible.

The last king, Thamada (1782–85), bearing as if in irony the name of the first king on earth, had less authority than ever, for he was of the despised race of Ramree. A band of lords went to Āva asking for intervention; perhaps they were patriots desiring to see their land at rest; perhaps they merely desired the sweets of office. Their request was granted with a vengeance, for Bodawpaya was now king in Burma. Many a village came out with bands of music to greet his armies as deliverers. But the methods of the Burmese were such that soon the very men who had invited them into the country were leading insurgents against them.[1]

THE TOUNGOO DYNASTY (1531–1752)

The Shan migration, lasting two centuries, had now ended, leaving Burma split into chieftainships. Tabinshwehti[2] set himself to revive the overlordship. Toungoo was thronged with refugees, so that he had no lack of men; he was in control of Kyaukse, the richest area in upper Burma and the key to Āva; and, to crown all, his opponents were Shans, a race which could not unite.

First he advanced against lower Burma. It was the richest part of the country and also it contained Portuguese adventurers who were willing to be hired. Sometimes he had as many as seven hundred. To

[1] See vol. v, p. 558. [2] See vol. III, p. 558.

obtain their services was to win the day, for they had firearms, hitherto unknown in Burma, and no race in Indo-China could stand up to them.

By 1541 he had annexed the Pegū state. He was able to enter Pegū city without a siege because the Talaings, after suffering several defeats, lost heart, and their king Takayutpi,[1] instead of putting heart into them, took to distrusting his officers and executing them; instead of leading his men to the end, Takayutpi deserted the city and lived in a stockade at Ingabu, Maubin district; a year later he died while hunting elephants and the fishermen there still worship a *nat* spirit called Po Yutpi. Martaban, a thriving port, rich with the accumulated stocks of merchants of many races, gave more trouble; it fought to the end, aided by seven Portuguese ships; these were small craft, manned largely by Eurasians and slaves, and Tabinshwehti drove them off with fire-rafts, while other rafts, with scaffolding higher than the ramparts, were run alongside the fortifications facing the river; the sack raged for three days.[2]

Tabinshwehti exercised his royal privilege of putting spires on the great Talaing pagodas; to the Shwedagon he offered his queen and redeemed her with 10 *viss* (1 *viss* = 3.65 lb.) of gold.[3] In 1542 he took Prome, although the Rājā of Arakan and the chiefs of upper Burma, headed by the Āva *sawbwa*, attacked him while he was besieging the town. In 1544 he annexed upper Burma as far as Minbu and Myingyan; he had already been crowned at Pegū as king of lower Burma, and now while halting at Pagan he was crowned as king of upper Burma. On returning home in 1546 he was crowned as king of both, using Talaing as well as Burmese rites. Only half his task was done, but the rest was sure, and men again beheld the glory of the ancient ritual; after three centuries of *sawbwas* (Shan chiefs) there was once more a king in Burma.

In the cold weather of 1546–47 he attacked Arakan. Many of his war-canoes were wrecked on the west coast. All his land forces arrived but Mrohaung was a strong town, and the only chance of taking it was when the walls were in disrepair. But Arakan was under an energetic raja (p. 477) who saw that his defences were in repair, and after a short time under the walls Tabinshwehti accepted the intercession of the monks and returned home.

He returned the more quickly because Siam, hearing that he and all his valiant men were away in Arakan, had raided Tavoy; and in 1547–48 the Burmese advanced against Siam.[4] The hosts crossed

[1] See vol. III, p. 556. [2] Pinto, *Voyages and Adventures*.

[3] Halliday, "Slapat Rajawan Datow Smin Ron", in *Journal Burma Research Society*, 1923.

[4] When, in 1767, the Burmese sacked Ayuthia (p. 515), they destroyed the palace archives, so that Siamese chronology before the eighteenth century is vague. Until recently the Siamese dates for the Burmese invasions of the sixteenth century were a decade or two earlier than the Burmese dates, which I follow. Recent research by Siamese gentlemen has, however, confirmed the Burmese dates, which are also borne out by contemporary Burmese inscriptions and European travellers. See the discussion in Harvey, *History of Burma*, p. 343; and Wood, *History of Siam*, pp. 23–25.

from Martaban to Moulmein on a bridge of boats over which they could ride their ponies at a gallop. His Majesty's elephant was ferried across on a raft, but the other elephants were sent upstream where the fords were shallow. Jingals were mounted on many of these elephants. The cannon were kept close to the king, and he moved in great state, surrounded by the choicest elephants, richly attired lords, and 400 Portuguese guards whose helmets and muskets were inlaid with gold, for they provided a bodyguard as well as artillery. Hundreds of workmen went ahead every day to pitch the wooden camp palace,[1] richly painted and gilded, and at each halt there was a *pwe* festival.

The Burmese advanced up the Ataran river, through Three Pagodas Pass and down the Meklawng river to Kanburi. Thence they struck at Ayuthia. The Siamese possessed cannon, made of the copper which was annually imported from China. The weakest part of the wall was defended by fifty Portuguese; Tabinshwehti tried to bribe them, but they treated the offer with derision and one of the Siamese commanders, flinging open the gate, dared Tabinshwehti to bring the money. After a month the Burmese withdrew and tried to plunder Kampengpet, a wealthy town; but here again were Portuguese, who used flaming projectiles so that the guns had to be kept under shelters of damp hide. Tabinshwehti, saying the Siamese were devils who, when their own weapons failed, used new ones never known since the beginning of the world, retreated, and it would doubtless have gone hard with him had he not captured the Siamese king's son and brothers in some open fighting. At once Siamese envoys came with red and green woollen cloths, *longyis* (men's skirts), and aromatic woods, offering friendship in return for the captive princes. Tabinshwehti released not only them but also his other prisoners, and was thereupon left unmolested in his retreat through Raheng.

Tabinshwehti dreamed of a united Burma. When conquering the Talaing kingdom he made no attempt to administer his new subjects by Burmese governors. Any Talaing lord who made timely submission could count on being left in his fief. Consequently from the first he had a large Talaing following; fully half his levies and best officers were Talaings. He left the beautiful buildings of the Talaing kings standing when he captured Pegū. Talaings had their full say in his councils, he took care to be crowned with the ritual of a Talaing king, and he gave way to the importunities of his Talaing princesses, letting them dress in their own fashion instead of the Burmese court dress. Finally, hearing an old prophecy that no king with a Burmese hairknot should rule the Talaing land, he bobbed his hair like a Talaing and wore the diadem of a Talaing king.[2]

[1] Faria y Sousa (Stevens), *The Portuguese Asia*, II, 135.
[2] Hmannan, II, 240.

On returning from Siam Tabinshwehti took to hunting with a young Portuguese captain, who had a gun and seldom missed his mark. Tabinshwehti thought a gun a miraculous thing, and in admiration gave him a royal handmaid to wife. The feringhi taught his bride to cook feringhi dishes for the king to eat, and gave him juice of the grape to drink, also spirits sweetened with honey. The king drank and his heart was glad, but he lost his wits, respecting not other men's wives, listening to evil tales and executing innocent men. Bayinnaung, his foster-brother and principal commander, remonstrated with him but he answered: "I have made friends with drink. Brother, do thou manage the affairs of state. Bring me no petitions. Leave me to my jollity." Sometimes he attended levees, sometimes he could not. The Burmese, Shan and Talaing lords at court combined to ask Bayinnaung to take the throne, but he was faithful, and would not.[1]

The king went to stay at Pantanaw, Maubin district, in the care of Talaing chamberlains, and Bayinnaung went to deal with a rebellion headed by a monk, a descendant of the fallen Talaing dynasty, who, flinging off the robe, assumed the title Smim Htaw, and occupied Dagon (Rangoon) and Dalla. The Talaing chamberlains enticed Tabinshwehti into a jungle saying a white elephant had been traced, and there they cut off his head;[2] they then raised the Talaings, seized Pegū, and set the leading chamberlain on the throne.

Bayinnaung (1551–81). The fiefs of central Burma all shut their gates and never lifted a finger to help Bayinnaung; his own brothers and kinsmen tried to set up as independent kings in such important charges as Prome and Toungoo itself. There he was, a king without a kingdom, grappling with one Talaing rebel in the west while another sat on his throne in the east, his Burmese people looked on with folded hands, and his own brothers seceded. At once he sent overseas for his Portuguese guards, who had rejoined their own people in Malaya; they came in haste, and in his unfeigned relief he greeted[3] their leader with the words: "Ah, brother Diogo, brother Diogo, we two, we happy two, I on my elephant and thou on thy horse, we could conquer the world together!" With them, and the few faithful levies that stood by him, he was safe, although little better than a fugitive in the jungles. But many joined him, including even Talaings, for men recognise character when they see it. As the months went by, he regained Toungoo and Prome, and finally he advanced on Pegū.

Smim Htaw had overthrown the usurping chamberlain and occupied the Pegū palace. When Bayinnaung's host came near the walls, the Talaings went out to meet it. The two chiefs fought hand to hand and finally Bayinnaung, freeing his elephant, drew back and charged,

[1] Hmannan, II, 268–70.
[2] He is worshipped as the Tabinshwehti Nat spirit, Temple, *Thirty-Seven Nats*, p. 64.
[3] Couto, *Da Asia*, vol. IV, part I, p. 136.

breaking the tusk of his foeman's elephant and driving him off the field followed by all his men. He then sacked Pegū, killing men, women, children and even animals.

Talaing opposition collapsed. Smim Htaw could get few more followers, but he made a gallant fight, hunted as he was throughout the Delta. Many a jungle there has its tradition of his hiding. Sometimes he would catch the Burmese boats stranded at low tide in a creek, and wipe them out, sometimes he would surprise an outpost. But as the months passed, the end drew near. His family fell into the hands of his pursuers. He fled alone in a canoe along the coast to Martaban. Once they fell on him during the evening meal, but he slipped away leaving his clothes in their hands. He hid in the hills round Sittaung, poor and unknown, till he took a village girl to wife and told her his secret; she guilelessly told her father, who reported to the village officer. Bayinnaung had him paraded through the jeering streets, and saying he had done evil put him to an evil death. Thus ended the lineage of Wareru.[1]

Having thus regained the position from which he should have started, Bayinnaung set out on his career of conquest. The size of his armies varied with the area of his kingdom for the time being. At its maximum, when it included upper Burma, the Shan States, and Siam, it supplied him with a mass levy approaching possibly one hundred thousand.[2] His efforts were on a bigger scale than had hitherto been known to Burma. Long records of faithful service, and the ties of ancient friendship, were pleaded in vain by officers who failed; the least they had to fear was deprivation of all titles and property, and exile to some fever-stricken spot. As for the rank and file, the severity they suffered was provoked by the fact that many of the levies were like herds of driven cattle, and the only way of keeping them together and bringing them to action was to use methods of frightfulness.

By 1555 he had annexed Āva, and by 1559 the whole of upper Burma, the present Shan States, Manipur, Chiengmai and Viengchang (Linzin). From this time dates Burmese suzerainty over the Shans; the Pagan monarchy had controlled little more than the foothills, and even now Burmese suzerainty was seldom more than nominal until the time of Alaungpaya (1752–60).

It is characteristic that while Bayinnaung was proceeding down the Salween against Chiengmai, his garrison in Mone was murdered

[1] See vol. III, p. 551.

[2] Elizabethan travellers who say they actually saw half a million men march out of Pegū are only repeating bazar talk. The Burmese chronicles give a list of Bayinnaung's levies totalling over a million men, but in the Anglo-Burmese wars of the nineteenth century our troops found Burmese commanders habitually overestimating numbers by at least one decimal. Even in the early nineteenth century the population of Burma can hardly have exceeded four millions. Harvey, *History of Burma*, p. 333, and Burney, *Population of Burman Empire*, in *Journal Statistical Society*, 1842.

and the bridge he had built across the Salween was destroyed by Mone, Yawnghwe and Lawksawk. Revolts were continuous. In 1562, 1572, 1574–76 he was campaigning against Mohnyin and Mogaung, and even to the north, wearing out his men in pursuits over snow-clad hills; finally the chiefs submitted, tired of starving in the wilderness. The Mogaung chief was exhibited for a week in fetters at the gates of Pegū; as for some scores of his principal followers, Bayinnaung, saying he was very merciful, refrained from executing them and sent them to be sold as slaves in the Ganges delta.

As was invariably the case, the Burmese no sooner occupied an area than they required levies, and the Burmese Shans were at once employed against the Siamese Shans. The chiefs presented daughters to the rival harem, sent their sons to be brought up in the palace, and paid periodic tribute; Momeik, the most valuable of all, paid rubies; Chiengmai paid elephants, horses, lacquer and silks. Everywhere he deported numbers of the people in order to populate his homeland. From Chiengmai he took artisans, especially her famous lacquer workers;[1] it is probably these who introduced into Burma the finer sort of lacquer ware called yun, the name of the Yun or Lao Shan tribes round Chiengmai.[2]

In the 1556 campaign he went by river as far as Katha district, accompanied by his harem and worshipping at the principal pagodas on the way. On the return journey in 1557 he set up at the Shwezigon pagoda, Pagan, the great bronze bell bearing in Pali, Burmese and Talaing an inscription every line of which breathes imperial pride in his conquests and in the steps he took to promote religion among the Shans, building monasteries, and suppressing funeral sacrifice. It had been customary to bury with a major *sawbwa* (Shan chief) as many as ten elephants, a hundred horses, and a hundred each of men and women slaves, the numbers being less for minor *sawbwas*.

He also suppressed the sacrifice of white animals (buffaloes, kine, goats, pigs, fowls) to the Mahagiri spirit on Popa Hill;[3] hitherto these animals had been killed for a feast, and their skulls were hung in strings all round the shrine; the worshippers drank intoxicants at the feast, and once a year the king and court shared in it as an act of state worship. Bayinnaung introduced prohibition and punished drunkenness with death. He enforced the divine command against taking life even to the extent of abolishing the Baqr 'Īd among Muslim settlers.

The king of Ayuthia, styled Lord of the White Elephants, had recently possessed no fewer than seven; it was the glory of these elephants which attracted white merchants from the ends of the

[1] See vol. III, p. 555.

[2] Morris, "Lacquerware industry of Burma", in *Journal Burma Research Society*, 1919; Kyaw Dun, "Lacquerware called Yun", in *ibid.* 1920.

[3] Hmannan, II, 312; Wawhayalinatta, p. 69.

earth and brought Siam unprecedented prosperity; there could be no other cause, for in the days of his predecessors, who had far fewer, there was less trade and European merchants had not come. He still had four, and Bayinnaung's soul was stirred to its depths at not having so many himself. He was considering not only his own glory but also the interests of his people; he believed it to be essential to their prosperity that he should acquire these elephants.[1] Therefore he invaded Siam. As he had a much larger area from which to get levies, his task was easier than Tabinshwehti's.

In 1563–64 the huge host captured Kampengpet and Sukhotai and then swarmed down on Ayuthia, losing considerably from the Siamese and their feringhi gunners, but capturing stockades, war-canoes and three foreign ships. The city quickly yielded in quite unnecessary terror of Bayinnaung's Portuguese artillery, which though noisy was too light to do real damage to the walls. The terms were the surrender of four white elephants, the captivity of the king and some princes as hostages, the presentation of a daughter, the cession of Tenasserim shipping tolls, and annual tribute of thirty war elephants. Bayinnaung left the Siamese king's son to rule as vassal with a Burmese garrison of 3000 men, and went home with the captive king and court, and with thousands of the population roped together in gangs with wooden collars; among them were actors and actresses, and it is probably these who introduced into Burma the songs and dances called Ayuthia. The loot included thirty crude images of men and elephants in bronze.

The captive princes of Ayuthia, Āva and Chiengmai were kept at Pegū and given reasonable treatment, even being allowed to live in double-roofed houses painted white, the prerogative of royalty.[2] But Siam was not settled with the fall of Ayuthia. Till the end of the reign the armies were constantly campaigning all over the country from the northern Laos downwards. Year after year Bayinnaung led a weary chase through trackless hills where his men were reduced to eating grass and died in thousands of starvation and disease. Year after year there was cruel fighting against the Siamese stockades, against their war-canoes and flaming rafts. He usually succeeded in occupying towns, setting his puppet with a Burmese garrison on their little thrones, and dragging away the population, when it had not hidden in the jungle, to work as slaves in Burma if they survived the long march. But he could do little more than this, he could give no settled government to the surviving victims, and some of the chiefs he never caught. He generously allowed the captive king of Siam, who had become a monk, to return home on pilgrimage; no sooner had he arrived than he flung off the robe and so another siege of Ayuthia became necessary. It lasted ten months

[1] For the significance of the White Elephant, see Harvey, *History of Burma*, p. 274.
[2] For Burmese sumptuary laws, see Shway Yoe, *The Burman, his Life and Notions*.

(1568–69). The Burmese losses were so heavy that the men used to take shelter under the piles of their comrades' corpses. The troops sickened of the carnage and officers were executed right and left for failure. The town could not be taken by storm and, although short of food, held its own until Bayinnaung employed treachery. He promised large rewards, and one of his prisoners, a Siamese lord, entered the town saying he had escaped from the Burmese. The Siamese gave him high command, and one night he opened the gates.

In 1560 the Portuguese captured the Buddha Tooth of Ceylon[1] and took it to Goa. Bayinnaung sent envoys on a Portuguese ship to Goa, offering, in return for the Tooth, eight lakhs of rupees and, whenever needed, shiploads of rice to provision the fortress of Malacca. Other Buddhist and Hindu kings made offers. The Portuguese wished to accept but were overridden by their archbishop who, in the presence of a large assembly including the Burmese envoys, ground the Tooth to powder, burnt the powder, and cast the ashes into the river. But soon men said that the Tooth was miraculously restored to its temple at Kandy.

Learning from his astrologers that he was destined to wed a princess of Ceylon, Bayinnaung sent envoys to find her. They went to Colombo and told of their master's glory. The chief there had no daughter, but his chamberlain had one whom the chief cherished as his own. He had no authority over the Temple of the Tooth at Kandy, where another chief ruled, but he showed the envoys a shrine which he said contained the Tooth. The envoys took the daughter and the Tooth. Bayinnaung sent gorgeous presents in return. The Tooth reached Bassein in 1576. Bayinnaung went to meet it in a great procession of magnificent canoes crowded with lords and ladies clad in court dress. He bathed ceremonially, scented himself, and bowed before the shrine. Princes waded into the river and bore it ashore at Pegū, walking over the state vestments which the lords took off and spread before them. It was encased in a golden casket studded with the gems of Dammazedi and the kings of old, and of Momeik and of Ayuthia, the vassal kings, and finally it was deposited at the Mahazedi pagoda, Pegū. This was the day of days in Bayinnaung's life; his wide conquests, even the white elephants from Siam, faded into insignificance; he said: "Heaven is good to me. Anawrahta could obtain only a replica Tooth from Ceylon, Alaungsithu went to China in vain, but I, because of my piety and wisdom, I have been granted this!"[2]

Bayinnaung's great Talaing officer, the *wungyi* (minister) Binnya Dala, compiled the Razadarit Ayedawpon chronicle.[3] Bayinnaung

[1] See vol. III, p. 548.

[2] Linschoten, *Voyage to the East Indies*, I, p. 293; Faria y Sousa (Stevens), *The Portuguese Asia*, II, 207–9, 251–2; Hmannan, III, 8, 33–35; Gerson da Cunha, "Memoir on the History of the Tooth Relic of Ceylon", in *Journal Bombay branch of the Royal Asiatic Society*, 1875.

[3] See vol. III, p. 553.

introduced a measure of legal uniformity by summoning distinguished monks and officials from all over his dominions to prescribe an official collection of law books; they prescribed the Wareru *dhammathat*[1] and compiled the Dhammathatkyaw and Kosaungchok. The decisions given in his court were collected in the Hanthawaddy Hsinbyumyashin *pyatton*.[2] He also tried to standardise weights and measures, such as the cubit, tical, and basket, throughout the realm.

Styling himself the king of kings, he governed only Pegū and the Talaing country directly, leaving the rest of the realm to vassal kings with palaces at Toungoo, Prome, Āva and Chiengmai. He regarded Chiengmai as the most important, having fifty-seven provinces; these, like the thirty-two provinces of Pegū,[3] were big villages. Chiengmai was a Shan state, and when he spoke of having twenty-four crowned heads at his command, he was referring to *sawbwas*. Each of the twenty gates of his new city at Pegū was named after the vassal who built it, such as the Prome gate, the Chiengmai gate, the Toungoo gate, the gates of Salin, Dalla, Mohnyin, Tavoy, Hsenwi, Linzin, Tenasserim, Ayuthia, Martaban, Pagan—it was the men of Pagan who had to plant the toddy palms all along the walls and at the street corners. As a model Buddhist king he distributed copies of the scriptures, fed monks, and built pagodas in Chiengmai, Koshanpye and other conquered states. Some of these pagodas are still to be seen, and in later ages the Burmese would point to them as proof of their claim to rule those countries still. He supervised mass ordinations at the Kalyānī *thein*.[4] Following a royal custom he would break up his crown and use its jewels to adorn the spire of a pagoda; he did this for the Shwedagon, the Shwemawdaw, and the Kyaiktiyo in Thaton district. Again, as at the Shwemawdaw, he would build as many surrounding monasteries as there were years in his life at the time, fifty-two; or he would bear the cost of ordaining a similar number of monks. After the 1564 earthquake, which coincided with his queen's death, he repaired the Shwedagon, and added a new spire. His chief foundation was the Mahazedi at Pegū, at which he enshrined a begging bowl of supernatural origin sent him in 1567 by some Ceylon kinglet, the Tooth (p. 489) and golden images of himself, the royal family, and such of the great officers of state as were in his inner circle.

Bayinnaung made no distinction of race in appointment to office. His best commander was a Talaing, Binnya Dala. As his predecessors had doubtless done for ages, he entered into artificial blood-brotherhood (*thwethauk*) with over a score of his principal officers, and the list includes Talaings. They penetrated his entourage to such an extent that the word used by European travellers for a court grandee

[1] See vol. III, pp. 551–2.
[2] Forchammer, *Jardine Prize Essay on Burmese Law*.
[3] See vol. III, p. 553.
[4] *Ibid*. p. 556.

is *semini*, an Italianisation of *smim*, the Talaing for lord. Such being his methods, he might have reconciled both races and founded a national dynasty. He failed to do so because he alienated human nature by his wars. The brunt fell on Talaings; hence while at first they followed him because they believed he could give them settled government, at last the only ones who followed him were hardy spirits desirous of foreign loot.

Unlike most Burmese kings, who lived in the backwoods (pp. 496, 513), Bayinnaung lived in a seaport and came into contact with the outer world. The extent to which overseas traders frequented the Delta indicates that his trade regulations were reasonable. Merchants sailing from India first sighted Negrais and saw there, as we see now, the superb Hmawdin pagoda flashing on the headland, a landmark for a whole day's sail.[1] They went upstream to Bassein and then, turning east, passed through the Myaungmya creeks to Pegū. Those creeks were, at least on the main route, crowded with villages almost touching each other, a teeming hive of happy people. Customs officers, though strict, were not obstructive, and there was free export of such commodities as jewels and rice, a thing subsequently forbidden by the benighted kings of Āva (p. 501). Bassein is scarcely mentioned, the chief ports being on the eastern side, Syriam, Dalla, Martaban, and above all Pegū, where the merchants were allowed, by special privilege, to have brick warehouses, the populace being restricted to houses of bamboo or timber. Ralph Fitch and the merchants of Venice never tire of describing Pegū city, the long moat full of crocodiles, the walls, the watch-towers, the gorgeous palace, the processions with elephants and palanquins and grandees in shining robes, the shrines filled with images of massy gold and gems, the unending hosts of armed men, and the vision of the great king himself receiving petitions as he sat throned on high amid his lords.

Yet despite its splendour, the kingship was not loved. Bayinnaung and the princes risked their lives freely at the head of the hosts conspicuously on elephants, and Bayinnaung shared many a hardship with his men. But what was sport to him was death to the common people. The disorganisation caused by his wars was such that Pegū sometimes starved. Even the fertile Delta cannot grow rice without men to plant it, and they were not there to plant it, having all been dragged away on foreign service. Of those that went, few returned, for if battle casualties were great, the wastage from hunger and dysentery was even greater. Even if they were not sent to fight, they were herded together and led away in one of the everlasting deportations which the kingship found necessary to re-populate ravaged areas.

At least once Bayinnaung had to hurry home from a Siamese campaign to deal with rebellion at his own capital. He had settled

[1] Hakluytus Posthumus, x, 150.

in the neighbourhood some twenty thousand Shans and Siamese. Talaings made common cause and led them when in 1564 they rose and burnt his palace, the palace which the Portuguese regarded as in itself a city, with roofs of solid gold. He penned thousands of the rebels in bamboo cages to be burnt alive according to immemorial custom, but ended by burning only seventy leaders, with their families, because the monks protested and popular feeling supported them.[1]

His campaigns were the price men had to pay for the unification of Burma. Thus far he succeeded. Beyond that he failed, because, like his age, he was not constructive. Every other year throughout his reign he was hastening somewhere to maintain himself in power. A ruler without an administration, he could not be everywhere at once, and no sooner did he turn his back than the chances were even that a rebellion would break out. The unity he gave was artificial and within a few years of his death it collapsed. If it rose again and endured for another century and a half, this was because his immediate successors happened to be men of character and because the listlessness of the people prevented organised opposition.

Bayinnaung died at the age of sixty-six leaving ninety-seven children. Although he already had more territory than he could hold, he was actually sending an expedition to annex Arakan when he died.

Rebellion at home compelled his son, Nandabayin (1581–99), to recall the expedition against Arakan. There was scarcely a year in which he was not campaigning from Mogaung in the north to Hmawbi in the south. He used his father's methods of terrible executions and wholesale conscription. Life was unbearable and men flocked to become monks, partly to seek religious consolation in their misery, partly to evade conscription.

The crown prince used Talaings for forced labour on his land, stored the crop, and made people buy from him alone. The king deported people from all over the country to populate Pegū. Distrusting the Talaings, he executed them in numbers; he branded them on the right hand with their name, rank and village, and sent those who were too old for service to be exchanged for horses in upper Burma; he exiled their monks to Āva and the Shan States. It is at this period that the periodic migrations[2] of the Talaings to Siam begin, migrations which lasted until the English conquest in 1824 and were due to the sustained severity of the Burmese.

The one hope of keeping the country together was to evacuate Siam and retrench in every direction. But neither Bayinnaung nor

[1] Hakluytus Posthumus, x, 160; Hmannan, III, 78.

[2] Halliday, *The Talaings*; and his "Immigration of the Mons [Talaings] into Siam", in *Journal Siam Society*, 1913; Ravenswaay, "Translation of Van Vliet's description of Siam", in *ibid.* 1910.

his son could see it. The only method by which the king could control remoter areas was by fighting them periodically, a process which used up the only people he could really call his own, the population round the capital. There were not sufficient left alive to till the soil there, and remoter areas would not send food. In 1596 a plague of field rats destroyed what little crop had been planted; there was a terrible famine, and it was only one of a series; wide stretches of country in lower Burma became a desert.

Nandabayin might have held the rest of his kingdom, but it was Ayuthia that ruined him. She found a leader in the famous prince Pra Naret. Year after year Nandabayin led his men into Siam; each incursion further reduced his remaining man-power but none succeeded in taking Ayuthia. He could never raise 25,000 men—a mere third of the number his father had led—and these were too few to surround Ayuthia, so that instead of the besieged it was the besiegers who starved. In 1593 his son was killed in hand-to-hand combat with Pra Naret; the Burmese fled in panic at the sight and were once more cut to pieces in a long and terrible retreat. After that there were no men left to invade Siam; indeed it is Ayuthia which invades Pegū.[1]

And now, in the hour of his utmost need, not one of the king's sons or brothers rallied to his side. If the king was not satisfactory they could have combined to set up someone who was; but instead of trying to keep the country together, each was out entirely for himself—it is doubtful how far the concept of a kingdom ever penetrated in a country where any brigand, who levied blackmail as far as eye can reach, was, within living memory, styled a king. The prince of Toungoo, first cousin to the king, actually wrote to Arakan proposing a joint attack on the king and a division of the spoil. He chose Arakan because it was farthest, and after getting its loot it would return home and not be a rival for the throne. The Arakanese shipped a force which occupied Syriam, effected a junction with the Toungoo levies, and with them besieged Pegū in 1599. The townsfolk and officers deserted. The king and a faithful son surrendered on a promise of good treatment and were put to death.

Hearing that there was a carcass, the king of Ayuthia came swooping down to see what he could get. As the victors would not share with him, he ravaged the country up to Toungoo and went home.

The Arakanese deported 3000 households of the wretched Pegū folk and went off with a white elephant and a daughter of the fallen king for their own royal harem; they also took brazen cannon and the thirty bronze images of Ayuthia (p. 488); and retaining Syriam they

[1] Faria y Sousa (Stevens), *The Portuguese Asia*, III, 120; *Peter Floris* (Moreland, Hakluyt Society, 1934), pp. 52–5; Frankfurter, "Events in Ayuddhya 686–966", in *Journal Siam Society*, 1909; Jones, "Siamese History", in the *Chinese Repository*, 1836–38; Saulière, "Jesuits on Pegu", in *Bengal Past and Present*, 1919; Hmannan, III, 97.

left it in charge of one of their Portuguese mercenaries, De Brito. The prince of Toungoo took away the Ceylon Tooth and begging bowl (p. 490) with more than twelve caravan-loads of loot.

Pegū was burnt. Bayinnaung's palace, his radiant buildings decked with the spoil of conquered kings, went up in flames. It was a pitiful ending. The misery in lower Burma beggared description: the bodies of those who died of wounds or starvation filled the rivers and impeded the passage of boats, and men ate human flesh.

The country south of Martaban paid homage to Ayuthia. Burma was once more a series of petty states, held by princes of the royal house. The best was the prince of Āva; a son of Bayinnaung, he reduced upper Burma and the Shan States; he induced China to extradite the fugitive Bhamo *sawbwa*, and the Chinese themselves admit that after 1628 Burma sent no more "tribute" missions.[1] His son Anaukpetlun (1605–28), having the north on which to draw for levies, found little difficulty in annexing the depopulated land of lower Burma. In 1607 he took Prome. In 1610 he took Toungoo, carrying home to Āva the Ceylon Tooth and begging bowl, two-thirds of the cattle, and many people, including all who had been deported from Pegū, Prome and Āva.

De Brito (p. 478) had made himself independent at Syriam, defeating all attacks whether by his old Arakanese master or by other chiefs. He had a hundred Portuguese, some negro and Indian slaves, and the Talaings who came in from the neighbourhood. He was liked, because he gave folk settled government. He had several ships cruising round the coast to prevent merchant vessels from putting in save at Syriam, where he could make them pay customs duty. He became so successful that the Portuguese viceroy at Goa acknowledged him as official Portuguese governor of Syriam. But he continued to do as he pleased, and he did wrong in pillaging pagodas. He would scrape the gold off images and beat it into gold-leaf for sale to pilgrims; and he melted down some of the beautiful bronze bells at the Shwedagon to save himself the expense of importing bronze to make cannon. He was allied to Martaban and Toungoo.

In 1613 Anaukpetlun advanced on Syriam. Success had made De Brito so careless that he had allowed himself to run out of powder when the king arrived with 12,000 men. However, the stockade was strong and the defenders beat off all attacks with boiling oil. Natshinnaung, the fallen prince of Toungoo and cousin to the king, was inside, having taken refuge with De Brito. The king especially desired to capture him, and offered De Brito friendship if he would surrender him. But De Brito replied: "We Portuguese keep faith. I have given my word to Natshinnaung and do not break it." The king cut off a prisoner's ears and sent him to De Brito saying: "Look at this, and consider whether it will pay thee to harbour mine enemy."

[1] Burney, "Wars between Burma and China", in *Journal Asiatic Society of Bengal*, 1837.

But De Brito never wavered. Once, when all the Portuguese were in church, the Burmese broke into the stockade, but the Portuguese came rushing out and none of the Burmese escaped alive. At the end of six weeks the Burmese mined the stockade and managed to pull out two of the posts; they poured in and captured the town. The king offered the two leaders their lives if they would beg pardon, but they refused, Natshinnaung saying: "You can kill my body, but my soul never. De Brito and I are brothers for we have entered into the *thwethauk* (p. 490) bloodbond. We have lived one life. Let us die one death." His wish was granted. De Brito was crucified and lingered three days. Perhaps he was still alive when some Portuguese relief ships arrived but went back, seeing that the town had fallen.[1]

The Portuguese, with Eurasians, women, and children, a total of 400, were enslaved and sent to live in the Shwebo villages called, after them, *bayingyi* (feringhi) villages. They were used as hereditary gunners to the king and were in charge of such cannon as he possessed. Their numbers were occasionally increased, as every white man who came into the power of the Burmese was sent there (p. 506), and by 1800 their descendants numbered two thousand, including women and children. Their chaplains were Goanese until 1721, when Italian Barnabites founded the European mission.

From about 1627 the Dutch, from 1647 the English, East India Companies had branches in Burma under junior representatives. These branches were closed from time to time, and, although profits were occasionally considerable, the disturbed state of the country made steady trade impossible. Both factories were at Syriam, and in 1677 the Dutch finally withdrew.[2]

Anaukpetlun tried to take Tenasserim, but the Siamese, aided by forty Portuguese, drove him off with heavy loss. He regained control down to Chiengmai and to Ye in Moulmein district. His methods were those of Nandabayin, and of many an energetic Burmese king. His people in delighted terror said that he had only to wave his sword and the tide would stop. Yet outside his palace at Pegū there hung a bell with an inscription in Burmese and Talaing calling on all who had a grievance to strike the bell and he would hear (p. 479).

When in his palace on the west side of the river at Pegū he detected his son Minredeippa in a love intrigue with one of the harem ladies, and told him he deserved roasting alive. Such punishment was not unusual, and Minredeippa, fearing it would really be inflicted, collected some friends, entered the king's room at night, and did him to death.

[1] Faria y Sousa (Stevens), *The Portuguese Asia*, III, 191; Pawtugi Yazawin and Furnivall, "A Forgotten Chronicle", in *Journal Burma Research Society*, 1912; *ibid.* 1926, pp. 101 *sqq.*; Hmannan, III, 118; Dinnyawadi Yazawinthit, p. 210.

[2] Hall, *Early English Intercourse with Burma.*

At once the ministers summoned a general assembly of the court. Early action was necessary, and they took it: they elected the parricide to the throne. Their reasoning was that the king's brothers, his natural successors, were away campaigning in the Shan States—at one time they had gone as far as Kenghung north-east of Kengtung—and the kingdom would be in turmoil before they could be recalled. Public morality apart, the reasoning was invalid, for young Minredeippa had not the wit to hold a throne, whereas his two uncles were mature men, each in command of an army, and the news reached them easily in nine days. So far from avoiding disorder, the court's decision caused it. The country respected the uncles, for they were men of authority; it knew nothing of Minredeippa, and half a dozen governors took the opportunity to revolt. Deprived of support from lower Burma, the two uncles had to waste sixteen months reducing the north country. Meanwhile they seized the families of the upper Burma companies in the palace guard, making the fact known in Pegū, and thus shaking the allegiance of Minredeippa's guards. He had not the courage to leave his palace and attack them. Town after town in upper Burma fell to them, and when they surrounded Āva, Minredeippa, foreseeing their success, decided to flee to Arakan; but his own followers, in disgust at his cowardice and tyranny, seized him and sent a deputation to Āva asking Thalun, one of the uncles, to take the throne. He did so, and immediately on arriving in Pegū executed Minredeippa, sternly rejecting his plea to be allowed to become a monk.

Thalun (1629–48) reigned with the help of his brother until the latter's death some years later. His coronation was scarcely over when Talaings rushed the palace; they were driven out, fled to Moulmein, and held it for some time before they migrated to Siam in large numbers. He moved the capital back to Āva and there it stayed. The Delta had lost its advantages now that the idea of attacking Ayuthia was dead, and Pegū ceased to be a seaport when, about 1600, the silting up of the river was complete. The proper site to move to was Syriam, but the court did not realise that the country's future lay on the sea coast (p. 513). The return to Āva signified the abandonment of Tabinshwehti's dream of a national kingship. The attempted union with the Talaings had failed, and the court relapsed into its tribal homeland, upper Burma.

The return to upper Burma restored Kyaukse to the importance it had lost so long as the kingship was situated among the Delta rice fields. Instead of dedicating prisoners of war as slaves to pagodas, Thalun found a new use for them: he settled them as tenants at Kyaukse, where their families supplied labour for the canals and they themselves served in the guard at court.

Indeed Thalun must rank as one of the best kings. The wars of his predecessors left the country bloodless for a century. He kept the peace and reorganised the administration. He may not have created, but at least he revived the old village and district administration which had been shattered; and he placed it on record in the great revenue inquest of 1638, the first in Burmese history. None of the record has been found, but probably it resembled Bodawpaya's 1784 inquest[1] and consisted of the sworn statements of every village headman throughout the country as to the number of people in his village, the area of cultivated land, the crops grown, the revenue paid, etc.

How destructive was the disorder which overwhelmed Burma is shown by the history of the Shwesettaw shrine in the Minbu district. It is one of the holiest imaginable, containing two of Buddha's reputed footprints. Yet, during the depopulation caused by the Siamese wars, so little was the intercourse with Arakan over the An Pass, the approach to which runs through Shwesettaw, that even this famous spot was forgotten. In 1638 a party of monks sent by the king succeeded in finding the footprints amid the jungle which enveloped them, and the shrine was restored.[2]

Thalun's minister Kaingsa Manu compiled the Manusarashwemin or Mahārājā *dhammathat*, the first law book written in Burmese instead of Pali. It is based on Bayinnaung's compilations (p. 490) and on the still earlier Talaing *dhammathats*, but it substitutes Burmese ideas on, for instance, inheritance, for theirs, which are largely Hindu.

Thalun's principal pagoda is the Yazamanisula (Kaunghmudaw) at Sagaing, of Cingalese pattern; here he enshrined the Ceylon Tooth and begging bowl (p. 494), dedicating Shan slaves from Chiengmai and elsewhere.

His son Pindale (1648–61) built the Ngatatkyi pagoda, Sagaing district, containing a very large sitting Buddha.

When the Ming dynasty of China was overthrown, Yung-li, the last Ming emperor, tried to maintain himself in Yünnan. But in 1658 he was defeated and fled to Bhamo with his family and seven hundred followers. He gave the Bhamo *sawbwa* 100 *viss* (1 *viss* = 3.65 lb.) of gold to send the king with a petition asking leave to live in Burma, and the king permitted him to live at Sagaing with his followers.

A plague of freebooter armies broke out in China during the change of dynasty. They swarmed over the provinces but, finding by bitter experience that it did not pay to plunder the Manchus, the new conquerors of China, they looked for easier prey. They occupied Mone and Yawnghwe and ravaged up to Āva, plundering the villages, killing men, carrying off women and burning monasteries, while the monks fled in terror to the woods. They could not take Āva, for it was a walled town, and one of their leaders was even killed by a shot from the feringhi gunners from the wall. But for

[1] Harvey, *History of Burma*, p. 269.
[2] Duroiselle, *Notes on the Ancient Geography of Burma*.

the next three years they ravaged upper Burma from Yawnghwe, occupying Wundwin in Meiktila district, raiding Pagan, defeating every army, and even capturing some of the princes.

The king ruled over much the same area as Bayinnaung and had the same resources at his disposal. Bayinnaung would have found a speedy remedy; he would have marched with a large force and taken such reprisals that no Chinaman would have dared show his face inside the frontier for a generation. But the king was spiritless and commanded no following outside his homeland.

He did indeed send for a levy of 3000 men from Martaban, but the Talaings had no heart in the business and deserted on the march. The punishment for desertion was burning alive in batches. Their indignant kinsmen rose, fired Martaban, drove the Burmese out, and went off into Siam, 6000 souls in all, including families and prisoners. The frontier guards reported to the king of Siam, who sent lords (*smim*) to greet them, men of their own race who had long since settled in Siam. He granted gracious audience to their eleven leaders in the palace at Ayuthia, and allotted them lands.

The Talaings had fled into Siam because they could not stand against Burmese vengeance. Thus, though there is some excuse for the king's failure to get levies from the Delta, there is none for his failure to get its rice, which could easily have been brought upstream. He needed that rice, for Kyaukse, the granary of upper Burma, was in the hands of the Chinese.

But he sat with folded hands while they roamed the land at will, the crops could not be sown, the city granaries ran low, and the guards and the palace staff were plunged into mourning by the massacre of their kinsmen in the villages. The guards could get no food to eat, and finally they found that the royal concubines had cornered what rice there was and were selling it at iniquitous prices. The king exercised no control and when they appealed to him he mournfully said he could not help them. They approached his brother Pye, who at once marched on the palace. Hearing the drums, the king sent eunuchs to see what was happening. They told him, and he went to hide while the queen with her son aged eight and grandson aged four remained on the couch of state. Pye and his men entered the palace cutting down some twenty men and women. Pye said: "Brother, I wish thee no harm, but these things cannot be. Many a time have the ministers called me, and now I must do as they say." The queen entreated him, saying: "Be king but spare our lives. We will end our days in religion. Let the children become monks." But Pye shook his head, saying: "When have our families been monks? They will only throw off the robe. Yet will I do you no harm, remembering the oath of brotherly love I took to our father." He kept them in a royal house, sending them food daily. But after a few weeks the court said: "There cannot be two suns in the sky", and he drowned[1] the king, queen and their son and grandson in the Chindwin river.

Pye (1661–72) was troubled in heart over these terrible events and after summoning the monks and listening to the scriptures he said to them: "I had no wish to be king but the ministers and captains insisted that they had no refuge but me. Even as the Lord himself is bound by his clergy, so must I hearken to the voice of my people." The monks did not gainsay him, for he spoke the truth. They represented the public conscience, and every good king strove to win their approval.

Pye stopped profiteering among the harem women, so that his guards did not have to go without food for three days at a time as under his predecessor. But otherwise his success was not perceptibly greater. The Siamese, with Martaban, Tavoy and Chiengmai levies in their army, raided Syriam and Pegū, carrying off the population in crowds.[2] The Chinese ravages continued with undiminished intensity.

Yung-li and his followers were helpless fugitives who only wished to be left in peace. But the court believed them to be implicated in the Chinese ravages, and summoned the followers to the Tupayon pagoda at Sagaing intending to split them into small parties and scatter them in distant villages. When they were being led away from the pagoda, the Chinese grew frightened and, though unarmed, resisted; they were slain to a man. Yung-li apologised pitifully, saying he was sure they were wrong.

In time, the Chinese freebooters wore themselves out and the iron hand of the Manchu dynasty fell on the remnants. In 1662 the Yünnan viceroy came with 20,000 men and, halting at Aungbinle in Mandalay district, he sent a herald summoning the king to surrender Yung-li or take the consequences. This was the pass to which things had come through lack of judgment in admitting Yung-li and lack of manhood in repelling the Chinese. The king called a council. He pointed out that there were precedents to show that fugitives ought to be surrendered[3] and accordingly Yung-li must be given up. The ministers agreed and, disregarding the solemn fact that Yung-li had been admitted to allegiance, they delivered him up to meet his doom.[4]

The reigns of Narawara (1672–73), Minrekyawdin (1673–98), Sane (1698–1714), and Taninganwe (1714–33), were uneventful save for the usual rebellions and frontier raids. When the Āva palace was rebuilt in 1676, human victims were buried as a foundation sacrifice.[5] In 1721 two Italian priests came to Āva and founded the Catholic

[1] For the taboo on shedding royal blood, and the convention whereby princes were drowned, see Harvey, *History of Burma*, p. 339.

[2] S. Smith, *History of Siam*, 1657–1767, pp. 22–30.

[3] See p. 494, vol. III, p. 547, and vol. v, p. 558.

[4] Hmannan, III, 261–82; Warry, *Précis*; Parker, *Précis*; and his "Letters from a Chinese Empress", in *Contemporary Review*, 1912; Anderson, *Expedition to western Yünnan*, pp. 19–20; Cordier, *Histoire générale de la Chine*, III, 240–4.

[5] See also vol. III, p. 551, and p. 509 below and Harvey, *History of Burma*, p. 320.

Mission;[1] hitherto the only clergy in the country had been the Goanese chaplains of the feringhi villages (p. 495), whose character may be inferred from the fact that it was largely at their instigation that two devoted priests of the Société des Missions Étrangères de Paris were martyred in 1693. The Jatapon, a collection of royal horoscopes, was compiled about 1680; it is of high chronological value as its dates are more reliable than those of the chronicles. In 1724 Nga Kala compiled the Yazawwingyi chronicle; it is an important work, based on earlier sources, and similarly large portions of its text are incorporated in the Hmannan chronicle. European trade centred in Siam and Malaya at places such as Tenasserim[2] (p. 488) which, save under Bayinnaung (1551–81), was in Siamese hands till 1760. The Portuguese ceased to count after 1641, when they were expelled from Malacca by the Dutch, but there is still a colony of their descendants, with high-sounding names they cannot pronounce, round the Catholic church at Mergui. The merchants of Golconda carried the India trade thither; the king of Siam and his minister, Phaulkon, a Greek, wishing to oust them and get the carrying trade for their own ships, employed English interlopers. Thus Burneby figures as governor of Mergui among the seven commissioners appointed by the king of Siam in 1686 to administer the port and province, and Samuel White, another of the commissioners, was port officer 1683–87. But the East India Company depended for its security on the king of Golconda, and persuaded its principal shareholder, James II, to claim Mergui in 1687. White outwardly professed compliance while secretly preparing to resist, but he had betrayed his Siamese employers as well as the East India Company, and the townsfolk now rose against him as well as against James II's frigate, drove them both out and massacred sixty other English who were ashore. James II was also actuated by a desire to forestall Louis XIV. Four companies of French infantry built a fort and garrisoned Mergui during 1688 by arrangement with the king of Siam, who played off the European nations against each other. The name French Bay, on the eastern side of King Island, the largest island in the Mergui group, commemorates the fact that it was for a few years about this time the rendezvous of French warships. With the death of the Siamese king and the murder of Phaulkon in 1688, the Siamese ceased to favour the French, and in any case the French before long had no energy to spare for the farther east.[3]

After 1687 the English continued to trade in Mergui. The Dutch remained predominant; they had the tin monopoly but based their

[1] *Purchas his Pilgrimage or Relations of the world*, p. 507; Herbert, *Some years travels into Africa and Asia*, p. 318; Launay, *Mémorial de la Société des Missions Étrangères*, II, 274, 332; Hamilton, *New Account of East Indies*, II, 63; Bigandet, *History of the Catholic Burmese Mission*.

[2] See vol. III, p. 556.

[3] Furnivall, *From China to Peru*; and his "Samuel White, Port Officer of Mergui", in *Journal Burma Research Society*, 1917; Anderson, *English Intercourse with Siam*; Collis, *Siamese White*.

trade on Malacca, and Mergui declined. Sea piracy was rife everywhere, some of the worst rogues being renegade Dutchmen.

The French Compagnie des Indes had a branch at Syriam in 1688; its existence continued intermittently for nearly a century.[1] The Burmese tried to make the English re-establish the branches which had been closed for many years (p. 495); as their efforts failed, they seized *St Antony and St Nicholas*, a ship affiliated to the English, which put into Syriam for wood and water in 1692. Thereupon governor Higginson of Madras consented to re-establish private trade, but a resident chief was not appointed to Syriam till 1722. The imports were firearms for the Burmese government, piece-goods, hats and other European wares, areca, and coconuts from the Nicobars; the exports were ivory, lac, pepper, cardamum, beeswax, fur, cutch, large quantities of raw cotton and silk, together with such jewels, silver, lead, copper, iron, tin and earth-oil as could be got in spite of the highly protectionist system of the Burmese, which prohibited the export of precious metal, jewels, rice, and indeed of most commodities. Moreover, they were allowed to use as much teak as they liked for building ships at Syriam, and they built many, the favourite type being brigantines of 40–50 tons.

The seizure of a ship was in accordance with Burmese customary law, which gave the king absolute rights over everything in his dominions. Seafaring men avoided Burmese ports. Although a shipmaster never pays his crew all the wages due to them before letting them go ashore in a foreign port, and naval regulations forbid it, the governor of Syriam would insist on crews being paid in full before landing, in order that he might encourage them to desert. If a sailor married a woman of the country, the governor would claim him as a Burmese subject, alleging that the husband takes the wife's nationality. If a ship was driven onto the coast by weather, the Burmese confiscated her and enslaved the crew, arguing that under their law anyone who saved another from drowning had the right to possess him as a slave. Nay, if a ship merely touched at a Burmese port for water, without being expressly consigned there, she was enslaved on the same reasoning.[2] But here, as in so much else, the harshness of the rulers was mitigated by the humanity of the monks: if the distressed mariner wandered into a monastery, he was safe, for the monks would tend his wounds, feed and clothe him, and send him as if in sanctuary with letters of commendation from monastery to monastery till he could reach Syriam, there to await the chance of some passing ship.[3]

Ruling a poor and thinly populated country, the king regarded

[1] Sonnerat, *Voyage aux Indes* (1782), II, 43–53; (1806), III, 40–43; Cordier, *La France en Chine*, I, p. xviii, and *Historique abrégé*, p. 6.

[2] Year 1755, Dalrymple, *Oriental Repertory*, I, 191; year 1781, Sonnerat, *Voyage aux Indes* (1806), III, 49; year 1782, Cordier, "Les Français en Birmanie", in *T'oung Pao* (1890), pp. 199, 205; year 1808, Sangermano, *Burmese Empire*, p. 61.

[3] Year 1727, Hamilton, *New Account of East Indies*, II, 62.

captives as a form of wealth. Any foreigner residing in the country was not merely allowed but publicly encouraged to take a temporary wife for the period of his stay; he had to pay her off before leaving, and never under any circumstances could he take his female children out of the country, though he might, on heavy payment, take his male children (p. 480); every ship on arrival was carefully searched for women, and if, on leaving, it contained one woman more than it did on arrival, that ship was seized and the crew enslaved: women could breed subjects for the king and they were not allowed to emigrate.[1]

Mahadammayaza-dipati (1733–52). Manipur had sent propitiatory tribute to Bayinnaung (1551–81) but thereafter went her own way, and occasionally made raids. The country bred famous ponies; in those days every man had two or three, and polo, played forty a side throughout the villages, produced a race of horsemen.[2] Under their raja, Gharīb Nawāz (1714–54), the Manipurī raiders became a terror; from 1724 till his death they came nearly every other year sweeping the country up to Ava and carrying off loot, cattle and thousands of people. Once they massacred two-thirds of a royal army including the commander, who was drunk. In 1738 they burnt every house and monastery under the walls of Āva and stormed the stockade built to protect the Kaunghmudaw pagoda, slaughtering the garrison like cattle in a pen and killing a minister of the Hluttaw council. They had recently been converted to Hinduism by preachers who said that if they bathed in the Irrawaddy river at Sagaing all blessedness would attend them. In 1744 their chief Brāhman actually came to Ava to convert the Golden Palace, but after staying a month he fell ill and died, whereupon his suite of Brāhmans returned home.[3]

Mahadammayaza-dipati, king of Burma, angered at his commanders' failure to repel the Manipurīs, used to expose them in the sun with a sword on their necks, saying: "If a failure like this comes to my golden ears again I will chastise you with my sword." Neither he nor his predecessors since 1648 ever took the field in person. In short, the kingdom was doomed. Unlike the mass of their subjects, the kings were polygamous and although, to preserve the fiction of an undiluted succession, the chief queen had to be the reigning king's half-sister, the heir was often not her son, or even the son of a queen, but any son who could intrigue or massacre his way to power. No dynasty lasted three centuries or preserved its vigour for three generations.

[1] Year 1592, Linschoten, *Voyage to East Indies*, I, 98; year 1727, Hamilton, *New Account of East Indies*, II, 51–3; year 1782, Cordier, "Les Français en Birmanie", in *T'oung Pao* (1890), p. 190 and (1891), p. 25; year 1795, Symes, *Embassy to Ava*, p. 329. Foreigners objected, but even in the 1826 treaty the victorious English could not get the restriction removed, Crawfurd, *Embassy to Ava*, II, Appendix, p. 14.

[2] Pemberton, *Report on Eastern Frontier*, p. 31.

[3] Hmannan, III, 380, 386.

The kingship was now like overripe fruit, ready to fall at the first touch. A crop of *minlaung* (pretenders) sprang up. Dacoity was rampant. A colony of Gwe[1] (i.e. Wa tribesmen) at Okpo, Mandalay district, were joined by captives at Madaya near by, built a stockade, and lorded it over the district, plundering whom they pleased. People took to migrating in hundreds to Arakan, complaining of drunkenness in the palace and famine in the villages.[2]

For a century the delta had given little trouble because the Talaings took time to recover from the depopulation caused by Bayinnaung's wars. But now that they had recovered, and repeopled the wilderness, trouble began. Provoked by grinding taxation—even the looms of old women were taxed[3]—they massacred the Burmese at Pegū, Syriam and Martaban and set up as king Smim Htaw Buddhaketi (1740–47), a monk who was a poor relation of the king of Āva. It was necessary for him to have a white elephant in order to prove himself a proper king, but as he spent too long in the jungles searching for one and would not attend to state affairs, he was replaced by his father-in-law Binnya Dala (1747–57). The Talaings held Prome and Toungoo and all the country to the south, and for years used to go raiding up the river to Āva with many thousands of men. They could not take Āva as it was a walled town.

The Burmese troops did little but run away. A few years later the same men were carrying all before them because they had found leaders; those leaders were there now, waiting to be used, but an effete despotism had not the means of selecting them.

As the years passed, the raids resulted in the ruin of agriculture in upper Burma. Feeling unsafe, men deserted their fields, and Talaings or dacoits burnt what little crop was left. The last hope of replenishing the royal granaries vanished when the Talaings occupied the Kyaukse canals. They then surrounded Āva; after a siege of some months, it starved; the Talaings were on the point of going home when they learnt this from deserters, and in April, 1752, they forced their way into the outer city. Two days later the inner city (p. 513) opened its gates; the Talaing *yuvarājā* (crown prince) rode to the palace in state, dismounted and entered barefoot; he found the king in a great hall surrounded by his women, and greeted him courteously;[4] the king replied: "In this mortal life there are happiness and woe. This is the hour of my woe. Take me and do with me as thou wilt, but spare my people." The Talaings seized the regalia, the royal treasures and the list of citizens, burnt the city to the ground, left a strong garrison, and returned with the captive king, court and people to Pegū.

They returned for fear of a Siamese attack on Martaban. They

[1] Harvey, "Gwe", in *Journal Burma Research Society*, 1925.
[2] Dinnyawadi Yazawinthit, pp. 230–4.
[3] Sayadaw Athwa, III, 139.
[4] Wood, *Précis*.

did not penetrate north of Āva, as they had not enough men; they had overthrown the dynasty which, founded by Tabinshwehti, and known as the Toungoo dynasty, had lasted 221 years, but they had not subjected the Burmese people.

THE ALAUNGPAYA DYNASTY (1752–1885)

Alaungpaya (1752–60) was born in 1714 at Shwebo (Moksobomyo, "Town of the Hunter Chief"), a village of 300 houses. Many of his followers were hunters, but he himself belonged to a better class, the landed gentry as it were; for generations his family had been *myothugyis* (major village headmen), and in later days he even claimed descent from the fifteenth-century Āva chiefs. The anarchy of the last few years led him and many another jungle chief to stockade their villages. Forty-six villages joined him, and between them they raised a few rusty muskets.

When Āva fell he was ready. The Talaings sent small detachments to administer *thissa-ye*, the holy water of allegiance.[1] One of these came towards Shwebo. Alaungpaya's father made ready to pay homage and offer half his property, saying: "We can do nothing. The Talaing army is too strong. We shall simply be overwhelmed. We may as well give in." "No," said Alaungpaya, "when fighting for your country it matters little whether you are few or many. What does matter is that your comrades have true hearts and strong arms." He went out and met those Talaings in the scrub jungle south of Halin. They got no homage; only such as were lucky got away with their lives.

They came back in a large detachment with orders to spare not even infants in the cradle. Alaungpaya built a state hut and sent ten horsemen to conduct them respectfully to it. But they were conducted along a hollow road and in the bushes on each side lay his musket men. The Talaings never reached that hut. A bare half dozen reached Āva alive to tell the tale.

Again they came back, several thousand strong this time, to extirpate Shwebo once and for all; but as they came without cannon the assault naturally failed and they had to undertake a siege. One night Alaungpaya burst out at the head of a general sortie. It was not a defeat but a rout. Word passed along the Burmese pursuers that men had seen Myinbyushin Nat, the spirit rider of the White Horse,[2] fighting on their side. The Talaings jumped into boats and, without stopping to report at Āva, fled straight home down the river.

The news spread. A dozen legends gathered round his name. Officers and men from the disbanded palace guard joined him with

[1] For *thissa-ye*, see Harvey, *History of Burma*, p. 339.

[2] Grant Brown, "Lady of the Weir", in *Journal Royal Asiatic Society*, 1916, pp. 492–3; *Gazetteer of Upper Burma and the Shan States*, part II, vol. I, p. 518.

such muskets as they had managed to keep. From half the villages of upper Burma lads of spirit came trooping in to take service under the new leader. Even the greater men, some of whom could trace royal blood and themselves had hopes as *minlaungs* (pretenders), decided to serve under him.

By the end of 1753 he had massacred the Gwes of Madaya-Okpo (p. 503), the survivors fleeing into the Shan States, and so harried the Talaings that they evacuated Āva. In 1754 the Talaings, having discovered a plot at Pegū, executed the captive Āva king; this so infuriated the Burmese deportees in the delta that they rose wholesale and seized Prome. Alaungpaya wrote telling them to hold out and promising the governorship of a district to any Burman who could make that district revolt against the Talaings. Finally he drove the Talaing besiegers away from Prome, and by 1755 he had annexed the country down to Lunhse (Kudut) in Henzada district, and to Rangoon; Lunhse he named Myanaung, "Speedy Victory", and Dagon Rangoon, "End of Strife". He went in procession with his great officers and returned solemn thanks at the Shwedagon for his victories.

In the fighting of a decade previously, when the Talaings were expelling the Burmese from the delta, the East India Company's buildings at Rangoon had been burnt to the ground. Thereupon the English avoided the mainland and in 1753 occupied Negrais Island, which was uninhabited save by fishermen, erecting a factory, with moat, glacis, walls and cannon. The French remained at Syriam and declared for the Talaings. The English were inclining towards the Burmese when Alaungpaya captured Rangoon; finding three English ships in the port, he seized their cannon as a matter of course but, hoping to enter into an agreement with them and thus secure more numerous cannon, he allowed the protest of Jackson, the captain of the ships, H.E.I.C.'s snow *Arcot*, and released the cannon. He then left for Shwebo, and the Talaings tried to recapture Rangoon. They bombarded it with the help of French ships, and finding Jackson ill ashore they put a prize crew on the *Arcot* and made her take part in the bombardment. Their attack failed and they would not let Jackson sail away till he had surrendered five of his cannon, probably nine pounders. The news of this reached Alaungpaya just when he was receiving the Company's envoy, Captain Baker, at Shwebo; he accepted Baker's repudiation, without believing it, and continued the negotiations, which ended in 1757 with an agreement whereby, in return for 700 lb. of powder, and one twelve pounder, annually, he ceded Negrais and a site at Bassein, in perpetuity, with the right to erect fortifications.[1]

Alaungpaya's advances in the delta involved heavy fighting not only on land but also on water; both sides had hundreds of great

[1] Dalrymple, *Oriental Repertory*, I, 133–226.

war-canoes, and these, driven by sixty paddles, would ram with terrific effect. On land his hardest task was yet to come, for his men were only a semi-armed mass levy, and so far he had not been confronted with a walled town. Moreover, Dupleix had regarded Syriam as his chief shipbuilding depot, and French ships lay in the river, defending the town. Alaungpaya invested it in 1755 but had to wait a year for starvation to do its work. In July, 1756, finding the defenders weak with hunger, he called for volunteers, fed them for days in his presence, and gave them leather helmets and lacquer armour. They numbered ninety-three and are known as the Golden Company. On the appointed night, the Burmese camp held a festival with drums and music. The sound, floating up to the Talaing city on the hill, induced the watchers to relax their vigilance. The Golden Company found their way over the walls, cut down the guards, and opened the gates. The Burmese poured in, and the town was theirs. To Alaungpaya's men from upper Burma it was a veritable Eldorado, and they glutted themselves with mirrors, candlesticks, lamps, chairs, clocks, and other European wonders. He made a heap of silver and let the survivors of the Golden Company take away as much as they could carry.

Bruno, the French agent at Syriam, had written to Pondicherry for help. Two ships, *Fleury* and *Galathée*, came. They arrived after the town had fallen and, knowing nothing, came up the river under a Burmese pilot who, under Alaungpaya's orders, stranded them; fire-rafts sealed their fate. Bruno was roasted alive; the ships' officers, numbering twelve and being gentlemen of quality, were beheaded.

The French were under no obligations to Alaungpaya, and as the Talaing state which they were helping was actually in existence they were entitled to treatment as prisoners of war. But it was customary among the races of Indo-China to give no quarter save to those they carried off into slavery, and Alaungpaya had to issue special orders[1] to prevent the killing, after capture, of Burmans and Shans whom the Talaings had taken and compelled to fight for them. Beheading was a merciful death, granted as a favour to officer prisoners.

The two ships contained thirty-five cannon (twenty-four pounders), five field guns, 1300 muskets, and ammunition. These were a godsend to Alaungpaya, and it was largely on their account that he gave the crews, over 200 men, their lives: white gunners were too valuable to execute. They were reasonably treated and given Burmese wives; some of them became captains of the guard; the rest were a *corps d'élite* who played no small part in major actions, and when too old to follow the armies they were allowed to retire in the feringhi villages of Shwebo district (p. 495): their descendants are indistinguishable from the surrounding population save by their religion and occasionally by the colour of their eyes.

[1] Konbaungset, p. 185.

Thus, until the gunners lost their man-of-war smartness, the Burmese had some good artillery. Alaungpaya had indeed already a number of cannon, mostly taken from the Talaings, but some of them were two hundred years old and the best of them was the gun used at Prome in 1754. This was a three pounder and it was the pride of the day, because when fired it went off, and when it went off it was the enemy that it hit, and the enemy whom it hit died; because of these things, it was coated with gold leaf, and men made offerings of spirit to it, reverently perfuming it with scents and wrapping it in fine raiment.[1] Alaungpaya was head of the church, but when he came to possess French gunners, he was not responsible for their souls, as they were unbelievers and it was their own concern if they chose to drink damnation. Besides, theologically speaking he did not countenance their use of intoxicants; he merely permitted the offering of spirits to the Gun Spirit, and the slaves of the Gun Spirit happened to consume the offering.

Alaungpaya burnt Syriam to the ground and henceforward its importance ceases. He made Rangoon the port of Burma, enlarging the stockade and appointing a senior governor. In 1756–57 he advanced on Pegū by land and water while a second army, mainly of Shan levies, moved towards it from Toungoo. His advance was slow, with grim losses, for the Talaings were now fighting literally with their backs to the wall and they were still superior in firearms, mainly jingals, a rough iron tube mounted on a bamboo tripod and throwing a one-pound ball. He left pots of poisoned intoxicants where the Talaings would find them, and so killed many.[2] They made desperate stands in forty stockades south of the city, especially near Mokkainggyi, at Kyaikpadaing and Zenyaungbin (Nyaungbin). At Zenyaungbin they captured many of Alaungpaya's jingals and turned them against him; it was a hornet's nest which he captured only by flinging in the Golden Company of Syriam, increased to three hundred; these pressed on through a hail of lead shouting "*Shwebotha!*", forced an entrance, and flung open the gate to their comrades. Finally the Burmese, devastating the country and deporting the population, closed around. A monastery at Sidi still shows a bell cast by Alaungpaya; he resided there, at the little fort of Zetuwadi, and was nearly driven out one night by some picked Talaings under the famous Talaban. But such efforts were vain. The Burmese, aided by their French artillery, and by war-boats which flung off the Talaings' fire-rafts, completed their lines round the doomed city.

The city starved. The Talaings sent monks asking for terms, and their king offered to become Alaungpaya's vassal. Alaungpaya replied that they had nothing to fear, for—it is the ambition of every great Buddhist king to become a Buddha—he was a divine incarna-

[1] Konbaungset, pp. 110–12. [2] Konbaungset, p. 198.

tion; and he gave the envoys two bunches of orchids, saying one was for offering, the other for adornment. The Talaings breathed more freely. They offered one to the Shwemawdaw pagoda, the other they twined in the tresses of their king's daughter, as for the bride of Alaungpaya. But she was beloved of Talaban, the soul of the defence; he was furious and, finding his advice, to sally forth and die like men, rejected, he collected his family and with some best troops broke through the Burmese lines and maintained himself at Sittaung in Thaton district. The trembling king sent his daughter to Alaungpaya's camp, borne in a gorgeous palanquin, and surrounded by a bevy of handmaidens and princes. After kneeling some time in homage, she was conducted into Alaungpaya's harem. Many of the Talaing captains and troops came to pay homage, and lived in Alaungpaya's camp, for they believed him.

Then, in May, 1757, Alaungpaya proceeded to storm the city and massacre the people. When the sack had subsided he made a state entry, gleaming aloft on his elephant, through the Mohnyin gate in the south wall, surrounded by ministers, his Guards and his French gunners. He returned solemn thanks at the Shwemawdaw pagoda and appointed governors to the conquered districts. He granted reasonable treatment to the fallen royal family; he sold the surviving population as slaves; and saying it was they who had led the city's resistance, he flung hundreds of Talaing monks[1] to the elephants.

He burnt the palace and razed the city wall. He made a desert and called it peace. For the Talaings it was the peace of the grave, and this is the end of them in Burma. Such as were not enslaved periodically migrated to Siam, where they rose to high office and furnished some of the best troops. Such as remained in Burma were prone to rebel, and whenever they dared to raise a head it was at once chopped off; they grew fewer and subsided, and their land relapsed into jungle.

The Burmese owed their civilisation to the Talaings: it was an older and apparently a gentler civilisation. Alaungpaya destroyed their manuscripts and we know too little to say with confidence why they went under. Probably it was because they received no reinforcements by immigration, unlike the Burmese who, lying to the north, were open to a constant trickle of immigration; moreover, Alaungpaya had Shan, Kachin and Kadu levies, whereas the Talaings had only their own little corner of Burma to draw on for men.

Several of Alaungpaya's court poets were also field officers, such as Letwethondara (p. 513), who served under the walls of Pegū; Letwethondara had been a writer to the Hluttaw council under the last king of Āva, and was one of the staff taken over by Alaungpaya. About 1750 the Sonta *sayadaw* (abbot) of Hsinbyugyun, Minbu district, compiled the Manu Ring *dhammathat* (law book), which

[1] Sayadaw Athwa, III, 148.

started the fashion of attributing the decisions of Kaingsa Manu (p. 497) to the ancient sage Manu. By Alaungpaya's order, his minister, the soldier Mahasiri-uttamajaya, compiled the Manu Kye *dhammathat*, a compilation of existing laws and customs which passed into general use owing to its encyclopaedic nature and to its being written in simple Burmese with very little Pali; one of its provisions is that no debt can be demanded when human victims are being offered at the foundation of a city (p. 499); and when in 1751 Tavoy was rebuilt, a condemned criminal was crushed in each post-hole of the city gates.[1]

In 1755 Alaungpaya sent an expedition to instil respect into the Manipurīs, who significantly call this, the first of his dynasty's inroads, "The First Devastation"; the Manipurīs found the Burmese on this occasion using firearms for the first time, their weapons, like those of the Manipurīs, having previously been only swords, spears, bows and arrows. In 1758–59 he himself led a force over the hills by the Khumbat route; at Pulel in the Imole pass the Manipurīs gave him battle and fled after a stubborn conflict; he entered Imphal, the capital, only to find it empty, as the inhabitants lay hiding in the woods; he left garrisons in permanent stockades at Tamu and Thaungdut, and returned home; in his capacity as a divine incarnation he promoted religion among the Kathe (Cassay, Manipur) Shans along his line of march; in his capacity as a king he massacred[2] more than four thousand of his Manipurī prisoners because they stubbornly refused to march away in his slave gangs. These incursions, lasting down to 1819, ended by depopulating the country and stamping out Manipurī civilisation so completely that we can no longer tell what their social and political conditions were like.[3] The Burmese valued Manipurī captives highly and settled them near the capital; they served the court as silversmiths; as silk-workers they introduced the *acheik* pattern;[4] they gave the Burmese army its best cavalry (the Cassay horse) and they supplied the bulk of the court astrologers, who stood robed in white, intoning benedictions, as the king took his seat on the throne.

Alaungpaya tried to dam the Mu river, and built the Mahananda lake to supply Shwebo town with water. The Mu canals were not successful and the work decayed after his death.

In May, 1759, the English, hard pressed in India, withdrew thirty-five Europeans and seventy Indians, almost the entire staff, from Negrais (p. 505). In October they sent a skeleton staff to retain a lien on the island. The governor of Bassein with Lavine, one of Bruno's men who was in high favour, and sixty followers, met the new staff on arrival saying they had a letter from the king to show,

[1] Mason, *Burmah, its People and Productions*, p. 106.
[2] Konbaungset, p. 303.
[3] Hodson, *The Meitheis*, pp. 4, 29, 58.
[4] Parlett, *Sagaing Settlement Report*, p. 4.

and the senior officers messed with the English in the fort. A day later, 6 October, 1759, at nine in the morning when they were sitting down to breakfast together, the senior guest, the governor of Bassein, gave a sign and some of the 2000 Burmans concealed in the woods rushed in, killed eight English and about a hundred Indians, turned the cannon of the fort on the two ships at anchor, and finally withdrew with all cannon, stores, and four English. A midshipman and sixty-four Indians escaped on board. What had happened was that the Armenians at court, jealous of the English, had told Alaungpaya that the English were fortifying their stations, supplying the Talaings with arms, and spoiling his revenue by preventing other traders from coming up the Bassein river. Alaungpaya sent the governor of Rangoon, brother to his queen, to extirpate Negrais. The governor returned saying there must be some mistake, he had found the English there to be innocuous. Alaungpaya regarded him as a traitor, flogged all his men, sent a second party which actually did the work, and before letting him return to his high office flung him into irons and pegged him out in the sun for days with three beams across his body so that a year later he was still suffering from the effects. The governor of Bassein subsequently admitted that the English had not intrigued with the Talaings, but had fed a few refugees, just as they fed Burmese refugees, and had made presents of four or five muskets which the Armenians represented to Alaungpaya as 500. The English had not prevented ships coming up the river, because they regarded Alaungpaya as too strong a raja to offend. Under the treaty (p. 505) he had expressly permitted them to erect fortifications.[1]

After the fall of Pegū, envoys from Chiengmai visited Alaungpaya. He told them they must make complete submission. They looked at those blackened ruins and went home; and before long Martaban, Tavoy, Chiengmai, Anan and other states in north-west Siam sent tribute.

Many Talaings had taken refuge in Siam; there were endemic slave raids on the border; and the Siamese had detained the captain of a Burma-owned ship which had been driven by weather into their port of Tenasserim. Moreover, seeing that after the conquest of the Delta he reigned over nothing but ruins, Alaungpaya wished to populate his realm with prisoners obtained in Siam. Early in 1760 he advanced with 40,000 men through Martaban and Tavoy. Capturing Tenasserim (which thereafter remained a Burmese possession) with the aid of some small ships managed by European captives, he went east over the hills to the shore of the Gulf of Siam and turned north. The Siamese came out to meet him but were

[1] Hall, "The Tragedy of Negrais", in *Journal Burma Research Society*, 1931, part III. The statement, sometimes made in recent English works, that the massacre was a dastardly deed, perpetrated by Alaungpaya's subordinates without his authorisation, disregards the standard Burmese account, Konbaungset, pages 144–7, which shows that Alaungpaya regarded the operation as high strategy and personally insisted on it throughout.

driven back. Approaching Ayuthia, he burnt some Dutch ships, massacred the defenceless population regardless of sex or age, and covered the surface of the rivers with their corpses.[1] Under the walls of Ayuthia he released prominent prisoners with this message to the king of Siam: "His Burman Majesty comes as a divine incarnation to spread true religion in your country. Come forth with respect and present him with elephants and a daughter."[2] But the Siamese had among them Talaing refugees who knew the story of Pegū (p. 508). Their feringhis and Muslims manned the war-canoes with cannon in the maze of canals which surrounded the city; the glacis and fords were strewn with caltrops; cannon frowned from the battlements, with thousands of resolute men behind. Alaungpaya had started much too late in the cold weather. The rains were at hand, when the whole country would be several feet under water. Half his men were down with dysentery, and he himself was far from well. It looked as if the ever victorious army was not going to be victorious. He sent another message to the king of Siam that he had no wish to dethrone him if only he would submit to religious reform. There was no reply, and Alaungpaya saw that the play was over; within a week of arrival the hosts were in full retreat, abandoning forty guns of three-inch calibre.

He selected the comrade of his youth, Minhkaungnawrahta, to command the rear-guard. These were the pick of the army—500 Manipur horse and 6000 foot, every man of whom had a musket. Minhkaungnawrahta spread them out, and it was some time before the Siamese realised that the main body had left; then they swept out upon him; his men, fearing to be cut off, watched the ring closing round them and begged him to let them fight farther back; but he said: "Friends, the safety of our Lord the King lies in our keeping. Let us not fight farther back, lest the sound of the guns should break his sleep." When they could stand they stood, and when they had to run they ran; they were defeated but never broken, and they withdrew in good order, collecting Alaungpaya's stragglers on the way.

Meanwhile Alaungpaya had gone ahead by forced marches. Perhaps, as he lay in pain jolting along in his litter, he longed for the sights and sounds of home; but he was destined never to see them, for whether he knew it or not the hand of death was upon him. Early in May, 1760, he reached Kinyua in Bilin township, Thaton district, and there at dawn he died (11 May, 1760).

The commanders, watching by his bedside, fearing to dishearten the troops, kept the death a close secret and sent their swiftest horsemen to Shwebo, so that the heir might be the first to know and secure the throne. The body, bound in sheets, was hidden in the curtained

[1] S. Smith, *History of Siam*, 1657–1767, p. 108.
[2] Konbaungset, pp. 315–18.

litter; and thus in death Alaungpaya still rode with his armies and the daily orders issued in his name. At Rangoon his death was made public and his body, placed on a state barge, was taken upstream. At Kyaukmyaung landing stage in Shwebo district the whole court came out to meet it, and bore it solemnly in through the Hlaingtha Gate of Shwebo. So he was buried with the ritual of the kings in the palace city which once had been his village, amid the mourning of a people. His grave, with an inscription in misspelt English, perhaps by some Negrais captive, is near the Shwebo Deputy Commissioner's court.

Naungdawgyi (1760–63) executed some of his father Alaungpaya's best officers on suspicion and drove Minhkaungnawrahta to rebel so that he had to be killed.

The East India Company sent Captain Alves to demand compensation for the Negrais murders, but were in no position to enforce it as their hands were full in India. The king told Alves that the Negrais victims were innocent, but they had to suffer for their predecessors who, he had no doubt, supplied arms to the Talaings, since, according to the law of nature, the innocent suffer with the guilty, just as, when a farmer clears the ground by burning the rank grass, the wheat burns along with the tares.[1] He refused compensation but permitted the Company to return provided they did not go to Negrais. He probably never saw the treaty by which Negrais had been ceded in perpetuity (p. 505) and had he seen it he would have regarded it as a grant revocable at pleasure: Burmese kings were not acquainted with the nature of treaties. Living inland, they could not understand what made the English prefer an island on their base, the sea, and they were firmly convinced that some deep plot was being hatched there. The Company had to come to Rangoon.

Talaban (p. 508) was able to maintain himself for years in the Kawgun caves, Thaton district, but finally his family was captured and, knowing what their fate would be, he gave himself up and when brought before the king claimed their lives in exchange for his own. Struck by his chivalry, the king released them all and took Talaban into his service.

Hsinbyushin (1763–76) himself raided Manipur in December, 1764, carrying away its people into captivity, for he wished to increase the population of his new capital, Ava, into which he moved in April, 1765. The gates of restored Ava were named after conquered states, some of them being—on the east side, Chiengmai, Martaban, Mogaung; on the south, Kaingma, Hanthawaddy, Myede, Onbaung (Hsipaw); on the west, Gandhalarit (Yünnan), Sandapuri (Viengchang, Linzin), Kenghung; on the north, Tenasserim, Yodaya (Siam). The various wards were, according to precedent, allotted on racial lines; thus the Indian traders lived in one, the Chinese in

[1] Dalrymple, *Oriental Repertory*, I, 373.

another, Christians in another, and in others were the Siamese and Manipur captives; such captives were often a source of suspicion, as in 1774 when the leading families of the Manipur colony were extirpated for alleged plotting. The wall, sixteen feet high, backed by earthwork, was of indifferent quality, but adequate to the only style of warfare it would have to meet. As was usual in Burmese capitals, the palace was an inner city, with its own moat, wall, and a massive teak stockade outside.[1]

To transfer to Āva was a wise step so far as it went, for it placed the king in direct communication along the Myitnge river with the Kyaukse granary, and it was on the great river, whereas Shwebo was landlocked. But the step did not go far enough. From the day that Vasco da Gama opened the sea route in 1498, the centre of gravity had shifted to the delta. The kings from Bayinnaung (1551–81) to Anaukpetlun (1605–28) acted as if they realised this, making Pegū their headquarters. But none of their successors realised it, and their failure to do so sealed the fate of the monarchy. Rangoon might have let a little fresh air from the outer world into the court. The delta was a foreign country to the Burmese and they did not feel safe among the Talaings. Hence there was some excuse for the earlier kings. But there was none for the Alaungpaya dynasty which exterminated the Talaings; their remnant continued to rebel for some time, but these rebellions were crushed with ease, and need not have occurred had the kings, instead of wasting their energy on wars in Siam and Assam, used half of it in giving the delta a good administration. As they would not move to the delta, the atmosphere of their palace was that of the upper Burma villages among which it lay. Their ideas remained in the nineteenth century what they had been in the ninth. To build pagodas, to collect daughters from tributary chiefs, to sally forth on slave raids, to make wars for white elephants—these conceptions had had their day, and a monarchy which failed to get beyond them was doomed. It is probably more than coincidence that Siam, which had its capital in a seaport, developed a more enlightened government than the Burmese kingship, and is independent to-day.

Nine Brāhmans whom the king obtained from Benares frequently assisted him with advice, and with their help the Maungdaung *sayadaw* (abbot) translated into Burmese various Sanskrit works on astrology, medicine, grammar, etc., known as *Vyākarana*. Letwethondara, whom the king exiled to Meza hill, Katha district, earned his recall by writing a poem, the well-known *Mezataungche*; in a subsequent reign he became one of the judges in the king's court nor did he die till the second decade of the next century.

The main armies spent 1764–67 against Siam. Starting from

[1] Konbaungset, p. 377; Crawfurd, *Embassy to Ava*, II, 1; Enriquez, "Capitals of the Alaungpaya Dynasty", in *Journal Burma Research Society*, 1915.

Kengtung with 20,000 men, mostly Shans, Thihapate slowly fought his way down from Chiengmai through Viengchang (Linzin), while another army of the same size under Mahanawrahta fought its way south-east from Tavoy to Petchaburi. Thihapate had to storm town after town, and found the villages stockaded against him. When roused, the men fought with spirit, vying among themselves as to who should mount the wall. They died like flies from preventible disease, and suffered ghastly wounds for which they got few thanks from the king, as the loss of a limb, even in honourable service, disqualified a man from entering the palace. They kept the field all the year round, a rare thing for Burmese levies, spending the rains in the towns they had won. At Chiengmai they had to resort to mining, with movable shelters under the wall; finally they captured part of the wall with its guns and turned them all night down into the terror-stricken population, who sent their monks to surrender in the morning. The prettiest girls and choicest loot were sent to the king at Āva.

Gradually they swept over the whole country, burning the towns and making the chiefs drink the water of allegiance. Such of the population as had not stampeded eastward ran a risk of having to contribute to the heads which the Burmese hacked off and piled up in great heaps[1] under the walls of the towns they besieged, in order to terrify the defenders. They were sometimes besieged themselves, for the Ayuthia armies came out and pressed them, trying hard to prevent their effecting a junction.

But finally the two commanders joined hands under the walls of Ayuthia. Mahanawrahta fixed his headquarters there at a pagoda built by Bayinnaung. In spite of wastage their hosts were as numerous as ever, as they had exacted contingents from the states which they had conquered, and according to Burmese custom their prisoners were made to fight for them. They were to spend fourteen months before Ayuthia. The rains came and flooded them out: they stood their ground. Their commanders died of hardship: they did not lose heart. Imperial armies from China invaded upper Burma: they were not recalled. During the first open season they could not get near the walls because of the numerous stockades outside the city; sometimes the whole plain was alive with swarms of Siamese working under the supervision of grandees, who were carried about in sedan chairs; both sides used bamboo matting between two uprights containing earth for temporary defence while they constructed permanent works. The Siamese had foreign adventurers fighting for them, one of their outworks containing four hundred Chinese. When the rains began to lay the whole country several feet under water, the commanders urged Mahanawrahta to withdraw, but he refused, and Thihapate

[1] Konbaungset, pp. 210–13, 381; cf. Alaungpaya Ayedawpon, p. 64; Laurie, *Pegū*, p. 461; Crawfurd, *Embassy to Ava*, II, 41.

supported him. The men stayed on knolls of rising ground or built dykes to keep out the water. The Siamese seeing them scattered in isolated groups attacked them in boats. In one of these attacks a Siamese leader, while waving his sword and hurling defiance in the bows of his boat, was brought down by a musket shot and fell into the water, and the whole flotilla fled. Ayuthia prided itself on its great guns, some of them 30 feet long with 30 *viss* (100 lb.) ball; one of these burst with an overcharge, but the shot killed several men on two Burmese boats. The Burmese had war-canoes in plenty, constructed by their lieges up the rivers, and so they were able to prevent provisions entering the city. When the dry season returned they reconstructed their earthworks. Some of these were higher than the walls, and the cannon were also mounted aloft on pagodas so as to fire down into the palace. Often the palace guns ceased fire, because the king yielded to the entreaties of his harem, who were terrified at the noise.[1]

The city starved. Shan states tributary to Siam sent an army which came down from the north and tried to raise the siege; they were swept away. The king and princes tried to cut their way out and escape; they were driven back. They asked what they had done to merit these horrors and were curtly told they were rebels and traitors and deserved all they were going to get. The commander-in-chief Mahanawrahta died; and by royal decree was buried with extraordinary honours; he deserved them. Thihapate had to finish the siege alone. The end was now near. At four in the afternoon on 28 March, 1767, the French guns opened for the last time. The wall had been mined; by nightfall the breach was practicable and the stormers effected an entry. The slaughter was indiscriminate. The king's body was identified next day among a heap of slain near the west gate. The houses, the temples, the great palace itself, went up in flames; the wall was razed to the ground; the city was never restored as a capital. The princes, the harem, the clergy, foreigners including a French Catholic bishop, and thousands of the population were carried away into captivity, so that many a private could boast of four slaves. There was gold, silver and jewels in abundance, for the royal treasure was immense. This is the secret of these continued Burmese attacks on Ayuthia: it was at once a thriving seaport and a king's palace, one of the wealthiest cities in Indo-China, so that its treasures were a standing temptation to the Burmese hordes.

The Lao and Shan levies were allowed to return home, probably because the long absence was rendering them unreliable, and many of them were prisoners serving under compulsion. But there was no rest for the weary Burmans. If Ayuthia had not fallen when it did, the siege would have had to be abandoned, as royal despatches now came urgently recalling the armies to take their place in the line

[1] Siamese palace tradition.

against the Chinese, whose attacks on Āva looked like breaking through; for the years 1765–69 saw a series of Chinese inroads.

The *sawbwas* (Shan chiefs) on the Yünnan border usually paid nominal tribute to both China and Burma. Some now ceased paying it to Burma, which therefore marched against them; one fled to Yünnan, and the Kengtung *sawbwa* made a foray there at the instigation of the Gwe (p. 505) in the course of their wanderings. Moreover, the Chinese were dissatisfied at the treatment their merchants received in Burma. At Bhamo a Chinese caravaneer, angry at delay in getting sanction to build a bridge, insulted the Burmese governor, who therefore arrested him; and when released he found that the Burmese officers had looted his caravan. At Kengtung a Chinaman was killed in a dispute about payment; the Burmese resident offered blood-money and even talked of executing the slayer, but would not hand him over, and the Chinese would not take less. These trivial incidents should not have caused a war, but the Burmese had no embassy system to arrange things peaceably, and China happened to be under an aggressive emperor.

The Chinese invaded in great strength with the active or passive co-operation of Hsenwi, Bhamo, Mogaung and Kengtung. The fighting was in the triangle Mogaung, Kenghung on the Mekong river, and down the Myitnge valley to within three marches of Āva. The Chinese had bases at Bhamo and Lashio and their line of advance was usually down the Shweli and Myitnge valleys. But the principal theatre was in Bhamo district, where Balamindin won fame by his great defence of Kaungton, twelve miles to the east of which, at Shwenyaungbin, the Chinese also had a gigantic stockade, "as big as a city".

The Burmese had better war-canoes than the Chinese, they received invaluable help from their captive French gunners, and they won most of the dozen major actions which were spread over four campaigns; but the suspense was terrible; as soon as one Chinese army was driven back, another came on in greater numbers than ever. The earth quaked, rending the national shrines; to placate the unseen powers, the king flung thousands of gold and silver images into the Shwezigon at Pagan and the Shwedagon.

The Chinese proved useless as soldiers, but the Manchu contingents were good troops who, with ladders, axes, hooks and ropes, would rush up to the stockades against a withering fire, while boiling lead poured down on them and their bodies were crushed by great beams of which the lashings were cut as soon as the stormers were underneath. The Chinese would have quickly disposed of the Burmese in the open, but the Burmese never allowed themselves to be caught there, giving battle only in their deadly stockades amid the jungle; and the Chinese, who described the climate as impossible, suffered severely from disease. Even so, they ought to have won; but whereas the Burmese commanders worked together hand in hand, the Chinese lacked co-ordination, and threw away the advantage of superior numbers by allowing themselves to be overwhelmed in detail. Moreover, they were handicapped by lack of topographical information; one of their armies spent two months wandering blindly through Mogaung and Mohnyin when it was urgently needed elsewhere: they did indeed study their staff record of the 1277–87 invasions, but found it useless as the place-names had changed. The best of their generals, Mingjui, son-in-law to the emperor, who had won distinction in Turkestān, fought his way from Lashio, smashing a Burmese army and driving it past the Gokteik gorge to Singaung three marches from Āva. The court in panic urged the king to flee but he scornfully refused, saying he and his brother princes, the sons of Alaungpaya, would face the Chinese single-handed if necessary. Mingjui's colleagues failed to support him, Burmese armies in his rear cut off his supplies, and he had to retreat beset by overwhelming odds; such was the slaughter that the Burmese could hardly grip their swords as the hilts were slippery with enemy blood. Mingjui fought in the rear-guard till he saw his men were safe and then, obeying the tradition of the Manchu officer corps, he cut off his plaited hair, sent it as a token to his emperor, and hanged himself on a tree; his servants hid his body with leaves lest the Burmese should desecrate it according to their wont.

At length in 1769, after losing, from first to last, 20,000 men and great stores of arms and ammunition which went to equip Burmes levies, the Chinese were driven out of their great stockade at Shwenyaungbin and their generals asked for terms. The Burmese staff was adverse to granting terms, saying that the Chinese were surrounded like cattle in a pen, they were starving and in a few days they could be wiped out to a man. Luckily the Burmese commander-in-chief, Mahathihathura, saw that the loss of a few armies so far from breaking China would only stiffen her resolution. He sent back the messenger with a conciliatory reply. At Kaungton the Burmese and Chinese officers met and drew up a written agreement whereby the Chinese were allowed to withdraw, trade was to be restored, and to prevent misunderstanding decennial missions were to pass between the sovereigns. The Chinese melted down their cannon and then, while the Burmese stood to arms and looked down, their columns marched sullenly away up the Taping valley, to perish by thousands of hunger in the passes.[1]

When he heard that the Chinese had been allowed to depart, the

[1] Konbaungset, pp. 425–92; Symes, *Embassy to Ava*, p. 69; Crawfurd, *Embassy to Ava*, II, p. 284; Burney, "Wars between Burma and China", in *Journal Asiatic Society of Bengal*, 1837; McLeod, *Journal*, p. 60; Cordier, *Histoire générale de la Chine*, III, 353; Huber, "Fin de la dynastie de Pagan", in *Bulletin de l'École Française d'Extrême Orient*, 1909, p. 669; Warry, *Précis*; Parker, *Précis*, and *Burma, Relations with China*, pp. 83–94; *Report of the Superintendent, Archaeological Survey, Burma*, 1918, p. 22.

king was angry; he thought they should all have been killed. So the armies, afraid to return home, went off to Manipur in January, 1770. Under a good raja, Manipur was recovering from the last devastation, and the commanders scented a fresh harvest of slaves and cattle with which to appease the king. The men of Manipur fought gallantly, but were overwhelmed in a three days' battle near Langthabal. The raja fled to Assam. The Burmese raised their own nominee to the throne and returned taking with them such of the population as were not hiding in the woods. The king's anger had subsided, and as after all they had won victories and preserved his throne, he was merciful; he sent Mahathihathura a woman's dress to wear, and exiled him and the commanders to the Shan States; he would not allow them to see him, and he also exiled the ministers who dared to speak on their behalf. Their wives, including the sister of his queen, were exposed in the sun at the western gate of the palace, with the Chinese presents of silk on their heads, a public mock for three days.

By granting honourable terms the Burmese gave the Chinese emperor a loophole to withdraw from a costly adventure in a country the trade of which was, as he minuted on the file, negligible, and what little there was went round by sea. Although pride prevented him from acknowledging the treaty, his silence gave consent, and soon the caravans of 400 oxen or 2000 ponies started coming down from Yünnan as of old, and the Burmese once more found a market for their raw cotton, of which China always bought appreciable quantities. Burma remained in possession of Koshanpye, the nine Shan towns above Bhamo. The Chinese prisoners taken in the war, numbering 2500, were settled in the capital as gardeners, and were given Burmese wives. But the material was as nothing to the moral gain. Their other victories were won over states on their own level, such as Siam; this was won over an empire. Alaungpaya's crusade against the Talaings was stained with treachery; the great siege of Ayuthia (1766–67) was a magnificent dacoity; but in the Chinese war the Burmese were waging a righteous war of defence against the invader.

The victory, coming as it did on top of a generation of continuous warfare which might well have exhausted the race, shows that the exploits of Alaungpaya were no mere flash in the pan but were broad-based on the energy of the race as a whole. His tradition was not only maintained, it was eclipsed. The chronicles for the period are verbose and pompous, but it is impossible to read them without being struck with their fierce pride. The Burman of those days knew that to the north lay a big country called China; to the east, Shans of various sorts some of whom had a kingdom called Siam; to the west a place called India and, further west still, a country of white people, which some people said was an island.

All these countries, except China, were uncivilised and not worth studying. The white people called themselves various names, such as Portuguese, Dutch, French and English, but they were all much the same just as the various Shans were much the same; and in any case they were not a numerous race and were usually crushed with ease. The Indians were more important, but even they could not count for much judging by the way the Manipuris had been exterminated. The Siamese and Chinese on the other hand were really great powers, but they had been defeated. Thus the whole world was accounted for, and the Burmese felt equal to anything. They had reason for their pride. They had no commissariat, and on the march they perished of underfeeding and disease. They were the ordinary people you can see in any village to-day, led by their *myothugyis* (major village headman), who ranked as lords. Yet their spirit carried their bare feet from Bhamo to Bangkok, they fought and died by hundreds and thousands, leaving their bones to bleach from Junkceylon to the banks of the Brahmaputra. They had bought those lands with their blood. Doubtless it was a small world, but it was the only world they knew, and a Burmese minister could say[1] with truth to his English suitor: "You do not realise. We have never yet met the race that can withstand us."

In 1773 Talaing levies, mustered for an expedition to Siam, mutinied. The Burmese commanders and guards fled, first to Martaban, and then to Rangoon. The mutineers failed to take the Rangoon stockade but fired the town and burnt several foreign ships which were building on the stocks. A week later the Burmese brought up reinforcements, seized a Dutch ship, and retook the town with the aid of her gunfire; they then robbed her of all guns and munitions and sent her to sea, where she foundered. The mutineers made off, collected their families and migrated to Siam, numbering three thousand. The general population could not flee, and on them, though not implicated, the Burmese wreaked vengeance, massacring both sexes.

In 1774 the king made a royal progress down the river to Rangoon in splendid barges with the queens, court, and captive Talaing princes, holding high festival at every halt, and worshipping at the pagodas on the way, especially the Shwezigon at Pagan and the Shwehsandaw at Prome.[2] He came to Rangoon to impress the Talaings in two ways because they continued rebelling and migrating to Siam. Firstly, he executed the captive Talaing king and princes; secondly, he raised the Shwedagon to its present height, 327 feet, regilded it with his own weight in gold, and erected a golden spire, studded with gems, to replace the one thrown down in the 1769 earthquake.

[1] Gouger, *Two Years Imprisonment in Burmah*, p. 104.
[2] Taw Sein Ko, "The Po-u-daung Inscription", in *Indian Antiquary*, 1893.

The king's prayers were for victory to his arms. Those prayers were needed, as the situation in Siam was serious. His supremacy there had begun to collapse almost before the ruins of Ayuthia ceased to smoulder. When the Burmese armies were sweeping down upon Ayuthia in 1765, there was a governor of a northern province who would not drink the water of allegiance. He was the son of a Chinese father and a Siamese mother, and his name was Paya Tak.[1] He collected a few hundred determined men like himself and withdrew to the hills. The Burmese repeatedly tried to dislodge him but he flung them back. He went east and gained Cambodia, vastly increasing his resources. The men of Siam, sick of oppression, rose and called on him to lead them, for their lawful princes were in captivity. In 1768 he destroyed several Burmese garrisons, reoccupied Ayuthia, and founded the present capital, Bangkok. He was now king, but his palace never saw him, as he lived in the field. The Burmese sent expeditions. He harried them in ambushes, cut them off, starved them out. He and his people were united in a just cause. Whether the Burmese could in any case have held Siam for long is doubtful, but whatever chances they had were ruined by the disunion which now became the curse of their armies in the field. For the spoilers fell out over their prey, and though captains like Mahathihathura, the hero of the Chinese war, and Thihapate, the conqueror of Ayuthia, continued to win occasional victories, they could achieve nothing permanent in the face of rampant insubordination. If a commander disapproved the plan of campaign, he showed his disapproval by simply withdrawing his levies and marching off elsewhere. Some of them were executed, but the harm had been done; the Burmese were driven across the frontier, and even at Chiengmai they were ill at ease, when the king died. He was succeeded by his son.

Singu (1776–82) at once finished the Siamese escapade by withdrawing the armies. His only wars were in Manipur. The rightful raja who fled from the Burmese in 1770 made four attempts to oust their nominee between 1775 and 1782; his base was in Cachār and they drove him back each time, but after 1782 they left him in possession, perhaps because the country was now so thoroughly devastated that nothing more could be wrung out of it. In the first two years, for which Singu was not responsible, the army was absent continuously, losing 20,000 men, partly by fever, and gaining barren victories in Cachār and Jaintia. These states had to present daughters and pay tribute of a tree with the earth still clinging to its roots in token that the king had seisin of the land; and henceforth he claimed these countries, although his suzerainty was, as usual, nominal.

The people liked Singu because he was peaceful. Except commanders who wanted titles and village ruffians who wanted loot,

[1] Pallegoix, *Description du Royaume Thai ou Siam*, II, 94–8.

everyone was made miserable by these everlasting wars, which indeed led to migrations. Thus, the Yaw folk fled from their original home to the remote Mu valley in Katha district in order to get out of the king's reach and escape conscription. If a town was depopulated by rebellion or by the slaughter of its levy on foreign service, a few hundred households would be transferred to it from another charge, sometimes a week's journey away, whether they wanted to go or not.

The people did not know that Singu was seldom sober; all they knew was that he left them alone, and they were deeply grateful. He built many pagodas, for he spent much of his time in prayer; he was an angler too, and had an eye for scenery, to judge from some of his favourite haunts, where the gleam of a golden spire is reflected in the green depths of the stream below. His chief queen had a talent for verse, and the tutor of his youth was the poet Nga Hpyaw, who now received the title Minyeyaza. Sleep, prayer, fishing, drink, the laughter of the palace ladies in some sequestered woodland—it was all very pleasant, far pleasanter than the hard life of the soldier in foreign fields.

He exiled Mahathihathura as soon as he arrived from Siam, and he executed great personages at court, including his queens, especially when he was angry as well as drunk. Had he been a man of ordinary character, such acts might have been accepted. But his habits deprived him and the ministers and swordbearers, most of whom followed his example, of respect. His fondness for making pilgrimages with only a small court, leaving the palace vacant for weeks at a time, and returning in slipshod fashion at any hour of night, gave conspirators their opportunity. While he was absent at Thihadaw pagoda on the Irrawaddy Island in Shwebo district, a party came to the palace at midnight. With them was a puppet of eighteen, Maung Maung, lord of Paungga in Sagaing district, dressed up so as to resemble the king his cousin. The guard passed them in, thinking it was the king; Mahathihathura returned from retirement and took command of the guard in Maung Maung's behalf.

When the news reached king Singu, his followers fled and he thought of taking refuge in Manipur; but his mother, the queen dowager, indignantly insisted on his playing the man. He went alone at dawn to the palace gate, and when challenged by the guard answered: "It is I, Singu, lawful lord of the palace." They fell back respectfully, and he entered the courtyard. There he saw a minister, father to one of the queens he had murdered. He made for him exclaiming: "Traitor, I am come to take possession of my right." The minister seized a sword and cut him down. At least he died royally.

Maung Maung was placed on the throne. Having spent most of his life in a monastery, he was terrified at his elevation and offered each of his seniors the crown, recalling them from the villages to which they had been exiled in the interests of his predecessor's safety. They all refused, suspecting some deep device. Soon, however, his impotence became apparent, and after seven days on his unhappy throne he was executed by one who had many faults but was no puppet. This was Bodawpaya (1782–1819), the eldest of Alaungpaya's surviving sons. The palace plots which were the bane of Burma proceeded in part from the lack of a clearly observed law of succession. Alaungpaya had expressed the wish that he should be succeeded by his sons in order of seniority, and this appears to have been in accordance with a recognised theory of succession[1] by the eldest agnate, but Hsinbyushin had disregarded it by nominating Singu.

[1] Temple, "Order of succession in the Alompra dynasty", in *Indian Antiquary*, 1892.

CHAPTER XVIII

MONUMENTS OF THE MUGHUL PERIOD

TO Bābur, fresh from the flourishing cities of his fatherland embellished with the magnificent buildings of the Timurids, the state of the cities and towns of Hindūstān must have afforded a striking contrast. Conditions in northern India for a long period had been such as to give little encouragement to the building art, few edifices of any importance had been constructed, and those monuments which told of the splendour of an earlier age had been suffered to fall into decay. Compared with the living culture that he had left, he found himself traversing a wilderness of neglect. Most of the towns through which he passed seem to have consisted of nothing more than mud forts. And the capital cities were but little better. Lahore, once adorned by the palatial residences of the Ghaznī and Ghorī sultans, was almost in ruins. Āgra, to which the Lodīs had moved their court, contained only a brick citadel in a state of disrepair. At Delhi, it is true, there remained substantial records of ancient architectural grandeur, "but now worn out and disfigured to the last degree". Bābur, from his camp near the river, made a tour of this historical site, much as a visitor would do the round of its various relics at the present day. He was compelled to pitch his tents here because the most recent city built by Fīrūz Tughluq had been abandoned some time before, and, except for its mosque, lay derelict. Everywhere in northern India it was much the same, and to complete the scene of desolation the severe earthquake of a few years previous had taken its toll. "Large and substantial buildings were utterly destroyed. The living thought the day of judgment had arrived; the dead the day of resurrection."[1] One place only seems to have moved Bābur to any degree of enthusiasm, and that was at Gwālior, where he "went over all the palaces of Man Sinh and Vikramajit", and remarked that "they were singularly beautiful, though built in different patches and without regular plan". These buildings, however, illustrated the prevailing type of secular architecture as practised by the Hindus early in the sixteenth century, and it was to such structures that the Mughuls turned when they began to build palaces of their own.

Bābur was a shrewd, but perhaps prejudiced, critic of the art of building in Hindūstān, as his *Memoirs* repeatedly indicate. Although he praises the remarkable dexterity of the Indian workman, especially the stonemasons, he complains of the slipshod manner in which they

[1] Tārīkh-i-Khān-Jahān Lodī (Elliot, v, 99).

designed their structures, without "regularity or symmetry", faults which would readily offend the inherent taste of the Mughuls for strict formality and balance. In spite of this he embarked on several building projects of a fairly ambitious order, for he states that "680 men worked daily on my buildings in Āgra,...while 1491 stone-cutters worked daily on my buildings in Āgra, Sīkrī, Biāna, Dholpur, Gwālior and Kiūl". Most of these craftsmen, however, appear to have been engaged on the construction of pleasaunces, pavilions, baths, wells, tanks and fountains, for as an out-of-doors man, such extemporary amenities appealed to him more than palaces or public buildings, and, having no religious or sentimental character, they were allowed to fall into decay and have entirely disappeared. Three mosques attributed to Bābur have survived. One of these in the Kābulī Bāgh at Pānīpat, and another, the *Jāmi' Masjid* at Sambhal, were both built in 1526. Although fairly large structures, neither of them possesses any special architectural significance, while of another mosque which he built about the same time within the old Lodī fort at Āgra, he himself complains that it "is not well done, it is in the Hindūstānī fashion".[1] Some of Bābur's dissatisfaction at the state of the building art may be traced to his having acquired in the course of his varied career a certain knowledge of the manner in which such things were done in Europe, as on one occasion he fortified his camp "in the Rūmī way", meaning no doubt in the western, or Byzantine, fashion. According therefore to one authority, in view of his frequently expressed dislike of the indigenous methods of building, he is said to have sent to Constantinople, for the pupils of the celebrated Albanian architect, Sinān, to advise him on his building schemes.[2] It is, however, very unlikely that this proposal ever came to anything, because had any member of this famous school taken service under the Mughuls, traces of the influence of the Byzantine style would be observable. But there is none; in no building of the dynasty is there any sign of the low segmental dome flanked by the slender pointed minaret which characterised the compositions of Sinān and his followers.

Had circumstances permitted, Bābur's son and successor, Humāyūn, would have left more than one monument as a record of his intermittent rule. But the political situation was unfavourable. As it was, one of his earliest undertakings was to build at Delhi a new city to "be the asylum of wise and intelligent persons, and be called Dīnpanāh (World-refuge)". It was to contain "a magnificent palace of seven storeys, surrounded by delightful gardens and orchards, of such elegance and beauty that its fame might draw people from the remotest corners of the world". The laying of the foundation stone

[1] *Memoirs*, II, 533. The third surviving mosque is at Ajodhya.

[2] Saladin, *Manuel d'art Musulman*, pp. 509, 561, quoting from Montani, *Architecture Ottomane*.

of this, the first Mughul capital, is thus described by one who was present.

> At an hour which was prescribed by the most clever astrologers and the greatest astronomers, all the great *mushāikhs* (religious men), the respectable *sayyids*, the learned persons, and all the elders, accompanied the King to the sacred spot, and prayed the Almighty God to finish the happy foundation of that city. First, His Majesty with his holy hand put a brick on the earth, and then each person from that concourse of great men placed a stone on the ground, and they all made such a crowd there that the army, people, and the artists, masons, and labourers found no room or time to carry stones and mud to the spot.[1]

As it is also related that "the walls, bastions, ramparts, and the gates of the city" were all nearly finished within the same year, it seems not unlikely that the work was pushed on with undue haste, without much consideration of its quality. In any case Humāyūn's capital is hardly traceable among the ruins of old Delhi, although its final demolition seems to have been one of the first acts of the Afghān usurper, Sher Shāh. Two mosques remain of those built during Humāyūn's reign, one in a ruinous condition at Āgra, and the other at Fathābād, Hissār, which indicate the methods of building in vogue at this period. They show no original features, being constructed of ashlar masonry covered with a coating of stucco, the only attempt at ornamentation consisting of geometrical patterns sunk in the surface of the plaster. It is probable that the city of Dīnpanāh was of the same simple unassuming character, rapidly "run up" to supply an immediate need.

The material records which have survived of both Bābur's and Humāyūn's contributions to the building art of the country are therefore almost negligible. On the other hand the indirect influence of their personalities and experiences on the subsequent art of the dynasty cannot be overlooked. Bābur's marked aesthetic sense, communicated to his successors, inspired them under more favourable conditions to the production of their finest achievements, while Humāyūn's forced contact with the culture of the Safavids is reflected in that Persian influence noticeable in many of the Mughul buildings which followed.

Although owing to the unsettled conditions of the country but little encouragement to architecture was possible during the early years of the Mughul dynasty, a few buildings of a private character which were erected in the neighbourhood of Delhi show that the style of the Sayyids and Afghāns as produced in the previous century still continued. A tomb, with its adjoining mosque, known as the Jamālī, built about 1530, illustrates the demand that was then arising for a richer and more decorative treatment of these rather sombre structures. The Jamālī mosque will be referred to later, as its connection with a phase of building which succeeded it is important. But the Sayyid-Afghān style was more suitable for tombs than for

[1] Humāyūn-nāma of Khondamīr, Elliot, v, 124–6.

any other purpose, as several mausoleums built near Delhi about this time testify. That of 'Īsā Khān, erected in 1547, is a well-balanced composition, standing within its own walled enclosure, and including a mosque on its western side. Enclosure, terrace, platform and mausoleum are all designed on an octagonal plan, with eight kiosks of the same shape rising above its crenellated parapet. Each angle of its pillared verandah is strengthened by a sloping buttress, the final instance of the use of this "batter", which, introduced by Fīrūz Tughluq, had now persisted for two centuries. In another large tomb in much the same style, that of Adham Khān, constructed some twenty years later, there is no sign of this characteristic slope, which evidently ceased with the tomb of 'Īsā Khān. Adham Khān's tomb is the last building of this type, and although it can hardly be described as decadent, its trite and uninspiring elevation conveys the impression that the potential growth of the style was at an end.

During the period, however, that the Sayyid-Afghān mode was approaching its logical conclusion at Delhi, it is significant of the unexpected course that events not infrequently take in Indian history, that in another and distant part of the country a group of buildings in this same style was being produced which are undeniably the finest of their kind. At Sasarām in Bihār, and in its neighbourhood, a series of tombs was erected, all probably within the decade before 1550, commemorative of the house of Sher Shāh Sūr and its association with the government of the lower Provinces. They are all buildings of noble proportions, the largest of them, that of Sher Shāh himself, being one of the most admirable monuments in the whole of India, and thoroughly expressive of the Indian genius. Much of this excellence is undoubtedly a tribute to the cultured intuition of Sher Shāh, which not only shows itself here, but, at a slightly later date, at Delhi also. From the imperial capital this Afghān governor obtained his ideas of what a royal mausoleum should be like, and from somewhat the same source he secured the services of the master-builder who was to put his plans into effect. The designer of these edifices was one Aliwāl Khān (whose tomb is one of the group), from his name apparently a native of the Punjāb, a skilled mason and evidently well acquainted with the art of tomb building as ordained by the court at Delhi. His first commission at Sasarām was the erection of a mausoleum for Hasan Khān Sūr, the father of Sher Shāh, a solid structure in much the same style as several of the royal or official tombs of the Sayyid or Lodī period. Viewed, however, as a whole this initial effort is not a complete success (Fig. 4). The uninteresting octagonal wall forming its middle story, unbroken by any opening, is a definite fault, and it seems not improbable that this tomb was of an experimental nature in view of what was to follow. Aliwāl Khān's next work, destined to be his *magnum opus*, was the mausoleum of his patron, a conception which, apart from its surpassing architectural merit, reveals an imagination of more than ordinary power. Standing in the midst of a spacious artificial lake, it forms an ideal funerary monument to such a remarkable soldier adventurer as Sher Shāh, a magnificent grey pile emblematic of masculine strength, and at the same time the embodiment of eternal repose.

The plan of isolating one's burial place from the outer world by means of a sheet of water had already occurred to Ghiyās-ud-dīn Tughluq some two centuries earlier, when he designed his tomb like a barbican thrown out from the fortress at Tughluqābād and surrounded it with a lake. Inspired no doubt by the originality and significance of this, by now, historical monument, Sher Shāh's mausoleum was designed on somewhat similar lines, except that instead of the irregular lake, it rises from a large rectangular tank, the cemented sides of which measure each approximately fourteen hundred feet in length. The tomb building itself occupies the centre of this body of water, forming a grand pyramidal mass of diminishing tiers, mounting up from a stepped plinth of over three hundred feet wide, and crowned by a semi-spherical dome. The plinth and the high terrace above it, which comprise the foundations of the composition, are square in plan, while the tomb building above is an octagonal structure in three storeys, a slightly elaborated form of the Lodī tombs at Delhi, but made vastly more imposing by its size, situation, and particularly by the massive and spacious character of its stepped and terraced basement. Much skill has been expended on the design and disposition of the architectural details, which break up the mass of the building with admirable effect. Flights of steps with entrance archways relieve the middle of each side of the terrace, and domed octagonal pavilions ornament each corner, with projecting oriel-balconies carried on heavy brackets in between. The upper surface of this immense sub-structure forms a courtyard, within which stands the mausoleum proper. This building is enclosed within an aisle of pointed arches, three to each of its octagonal sides, and shaded all round by a wide eave surmounted by a crenellated parapet. This constitutes the lower storey. Above, the two upper storeys are decorated by means of pillared kiosks, one at each angle and alternating with oriel windows, while the dome crowning the whole is crested by a solid lotus finial. The interior of the tomb consists of one large vaulted hall, octagonal in shape and surrounded by an arcade of arches; it is somewhat bare and plain, and may be unfinished. Seen across the rippling waters of the tank, the entire composition now appears grey and sombre, but this was by no means the original intention. It is the greyness of age, as, when first built, its walls displayed patterns of glowing colour, and the dome was set brilliantly white against the blue sky. Traces of this glazed decoration still remain, fine bold borders of blues, reds and yellows, in keeping with the grand scale of the building itself. Access to the mausoleum is obtained by means of a causeway built across the water, the entrance to which is through a square domed guardroom on the northern side of the tank. The causeway has become much ruined, but its original character may be judged from a somewhat similar approach to the remains of Salīm Shāh's tomb, another monument of the group, also located in a large artificial lake. Although resembling a bridge it contains no arches, but consists of a succession of piers with the intervening spaces spanned by lintels and corbels, the piers being ornamented by kiosks and projecting balconies. In the course of building the mausoleum of Sher Shāh a curious error in orientation seems to have occurred, there being a difference of eight degrees between the alignment of the stepped plinth and that of the terrace above. The latter faces the true north, but the mistake in the direction of the foundations was evidently discovered and the required correction made while the building was in progress, a fact which must have added considerably to the difficulties of its construction; although noticeable, it does not materially detract from the general appearance (Fig. 5). The other tombs of the Sūrī group, five in number, all in the Shāhābād district, are of the same general type, but each one has some distinguishing feature, such as the specially designed gateway of Aliwāl Khān's, the architect, or the entrance to the enclosure of Hasan Khān's, while the others show variations in the composition of their façades. Excellent though they all are, none of them approaches the solemn grandeur of Sher Shāh's last resting-place, which takes first rank in magnificence of conception. Its pyramidal mass, the silhouette of which seen at sunset is something to be remembered, the sense of finely adjusted bulk, the proportions of its diminishing stages, the harmonious transitions from square to octagon and octagon to circle, the simplicity, breadth and scale of its parts, all combine to produce an effect of great beauty. India boasts of several mausoleums of more than ordinary splendour; the Tāj at Āgra in some of its aspects is unrivalled; over Muhammad 'Ādil Shāh's remains at Bijāpur spreads a dome of stupendous proportions, but Sher Shāh's island tomb at Sasarām, grey and brooding, is perhaps the most impressive of them all.

The architectural activities of the house of Sūr were not, however, confined to Bihār. With Sher Shāh elevated to the throne vacated by Humāyūn, the building art was again revived at the imperial capital, where it was undergoing an interesting state of transition. Delhi had for some time established a tradition somewhat parallel to that of classical Rome, in that it maintained an imperial style of its own as distinct from that of the provinces. Towards the middle of the sixteenth century there were signs of a renaissance. The art was beginning to throw off that puritanical influence which had fettered it since the time of Fīrūz Tughluq, and apparently was attempting to return to the more ornate style of the Khaljīs. For two hundred years this austere method of building had prevailed, preventing the Indian artisan from exercising his natural aptitude for fine ashlar masonry, and from decorating the edifices thus constructed with rich carving, both of which were his birthright. Already indications of such a movement are observable in buildings dating from the beginning of the sixteenth century, as for instance in the Moth-kī-Masjid, where, among other innovations, in place of the "beam and bracket" opening in the centre of the façade, ordained by Fīrūz and continued by his successors, there emerges again the recessed archway of the early Tughluqs and Khaljīs. Some twenty years later a further step is seen in the treatment of the Jamālī Masjid, with its ashlar masonry laced with white marble, and, more important still, its double recessed arch enriched with "spear heads", signifying a definite attempt to pick up the threads of the older style. What was required at this stage was intelligent patronage to stimulate the movement, now well begun, into further effort. This was supplied by the building predilections of Sher Shāh, who, had he lived longer, would undoubtedly have influenced very profoundly the character and course of the art. As it was, during the short time that he ruled at Delhi a form of architecture was initiated which was not only of a high character in itself, but was destined to affect considerably the styles which followed.

The Afghān ruler's first act was, however, destructive, as he razed to the ground Humāyūn's city of Dīnpanāh, founded so auspiciously a few years previously, and in its place, on the site of Indarpat, began to build a new walled capital containing within it a strong citadel for his own accommodation. Owing to his untimely death the city itself was never finished—only two gateways remain—but the citadel known as the Purānā Qil'a, although now little more than a shell, is still intact, and its walls and gateways, together with one building in its interior, form an important landmark in the architectural development of the period. Its bastioned ramparts, massively constructed of rubble masonry, are marvels of strength, while the bold battlements protect a wide parapet walk, underneath which is a spacious double arcade carried around its entire circuit. On their outer side these plain rugged walls are relieved by ornamental machicolations at frequent and regular intervals, with an occasional balcony projected on brackets. As a contrast to the severely practical nature of these defences, and also to their rough rubble construction, are the gateways built of fine sandstone ashlar decorated with white marble inlay and coloured glaze. In the design and execution of these gateways we seem to see the beginnings of a more refined and artistically ornate type of edifice than had prevailed for some time. That a development of this kind was taking place is proved by the character of the only building of any note now left within the walls.

This is a mosque, the Qil'a-i-Kuhna Masjid, a structure of such admirable architectural qualities as to entitle it to a high place among the buildings of northern India.

Reference has been already made to the Jamālī Masjid, and it was out of this that the Qil'a-i-Kuhna Masjid was evolved. Each mosque has a double arch for its fronton, with two archways in each of its wings. The interiors of both consist of one large hall divided into five bays, there is one central dome, and the systems of pendentives supporting the roof have much in common. The Qil'a-i-Kuhna was built in 1545, some fifteen years after its prototype, and depicts in a most decisive manner the advance that took place in that short period. Every feature, somewhat crudely fashioned in the earlier example, was carefully refined, improved or amplified during this time, in order to fit it for its place in the finished composition of the Qil'a-i-Kuhna. This mosque was evidently the Chapel Royal of Sher Shāh and the perfection of its parts may be due to his personal supervision. It has no cloisters, although there is a courtyard in front, with an octagonal tank in its centre, and at the side is a doorway to serve as the royal private entrance. The mosque is not large, occupying a rectangle of 168 feet by 44½ feet, and its height is 66 feet. There is a handsome stair turret at each of its rear corners, with oriel windows on brackets at intervals. All these features have been carefully disposed, but the chief beauty of the building lies in the arrangement of its façade. This is divided into five arched bays, the central one larger than the others and each having an open archway recessed within it. With these as the basis of his scheme, the designer has enriched each part with mouldings, bracketed openings, marble inlay, carving and other embellishments all in such good taste that the effect of the whole is above criticism. The interior is equally pleasing. Archways divide it into five compartments which correspond to the five façade openings, and recessed in the west wall of each is an elegant *mihrāb*. In the support of the roof three different methods have been exploited. The central bay, roofed by the dome, has the usual squinch-arch as a pendentive, but the others, although they have no domes, have vaulted ceilings necessitating some kind of support in the angles. In one instance this support is formed of diminishing rows of brackets with small ornamental arches in between, a most artistic solution of this constructive problem (Fig. 10). But the method adopted in the end bays shows more originality; a flattened arch is thrown across, leaving a space at the back which is filled in with a semi-dome, pendentives supporting the corners, a daring experiment and not perhaps one to be repeated, but the whole building proclaims the artistic and inventive skill of the architect. Where, however, this craftsman excelled was in the design of the *mihrābs*, which, of their kind, can have no equal in any other mosque in India. An arched niche is commonly the form these take, but by sinking one recess within another, and by doming them over, he provided himself with a foundation inviting decoration. His material was marble, and the sure manner in which he has manipulated this, and the effect produced, is beyond praise.

With the Qil'a-i-Kuhna mosque, however, this mode of building virtually begins, and also ends; it stands as an isolated example among the different types of structure which lie around old Delhi. Sher Shāh, as both Sasarām and the Qil'a-i-Kuhna Masjid seem to prove, had either the gift of discovering genius and making full use of it, or he was of a nature that inspired those he employed to their highest affords. History indicates the latter, because with his death in 1545 the art also appears to have died. And with his last breath he regrets that fate had not spared him longer to put into effect other ambitious building schemes which he specifies.[1] For the following twenty years little building of any importance is recorded, the few structures that were erected reflecting the unstable political conditions that then prevailed. The only contribution of his successor Salīm Shāh consisted of a fort, named after him, on the banks of the Jumna, a group of frowning bastions of no architectural merit, now considerably dismantled, and converted into an outwork to Shāh Jahān's more famous palace-fortress. Somewhat later, about 1560, two buildings were raised at Delhi, and it is perhaps significant of the times that they were not founded by men, all of whom were engaged in less peaceful pursuits, but by women, members of the royal household. One of these is the mosque of Khair-ul-manāzil and the other a large hostel known as the Arab Sarai. Neither, in itself, is a work of much importance, but portions of them show that the mode initiated by Sher Shāh was still remembered. The mosque is unusual because it has an upper storey of classrooms enclosing the courtyard within a high screen, an arrangement for strict seclusion which suggests that the school was for girls, and the mosque for the use of women only. Its architectural interest, however, lies in the handsome gateway by which it is entered (Fig. 11). This consists of a doorway recessed within a larger arched alcove, similar in many respects to those in the buildings of Sher Shāh. But there is one notable difference. The wall containing the doorway is joined above on to the outer archway by means of a semi-dome, a stage in the development of a prominent feature common in the façades of the Mughuls. This, however, is only one instance of the influence that the able craftsmen under the Sūr dynasty exercised on the architecture that followed. Much of the character of the works carried out under Akbar and Jahāngīr may be traced to the genius of the master-builder who produced the remarkable little mosque in the citadel of Sher Shāh.

[1] Tārīkh-i Khān-Jahān Lodī, Elliot v, 108–9.

It was not until Akbar had occupied the throne for eight years that the country became sufficiently settled to enable any large building projects to be contemplated. Then the encouragement of the arts began in real earnest. About the year 1564 at least five building schemes of varying importance were commenced in different parts of the empire, three of them of the first rank, and the others illustrating in a marked manner certain developments that were then taking place. Of the larger schemes, Humāyūn's tomb at Delhi is the most noteworthy, although Akbar's fortress-palaces at Āgra and Lahore were stupendous undertakings. Compared with these imperial enterprises the tomb of Muhammad Ghaus at Gwālior appears a small affair, but the peculiarities of its design are of some interest, while the tomb of Adham Khān at Delhi, previously described, is significant because it rings down the curtain on the "Lodī" style, a mode which had persisted for nearly two centuries. It is a coincidence that at practically the same time that this final example of the puritanism originated by Fīrūz Tughluq was being constructed, four miles away, in the building of Humāyūn's tomb, an entirely new movement was being begun. In other words Adham Khān's tomb marks the death of one tradition, and Humāyūn's tomb the birth of another. The latter, besides being a composition of more than ordinary breadth and power, introduces a new era into the history of architecture in northern India. Some of its parts, notably the shape and construction of its dome, are clearly adaptations of somewhat similar buildings in the cities of the Timurids in Persia. This attribution is readily explained. The tomb was built by Humāyūn's widow, Hājī Begam, who shared his long exile at the court of the Safavids. Moreover, as architect she employed Mirāk Mīrzā Ghiyās, almost certainly of Persian extraction and therefore trained in the Timurid tradition. He, with others having somewhat similar affinities, formed part of a small colony of the Begam's retainers who had settled in Delhi. The influence of their culture shows itself in the character of Humāyūn's tomb. But in the process of transforming the style of one country to suit the conditions of another, certain changes became necessary. Some of these changes are due to the differences of material; the Persians built almost entirely of brick with decorations of terra-cotta and glaze, and the Indian masons had to translate these fictile forms into chiselled marble and stone. But the design of Humāyūn's tomb did something more than introduce other elements into the architecture of Hindūstān; it suggested new principles, wider possibilities, greater flexibility, and generally infused the building art with fresh life. There were subsequent occasions when the Mughul artizans received inspiration from the same source, but the main Persian incentive came to the building art of the Mughuls through Hājī Begam's conception of her royal consort's mausoleum.

One of the most attractive features of this composition as a whole is the innovation of placing the building in the centre of a large park-like enclosure. It had already become the custom to surround the tomb by a walled-in space, but the idea of expanding this into an extensive formal garden was entirely that of the Mughuls. The garden around a Mughul tomb, with its paved pathways, flowered parterres, avenues of cypress trees, ornamental watercourses, tanks and fountains, was considered by them an essential complement to the mausoleum building in its centre. Added to this the entrance gateways, one in the middle of each side of the perimeter wall, were structures of fairly generous proportions, so disposed and designed as to serve as a prelude to the monument within, the arched shape of the main portal being of such dimensions as to frame in a most striking manner the distant tomb. The principal entrance to the enclosure of Humāyūn's tomb is on the western side, and the doorway is recessed, instead of being embowed as was usual in all subsequent doorways, but this was done in order to repeat, like a refrain, a similar recessed effect in the façade of the main building. This main building stands on a high and wide-spread terrace, the sides of which are arcaded, each arcade leading to a small room within for the accommodation of visitors to the tomb. On the broad platform formed by the upper surface of this terrace the mausoleum stands, occupying a square of 156 feet side. This square plan is recessed in the middle of each side, and its corners are chamfered, thus producing in the elevation of the building a variety of contrasting planes and shade effects. All four façades, save for a slight deviation on the north side, are similar, their main characteristic being a large rectangular fronton set back in the centre, and containing a deeply recessed archway, with smaller corresponding archways in the projecting wings on each side. Much of the attractive appearance of the building is due to the size and excellent spacing of these recesses in relation to the remainder of the façade, the apportionment of solid to void being most skilfully regulated. Above the façade rises the great dome mounted on a high drum, with a combination of kiosks roofed by small cupolas and slender turrets breaking the skyline at its base. The arrangements in the interior comprise a spacious central hall, rising to a vaulted roof, and around this main hall are grouped several subsidiary chambers on a regular plan, and connected one with another by galleries and corridors. Light is obtained through clerestory windows of perforated screens fitted within the recessed archways of the façade.

Apart from the simple comprehensiveness of the total conception, proclaiming it a building of exceptional merit, the principal architectural feature which distinguishes it from anything previously attempted is the design and construction of the dome. In shape the dome, with its finial rising straight from the apex without any intervening *āmalaka*, was clearly derived from a type not uncommon at Bukhārā and Samarqand in the fifteenth century, of which the tombs of Tīmūr and Bībī Khānum are examples. It is not, however, a copy of either of these, but there is a fairly strong family likeness. The slightly constricted neck with its decorated cavetto is from the same source, but the Timurid domes usually finish at the base in a stalactite moulding, which the Indian mason converted into a course of small brackets. Further, the white marble casing, with which the whole of the latter is covered, is in marked contrast to the brilliantly coloured tiles which invariably supplied the finish to the Persian type. But it is in the constructive principle adopted in the dome of Humāyūn's tomb that the main concession is made to the ingenuity of the Timurid builders and their predecessors. Here we see for the first time in India the use of the double dome, a method of building these structures which had been practised in western Asia over a considerable period. One or two of the low-pitched domes of the previous style, notably that of the tomb of Sikandar Lodī, show attempts at this system of construction, but their flattened shape did not encourage its use, and it apparently found no favour. In Humāyūn's tomb the principle was correctly applied, the dome being composed of two separate shells, an outer and an inner, with a vacant compartment between; the outer shell supports the white marble exterior casing, while the inner forms the vaulted ceiling of the mortuary chamber below. In addition to the character and technical details of the dome, other features of the building show a similar influence. Among these is the large recessed archway with its surrounding rectangular fronton, the central element on most Mughul façades, and one which in an immature form had appeared during the previous period. In Humāyūn's tomb this effective conception was fully developed, showing, together with other motifs, its designer's further obligations to the architectural traditions of Persia. While adapting, however, the Timurid type of building to suit the materials and methods of the Indian workman, one factor was overlooked. In the Persian style almost all mouldings were purposely omitted, in order that the surfaces of the buildings should be kept clear for the application of coloured tiles, to the brilliancy of which they owed their principal effect. The bare, almost frigid, appearance of Humāyūn's tomb, in its decorative aspect, may be traced to its designer's inability to replace successfully this colour scheme by a suitable one in stone and marble. That the effort was made is shown by the borders and panels of white marble inlay applied with such good results, but in outlining the archways with the same material the severity of the façade is emphasised. As to the disposal of the rooms in the interior, this appears to be an elaboration of the plan generally adopted in Muslim tombs in India, but the diagonal connecting passages may have been suggested by a similar arrangement in

Persia, as seen in the tomb of Sāfī-ud-Dīn at Ārdabīl. The fact that the design of Humāyūn's tomb did not immediately commend itself to the Mughuls and thus revolutionise the building art of India seems to indicate that it was in advance of its time. A small tomb, however, near by, enshrining the remains of Atga Khān, is of somewhat the same type in miniature, and was produced at this time probably by those employed on the royal mausoleum. But although the superior style of the latter could not fail to influence the later work of Akbar's reign, it was not until more than sixty years had elapsed before the Mughul builders were sufficiently inspired to attempt another tomb of the same type.

That even in the production of works to serve a utilitarian purpose the Mughuls at this time were inclined to employ labour drawn from sources not far removed from Persia is shown in a famous bridge built at Jaunpur. Begun as early as 1564 to conduct the road across the Gumtī, it was devised and carried out by workmen imported from Hazāra in Afghānistān, noted for their engineering skill. Into the design of this bridge the builders introduced appropriate decorative elements which have made it a handsome structure of good architectural appearance (Fig. 14). It consists of ten spans of pointed arches with substantial piers carried up into pillared pavilions partly projected over the water on brackets. The whole composition provides an excellent illustration of the aesthetic spirit that then prevailed, and of the manner in which an object primarily intended for use, can with correctly applied taste become also a work of art.

Meanwhile in the somewhat distant and hitherto Hindu environment of Gwālior the tomb of Muhammad Ghaus was being constructed, the unusual character of its design lending this building a certain interest. Erected over the remains of a Muslim saint who flourished under the early Mughuls, it combines characteristics of the "Lodī" style, together with others associated more with the kind of building that found favour in western India. This admixture was no doubt due to the actual workmanship being entrusted to the local masons more accustomed to the requirements of Mālwā patrons than to the demands of their new Muslim overlords. The building shows a lack of co-ordination, the two phases, the Mughul and Mālwā, having not yet coalesced, a condition to be attained later under the tolerant policy of the emperor Akbar. None the less it contains some choice details, especially in its perforated screens, but the attachment of the hexagonal corner-turrets by their angles causes the general effect of the elevation as a whole to appear disconnected (Fig. 15).

After Humāyūn's tomb, however, the most important building projects of this time were the two palace-fortresses begun by Akbar at Āgra and Lahore. These were the first notable efforts made by this emperor, and were executed "under the superintendence of

Qāsim Khān, the overseer of buildings and ships".[1] Of the fort at Āgra it was said that no such walls had ever been raised before, "from top to bottom the fire-red hewn stones are joined so closely that even a hair cannot find its way into their joints." They were composed of a massive interior core of rubble and concrete faced with carefully worked blocks of sandstone "linked together by iron rings". These blocks of stone were laid in alternate courses, a wide course separated by narrow bond-stones, a method of construction which is found in nearly all the buildings of Akbar's time. The walls of Āgra fort, just under 70 feet high, consist of a continuous stretch of almost unbroken masonry nearly one and a half miles in circuit, the first conception of dressed stone on such a large scale. The somewhat irregular plan of the fort is probably due to the walls having followed the lines of the original Lodī defences of which it took the place, and its position in relation to the river Jumna had also to be considered. From a distance across the river it resembles the stranded hull of a rusty red battleship, its sombre mass relieved by the group of white domes and kiosks of the Motī Masjid rising like armoured turrets above. It is entered by two gateways, the main entrance on the western side, known as the Delhi Gate, being undeniably one of the most impressive portals in all India (Fig. 18). It is the ceremonial entrance to the fortress (the other and smaller gateway of Amar Singh being for private use), and originally its main archway was flanked by two statues of elephants; hence it was often referred to as the *Hāthī Pol* or "Elephant Gate". As it was finished in 1566 it is one of the earliest of Ākbar's productions, and shows that that emperor's builders had already realised the high standard that was required of them. It is devised on the usual plan of an archway flanked by two bastions, but it is the masterly manner in which this simple scheme was handled that gives it such an imposing and at the same time artistic appearance. Taking the octagon as his theme, the designer has made the bastions, the vaulted chamber between, and the domed kiosks crowning the battlements all eight-sided in plan. Height was obtained by the whole being in two storeys, with the bastions divided transversely by a balcony on brackets, a projection which gives a most useful line of interruption to the façade. Openings below would only weaken the appearance of a building obviously required for strength, so that except for the main archway the lower storey has no voids, but above the balcony are arched recesses producing the necessary effect of depth and substance. Considerable interest attaches to the manner in which the entire surface of the gateway was decorated; patterns in white marble inlay enrich the arcades and panels, while coloured tiles of winged dragons, elephants and foliated birds add vitality to a composition which in itself is remarkable for animation and strength.

[1] Akbar Nāma, II, 246–7.

Within the Āgra fort enclosure, the "Āīn" states that Akbar built "upwards of five hundred edifices of red stone in the fine styles of Bengal and Gujarāt". Many of these structures were demolished later to make room for Shāh Jahān's white marble pavilions, but enough remain to show the general character of these early Mughul palaces. They now consist of a group of buildings in the south-east corner of the fort, but originally they extended along the greater portion of the east wall overlooking the river. Apparently built and added at different periods during the long course of Akbar's reign, that known as the Akbarī Mahall, with the Bangālī bastion, is the earliest, as it is contemporary with the fort-wall of which it forms the upper part. At a later date, probably towards the end of the sixteenth century, considerable alterations appear to have taken place, and a section of the outer wall was dismantled in order to accommodate another palace, that of the Jahāngīrī Mahall, intended as a residence for the heir apparent and his family. Both palaces, however, are designed on the usual plan of a central square court-yard, with ranges of double-storeyed rooms on each of the four sides. They are almost entirely of red sandstone, with insertions of white marble on the exterior, and the principle of construction is the "beam and bracket", the arch being sparingly used and then only in its ornamental capacity. There is little difference in the character of these two palaces, the older one being perhaps a little coarser and bolder in its treatment compared with the finer and more ornate handiwork on the Jahāngīrī Mahall. In the latter one is struck by the elaborate character of the carved stone brackets which support the stone beams, wide eaves and flat ceilings in all parts of the building. In no other structure, except in a range of similar pavilions in the fort at Lahore being built about the same time, has such ingenuity been shown in the design of these supporting brackets, or have they been applied in such profusion. Apart from this feature, which, as a constructional motif, is itself of wooden origin, several of the details in this palace suggest a derivation from a phase of wooden architecture which may have preceded it. This is particularly noticeable in the treatment of the portico of the eastern façade, and also in the use of struts in the northern hall. In the former the two slender pillars with their expanding caps and bases and the arrangement of brackets above would be much more appropriate in wood than in stone (Fig. 22); as regards the latter the struts supporting the ceiling are obviously copies of wooden beams; in fact the whole design of this hall resembles the wooden interior of some of the large houses in the city of Lahore of a slightly earlier date (Fig. 23). That those who worked under Akbar borrowed readily and from a variety of sources is obvious. In the general character of the fort at Āgra there is a resemblance to the fortress at Gwālior, with its palaces of Mān Singh built early in the century, which cannot be accidental.

The elephant gateway, the cupolas of Amar Singh's gateway, the palaces rising out of the fort-walls, the planning of these palaces, and also some of the carved details, all indicate that the Rājput citadel, which had moved Bābur to admiration some forty years before, was used freely as a model by his more fortunately placed grandson.

Although Lahore was regarded as only the secondary capital of the empire, the fort that Akbar constructed there almost at the same time as that at Āgra was conceived and carried out on practically the same grand scale. It may be remarked, however, that its lay-out generally indicates an advance on that of the more southerly capital, as it is rectangular in plan and the interior arrangements are more regularly aligned. It was, however, altered even to a greater extent by Shāh Jahān, and subsequent rulers, including the Sikhs, have also changed its appearance. What is left of the palace buildings, dated from the time of Akbar, and possibly Jahāngīr, show that the style of these was similar in most respects to the Jahāngīrī Mahall at Āgra, except that the carved decoration was, if anything, more vigorous and unrestrained. Elephants and lions figure in the brackets and peacocks on the friezes, from which it may be inferred that Hindu craftsmen predominated, and that the supervision of the Mughul overseers was of a very tolerant order. One other fort of the first rank was built by Akbar some twenty years later at Allahābād, which still shows remains of considerable architectural merit, but its outer walls have been partly dismantled, and its interior structures have been very roughly treated, so that little is left of its original appearance. It is of the same irregular plan as the fort at Āgra, but this again may have been partly due to its position at the junction of the Jumna and Ganges. One noble pavilion, however, still remains intact, the Zanāna Palace, from which the character of the whole may be surmised. The pillars enclosing the verandah of this structure are in pairs, with two groups of four at each corner, a columniation of an unusually rich kind. Above, the pillars branch out into bracket-capitals forming elaborate clusters of forms which break up the deep shadow of the eaves that they support. For its effect it depends very largely on the number and distribution of its pillars with their superstructures, and records of other buildings in this fort indicate that a peristylar arrangement was much favoured by its architect.

It is characteristic of Akbar's almost insatiable passion for building, that even before the forts of Āgra and Lahore were completed, he began to contemplate a scheme which eventually matured into the greatest of all his architectural projects. This was the construction of an entirely new capital city on an elevated site at Fathpur Sīkrī, some twenty-six miles distant from Āgra. No sooner was the idea formed than plans were prepared, artizans summoned from all parts of his dominions, and the work pushed on with such lightning rapidity that not only its splendour but the almost magical speed with which it was completed was a matter of contemporary comment. Jahāngīr writes that "in the course of fourteen or fifteen years that hill, full of wild beasts, became a city containing all kinds of gardens and buildings, and lofty elegant edifices and pleasant places attractive to the heart";[1] while Father Monserrate, after giving details of the extraordinary expedition with which certain buildings were finished, remarks that "all the material, prepared according to specification, was brought complete and ready to the place where it was to be used",[2] reminding him of the scriptural precedent "and the house, when it was in building, was built of stone made ready before it was brought thither: so that there was neither hammer nor axe nor any tool of iron heard in the house, while it was in building" (1 Kings vi. 7). Such, however, was the common practice of masons in the east. In India, although at certain times and in some localities the carving was apparently done on the walls, as a rule the stones were separately prepared, carved into pattern and then conveyed as a finished product to the building to be placed in position. The latter was evidently the system in vogue in Mughul times. At Akbar's new capital the method would present no difficulties, as there was an unlimited supply of good building material to be quarried on the site itself. In the words of the "Āīn": "Red sandstone...is obtainable in the hills of Fathpur Sīkrī, His Majesty's residence, and may be broken from the rock at any length or breadth. Clever workmen chisel it so skilfully as no turner could do with wood." Most of the labour was done in a kind of open-air workshop on a level space towards the western limits of the ridge. Here the masons erected for their own worship a mosque called the "Stone-cutters' Masjid", which is probably one of the earliest buildings on the site.

The ridge at Fathpur Sīkrī is a rocky eminence running north-east and south-west. Along and astride it was marked out a rough rectangle approximately two miles long and one mile broad, three sides of which were walled, while the remaining side was protected by a large artificial lake. The encircling walls were not very substantially built, being merely a symbol of demarcation and of little military value. In an emergency Akbar and his court could readily fall back on the strong fortress of Āgra, to which it was connected by a broad thoroughfare, the conditions being somewhat similar to those of Windsor Palace and its relation to the Tower of London. Nine gates were constructed, but only four of these were of importance, while there was the usual "Elephant Gate" or *Hāthī Pol*, but this was a ceremonial gateway to the palace precincts and not in the city walls. The principal entrance was by the Āgra gate which faced

[1] *Memoirs*, I, 2.
[2] First Jesuit Mission to Akbar by Father Monserrate. *Memoirs of Asiatic Society of Bengal*, III, 560, 642.

that city, and from this the main road bifurcated, one branch leading up to the palaces, the other continuing lower down the hill to the suburb of Fathpur.

The chief buildings of the capital occupy a comparatively small portion of the centre of the walled area, the crest of the ridge having been levelled into an irregular flat space about half a mile long and an eighth of a mile broad. On this plateau the palaces and other civil edifices form one compact group, with the Jāmi' Masjid standing slightly detached; a separate road leads to each. Around and at lower levels were various supplementary structures such as *sarais*, baths, wells, offices, the treasury and the mint. All the principal buildings on the ridge are not aligned parallel but diagonally to the rectangle of the encircling walls, facing accordingly east and west. This plan was necessary in order to ensure regularity, and to be in accordance with the fixed orientation of the Jāmi' Masjid, the largest and most important building on the site. The main road from the Āgra gate led directly into the large courtyard of the Dīwān-i-'Ām, as this was a semi-public enclosure to which most visitors to the capital would have the right of admittance. But the far wall of the Dīwān-i-'Ām, with its extension, marks the dividing line between the public and private portions of the palace precincts. Behind this are the royal palaces, residences, retiring rooms and offices of state, each within its own courtyard or enclosure, regularly disposed but apparently on no particular plan except that from Akbar's own apartments access could readily be obtained to all parts.

Although all the buildings at Fathpur Sīkrī conform to the general style of architecture which was developed during Akbar's reign, the Jāmi' Masjid, on account of the special purposes for which it was intended, and the traditional character which it was required to maintain, was treated in a somewhat different manner from the other edifices. The latter, comprising the secular or civil buildings, such as palaces, residences, state compartments and offices, are as a whole similar to those already referred to in the forts of Āgra and Lahore. They are mainly trabeated in their construction and the indigenous methods and motives prevailed. But a few of them are even more "Hindu" than those already described, and it is quite clear that some of their decorative features are copies of those seen in the temples of the Jains and Hindus. Akbar's tolerance, and his sympathies with Indian culture as a whole, partly account for these unorthodox intrusions, but there is another explanation. The magnitude of the undertaking, and the haste with which it was accomplished, necessitated an immense staff of workmen drawn from all possible sources. Numbers were drafted from distant provinces, and it is clear that in their personnel the Hindu element predominated. Each group brought with it the characteristics of its own particular school, and more than one of these can be distinguished by certain unmistakable motifs and methods. As in the production of the secular buildings racial and religious considerations were of little consequence they were employed on these, as their style plainly shows. On the other hand the local craftsmen, having for generations been more closely concerned with Islamic usage, were concentrated on the production of the great mosque.

Most important of the residential buildings is that known as Jodh Bāī's palace, one of the first structures to be erected, and one in which the Hindu influence is mainly in evidence. Like many large dwellings in the east, particularly those in contact with Islām, it is planned with the object of ensuring privacy and protection. Its double-storeyed rooms face inward on to a quadrangle, their continuous rear walls acting as a high screen all round. The lower storey of its exterior walls is almost forbiddingly plain, but, above, balcony windows project near the angles, and there is a handsome gateway on the east side also decorated with balconies, while kiosks rise over its parapet. Over the high walls appear the gabled roofs of the interior apartments, bright with coloured tiles, and at each corner is a low-pitched dome. The regularity of its exterior is broken on one side by an annex for baths and service purposes, and on the opposite side a double-storeyed pavilion is attached called the *Hawā Khāna* or "House of Air". The design of the entrance is characteristic. With a porter's lodge at one side, the shallow arched porch leads into a vestibule for the accommodation of an inner guard. The doorway on the opposite side, giving admission to the interior courtyard, is not in line but to one side, thus entirely preventing any one outside from seeing within. Around the paved courtyard of the interior of the palace is carried a one-storeyed corridor, but imposed in the middle of each side is a substantial building two storeys in height consisting of a pillared portico in front and an arrangement of rooms in the rear. In each corner is also a double-storeyed structure surmounted by the low dome mentioned above. From the courtyard the appearance of the whole building is remarkable for its two rows of wide eaves which cast immense shadows over every frontage, and also for the shape and variety of the angular roofs, which, with the parapets, still retain traces of a considerable amount of colour.

The two-storeyed buildings in the centre of each side are commodious apartments, each more or less a self-contained suite, but connected with the corner rooms and also with one another by the continuous corridor below. They are sufficiently large to serve a variety of purposes, some of them being evidently reception rooms, while others are dining rooms or retiring rooms and for promenades. More than one of the chambers of the upper storey is covered by a waggon-vaulted roof of stone. But it is when some of the carved features inside these rooms are examined that special interest is aroused. There are pillars, balconies, grilles, niches, and such details as volutes and the "chain and bell", all copied exactly from these well-known elements in the temple architecture of western India, notably Gujarāt. So marked is this influence that there are good reasons for assuming that the task of constructing Jodh Bāī's palace was entrusted to the descendants of the craftsmen who built the temples at Mount Ābū, Somnāth, Modhera, and other famous shrines of those parts.

There are two other residences at Fathpur Sīkrī, besides the palace of Jodh Bāī, presumed to have been built for the accommodation of Akbar's queens. Neither of these, however, equals in size and importance that of the Rājput princess, as they are little more than pavilions, but they are structures which in style and decorative treatment have considerable individuality. It has been shown that Jodh Bāī's palace was apparently the handiwork of one group of artizans, and there seems little doubt that the construction of each of the other queen's houses was assigned to similar groups of craftsmen to produce these after their own particular fashion. The one known as Miriam's house is almost too slight to have any distinctive architectural character, as it consists merely of a suite of rooms, a portico, and a kiosk on its roof. But on the other hand the interior was ornamented with pictures, scenes painted on the walls of various subjects drawn with great vigour. Only traces of these have survived, but it is clear that several of the leading exponents of Akbar's school of miniature painting were engaged on this mural decoration. The other house, that of the "Turkish Sultāna", is also structurally of no special significance, except that it is a pleasing little retiring room surrounded by a piazza, but the manner in which this is embellished and the nature of its carving calls for remark. Every portion of its surface inside and out is chiselled in a variety of designs and patterns, some of the usual conventional order common to Islāmic art in India, while others are based on natural foliage, such as the vine and the pomegranate. A series of panels forming the dado of the interior depicts with remarkable spirit and grace "jungle" scenes of trees and animals in a very specialised plastic style (Fig. 34). All the designs are notable for the refinement of their treatment, and are executed in a delicate method of low relief, the only fault of which is that it is almost timid in its handling. The whole of this structure seems to have been produced by a group of craftsmen of marked artistic and creative ability, but the constrained manipulation of their material shows that stone had not always been their métier, and the probability is that they were originally wood-workers from Lahore.

In addition to these apartments of the queens there are two other secular buildings of outstanding character. One of these is Bīrbal's house, and the other the Dīwān-i-Khāss. Although each was designed for a very different purpose, the exteriors of both are of the style which defines the majority of the buildings of Fathpur Sīkrī. Bīrbal's house attracts the eye on account of the exuberance of its carved decoration, both inside and out, every surface displaying sculptured patterns, while the brackets of its exterior are amazingly ornate. Its roof is surmounted by two domes, in the construction of which a hollow space has been left between the inner and outer shells, showing that the principle of the double dome, even in its low-pitched form, was already being put into practice. The other structure, the Dīwān-i-Khāss, a hall provided for audiences of a special nature, has a comparatively plain exterior, but the arrangements inside are unique. Externally the building appears to be in two storeys, but the interior is really one lofty room. This is divided at about half its height by a gallery on brackets continued around its four sides, with other narrow hanging galleries thrown diagonally from corner to corner. Where the diagonal galleries meet in the centre of the room, a circular platform has been inserted, the entire construction being supported on an immense cluster of brackets forming the capital of a column which rests on the ground. The intention of this complicated contrivance was to enable the emperor to sit on a throne in the central platform and hear disputants from all sides, the whole arrangement symbolising his "dominion over the four quarters". This freakish notion the designer has worked out to the best of his ability, and the main feature, the central pillar with its huge circular array of brackets, in spite of its top-heavy appearance, has considerable dignity of effect (Fig. 36). Akbar's ideas were usually sound, and his good taste almost instinctive, but occasionally, as in this instance, his desire for the bizarre prevailed. A similar weakness is observable in two other structures near the Dīwān-i-Khāss; one, a square canopy standing on a platform, and known as the "Astrologer's Seat", has excessively large voluted struts peculiar to the Jain temples of western India. The other is a tall pyramidal structure in five storeys known as the Pānch Mahall, a somewhat fantastic erection with the many pillars comprising one of its stages elaborately carved each in a wholly different design.

But undoubtedly the most imposing building at Akbar's capital and the one on which the highest architectural skill was concentrated is the Jāmi' Masjid. Additional interest attaches to this structure because it was the first of those grand congregational mosques which adorn the chief cities of the Mughuls and for which it furnished the original model. The main façade forming the exterior of the sanctuary hall may not be equal to that of the Jāmi' Masjid at Delhi, the largest and finest of its type, but the planning and arrangements of its interior aisles are far superior. The difference in the architectural treatment of the mosque at Fathpur Sīkrī compared with that of the civil buildings just described is notable. The two principal divergences are that whereas the construction of the latter is trabeated, on the other hand the mosque is mainly arcuate, and secondly in place of carving inlaid marble and plaster relief in colour were freely used. When completed in 1571 it displayed a perfectly regular plan, symmetrical in all its parts with the courtyard entered by gateways, one in the middle of three of the sides. Shortly afterwards, however, three additions were made, which, although they have increased its interest, have tended to disturb the balance of the composition as a whole. The first of these was the tomb of Salīm Chishtī, the saint whose long residence on the site is commemorated by a very chaste marble structure placed on the north side of the quadrangle. A little later the south gateway was replaced by the magnificent portal known as the Buland Darwāza, a triumphal archway to commemorate Akbar's conquest of Gujarāt. In 1612 a further encroachment was made on the north side of the courtyard by the inclusion of Islām Khān's large tomb, causing the entrance-gateway to the mosque on that side to be dismantled and closed. Admirable though these additions are in themselves, they are not part of the scheme as at first planned. The two tombs, although that of Salīm Chishtī is a gem of craftsmanship, as will be described later, obstruct the fine spatial effect of the great quadrangle, while the Buland Darwāza, which, as will be shown, is equalled by no other gateway in India, dominates not only the entire mosque but even much of the city itself by the immensity of its mass.

The mosque is contained within a high wall crowned by a crenellated parapet and enclosing a rectangle of 438 feet by 515 feet. Against the inside of this retaining wall is a continuous range of arcaded cloisters ornamented above by a series of small kiosks. The only original doorway to the courtyard now remaining is the Bādshāhī, or "King's Gate", on the east side, the private entrance of the emperor, a structure according so perfectly with its surroundings that its excellent proportions and carefully adjusted parts may quite readily pass unnoticed. But the most important feature of the whole conception is the sanctuary hall on the opposite side of the quadrangle. Hitherto the Indian builders had generally considered it sufficient merely to enlarge and amplify the western aspect of the mosque enclosure in order to make a hall suitable for its purpose. At Fathpur Sīkrī the plan was adopted of designing the sanctuary in the form of a spacious self-contained place of worship, a separate structure provided with a nave, aisles and chapels so combined as to produce a unity in itself. The façade of this fine prayer hall resolves itself into two parts consisting of a large arched portico in the centre, with arcaded wings extending on each side (Fig. 38). Above this façade rise three domes, of the flattened "Lodī" type, but considerably stilted in order to add to their height; the central one roofs the principal prayer chamber, corresponding to the nave, while the others are over the side chapels. As usual there is the unavoidable masking of the main dome owing to the height of the parapet over the portico, but this is a failing in nearly all Indian mosque elevations, the heritage of the *maqsūra* or arched screen prescribed by ancient tradition. The qualities of simplicity and largeness which distinguish the exterior of this sanctuary are maintained in the treatment of the interior. This resolves itself into several major compartments, the most important of which is the central hall or nave, divided off from the wings by solid walls but communicating with them by side arches. This central hall, approached by archways from the portico, is the principal prayer chamber, and consists of a square room with a high domed roof. On each side of this central compartment are the other main divisions of the interior comprising the wings. These wings are not enclosed by walls as is the central hall, but open on to the quadrangle by means of an arcaded piazza, behind which are the pillared aisles. Within these aisles are the two side chapels, the position of each being indicated exteriorly by the smaller domes. Occupying an upper storey at the extreme ends of the wings are chapels for the *zanāna*. Much of the effective appearance of the interior is obtained by the long receding vistas of the aisles, the contrast of the pillars and their brackets with the graceful pointed archways, the inlaid geometrical patterns which decorate the piers, and the brilliantly painted ornament on the *mihrāb* walls. The *mihrābs* themselves, twenty-one in number, are inferior in design to those of the Qil'a-i-Kuhna Masjid, produced nearly twenty-five years before, but they endeavour to vie with these in the diversity and richness of their painted surfaces. An unorthodox motive is introduced into one of these prayer niches in the form of a border containing a grape vine.

In spite of the fine symmetrical effect of the sanctuary façade the eye of the spectator as he enters the enclosure naturally turns to the southern entrance of the mosque formed by the Buland Darwāza, the immense bulk of which throws its shadow all day long across the courtyard. This is a superb structure, and thoroughly characteristic of the period. Each art culture has usually one form of utterance in which it finds the readiest means of expression, and with the Mughuls this was the entrance gateway. To the gardens of their tombs, the quadrangles of their mosques, the walls of their forts, the courtyards of their palaces, the entrance gateway was always a prominent feature, excellently proportioned in itself and at the same time in complete harmony with its surroundings. These gateways were essentially an Islāmic heritage derived from the earlier days of the Faith when life was mainly spent in fortresses of which the most vital parts were the entrances. Experience in designing these in time of war bore fruit in times of peace. Under the Mughuls its culmination is seen in this magnificent triumphal archway and entrance-gateway combined. Seen from any point of view, but specially from a distance, its great size and commanding height present a most imposing appearance. Its measurements are significant. From the platform in front of the doorway to the finial at the top is 134 feet, but including the flight of steps leading up to it, its total height is 176 feet. Across the main front it measures 130 feet, while its greatest depth from front to back is 123 feet. Such an unpremeditated addition to the mosque presented certain constructional difficulties on this side of the courtyard, as the ridge slopes away sharply, thus necessitating an unusually long and steep flight of steps at its foot. Its approach and outlook also emphasise the fact that the whole project was an afterthought, as it overlooks the *hammām*, beyond which are the quarters of the servants. And further, its boldly projecting façade, towering height and almost aggressive strength would be more appropriate to a citadel than the peaceful and sacred precincts of a mosque. Yet it fulfils its double purpose as a triumphal arch and a mosque gateway combined in a remarkably effective manner. The method by which this monumental edifice is gradually diminished in its parts until it is finally reduced to an ordinary-sized doorway, as was its secondary intention, has been well described by Fergusson,[1] who correctly attributes the result to long experience in working on right principles.

Few buildings could furnish a more marked contrast to the one referred to above than the tomb of Salīm Chishtī, situated only a short distance away on the opposite side of the courtyard. Each structure makes a separate appeal, the gateway in view of its size and majestic proportions, the tomb by its casket-like appearance and the richness and delicacy of its detail. The date of the latter is 1571, but as it is constructed wholly of white marble it appears to belong to a later period. What, however, has happened is that the original tomb was built of sandstone, as were all the buildings of this time, but subsequent devotees, feeling that the shrine of their saint should be made of something more precious than common stone, converted it into its present state by substituting marble for certain parts, and covering others over with thin slabs of the same material like a veneer. It may therefore be described as an architectural palimpsest. But although the material has been changed its design cannot be far different from what it was when first erected. In the course of conversion the dome may have lost its original contour through being covered with slabs of marble, while in the process of copying the pillars and perforated screens some extra play of fancy may have been indulged in. The plan and general arrangements of the tomb building call for no special remark; there is the square-domed cenotaph chamber surrounded by a verandah and with a projecting pillared portico. Painted patterns cover the walls of the interior, semi-precious stones of artistic colours decorate the floors, and the pierced screens of the verandah are of exceptionally fine workman-

[1] *Indian and Eastern Architecture* (1910), II, 297.

ship. A wooden canopy over the sarcophagus is inlaid with arabesques in ebony and mother-of-pearl of exquisite design, probably executed by artizans of the northern Punjab noted for their skilled inlay. What, however, distinguishes this building from all others is the character of its pillars and pilasters, and, more particularly, the style of the large and elaborate struts which support the wide-spreading eaves. The shape of the pillars themselves is unusual; a zigzag pattern covers their shafts, and their capitals recall those of the stalactite order. But the convoluted struts with perforated ornament between the scrolls springing from half-way down their shafts and carried right up to a bracket under the eaves are unique. Based on somewhat similar supports in the temples of Gujarāt, the Mughul craftsmen elaborated this idea to the extent here seen. Much of the marble work is, however, attributed to the early years of Jahāngīr's reign, when the style was losing its quality of direct simplicity, an appearance which in the West would be regarded as a form of the baroque.

The methods perfected by the builders of Akbar's time had one comparatively small but interesting repercussion. It has been shown that the early Mughul buildings owed not a little of their character to the indigenous temple architecture, elements from which were freely borrowed. To find therefore at the sacred Hindu retreat of Brindāban near Muttra several temples assimilating in their turn much of the contemporary style of the Mughuls is some measure of its vigorous nature. Of these temples that of Govind Deo erected in 1590 is the most notable, and testifies not only to its adaptability to other purposes but is also a tribute to the versatility of the Indian masons who built it (Fig. 45). There is a wide difference between the needs of a Mughul palace or mosque and those of a Hindu temple, but any difficulties this interchange presented were readily overcome. The temple was never quite finished, but the plan and intention of its designers can be understood from what now appears. As far as the exterior is concerned this suggests certain aspects of the architecture of western India, the exuberance common to that style, however, having been restrained by its contact with the more sober style of the Mughuls; it shows a sense of refinement and an appreciation of the value of plain surfaces not often seen in temple design. The contrast between the horizontal lines of its richly moulded buttresses and the perpendicular effect of the pillared openings between has been well maintained. A still more advanced treatment is observable in the interior as its cruciform plan, "Tudor" arched transepts, and groined and vaulted hall would not be out of place in a Gothic church. Here the builders seem to have gone farther afield for inspiration, as the principle of the intersecting arches supporting the domed roof is allied to that employed in the provincial style of Bijāpur, while the roofing of the aisles was apparently borrowed from the transepts of the Jāmi' Masjid[1] at Jaunpur, where the application of the waggon vault and groin had been already mastered. But the pillared cloisters in two stories with their lintels and carved brackets are reminiscent of the palaces of Fathpur Sīkrī. There is much that is original in the temples of Brindāban, but in few other Hindu buildings is the influence of the prevailing style of the Muslims more obvious than in the temple of Govind Deo.

Yet the secular architecture also of the Hindus did not remain unaffected by the building activities of Akbar and his successors, as is shown by several palaces and other important structures erected in Rājputāna and Mālwā about this time. Chief among these are the royal residences and other state buildings in the romantic city of Amber which were begun about 1600, and the palace of Bīkāner, also begun towards the end of the sixteenth century. These were followed by the palace-fortresses of Jodhpur and Orchha, with the stately palace of Datia, all dating from the early part of the seventeenth century, and finally by the palace at Dīg commenced about 1725. All these palatial retreats of the Rājput princes show by their style an association with the building art as evolved by the Mughuls, but with elaborations of their own. Apart from the richness of their decoration, they display a fancifulness expressive of the imaginative Hindu mind, together with evidences of a survival of the ancient craft traditions of the country. This Mughul foundation breaking out into Hindu exuberance is well illustrated in its most florid aspect by the Durbar buildings of Amber (Fig. 47), and perhaps with slightly more restraint by the fluted pavilions of the citadel at Jodhpur. It is not difficult to see in such buildings how the stone structures of the early Mughuls by the addition of engrailed arches, glass mosaics, painted plaster, gilded gesso and sgraffito were adapted to the more colourful requirements of the Hindu princes.

After the death of Akbar in 1605 there was a pause in the building operations of the Mughuls. The strenuous and unceasing activity of this great building monarch was followed by a period of partial inertia. His successor's chief interests lay in fields other than that of architecture. Under Jahāngīr the art of miniature painting flourished exceedingly, and owing to his patronage it reached great heights. But perhaps this emperor's principal delight was in the laying out of large formal gardens, the romantic beauty of which has contributed not a little to the aesthetic reputation of the Mughul dynasty. Bābur had already introduced this type of garden in India by devising the Rām Bāgh at Āgra, and Akbar had a similar large enclosure planted at Sikandra, where afterwards he planned his tomb. Through Jahāngīr's love of nature, inherited from his progenitor Bābur, the Mughul garden was brought to perfection, and at all places where this emperor sojourned for any length of time one

[1] See vol. III, p. 628.

of these pleasaunces was generally prepared. Some of his courtiers also built retreats of this kind, as for instance Āsaf Khān's Nishāt Bāgh in Kashmīr, and, later, the emperor Shāh Jahān had a very large one constructed at Shālamār near Lahore. The Mughul garden is a conventional arrangement of squares, usually in the form of terraces placed on a slope for the easy distribution of the water which is an essential part of the scheme. Each terrace is divided into four lesser squares in order to conform to the traditional plan of what is known as the *chār bāgh* or fourfold plot, the whole being a combination of rectangles and straight lines, no curved paths or even circular parterres being found. Artificial pools with numerous fountains play an important part in the composition, while in an inconspicuous spot a bath or *hammām* is sometimes introduced. Pavilions occupy central positions, and the flagged causeways are shaded by avenues of trees. One of the loveliest of these gardens is the Shālamār Bāgh in Kashmīr constructed by Jahāngīr, which, however, owes not a little of its charm to the wonderful situation with a background of mountains and a view over the crystal waters of the Dal lake. Immense *chanār* trees grace its walks and green swards, water ripples and cascades down its sloping channels, lotus-bud fountains dance in the sunshine and beds of flowers give colour and fragrance to the whole.

It was in the production of scenes of this kind that the emperor Jahāngīr excelled, but nevertheless his predecessor had given such an impetus to the art of significant building that in spite of any indifference he may have shown towards the subject, it was carried along by its own momentum. The incentive was in a manner supplied by a solemn obligation laid upon Jahāngīr, namely the construction of his august father's mausoleum. Whether Akbar or his son was responsible for the design of this structure is not clear, but that practically the whole of the actual building was carried out in Jahāngīr's reign is now fairly well established. The site, which was on a garden prepared by Akbar at Sikandra near Āgra, and also very probably some idea of the design of the tomb, were settled before his death. In all his building schemes, although some of these may have been fanciful, Akbar made no serious mistakes, and it is singular that the least successful monument associated with his name is his mausoleum. The inference is that had this "Great Mogul" taken the precaution of erecting his tomb in his own lifetime the result might have been different. Under Jahāngīr's spasmodic supervision, which on occasion looked like undue interference, and with his dilettante temperament, the final state of the structure is perhaps largely due. Jahāngīr had a trained eye for a picture, but not a mind that could understand the largeness and breadth required for architectural effect. When on one of his hasty visits to Sikandra he relates that he was not satisfied with the work, and ordered the mason "once more to knock down some parts", some of the reasons for its defects may be apparent.

Spatial effect is the key-note of Akbar's tomb, and the great square garden with which it is surrounded emphasises this quality. This garden, itself an important accessory to the composition as a whole, is a formal arrangement of squares, but much of its original intention is now lost. It was divided into four quarters by broad paved causeways raised 8 feet above the surrounding parterres. The sweep of each of these wide approaches is interrupted in the middle by being expanded into a terrace containing an ornamental tank and fountain. Aqueducts traverse these causeways, and in convenient places flights of steps lead down to flower beds at a lower level. A fine gateway is introduced into the centre of each side of the high embattled wall enclosing the whole garden area, that on the south side and the largest of all forming the main entrance, the others being false doorways added to ensure symmetry. Each of these portals is a minor monument in itself, as they are charmingly proportioned and the variety of their carved, painted and inlaid decoration makes each one a work of art. Specially does this apply to the main entrance, which, apart from its elegant appearance and the boldness of the arabesques decorating its surfaces, is distinguished by the addition of a tall white marble minaret rising from each of its four corners. The presence of these minarets marks a notable step in the development of Islamic architecture in Hindūstān, as in no other instance does this characteristic feature appear in upper India since the erection of the Qutb Minār four centuries previously. And here it emerges, not as an experiment, but fully developed with all its parts in perfect harmony and in exact and final form.

The mausoleum building itself is a huge structure occupying a square of 340 feet side, and consists of five terraces diminishing as they ascend, thus approximating a low truncated pyramid. Muslim tombs in India are invariably designed on the plan of a crypt in which the body is buried, and a building above containing the tomb-chamber with its cenotaph. As might be expected in view of Akbar's unconventional nature his tomb is a departure from this orthodox arrangement. Instead of the subterranean vault there is a high domed hall, almost on ground level, which takes the place of crypt and tomb-chamber combined. Around this domed hall was built the lowest terrace, a stupendous mass of masonry 30 feet high, and almost solid except for a range of cloisters continued all round its outer sides. Externally, as part of the façade, these outer sides of the terrace are arcaded, and in the centre of each is inserted a large portico with a deeply recessed archway. The portico on the south side forms the entrance to the domed mortuary chamber, which is reached by a long and slightly descending corridor, light being admitted through clerestory windows by means of shafts from above.

The roof of this terrace provides a wide platform, in the centre of which rises the superstructure comprising the four remaining storeys. Three of these storeys consist of superimposed tiers of pillared arcades and kiosks built mainly of red sandstone. The arcades lead to ranges of rooms in the interior, but they also act as a façade to the masonry which encloses the dome of the mortuary chamber below. Supported on these rows of sandstone arcades is the topmost storey of white marble, its perforated lattices forming the cloisters of an open court with a cenotaph in the centre; each corner of this storey is surmounted by a slender marble kiosk.

Although there is much that calls for admiration in this vast structure, particularly in the treatment of its final storey, which for delicacy and finish is unsurpassed in any other Mughul monument, as a whole it is disappointing. It is unimpressive because it lacks the quality of mass which is one of the principles of beauty, and of coherence which is the basis of style. The lowest terrace is a noble conception, substantial yet not heavy, a suitable foundation inviting an imposing superstructure to be erected on its broad platform. But the opportunity was not taken. Instead of a solid and dignified building above, consistent with this ponderous base, there arises a light and almost frivolous array of arcades and kiosks, more appropriate in a summer palace than forming the principal part of a royal mausoleum. Here it may have been that Jahāngīr interposed, ordered what had previously been approved to be demolished and "reconstructed at a cost of fifteen lakhs of rupees". It was at this critical stage that those concerned in the production of the building seem to have become confused and lost their aesthetic propriety in a maze of little arches, balconies and pillared pavilions. They recaptured it in the chaste and elegantly designed marble storey above, but by that time it was too late to present this ambitious monument as a complete and balanced unity.

Much the same criticism applies to Jahāngīr's own mausoleum built at Shāhdara near Lahore some twenty years later, which is conceived on somewhat similar lines. But it lacks even the lofty effect of the earlier example, as there is no superstructure, the body of the building consisting of a single story in the form of a square terrace 22 feet high. It is true some appearance of height is obtained by a handsome minaret rising from each corner, and there was originally a marble pavilion placed in the middle of the platform above, which, when *in situ*, would have offered a central point of interest. Now shorn of this feature, which was removed during the Sikh supremacy, the whole composition is singularly ineffective. Efforts were made to improve its appearance by the lavish application of inlaid marbles, glazed tiles, and painted patterns, some of which are remarkably good examples of mural decoration, but no amount of embellishment of this nature can redeem its obvious architectural defects. As a contrast to the somewhat affected grandeur of both these royal mausoleums, and also as a proof that probably under less exacting conditions the craftsmen of the time were capable of first-rate workmanship, are two tombs erected towards the end of Jahāngīr's reign, one at Delhi and the other at Āgra. Apart from the high character of their design both of these structures mark a definite stage in the evolution of the style, and forecast plainly its subsequent attainments. The tomb of Khān Khānān at Delhi, a nobleman who died in 1627, shows a return to the Persian mode initiated in the mausoleum of Humāyūn some sixty years before. Unfortunately in the eighteenth century it was stripped of much of its marble covering, so that now it is little more than a shell, but even in a mutilated state it is possible to see that in many of its particulars it is a copy to a smaller scale of the emperor's tomb near by. In one notable respect it differs, however, from its prototype, in that the wings of the façade have been simplified so that the plan, instead of being octagonal, is a plain square; in all other directions both designs are almost identical. Each stands on a terrace with seventeen arched recesses on each side. The mausoleum building which rises above the platform formed by the terrace has much the same distribution of parts in both examples; there is the large central arched recess, the arrangement of kiosks above, and the double Timurid dome over all. The tomb of Khān Khānān therefore indicates that the Persian attribution even after this considerable passage of time was still definitely alive (Fig. 58).

The other tomb of this date, that enshrining the remains of I'timād-ud-daula at Āgra, is a very different conception. It was built by this high official's daughter Nūr Mahall, the brilliant consort of Jahāngīr, who, it should be added, was also responsible for the construction of that emperor's mausoleum at Shāhdara. No two buildings could be more dissimilar, and the wide divergence of style seems to show that while on the one hand the royal tomb of Shāhdara was no doubt originally planned by Jahāngīr himself, the tomb at Āgra bears in every part of it the imprint of the refined feminism of this remarkable queen. There is no other building like it in the entire range of Mughul architecture, the delicacy of treatment and the chaste quality of its decoration placing it in a class by itself. It is a comparatively small structure, the tomb building measures only 69 feet wide, and as it is constructed in the purest white marble with much of its ornamentation of inlaid semi-precious stones it conveys the impression of a rich article of jewellery magnified into architecture. Situated in the middle of a square enclosure, recalling in some respects the pleasant repose of a cloister garth, this brilliant little edifice stands out in strong contrast to its surroundings of dark cypress trees and red sandstone gateways. The latter in themselves are charmingly designed entrances, notably that on the western side by which the mausoleum is approached from the river (Fig. 55). All these essential appendages are in the best of taste and skilfully subordinated to the marble edifice enthroned in the centre amidst parterres, tanks and fountains. The mausoleum consists of a square lower storey with a gracefully proportioned turret like a dwarf minaret thrown out from each corner, while above a smaller second storey rises in the form of a traceried pavilion; the interior is a simple arrangement of a central chamber containing the cenotaphs, surrounded by connected rooms corresponding to an enclosed verandah. Light everywhere is obtained through perforated screens, a "gossamer of fretted grilles" which give an exquisite texture to all the openings. And over the whole, delicately modifying the dazzling effect of the white marble, is laid with deft fingers a diaphanous veil of coloured inlay in patterns of bewildering diversity. Whether regarded as an architectural composition of matchless refinement, as an example of applied art displaying rare craftsmanship, or as an artistic symbol of passionate filial devotion, the tomb of I'timād-ud-daula expresses in every part of it the high aesthetic ideals that prevailed among the Mughuls at the time. But this building in addition to its intrinsic beauty has another interest. It is the first structure of the Mughuls to be composed entirely of white marble, and also the first in which that form of inlaid decoration known as *pietra dura* makes its appearance. In its technical aspect therefore it denotes a turning-point in the evolution of the building art, marking the change from the sandstone construction and *opus sectile* ornamentation which satisfied the simpler taste of Akbar and Jahāngīr to the sumptuous white marble pavilions and *pietra dura* of Shāh Jahān.

Augustus's boast that he found Rome of brick and left it of marble has its counterpart in the building productions of Shāh Jahān, who found the Mughul cities of sandstone and left them of marble. In the forts of Āgra and Lahore, and at other places besides, this emperor swept away many of the sandstone structures of his predecessors and in their places erected marble palaces. The quarries of Makrāna in Rājputāna provided unlimited supplies of this finely textured building material, so that pavilions, courts and columned halls were all constructed in pure white marble; when for various reasons this was not made use of, the stone which took its place was faced with stucco, the plastered surfaces being polished to an egg-shell whiteness in keeping with the marble masonry. Such a definite change of material naturally implied a corresponding change in architectural treatment. The building art acquired a new sensibility. Instead of the rectangular character of the previous period there arose the curved line and flowing rhythm of the style of Shāh Jahān, while the chisel of the stone carver was replaced by the finer instruments of the marble cutter and polisher. No longer was effect dependent on bold string-courses and intricate carving; the chaste texture of the marble itself was sufficient to give quality to any building, and any relief decoration required to be of the most refined order and sparingly applied. Variety of surface was obtained by panels in correct proportions outlined by mouldings fine and rare in their contours. Most of the ornamentation was, however, of a much more subtle nature, colour and gilding being introduced, while patterns inlaid in semi-precious stones—the *pietra dura* already mentioned—were a special feature. But perhaps the most striking innovation was the change in the shape of the arch, which in almost all buildings of Shāh Jahān's reign is foliated or cusped in its outlines, so that white marble arcades of engrailed arches became the distinguishing characteristic of the period. During the governance of this emperor, Mughul architecture undoubtedly found its golden age. Of a highly artistic nature he satisfied his desires by the building of sumptuous edifices of all kinds, not waiting to complete one piece of self-expression before committing himself to another. All other forms of culture not dependent on the mason's art, such as literature, the school of miniature painting encouraged by Akbar and Jahāngīr, and similar intellectual pursuits, were disregarded, his entire patronage being concentrated on building. And it was building of the most sensuous, even voluptuous order. The productions of his predecessors were looked upon as almost barbaric, the court chronicler comparing certain of their "abominations" with the masterpieces of "this august reign, when. . .lovely things reached the zenith of perfection".[1] At Āgra and Lahore the palaces within the forts were largely reconstructed, and all the cities of the Mughuls display examples of Shāh Jahān's building predilections. In the fort at Āgra the greatest changes are recorded, the whole of the structures north of the Jahāngīrī Mahall being dismantled and their places taken by marble edifices such as the Dīwān-i-'Ām, Dīwān-i-Khāss, the Khāss Mahall, the Shīsh Mahall, the Musamman Burj, the Angūrī Bāgh, the Machhī Bhawan and the Motī Masjid. Details of all these alterations and additions are to be found in contemporary accounts written in the flowery language of the time. But even the most ardent flatterer, trained in poetical analogies, could barely do justice to the surpassing beauty of some of these structures, which in spite of vicissitudes still hold their own as the most elegant of their kind. What could be more graceful than the hall of the Dīwān-i-Khāss with its series of double columns, or the Musamman Burj hanging like a fairy bower over the grim ramparts? Even these, however, are excelled by the peerless refinement of the Motī Masjid or "Pearl Mosque", one of Shāh Jahān's latest additions, as it was erected in 1654 when the art had attained its ripest state. Few religious edifices convey to the beholder a finer sense of purity than this chapel royal, which, both on account of the flawless quality of its material,

[1] Bādshāh Nāma, I, 221.

and the skilfully modulated disposition of its elements, represents the Mughul style at its zenith. The subordination and contrast of the entrance archways to the arcading of the sanctuary, the proportions and arrangement of the kiosks surmounting the cornices, and, notably, the subtle raising of the drum of the central dome in relation to those on each side, are a few only of the aspects of this structure which show in the most emphatic manner that the principles of balance and rhythm were by this time thoroughly appreciated by the Mughul builders.

Similar alterations were effected by Shāh Jahān in the interior arrangements of the fort at Lahore, where this ruler's additions mainly in marble may be readily distinguished from the sandstone structures of his predecessors. The "Hall of Forty Pillars", now called the Dīwān-i-'Ām, the Musamman Burj, including the Shīsh Mahall, the Naulākha, the Khwābgāh, and all the buildings towards the north-west portion, were erected at this time. But the remodelling of the palaces of his forefathers did not satisfy the ardent building propensities of Shāh Jahān, and accordingly in 1638 he began at Delhi the construction of an entirely new capital city of his own. Within its walls was to be included a large citadel or palace-fortress, the whole resting on the right bank of the Jumna. No regular plan seems to have been followed in working out this scheme, except that the city is roughly in the shape of a quadrant with the fortress at its apex overlooking the river. Two wide thoroughfares radiate from the main gates of the fortress to those in the city walls, and in the angle thus formed was placed the Jāmi' Masjid. As a contrast to this apparently casual lay-out of the walled city, the fort itself is a fairly orderly production in the shape of a parallelogram running north and south, with its corners chamfered and its northern side set at an angle to accommodate the existing fortress of Salīmgarh, which then became a barbican to the newer construction. The rectangle thus formed measures 1600 feet by 3200 feet and is enclosed by a formidable wall of the same type as that at Āgra fort, but lacking its bold rugged strength; within this area the designers proceeded to plot out the interior arrangements under the personal supervision of the emperor himself. These arrangements included such essential requirements as three entrances consisting of a ceremonial, a private, and a river gateway; barracks for the guard, and accommodation for the immense retinue attached to the court, together with shops and similar facilities for their personal convenience; an official portion for public and private durbars and affairs of state; a private enclosure to contain the palaces of the emperor and the residences of the royal family, with ornamental gardens attached; royal store rooms, regalia chambers, kitchens, horse and elephant stables, and other minor amenities appertaining to the imperial establishment. It is possible to see in the typical disposition of these requirements within the fortified area traces of very early traditions, beginning with the palaces of the Assyrians, through those of Ecbatana, Susa, Persepolis, and, then further west, to the palace of Diocletian at Spalato, the resemblance of which to a Mughul palace-fort points to a common origin. The hypostyle hall of ancient Persia may well be the prototype of the hall of audience of the Mughuls, which in its turn suggests the Roman forum, for in all these rectangular pillared courts it was customary to transact judicial and political business. Turning again to the east in ancient India the Mauryas copied at Pātaliputra the columned halls of the Achaemenid Persians, and much of Dhammapāla's description of Asoka's palace of the third century B.C. might apply to Shāh Jahān's fortress at Delhi.

This magnificent royal residence, the last and finest of its kind, is unique because the whole of it was the conception of one mind, and carried out on a systematic and uniform plan. The scheme of this plan was an arrangement of rectangles, generally squares, no curved or oblique lines being introduced, in accordance with that quadrangular convention so deeply rooted in the Mughul mind. Immediately within the main gate a large space was divided off to contain the habitations of the palace retinue, who although residing within an enclosure assigned to them, would thus have easy access to both the city outside and the palace within. Through this service area a wide vaulted passage led directly from the main gate to the official portion, admission to which was obtained through the *naubat khāna* or music gatehouse. This official portion, occupying a large rectangle in the centre of the fort, consisted of an arcaded courtyard with the columned hall of the Dīwān-i-'Ām at the far side, where affairs of an official nature were administered. Around this central enclosure the entire area remaining was reserved for the accommodation and personal use of the royal household, including also the Dīwān-i-Khāss where private audiences were held. One half of this private part was occupied by the residences and living rooms of the emperor's family, while the corresponding space on the other side was divided up into a series of formal gardens. And along the whole length of the retaining wall overlooking the river was aligned that range of marble pavilions and palaces each one more chaste than the other, proving by their combined beauty the truth of the couplet with which one of them is inscribed, that "if there is a paradise on earth, it is this, it is this, it is this".

Although there is much that is very fine in the external appearance of this fortress as a whole with its steep insurmountable defences and strong but elegantly designed gateways, the highest skill of its architects was undoubtedly expended on the design, construction and decorative treatment of this range of royal palaces, together with the Dīwān-i-'Ām. Each of the palaces on its side looking into the fort was fronted by a garden divided into parterres by watercourses with an ornamental fountain in the middle, while on their outer side they crowned the sandstone ramparts with a succession of turrets, kiosks, gilt domes, hanging balconies, oriel windows, arcades and perforated screens, which if not exactly orderly in their arrangement, were remarkably picturesque and breathed the very spirit of romance. Along this wall there were something like twelve separate pavilions, all connected with one another and each designed for a different purpose and bearing a distinctive name, such as the *Motī Mahall* or "Pearl Palace", the *Hīra Mahall* or "Diamond Palace", and the *Rang Mahall* or "Painted Palace". The style of each is much the same, although there is a pleasing variety of plan, each consisting of a single-storeyed hall usually open on all sides, divided into bays by massive piers and the roof supported by foliated arches. Above are flat coffered ceilings at one time plated with silver or gilt, and the piers, walls and all interior surfaces are decorated either with inlay, low relief carving or patterns in colour and gold. The floors are paved with marble, and provision is made for a system of aqueducts to pass along the entire length of the buildings, partly to supply water for the numerous *hammāms*, but with the main object of adding to each apartment all the refreshing accompaniments of a water-palace. A constant supply of water was obtained by tapping the river Jumna at a point seventy miles up stream and bringing it by canal to the fort, where its inlet was at the northern angle. Here the Nahr-i-Bihisht, or "Stream of Paradise", as it was called, entered by a scalloped marble cascade in the open central arcade by the Shāh Burj or "King's Tower", and from there was distributed by stone or marble channels in all the required directions. In some of the pavilions it was diverted into fountains, the finest of which is the one completely filling the central compartment of the Rang Mahall (Fig. 72), and, in the words of Sayyid Ahmad, its

> beauty baffles description. It is made of marble and fashioned in such a way that it resembles a full blown flower,...yet it is of little depth...just like the palm of a hand. The particular beauty of this is that, when it is full of rippling water, the foliage of the inlay appears to wave to and fro. In its centre is a beautiful flower like a cup of marble; moreover, on each curving point and arched cusp, flowers and leaves of coloured stones spring from creeping plants, and creeping plants from flowers and leaves. Within the cup you will find a hole through which the water bubbles up from a hidden channel underneath. The sheet of water falling from the edges of the cup and the waving of the plants and flowers under the dancing water are nothing less than a scene of magic.[1]

From the palaces the water was conveyed to the gardens, of which that known as the Hayāt Bakhsh was the largest and most enchantingly laid out. Here, in a strictly formal pattern of square flower beds amidst flowing watercourses, are two pavilions named after the two months of the rainy season, Sāwan and Bhādon, both

> decorated with pictures and paintings like the enamelled throne of the Queen of Sheba, or like Solomon's throne studded with emeralds. Through the two

[1] Āsār-us-Sanādīd, Sayyid Ahmad Khan, Cawnpore 1904, chap. II, p. 54.

waterways of the tanks which are made in the centre of these buildings, the water is always issuing gracefully, and from the edge of their platforms,...it is falling into the tank below, in the form of a cascade. In the niches, flower vases of gold and silver, full of golden flowers, are placed during the day time, and at night, white wax candles, which look like stars amid fleecy clouds, are lighted inside the veil of water.[1]

This imaginative treatment of the private portions of the fort and of the palaces wherein the emperor took his ease differed, however, from the more sedate character of the official portion where he held durbars and conducted publicly the affairs of state. The Dīwān-i-'Ām or "Hall of Public Audience" is an expansive columned hall of sandstone with its central bay occupied by a large and stately throne of marble carved and inlaid in the manner of the time. The wall at the back of the throne is also embellished with inlaid decoration, in the form of *pietra dura,* but much of this ornamentation differs materially, both in design and technique, from that in any other Mughul building. One scene particularly is a characteristically occidental representation of Orpheus sitting under a tree and fiddling to a circle of listening animals. It has now become clear that this and several of the surrounding panels of birds and foliage were originally fashioned in Italy, and in the course of commercial relations found their way to India to be acquired as objects of art by someone at the Mughul court. The artistic character of these pieces suggested their inclusion in the scheme of decoration at the back of the throne, where, surrounded by other panels of obviously Indian handiwork, their exotic appearance has given rise to some speculation.

Almost contemporary with the building of the fort at Delhi was the construction of the Jāmi' Masjid, which, as already shown, was an essential part of the scheme of Shāh Jahān's new capital. This grand mosque, the largest and most eminent in all India, was begun in A.D. 1644, but was not completed until fourteen years later. In the meantime a somewhat similar congregational mosque was being erected under the emperor's patronage at Āgra, which, although not on the same majestic scale as the Delhi example, was nevertheless a structure of considerable size and importance. Both mosques are planned according to tradition and follow the same broad principles as regards arrangements and general style. But given all these common factors they show in the most marked manner how widely two buildings of the same type may be made to differ in effect. Nothing could be more severely dignified or imperious in appearance than the Jāmi' Masjid at Delhi, or more suitable for its purpose, as it was obviously designed primarily for the ceremonial attendance of the emperor and his retinue, the imposing royal portal on the east with its arcading effectually screening the congregation within from

[1] Amal-i-Sālih, fols. 580–83 (Delhi Fort, *Arch. Survey of India,* 1929).

outside observation. An example of the highest type of religious architecture, precise and perfect, it forms a noble pile; the endless flights of steps before each entrance, the lofty white domes and tapering minarets with the broad arch of the façade are admirably disposed. The courtyard, 325 feet side, is in keeping with the great scale of the rest of the building, while the cloisters around the three sides and the symmetrical range of arches comprising the sanctuary are of the same generous proportions. But in spite of its great size, the orderly distribution of its parts and its undeniable grandeur, the building as a whole leaves the aesthetic sense only moderately stirred; it fails to arouse the highest emotions on account of its impersonality and aloofness. The uncompromising rigidity of its long horizontal lines, the harsh black and white inlay of its domes and minarets, its very vastness which necessitates the unending repetition of each detail, all combine to give this otherwise magnificent structure a character which never wholly attracts. On the other hand the mosque at Āgra, owing to its humanist values, makes a definitely intimate appeal. Although it lacks the perfection of the Delhi structure—the low position and timid contours of the domes are obvious defects—its free open frontage bringing everything into view, its rippling succession of kiosks of varying sizes which crown its parapets, the interesting passages of shadow thrown by its *chattris* and turrets, the warm broken colour of its masonry produce an effect of a singularly pleasing kind. It is a mosque evidently built for the benefit of the people; its shady cloisters, informal resting-places and alcoved retreats are an open invitation to all and sundry to spend a quiet hour within its precincts.

While at the principal seats of the Mughuls the white marble style was being maintained, a different phase of building was becoming manifest in the Punjab, notably at Lahore. This took the form of brick construction, with occasional sandstone additions, but owing its distinctive character to the glazed tile decoration with which its entire surfaces were often covered. The fact that Lahore was situated in an alluvial plain, and somewhat remote from any outcrop of stone, partly accounts for this brick and tile development, but not entirely. Since the days of the Ghaznavid occupation, the Punjab capital had been inclined to cultivate an independent architectural tradition, and instinctively to look to the north-west and beyond for its aesthetic inspiration. In the first half of the seventeenth century the Safavid art of Persia had attained its zenith, and for a time Lahore appears to have come under its powerful spell. It was not that the buildings of the Punjab were exact reproductions of those of Shāh 'Abbās the Great; they displayed a certain individuality, but the brick construction was based on that prevailing in Persia, and the glazed tiles were of the same type as those produced in the famous kilns of Kāshān and other places on the Irānian plateau. The outstanding characteristic of this style of building, both in Persia and the Punjab, is its accentuation of colour, as it depends almost entirely for its expression on the brilliant display of patterns in faience. To such an extent was this colour scheme allowed to dominate the entire fabric that one of the fundamental principles of good building has been sacrificed, inasmuch as the designers subordinated intentionally all constructional emphasis in order to give precedence to the applied art. Eliminate this ornamentation and the building becomes a bald arrangement of flat surfaces without shadow or any form of relief, mouldings and string-courses are at a discount, the whole structure resolving itself into a mere background on which the tile-setter was encouraged to squander his art unrestrained. That such a procedure produced buildings having any claim to architectural merit is mainly due to the quality of this tile decoration, which is of the highest order, as the brilliantly designed arabesques in variegated hues lit by the eastern sun produce a vitality of effect disarming all criticism. In Lahore and its neighbourhood a large number of buildings were erected in this style during the reign of Shāh Jahān, but owing to the impermanent nature of their construction many of them are in ruins or have almost entirely disappeared. The immense mounds of spoil from the brick kilns of this period testify to the importance this industry assumed, so much so that one Buddhu whose tomb is near Lahore was appointed chief purveyor of bricks to the royal establishment. But in all these rubbish mounds, several of which have been excavated, not a trace has been discovered of the glazed tiles nor are there any definite records of such a craft ever having existed in this locality in the past. Panels of faience decorate the exterior of Rājā Mān Singh's palace at Gwālior, and the glazed earthenware of Multān and Sindh has long been a thriving handicraft, but it is clear from their style and technique that both these are the offspring of an entirely different art tradition. The Lahore tiles are of a type which is unmistakeable, and are of two distinct kinds, the "mosaic" and the "square". The former consist of pieces of a glazed composition cut to the shape and colour of the design, and are set together like the tesserae of a mosaic; the latter are usually 6 inches square and the pattern painted on them is carried across the joints to fill the required space. Exactly similar glazed decoration of both kinds is seen in profusion in the seventeenth-century buildings of Persia and 'Irāq, most of it being made at the town of Kāshān, where the name for it is Kāshī, which is also the name by which this art is commonly known in Lahore. Some of the designs, notably those in the outer wall of Lahore fort, are much more Persian than Mughul in character, and include suggestions of Mithraic symbolism. Chardin, the French traveller, mentions at this time that Persia supplied India with large quantities of "earthenware", most probably referring to this trade in glazed tiles.[1] It seems not unlikely therefore that most if not all of this decoration was imported in bulk from Kāshān.

The finest example of this phase of Mughul building is Wazīr Khān's mosque erected in 1634, but there are many others, such as the Gulābi Bāgh, the Chauburjī, and 'Alī Mardān Khān's tomb, all at Lahore, while as far distant as Āgra the tomb of Afzal Khān of Lahore known as the "Chīnī kā Rauza" is of the same type. The mosque of Wazīr Khān, a most picturesque structure, consists of the customary arrangement of buildings enclosing a brick-paved court-yard, with the entrance-gateway, cloisters and sanctuary all in their accepted positions. Four octagonal minarets rise from the corners, and the domes which roof the sanctuary and the gateway are of the low-pitched "Lodī" order. Much of the surface decoration, which comprises not only tiles but in the interior patterns painted in distemper, has become considerably abraded, although sufficient remains to show what a gorgeous glow of colour this building presented when first erected. The walls are flat except for an occasional cornice, oriel window, or balcony, and are divided up into shallow sunk compartments for the reception of the glazed patterns. The fertility of design and the diversity of colour in the scheme are amazing, and although in its present state a somewhat vivid yellow is inclined to predominate, each panel, spandrel and border is in itself a work of art, rivalling in the brilliancy of its hues the sheen of the blue jays and green parrots which flit about its walls. There could be no finer illustration of that ardent desire for a display of exuberant colour innate in the east than these glazed tile buildings of the Punjab.

All such forms of architectural expression, however, and even those possessing the formal elegance of the royal palaces, take second place when compared with that masterpiece of Mughul architecture, the Tāj Mahall. During the first three years of his reign, Shāh Jahān had already provided in the fort at Āgra a palace for the accommodation of his consort, described in the Shāh-Jahān Nāma as "the Paradise-like buildings of Her exalted chaste Majesty, the Queen of the world, the Begam Sāhiba", and identified as the Khāss Mahall, the most sumptuous of all edifices up to that time. And as during life no building was considered too splendid, so on her death it was fitting that her remains should be enshrined within a monument of matchless beauty. Architects were therefore summoned to prepare designs for a mausoleum which to be worthy of her memory should surpass all others in artistic dignity and stateliness. Of the manner in which the design was obtained and who was responsible for the noble building which eventually matured, there are no direct records. What evidence there is is contradictory. On the one hand, there is the contemporary statement of Father Manrique, who definitely

[1] Langlès, *Voyages du Chevalier Chardin* (Paris, 1811), IV, 165.

affirms that models were prepared and submitted to the emperor by a certain Geronimo Verroneo, a Venetian, who was residing in the Mughul capital at the time.[1] On the other hand, indigenous documents have been preserved containing a detailed account of those employed on the building, all of whom were Asiatics, with no indication of any European intervention. And as an answer to the Jesuit father's contention there is the standing testimony of the Tāj Mahall itself, which shows in all its aspects that it was the natural evolution of the style, true to tradition and entirely unaffected by occidental influence. The truth seems to be that Verroneo was invited, as were others, to produce designs, but that prepared by the Mughul master-builders was the one eventually selected.

Particulars of those who took part in the production of this incomparable masterpiece indicate that no effort was spared to obtain the services of specialists in every phase of the work. Several of these were indigenous craftsmen from Delhi, Lahore, Multān and similar art centres of the Mughul empire, while others were drawn from more distant sources, such as a calligraphist from Baghdād and another from Shīrāz, to ensure that all the inscriptions were correctly carved or inlaid; a "flower carver" from Bukhārā; an expert in dome construction, Isma'īl Khān Rūmi, who by his name may have come from Constantinople; a pinnacle maker from Samarqand, a master-mason from Qandahār, and, lastly, an experienced garden planner. The chief supervisor who co-ordinated the entire work was one Ustād 'Īsā, "the best designer of his time", and, according to one account, originally an inhabitant of Shīrāz. It may be noted that while the structural portions seem to have been principally in the hands of Muhammadans, the decoration was mainly the work of Hindu craftsmen, the difficult task of preparing the *pietra dura* specially being entrusted to a group of the latter from Kanauj.

The design finally approved was based largely on the recently completed tomb of Khān Khānān at Delhi, which in its turn was a reduced and modified copy of the mausoleum of the emperor Humāyūn. But the large edifice enclosing the tomb-chamber of the Tāj Mahall, although the main feature of the composition, is only a portion of the scheme as a whole. It is supplemented by certain essential accompaniments leading up to the main building, comprising a garden, entrance-gateways, a mosque, and other accessories that would surround the mausoleum with an appropriate setting. In the preliminary thought expended on these amenities the Mughul architect excelled, every need was provided for and no incongruous changes were afterwards introduced to mar the effect. The result was that before the actual construction was even begun every minute detail, useful or ornamental, was correctly specified. Outside the

[1] See note, pp. 174–7, vol. II, *Travels of Sebastian Manrique*, trans. by C. E. Luard and H. Hosten.

precincts of the Tāj itself among other annexes were buildings for the accommodation of visitors, their attendants and conveyances, a bazar for their maintenance and a forecourt with wide approach to avoid congestion of traffic. Nothing was omitted; a more complete lay-out it would be impossible to conceive. The position of the building was also carefully considered. The site selected was on a high bank of the river at a bend, so that from every point of view there was a pleasing effect; on the one side its reflections in the water gave it an added charm, while on the other, from the garden, its white marble façades stand out clearly, having no background except the sky. At the same time its proximity to the river demanded special care in the preparation of the foundations, which it was the practice of the Mughul builder to support on masonry cylinders sunk in the soil at close intervals. Some such system was no doubt employed in the substructure of the terrace, as the entire building including the minarets apparently rests on one firm compact bed of masonry. That the method adopted was a sound one is shown by the condition of the building, for after three centuries, during which it has suffered serious neglect, its lines and angles are still as accurate as when first produced; any deviation from the true in a structure which relies for much of its beauty on the mathematical precision of its outlines would of course be fatal.

The whole scheme, including the garden, is laid out in the form of a rectangle with its long axis lying north and south, the mausoleum standing at the northern end, a departure from the traditional square plan with the main building in the centre. This rectangle is enclosed by a high wall with broad arcaded turrets at each corner, and is entered on the south side by a monumental gateway, in itself an admirable composition. Within the enclosure is the conventional garden, so designed as to comprise an intrinsic part of the architectural effect, the avenue of cypress trees being planted to harmonise with the lines of the building, and the watercourses with their ornamental pools elevated in such a manner as to reflect the most attractive points of view. At the northern end of the enclosure is a wide terrace with the mausoleum occupying the centre and balanced by subsidiary buildings on either side. The latter consist of a mosque on the west and a corresponding structure of no special religious significance on the east, but added in order to maintain strict symmetry. Although naturally intended as the predominating feature in the scheme, the mausoleum building in itself is remarkable for the vivid simplicity of both its plan and elevation. It rises almost abruptly from the high marble terrace, with no noticeable flight of steps leading up to it, for the stairway is concealed within a passage, thus unconsciously adding to that atmosphere of reserve in keeping with its chaste character. The plan is square with chamfered corners, each side being 186 feet long, so that the width of the façade is equal to the entire height of the building. Its elevation is divided approximately into two parts of equal height, the lower half consisting of the rectangular ground storey, the upper half of the great dome and its accompanying kiosks. Externally each façade of the lower rectangular portion is relieved by an arrangement of arched recesses, and to the rich shadows within these voids the whole structure owes much of its charm of effect. But its crowning glory is the great dome, which hangs in the sky like a shapely white cloud, its soaring height being mainly due to the tall drum at its base. The body of the dome is spherical, so that it rests on this drum like a ball on a cup, but its upper curve by means of a carefully calculated tangent gracefully tapers off into a foliated crest. To give a finish to the whole composition as well as to draw the eye of the spectator imperceptibly from undue concentration on the central structure, at each corner of the terrace rises a slender minaret.

The interior arrangements of the mausoleum building consist of a crypt below and a vaulted tomb-chamber above, with other rooms one in each angle all connected by corridors, light to every part being obtained by means of perforated grilles set in the arched recesses of the exterior. At a height corresponding to the parapet of the façade outside, the tomb chamber is ceiled over so that above this the whole of the interior of the great dome becomes a hollow space, a notable illustration of the system of double dome construction. As to the scheme of decoration, both inside and out, this is everywhere in keeping with the broad unity of the building and the chaste white marble of which it is composed. Certain portions are enriched with patterns carved in low relief, but the principal embellishment is obtained by arabesques of inlaid coloured stones—*pietra dura*.[1] Of the former method the square borders of inscriptions around the main archways are artistically designed and chiselled, and the dados in the interior of conventional plant-forms are modelled with exquisite feeling. But it is in the finished quality of the *pietra dura* that the inimitable patience and skill of the Indian inlayer is most plainly shown, as his share in the decorative effect ranges from the bold scrollwork in the spandrels above the great arches to the minute flowers on the cenotaphs and the perforated marble screen which encloses these. This perforated marble screen is said to have replaced a gold and jewelled railing, so that it is not part of the original design, but if a later introduction it shows that the high character of craftsmanship was maintained. The delicate carving of the marble into a grille of graceful volutes and the enrichment of each scroll with inlaid precious stones has produced a work of art of entrancing beauty, but even this is surpassed by the *pietra dura* on the cenotaphs themselves, which is cut with the fineness of a cameo. Diapers and

[1] For specimens see plates 25–30, W. Sleeman, *Rambles and Recollections*, 1844, and *Journal of Indian Art*, 1885, p. 61.

borders of pendant flowers, sprays of foliage with lilies and other floral forms either in detached repeats or contained within curved panels, are evenly distributed over their marble surfaces. So sensitive and yet so firm is the drawing that it resembles the spirited sweep of a brush rather than the slow laborious cutting of a chisel.

In addition, however, to its artistic merit, the scientific thought and technical skill expended in the construction of this monument is remarkable. Particularly is this noticeable in the subtle overhang of the great dome, which shows that the builders were conversant with the principles of tension, stress and strain, so that this problem presented no difficulties. The contrast in the character of the large dome with the cupolas over the kiosks denotes that two different traditions here meet in the same building. The main dome by its shape is plainly of Timurid extraction, its remote ancestor being the Dome of the Rock at Jerusalem; on the other hand the cupolas with their wide eaves are of indigenous origin, being derived from the overlapping rings of masonry which formed the vaulted ceiling of the Hindu temple. For the centering of the dome timber scaffolding supplemented by brick was employed, as noted by Tavernier.[1] Although details are lacking, light is thrown on this aspect of the work from an interesting source, for some of the miniature paintings of the time depict in a lively manner the various methods then in use, including that of centering[2] (Figs. 24, 25). The design of the minarets was suggested by those over the entrance to Akbar's tomb at Sikandra, although there is a notable difference in their surface treatment. In the minarets of the Tāj the face joints are countersunk, forming a kind of rustication not seen in any other part of the structure, and so by a subtle contrast in texture aiding in their detachment from the main building. In this manner by a combination of the finest art and the most expert construction the Mughul craftsmen have produced in the Tāj Mahall a monument which has most nearly reached the utmost height of perfection. Added to this the building owes not a little of its sensuous charm to the extraneous effects of the atmosphere, and the variations in the light on its marble surfaces. The marble when first won from the uninspiring mounds of Makrāna is itself of a superb texture—white with a delicate grey grain. In the course of centuries, mellowed by the sun, and sandblasted by the red dust of the surrounding country driven into it by the monsoon rains, it has acquired a patina, almost imperceptible but sufficient to affect its colour values. The result is that the building assumes at different times a variety of tints, from a cold grey at dawn, shimmering white at noon, and suffused with a tender blush rose in the afterglow, with a wide range of half-tones in between.

[1] Book 1, p. 111.

[2] Victoria and Albert Museum, South Kensington, Indian Section, No. 1896 (I.S.), 86/117, etc.

And in the light of the moon another and entirely changed palette is called into requisition. On some of these occasions, with the flowers in the garden painting the foreground with their vivid colouring, it seems as if the hand of nature and the hand of man had united and done their utmost to produce a spectacle of supremely moving beauty.

The mausoleum of Shāh Jahān's queen, although apparently complete in itself, was intended, however, as only one part of a more comprehensive architectural scheme. On the opposite side of the river, where is now the Mahtāb Bāgh, the emperor planned his own tomb, a replica of the Tāj but in black marble, the two monuments to be connected by a bridge. Tavernier definitely states that "Shāh Jahān began to build his own tomb on the other side of the river, but the war which he had with his son interrupted his plan, and Aurangzīb, who reigns at present, is not disposed to complete it".[1] And in support of this contemporary record there is the testimony of the cenotaphs themselves and their position in the tomb-chamber of the Tāj. Here Mumtāz Mahall lies proudly in the centre, a fairly clear proof that the building was intended for her remains alone; subsequently, and on one side, was inserted the cenotaph of the emperor, evidently an afterthought because his own separate resting-place never matured. That Aurangzīb's unfilial actions and bigotry generally were responsible for this project being abandoned there seems little doubt, and owing to these personal failings humanity has been deprived of an architectural composition which for romance, imagination and magnificence would have had no equal. With this emperor's accession to power the course of the building art under the Mughuls came to an end. Aurangzīb added a few structures, some of them large and pretentious, to the long series of monuments erected by this dynasty, but compared with those of his predecessors they are decidedly inferior. The sudden decline of the art towards the middle of the seventeenth century may be traced to several causes. There is the obvious reason that at this time the Mughul empire itself had begun to totter, and with it the cultural activities patronised by the dynasty suffered neglect. Associated with this political and artistic decadence was the personality of Aurangzīb himself, whose philistinism and narrowness of outlook were largely responsible for the disintegration. On the other hand, the decline of the style may have been due to the natural progress of events. Under Shāh Jahān the country had experienced a period of unrestrained production, during which its exponents had reached the summit of achievement. The usual sequence to such a condition is a marked reaction, of which art history provides several notable instances, including among others that of the great schools of painting in Europe of the seventeenth century, whose finest efforts were followed by an interval of

[1] Tavernier, I, 110, 111.

profound exhaustion. And so it was with the architecture of the Mughuls. It had endured its golden age, run its course, and even before the reign of Aurangzīb had begun to show signs of decadence. The shallow elegance of some of Shāh Jahān's later buildings, as for example the Machhī Bhawan in Āgra fort, is a forecast of what was about to take place. Its energies dissipated by the very number and grandeur of its conceptions, with nothing further possible, a period of sterility was inevitable. It is questionable whether any human power, even that of vigorous imperial patronage, could have changed the course of destiny or prolonged its life another span.

One of the few large buildings of Aurangzīb's reign, but one which fully illustrates the change that was then taking place, is far removed, however, from the majority of the Mughul monuments, as it is in the Deccan. Near the town of Aurangābād, now in the Nizām's dominions, this emperor caused to be erected in 1679 by "'Atā-ullah, Chief Architect", the mausoleum of his wife Rābi'a-ud-Daurānī. A frank copy of the Tāj Mahall, although approximately only half its size, it shows in the thirty years that intervened the extent to which taste had deteriorated and the style become impoverished. With inadequate knowledge the architect had evidently endeavoured to improve on the proportions of the Tāj, and also to enrich it with considerable superfluous ornament. The result, as would be expected, is a very mediocre production, the relation of height to width being unpleasing, leading to a loss of dignity and a congestion of the structures around the base of the dome. Almost every arch is demeaned with miniature cusps, the cornices garnished by insipid mouldings, and the surfaces are aggravated by spiritless arabesques. Those outstanding qualities of simplicity and breadth which make the Tāj so profound and satisfying have been disregarded, and meaningless efforts at embellishment have been applied all over the building. But although the structure as a whole shows such marked evidences of debasement, the same cannot be said of some of the applied art with which it is decorated. The fine quality of some of the accessories proves that good craftsmen were still available. The octagonal screen of white marble enclosing the sarcophagus is carved in a perforated pattern equal in workmanship to that of the previous reign, while some of the designs in bas relief are exquisitely modelled. But the finest ornament is in metal, some of the doors being of beaten brass with bold floral panels and borders hammered and chiselled in masterly fashion. The hand of the craftsman was still effective, it was the spirit of the art that had declined.

Owing perhaps to being in one of the Mughul cities of Hindūstān, and not so distantly situated as the previous monument, fewer defects are observable in the Bādshāhī mosque at Lahore. Its production was the work of Fidāi Khān Kūka, Aurangzīb's Master of Ordnance, whose engineering experience enabled him to plan and erect a building of sound construction and great size. But even his technical skill could not build to withstand the earthquake which in 1840 shattered its four minarets, the principal feature of the design. Without these the building loses much of its effect, but there is a certain dignity in its broad quadrangle leading up to the façade of the sanctuary, a scheme in red sandstone laced with marble. The three bulbous domes are well-proportioned, and rise into a grand mass of white marble above the western wall, which presents an almost unbroken surface of masonry of imposing appearance. As a contrast to the excess of decoration in the mausoleum referred to above this mosque marks the other extreme; its ornamentation, although boldly conceived, is sparingly introduced, so that the general impression it conveys is uninteresting, the attempt at economy of detail defeating its own purpose. Another and entirely opposite example of the Mughul style, as manifested in the time of Aurangzīb, is the mosque at Benares, the minarets of which dominate the city with their slender prettiness but entirely lack stability or strength. It illustrates with the other buildings executed during this emperor's reign the inconsistent nature of the art and the extent to which it had fallen away from its previous standard towards the end of the seventeenth century. The final state of the style in the eighteenth century is seen in the tomb of Safdar Jang, a large and pretentious structure erected in Delhi as late as 1753. As it is situated a comparatively short distance from the mausoleum of the emperor Humāyūn it is an easy matter to compare the two monuments, the first and the last of their kind. A period of nearly two hundred years separates the one from the other, and the change that has taken place is illuminating. They represent the extremes of their style, that of the emperor expressing in every line its power and exultant vitality, and that "dew of the morning" which marks the beginning of every new movement. On the other hand, the tomb of Safdar Jang seems to be striving by artificial means to reproduce the original vigour, while in reality it is enfeebled and decadent. Gone are the balanced proportions with broad simple planes, and in their place is an ostentatious and affected structure, each part embarrassed with repetitions of weak and tasteless motifs. It was a final effort to recapture the old spirit of the Mughul style as seen in the royal tombs when the dynasty was a living force; but by this time the art had gone beyond any hope of recall.

During this period, while the building art of the Mughuls was pursuing its course in Hindūstān, a somewhat independent development of the style established itself in Sind, when that part of the country was eventually incorporated in the empire under Akbar. Lower Sind, where most of the buildings are found, lies in the direction of an art current which very early set in from the west, a stream of no great strength but which persisted intermittently for several centuries. It brought with it first the influence of the Arab culture, such as it was in so remote a possession, and afterwards that of Persia. Buildings in brick therefore are characteristic of the towns of Sind, a method of construction which continues all along the Indus and beyond to Multān, encouraged by the alluvial formation of the country. Such a monochromatic prospect which this vast plain presents cries out for colour, so that it became the custom to decorate all buildings with brilliant schemes of glazed tiles. This method of ornamentation was probably first introduced by the Arabs, and was revived later by intercourse with Persia at a time when that country was enriching all its larger towns with brick buildings covered with patterns in coloured faience. Sind tiles are, however, not copies of the Persian model, nor are they similar even to those of the Punjab, a much nearer neighbour. They have a special character which is easily recognised. Most of the patterns are geometrical, and where foliage is interposed it is of a strictly conventional order. In technique the tiles are rarely square or rectangular but cut in geometrical shapes corresponding to the details of the design. With such a long tradition for brick and glaze it seems an anomaly to find in the town of Tatta, once the old capital of lower Sind, a group of tombs constructed entirely of stone and carved in a style which suggests that of Akbar's buildings at Fathpur Sīkrī. Most of these tombs appear to have been erected when the country was first included within the empire of the Mughuls under Mīrzā 'Īsā Tarkhān, who was governor of Tatta between A.D. 1627 and 1644. Some of the graves, however, bear an earlier date, and it is therefore fairly evident that the influence of Akbar's expansive building operations at the end of the sixteenth century found an echo in this rather distant part of his dominions. The most important of the tombs at Tatta is that of 'Īsā Tarkhān himself, a two-storeyed building standing on a raised platform in the centre of an enclosed courtyard. Its chief architectural feature is a double arcade surrounding the building, each pillar of which is a monolith, those of the inner row, together with the interior walls, being elaborately carved. The general character of the structure has much of the temperament of Akbar's capital, and this especially applies to the low relief patterns with which all the surfaces are profusely adorned. But as with the tiles this carving is not a servile imitation although it has the same manipulative texture as that at Fathpur Sīkrī, yet none the less expressing the individuality of the local artizans, who seem to have speedily acquired a marked aptitude in the use of the chisel.

This phase of sandstone building in Sind endured only, however, for a time, for in the reign of Shāh Jahān the builders returned again to their customary creations in brick and tile. In 1644 this emperor caused to be begun at Tatta a Jāmi' Masjid, one of the largest buildings in Sind and decorated with the finest type of coloured glaze. It occupies a rectangle of 305 feet by 170 feet, the plan being remarkable for the great depth of its aisles and for two small square courtyards that are placed on each side of the entrance hall. Consisting of large flat surfaces unrelieved by any serious attempt at contrasting planes or mouldings, it relies for effect on an unlimited display of broken colour, every portion of the interior being covered with tiles. From floor to ceiling and right up into the main dome geometrical patterns are crowded together, with panels of inscriptions along the cornice and arabesques in the spandrels. The principal colours are two varieties of blue, light and dark, and white, while the minute character of the workmanship may be judged by the smallness of the tiles, many of them being only half an inch wide, over a hundred being used in a square foot of pattern so that it resembles a mosaic. But with all this expenditure of skilled labour in the production of the colour scheme the general appearance of the building arouses little enthusiasm, and although the prodigality of the decoration has its attractions there is such a surfeit of it that it becomes cloying. Other buildings, chiefly tombs of this type, are found in various parts of Sind, at Haidarābād, Khudābād and Sukkur, but most of these were erected after the period of the Mughul ascendancy.

Distinct in character from the architecture of the Mughuls, but simultaneous with that dynasty during the first century of its rule, a provincial style prevailed in a part of the Deccan represented by a large and important group of buildings of pronounced appearance and rare architectural merit. This independent development of the art of building was due to the power and artistic patronage of the sultans of the 'Ādil Shāh dynasty, who, until absorbed into the Mughul empire in the middle of the seventeenth century, made their capital at Bijāpur one of the most magnificent cities in the whole of India. Unlike Akbar's capital at Fathpur Sīkrī, with which many of its buildings were contemporary, instead of being the result of an autocratic impulse to provide an architectural setting for the pageantry of the court, Bijāpur grew out of a real need for a large town, strongly fortified, essential for the permanent accommodation of its rulers and their retinue, and from which the province could be properly administered. It consists therefore of a wide circular area enclosed by a wall having a citadel towards the centre, and the remainder of the space occupied with all the constituent buildings of a state capital, such as palaces, mosques, tombs, mint and gateways. Compared also with the cities of the Mughuls bright with red sandstone and white marble, the capital of the 'Ādil Shāhs, constructed almost entirely of a local trap, dark brown in colour, presents in spite of its many fine monuments a somewhat monotonous and sombre effect. Attributing to themselves a Turkish origin denoted by the crescent-finial surmounting several of the state buildings, the 'Ādil Shāhs brought into the style of these structures a new and vigorous infusion, with remarkable results. This is shown in the wide range of their types of building, combined with a knowledge of construction which equals, if it does not exceed, that of the master-masons of the Mughuls. As an instance of the versatility of the Bijāpur workmen, the contrast between the majestic proportions and breadth of treatment of the Gol Gumbaz, Muhammad 'Ādil Shāh's tomb, and the exquisite detail of the miniature Mihtar Mahall, is noteworthy. The former building is a *tour de force*, as its dome, in some of its dimensions, is one of the largest of its kind, the total area that it covers being over eighteen thousand square feet. Under Muhammad (1627–56), the 'Ādil Shāh dynasty reached the height of its power, a circumstance which is marked by this immense mausoleum, unquestionably the most striking monument in Bijāpur, and one of the most impressive in the whole of India. Seen in the gathering dusk of evening its great bulk rises above the surrounding plain like mountain scenery rather than the product of the puny hand of man. The Gol Gumbaz is, however, only the central portion of a considerable architectural complex which was intended to include a mosque, a gateway and musicians' gallery, a hostel and other annexes essential to a royal tomb, all disposed within an extensive walled enclosure. Some of these buildings still exist, but it is doubtful whether the entire scheme was ever quite completed, the bareness of the interior of the mausoleum, which was evidently intended to be decorated, being a significant omission. The design of the tomb building itself is comparatively simple as it encloses one chamber only, but this is a hall of noble proportions, and like the Pantheon at Rome and the Basilica of Constantine one of the largest single cells ever erected. Externally, apart from the vast size of the dome, the most arresting features are the octagonal turrets which project at each angle, and the ponderous bracketed cornice below the parapet. The wall space between these is relieved only by three sunk arches, and it is here that the design seems to have been left unfinished; a little detail judiciously applied would have given more interest to these façades. Above the corbelled cornice is an arcade, and the parapet is surmounted by ornamental crenellations, while as in all the domes at Bijāpur the low drum is encircled by a foliated band. In the interior, except for the wooden pavilion in the centre under which the cenotaph is placed, the only other noticeable features in this great bare hall are the tall pointed arches supporting the dome. And in the arrangement of these arches the builder showed his consummate skill in solving a difficult problem of construction in a scientific and at the same time artistic manner. The intention of the building required him to lay out the foundations of the hall on a square plan, and, as the walls gained height, gradually to change this square so that the summit of the walls finished in a circle; on this circular cornice he could readily construct his dome. By an ingenious combination of eight intersecting arches, the foot of each standing within the square plan but its plane set at an angle, the corner was bridged over, the whole construction eventually forming a broad circular gallery or platform of masonry some 24 feet wide and more than 100 feet from the ground. With this platform as a base the builders proceeded to erect the huge inverted bowl of the dome. The materials used for this purpose were bricks and mortar, and a noticeable fact is the great thickness of the mortar between each course, so much so that the dome may be described as consisting of a hollow mass of concrete reinforced with layers of brick set in level courses. Of a somewhat similar composition most large domes have been built, as for instance that of St Sophia and also the Pantheon, and here may be suspected slight evidence in support of that Turkish attribution to which the 'Ādil Shāh dynasty laid claim, as this method of construction was probably derived from Ottoman sources. Another indication that the builders of Bijāpur may have sought far and wide for inspiration is shown by the device of intersecting arches referred to above, which made the raising of this great dome in such a manner a practical expedient. For probably the only other example of this particular system by which a dome may be supported is in the cupola of the *mihrāb* vestibule at Cordova in Spain erected considerably over six hundred years before.

The Gol Gumbaz, however, is a building which depicts the Bijāpur style in what may be termed its masculine aspect, while its colossal size is perhaps its most distinctive characteristic. For the opposite of all these qualities there is the comparatively small edifice known as the Mihtar Mahall erected in 1620, one of those rich gems of the builder's art which the Indian's mind at times found such delight in producing, and in the decoration of which his most skilled craftsmen expended their ungrudging care. Although called a *mahall*, or palace, this structure is really a gateway to the inner courtyard of a mosque which lies a little way behind it. But it is something more than a mere entrance, for it is a tall graceful building with an upper storey containing an assembly room, and above this again is an open terrace surrounded by a high wall with oriel windows and a perforated parapet. On each side of the façade are two slender ornamental minarets of a type characteristic of the Bijāpur style, but it is the projecting balcony window filling in the entire space between that is the most striking feature. It is thrown out from the wall on a series of closely set carved brackets, and the wide eaves-board is supported by struts of stone so finely wrought with the chisel as to have every appearance of wood. Perhaps in its imitation of other and more plastic materials, and its delicate prettiness as a whole, this charming little structure is open to criticism; it conveys the impression that its designer had been commissioned to prepare a miniature masterpiece complete in every detail regardless of time or cost, and had been allowed a free hand in the matter. The manner in which he played with the stone as if it were clay in reproducing mouldings, joggled joints, and particularly the sunk coffers in the ceiling of the ground storey, show the exuberance of his fancy and the sheer delight he took in his task.

One of the first buildings of importance to be erected in the city of Bijāpur, and thus illustrating the style in its formative state, was the Jāmi' Masjid begun by 'Alī 'Ādil Shāh I about 1565. Never quite finished it still lacks the frontage of the courtyard and two minarets which were to complete this portion of its outer façade. An endeavour was made by the Mughul emperor Aurangzīb to supply this deficiency, and under his orders an eastern entrance gateway was added, but on this side of the structure much still remains to be done. The exterior shows a large rectangular building of plain aspect but powerful proportions rising at its western end into a low square battlemented tower supporting a fine dome. As usual this dome is over the central prayer hall of the sanctuary, and it is in the remarkable depth of space covered by the sanctuary that this mosque differs from many others. This arcaded prayer hall consists of five aisles separated by piers, thus dividing the whole into a series of square bays of wide pointed arches; the effect of this great expanse, with its perspective of piers and arches, is very impressive. The appearance of the entire building is forceful and uninvolved, a consummation achieved by the correct relation of its parts and the skilful subordination of the lesser to the larger forms of the composition. Ornament has been sparingly introduced and then only to enrich a shadow or emphasise a line, as may be seen in the cusping of the central arch of the façade, the elaboration of the brackets between the arches, and other features that called for decorative accentuation. All the surfaces have been treated to a coat of plaster, the interior walls having been finished with a layer of very fine quality which has mellowed to a pleasing creamy tint. Amidst this display of austere refinement, on the removal of a heavy protecting curtain covering the central bay containing the principal *mihrāb*, it is surprising to find this particular space embellished with the most gorgeous array of patterns in colour and gold. Although there is much to admire in this unexpected blaze of colour, which depicts arcades and minarets, lamps, arabesques and inscriptions all conventionally treated, it is not in exact harmony with its surroundings and is the work of a later hand.

That the Bijāpur master-masons could, however, produce a highly ornate type of architecture on a large scale is shown by the Ibrāhīm Rauza, a group of buildings erected towards the end of the sixteenth century. The Rauza consists of the tomb of Sultān Ibrāhīm II together with its mosque, the two structures confronting one another on a raised terrace, the whole being contained within the usual square-walled enclosure. Rivalling even the finest buildings of the Mughuls in this respect, the premeditated completeness of this mausoleum and its appurtenances is astonishing, every detail of the scheme from the lettering of the inscriptions to the stone hooks in the stables having evidently been determined before the first stone was laid. Great ingenuity has been shown by the manner in which the designer has disposed the two main structures, each widely different in plan and purpose, so that together they form a symmetrical unity. Both are arcaded edifices with wide eaves on carved brackets, ornamental minarets at each angle as turrets, and each is surmounted by a bulbous dome. The mausoleum, as was intended, is the more important building, and on this the workmen have exercised their exceptional artistic ability, so that in design, construction and ornamentation it leaves little to be desired. Enclosed within a double verandah the tomb-chamber is square in shape with a flat coffered ceiling composed of stones set together edge to edge, having apparently no means of support, but evidently with concealed joggled joints. Above this ceiling is the vaulted void of the double dome, a large empty upper-storey chamber entered from the roof but having no particular use. The mosque which faces the tomb across a courtyard is in the same ornate style but slightly modified, and consists of an open arcaded prayer chamber of three pillared aisles with a deeply sunk *mihrāb* in the western wall. Where, however, both these buildings excel is in the individual character of the carved decoration, which, like the Bijāpur architecture itself, denotes the presence of a definite school. The substance of this ornamentation is similar to that found in all Islamic art, but certain factors have been introduced, such as a special kind of bracket supporting a medallion, which are as original as they are graceful. Unlike the somewhat hybrid designs which satisfied the Mughuls, the Deccani patterns exhibit little extraneous influence; they are clearly the creation of the fertile imagination of the Bijāpur craftsmen. Equally distinctive are the buildings themselves, the typical features of which may be readily recognised. These consist of the bulbous dome with its foliated drum, the tall slender turret or pinnacle in the form of an ornamental minaret, and the almost invariable preference for the pier instead of the pillar. In their methods the Bijāpur builders were often bold and daring, but this adventurous spirit was accompanied by no little engineering experience and scientific knowledge. This has been already noticed in referring to the technical skill displayed in the construction of the Gol Gumbaz and the ceiling of the Ibrāhīm Rauza, but it is similarly shown in the immense size and spread of some of the archways, as for instance that of the Gagan Mahall and a viaduct which leads to the Athar Mahall. These *mahalls* are two of the several palaces built in or near the citadel and illustrate the secular buildings of the 'Ādil Shāhs, but none of them compares in architectural character with their mosques and tombs, nor are they in the same class as the noble marble pavilions of the Mughuls.

One other style of building of a quasi-independent order manifested itself in the Deccan both before and during the Mughul ascendancy, in the state of Khāndesh. Here in the local capitals of Burhānpur and Thālner several monuments were erected in the fifteenth and sixteenth centuries by the Fārūqī dynasty; later, in the seventeenth century, the Mughul governors were responsible for a number of tombs of a particular kind. The geographical position of this comparatively small state, surrounded as it was by a number of powerful kingdoms each with its own form of artistic expression, rendered it specially liable to external influences. These show themselves unmistakably in the character of many of its buildings. Yet although these borrowings are discernible they do not entirely dominate the style, as the architecture of Khāndesh in some of its phases displays certain originality. One of the first buildings erected by the Fārūqī rulers was a large palace on a commanding situation above the Tāptī river at Burhānpur, followed by a group of tombs at the same place and another group at Thālner, all dating from the first half of the fifteenth century. Although the palace is now in ruins, enough remains to indicate that this edifice, and perhaps more noticeably the tombs, owed not a little of their appearance to similar buildings being then raised in the neighbouring city of Māndū, the capital of Mālwā. The tombs of the founders of the Fārūqī dynasty, such as that of Nāsir Khān (1399–1437) at Burhānpur, and Mīrān Mubārak I (deceased 1457) at Thālner, show a marked affinity to the more famous mausoleum of Hūshang at Māndū in the solidity of their effect and proportions generally. The Khāndesh masons have, however, endeavoured to lighten the mass of the structure by the introduction of projecting openings on each side of the central doorway, and have also provided more height by raising the dome on a well-proportioned drum, which, together with other features, constructive and decorative, give these Fārūqī tombs an air of no little distinction. At a later date two mosques were erected at Burhānpur, the Jāmi' Masjid built by 'Alī Khān in 1588 being the larger and more important, while the Bībī-kī-Masjid is better designed. The former is a comparatively plain structure, the fifteen pointed arches comprising its façade being flanked by two lofty minarets, a simple conception, but the symmetry and disposition of its parts has been carefully considered. It is not unlikely that the construction of this building was interrupted by the subjection of the state by Akbar, its completion being undertaken by the Mughuls, so that its final appearance may not be as originally intended. As an example of a coherent composition the Bībī-kī-Masjid is much superior, but it is too obviously dictated by similar structures in Ahmadābād and Chāmpāner to be commended for its originality, although the minarets are a departure from the Gujarātī type, particularly the projecting windows and rounded cupolas. The concluding phase of the style, when it came under the influence of the Mughuls, is seen in the tomb of Shāh Nawāz Khān, one of its provincial governors in the seventeenth century. Much of this building is frankly a composite conception displaying elements acquired from a variety of sources. Its square design in two storeys is suggestive of some of the royal tombs of the Ahmad Shāh dynasty, the pinnacles are those introduced by Fīrūz Tughluq but ornamented with foliations from Bijāpur, and, finally, the whole is surmounted by a "Lodī" dome. Yet these attributions are combined with no little skill, and the general appearance of the structure is not unattractive. At the same time it is clear that the style had no further resources of its own, and could only be maintained by appropriating the ideas of others. In such circumstances it naturally follows that no more buildings of any consequence were erected in Khāndesh.

BIBLIOGRAPHY

GENERAL

A. HISTORICAL

BURGESS, J. The Chronology of Modern India. Edinburgh, 1913.
ELLIOT, H. M. and DOWSON, J. The History of India, as told by its own Historians. 8 vols. 1867–77.
HODIVALA, S. H. Historical Studies in Mughal Numismatics. Calcutta, 1923.
KEENE, H. G. Fall of the Moghul Empire. 1887.
LANE-POOLE, S. Mediaeval India under Muhammadan rule. 1902.

B. NUMISMATIC

Catalogues of Mughul coins in Museums:
British Museum. By S. Lane-Poole. 1892.
Calcutta. By H. Nelson Wright. 1908.
Lahore. By R. B. Whitehead. 1914.
Lucknow. By C. J. Brown. 2 vols. 1920.
Numismatic Supplement to the *Journal, Asiatic Society of Bengal*. Calcutta, from 1904.
Index to Num. Supp. I–XV. Allahabad, 1912.
WHITEHEAD, R. B. Coins of Nādir Shāh and the Durrānī Dynasty. 1934.

CHAPTER I

BĀBUR

1. ORIGINAL SOURCES

Memoirs of Bābur:
Turkī text.
(*a*) Edited by N. Ilminski. 1857.
(*b*) Facsimile of Hyderābād Codex, edited by A. S. Beveridge. 1905.
Persian Versions.
(*a*) By Pāyandah Hasan.
(*b*) By Mīrzā 'Abdu'r-Rahīm.
European translations.
(*a*) By J. Leyden and W. Erskine of 'Abdu'r-Rahīm's Persian version. 1826. Revised by Sir L. King. 1921.
(*b*) By A. Pavet de Courteille, from Ilminski's text. 1871.
(*c*) By A. S. Beveridge, from the Hyderābād Codex. 1921.
Tārīkh-i-Rashīdī. By Muhammad Haidar Dughlāt.
Translation of the Persian text by N. Elias and E. Denison Ross. 1895.
Habīb-us-Siyar. By Khvānd Amīr.
Persian text, lithographed. Teheran, 1855 and Bombay, 1857.
Ahsan-us-Siyar. By Mīrzā Barkhwardār Turkmān.
Shaibānī-nāma. By Muhammad Sālih.
Turkī text and German translation by H. Vambéry. 1885.
Text edited by P. M. Melioransky and A. N. Samoïlovich. 1908.
Tārīkh-i-'Ālamārāi 'Abbāsī. By Iskandar Munshī.
Persian manuscript in the Bodleian. (Fraser 144, 147, 145.) Lithographed. Teheran, 1896.
Humāyūn-nāma. By Gulbadan Begam.
Persian text, edited and translated by A. S. Beveridge. 1902.

Tārīkh-i-Haqqī. By 'Abdul-Haqq ibn Saif-ud-Dīn Dihlavī.
Persian manuscript in the Bodleian. (Fraser 132.)
Ahsan-ut-Tawārīkh. By Hasan.
Persian manuscript in the Bodleian. (Ouseley 232.)
Tārīkh-i-Firishta. By Muhammad Qāsim called Firishta.
Persian text, edited by J. Briggs. 1831. Lithographed edition, Lucknow, 1864.
Translation by J. Briggs. London, 1829; reprinted Calcutta, 1908.
Tabaqāt-i-Akbarī. By Nizām-ud-Dīn Ahmad ibn Muhammad Muqīm.
Persian manuscript in Bodleian. (Elliot 381.)
Edited and translated by B. De. (*Bibliotheca Indica.*) In progress, 1913–
Akbar-nāma. By Abu-'l-Fazl.
Persian text, edited by Āghā Ahmad 'Alī and Maulavī 'Abd-ur-Rahīm. (*Bibliotheca Indica.*) 1877–87.
Translation, by H. Beveridge. (*Bibliotheca Indica.*) In progress, 1903–

2. MODERN WORKS

Caldecott, R. M. The life of Baber. 1844.
Edwardes, S. M. Bābur: diarist and despot. 1926.
Erskine, W. A history of India under...Bāber and Humāyūn. 1854.
Grenard, Fernand. Baber, first of the Moguls. Translated and adapted by Homer White and Richard Glaenzer. 1930.
Poole, S. Lane. Bābar. (Rulers of India.) 1899.
Williams, L. F. Rushbrook. An empire builder of the sixteenth century...Babur. (Allahabad University Publications, no. 3.) 1918.

CHAPTER II

HUMĀYŪN

1. ORIGINAL SOURCES

Memoirs of Bābur, see chap. 1.
Tārīkh-i-Rashīdī, see chap. 1.
Humāyūn-nāma, see chap. 1.
Humāyūn-nāma. By Khvānd Amīr. Partly translated in Elliot and Dowson, v, 116–26.
Tārīkh-i-Gujarāt. By 'Abdullah Muhammad. Edited by E. Denison Ross. 1910, 1921 and 1928.
Tezkereh-ul-Vákiát. By Jauhar. Translated by C. Stewart. 1832.
Memoirs of Bāyazīd. (India Office Library, MS. 216, 223.) Abstract in English by H. Beveridge, *J.A.S.B.* 1898, p. 296.

2. MODERN WORKS

Erskine, W. History of India, see chap. 1.

CHAPTER III

SHER SHĀH

1. ORIGINAL SOURCES

Tārīkh-i-Sher Shāhī. By 'Abbās Sarwānī. Translated in Elliot and Dowson, iv, 305–433.
Makhzan-i-Afghāna. By Ni'mat-Ullah. Translated by B. Dorn in *History of the Afghāns.* 1829.

Tārīkh-i-Dāūdī. By 'Abdullah. Partly translated in Elliot and Dowson, IV, 434–513.

Memoirs of Bābur, Tārīkh-i-Rashīdī, Humāyūn-nāma, Tabaqāt-i-Akbarī, Akbar-nāma, see chap. I.

2. MODERN WORKS

BHATTASALI, N. K. The date of Sher Shāh's accession. *Islamic Review*, 1936, p. 127.

ERSKINE, W. History of India, see chap. I.

KĀLIKĀRANJAN QĀNŪNGO. Sher Shāh. Calcutta, 1921.

PARAMATMA SARAN. The date and place of Sher Shāh's birth. *Journal, Bihar and Orissa Research Society*, 1934, p. 108.

CHAPTERS IV AND V

AKBAR

I. ORIGINAL SOURCES

Akbar-nāma. By Shaikh Abu-'l-Fazl. Published by the A.S.B. in the *Bibliotheca Indica* series. Text, 3 volumes.

A most valuable chronicle of Akbar's reign and the principal authority for dates and bare facts. When it goes beyond these it is highly coloured by Abu-'l-Fazl's adulation of his master.

The *Akbar-nāma* has been translated into English by Mr H. Beveridge and published by the A.S.B. in the same series.

Āīn-i-Akbarī. By Shaikh Abu-'l-Fazl. Published by the A.S.B. in the *Bibliotheca Indica* series. Text, 3 volumes.

English translation in the same series, three volumes, vol. I by Blochmann and vols. II and III by Jarrett. The translation of vol. I is generally accurate but its chief value lies in the copious notes and appendices with which the erudition of Mr Blochmann has enriched it. The translation of vols. II and III is excellent and the notes are ample,[1] but the statistical account of the provinces in vol. II is marred by failure to identify place names.

The *Āīn-i-Akbarī* contains a code of Akbar's regulations in all departments and on all subjects and includes, besides some extraneous matter, a valuable and minute statistical account of his empire, with historical and other notes.

Muntakhab-ut-Tawārīkh. By 'Abdul-Qādir Badāūni. Also known as *Tārīkh-i-Badāūni*. Published by the A.S.B. in the *Bibliotheca Indica* series. Text, 3 volumes.

English translation in the same series. Vol. I by Lt.-Col. Ranking, vol. II by the Rev. W. H. Lowe, vol. III by Lt.-Col. Haig.

The book, being written from the point of view taken by a bigoted Sunnī, is of the highest value as a check on the turgid panegyric composed by the latitudinarian Abu-'l-Fazl.

Tabaqāt-i-Akbarī. By Khvāja Nizām-ud-dīn Ahmad. Text, Lucknow lithographed edition of A.H. 1292 (A.D. 1875).

A dry chronicle of events, without comment, written by a highly placed and therefore cautious official. The chronology is faulty but the work is specially valuable for a record of events in Gujarāt, where the author was much employed. It is brought down to the thirty-ninth year of the reign.

Tārīkh-i-Firishta. Bombay lithographed text of 1832.

A mere compilation, which contains, however, a few interesting items of information, especially relating to the Deccan, contributed by the author from his own personal knowledge.

Darbār-i-Akbarī (in Urdu). By Shams-ul-'Ulamā Maulānā Maulavī Muhammad Husain, Āzād. Rifāh-i-'Āmm Press, Lahore, 1898.

A useful compilation, based chiefly on the works of Abu-'l-Fazl.

[1] Except on administrative matters [Ed.].

Inshā-i-Abu-'l-Fazl. A collection of official dispatches written by Shaikh Abu-'l-Fazl, and interesting as throwing much light on Akbar's relations with his neighbours and with his own nobles and officers, but prolix, pompous, and tedious. Lucknow lithographed edition of A.H. 1279 (A.D. 1862).

Zubdat-ut-Tawārīkh. By Shaikh Nūr-ul-Haqq. MSS.

Tārīkh-i-Haqqī. By Shaikh 'Abdul-Haqq, father of the preceding. MSS. (A.D. 1596–7).

Mongolicae Legationis Commentarius. By Fr. Anthony Monserrate, S.J. Latin text published in *Memoirs of the Asiatic Society of Bengal*, III, no. 9, 1914. English translation by J. S. Hoyland, 1922.

Travels of Ralph Fitch (1583–91) and John Mildenhall (1599–1606) in *Early Travels in India*. Edited by W. Foster. 1921.

2. MODERN WORKS

BINYON, L. Akbar. 1932.

IRVINE, W. Army of the Indian Moguls. 1903.

MACLAGAN, Sir E. The Jesuits and the Great Mogul. 1932.

MALLESON, G. B. Akbar. (Rulers of India Series.) 1890.

MODI, J. J. Parsees at the court of Akbar. Bombay, 1903.

MORELAND, W. H. India at the death of Akbar. 1920.

—— The agrarian system of Moslem India. 1929.

NOER, Count VON. Kaiser Akbar. 1880 and 1885.

SMITH, V. A. Akbar the great Moghul. 1917 and 1919. This contains a fuller bibliography with description of sources.

CHAPTER VI

JAHĀNGĪR

1. ORIGINAL SOURCES

Tūzuk-i-Jahāngīrī. By Jahāngīr himself to the seventeenth year of his reign (1622–3), and continued under his direction to the nineteenth year by Mu'tamid Khān. Lithographed at 'Aligarh, 1864.

English translation by A. Rogers, edited by H. Beveridge, vols. I (1909) and II (1914).

Iqbāl-nāma. By Mu'tamid Khān. Persian text in *Bibliotheca Indica* series. Calcutta, 1865. Partly translated in Elliot and Dowson, VI, 393–438.

Tatimma Wāqi'āt-i-Jahāngīrī. By Muhammad Hādī. Partly translated in Elliot and Dowson, VI, 393–9.

Maāsir-i-Jahāngīrī. By Khvāja Ghairat Khān. Partly translated in Elliot and Dowson, VI, 442–5.

Intikhāb-i-Jahāngīr Shāh. Partly translated in Elliot and Dowson, VI, 447–52.

Shash Fath-i-Kāngra. By Muhammad Jalāl Tibātibā. Partly translated in Elliot and Dowson, VI, 518–31.

Maāsir-i-Rahīmī. By Muhammad 'Abdul-Bāqī. Part I printed by Asiatic Society of Bengal, Calcutta.

Khulāsat-ut-Tawārīkh. By Sujān Rāy. Edited by M. Zafar Hasan and lithographed at Delhi, 1918.

Muntakhab-ul-Lubāb. By Muhammad Hāshim Khāfī Khān. Printed in *Bibliotheca Indica*. Calcutta, 1869.

Bahāristān-i-Ghāibī. By Mīrzā Nathan. Abstract translation by Professor Srī Rām Sharma, *Journal of Indian History*, 1932, pp. 334 *sqq*.

Bīr Singh Deo Charitra. By Kesho Dās.

The annual Relation of Father Fernão Guerreiro, S.J. for 1607–8. Abstract translation by H. Hosten, S.J. in *Journal of Punjab Historical Society*, VII, 50.

Early Travels in India (W. Hawkins, 1608–13), W. Finch (1608–11), N. Withington (1612–16), T. Coryat (1612–17), E. Terry (1616–19). Edited by W. Foster. 1921.

The Embassy of Sir Thomas Roe to India, 1615–19. Edited by W. Foster. Hakluyt Society, 1899; revised edition, 1926.
Jahāngīr's India (The Remonstrantie of F. Pelsaert). Translated from the Dutch by W. H. Moreland and P. Geyl. Cambridge, 1925.
Letters received by the East India Company from its servants in the East, 1602–17. Vols. I to VI, 1896–1902.
English Factories in India. Edited by W. Foster. (1618–21) 1906, (1622–3) 1908, (1624–9) 1909.
Voyage of Peter Floris to the East Indies (1611–15). Edited by W. H. Moreland. Hakluyt Society. 1934.
Voyage of Thomas Best (1612–14). Edited by Sir W. Foster. Hakluyt Society. 1934.

2. MODERN WORKS

DE LAET. De Imperio Magno Mogoli, sive India vera, Commentarius ex variis Auctoribus Congestis. Leyden, 1631. Translated into English by J. S. Hoyland. Bombay, 1928.
GLADWIN, F. Reign of Jahāngīr. Calcutta, 1788.
MORELAND, W. H. From Akbar to Aurangzeb. 1923.
PRASAD, BENI. History of Jahāngīr. 1922, with a very full bibliography.

CHAPTER VII

SHĀH JAHĀN

1. ORIGINAL SOURCES

Makhzan-i-Afghāna, see chap. III.
Tūzuk-i-Jahāngīrī, see chap. VI.
Maāsir-i-Jahāngīrī, see chap. VI.
Iqbāl-nāma, see chap. VI.
Pādshāh-nāma. By Mīrzā Amīnāī Qazvīnī.
Pādshāh-nāma. By Jalāl-ud-dīn Tabātabāī.
Pādshāh-nāma. By 'Abdul-Hamīd Lāhaurī. Printed in *Bibliotheca Indica*, 1867.
Pādshāh-nāma. By Muhammad Wāris.
Shāhjahān-nāma. By Muhammad Sādiq.
'Amal-i-Sālih. By Muhammad Sālih Kambū. Being printed in *Bibliotheca Indica*.
Zafar-nāma-i-'Ālamgīrī. By Mīr Khān.
English Factories in India, see chap. VII. (1624–9) 1909, (1630–3) 1910, (1634–6) 1911, (1637–41) 1912, (1642–5) 1913, (1646–50) 1914.
The Travels of Peter Mundy. Edited by Sir R. Temple. Hakluyt Society. Vol. II (1628–34), 1914.
The travels of Sebastian Manrique (1629–43). Edited by C. E. Luard and Father H. Hosten, S.J. Hakluyt Society. 1926 and 1927.

2. MODERN WORKS

BANĀRSĪ PRASĀD SAKSENA. History of Shāh Jahān of Dihlī. Allahabad, 1932, with a very full bibliography.
MORELAND, W. H. From Akbar to Aurangzeb, see chap. VI.

CHAPTERS VIII AND X

AURANGZĪB

1. PRIMARY SOURCES

PERSIAN

'Ālamgīr-nāma. By Mīrzā Muhammad Kāzim. Official history of the first ten years of Aurangzīb's reign, based upon State records. (*Bibliotheca Indica.*)

Maāsir-i-'Ālamgīrī. By Muhammad Sāqī Musta'idd Khān. A complete history of Aurangzīb's reign, based upon state-papers but very condensed, the first ten years being abridged from *'Ālamgīr-nāma.* Edited by Ahmad 'Alī and printed in *Bibliotheca Indica*, 1870–3.

'Amal-i-Sālih, see chap. VII.

Zafar-nāma (*also* Wāqi'āt *or* Hālāt)-i-'Ālamgīrī. By 'Āqil Khān Rāzī. Covers 1657–63. MSS. O.P.L.,[1] A.S.B.[2]

Tārīkh-i-Shāh Shujā'ī. By Mīr Muhammad Ma'sūm (an old servant of Shujā'). Invaluable for Bengal occurrences; ends abruptly on 18 April, 1660. MSS. I.O.L.,[3] O.P.L.

Aurang-nāma. A poem by "Haqīrī" (a Roz-bihānī soldier posted in Bengal), often agrees with Ma'sūm; ends with execution of Dārā. Hyderābād Āsafiya Library MS. (only copy extant).

Fathiyya-i-'ibriyya. By Shihāb-ud-dīn Ahmad (*bin* Muhammad) Tālish. A diary of Mīr Jumla's invasion of Kuch Bihār and Assam. Printed in Calcutta, A.H. 1265=A.D. 1848–9. MSS. O.P.L., A.S.B. Abridged in English by Blochmann, *J.A.S.B.* 1872; two sections translated by Jadunāth Sarkār in *J.B.* and *O.R.S.* "Continuation" (Bodleian MS. 589) gives the history of Bengal from the death of Mīr Jumla to the conquest of Chatgāon (1663–6); ends abruptly. Four long sections of the "Continuation" translated by Jadunāth Sarkār in *J.A.S.B.* 1906 and 1907.

Nuskha-i-Dilkushā. By Bhīmsen. Invaluable as an eye-witness of Deccan affairs 1670–1707. Br. Mus. Or. 23. See J. Sarkār's *Studies in Mughal India* for life of author and analysis of contents.

Futūhāt-i-'Ālamgīrī. By Ishwar Dās (a Nāgar Brāhman of Pattan and a Mughul civil officer in Jodhpur). First-rate authority for events in Rājputāna only. Covers 1657–98. Br. Mus. Add. 23,884 only MS. extant. See J. Sarkār's *Studies in Mughal India* for life of author and analysis of contents.

Waqāi'. By Ni'mat Khān 'Alī. Describes in highly rhetorical prose, interspersed with verse, four episodes of the siege of Golkonda in 1687. Text edited by Scholfield; also lithographed A.H. 1248 and printed (Lucknow) 1259.

Mirāt-i-Ahmadī. By 'Alī Muhammad Khān (the last Mughul *dīwān* of Gujarāt). Completed in 1754, 3 vols. (Gaekwad's Oriental Series.) Original source only in respect of Gujarāt affairs, the wealth of *farmāns*, etc. quoted *in extenso* and the economic data supplied. From 1730 onwards gives very useful details of political history not to be found elsewhere. First part, ending with 1605, translated as Bird's *History of Goozerat*; second part summarized in Campbell's Bombay Gazetteer; third part translated in Gaekwad Series.

Akhbārāt-i-darbār-i-mu'alla. Daily news-letters from the imperial camp. Tod MS. in R.A.S., and the residue in Jaipur State archives. Earlier years of Aurangzīb's reign very scanty, with a long gap *annis* 23–34; last thirteen years of the reign very copious. Similar *Akhbārāt* of Muhammad A'zam's viceroyalty of Gujarāt (*annis* 46–9 of Aurangzīb) and second regnal year of Bahādur Shāh I in R.A.S.; many sheets for 1707–22 in Jaipur State archives; twenty sheets for 1742 in Paris Bib. Nat.; many of Shāh 'Ālam II in Poona and elsewhere.

[1] Oriental Public Library (Patna).
[2] Asiatic Society of Bengal.
[3] India Office Library.

Ahkâm-i-'Âlamgîrî. Ascribed to Hamîd-ud-dîn Khân Bahâdur, Nimcha-i-'Âlamgîr Shâhî. Text edited by Jadunāth Sarkār (2nd ed.). English translation by same, *Anecdotes of Aurangzib* (2nd ed.). Very characteristic anecdotes and caustic remarks and orders of Aurangzīb.

Zawâbit-i-'Âlamgîrî. Br. Mus. Or. 1641. The best *dastūr-ul-'amal* (i.e. official manual, containing statistics, office procedure, administrative regulations and miscellaneous information regarding the Mughul empire), *c.* 1689.

Tārīkh-i-'Alī 'Ādil Shāh Sam. By Sayyid Nūr-ullah. Ends 1667. I.O.L. MS. 3052.

Muntakhab-ul-Lubāb. By Muhammad Hāshim Khāfī Khān. See chap. VI.[1]

Tavārīkh-i-Bangāla. By Salīm-ullah. English translation by F. Gladwin as *Narrative of Transactions in Bengal* (Calcutta, 1788), reprint 1918.

Letters

The letters of Aurangzīb have survived in (*a*) four compact and clearly defined collections made by his secretaries and one by a personal attendant, (*b*) certain compilations made after his death by selection from various earlier sources, and (*c*) stray letters and orders scattered through a large number of other books or as separate pieces.

Ādāb-i-'Ālamgīrī. A collection of fully drafted letters from Aurangzīb (1650–8) written by his first secretary Abu-'l-Fath Qabīl Khān (d. May 1662), together with (i) Abu-'l-Fath's own letters, (ii) letters written by Sādiq of Ambāla on behalf of Prince Muhammad Akbar, *c.* 1675–80, and (iii) a history of the war of succession. Put together in 1704. Excellent O.P.L. MS. In course of publication, ed. by S. Ashraf Nadavī at Azamgarh.

Ahkām-i-'Ālamgīrī. By 'Ināyat-ullah Khān (Aurangzīb's last secretary). Containing a *précis* of the points which the emperor dictated to his secretary for inclusion in the letters; covers *c.* 1700–5. Rāmpur State Library and Patna O.P.L. MSS. only copies known.

Kalimāt-i-Tayyibāt. Compiled by the same 'Ināyat-ullah in 1719. Very brief and obscure *précis*, overloaded with Arabic texts; covers *c.* 1699–1704. MSS. A.S.B., O.P.L.

Kalimāt-i-Aurangzīb. By the same 'Ināyat-ullah. Same style; covers *c.* 1703–6. Complete copy in Rāmpur State Library; a fragment in I.O.L. 3301, ff. 33a–60b.

There are certain later and shorter collections of Aurangzīb's letters, mostly selected from 'Ināyat-ullah and bearing various titles, e.g. *Raqāim-i-Karāim* (compiled by Sayyid Ashraf Khān Mīr Muhammad Husainī *bin* 'Abdul Karīm), *Dastūr-ul-'amal-i-Āgāhī* and *Rumūz-wa-Ishārahā-i-'Ālamgīrī* (both compiled by Rājā Āyā Mal, the *dīwān* of Jay Singh Savāī, in 1738 and 1742 respectively). Several letters from these selections constitute the lithographed *Ruq'āt-i-'Ālamgīrī*. The MSS. are very numerous and seldom exactly correspond in their contents or titles.

Other letters of Aurangzīb are to be found in Jaipur State archives:

Paris Bib. Nat. MS. Persan Suppl. 476 (Blochet, no. 704).

Faiyyāz-ul-qawānīn (11 letters).

Mirāt-i-Ahmadī, vol. II (edicts only).

Khatūt-i-Shivājī. R.A.S. MS. 71.

Zāhir-ul-Inshā, lithographed.

Bahār-i-Sakhun (completed 1663). I.O.L. MS. Ethé 2090, I.O.L. MS. 549, f. 50, and numerous other volumes.

Letters of other historical personages:

Haft Anjuman. Compiled by Udirāj (afterwards Tala'-yār), the secretary of Rustam Khān and of Mīrzā Rājā Jay Singh. Paris Bib. Nat. no. 37, a fragment; two complete MSS. in India.

Ruq'āt-i-Shāh 'Abbās Sānī.

[1] For a suggestion that Khāfī Khān borrowed from another writer, Abu-'l Fazl Ma'mūrī, see Sri Ram Sharma, *J.R.A.S.* 1936, p. 279. [Ed.]

Khatūt-i-Shivājī. R.A.S. MS. 71. Containing letters of Shivājī, Aurangzīb, prince Akbar, Shambhūjī, Shāhū, etc. (Two of Akbar's letters are printed in Zāhir-ul-inshā.)

Faiyyāz-ul-qawānīn. 266 folios, containing 25 letters from Shāh Jahān, 8 from Dārā, 6 from Shujā', 47 from Murād Bakhsh, 9 from *vazīr* Ja'far Khān, others from Shāh 'Abbās II, 'Ādil Shāh, Qutb Shāh, Jay Singh, etc.

Ruq'āt-i-Hamīd-ud-dīn Khān (a servant of Aurangzīb's mother-in-law Nauras Bānū and afterwards *faujdār* in Mālwā). Two incomplete MSS. in India.

Ruq'āt-i-Nawāzish Khān (*faujdār* of Māndū, later governor of Kashmīr).

Inshā-i-Mādhu Lāl. Lithographed letters of Mu'izz-ud-dīn and others.

Kārnāma-i-waqāi', being the letters of Ma'tabar Khān (*faujdār* of Kalyān) by his secretary Jethmal ("Hindu"). I.O.L. MS. 2007.

Muraqa'āt-i-Hasan. By Maulānā Abu'l-Hasan, a civil officer in Bengal and Orissa, 1655–67. Rāmpur State Library, Inshā, no. 182.

Majmū'a-i-munshāt-va-ghaira. Letters from and to Bīdār Bakht, from Mukhlis Khān Rūh-ullah Khān, Asad Khān, to Muhammad Murād Khān, etc. Rāmpur State Library, Inshā, no. 176.

I.O.L. MS. 150. *Surat English Factory letters*, 1695–6. English summary in *Proceedings of Indian Historical Records Commission*, Calcutta session.

Inshā-i-Raushan-Kalām. By Bhūpat Rāy, servant of Ra'dandāz Khān, *faujdār* of Baiswāra. Irvine MS. in I.O.L. Br. Mus. Add. 6600. Letters from 'Abdullah Qutb Shāh, etc.

Bahār-i-sakhun. I.O.L. Ethé 2090.

Br. Mus. Sloane MS. 3582, ff. 101–24. Letters and official papers relating to the Karnātak.

I.O.L. MS. 2678, ff. 72–128.

I.O.L. MS. 549.

I.O.L. MS. Land orders.

Pārasnīs MS. Letters from Shivājī, Murād Bakhsh, etc. Marāthī translation published by Rājwāde; an English translation (in MS.) in Pārasnīs Collection, Sātārā.

Secondary Persian Sources

Basātīn-us-salātīn, a history of Bijāpur. By Mīrzā Ibrāhīm Zubairī. 1824. Very valuable and accurate in spite of being a later compilation. Lithographed at Hyderābād.

Qutb-numā-i-'Ālam (Golkonda history). By Sayyid Muhammad Mīr Abū Turāb. 1806.

Maāsir-ul-Umarā, a biographical dictionary of the peerage of the Mughul empire, 1742–79. Edited by 'Abdur-Rahīm and Ashraf 'Alī and printed in *Bibliotheca Indica*, 1887–95. Translation by H. Beveridge in progress from 1912. Contains much valuable information from correct tradition and certain works now lost.

MARĀTHĪ

Shiva-Chhatrapatichen Charitra. By Krishnājī Anant Sabhāsad, edited by K. N. Sane (3rd ed. 1912). Translated by Mankar (1884 and 1886) and by S. N. Sen (2nd ed. 1925).

Jedheyānchi Shakāvali. Text in *Shiva-charitra-Pradīp*. Translation by Jadunāth Sarkār in *Shivājī Souvenir*, 1927.

Il-Qalmī Bakhar. By Dattājī (the chronicler of Shivājī) and transcribed (with modifications) by Khandojī R. Malkare. Edited by Rājwāde and Pārasnīs. Rough translation by Frissel, as "the Raigarh Life" in Forrest's *Selections... Bombay...Maratha Series*. Expanded Persian version, *Tarīkh-i-Shivājī* (I.O.L. 1957, also Rieu, i, 327), by Jadunāth Sarkār in *Modern Review*, 1907 and 1910. (For a critical bibliography of early Marāthā history, see Jadunāth Sarkār's *Shivājī*, 3rd ed.)

HINDĪ

Chhatra-prakāsh. By Lal Kavi. Text edited by W. Price, Calcutta, 1829; translated in Pogson's *History of the Boondelahs*, 1830.

ASSAMESE

Buranji from Khunlun and Khunlai. English translation in MS. from the Ahom language, in Assam Government Secretariat.
Kāmrūpar Buranji. Edited by S. K. Bhuyan, Assamese text.
Purāni Āsām Buranji. Gauhati. 1930.

EUROPEAN RECORDS AND WORKS

English Factories in India, see chap. VII. (1651–4) 1915, (1655–60) 1921, (1660–4) 1923, (1665–7) 1925, (1668–9) 1927, thereafter in MS. at the India Office, London.
Diary and Consultation Books of Fort St George, 1681–5. Edited by A. T. Pringle. 5 vols. Madras, 1893–5.
Early Annals of the English in Bengal. By C. R. Wilson. 3 vols. Calcutta, 1895–1917.
The Diary of W. Hedges. Edited by Colonel H. Yule. 2 vols. Hakluyt Society. 1887–9.
The Diaries of Streynsham Master, 1675–80. Edited by R. C. Temple. 2 vols. Indian Records Series. 1911.
Storia do Mogor. By N. Manucci. Translated and edited with valuable notes by W. Irvine. 4 vols. 1907–8.
The Dutch records are in *Hague Transcripts* (in the India Office Library) and the *Dagh Register*, which covers the period 1624–93 and is still being published at the Hague. The Portuguese records are in Biker's *Collecção de Tratados*, 14 vols. Lisbon, 1881–7, and the writings of Panduranga S. Pissurlencar (Nova Goa).

2. MODERN SOURCES

BERNIER, F. Travels. Edited by Constable. 2 vols. ed. 1914.
BHATTĀCHĀRYA, S. N. History of the Mughal N.E. Frontier Policy. A minutely detailed study. Calcutta, 1928.
BIDDULPH, C. E. Afghan Poetry of the seventeenth century. 1890.
BIDDULPH, Col. J. Pirates of Malabar. 1907.
CARERI, GEMELLI, Travels of. In Churchill's *Voyages*, vol. IV.
GAIT, E. A. History of Assam. 2nd ed.
KAEPPELIN, P. La Compagnie Indes Orientales et François Martin. Paris, 1908. The best guide to the French records and history of the French in India in the seventeenth century.
SARKĀR, JADUNĀTH. History of Aurangzīb. Based on original sources. 5 vols. Vols. I and II (1st ed. 1912, 2nd ed. 1925), vol. III (1st ed. 1916, 3rd ed. 1928), vol. IV (1st ed. 1919, 2nd ed. 1930), vol. V (1925).
—— Shivājī and His Times. 1st ed. 1919, 3rd ed. 1929.
—— Mughal Administration. 2nd ed. 1924.
—— Studies in Mughal India. 1919, being the 2nd ed. of *Historical Essays* published in 1913.
—— Anecdotes of Aurangzīb. 2nd ed. 1925.
—— India of Aurangzīb: Statistics, topography and roads. 1901.
WRIGHT, ARNOLD. Annesley of Surat. 1918.

CHAPTER IX

THE KINGDOMS OF THE DECCAN DURING THE REIGNS OF JAHĀNGĪR, SHĀH JAHĀN AND AURANGZĪB, AND THE RISE OF THE MARĀTHĀS

1. ORIGINAL SOURCES

Tārīkh-i-Firishta, see chaps. IV and V. For the reigns of Ibrāhīm 'Ādil Shāh II and the history of the Deccan generally, to the fall of Ahmadnagar.

Tūzuk-i-Jahāngīrī, see chap. VII. For an account of Jahāngīr's dealings with the Deccan.

Iqbāl-nāma-i-Jahāngīrī, see chap. VII.

Pādshāh-nāma. By 'Abdul-Hamīd Lāhaurī, see chap. VII. For the affairs of the Deccan during the reign of Shāh Jahān.

Muntakhab-ul-Lubāb, see chap. VI. For the affairs of the Deccan during the reigns of Jahāngīr, Shāh Jahān, and Aurangzīb and the history of the independent kingdoms of the Deccan.

Basātīn-us-Salātīn. By Mīrzā Ibrāhīm. Hyderabad lithographed edition. A history of the 'Ādil Shāhī kings of Bijāpur.

Tārīkh-i-Muhammad Qutb Shāhī. MS. in author's possession. A history of the Sultāns of Golconda to A.D. 1617.

Hadiqat-us-Salātīn. A history of the reign of 'Abdullah Qutb Shāh of Golconda. MS. in India Office Library.

Hadīqat-ul-'Ālam. By Mīr Abu-'l-Qāsim, Mīr 'Ālam. Hyderābād lithographed edition of A.H. 1309. A history of the Sultāns of Golconda.

History of the Mahrattas. By James Grant Duff. Bombay reprint of 1878. The leading authority on the history of the Marāthās.

The Portuguese in India. By F. C. Danvers. 1894. For the relations between the Portuguese and the native powers in the Deccan.

Bernier's Travels, see chaps. VIII and X. Deals with Aurangzīb's relations with the independent kingdoms of the Deccan and the Marāthās.

Tavernier's Travels. Edited, by V. Ball. 1889. Ditto.

Storia do Mogor, see chaps. VIII and X. Treats in considerable detail of Aurangzīb's relations and dealings with the independent kingdoms of the Deccan and the Marāthās. A most valuable work.

Relations of Golconda in the early seventeenth century. Edited by W. H. Moreland. Hakluyt Society. 1930. Contains valuable descriptions of the country in the early seventeenth century.

2. MODERN WORKS

HAIG, Major T. W. Historic Landmarks of the Deccan. Allahabad, 1907. Treats of episodes in the history of the Deccan. Drawn exclusively from original sources.

SAYYID NŪH-ULLAH QĀDIRĪ, Tārīkh-i-'Alī 'Ādil Shāhī. An exceedingly turgid and bombastic history of the reign of 'Alī 'Ādil Shāh II. Of slight value. MS. in author's possession.

CHAPTER XI

BAHĀDUR SHĀH, JAHĀNDĀR SHĀH, FARRUKH-SIYAR, RAFĪ'-UD-DARAJĀT AND RAFĪ'-UD-DAULA

1. ORIGINAL SOURCES

Persian

Bahādur Shāh-nāma. By Dānishmand Khān (Ni'mat Khān 'Alī). Covering 1707–9. I.O.L.[1] MS. Ethé 385.
Muntakhab-ul-Lubāb, see chap. vi.
Nuskha-i-Dilkushā, see chap. viii.
Maāsir-ul Umarā, see chap. viii.
Tazkira *or* Tārīkh. By Irādat Khān (Mīrzā Mubārak-ullah). Covering 1707–13. I.O.L. MS. Ethé 389. English translation by Jonathan Scott as *Memoirs of Eradut Khan* in vol. ii of his translation of Firishta, 1794.
A'zam-ul-harb. By Kām Rāj. 1707 only. Br. Mus. Or. 1899.
'Ibrat-nāma. By Kām Rāj. 1707–19. I.O.L. MS. Ethé 391.
'Ibrat-nāma. By Muhammad Harīsī, Mīrzā. Ends 1721. I.O.L. MS. 50.
'Ibrat-nāma. By Muhammad Qāsim Lāhaurī. *c.* 1721. I.O.L. MS. 194, Lahore Public Library.
Tārīkh-i-Farrukh-siyar. By Muhammad Ihsān Ijād. Br. Mus. Or. 25.
Mirāt-i-Wāridāt. By Muhammad Shafī' Wārid. Ends 1734. Br. Mus. 6579, O.P.L.[2] MS.
Tazkirat-us-salātīn-i-Chaghtaia. By Muhammad Hādī Kāmwār Khān. Ends 1724. MS. O.P.L., I.O.L., Br. Mus.
Tārīkh-i-Hind. By Rustam 'Alī. Ends 1736. Br. Mus. Or. 1628.
Tazkirat-ul-mulūk. By Yahya Khān. 1712–36. Very brief for the later Mughul emperors. I.O.L. MS. 1149.
Dastūr-ul-inshā (*c.* 1757). By Yār Muhammad. Printed Calcutta, A.H. 1253.
Jang-nāma of Farrukh-siyar and Jahāndār Shāh. By Ni'mat Khān 'Alī. Translated by W. Irvine, *J.A.S.B.* 1900.
Nādir-uz-Zamānī. By Khush-hāl Chand. Vol. i (1679–1719) (mostly a compilation). Lahore Public Library.
Ahwāl-ul-Khawāqīn. By Muhammad Qāsim. Br. Mus. Add. 26,244. Vol. i (1707–19), vol. ii (1719–38).
Muntakhab-ut-Tavārīkh. By Jagjīvan Dās. Written in 1708; gives useful statistics of all the *sūbas* in 1707. Br. Mus. Add. 26,253.
Chahār Gulshan. By Chatarman, Rāj. Gives useful statistics. Partly translated in Jadunāth Sarkār's *India of Aurangzīb* (1901). I.O.L. and O.P.L. MSS.
Jaipur State Records. A very large mass of Persian *farmāns*, *hasb-ul-hukms*, *parwānas*, news-letters, *vakīls'* reports and business papers of the period 1707–*c.*1723. The imperial letters have been preserved with their seals and silk bags (*Kharītas*) intact (except for a slit), and the ordinary letters with their (open) paper envelopes and belts. A unique collection.

Urdū

Shamsher-i-Khālsa. By Gyān Singh and Rajindar Singh. Lithographed, 1891.

Dutch

Diary of E. Conraad Graaf for embassy of 1712–13. State Record Office at the Hague. Translated by Mrs Kuenen-Wicksteed and J. Ph. Vogel, *Journal, Panjab Historical Society*, x, 1.

2. MODERN WORKS

Cunningham, J. D. History of the Sikhs. 1840 and 1918.
Downing, Clement. History of the Indian Wars. Edited by W. Foster. 1924.

[1] India Office Library. [2] Oriental Public Library (Patna).

DUFF, J. G. History of the Mahrattas, see chap. IX.
IRVINE, W. Later Mughals. Edited and continued by Jadunāth Sarkār. Vol. I (1707–19), vol. II (1719–39). Calcutta, 1921–2. All the Persian sources have been exhausted in it, and chap. XI is mostly an abridgement of it, with a few additions.
MACAULIFFE, M. A. The Sikh Religion. 6 vols. 1909.
WILSON, C. R. Early Annals of the English in Bengal, see chap. VIII.
A French account of the Jāts, written about 1774, most probably by Father F. Xavier Wendel, in Orme MSS., I.O.L. (vol. CCXVI, no 2, copy in vol. XV, no. 11).

CHAPTER XII

MUHAMMAD SHĀH

The authorities quoted for chap. XI cover this chapter also, except those which are shown to cease at earlier dates. For authorities on the Marāthās see chap. XIV. The following additions may be made.

1. ORIGINAL SOURCES

Tārīkh-i-Shahādat-i-Farrukh-siyar wa Julūs-i-Muhammad Shāh. By Muhammad Bakhsh, Āshob. Extract in Elliot and Dowson, VIII, 232.
Tārīkh-i-Faiz Bakhsh. By Shiva Prasād. For contents see Elliot and Dowson, VIII, 175.
Shāhnāma or Munavvar-ul-Kalām. By Shiva Dās of Lucknow.
Bayān-i-Waqāi'. By Abdul Karīm, Kashmīrī. Extracts translated in Elliot and Dowson, VIII, 124.
Tarīkh-i-Jahānkushā-i-Nādirī. By Mīrzā Mahdī. Lithographed at Bombay.
Nādir Shāh aur Muhammad Shāh. Hindī poem by Tilok Dās. Edited and translated by W. Irvine. *Journal, Asiatic Society Bengal*, 1897, p. 24.
Historical relation of the Rohilla Afgans. By W. Hamilton. 1787. Practically a translation of *Tārīkh-i-Faiz Bakhsh, supra.*
Revolutions of Persia. By J. Hanway. 1762.
History of Nādir Shāh. By J. Fraser. 1741.
Goolistan-i-Rehmut or Life of Hāfiz Rahmat Khān. Translated by C. Elliott. 1831.

2. MODERN WORKS

IRVINE, W. The Bangash Nawabs of Farrukhābād. *Journal, Asiatic Society Bengal*, 1878–9.
MUHAMMAD ABDUS-SALĀM KHĀN. Sarguzasht-i-Nawāb Najīb-ud-daula. Lithographed, Aligarh and Rampur, 1924.
SRIVĀSTAVA, A. L. The first two Nawabs of Oudh. Lucknow, 1933. Contains a full critical bibliography.

CHAPTER XIII

THE HYDERĀBĀD STATE, 1724–1762

No detailed history of Āsaf Jāh I on the lines of the court annals of the Delhi emperors was ever written. The sources of his career up to 1724 are given in W. Irvine's *Later Mughals* (see chap. XI), as a part of the general history of the Mughul empire. For his independent rule in the Deccan (1724–48) the contemporary recorders are Khāfī Khān, Ghulām 'Alī Āzād, and Shāh Nawāz Khān—all in his service. They are extremely brief, giving merely a list of important events with a short character-sketch. The later histories in Persian worth mentioning are the *Maāsir-i-Āsafī* of Lachmī Nārāyan (a hereditary revenue official), compiled in 1792–3, and the *Hadīqat-ul-'Ālam* of the famous minister Mīr 'Ālam, completed in 1802. The former gives a short summary of events from well-known sources, with a very large number of anecdotes illustrating Āsaf Jāh's virtues. The *Hadīqat* remains the best and longest Persian authority for the period 1724–62. Its author professedly borrows from the three contemporary writers named above, but he gives much fresh information in detail, which, however, requires correction. The English and French factory records attain to primary value for Carnatic affairs—and only incidentally for Hyderābād affairs—from 1740 onwards. The printed documents in these two languages have been co-ordinated and corrected, and the mass of manuscript correspondence analysed with admirable skill and success in Dodwell's *Dupleix and Clive*, without the help of which guide these documents cannot be properly utilized, nor the prevalent heresies corrected. But by far the most valuable original material for the history of the earlier Nizāms has been recently published in the form of Marāthī news-letters from their court, despatches from Marāthā officers, and reports from the Peshwās' agents. These give, month after month and even oftener, the minutest information about the movements of the Nizāms, their policy, the discussions in their councils, their campaigns, and the doings of their opponents, exactly as recorded at the time. These enable us to correct many errors and fill up many gaps in the current histories of that period, such as Grant Duff's. When these original sources are used, later histories like those of Briggs and Gribble may be safely discarded.

1. ORIGINAL SOURCES

Persian

Muntakhab-ul-Lubāb, see chap. vi.

Khazāna-i-'Āmira. By Ghulām 'Alī Āzād. Lithographed, Cawnpore; repeated in his *Sarv-i-Āzād* (ditto).

Maāsir-ul-Umarā.

Hadīqat-ul-'Ālam. By Mīr Abu'l-Qāsim, Mīr 'Ālam. Lithographed, Hyderābād, A.H. 1310. Vol. II.

Maāsir-i-Āsafī. By Lachmī Nārāyan Khattrī. I.O.L. MS., Ethé 468. I have used the Hyderābād Record Office MS., entitled *Maāsir-i-Nizāmī*.

Jagjīvan Dās. Revenue returns of Hindustan and Deccan in A.H. 1200. I.O.L. MS., Ethé 434. Other (earlier) returns translated in Jadunāth Sarkār's *India of Aurangzīb: Statistics, topography and roads*. 1901.

Khatūt-i-Shivājī. R.A.S. MS. Persian 71. Gives three letters from Shāhū to Āsaf Jāh I.

Marāthī

Selections from the Peshwās' Daftar. Edited by G. S. Sardesai (Bombay):

Vol. I. Battle of Udgīr. 1930.

Vol. X. Early strife between Bājī Rāo and the Nizām. 1931.

Vol. XXV. Bālājī Bājī Rāo and the Nizām, 1740–61. 1932. Greatly supplements vol. I.

Vol. XXVIII. Peshwā Bālājī Rāo: Karnātak Affairs, 1740–61. 1933.

Vol. XX. Bhonsles of Nāgpur. 1931.

Vol. XXXV. Peshwā and Nizām, supplementary. 1934.

Aitihāsik Patren Yādi waghaira Lekh. 2nd ed. Edited by G. S. Sardesai and others. 1930.

Aitihāsik Patravyavahār. Edited by G. S. Sardesai and others. 1933.

Marāthyānchya Itihāsāchī Sādhanen. By V. K. Rājwāde. Vols. I (1898), III (1901), and VI (1905).

Selections from the Sātārā Rājās' and the Peshwās' Diaries. By G. C. Wad and D. B. Pārasnis. Vols. I (Shāhū), II and III (Bālājī Rāo), IV–VI (Mādhav Rāo). Vol. II gives the Peshwās' itineraries with dates.

Marāthī Riyāsat. By G. S. Sardesai, Madhya Vibhāg. Vols. I, II and IV (Bombay).

2. MODERN WORKS

DODWELL, H. H. Dupleix and Clive. London, 1920.

—— Calendar of the Madras Records, 1740–44. Madras, 1917.

DUFF, J. G. History of the Mahrattas, see chap. IX.
IRVINE, W. Later Mughals, see chap. XI.
ORME, R. History of...Indostan. 4th ed. vol. I. London, 1803.
SARKĀR, Sir JADUNĀTH. Fall of the Mughal Empire. Vol. I. Calcutta, 1932.
WHEELER, J. T. Madras in the Olden Time. Vol. III reproduces the diary o. T. Eyre's embassy to Āsaf Jāh at Trichinopoly. Madras, 1862.
Lettres et Conventions des gouverneurs de Pondichéry avec différents princes hindous, 1666–1793. Pondichéry, 1914.
Mémoire pour Bussy, expositif de ses créances.... Paris, 1764.
Letters of François Raymond. Translated into English by Jadunāth Sarkār in *Islamic Culture* (Hyderābād, 1932), describing the military and financial conditions under Nizām 'Alī.

CHAPTER XIV

THE RISE OF THE MARĀTHĀ EMPIRE, 1707–1761

I. ORIGINAL SOURCES

(a) MARĀTHĪ

The vast collection of MSS., State Papers, and other documents in the Alienation Office, Poona (the Poona Daftar), and the collections made by V. K. Rājwāde, D. B. Pārasnīs, and other scholars, and housed in the Bhārata Itihāsa Mandala at Poona and the Historical Museum at Sātārā, together with the Daftars of the various Marāthā States, constitute the chief original sources for the period in Marāthī. The State Papers in the Poona Alienation Office have now been thoroughly sifted by Mr G. S. Sardesai, and forty-six volumes of Selections have been published under the auspices of the Government of Bombay. At the time of writing (1935) the papers in the Poona Residency Records are also being examined by Sir J. Sarkār and Mr Sardesai, with a view to the publication of similar volumes of Selections. The chief volumes of Selections at present printed are as follows:

Marāthyānchyā Itihāsāchī Sādhane. By V. K. Rājwāde, 22 vols. Poona, 1898–1902.
Itihāsa Sangraha. By D. B. Pārasnīs. 7 vols. Poona, V.D.
Selections from the Peshwā's Daftar. By G. C. Wād. 9 vols. Poona, V.D. (Introduction by M. G. Rānade.)
Selections from Shāhu Rājā's Daftar. By V. K. Pārasnīs. Poona, 1904.
Selections from the Chitnīsi and other Daftars. By V. K. Pārasnīs. Published in *Itihāsa Sangraha*. 7 vols. Bombay, V.D.
Selections from the Poona Daftar (Letters and Despatches relating to the Battles of Udgīr and Pānīpat). By G. S. Sardesai. Government Central Press, Bombay, 1930.
Treaties, Agreements and Sanads. By D. B. Pārasnīs and P. V. Māvjī. Poona, 1908–14.
Selections from the Peshwā Daftar. Edited by G. S. Sardesai, B.A. 45 vols. Government Central Press, Bombay, 1933. With Indexes, and a foreword by Sir Jadunāth Sarkār, C.I.E. This includes a Handbook to the records in the Alienation Office, Poona.

(b) ENGLISH

The Papers in the Bombay Secretariat are described in Kindersley's *Handbook*. *Selections from the State Papers in the Bombay Secretariat* (Home Series, 1887; Marāthā Series, 1885) have been published by Sir G. W. Forrest. For the India Office Records, Foster's *Guide*, and for the papers in the Imperial Record Department, the *Handbook to the Records of the Government of India* (1748–1859), Calcutta, 1925, should be consulted.

(c) PERSIAN

The Persian correspondence in the Imperial Record Department will be found in the *Calendar of Persian Correspondence* issued by the Government of India, Calcutta, V.D. Many Persian documents, *farmāns*, etc. in the various daftars and in private possession require investigation. Detailed references to the Persian sources for the period are given in Sir Jadunāth Sarkār's *Fall of the Mughal Empire*, and his edition of Irvine's *Later Mughals*, see chap. XI; the leading Muhammadan historians of the period are translated in Elliot and Dowson's *History of India as told by its own Historians* (q.v.).

II. SECONDARY SOURCES

(a) English

Agworth, H. A. Ballads of the Marāthās. London, 1894.
Autobiographical Memoir of the Early Life of Nānā Farnavīs. Trans. Briggs. *Transactions, Royal Asiatic Society*, vol. II. 1829.
Bombay Presidency Gazetteer. Edited by J. M. Campbell. Bombay, 1877–94.
Casi Raja Pundit, see Kāsīrāj Pandit.
Downing, Clement. History of the Indian Wars, see chap. XI.
Elphinstone, Mountstuart. History of India. Edited by E. B. Cowell. 6th ed. 1874.
Forbes, A. K. Rās Mālā: Hindoo Annals of the Province of Goozerat. Edited by H. G. Rawlinson. 1924.
Ghulām Husain Khān. Siyar-ul-Mutaākhkhirīn. English translation. Reprint, 4 volumes, Calcutta, 1902.
Grant Duff, J. C. History of the Mahrattas, see chap. IX.
Gwalior State Gazetteer. Gwalior, 1908.
Ives, E. A Voyage from England to India in the Year 1754. 1773.
Jervis, T. B. Geographical and Statistical Memoir of the *Konkan*. Calcutta, 1840.
Kāsīrāj Pandit (Casi Raja Pundit). An Account of the Last Battle of Pānīpat. (Trans. J. Browne, *Asiatic Researches*, vol. III.) Reprint, edited by H. G. Rawlinson, 1926. The original MS. has now been discovered by Sir Jadunāth Sarkār, and a revised translation appeared in the *Indian Historical Quarterly*, 1934.
Kincaid, C. A. and D. B. Pārasnīs. A History of the Marāthā People. 3 vols. 1918–25. Edition in one volume, 1931.
Malcolm, Sir J. Memoir of Central India. 2 vols. London, 1823.
Malleson, G. B. History of the French in India. London, 1868.
—— Native States of India. 1875.
Orme, R. Historical Fragments of the Moghul Empire. London, 1782.
Pārasnīs, D. B. Mahableshwar. Bombay, 1916.
—— Poona in Bygone Days. Bombay, 1921.
Rānade, M. G. Rise of the Marāthā Power. Poona, 1900.
—— Miscellaneous Writings. Poona, 1900.
—— Introduction to the Peshwa's Diaries. Poona, 1900.
Sardesai, G. B. Main Currents of Marāthā History. Calcutta, 1926.
Sarkar, Sir J. Fall of the Mughal Empire, see chap. XIII.
Sen, S. The Administrative System of the Marāthās. Calcutta, 1923.
Subramanian, K. R. Marāthā Rājās of Tanjor. Madras, 1928.
Waring, E. S. History of the Mahrattas. London, 1810.

(b) Marāthī

In Marāthī, the chief secondary sources are the *bakhars* or prose-chronicles. They are of varying value, but the early ones especially contain a great deal of information gleaned at first hand. Many of them were published by R. N. Sane in the historical journal *Kavyetihāsa Sangraha* (1878–89), and have since been separately printed. Some of the most important for the period are:

1. The Pānīpat Bakhar. By Raghunāth Yādāv. 1763.
2. The Peshwā's Bakhar. By Sohoni. 1822.
3. The Bhāo Sāhib's Bakhar. N.D.
4. Dābhāde Gāikwādāchī Hakīkat (History of the Dābhādes and Gāikwārs). 1818.
5. Holkarānchi Kaifiyat (Narrative of the Holkar family).
6. The Nāgpur Bhonsles' Bakhar. 1818.
7. The Bakhar of Shāhū Mahārājā. By Govindrāo Chitnīs.

8. Thorle Shāhuche Charitra (Life of Shāhū I). By Malhārrāo Chitnīs. 1810.
9. Dhākte Rāmrājāche Charitra. By Malhārrāo Chitnīs. 1810.
Malhārrāo Holkar Yānche Charitra. By M. M. Atre. Poona, 1893.
Marāthyānche Parākrama. By D. B. Pārasnis. Bombay, 1895.
Brahmendraswāmī Yānche Charitra. By D. B. Pārasnīs. Bombay, 1903.
Marāthyānche Ārmār (Marāthā Navy). By D. B. Pārasnīs. Bombay, 1904.
The Standard History of the Marāthās in Marāthī is *Marāthī Riyāsat*, by G. S. Sardesai, 7 vols. Bombay, V.D., 1915–29.

CHAPTER XV

AHMAD SHĀH, 'ĀLAMGĪR II AND SHĀH 'ĀLAM

1. ORIGINAL SOURCES

Most of the authorities quoted for chaps. XI, XII, XIII and XIV also cover this period. The following additions should be made:

Miskīn or memoirs of Tahmāsp Khān, *Miskīn*, see Elliot and Dowson, VIII, 100.
Mujmil-ut-tawārīkh ba'd Nādiriya. By Ibn Muhammad Amīn Abu-'l-Hasan Gulistānī. Edited by O. Mann. Leyden, 1896.
Tārīkh-i-Muzaffarī. By Muhammad 'Alī Khān. Extract translated in Elliot and Dowson, VIII, 316.
Riyāz-us-Salātīn. By Ghulām Husain Salīm. Persian text printed in *Bibliotheca Indica*. English translation by M. Abdus-Salām. Calcutta, 1902.
Siyar-ul-Mutaākhkhirīn. By S. Ghulām Husain Tabātabāī. English translation, Calcutta reprint, 1902.
Tārīkh-i-Ahmad Shāh. Anonymous. See Elliot and Dowson, VIII, 104.
Tuhfa-i-tāza. By Khair-ud-dīn Khān. Translated by F. Curwen under title "Bulwunt-nama." Allahabad, 1875.
Sujān Charitra. By Sūdan. Printed at Benares.

2. MODERN WORKS

KEENE, H. G. The Fall of the Moghul Empire. 1887.
SARKĀR, Sir JADUNĀTH. Fall of the Mughal Empire. 2 vols. Calcutta, 1932 and 1934.

CHAPTER XVI

THE REVENUE SYSTEM OF THE MUGHUL EMPIRE

1. ORIGINAL SOURCES

(*a*) INDIAN

Āīn-i-Akbarī, see chaps. IV and V.
Akbar-nāma, see chap. I.
Tārīkh-i-Sher Shāhī, see chap. III.
Tārīkh-i-Dāūdī, see chap. III.
Aurangzīb's Revenue orders. Text, with translation, by J. Sarkār. *Journal, Asiatic Society Bengal*. 1906, p. 223.
Tārīkh-i-Humāyūn. By Bāyazīd, see chap. II.
Muntakhab-ut-Tawārīkh, see chaps. IV and V.
Tūzuk-i-Jahāngīrī, see chap. VI.
Muntakhab-ul-Lubāb, see chap. VI.
Pādshāh-nāma. By 'Abdul-Hamīd Lāhaurī, see chap. VII.
Iqbāl-nāma-i-Jahāngīrī, see chap. VI.
Makhzan-i-Afghāna, see chap. III.
Tabaqāt-i-Akbarī, see chap. I.

'Amal-i-Sālih, see chap. vii.
Ma'āsir-ul-Umarā, see chaps. viii and x.

Specimen of Akbar's grants of land:
(1) S. H. Hodivala, Studies in Parsi History, Bombay, 1920; (2) J. J. Modi, Journal of the Bombay Branch of the Royal Asiatic Society, 1902, p. 69 and 1920, p. 419.

(b) Foreign

Bernier, François. Travels in the Mogul Empire. Translation, ed. A. Constable. London, 1891.
Geleynssen de Jongh, W. Remonstrantie. Ed. W. Caland for the Linschoten Vereeniging. The Hague, 1929.
Manrique, Fray Sebastien. Itinerario de las Missiones orientales. Translation by C. E. Luard and H. Hosten. Hakluyt Society. 1927.
Pelsaert, Francisco. Remonstrantie, see chap. vi.
Purchas, Samuel. Purchas his Pilgrimes. London, 1625.
van Twist, Jan. Generale Beschrijvinge van Indien. Amsterdam, 1648.

(c) Early Records of the British Period

Early Annals of the English in Bengal, see chaps. viii and x.
Selections from the Duncan Records. Edited by A. Shakespear. Benares, 1873.
Fifth Report from the Select Committee of the House of Commons on the Affairs of the East India Company. London, 1812. Also, new edition, edited by W. K. Firminger. Calcutta, 1917.
North-Western Provinces. Selections from the Revenue Records. Vol. i, Calcutta, 1866; vol. ii, Allahabad, 1872.
Punjab Government Records. Vol. i, Lahore, 1911.

2. MODERN WORKS

Ascoli, F. D. Early Revenue History of Bengal. Oxford, 1917.
Briggs, John. The Present Land-Tax in India. 1830.
Elliot and Dowson. The History of India, as told by its own Historians, see "General".
Moreland, W. H. The Agrarian System of Moslem India. Cambridge, 1929.
Qanungo, K. Sher Shah, see chap. iii.
Ramsbotham, R. B. Studies in the Land Revenue History of Bengal. Oxford, 1926.
Sarkār, J. Studies in Mughal India, see chaps. viii and x.

CHAPTER XVII

BURMA (1531–1782)

For Burmese sources, see note at beginning of bibliography, vol. iii, p. 656. Inscriptions are rarer than in the period covered by that chapter, epigraphy apparently yielding, with the spread of literacy, to palm-leaf writing. *Hmannan Yazawin* stops with the fall of Ava in 1752, at which point the narrative is taken up by the portentously verbose *Konbaungset Yazawin* of nearly 2000 pages, published in 1905 by a Burmese officer in the provincial civil service; it is a compilation from official records and has not been translated; for its quality, see Harvey, *History of Burma*, p. 355. *Alaungpaya Ayedawpon* is a chronicle-biography of Alaungpaya.

Siamese material is hard to get. A glance at Jones, *Siamese History* and S. Smith, *History of Siam*, which are translations of Siamese royal chronicles, will show the quality of the record; see also p. 288, n. 1. Other sources are Anderson, Frankfurter, Pallegoix, Ravenswaay. The best general history is Wood, and he has in addition furnished me with a MS. précis of references in the Siamese chronicles to Burma.

For Arakanese sources, see Harvey, *History of Burma*, pp. xviii–xix.

For Shan, Talaing, Chinese, see vol. III, p. 656, and Warry.

The European sources speak for themselves. Hall, *Early English Intercourse with Burma*, is the best authority on its subject.

* indicates a vernacular work

Alaungpaya Ayedawpon. Hanthawaddy Press, Rangoon, 1900.

ANDERSON. English Intercourse with Siam in the Seventeenth Century. Kegan Paul, 1890.

—— Expedition to Western Yünnan via Bhamo. Supt. Govt. Printing, Calcutta, 1871.

BERNIER, F. Travels in the Mogul Empire. Edited by Constable and Vincent Smith. 1914.

BIGANDET, P. Outline of the History of the Catholic Burmese Mission from the year 1720 to 1887. Hanthawaddy Press, Rangoon, 1887.

BOWREY, T. Geographical Account of Countries round the Bay of Bengal, 1669–79. Edited by Sir Richard Temple. Hakluyt Society. 1905.

BURNEY, H. Wars between Burma and China. *Journal, Asiatic Society Bengal.* 1837.

Chittagong Gazetteer. Bengal Secretariat Book Depot, Calcutta, 1908.

CORDIER, P. La France en Chine au Dix-huitième Siècle. Paris, 1883.

—— Historique Abrégé des Relations de la Grande-Bretagne avec la Birmanie. Paris, 1894.

—— Histoire générale de la Chine. Paris, 1920.

—— Les Français en Birmanie au Dix-huitième Siècle. *T'oung Pao.* 1890 and 1891.

COUTO, B. DE. Da Asia. His Majesty's Press, Lisbon, 1778–88.

CRAWFURD, J. Journal of an Embassy from the Governor-General of India to the Court of Ava. 1834.

Dagh Register. Dagh-Register gehouden int Casteel Batavia. Series edited by J. A. van der Chijs. Nijhoff, 's Hage, 1889 onwards.

DALRYMPLE, A. Oriental Repertory. 1795–7.

DE JONGE, J. K. J. De Opkomst van het Nederlandsche Gezag in Oost-Indie. Series. Nijhoff, 's Gravenhage, 1862–88.

*Dinnyawadi Yazawinthit. Pyegyimantaingpitaka Press, Rangoon, 1910.

DUROISELLE, C. Catalogue of Coins in the Phayre Museum [Rangoon]. Supt. Govt. Printing, Rangoon, 1924.

—— Notes on the ancient Geography of Burma. Supt. Govt. Printing, Rangoon, 1906.

ENRIQUEZ, C. M. Capitals of the Alaungpaya Dynasty. *Journal, Burma Research Society.* Rangoon, 1915.

FARIA Y SOUSA. The Portuguese Asia. Translated by Stevens. 1695.

FLORIS. Peter Floris, His Voyage to the East Indies in the *Globe* 1611–15. Edited by W. H. Moreland. Hakluyt Society. 1934.

FORCHAMMER, E. The Jardine Prize; an essay on the Sources and Development of Law. Supt. Govt. Printing, Rangoon, 1885.

FRANKFURTER, O. Events in Ayuddhya 686–966. *Journal, Siam Society.* Bangkok, 1909.

FURNIVALL, J. S. A Forgotten Chronicle. *Journal, Burma Research Society.* Rangoon, 1912.

—— From China to Peru. *Journal, Burma Research Society.* 1917.

—— Samuel White, Port Officer of Mergui. *Journal, Burma Research Society.* 1917.

Gazetteer of Upper Burma and the Shan States. Supt. Govt. Printing, Rangoon, 1900.

GERSON DA CUNHA. Memoir on the History of the Tooth Relic of Ceylon. *Journal, Bombay branch Royal Asiatic Society.* 1875.

GOUGER, H. Personal Narrative of Two Years Imprisonment in Burmah. 1860.

GRANT BROWN, R. The Lady of the Weir. *Journal, Royal Asiatic Society.* 1916, p. 491.

Hakluytus Posthumus. Hakluytus Posthumus, or Purchas His Pilgrimes. Glasgow, 1907.
Hall, D. G. E. Early English Intercourse with Burma. Longmans, London, 1928.
—— The Tragedy of Negrais. *Journal, Burma Research Society.* 1931, part III.
Halliday, R. Immigration of the Mons into Siam. *Journal, Siam Society.* Bangkok, 1913.
—— Slapat Rajawan Datow Smin Ron. *Journal, Burma Research Society.* Rangoon, 1923.
—— The Talaings. Supt. Govt. Printing, Rangoon, 1917.
Hamilton, A. A New Account of the East Indies. Edinburgh, 1727.
Harvey, G. E. Fate of Shah Shuja. *Journal, Burma Research Society.* Rangoon, 1922.
—— Gwe. *Ibid.* 1925.
—— History of Burma. 1925.
Herbert, Sir Thomas. Some Years Travels into Africa and Asia. 1638.
*Hmannan Yazawin. Upper Burma Press, Mandalay, 1908.
Hodson, T. C. The Meitheis. Nutt, London, 1908.
Hosten, H. The Twelve Bhuiyas or Landlords of Bengal. *Journal, Asiatic Society Bengal.* 1913, p. 437.
Huber, E. Fin de Dynastie de Pagan. *Bulletin de l'École Française d'Extrême Orient.* Hanoi and Paris, 1909.
India Office:
Hague Transcripts.
Mackenzie Collection.
Jadunāth Sarkār. The Conquest of Chatgaon. *Journal, Asiatic Society Bengal.* 1907, p. 405.
—— The Feringhi Pirates of Chatgaon. *Journal, Asiatic Society Bengal.* 1907, p. 419.
—— History of Aurangzib. Sarkar, Calcutta, 1912–19.
Jones, J. T. Siamese History; Distinction of Sacred and Common Eras; with Historical notices from A.D. 1351 from a Correspondent [J. Taylor Jones]. Chinese Repository, Canton, 1836–8.
*Konbaungset Yazawin. Mandalay Taing Press, Mandalay, 1905.
Kyaw Dun. Lacquerware called Yun. *Journal, Burma Research Society.* Rangoon, 1920.
Launay, A. Mémorial de la Société des Missions Étrangères. Paris, 1912–16.
Laurie, W. F. B. Pegu, being a Narrative of Events during the Second Burmese War. 1854.
Linschoten, J. H. Voyage to the East Indies. Hakluyt Society. 1885.
McLeod, W. C. Journal of a Mission from Moulmein to the Frontiers of China, 1836–37. 1869.
Manrique. Itinerario de las Missiones del India Oriental. Rome, 1649 and Hakluyt Society translation by Luard and Hosten, London, 1926–7.
Manucci. Storia do Mogor. Trans. Irvine, India Text Series. 1907.
Mason, F. Burmah, its People and Natural Productions. 1860.
Morris, A. P. Lacquerware Industry of Burma. *Journal, Burma Research Society.* Rangoon, 1919.
*Nga Me. MS. History of Arakan.
Pallegoix, D. J. B. Description du Royaume Thai ou Siam. Mission de Siam, Paris, 1854.
Parker, E. H. Burma with Special Reference to her relations to China. Rangoon Gazette Press, Rangoon, 1893.
—— Letters from a Chinese Empress and a Chinese Eunuch to the Pope in the Year 1650. *Contemporary Review.* 1912.
—— *Précis* of Chinese records, printed in the political files of the Rangoon Secretariat.
Parlett, L. M. Sagaing Settlement Report. Supt. Govt. Printing, Rangoon, 1903.
*Pawtugi Yazawin. Sun Press, Rangoon, 1918.
Pemberton, R. B. Report on the Eastern Frontier of British India. Printed by order of the Supreme Government. Calcutta, 1835.
Phayre, A. P. Coins of Arakan, of Pegu and of Burma. *International Numismata Orientalia.* 1882.

PINTO, F. M. Voyages and Adventures of Ferdinand Mendez Pinto. 1612, 1829.
PURCHAS. Purchas His Pilgrimage or Relations of the World. 1626.
RAVENSWAAY, L. F. VAN. Translation of Van Vliet's description of Siam. *Journal, Siam Society.* Bangkok, 1910.
Report of the Superintendent Archaeological Survey Burma. Published annually by the Supt. Govt. Printing, Rangoon.
SANGERMANO, FR. Description of the Burmese Empire. Supt. Govt. Printing, Rangoon, 1885.
SAULIÈRE, Rev. A. Jesuits on Pegu. *Bengal Past and Present.* Calcutta, 1919.
*Sayadaw Athwa. Burmese translation of his Talaing History of Pegu used by Phayre, now in the British Museum, being MSS. Or. 3462–4.
SCHOUTEN, J. Voyage aux Indes Orientales commencé l'An 1658 et fini l'An 1665. Amsterdam, 1707.
SHWAY YOE (Sir George Scott). The Burman, His Life and Notions. 1896.
SMITH, S. History of Siam 1657–1767. Being reigns of the kings translated by him and printed at his office. Bangkok, 1880–1.
SMITH, VINCENT. Catalogue of the Coins in the Indian Museum, Calcutta. Clarendon Press, 1906.
SONNERAT, P. Voyage aux Indes Orientales et à la Chine. Paris, 1782. 1806 edition.
SYMES, M. An Account of an Embassy to the Kingdom of Ava. 1800.
TAW SEIN KO. Preliminary Study of the Pe-u-daung Inscription. *Indian Antiquary.* 1893.
TEMPLE, SIR RICHARD. Buddermokan. *Journal, Burma Research Society.* 1925.
—— The Thirty Seven Nats, a Phase of Spirit Worship prevailing in Burma. Griggs, 1906.
—— The Order of Succession in the Alompra Dynasty. *Indian Antiquary.* 1892.
TENNENT, J. E. Christianity in Ceylon. Murray, 1850.
Twenty-four Parganas Gazetteer. Calcutta, 1914.
VALENTYN, F. Oud en Nieuw Oost-Indien. Dordrecht and Amsterdam, 1724–6.
WARRY, W. *Précis* of Chinese records, printed in the political files of the Rangoon Secretariat.
*Wawhayalinatta Dipani-kyan. Myammataya Press, Mandalay, 1899.
WOOD. *Précis* of Siamese Chronicles, and of Talaing Chronicles in Siam, written for me by Mr W. A. R. Wood, H.B.M.'s Consul General, Chiengmai.
—— History of Siam. London, 1926.
WROUGHTON, Capt. Inscription of the large Arakan Bell. *Journal, Asiatic Society.* Bengal, 1838, p. 287.

CHAPTER XVIII

THE MONUMENTS OF THE MUGHUL PERIOD

1. ARCHITECTURE

GENERAL

FERGUSSON, J. History of Architecture in all countries. London, 1865.
—— History of Indian and Eastern Architecture. London, 1910.
FLETCHER, B. F. A History of Architecture on the Comparative Method. London, 1921.
LETHABY, W. R. Architecture, An Introduction to the History and Theory of the Art of Building. London, 1929.
SIMPSON, F. M. A History of Architectural Development. London, 1905.

2. MUSLIM ART AND ARCHITECTURE

GENERAL

MAINDRON, M. L'Art indien. Paris, 1898.
MIGEON. L'Art Musulman. 2 vols. Paris, 1907.
NIEDERMAYER, OSKAR VON. Afghanistan. Leipzig, 1924.

OLFUSEN, O. Old and New Architecture in Khiva, Bokhara and Turkestan. Copenhagen, 1904.
RICHMOND, E. T. Moslem Architecture. Royal Asiatic Society. 1926.
—— The Dome of the Rock in Jerusalem. Oxford, 1924.
RIVOIRA, G. T. Moslem Architecture. Oxford, 1918.
SALADIN, H. Manuel d'Art Musulman. Paris, 1907.
SARRE, F. Denkmäler Persischer Baukunst. Berlin, 1901.
SIMAKOFF, N. L'Art de l'Asie Centrale. St Petersburg, 1883.

3. MUSLIM ART AND ARCHITECTURE IN INDIA

GENERAL

COLE, H. H. Illustrations of Buildings near Muttra and Delhi. London, 1872.
CUNNINGHAM, A. Archaeological Survey of India. Vols. I–XXIII. Simla and Calcutta, 1865–77.
FANSHAWE, N. C. Delhi: Past and Present. London, 1902.
GRIGGS, W. India. Photographs and Drawings of Historical Buildings. London, 1896.
HAVELL, E. B. Indian Architecture, from the first Muhammadan invasion to the present day. London, 1913.
HEARN, H. C. The Seven Cities of Delhi. London, 1906.
KEENE, H. G. Handbook to Delhi. Calcutta, 1906.
LA ROCHE, E. Indische Baukunst. Folio. 3 vols. München. 1921.
LATIF, S. M. Agra, Historical and Descriptive. Calcutta, 1896.
—— Lahore, Historical and Descriptive. Lahore, 1892.
LE BON, G. Les Monuments de l'Inde. Paris, 1893.
MARSHALL, Sir JOHN. Annual Reports of the Archaeological Survey of India, 1902–3 to 1930. Calcutta.
SHARP, Sir HENRY. Delhi: Its Story and Buildings. Bombay, 1921.
SMITH, E. W. Portfolio of Indian Architectural Drawings. London, 1897.
SMITH, V. A. A History of Fine Art in India. Oxford, 1911; 2nd ed. 1930.
STEPHEN, CARR. Archaeology of Delhi. Calcutta, 1906.
THORNTON, T. H. History and Antiquities of Lahore. Lahore, 1873.
Transactions of the Archaeological Society of Agra, January to June 1874. Delhi.
WETZEL, F. Islamische Grabbauten in Indien, 1320–1540. Leipzig, 1918.

4. MUGHUL ART AND ARCHITECTURE

ANDREWS, F. H. Mosque of Wazir Khan, Lahore. *Journal of Indian Art*, vol. X.
BROWN, PERCY. Indian Painting under the Mughals. Oxford, 1924.
CHISHOLM, R. F. Journal of the Royal Society of Arts, January, 1911.
Delhi Fort, a Guide to the Buildings and Gardens (Archaeological Survey of India). Calcutta, 1929.
GROWSE, F. S. Mathura, a district Memoir. 1883.
HAVELL, E. B. Handbook to Agra and the Taj. Longmans, 1912.
—— The Taj and its Designers. *Nineteenth Century and After*. June, 1903.
HANKIN, E. H. The Drawing of Geometric Patterns in Saracenic Art. (Memoir 15, Archaeological Survey of India, 1925.)
Journal of the Punjab Historical Society, vol. I. Calcutta, 1911.
KIPLING, J. L. The Mosque of Wazir Khan at Lahore. *Journal of Indian Art*, vol. II, no. 19.
MOIN-UD-DIN, MUHAMMAD. History of the Taj. Agra, 1905.
SMITH, E. W. Akbar's Tomb, Sikandarah, near Agra. Allahabad, 1909.
—— Archaeological Survey of India. Vol. XVIII, Mughal Architecture of Fathpur-Sikri. 4 vols. Allahabad, 1896.
—— Moghul Colour Decoration of Agra. Allahabad, 1901.
VOGEL, J. PH. Tile-mosaics of the Lahore Fort (Archaeological Survey of India, vol. XLI). New Imperial Series. Calcutta, 1920.

BIJAPUR

COUSENS, H. Bijapur and its Architectural Remains (Archaeological Survey of India, vol. XXXVII, Imperial Series). Bombay, 1916.
—— Guide to Bijapur. Poona, 1905.
FERGUSSON, J.
(a) Architectural Splendour of Bijapur.
(b) The Great Dome of Sultan Mahammad.
(*Transactions, Royal Institute of British Architects*, 1st Series, vol. v.) 1854–5.
FERGUSSON, J. and HART, P. D. Architectural Illustration of the Principal Mahomedan Buildings of Beejapore. London, 1859.
MEADOWS TAYLOR and FERGUSSON, J. Architecture of Bijapur.

SIND

COUSENS, H. Antiquities of Sind (Archaeological Survey of India. Vol. XLVI, Imperial Series). Calcutta, 1929.
—— Portfolio of Illustrations of Sind Tiles. London, 1906.

5. GARDENS

VILLIERS-STUART, C. M. Gardens of the Great Mughals. London, 1913.

CHRONOLOGY

INDIA

A.D.

1483 Birth of Bābur (p. 3).

1489 (or earlier)[1] Birth of Farīd Khān (Sher Shāh) (p. 45).

1494 Bābur succeeds his father in Farghāna (p. 4).

1497 Bābur captures Samarqand (p. 4).

1504 Bābur occupies Kābul (p. 5).

1505, 1507 Bābur raids into India (pp. 5, 6, 10).

1508 Birth of Humāyūn (p. 5).

1511 Bābur seizes Samarqand again (p. 7).

1512 Bābur abandons attempts on trans-Oxiana (p. 8).

1516 'Askarī born.

1519 Bābur takes Bājaur (p. 10). Birth of Abu-'n-Nāsir Hindāl.

1520 Humāyūn appointed governor of Badakhshān (p. 43).

1525 Bābur leaves Kābul for India (p. 12).

1526 Humāyūn takes Hissār Fīrūza (p. 12).
Battle of Pānīpat (p. 13).

1527 Battle of Khānua (p. 17).

1528 Chanderī taken (p. 17).

1529 Battle of the Gogra (p. 17).

1530 Death of Bābur and succession of Humāyūn (p. 18).

1531 Battle of Daunrūā (pp. 21 and 49).

1533 Rebellion of the Mīrzās (p. 22).

1534 Humāyūn moves to Gwalior (p. 22).

1535 Bahādur Shāh of Gujarāt defeated and flies to Māndū (p. 23).
Capture of Chāmpāner (p. 25).

1536 'Askarī leaves Gujarāt (p. 26).
Mālwā abandoned (p. 27).

1537 Death of Bahādur Shāh of Gujarāt (p. 28).
Capture of Chunār (p. 29).

1538 Sher Khān defeats Mahmūd Shāh of Bengal (p. 29).
Humāyūn enters Gaur (p. 30).

1539 Sher Khān defeats Humāyūn at Chausa and assumes sovereignty (pp. 33, 51).

1540 Humāyūn again defeated near Kanauj (p. 34).
Humāyūn retreats towards Sind (p. 36).

1541 Humāyūn marries Hamīda Begam (p. 38).

1542 Birth of Akbar (p. 39). Death of Mahmūd Lodī (p. 49). Sher Shāh invades Mālwā (p. 52).

1543 Sher Shāh takes Rāisen (p. 53) and invades Rājputāna (p. 54).
Humāyūn, defeated by Shāh Mīrzā Husain, leaves Sind (p. 40).

1544 Humāyūn arrives in Persia (p. 40).

1545 Death of Sher Shāh (p. 55). Succession of Islām Shāh (p. 58).
Humāyūn takes Qandahār (p. 40) and Kābul (p. 41).

[1] Possibly as early as 1472. *Vide Journal Bihar and Orissa Research Society*, 1934, p. 113.

A.D.

1546 Kāmrān recovers Kābul (p. 41).
Khavāss Khān murdered (p. 59).
1547 Humāyūn re-takes Kābul (p. 41).
Shujā'at Khān rebels in Mālwā (p. 60).
1548 Kāmrān submits to Humāyūn (p. 42).
Death of Shaikh 'Alāī (p. 63).
1549 Humāyūn's campaign against the Uzbegs (p. 42).
1550 Kāmrān rebels and occupies Kābul but is ejected (p. 42).
1551 Death of Hindāl in battle (p. 42).
1552 Kāmrān visits Islām Shāh (p. 43).
1553 Kāmrān surrenders to Humāyūn and is blinded (p. 43).
1554 Death of Islām Shāh (p. 61). Succession of Muhammad 'Ādil Shāh (p. 64).
Humāyūn arrives at Peshāwar (p. 67).
1555 Ibrāhīm Shāh assumes royal title (p. 65), and is defeated by Ahmad Khān who styles himself Sikandar Shāh (p. 66).
Humāyūn defeats Sikandar Shāh's army (p. 67) and enters Delhi (p. 68).
1556 Death of Humāyūn and proclamation of Akbar (p. 69).
Second battle of Pānīpat (p. 72).
1557 Death of Kāmrān (p. 43).
Sikandar Shāh surrenders (p. 73).
1558 Death of 'Askarī (p. 42, n. 1).
Akbar moves to Āgra (p. 75).
1559 Capture of Gwalior (p. 77).
1560 Akbar breaks with Bairam Khān (p. 77), who is assassinated (p. 78).
1561 Invasion of Mālwā (p. 79).
Revolt in eastern provinces crushed and Chunār captured (p. 81).
1562 Akbar visits Ajmer and marries daughter of Rājā Bihārī Mal of Amber (p. 81).
Merta surrendered (p. 82). Reverses in Mālwā (p. 82).
Atga Khān and Adham Khān murdered (p. 83).
Akbar frees himself from harem influence (p. 84).
Revolt in Kābul (p. 84).
1563 Expedition against Gakkhars (p. 86).
1564 Attempt on Akbar's life (p. 87).
Execution of Shāh Abu-'l-Ma'ālī (p. 86).
Muzaffar Khān appointed revenue minister (p. 87).
Jizya abolished (p. 87).
Gond kingdom annexed (p. 88).
Rebellion in Mālwā crushed (p. 89).
Campaign in Bihār (p. 90).
1565 Revolt of Uzbegs in India quelled (p. 91).
1566 Akbar visits Jaunpur, Chunār and Benares (p. 93).
Muhammad Hakīm invades the Punjab (p. 94).
Valuation of assignments (p. 461).
1567 Revolt of Mīrzās in Rohilkhand (p. 94).
Final suppression of Uzbegs (p. 96).
Akbar attacks the Rānā and besieges Chitor (p. 97).
1568 Capture of Chitor (p. 98).
Sulaimān of Bengal recognizes Akbar's supremacy (p. 99).

A.D.

1568 The Mīrzās invade Mālwā and Gujarāt (p. 99).
"The foster-father cohort" dispersed (p. 100).

1569 Capture of Ranthambhor and Kālinjar (p. 101).
Birth of prince Salīm (Jahāngīr) (p. 102).

1570 Birth of prince Murād (p. 102).

1571 Foundation of Fathpur Sīkrī (p. 103).

1572 Invasion of Gujarāt (p. 103).
Operations against the Mīrzās (p. 104).
Birth of prince Dāniyāl (p. 102).
Death of Sulaimān of Bengal (p. 110).

1573 Surat surrenders to Akbar (p. 105).
Understanding with Portuguese (p. 105).
Cash salaries introduced (p. 461).
Akbar doubts sufficiency of Islam (p. 107).
Revolt in Gujarāt (p. 108).
Dāūd, king of Bengal, invades Bihār (p. 111).

1574 Akbar takes Bihār and orders invasion of Bengal (p. 112).

1575 Famine in Gujarāt (p. 112).
Mīrzā Sulaimān expelled from Badakhshān (p. 115).
Dāūd surrenders Bengal (p. 113), but rebels (p. 115).

1576 Campaign against the Rānā (p. 115).
Dāūd slain and Bengal subdued (p. 116).

1577 Khāndesh taken (p. 117).
Rebellion in Gujarāt (p. 118).

1578 Portuguese mission arrives at Āgra (p. 121).

1579 Muzaffar Khān appointed viceroy of Bengal (p. 121).
Akbar's infallibility decree prepared (p. 122).
Assignments restored (p. 462).

1580 Yūsuf Shāh recovers Kashmīr (p. 124).
First Jesuit mission arrives at Āgra (p. 124).
Muslim plot to replace Akbar by Muhammad Hakīm (p. 125).
Rebellion in Bihār and Bengal (p. 125).

1581 Akbar marches against Muhammad Hakīm (p. 127).
Execution of Shāh Mansūr (p. 127).
Reconciliation with Muhammad Hakīm (p. 128).

1582 Abortive attack on Portuguese in Damān (p. 128).
Jesuit mission recalled from Āgra (p. 129).
"Divine Faith" promulgated (p. 129).

1583 Muzaffar III unsuccessfully rebels in Gujarāt (p. 133).
Administrative reforms (p. 133).
Foundation of fort at Allahābād (p. 134).

1584 "Divine era" introduced (p. 134).

1585 Death of Muhammad Hakīm (p. 134).
Newbery, Fitch and Leedes arrive at Āgra (p. 135).
Expeditions against Kashmīr and the Yūsufzāīs (p. 135).

1586 Kashmīr annexed (p. 136).
The Raushanāīs defeated (p. 136).
Unsuccessful raids into Berār and Sind (p. 137).

1587 Mān Singh recalled from Kābul (p. 137).

A.D.

1589 Akbar visits Kashmīr (p. 138).
Burhān Nizām Shāh II becomes king of Ahmadnagar (p. 138).
Death of Todar Mal and Bhagwān Dās (p. 138).

1590 Rebels in Bengal, Bihār and Orissa finally crushed (p. 139).

1591 Second Jesuit mission to Āgra (p. 139).
Envoys sent to courts in the Deccan (p. 139).

1592 Rebellion in Kashmīr which Akbar visits again (p. 140).
Orissa finally subdued (p. 140).

1595 Qandahār surrendered to Mughuls (p. 141).
Third Jesuit mission to Lahore (p. 141).

1596 Berār ceded to Akbar (p. 143).

1597 Mughul victory over troops of Deccan (p. 143).

1598 Surrender of Gāwīlgarh and Narnāla (p. 143).
Death of 'Abdullah Shaibānī (p. 144).

1599 Death of prince Murād (p. 144).
Akbar sets out for Deccan (p. 145).
Rebellion in Bengal (p. 146).
Prince Salīm revolts (p. 147).

1600 Ahmadnagar stormed (p. 147).

1601 Asīrgarh surrendered and Khāndesh annexed (p. 148).
Prince Dāniyāl appointed viceroy of the Deccan (p. 148).

1602 Murder of Shaikh Abu-'l-Fazl (p. 149).

1603 Salīm reconciled with Akbar (p. 150).
John Mildenhall arrives in Āgra (p. 151).

1604 (or 1605) Death of prince Dāniyāl (p. 151).

1605 Death of Akbar (p. 153) and succession of Salīm as Jahāngīr (p. 156).

1606 Khusrav's revolt (p. 156).
Parvīz and Āsaf Khān sent to invade Mewār (p. 158).
Qandahār invested by Persians (p. 158).

1607 Qandahār relieved by Mughuls (p. 158).
Sher Afgan, first husband of Nūr Jahān, killed (p. 160).
Second revolt by Khusrav (p. 158).

1608 Mahābat Khān supersedes Āsaf Khān in Mewār campaign (p. 158).
Khān Khānān sent to command in Deccan (p. 159).
Ahmadnagar taken by Malik 'Ambar (p. 159).

1609 Hawkins arrives at Āgra (p. 162).
'Abdullah Khān replaces Mahābat Khān in Mewār (p. 158).

1610 Riot at Patna caused by youth impersonating Khusrav (p. 160).
Parvīz arrives in Deccan with Āsaf Khān, Khān Khānān (pp. 159, 260).
Khān Khānān, defeated in Deccan, loses Ahmadnagar (pp. 159, 260).
Khān Khānān recalled, and Khān A'zam sent to Deccan (p. 159).

1611 'Abdullah Khān defeats Mewār forces, and is appointed governor of Gujarāt (p. 158).
Jahāngīr marries Mihr-un-Nisa (Nūr Jahān) (p. 163).
Failure of attack on Deccan by 'Abdullah Khān, Khān Jahān and Mān Singh (p. 160).

1612 Mughul governor of Bengal defeats rebellious Afghāns (p. 161).
Khurram marries Arjumand Bānū Begam (Mumtāz Mahall) (p. 163).
First English factory at Surat (p. 306).

A.D.

1612 Mughuls annex Kuch Hājo (p. 233).
1613 Jahāngīr leaves Āgra for Ajmer (p. 161).
Portuguese capture Mughul ships (p. 162).
1614 Khurram deputed to Mewār campaign (p. 161).
First mention of English in Mughul records (p. 162).
1615 Portuguese attack on British ships repulsed by Downton (p. 162).
Rānā of Mewār submits to Khurram (p. 161).
Birth of prince Dārā.
Sir Thomas Roe arrives in India (p. 162).
1616 Roe received by Jahāngīr (p. 162).
Khurram appointed to Deccan (p. 164).
Persian embassy received at Ajmer (p. 170).
Khusrav placed in charge of Khurram (p. 164).
Plague breaks out in N. India (p. 167).
1617 Khurram makes peace in Deccan and receives title of Shāh Jahān (p. 165).
Jahāngīr leaves Māndū for Gujarāt (p. 166).
1618 Jahāngīr leaves Gujarāt (p. 166).
Roe, after obtaining *farmāns* for English trade, leaves court (p. 166).
Aurangzīb born at Dohad (p. 166).
1619 Jahāngīr arrives at Āgra, and leaves for Kashmīr (p. 167).
Campaign in Kishtwār (p. 167).
1620 Kāngra fort taken (p. 167).
Shahryār betrothed to Nūr Jahān's daughter (by Sher Afgan) (p. 168).
Malik 'Ambar revolts in Deccan (pp. 168, 261).
Shāh Jahān again deputed to Deccan (p. 168).
1621 Shāh Jahān successful in Deccan (p. 169).
Jahāngīr leaves Āgra for Hills (p. 169).
I'timād-ud-daula dies (p. 169).
1622 Khusrav dies or is murdered (p. 169).
Shāh 'Abbās of Persia besieges and takes Qandahār (p. 170).
Shāh Jahān ordered to recover Qandahār but rebels (p. 170).
Malik 'Ambar takes Bīdar (p. 262).
1623 Shāh Jahān defeated by imperial army at Bilochpur (p. 171).
Shāh Jahān's forces defeated in Central India (p. 171) and he flies to Golconda territory, and Orissa (p. 172).
1624 Shāh Jahān successful in Bengal and Bihār, and Parvīz and Mahābat Khān return from Deccan to meet him (p. 172).
Shāh Jahān, defeated near Allahābād, returns through Bengal and Golconda (p. 173).
Birth of Murād Bakhsh (p. 173).
Malik 'Ambar attacks Bijāpur (pp. 173, 262).
1625 Shāh Jahān joins Malik 'Ambar and unsuccessfully besieges Burhānpur (pp. 173, 263).
Parvīz and Mahābat Khān return to Deccan and Shāh Jahān retires to Bālāghāt and offers submission (p. 173).
Mahābat Khān appointed governor of Bengal and summoned to court (p. 174).
1626 Jahāngīr starts for Kābul, and is seized by Mahābat Khān (p. 174).
Death of Malik 'Ambar (p. 176).

A.D.

1626 Shāh Jahān moves north towards Sind to meet Mahābat Khān, who leaves the emperor (p. 177).
Parvīz dies at Burhānpur (p. 177).

1627 Jahāngīr starts for Kashmīr, and dies on return journey (p. 178).
Dāwar Bakhsh proclaimed successor (p. 183).
Birth of Shivājī.

1628 Shāh Jahān proclaimed emperor (p. 183).
Dāwar Bakhsh murdered (p. 183).
Jujhār Singh's rebellion (p. 184).

1629 Rebellion of Khān Jahān Lodī (p. 185).
Shāh Jahān leaves Āgra for Deccan (pp. 186, 264).

1630 Shāh Jahān invades Ahmadnagar territory (pp. 186, 264).

1631 Khān Jahān finally defeated and slain (p. 188).
Death of Mumtāz Mahall (p. 189).

1632 Mughuls invade Bījāpur (pp. 189, 264).
Sack of Hooghly (p. 191).

1633 English factories opened at Balasore and Hariharpur (p. 306).
Daulatābād stormed and end of Ahmadnagar dynasty (pp. 193, 265).

1634 Abdāl of Bāltistān submits (p. 198).
Unsuccessful siege of Parenda (pp. 194, 266).
Death of Mahābat Khān (p. 194).
Insurrection in Bundelkhand (p. 194).

1635 Expedition against Garhwāl (p. 207).

1636 Peace made with Bījāpur (pp. 197, 267).
Shāhjī submits, and enters service of Bījāpur (pp. 198, 267).

1637 Aurangzīb appointed viceroy of Deccan (p. 267).
Annexation of Bāglān (p. 200).

1638 Peace between Mughuls and Āhom king (pp. 200, 233).
Qandahār recovered by Mughuls (p. 199).

1639 Invasion of Balkh planned (p. 202).
Foundation of new Delhi laid (p. 220).

1640 Foundation of Fort St George, Madras (p. 306).

1641 Revolt in Kāngra (p. 200).
Cheros in Palāmau subdued (p. 201).
Death of Āsaf Khān (p. 201).

1644 Aurangzīb resigns viceroyalty of Deccan (p. 268).

1645 Death of Nūr Jahān (p. 202) and of Gurū Har Govind (p. 245).
Invasion of Balkh (p. 202).

1646 Shivājī captures Torna (p. 268).
Balkh taken by Murād Bakhsh (p. 203).

1647 Aurangzīb replaces Murād Bakhsh but withdraws to Kābul (p. 204)
Shivājī captures Kondhānā (Sinhgarh) and other forts (p. 268).

1648 Shāhjī imprisoned in Bījāpur (p. 268).
Ruler of Bījāpur recognized as "Shāh" (p. 208).

1649 Persians recover Qandahār (p. 205).
Inauguration of new Delhi (p. 205).

1651 Aurangzīb re-appointed to Deccan (p. 269).
English factory opened at Hooghly (p. 306).

1652 Shujā' grants permission to English to trade in Bengal (p. 306).

A.D.
1652 Aurangzīb fails to recover Qandahār (p. 206).
1654 Expedition against Garhwāl (p. 207).
1655 Aurangzīb attacks Hyderābād and Golconda (pp. 208, 270).
1656 Golconda princess marries Aurangzīb's son (pp. 208, 270).
Garhwāl submits (p. 207).
Aurangzīb interferes in succession to Bijāpur (pp. 209, 270).
1657 Shivājī raids Ahmadnagar and Junnar, but is pardoned (pp. 210, 272).
Aurangzīb takes Bīdar, Kalyānī and Gulbarga (p. 271).
Illness of Shāh Jahān (p. 211).
Murād and Shujā' rebel (p. 211).
1658 Shujā' defeated near Benares (p. 211).
Aurangzīb defeats royalists at Dharmatpur (p. 212).
Battle of Sāmogarh (p. 213).
Aurangzīb crowned at Delhi (pp. 215, 222).
1659 Shujā' defeated at Khajuhā (p. 224).
Dārā defeated at Deorāī and executed at Delhi (p. 227).
Second coronation of Aurangzīb (p. 228).
Shivājī murders Afzal Khān (p. 272).
1660 Shujā' driven from Bengal flees to Arakan (pp. 226, 480).
Mīr Jumla appointed to Bengal (p. 234).
Mughuls occupy Poona and Chākan (p. 257).
1661 Shujā' killed in Arakan (pp. 226, 481).
Murād Bakhsh executed (p. 228).
Capture of Cooch Behār (p. 234).
1662 Assam occupied (p. 234). Cooch Behār recovered by its Rājā (p. 236).
Peace with Āhoms (p. 235).
1663 Death of Mīr Jumla (p. 235).
Shivājī raids Poona (p. 257).
1664 Shivājī assumes royal title (p. 273) and sacks Surat (p. 258).
1665 Jay Singh defeats Shivājī (p. 258).
1666 Death of Shāh Jahān (p. 233).
Chittagong captured (pp. 237, 481).
Shivājī visits Āgra, and escapes (p. 258).
1667 Yūsufzāīs rebel (p. 238).
Āhoms recover Assam (p. 235).
1668 Intolerant religious ordinances issued (p. 230).
Sholāpur ceded to Mughuls (p. 273).
1669 Destruction of temples ordered (p. 241).
Jāt rebellion (p. 243).
1670 Shivājī rebels and again sacks Surat (p. 258).
Chhatra Sāl becomes leader of Bundelās (p. 313).
1672 Rebellion of Afrīdīs (p. 238), and of Satnāmīs (p. 243).
Civil war in Bijāpur (p. 255).
1673 Shivājī sacks Hublī (p. 275).
1674 Aurangzīb conducts campaign against Afghān tribes (p. 239).
Shivājī assumes title of *Chhatrapati* (pp. 259, 275).
1675 Gurū Tegh Bahādur executed (p. 245).
1676 Unsuccessful invasion of Bijāpur (p. 255).
1677 Shivājī conquers Carnatic and Mysore (pp. 259, 276).

A.D.
1678 Mārwār occupied by Mughuls (p. 247).
1679 Gauhātī temporarily recovered by Mughuls (p. 236).
First English ship enters Ganges (p. 307).
Jizya re-imposed (p. 242).
Mughuls again invade Bijāpur unsuccessfully (pp. 259, 278).
Attack on Mewār (p. 248).
1680 Death of Shivājī and succession of Shambhūjī (pp. 259, 278, 279).
1681 Kāmrūp finally lost by Mughuls (p. 236).
Prince Akbar rebels (p. 250).
Mewār regains freedom (p. 252).
Aurangzīb sets out for Deccan (p. 281).
1682 Aurangzīb attacks the Marāthās (p. 282).
1685 Siege of Bijāpur (p. 285).
King of Golconda submits to Aurangzīb (p. 287).
Jāt rebellion (p. 305).
1686 Fall of Bijāpur (p. 287).
English sack and burn Hooghly (p. 308).
1687 Prince Akbar sails for Persia (p. 284).
Shāh 'Ālam imprisoned (p. 287).
Golconda captured (p. 289).
Durjan Sāl seizes Būndī (p. 303).
English expelled from Hijilī (p. 308).
1688 Marāthās plunder Conjeveram (p. 291).
Jāts rob Akbar's tomb at Sikandra (p. 305).
English factors imprisoned at Surat (p. 309).
1689 Shambhūjī captured and executed. Rājā Rām succeeds (p. 284).
Aurangzīb supreme in north India and Deccan (p. 284).
English abandon Bengal (p. 308) and are besieged in Bombay (p. 309).
1690 Mughuls besiege Rājā Rām in Gingee (p. 292).
Marāthā successes near Sātārā (p. 293).
Peace made between Mughuls and English (p. 309).
1692 Renewed Marāthā activity in Deccan (p. 294).
1693 Marāthās raid Berār (p. 294).
1694 Shāhjī II of Tanjore makes peace with Mughuls (p. 293).
1695 Mughul army defeated by Marāthās near Chitaldroog (p. 294).
Shāh 'Ālam appointed viceroy of Punjab and Sind (p. 296).
Mughul ships taken by English pirates (p. 309).
1696 Marāthā dissensions (p. 295).
Rebellion in Gondwāna (p. 314).
1697 Santājī Ghorpare murdered (p. 295).
1698 Gingee stormed (p. 293).
Ajīt Singh of Mārwār pardoned (p. 304).
English and Dutch piracy (p. 310).
1699 Rājā Rām defeated by Bīdār Bakht (p. 295).
Siege of Sātārā (p. 297).
First Marāthā raid in Mālwā (p. 313).
1700 Death of Rājā Rām (p. 295) and disputes over succession (p. 392).
Sātārā taken by Mughuls (p. 297).
1701 Aurangzīb takes Parlī and other forts (pp. 297, 298).

A.D.

1701 Ja'far Khān appointed revenue minister of Bengal (p. 312).

1702 Durgā Dās rebels (p. 304).

1703 Sinhgarh taken by bribery (p. 298).
Marāthās stop Mughul communications between northern and southern India (p. 313).

1704 Death of Muhammad Akbar (p. 302).

1705 Chhatra Sāl recognized by Aurangzīb (p. 314).
Serious illness of Aurangzīb (p. 299).
Durgā Dās restored to office (p. 304).

1706 Barodā sacked by Marāthās and Kolīs (pp. 306, 315).
Marāthā raids in southern India (p. 301).

1707 Aurangzīb separates his sons (p. 301).
Death of Aurangzīb (p. 302).
Rāthor war of independence (p. 303).
Prince Mu'azzam becomes emperor as Bahādur Shāh (p. 319).
Prince A'zam asserts claim in Deccan (p. 319).
Prince Kām Bakhsh crowns himself (p. 321).
A'zam defeated near Jājau and slain (p. 320).

1708 Shāhū recognized as Marāthā king (p. 392).
Ajīt Singh submits to Bahādur Shāh (p. 321).
Bahādur Shāh marches against Kām Bakhsh (p. 321).
Rājputs again rebel (p. 321).
Death of Gurū Govind Singh and revolt of Banda (p. 322).

1709 Kām Bakhsh defeated and killed (p. 321).

1710 Rājputs pardoned (p. 322).
Bahādur Shāh attacks Sikhs (p. 323).

1711 Sirhind recovered by Mughuls (p. 323).
Shiah-Sunnī dissension at Delhi (p. 324).

1712 Death of Bahādur Shāh (p. 324) and contest for succession (p. 325).
Jahāndār becomes emperor (p. 326).
Farrukh-siyar with help of Sayyid brothers gains battle of Khajuhā (p. 327).

1713 Farrukh-siyar defeats Jahāndār near Āgra (p. 328), and is enthroned (p. 330).
Jahāndār murdered (p. 330).
Expedition against the Sikhs (p. 335).

1714 Mughuls invade Mārwār (p. 333).
Intrigues against the Sayyids (p. 334).
Sayyid Husain 'Alī appointed viceroy of Deccan (p. 334).

1715 William Hamilton visits Delhi (p. 335).
Surrender of the Sikhs (p. 335).

1716 Execution of Banda (p. 335).
Rājā Jay Singh attacks Jāts (p. 336).

1717 *Jizya* re-imposed (p. 337).

1718 Churāman Jāt visits Delhi (p. 336).
Plot to seize Sayyid 'Abdullah (p. 337).

1719 Husain 'Alī returns to Delhi and proposes concessions to Marāthās (pp. 338, 395).
Farrukh-siyar deposed and strangled and Rafī'-ud-Darajāt succeeds (p. 339).
Jizya abolished (p. 340) and re-imposed (p. 346).

A.D.

1719 Death of Rafī'-ud-Darajāt, and of his successor Rafī'-ud-Daula (Shāh Jahān II) (p. 340).
Raushan-Akhtar succeeds as Muhammad Shāh (p. 340).

1720 Quarrels between Sayyid brothers (p. 342).
Death of Bālājī Peshwā and succession of Bājī Rāo (p. 396).
Nizām-ul-Mulk invades Khāndesh (p. 343) and defeats Sayyid forces in Berār (pp. 343, 399).
Assassination of Sayyid Husain 'Alī (p. 344).
Sayyid 'Abdullah proclaims Ibrāhīm as emperor, but is defeated by imperial army (p. 345).
Jizya abandoned (p. 346).
Marāthās obtain hold on Gujarāt (p. 398).

1721 Ajīt Singh rebels but submits (pp. 346, 347).

1722 Nizām-ul-Mulk returns to Delhi and becomes minister (p. 347).
Sayyid 'Abdullah poisoned (p. 348).
Sa'ādat Khān, Burhān-ul-Mulk, appointed viceroy of Oudh (p. 348).

1723 Nizām-ul-Mulk leaves Delhi (p. 349).

1724 Qamar-ud-dīn becomes minister (p. 349).
Abhay Singh succeeds Ajīt Singh (p. 352).
Battle of Shakarkhelda, Nizām now independent (pp. 350, 377, 399).
Bājī Rāo crosses Narbadā (p. 397).

1725 Nizām-ul-Mulk receives title of Āsaf Jāh and comes to terms with Marāthās (pp. 350, 379).
Muhammad Khān Bangash becomes governor of Allahābād (p. 353).
Nizām-ul-Mulk's attempts on Gujarāt (p. 351).

1726 Death of Ja'far Khān (p. 364).
Nizām-ul-Mulk supports Shambhūjī (pp. 380, 400).

1727 Khān Daurān becomes minister (p. 351).
Abhay Singh appointed governor of Gujarāt (p. 352).
Arakanese raid in Bengal (p. 479).

1728 Nizām-ul-Mulk takes Poona but compelled to evacuate it (pp. 381, 400).
Treaty of Mungī Shevgāon (pp. 381, 400).

1729 Marāthās defeat Muhammad Khān Bangash in Bundelkhand (p. 353).
Nādir Qulī expels Afghāns from Persia (p. 357).

1730 Sarbuland Khān's contest with Abhay Singh (p. 352).
Shāhū's army defeats Shambhūjī (p. 401).

1731 Muhammad Khān Bangash appointed to Mālwā (p. 354).
Nizām-ul-Mulk incites Marāthās to invade northern India (pp. 351, 382).
Bājī Rāo establishes Marāthā authority in Gujarāt (p. 401).
Treaty of Warnā between Shāhū and Shambhūjī (p. 401).

1732 Bājī Rāo invades Mālwā (p. 402).
Rājā Jay Singh replaces Muhammad Khān in Mālwā (p. 354).

1734 Marāthās capture Hindaun (p. 354).

1735 Marāthās sack Sāmbhar (p. 354).
Bājī Rāo recognized by emperor as governor of Mālwā (pp. 354, 402).
Rebellion in Korā (p. 355).

1736 Bājī Rāo's claims for territory and tribute (p. 355).
Nādir Shāh becomes king of Persia (p. 357).

1737 Mughuls attack Holkar near Bhadāwar (p. 356).

A.D.

1737 Bājī raids almost to Delhi and is formally appointed governor of Mālwā (pp. 356, 403).
Nizām-ul-Mulk visits Delhi (p. 382).
Marāthās over-run Konkan and besiege Bassein (p. 405).
Chanda Sāhib seizes Trichinopoly (p. 384).

1738 Nizām-ul-Mulk makes terms with Marāthās (p. 357).
Nādir Shāh takes Kābul and invades India (p. 357).
Marāthā depredations in Berār (p. 383).

1739 Nādir Shāh defeats Mughuls near Karnāl (p. 360), enters Delhi and orders massacre (p. 361).
Burhān-ul-Mulk dies and is succeeded by Safdar Jang (p. 362).
Mughuls lose Kābul and trans-Indus territory (p. 362).
Death of Shujā'-ud-Daula of Bengal (p. 364).
English obtain rights to trade in Deccan (p. 406).

1740 'Alī Vardī Khān appointed to Bengal (p. 364).
Marāthās invade Arcot. Dost 'Alī killed (p. 384).
Death of Bājī Rāo and succession of Bālājī Rāo (pp. 365, 407).
Nizām-ul-Mulk finally leaves Delhi (p. 383).
Nāsir Jang rebels against Nizām-ul-Mulk (pp. 366, 383).

1741 'Alī Vardī Khān reduces Orissa (p. 366).
Marāthās capture Trichinopoly and Chanda Sāhib (p. 384).
Death of Chimājī Appa (p. 407).

1742 Bhāskar Pant invades Bengal (p. 367) and is driven out by 'Alī Vardī Khān (p. 368).
"Marāthā ditch" dug round Calcutta (p. 408).

1743 Raghūjī Bhonsle invades Bengal. *Chauth* of Bihār granted to Peshwā (p. 368).
Nizām-ul-Mulk takes Arcot and instals Anvar-ud-dīn (p. 384).
Death of Rājā Jay Singh (p. 368), and of Muhammad Khān Bangash (p. 429).

1744 Treaty between Nizām-ul-Mulk and Marāthās (p. 384).
Raghūjī Bhonsle's troops invade Bengal (p. 441).

1745 Rohilla insurrection under 'Alī Muhammad Khān (p. 370).
Raghūjī Bhonsle occupies Orissa, but is defeated at battle of Katwa (p. 441).

1746 Mīr Ja'far appointed to Orissa (p. 442).

1747 Murder of 'Umdat-ul-Mulk (p. 371).
'Alī Vardī Khān defeats Marāthās near Burdwān (p. 442).
Nādir Shāh assassinated (p. 371).
Famine in Gujarāt (p. 384).
Ahmad Shāh Abdālī crosses Indus (p. 372).

1748 Death of Qamar-ud-dīn Khān (p. 373).
Ahmad Shāh Abdālī retreats to Kābul (p. 373).
Death of Muhammad Shāh and succession of Ahmad Shāh Bahādur (p. 373).
Death of Nizām-ul-Mulk and succession of Nāsir Jang (pp. 384, 385).
Muzaffar Jang and Chanda Sāhib seize Arcot (p. 387).
Qāim Jang Bangash killed by Rohillas (p. 429).

1749 Death of Shāhū and succession of Rām Rājā (p. 410).
Ahmad Shāh Abdālī invades Punjab (p. 429).

A.D.

1749 Ahmad Khān Bangash defeats Naval Rāi and Safdar Jang (p. 430).
1750 Nāsir Jang defeats Muzaffar Jang but is killed. Muzaffar Jang recognized by French (p. 387).
Rām Rājā imprisoned by Tārā Bāī (p. 411).
1751 Muzaffar Jang killed and succeeded by Salābat Jang (p. 387).
Peshwā favours succession of Ghāzī-ud-dīn at Hyderābād but is defeated by Salābat Jang with aid of French (pp. 387, 410).
Safdar Jang invites Marāthās to Dūāb and defeats Bangash and Rohilla Afghāns (pp. 415, 431).
Orissa surrendered to the Marāthās (pp. 408, 443).
1752 Punjab and Multān ceded to Ahmad Shāh Abdālī (p. 434).
Ghāzī-ud-dīn sets out for Deccan. Alliance between Salābat Jang and Marāthās. Ghāzī-ud-dīn poisoned (pp. 388, 412, 434).
1753 Shāh Nawāz Khān appointed regent in Deccan (p. 388).
Safdar Jang's revolt at Delhi (p. 435).
Gāikwār establishes himself in Gujarāt (p. 411).
1754 Ahmad Shāh Bahādur deposed and succeeded by 'Ālamgīr II (p. 436).
Shāh Nawāz exacts tribute from Raghūji Bhonsle of Nāgpur (p. 389).
Peshwā invades Carnatic (p. 412).
Death of Safdar Jang and succession of Shujā'-ud-daula (p. 439).
Mughul attempt to recover Punjab (p. 437).
1755 Clive and Watson defeat Angrias (p. 394).
1756 Attempt by Shāh Nawāz to dismiss French (p. 389).
Death of 'Alī Vardī Khān and succession of Sirāj-ud-Daula (p. 443).
1757 Ahmad Shāh Abdālī sacks Delhi and Muttra (pp. 416, 438).
Shāh Nawāz replaced by Basālat Jang and later by Nizām 'Alī (p. 389).
'Ālī Gauhar escapes from Delhi (p. 440).
Clive's victory at Plassey (p. 443).
1758 Marāthās invade Punjab (pp. 416, 445).
Shāh Nawāz murdered. French influence at Hyderābād wanes and Bussy departs (pp. 390, 412).
'Ālī Gauhar invades Bihār (p. 443).
1759 Ahmad Shāh Abdālī expels Marāthās from Punjab (pp. 416, 445).
Marāthās attack Najīb-ud-daula (p. 444).
'Ālamgīr II assassinated and succeeded by Shāh Jahān III (p. 444).
1760 Ahmad Shāh Abdālī defeats Sindia at Barārī Ghāt and Holkar at Sikandarābād (pp. 416, 446).
Marāthās invade Hyderābād (p. 390).
Battle of Udgīr (pp. 390, 413).
Marāthā army sets out for north (pp. 417, 446).
Shāh Jahān III deposed and Javān Bakht nominally enthroned (p. 447).
1761 Battle of Pānīpat (pp. 420, 448).
'Ālī Gauhar becomes emperor as Shāh 'Ālam II (p. 448).
Shujā'-ud-Daula appointed minister (p. 448).
Nizām 'Alī invades Mahārāshtra (p. 391).
Death of Bālājī Peshwā (p. 425).
1762 Nizām 'Alī imprisons Salābat Jang and recognized by emperor as viceroy (p. 391).

BURMA

A.D.

1404 Narameikhla flies from Arakan to Bengal (p. 477).
1430 Narameikhla re-instated (p. 477).
1434 Narameikhla dies and 'Alī Khān succeeds (p. 477).
1459 'Alī Khān succeeded by Basawpyu (p. 477).
1531 Minbin (Zabauk Shāh) succeeds (p. 477).
1541 Tabinshwehti annexes Pegū (p. 483).
1542 Tabinshwehti annexes Prome (p. 483).
1544 Tabinshwehti annexes upper Burma (p. 483).
1546 Tabinshwehti crowned king of all Burma and annexes Arakan (p. 483).
1547 Burmese expedition against Siam (p. 483).
1551 Tabinshwehti murdered and succeeded by Bayinnaung (p. 485).
1556 Expedition to Katha (p. 487).
1560 Envoys sent to Goa to recover Buddha tooth (p. 489).
1563 Invasion of Siam (p. 488).
1564 Rebellion in Burma (p. 492).
1568 Siege of Ayuthia (pp. 488, 489).
1576 Arrival of Buddha tooth in Burma (p. 489).
1581 Nandabayin succeeds Bayinnaung (p. 492).
1593 Minrazagyi (Salīm Shāh) succeeds in Arakan (p. 478).
1599 Arakanese and Siamese invade Pegū (p. 493).
1605 Anaukpetlun succeeds Nandabayin (p. 494).
1607 Anaukpetlun takes Prome (p. 494).
1610 Anaukpetlun takes Toungoo (p. 494).
1613 Anaukpetlun attacks De Brito in Syriam (p. 494).
1617 Minhkamaung (Husain Shāh) expels Portuguese from Sandwīp (p. 478).
1622 Thirithudamma succeeds Minhkamaung (p. 479).
1627 Dutch establish factory in Burma (p. 495).
1628 Last payment of tribute by Burma to China (p. 494).
Anaukpetlun murdered by Minredeippa (p. 495).
1629 Minredeippa executed and succeeded by Thalun (p. 496).
1638 Narapatigyi succeeds Thirithudamma (p. 480).
1647 British establish factory in Burma (p. 495).
1648 Pindale succeeds Thalun (p. 497).
1652 Sandathudamma becomes king of Arakan (p. 480).
1658 Yung-li, last Ming emperor of China, flies to Bhamo (p. 497).
1661 Shujā' executed in Arakan (p. 481).
Pindale drowned and succeeded by Pye (p. 499).
1662 Yung-li surrendered to viceroy of Yünnan (p. 499).
1666 Chittagong captured by Mughuls (p. 481).
1670 Massacre of Dutch at Mrohaung (p. 480).
1672 Narawara succeeds Pye (p. 499).
1673 Minrekyawdin succeeds Narawara (p. 499).
1677 Dutch withdraw from Burma (p. 495).
1680 Jatapon horoscopes compiled (p. 500).
1687 English unsuccessfully claim Mergui (p. 500).
1688 French build fort at Mergui (p. 500).
1692 English ship seized at Syriam (p. 501).
1698 Sane succeeds Minrekyawdin (p. 499).

A.D.

1710 Sandawiziya becomes king of Arakan (p. 482).
1714 Taninganwe succeeds Sane (p. 499).
1721 Italian mission founded at Āva (p. 500).
1722 English factory established at Syriam (p. 501).
1724 Yazawwingyi chronicle compiled (p. 500).
Manipurī raids begin (p. 502).
1731 Sandawiziya murdered (p. 482).
1733 Mahadammayaza succeeds Taninganwe (p. 502).
1738 Manipurī raids extend to Āva (p. 502).
1740 Talaings set up Htaw Buddhaketi as king (p. 503).
1747 Htaw Buddhaketi replaced by Binnya Dala (p. 503).
1750 Manu Ring *dhammathat* compiled (p. 508).
1752 Talaings take Āva (p. 503).
Alaungpaya founds new dynasty (p. 504).
1753 Alaungpaya expels Talaings (p. 504).
English occupy Negrais (p. 505).
1754 Talaings execute captive king of Āva (p. 505).
1755 Alaungpaya annexes country as far as Rangoon (p. 505).
Expedition against Manipur (p. 509).
1756 Burmese capture Syriam (p. 506).
Alaungpaya advances on Pegū (p. 507).
1757 Negrais and site at Bassein ceded to English (p. 505).
1758 Alaungpaya enters Imphal (p. 509).
1759 Massacre of English at Negrais (p. 510).
1760 Alaungpaya takes Tenasserim and invades Siam (p. 510).
Death of Alaungpaya and Naungdawgyi succeeds (pp. 511, 512).
1763 Hsinbyushin succeeds Naungdawgyi (p. 512).
1764 Invasion of Siam (p. 513).
1765 Āva becomes capital (p. 512).
1767 Ayuthia stormed (p. 515).
1768 Paya Tak reoccupies Ayuthia and founds Bangkok (p. 520).
1769 Chinese invasion repelled (p. 517).
1770 Fresh expedition against Manipur (p. 518).
1773 Talaing rebellion (p. 519).
1776 Singu succeeds Hsinbyushin (p. 520).
1782 Singu killed and succeeded by Bodawpaya (p. 522).
Thamada becomes last king of Arakan (p. 482).

DYNASTIES AND GENEALOGICAL TABLES

1. THE MUGHUL EMPERORS OF INDIA

A.H.		A.D.
932	Bābur, Zahīr-ud-dīn	1526
937	Humāyūn, Nasir-ud-dīn	1530
(945	[Sher Shāh, Sūr]	1538)
962	Humāyūn (restored)	1555
963	Akbar, Jalāl-ud-dīn	1556
1014	Jahāngīr, Nūr-ud-dīn	1605
1037	Dāwar Bakhsh	1627
1037	Shāh Jahān, Shihāb-ud-dīn	1628
1068	Murād Bakhsh	1657
1068	Shāh Shujā‘	1657
1068	Aurangzīb ‘Ālamgīr, Muhīy-ud-dīn	1658
1118	A‘zam Shāh	1707
1119	Kām Bakhsh	1707
1119	Shāh ‘Ālam Bahādur, Qutb-ud-dīn	1707
1124	‘Azīm-ush-Shān	1712
1124	Jahāndār Shāh, Mu‘izz-ud-dīn	1712
1124	Farrukh-siyar, Muhīy-ud-dīn	1713
1131	Rafī‘-ud-Darajāt	1719
1131	Shāh Jahān II (Rafī‘-ud-Daula)	1719
1131	Muhammad Shāh, Nasīr-ud-dīn	1719
(1132	Ibrāhīm	1720)
1161	Ahmad Shāh Bahādur, Mujāhid-ud-dīn	1748
1167	‘Ālamgīr II, ‘Azīz-ud-dīn	1754
1173	Shāh Jahān III	1759
1173	Shāh ‘Alam II, Jalāl-ud-dīn	1759
(1202	Bīdār Bakht	1788)
1221	Muhammad Akbar II, Mu‘īn-ud-dīn	1806
1253	Bahādur Shāh II, Sirāj-ud-dīn	1837

1. GENEALOGY OF THE MUGHUL EMPERORS OF INDIA[1]

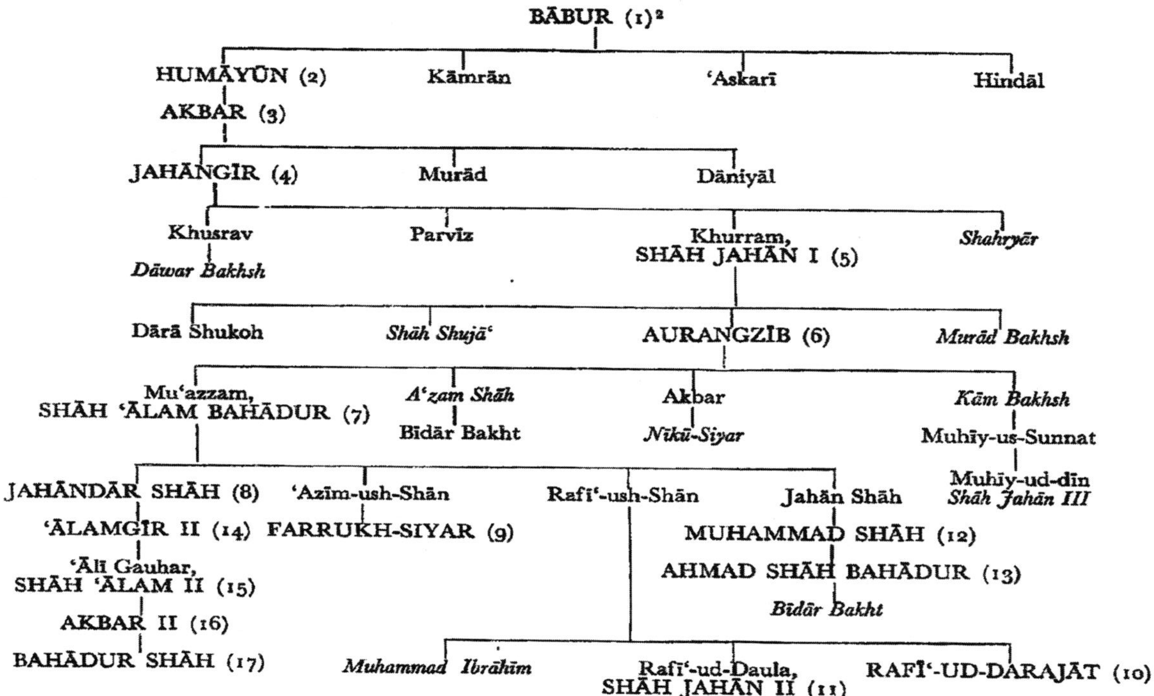

[1] The names of pretenders or puppet kings are shown in italics.

[2] For the Chaghatāī and Turkī ancestry of Bābur see tables opposite pp. 49–50, Elias and Ross, *History of the Moghuls of Central Asia*.

2. THE SŪR DYNASTY

A.H.		A.D.
945[1]	Sher Shāh	1538–9
952	Islām Shāh	1545
961[2]	Muhammad ʻĀdil Shāh	1554
962	Ibrāhīm Shāh	1555
962	Sikandar Shāh	1555

[1] See N. K. Bhattasali, "The date of Sher Shāh's accession" in *Islamic Culture*, 1936, p. 127.

[2] The histories (Elliot, IV, p. 505) give this date, but the latest date known on coins of Islām Shāh is 960, which is also found on coins of Muhammad ʻĀdil Shāh.

2. GENEALOGY OF THE SŪR DYNASTY

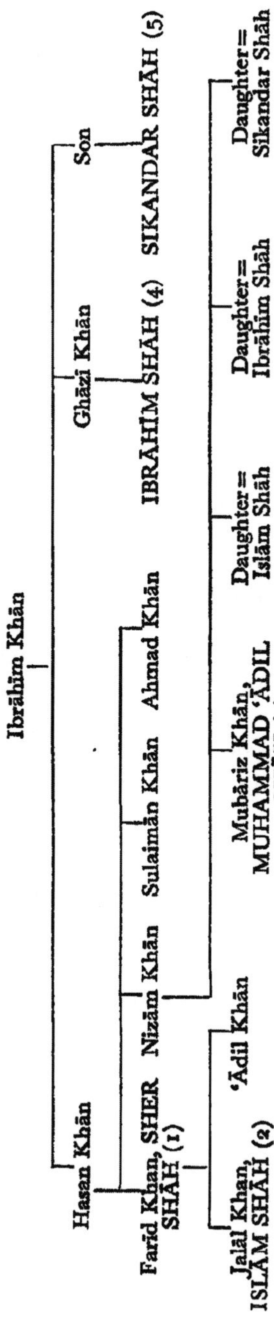

Names of rulers are shown in capitals.

3. THE MARĀTHĀ DYNASTY

	A.D.
Shivājī	1674
Shambhūjī	1680
Rājā Rām (regent)	1689
Tārā Bāī	1700
Shāhū	1708
Rām Rājā	1749
Shāhū	1777
Pratāp Singh	1810

3. GENEALOGY OF THE MARĀTHĀS

A. THE BHONSLES

Mālojī Bhonsle

Shāhjī

Sambhājī | SHIVĀJĪ (1) (*b.* 1627 (?), *d.* 1680) | Vyankājī (Rājā of Tanjore, 1676–83)

SHAMBHŪJĪ (2) (Rājā 1680–9)

SHĀHŪ (5) (Rājā 1708–49)

TĀRĀ BĀĪ (4) (Regent 1700–8; *d.* 1761) = RĀJĀ RĀM (3) (Regent, 1689–1700) = Rājas Bāī

Shambhūjī (Rājā of Kolhāpur, *b.* 1693, *d.* 1760)

Shivājī (*b.* 1691, *d.* 1723)

RĀM RĀJĀ (6) (*b.* 1723, *d.* 1777. Rājā, 1749)

SHĀHŪ (7) (titular Rājā 1777–1810)

PRATĀP SINGH (8) (restored to throne 1816: deposed 1839) | Shāhjī (Rājā 1839–48)

B. THE SINDIAS

Rānojī, *d.* 1750

Jayappa (murdered at Nagaur, 1759) | Dattājī (killed at Barārī Ghāt, 1760) | Jyotbā (killed at Barārī Ghāt, 1760) | Tukojī (illegitimate: killed at Pānīpat, 1761) | Māhādjī (illegitimate), *d.* 1794

Jānkojī (killed at Pānīpat, 1761)

4. THE PESHWĀS

	A.D.
Bālājī Vishvānāth	1714
Bājī Rāo I	1720
Bālājī Bājī Rāo	1740
Mādho Rāo I	1761
Nārāyan Rāo	1772
Mādho Rāo II	1774
Bājī Rāo II	1796

4. GENEALOGY OF THE PESHWĀS

(1) BĀLĀJĪ VISHVĀNĀTH
Peshwā, 1714–20

- (2) BĀJĪ RĀO I, Peshwā, 1720–40
    - (3) BĀLĀJĪ BĀJĪ RĀO, Peshwā, 1740–61
        - Vishvās Rāo, killed at Pānīpat, 1761
        - (4) MĀDHO RĀO I, Peshwā 1761–72
        - (5) NĀRĀYAN RĀO, Peshwā 1772–3
            - (6) MĀDHO RĀO II, Peshwā, 1774–95
    - Raghunāth Rāo (Ragoba), *b.* 1734, *d.* 1784
        - (7) BĀJĪ RĀO II, last Peshwā, 1796–1818
- Chimājī Appa, the conqueror of Bassein, *b.* 1708, *d.* 1741
    - Sadāshiv Rāo (the Bhāo Sāhib), killed at Pānīpat, 1761

5. THE NAWĀBS OF OUDH

A.H.		A.D.
1136	Sa'ādat Khān	1724
1152	Safdar Jang	1739
1167	Shujā'-ud-Daula	1754

5. GENEALOGY OF THE NAWĀBS OF OUDH[1]

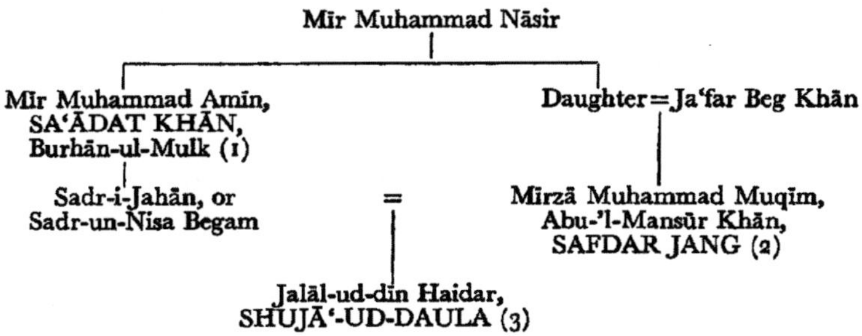

[1] See A. L. Srivastava, *The First Two Nawabs of Oudh*, Lucknow, 1930.

6. THE NIZĀMS OF HYDERĀBĀD

A.H.		A.D.
1137	Nizām-ul-Mulk, Āsaf Jāh	1724
1161	Nāsir Jang	1748
1164	Muzaffar Jang	1750
1164	Salābat Jang	1751
1175	Nizām 'Alī	1762
1217	Sikandar Jāh	1802

6. GENEALOGY OF THE NIZĀMS OF HYDERĀBĀD

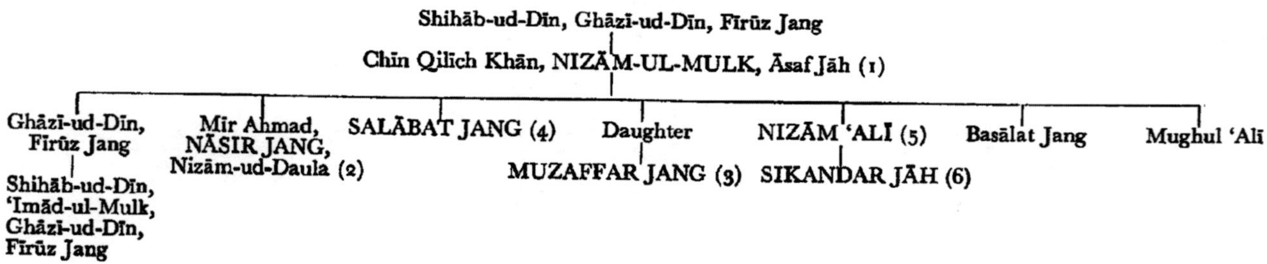

7. THE TOUNGOO DYNASTY IN BURMA

	A.D.
Bayinnaung	1551
Nandabayin	1581–99
(Petty rulers)	
Anaukpetlun	1605
Minredeippa	1628
Thalun	1629
Pindale	1648
Pye	1661
Narawara	1672
Minrekyawdin	1673
Sane	1698
Taninganwe	1714
Mahadammayaza-Dipati	1733–52

7. GENEALOGY OF THE TOUNGOO DYNASTY

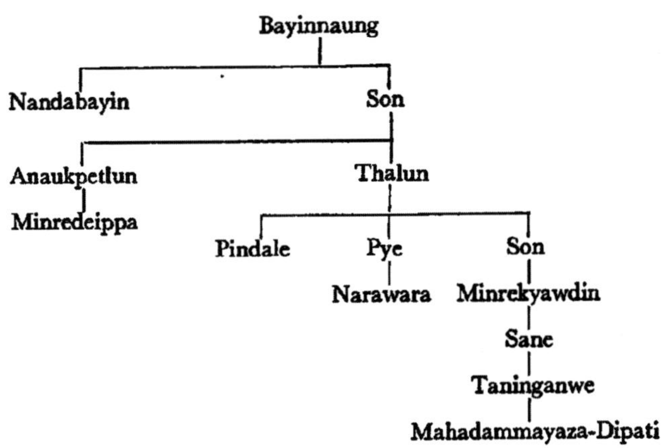

INDEX

CAMBRIDGE: PRINTED BY WALTER LEWIS, M.A., AT THE UNIVERSITY PRESS

1. Delhi, Jamālī Masjid (*cir.* 1530)

2. Delhi, Tomb of 'Īsā Khān (1547)

3. Delhi, Tomb of Adham Khān (dec. 1561)

4. Sasarām, Tomb of Hasan Khān Sūr (*cir.* 1540)

5. Sasarām, Tomb of Sher Shāh Sūr (*cir.* 1545)

6. Sasarām, Tomb of Sher Shāh Sūr, Northern Entrance

7. Delhi, Main Entrance to Purāna Qil'a (*cir.* 1545)

8. Delhi, Qil'a-i-Kuhna Masjid in the Purāna Qil'a (*cir.* 1545)

9. Delhi, *Mihrāb* in the Qil'a-i-Kuhna Masjid

10. Delhi, Pendentive in the Qil'a-i-Kuhna Masjid

11. Delhi, Entrance Gateway to the Khair-ul-manāzil (*cir.* 1560)

12. Delhi, Tomb of Humāyūn (1564)

13. Delhi, Tomb of Atga Khān (dec. 1561)

14. Jaunpur, Bridge over river Gumti (1564–8)

15. Gwalior, Tomb of Muhammad Ghaus (*cir.* 1564)

16. Gwalior, Perforated stone screen in tomb of Muhammad Ghaus

17. Āgra Fort

18. Āgra Fort, Delhi Gate (1566)

19. Āgra Fort, Jahāngīrī Mahall, east façade

20. Āgra Fort, Jahāngīrī Mahall, detail of east façade

21. Āgra Fort, Jahāngīrī Mahall, brackets in courtyard

22. Āgra Fort, Jahāngīrī Mahall, interior of northern hall

23. Lahore, Wooden doorway of a house (16th cent.?)

24. Mughul miniature painting, probably depicting the construction of the Elephant Gateway of Āgra Fort (painted *cir.* 1580)

25. Mughul miniature painting, depicting building under construction (painted *cir.* 1580)

26. Fathpur Sīkrī, Entrance gateway to palace of Jodh Bāī (*cir.* 1572)

27. Fathpur Sīkrī, Jodh Bāī's palace, west side of courtyard

28. Fathpur Sīkrī, Jodh Bāī's palace, west side of courtyard

29. Fathpur Sīkrī, House of Miriam

30. Fathpur Sīkrī, Jodh Bāī's palace, interior of northern hall

31. Fathpur Sīkrī, Rājā Bīrbal's house, detail of brackets on exterior

32. Fathpur Sīkrī, Rājā Bīrbal's house

33. Fathpur Sīkrī, Sultāna's house

35. Fathpur Sīkrī, Sultāna's house, carved sandstone detail of exterior

34. Fathpur Sīkrī, Sultāna's house, carved sandstone panel in interior

36. Fathpur Sīkrī, the Dīwān-i-Khāss, interior with pillar

37. Fathpur Sīkrī, the Dīwān-i-Khāss

38. Fathpur Sīkrī, Jāmi' Masjid, façade (finished 1571)

39. Fathpur Sīkrī, Jāmi' Masjid, central *mihrāb*

40. Fathpur Sīkrī, Jāmi' Masjid, interior showing brackets

42. Fathpur Sīkrī, Buland Darwāza, interior view

41. Fathpur Sīkrī, Buland Darwāza, exterior (1575–6)

43. Fathpur Sīkrī, Tomb of Shaikh Salīm Chishtī

44. Fathpur Sīkrī, Tomb of Shaikh Salīm Chishtī, portico

45. Brindāban, Temple of Govind Deo (1590)

46. Brindāban, Temple of Govind Deo, detail of arcades

47. Jaipur, Amber, Courtyard of Durbar Hall

48. Sikandra, Akbar's Tomb (finished 1612–13)

49. Sikandra, Akbar's Tomb, entrance gateway

50. Sikandra, Akbar's Tomb, inlaid stonework on entrance gateway

51. Sikandra, Akbar's Tomb, entrance to tomb chamber

52. Sikandra, Akbar's Tomb, upper storey

53. Āgra, Tomb of I'timād-ud-Daula (finished 1628)

54. Āgra, Tomb of I'timād-ud-Daula, detail of inlay

55. Āgra, Tomb of I'timād-ud-Daula, river entrance gateway

56. Āgra, Tomb of I'timād-ud-Daula, interior of upper storey

57. Lahore, Tomb of Jahāngīr at Shāhdara (1627)

58. Delhi, Tomb of Khān Khānān (1627)

59. Āgra Fort, the Dīwān-i-Khāss

60. Āgra Fort, the Khāss Mahall

61. Āgra Fort, the Musamman Burj

62. Āgra Fort, Motī Masjid, interior

63. Āgra Fort, the Musamman Burj, interior

64. Āgra Fort, Motī Masjid, exterior

65. Lahore Fort, Shīsh Mahall

66. Lahore, Mosque of Wazīr Khān (1634)

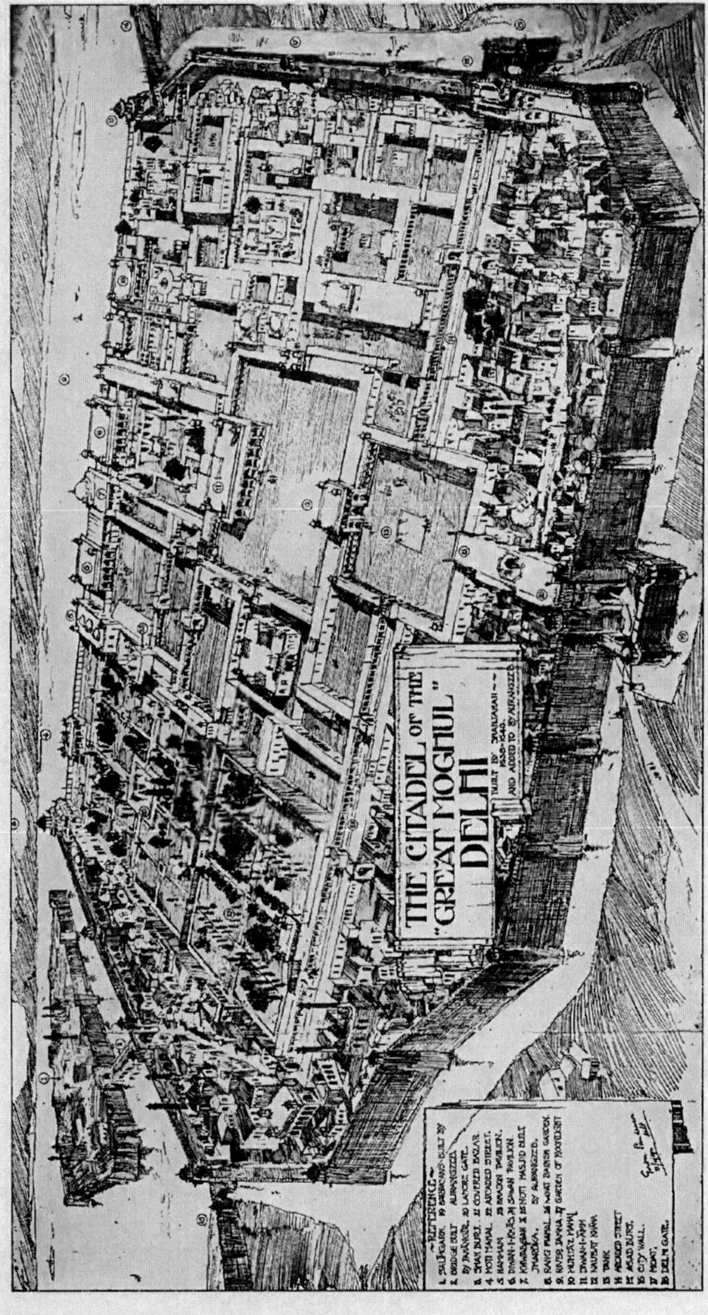

67. Delhi Fort, "The Citadel of the Great Moghul" (1639–48)

68. Delhi Fort, the Dīwān-i-ʻĀm, the throne

69. Delhi Fort, the Dīwān-i-'Ām

70. Delhi Fort, the Dīwān-i-Khāss

71. Delhi Fort, the Diwān-i-Khāss, interior

72. Delhi Fort, the Rang Mahall

73. Delhi Fort, the Pearl Mosque

74. Delhi Fort, Screen "Scales of Justice" in *Rang Mahall*

75. Delhi Fort, interior of the Pearl Mosque

76. Delhi, the Jāmi' Masjid (1644–58)

77. Delhi, the Jāmi' Masjid from the courtyard

78. Delhi, the Jāmi' Masjid, the *mihrāb*

79. Āgra, the Jāmi' Masjid (1648)

80. Āgra, the Jāmi' Masjid from the courtyard

81. Āgra, the Tāj Mahall, entrance gateway

82. Āgra, the Tāj Mahall (begun 1632)

83. Āgra, the Tāj Mahall from the river

84. Āgra, the Tāj Mahall, the mosque

85. Āgra, the Tāj Mahall, interior

86. Aurangābād, Tomb of Rābi'a-ud-Daurānī (*cir.* 1679)

87. Lahore, the Jāmi' Masjid (Bādshāhī Masjid, 1674)

88. Tatta, Sind, Tomb of 'Īsā Tarkhān (*cir.* 1640)

89. Tatta, Sind, Tomb of 'Īsā Tarkhān, detail of arcade

90. Tatta, Sind, Jāmi' Masjid (begun 1644)

91. Bijāpur, Jāmi' Masjid (1576)

92. Bijāpur, Jāmi' Masjid, interior

93. Bijāpur, Tomb of Sultān Muhammad (dec. 1656)

94. Bijāpur, the Ibrāhīm Rauza, the Tomb (1627)

95. Bijāpur, the Ibrāhīm Rauza, the Mosque

96. Bijāpur, the Mihtar Mahall (*cir.* 1620)

97. Burhānpur, the Bībī-kī-Masjid (*cir.* 1590)

98. Delhi, Tomb of Nawāb Safdar Jang (dec. 1754)

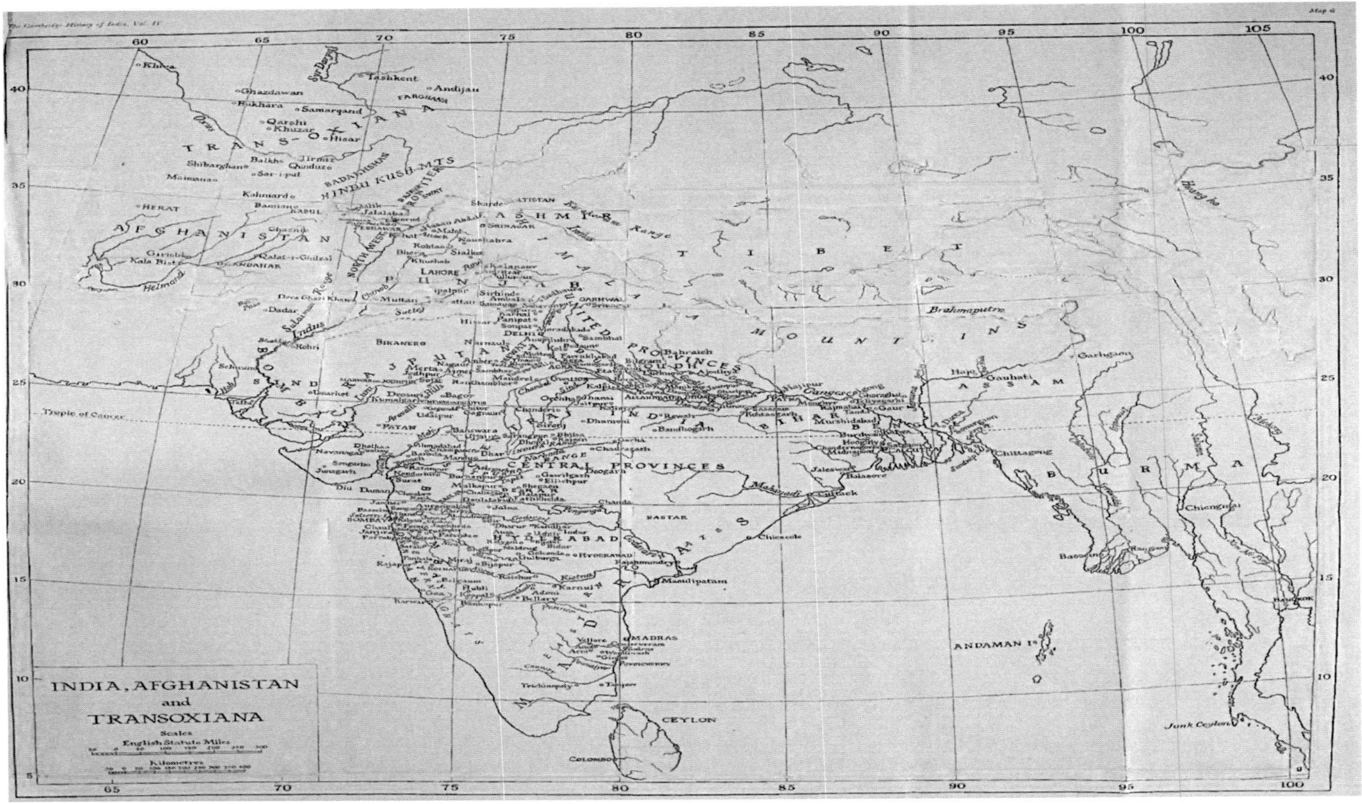
The Cambridge History of India, Vol. IV
Map 6
INDIA, AFGHANISTAN
and
TRANSOXIANA
Scales
English Statute Miles
Kilometres
TRANSOXIANA
AFGHANISTAN
HINDU KUSH MTS
BADAKHSHAN
NORTH WEST FRONTIER
KASHMIR
PUNJAB
HIMALAYA MOUNTAINS
TIBET
UNITED PROVINCES
OUDH
RAJPUTANA
SIND
BOMBAY
CENTRAL PROVINCES
HYDERABAD
BIHAR
BENGAL
ASSAM
BURMA
ORISSA
CEYLON
ANDAMAN Is
Tropic of Cancer
Tashkent
Andijan
FARGHANA
Samarqand
Bukhara
Ghazdawan
Qarshi
Khuzar
Hisar
Balkh
Shibarghan
Maimana
HERAT
KABUL
Ghazni
KANDAHAR
Qalat-i-Ghilzai
LAHORE
Multan
DELHI
Sirhind
Panipat
Sonpat
Hissar
BIKANER
Narnaul
Ajmer
Udaipur
PATAN
Chitor
Ujjain
Mandu
Dhar
Surat
Broach
Cambay
Ahmadabad
Junagarh
Diu
Daman
BOMBAY
Chaul
Goa
Belgaum
Bijapur
Gulbarga
Bidar
Golconda
HYDERABAD
Daulatabad
Ahmadnagar
Jalna
Ellichpur
Gawilgarh
Deogarh
Chanda
BASTAR
Masulipatam
Rajahmundry
Chicacole
Cuttack
Balasore
Jaleswar
Karnul
Adoni
Bellary
Raichur
MADRAS
Vellore
Conjeveram
Pondicherry
Tanjore
Trichinopoly
COLOMBO
Srinagar
Skardo
Jalalabad
Peshawar
Attock
Rohtas
Bhera
Sialkot
Kalanaur
Dera Ghazi Khan
Dadar
Rohri
Bhakkar
Sehwan
Umarkot
Jodhpur
Merta
Nagaur
Ambala
Saharanpur
Sambhal
Budaun
Bahraich
Ajodhya
Kalpi
Chanderi
Sironj
Bhilsa
Dhamoni
Bandhogarh
Rewah
Rohtasgarh
Murshidabad
Rajmahal
Gaur
Burdwan
Hooghly
Satgaon
Midnapur
Chittagong
Sandwip
Hajipur
Gauhati
Hajo
Garhgaon
Chiengmai
Rangoon
Bassein
BANGKOK
Junk Ceylon
Brahmaputra
Ganges
Indus
Sutlej
Chenab
Ravi
Helmand
Oxus
Syr Darya
Hwang ho
Salween
Narbada
Tapti
Godavari
Kistna
Mahanadi
Penner
Cauvery